Reading and Study Skills

Tenth Edition

John Langan

Atlantic Cape Community College

Praise for *Reading and Study Skills*

"*Reading and Study Skills* is thorough and step-by-step. Students really like the introductions from other students; I think it helps them realize that other people have been in their situation before."

Shannon Fernandes, Yakima Valley Community College

"I LOVE the readings Langan uses. . . . They cover engaging, relatable, and memorable topics. Their readability proves to students, especially reluctant readers, that they can and will enjoy reading, especially when the topic is interesting."

Margo N. Kourkoutas-Morea, Ramapo College of New Jersey

"I am thrilled about your motivational section; you devote more pages than many texts do to that area."

Shawn Bixler, University of Akron

"I have always been impressed with Mr. Langan's ability to break skills down to specific points, explain those points in a clear and concise manner, provide massive amounts of practice on the specific points, and then expand the practice into longer readings with comprehensive reading skills."

Joycelyn Jacobs, Lee College

"The text is one with which students can relate because of the style, tone, and level of this text. Often my students say that they are going to keep the text as a handbook. I am glad to have found such a helpful book."

Betty Perkinson, Tidewater Community College

"Over the years I've tried using other texts, for variety's sake, but have found them to be less useful overall than *Reading and Study Skills*. I choose this text because of its comprehensive coverage of reading and study skills, and because its layout and format are appealing to readers. The chapters are of reasonable length, and the quantity and variety of practice exercises, and of review and mastery tests, offer students frequent opportunities to apply newly learned skills and to test their own competency."

Jamie T. Barrett, Holyoke Community College

"I believe that this book can be very useful throughout my students' college careers. I once had a student tell me she was going to graduate school and was still using PRWR—wow!"

Denis J. Davis, Widener University

"The way Langan personalizes the approach and his insistence from the beginning on the importance of attitude in any endeavor certainly focus the concerns of the text clearly for both student and instructor. I think students would enjoy learning from this text for these reasons, just as instructors would enjoy teaching from it for the same reasons."

Larry D. Griffin, Dyersburg State Community College

"Langan introduces each new concept with clear examples, and the practice exercises provide immediate feedback about student understanding. Concepts are related to students' experiences and linked to academic success. Additional readings that emphasize various college disciplines link the content to other courses of study."

Patricia R. Grega, University of Alaska, Anchorage

"The book is non-intimidating for both the student and the instructor. A well-organized and fully developed reading and study skills text."

Carolyn Brown, University of South Alabama

About the Author

As a teacher, writer, and publisher, John Langan has commit-ted himself to improving reading and writing skills instruction for more than thirty years. The author of a popular series of college textbooks on both reading and writing, John enjoys the challenge of developing materials that teach skills in an especially clear and lively way. Before teaching, he earned advanced degrees in writing at Rutgers University and in reading at Rowan University. He also spent a year writing fiction that, he says, "is now at the back of a drawer waiting to be discovered and acclaimed posthumously." While in school, he supported himself by working as a truck driver, a machinist, a battery assembler, a hospital attendant, and an apple packer. John now lives with his wife, Judith Nadell, near Philadelphia. In addition to his wife and Philly sports teams, his passions include reading and turn-ing nonreaders on to the pleasure and power of books. Through Townsend Press, his educational publishing company, he has developed the nonprofit "Townsend Library"—a collection of more than a hundred new and classic stories that appeal to readers of all ages.

The Langan Series

TWO-BOOK SERIES

Exploring Writing: Paragraphs and Essays, Second Edition
ISBN: 0-07-337185-8 © 2010

Exploring Writing: Sentences and Paragraphs, Second Edition
ISBN: 0-07-337186-6 © 2010

ESSAY-LEVEL

College Writing Skills with Readings, Eighth Edition
ISBN: 0-07-337166-1 © 2011

College Writing Skills , Eighth Edition
ISBN: 0-07-337165-3 © 2011

PARAGRAPH-LEVEL

English Skills with Readings, Ninth Edition
ISBN: 0-07-337168-8 © 2012

English Skills, Ninth Edition
ISBN: 0-07-353330-0 © 2012

SENTENCE-LEVEL

Sentence Skills with Readings, Fourth Edition
ISBN: 0-07-353326-2 © 2010

Sentence Skills: A Workbook for Writers, Form A, Ninth Edition
ISBN: 0-07-337169-6 © 2011

Sentence Skills: A Workbook for Writers, Form B, Eighth Edition
ISBN: 0-07-353327-0 © 2009

STUDENT SUCCESS, STUDY SKILLS AND REVIEW

Reading and Study Skills , Ninth Edition
ISBN: 0-07-337164-5 © 2010

English Brushup, Fifth Edition
ISBN: 0-07-742836-6 © 2011

English Essentials, Third Edition
ISBN: 0-07-353332-7 © 2013

Ten Skills You Really Need to Succeed in College, First Edition
ISBN: 0-07-281955-3 © 2003

Contents

To the Instructor   xi

Introduction   1

Part One: Motivational Skills   9

Preview   10

Your Attitude: The Heart of the Matter   11

Setting Goals for Yourself   21

Learning Survival Strategies   29

Part Two: Study Skills   39

Preview   40

Taking Classroom Notes   41

Time Control and Concentration   73

Textbook Study I: The PRWR Study Method   95

Textbook Study II: Using PRWR   115

Textbook Study III: Applying PRWR to a Textbook Chapter   151

Building a Powerful Memory   201

Taking Objective Exams 219

Taking Essay Exams 237

Using Research Skills 249

Part Three: A Brief Guide to Important Word Skills 263

Preview 264

Using the Dictionary 265

Understanding Word Parts 277

Vocabulary Development 297

Part Four: Reading Comprehension Skills 313

Preview 314

Introduction 315

Ten Key Skills 315

Comprehension and Rapid Reading 316

Skill 1: Recognizing Definitions and Examples 317

Skill 2: Recognizing Enumerations 324

Skill 3: Recognizing Headings and Subheadings 334

Skill 4: Recognizing Signal Words 347

Skill 5: Recognizing Main Ideas in Paragraphs
and Short Selections 358

Skill 6: Knowing How to Outline 367

Skill 7: Knowing How to Summarize 382

Skill 8: Understanding Graphs and Tables 398

Skill 9: Making Inferences 409

Skill 10: Thinking Critically 422

Part Five: Skim Reading and Comprehension   435

Preview   436

Introduction   437

How to Skim-Read   438

Selection 1: Visual Assertion   439

Selection 2: Science and the Search for Truth   442

Selection 3: The Nature of Power   446

Selection 4: Defense Mechanisms   449

Selection 5: Fatigue   453

Skim-Reading Progress Chart   457

Questions on the Skim-Reading Selections   458

Part Six: Rapid Reading and Comprehension   461

Preview   462

Introduction   463

Selection 1: From *The Autobiography of Malcolm X*   467

Selection 2: Learning to Keep Your Cool during Tests   470

Selection 3: Wired for Touch   474

Selection 4: The Scholarship Jacket   479

Selection 5: Dare to Think Big   486

Selection 6: Winning the Job Interview Game   491

Selection 7: A Door Swings Open   496

Selection 8: From Nonreading to Reading   501

Selection 9: The Certainty of Fear   507

Selection 10: What You Need to Know to Succeed at Math   514

Rapid Reading Progress Chart   521

Reading Rate Table   522

Part Seven: Mastery Tests   525

Preview	526
Motivational Skills	527
Taking Classroom Notes	529
Time Control and Concentration	531
Textbook Study I	533
Textbook Study II	535
Textbook Study III	537
Building a Powerful Memory	540
Taking Objective Exams	542
Taking Essay Exams	544
Taking Objective and Essay Exams	546
Using Research Skills	549
Using the Dictionary	551
Understanding Word Parts	552
Vocabulary Development	553
Definitions and Examples	556
Enumerations	558
Headings and Subheadings	560
Signal Words	562
Main Idea	564
Outlining	566
Summarizing	568
Understanding Graphs and Tables	572
Making Inferences	574
Thinking Critically	576

Skim Reading   578

Rapid Reading Passage   580

Part Eight: Additional Learning Skills   585

Preview   586

Studying Mathematics and Science   587

Reading Literature and Making Inferences   599

Reading for Pleasure: A List of Interesting Books   609

Writing Effectively   615

Acknowledgments   635

Index   637

To the Instructor

Key Features of the Book

Reading and Study Skills will help students learn and apply the essential reading and study skills needed for success in college work. The book also provides a brief review of important word skills that students must have. And it will help students examine their attitudes about college and about studying, set goals for themselves, and take responsibility for their own learning.

The book covers a good number of skills because, quite simply, students often need to learn or review that many. In the best of academic worlds, students would have an unlimited amount of time to spend on study skills, word skills, motivation for achievement, and so on. In such an ideal scheme of things, they could use a series of books over several semesters to strengthen their learning ability. But in reality, students usually have only one or two semesters for improving their reading and study skills, and all too often they are asked to handle regular academic subjects at the same time as their developmental course. They should, then, have a book that presents all the central skills they need to become more effective learners. The book should also be organized in self-contained units so that students can turn quickly and easily to the skills needed in a given situation.

With *Reading and Study Skills*, an instructor can cover a wide range of skills and activities that might otherwise require several books or one limited book and a bundle of handouts and supplementary exercises. In addition to its comprehensiveness, *Reading and Study Skills* has a number of other important features:

- The book is highly *versatile*. Its eight parts, and many sections within these parts, are self-contained units that deal with distinct skills areas. An instructor can present in class those areas most suited to the general needs of students and then assign other sections for independent study. Also, because the book is so flexible, an instructor can more easily sustain students' attention by covering several skills in one session. For example, in a three-hour class period, work could be done on a study skill such as time control, a motivational skill such as setting goals, and a reading skill such as locating main ideas in short selections.

- The book is *practical.* It contains a large number and wide range of activities so that students can practice skills enough to make them habits. There are, for instance, more than sixty separate exercises in the section on study skills, more than fifty activities in the section on reading comprehension skills, and twenty-six mastery tests that cover most of the skills in the book. No instructor is likely to cover all the exercises in the book, but the chances are good that an instructor will be able to select the combination of skills best suited to the needs of a reading class or individual students.

- The book is *easily used.* It has a simple conversational style and explanations that are friendly and nonpatronizing. It presents skills as processes that can be mastered in a step-by-step sequence. Besides its many activities, the book uses a question–answer format to help students learn the material. After a set of ideas is presented, one or more questions may follow so that students can check their understanding of those ideas. Such questions are signaled in the text with a bullet (•). Finally, the book features high-interest materials. For instance, activities and selections on how people cope with conflict, on the need for human touch, on eating disorders, on the hazards of cellphone use, on fatigue in everyday life, and on the importance of education are used to practice reading skills.

- The book is *realistic.* It uses material taken from a variety of college text-books (in one instance, an entire textbook chapter) and gives practice in common study situations. Wherever possible, students are asked to transfer skills to actual study and classroom activities. A particular value of *Reading and Study Skills* for instructors should be its emphasis on activities that help students practice and apply study skills; the lack of such activities is a drawback in many currently available texts. In the past, too much attention has been given to increasing students' skill in reading selections rapidly and answering questions about the selections. Such drill has some value, but it does not prepare students to cope with an essay, control their study time, memorize material effectively (on those still-too-frequent occasions when memory work is emphasized), take useful classroom notes, or carry out the study assignments in a textbook chapter. *Reading and Study Skills* treats all the study skills that students need to survive in their courses at the same time they are working in other parts of the book to improve their reading skills.

Changes in the Tenth Edition

The helpful comments of reading and study skills instructors who have used previous versions of *Reading and Study Skills* have prompted changes to the new edition.

- Two new readings—"Wired for Touch" and "A Door Swings Open"—have been added to Part Six, offering a moving look at the importance of human touch to our everyday lives and an inside view of how one woman coped with a life-threatening illness. These additions, along with eight other readings in Part Six, give students further practice in reading comprehension while providing thought-provoking subject matter.

- Part Two: Study Skills includes a newly revised textbook chapter from the popular introductory sociology text, Hughes and Kroehler's *Sociology: The Core*. The chapter covers marriage and family issues in the United States with a focus on the special challenges that American families and society face as a whole. This chapter—presented in its entirety—is accompanied by activities giving students extensive practice in reading, responding to exercises, understanding various graphics (such as tables and graphs), and taking study notes on a full-length chapter.

- Part One: Motivational Skills now includes a useful set of tips and strategies to help students develop self-motivation so that they can be more effective learners and participants in their everyday lives.

- Throughout, examples, activities, and exercises have been revised to reflect contemporary issues and popular culture. New subject matter includes coverage of the hazards of cellphone use, eating disorders, and dealing with anger.

About the Media Links

This edition of *Reading and Study Skills* includes icons that link the text and its class-tested Online Learning Center. Each chapter in this edition features marginal icons that alert students to additional exercises and supplemental resources for the topic at hand.

Learning Objectives/Visuals: A list of learning objectives and PowerPoint slides supplement each chapter of the textbook.

Exploring and Writing Activities: Exercises encourage students to explore sites on the Web related to each chapter topic, and journal activities prompt students to write about what they have learned from a chapter.

Interactive Quizzes: Multiple-choice questions reinforce comprehension of key concepts and skills.

Additional Resources: Offerings include a learning styles assessment, a guide to using the Internet, a guide to avoiding plagiarism, a study skills primer, and more.

Helpful Learning Aids Accompany the Book

Supplements for Instructors

- An *Instructor's Edition* (ISBN 0-07-742694-0) consists of the student text complete with answers to all activities and tests, followed by an Instructor's Guide featuring teaching suggestions and a model syllabus.

- An *Online Learning Center* (**www.mhhe.com/langan**) offers a host of instructional aids and additional resources for instructors, including a comprehensive computerized test bank, a downloadable Instructor's Manual and Test Bank, online resources for writing instructors, and more.

- The online content of *Reading and Study Skills* is compatible with WebCT, eCollege.com, and Blackboard. To find out more, contact your local McGraw-Hill representative or visit **http://www.mhhe.com/solutions.**

Supplement for Students

- An *Online Learning Center* (**www.mhhe.com/langan**) offers a host of instructional aids and additional resources for students, including self-correcting exercises, writing activities for additional practice, a PowerPoint grammar tutorial, guides to doing research on the Internet and avoiding plagiarism, useful Web links, and more.

Dictionary and Vocabulary Resources

- McGraw-Hill is proud to offer a variety of dictionary and vocabulary resources from **Merriam-Webster**. You can contact your local McGraw-Hill representative or consult McGraw-Hill's Web site at **www.mhhe.com/langan** for more information on these resources as well as any other supplements that accompany *Reading and Study Skills,* Tenth Edition.

Acknowledgments

Reviewers who have contributed to this and previous editions of *Reading and Study Skills* through their helpful comments include Rane Arroyo, University of Toledo; Jamie T. Barrett, Holyoke Community College; Karen Becker, Youngstown State University; Shawn Bixler, University of Akron; Carolyn Brown, University of South Alabama; Delores J. Cabezut-Ortiz, Merced College; Betty J. Conaway, Baylor University; Sandra Connelly, Delaware County Community College; Denis J. Davis, Widener University; Deborah Edson, Tidewater Community College, Virginia Beach; Ann Engle, Iowa Western Community College; Shannon Fernandes, Yakima Valley Community College; Jennifer Fleischer, State University of New York, Albany; Daniel Ford, Arkansas Community College at Hope; Dennis Gill, Treasure Valley Community College; Brent Green, Salt Lake Community College; Patricia Grega, University of Alaska, Anchorage; Larry D. Griffin, Dyersburg State Community College; Jeff Gundy, Bluffton College; Beth Healander, Lexington Community College; Nancy Holmes, Southwest Mississippi Community College; Maurice Hunt, Baylor University; Joycelyn Jacobs, Lee College; Eleanor James, Montgomery County Community College; Ellen Kaiden, Ramapo College of New Jersey; Muata Kamdibe, Rio Hondo College; Sandra Kelley, Leeward Community College; Martin Kenney, Community College of Philadelphia; Barbara Maurer, Chestnut Hill College; Elizabeth McConnell, Massachusetts Communications College; Natalie McLellan, Holmes Community College; Margo Kourkoutas-Morea, Ramapo College of New Jersey; Pratul Pathak, California University of Pennsylvania; Betty J. Perkinson, Tidewater Community College; Karen Pinter, Sauk Valley Community College; Michelle Powell, Baylor University; Sol Rabushka, St. Louis Community College at Forest Park; Ron Reed, Hazard Community College; Linda Robitzsch, University of South Alabama; Thomas Sadowski, Allan Hancock College; Charis Sawyer, Johnson County Community College; Dianne Belitsky Shames, Delaware County Community College; Jan Strever, Spokane Community College; Claudia H. Stokes, DeKalb Technical College; Betty Thomas, Southwest Missouri State University; Joyce Washburn, Colby Community College; Gail Watson, County College of Morris; Patricia Wells, Morgan State University; Barbara Wilan, Northern Virginia Community College.

I am also grateful for help provided by Janice Wiggins-Clarke and Jessica Cannavo as well as for the support of my McGraw-Hill editor, John Kindler.

John Langan

Introduction

While working my way through school, I had all kinds of summer and part-time jobs. One of my first summer jobs was as a drill-press operator in a machine shop. When I reported to begin work, the supervisor said to me, "Langan, I want you to spend the first couple of nights going around and observing the operators and picking up everything you can. Then I'll put you on a machine." So for three nights, I walked around and watched people, was bored stiff, and learned very little. I didn't learn the skill of operating a drill press until I was actually put on a machine with a person who could teach me how to run it and I began practicing the skill. I have found that my experience in the machine shop holds true for skill mastery in general. One picks up a skill and becomes good at it when a clear explanation of the skill is followed by plenty of practice. This book, then, tries to present clearly the reading and study skills that you will need to succeed in your school or career work. And it provides abundant activities so that you can practice the skills enough to make them habits.

The skills in this book should help make you an independent learner—a person able to take on and master almost any learning challenge. However, the book cannot help you at all unless you have a personal determination to learn the skills. Back in the machine shop, I quickly learned how to run the drill press because I had plenty of motivation to learn. The job was piecework, and the more skilled I became, the more money I could make. In your case, the more reading and study skills you master, the more likely you are not only to survive but also to do well in your college courses.

1

Overview of the Book

Here are the eight parts into which this book is divided.

- *Part One: Motivational Skills*   This part describes important steps you must take to get off to a strong start with your college career and offers tips on how to develop self-motivation.
- *Part Two: Study Skills*   Part Two explains and gives practice in all the key study skills you need to do well in your courses.
- *Part Three: A Brief Guide to Important Word Skills*   The information here will help you quickly brush up on important word skills.
- *Part Four: Reading Comprehension Skills*   Part Four explains and offers practice in comprehension skills that will help you read and take notes on your textbooks and other college materials.
- *Part Five: Skim Reading and Comprehension*   Here you will learn how to do skimming, or selective reading.
- *Part Six: Rapid Reading and Comprehension*   This part of the book will suggest a method for increasing your reading speed.
- *Part Seven: Mastery Tests*   Part Seven consists of a series of mastery tests for many of the skills in the book.
- *Part Eight: Additional Learning Skills*   This last part of the book presents other learning skills that can help you with your college work.

What Skills Do You Need to Master?

Which learning skills do you need most? To help yourself answer this question, respond to the groups of statements that follow. The statements will tell you important things about yourself as a student.

They will make you aware, first, of your attitude toward study. By recognizing negative feelings you may have about yourself or about student life, you can begin to deal with those feelings. The statements will also make you aware of important reading and study skills you have—or do not have—right now. You can then use the book to master the skills you need.

Read and consider each statement carefully. Check the space for *True* if a statement applies to you most of the time. Check the space for *False* if a statement does not apply to you most of the time. Remember that your answers will be of value only if they are honest and accurate.

True	False	*Attitude about Studying*
____	____	1. I feel there are personal problems that I have to straighten out before I can be a good student.
____	____	2. I seem to be so busy all the time that I don't have a chance to do my school-work regularly.
____	____	3. If a subject is boring to me, I don't make the full effort needed to pass the course.
____	____	4. I often get discouraged about how much I have to learn and how long it's going to take me.
____	____	5. I will let myself be distracted by almost anything rather than study.
____	____	6. I want to be a successful student, but I hate studying so much that I often don't bother.
____	____	7. I often get moody or depressed, and then I am not able to study.
____	____	8. I keep trying to do well in school, but I don't seem to be making any progress.
____	____	9. I am still trying to develop the willpower needed to study consistently.
____	____	10. I am not completely sure that I want to be in school at this time.

Evaluating Your Responses   If you answered *true* more than twice in questions 1 to 10, you should read and work through all of Part One in this book. Part One will encourage you to think about the commitment you must make to become an independent learner. It will also help you set goals for yourself, show you five important survival strategies, and offer you tips on being self-motivated.

It may also be important for you to discuss your situation with a counselor, a friend, a teacher, or some other person whose opinion you respect. All too often, people try to keep problems closed up inside themselves. As a result, they may limit their potential unnecessarily and waste valuable time in their lives. Talking with another person can help you get a perspective on your own situation and so help you deal better with that situation. If you care about making yourself a strong and successful person, you should take the risk of sharing your feelings and concerns with someone else.

True	False	*Taking and Studying Classroom Notes*
		When I must take classroom notes,
____	____	11. I have trouble deciding what to write down.
____	____	12. While I am writing down an earlier point, I sometimes miss a new point the instructor is making.

True   False

____ ____   13. I often get sleepy or begin to daydream when the instructor talks for long periods.

____ ____   14. I don't know how to organize my notes, and so they are often hard for me to understand later.

____ ____   15. I write down what the instructor puts on the board, but I usually don't take notes on anything else.

____ ____   16. I seldom go over my notes after a class to make them easy to understand or to fill in missing points.

____ ____   17. I don't have an effective way of studying my notes for a test.

Evaluating Your Responses   If you answered *true* more than twice in questions 11 to 17, you should read and work through the first chapter on study skills, "Taking Classroom Notes" (pages 41–71). The chapter will show you how to take effective notes in class and how to study those notes. If you are taking any content course such as business, psychology, sociology, or a science at the same time as your course in reading and study skills, you should *read this chapter first.*

True   False   *Time Control and Concentration*

____ ____   18. I never seem to have enough time to study.

____ ____   19. I don't have a schedule of regular study hours.

____ ____   20. I never make up a list of what I need to study in a given day or week.

____ ____   21. I don't write down test dates and paper deadlines in a place where I will see them every day.

____ ____   22. When I sit down to study, I have trouble concentrating.

____ ____   23. I often end up having to cram for a test.

Evaluating Your Responses   If you answered *true* more than twice in questions 18 to 23, you should read and work through "Time Control and Concentration" (pages 73–94) early in the semester. You'll learn how to use your time effectively—a key to success in college as well as in a career—and to develop consistent study habits.

True   False   *Textbook Study*

____ ____   24. I'm not sure how to preview a textbook chapter.

____ ____   25. It takes me a very long time to read and understand a textbook chapter.

____ ____   26. I'm never sure what is important when I read a textbook.

True   False

27. I don't have a method for marking important passages while reading a textbook chapter.

28. I don't have a really good way of taking notes on a textbook chapter.

29. I don't have a really good way of studying my notes on a textbook chapter.

30. I have trouble understanding tables and graphs.

Evaluating Your Responses   If you answered *true* more than twice in questions 24 to 30, you should read and work through the entire chapter "Textbook Study I" on pages 95–114. This chapter will provide immediate help to you as you begin getting textbook assignments in other courses. Then go on to "Textbook Study II" and "Textbook Study III."

As time permits, you will then want to work through Part Four of the book, which explains and offers practice in eight key reading comprehension skills. Students often ask, "What can I do to understand and remember more of what I read?" The first five skills (pages 317–366) will help you locate and understand important points in articles and textbook chapters. The sixth and seventh skills (pages 367–397) will enable you to take down and remember those key points in the form of clear, concise study notes. The eighth skill (398–408) will enable you to decipher the material displayed in tables and graphs. The ninth and tenth skills will teach you how to make inferences and improve your critical thinking skills.

True   False   *Memory Training*

31. I have trouble concentrating and often "read words" when I try to study.

32. I don't know any techniques to help me remember material.

33. I often forget something almost as soon as I have studied it.

34. I usually don't organize material in any special way before I try to study it.

35. I don't know how to study and remember a large amount of material for a test.

Evaluating Your Responses   If you answered *true* more than twice in questions 31 to 35, you should read and work through "Building a Powerful Memory" on pages 201–217. That chapter presents techniques to help you remember both classroom and textbook notes.

True   False   *Taking Tests*

36. When I take a test, I often panic and forget what I have learned.

37. Before a test, I never make a careful, organized review.

38. When I prepare for a test, I am never sure what is important enough to study.

True   False

____   ____   39. I don't know how to go about preparing for an essay test.

____   ____   40. When I write an essay answer, I have trouble organizing my thoughts.

____   ____   41. I sometimes misread test questions and give an answer other than the one called for.

____   ____   42. I don't know any hints to keep in mind when taking a true–false or multiple-choice test.

____   ____   43. I sometimes spend too much time with some questions on a test and don't have enough time for others.

Evaluating Your Responses   If you answered *true* more than twice in questions 36 to 43, you should read and work through "Taking Objective Exams" (219–235) and "Taking Essay Exams" (237–248). These chapters show you how to prepare for both kinds of exams and explain test-taking techniques. Use them whenever exams are approaching.

True   False   *Using the Internet and the Library*

____   ____   44. I don't know how to use the search engine Google.

____   ____   45. I don't know how to narrow a research topic by using key words.

____   ____   46. I don't know how to use an online bookseller such as Amazon to look for books on a topic.

____   ____   47. I'm not sure how to look up or find a book in my library.

____   ____   48. I don't know the basic steps in preparing a research-based paper.

Evaluating Your Responses   If you answered *true* more than once in questions 44 to 48, you should read and work through "Using Research Skills" on pages 249–262. You'll learn all the basics you need to know in order to use the Internet and the library for researching a topic and preparing a research paper.

True   False   *Word Skills*

____   ____   49. I'm not sure how to use the dictionary for spelling and pronouncing words.

____   ____   50. I don't know how to use an online dictionary.

____   ____   51. I have trouble pronouncing unfamiliar words.

____   ____   52. I'm not sure how to use prefixes, suffixes, and roots to improve my pronunciation and spelling of words.

True   False

___ ___   53. If I see an unfamiliar word, I'm not able to guess its meaning by looking at the rest of the sentence.

___ ___   54. I feel that my vocabulary is limited and that this keeps me from understanding my textbooks.

___ ___   55. I have never really thought about the value of regular reading.

Evaluating Your Responses   If you answered *true* more than twice in questions 49 to 55, you should read and work through all of Part Three of the book. Part Three will help you improve your spelling and show you how to pronounce unfamiliar words, including specialized terms in your various subjects. You'll also learn ways to develop your vocabulary—a vital matter, because a small word base will limit your understanding of what you read. The concise information about word skills in Part Three can be supplemented with practice materials that are probably available in your college learning center.

True   False   *Other Reading Skills*

___ ___   56. I have trouble locating definitions when I read.

___ ___   57. I have trouble locating examples of ideas when I read.

___ ___   58. I have trouble locating enumerations (lists of items) when I read.

___ ___   59. I don't know how to use headings or subheadings when I read.

___ ___   60. I don't know what kinds of words are used to signal important facts or ideas.

___ ___   61. I have trouble locating main ideas in what I read.

___ ___   62. I would benefit from practice in outlining and summarizing.

___ ___   63. I don't know how to skim-read a textbook chapter effectively.

___ ___   64. I think learning how to speed-read would help me.

___ ___   65. I feel my lips moving as I read silently.

___ ___   66. My eyes go back a lot to reread earlier lines on a page.

Evaluating Your Responses   If you answered *true* more than twice in questions 56 to 66, you should read and work through Parts Four, Five, and Six of the book. The chapters on textbook study in Part Two offer a quick course in becoming a better reader and note-taker; the chapters in Part Four provide a more detailed step-by-step process to strengthen your textbook reading and note-taking skills.

Part Five gives you practice in skim reading—going through a selection quickly and selectively to find important ideas. Skimming is a valuable technique when it is not necessary to read every word of a passage.

Part Six introduces you to rapid reading—processing words at a faster rate than is your normal habit. You will learn that rapid reading is not a cure-all for reading problems but simply one technique used by effective readers.

The overall purpose of Parts Four, Five, and Six is to make *you* an effective, flexible reader—able to apply "study reading," skim reading, or speed reading (or all three), depending on your purpose for reading and on the nature of the material. You will improve your comprehension, slowly but surely, if you isolate and work on important reading skills in a systematic way.

Other Reading and Study Skills

True False

___ ___ 67. I find it especially hard to deal with a math or science textbook.

___ ___ 68. I would like tips on reading short stories, poems, and other literary works.

___ ___ 69. I need to know just how to go about doing a research paper.

___ ___ 70. The connections between reading and writing are not clear to me.

___ ___ 71. I'd like to start reading some good books but have no idea what to read.

Evaluating Your Response   If you answered *true* to any of questions 67 to 71, read and work through the appropriate chapter in Part Eight of the book.

Achieving Your Goal

You should now have a good sense of just what skills you most need to work on. Many students, I find, say that they want to improve in almost *all* the areas listed above. Whatever your specific needs, the material in this book should help.

Your goal as you begin your work is to become an independent learner—a person who can take on the challenge of any college course. Achieving the goal depends on your personal determination to do the work it takes to become a successful student. If you decide—something that only you can decide—that you want to make your college time productive and worthwhile, this book will help you reach that goal. I wish you a successful journey.

Part One
Motivational Skills

Preview

Part One is about important steps you must take to get off to a strong start in your college career. The point stressed throughout the first chapter, "Your Attitude: The Heart of the Matter," is that you must make a personal decision and commitment to do the diligent work that learning requires. The chapter describes several students who made or failed to make this commitment, and also asks a series of questions that will help you measure your own willingness to make it. The second chapter, "Setting Goals for Yourself," will encourage you to think actively about your eventual career goal and the practical steps you should take to start working toward that goal. In the third chapter, "Learning Survival Strategies," a successful student talks about the importance of planning for a realistic career, of getting organized, of learning how to persist, of being positive, and of remaining open to growth.

Your Attitude:
The Heart of the Matter

This book is chiefly about the reading and study skills you need in order to do well in your college work. But your *attitude* toward college work is even more crucial than any reading or study skill. Without the proper frame of mind, you might as well throw this book in the trash. And without the proper frame of mind, you may be wasting your time in school.

Doing the Work

Your attitude must say, "I will do the work." I have found that among the two hundred or so students I meet each year, there is almost no way of telling at first which students have this attitude and which ones do not. Some time must pass for people to reveal their attitude by what they do or do not do. What happens is that, as the semester unfolds and classes must be attended and work must be done, some people take on the work and persist even if they hit all kinds of snags and problems; others don't take on the work or don't persist when things get rough. It becomes clear which students have determined inside themselves, "I will do the work," and which have not.

The crucial matter is seldom the speed at which a person learns; the crucial matter is his or her determination—"I *will* learn." I have seen people who had this quality of determination or persistence do poorly in a course, come back and repeat it, and eventually succeed. And two years or so later, in June, I have heard their names being called out and have seen them walking up to the commencement stage to get their degrees.

For example, I saw the woman who wrote the following piece as her first assignment in a reading and writing class go up to receive her associate of arts degree:

> Well its 10:48 and the kids are all in bed. I don't know yet what Im going to write about but I hope I think of something befor this ten minutes are up. boy I don't even like to write that much. I never send my letters or cards because I dislike writing, may be because I never took the time to sit down and really write, I've always wishes I could, put thing on paper that were in my mind. but my spelling isn't at all good, so when I had to take the time to look up a word or ask one of my children how to spell it, I said to heck with it, but, I can't do that with this any way I don't believ I can write for ten mintes straght, but Im trying I refus to stop until Ive made It. Ive always given my self credit for not being a quiter, so I guess I have to keep fighting at this and every thing else in the future, If I wish to reach my gols wich is to pass my GED and go in to nursing. I know it will take me a little longer then some one who hasen't been out of school as long as I have but no matter how long it takes I'm shure I will be well worth It and I'll be glad that I keep fighting. And Im shur my children will be very prowd of ther mother some day.

Through knowing such determined people as this woman, I have come to feel that the single most important factor for survival and success in college is not a high IQ, or plenty of money, or an easy balance between school, work, and family life. Instead, it's *an inner commitment to doing the work*. When the crunch comes—and the crunch is the plain hard work that college requires—the person with commitment meets it head-on; the person without commitment avoids it in a hundred different ways.

Doing the Work Despite Difficulties

The person who is committed to doing the work needed to succeed in college is not necessarily someone without confusion and difficulties in his or her life. A joke that is sometimes made about freshman orientation—the day or so preceding the start of the first semester, when the student is introduced to college life—is that for some people freshman orientation takes a year or more. The joke is all too often true. I can remember my own confusing first year at LaSalle College in Philadelphia. I entered as a chemistry major but soon discovered that I could not deal with the mathematics course required. As hard as I tried, I couldn't pass any of the weekly quizzes given in the class. I felt that the instructor was poor and the text unclear, but since other people were passing the tests, I felt that the problem was in me, too. It was a terribly confusing time. Because I doubted my ability to do the work, I began questioning my own self-worth.

At the same time that I doubted whether I *could* do the work in mathematics, I began to know that I did not *want* to do the work. Even if I eventually passed the course and the other mathematics courses I would have to take, I realized I did not want to spend my life working with numbers. Very quickly my career plans disintegrated. I was not going to be a chemist, and I was left in a vacuum, confused and anxious, wondering what I *was* going to be.

My career identity was not my only problem. My social identity was precarious as well. The one male friend that I had from high school had gone into the Army and was in Germany. And because I was shy, I found no one immediately at the college to share experiences with. My one female friend—or supposed friend—from high school had gone off to a school in Chicago, and we did not bother to write to each other. I realized dismally that we didn't write because we didn't really know each other anyway. We had gone together in high school for the sake of form and convenience—so we would each have a partner for social events. There had never been real communication and sharing between the two of us. I had no one to help me shape my fragile social and sexual identities, and I felt very alone. To make matters worse, in the midst of all this, my blood was burning. I yearned desperately for someone to burst into flame with—and felt lost that I had no one. In sum, my first college year was a very worried, confused, and anxious time.

I responded to my general unhappiness partly by trying to escape. One way I did this was by resorting to games. In some respects my real major that first year at LaSalle was the game room located in the student center. Before and after classes I went there to play endless games of chess and Ping-Pong. I played, I now realize, not only to find relief from my worries but also as an indirect way of trying to meet other people. For a while I had a roommate who was in college only because his parents wanted him to be; he too was desperately unhappy. We seldom talked because we had very little in common, but we would spend entire evenings playing chess together. One day, soon after midsemester grades were sent out, I came back to the dorm to find that my roommate, his clothes, his chessboard—everything—had disappeared.

The games were not enough escape for me, and so I decided to get a job. I did not absolutely need a job, but I told myself I did. Not only did I need an excuse to get away from my dismal days at the college; I also wanted to shore up my unsure self-image. If I could not be a successful student or friend or lover, I could at least be a successful wage earner. Fortunately, I did not get a full-time job but instead began working as a graphotype operator two nights a week in downtown

Philadelphia. The job made me feel a little older and closer to being independent, so it helped lift my spirits.

Had I gotten a full-time job, it might have provided enough excuse for me to drop out of school, and I might have done so. As it was, I stayed, and—despite general unhappiness and partial escape through games and my part-time job—I did the work. Mathematics was hopeless, especially because there was no tutoring program or mathematics lab at the college, so I dropped the course. But I knew I would need the chemistry course that I was taking as a basic science requirement for graduation. The course meant a massive amount of work for me, and I studied and studied and went into each test hoping to get a grade that would reflect all the studying I had done. Instead, I always came out with D's. The grades were all the more discouraging because I felt so generally displeased with myself anyway. They seemed to be saying to me, "You are a 'D' person." However, I kept studying. I read and underlined the text, took lots of notes, and studied the material as best I could. I was determined to get the course behind me and, with a final grade of low C, I did.

I have known students who experienced a far rougher personal time at college than I did in my first year. And those people *who were determined to do the work,* despite all their difficulties, were the ones who succeeded. To overcome the worries, fears, and demands that may seem overwhelming during a semester, you must make a firm decision to do the work. Running from the work, you may lose precious time and opportunities in your life.

It is true that in a given situation you may decide it is better to drop a course or drop out for a semester rather than to try to do the work. You may be right, *but* it is important that you first talk to someone about your decision. One of the things that helped me stay in school during the hard first year was talking to an instructor I liked and felt I could trust. At your school you will find there are people—counselors, instructors, and others—who will care about your special situation. Talking with someone about your concerns will enable you to do something you cannot possibly do alone—get a perspective on yourself. From time to time we all need the insights into ourselves that can come from such a perspective. So, if you are having trouble making yourself do the work that college requires, it is in your best interest to talk to someone about it.

Discovering the Commitment to Do the Work

I have often seen people come to college almost accidentally. Perhaps they are in doubt about what to do after high school, or are discontented with their limited job opportunities, or are looking for other interests to fill the time they once spent with their children. So they come to college uncommitted, vaguely looking for a change of pace in their lives. Without a commitment, they often drift along for a couple of weeks or months or semesters and then fade away—silent, shadowy figures in both their coming and their going.

But in some instances a spark ignites. These people discover possibilities within themselves or realize the potential meaning that college can have in their lives. As a result, they make the commitment to do the work that is absolutely essential to success in college. Here is one student's account of such a discovery:

My present feeling about college is that it will improve my life. My first attitude about college was that I didn't need it. I had been bored by high school, where it seemed we spent grades 9 to 12 just reviewing everything we had learned up through grade 8. I had a job as a bottle inspector at Wheaton's and was taking home over $225 a week. Then I was laid off and spent whole days hanging around with nothing to do. My roommate was going to Atlantic Community College and talked me into going, and now I hope I'll be thanking her one day for saving my life.

When I entered college in January I thought it was fun but that's all. I met a lot of people and walked around with college textbooks in my hand playing the game of being a college student. Some weeks I went to class and other weeks I didn't go at all and went off on trips instead. I didn't do much studying. I really wasn't into it but was just going along with the ball game.

Then two things happened. My sociology class was taught by a really cool person who asked us questions constantly, and they began getting to me. I started asking *myself* questions and looking at myself and thinking, "What am I about anyway? What do I want and what am I doing?" Also I discovered I could write. I wrote my own version of the Red Riding Hood story and it was read in class and everyone, including the instructor, roared. Now I'm really putting time into my writing and my other courses as well.

After reading my first version of this paper, the instructor asked me, "What is the point at which you changed? When was the switch thrown to 'On' in your head?" I don't know the exact moment, but it was just there, and now it seems so real I can almost touch it. I know this is my life and I want to be somebody and college is going to help me do it. I'm here to improve myself, and I'm going to give it my best shot.

Earlier in the semester things seemed so bad to me. I was busted for drugs, I got an eviction notice, and I was having man trouble too. I was going to quit school and get a job and try to get a new start. But then I realized this is my start and this is where I will begin. I can tell you with a strong mind that nothing will discourage me, and that I will make it.

Running from the Commitment to Do the Work

I said earlier that as a semester unfolds and the crunch of work comes, people are put up against the wall. Like it or not, they must define their role in college. There are only two roads to take. One road is to do the work: to leave the game table, click off the stereo or television, turn down the invitation to go out, get off the telephone, stop anything and everything else, and go off by oneself to do the essentially lonely work that study is. The other road is to avoid the work, and there are countless ways of doing this. Here is one student's moving account of the avoidance pattern in his life and his discovery of it:

> Somewhere, a little piece of me is lost and crying. Someplace, deep in the shadows of my subconscious, a piece of my soul has sat down and anchored itself in defeat and is trying to pull me down into the darkness with it. This might sound strange to someone who is not familiar with the inner conflicts of a person that can tear and pull at his soul until he begins to stop and sink in his own deep-hollow depths. But sinking doesn't take much. It takes only one little flaw which left unattended will grow and grow . . . until like cancer it consumes the soul.
>
> My flaw, the part of me that has given up, is best seen when it is winning. Then I am lost like a rudderless ship after the storm has abated, motor gone, drifting . . . pushed about by the eddying currents in little circles of lassitude and self-doubt, just waiting . . . just waiting . . . peering at the ominous dark clouds in the sky, waiting for help to arrive.
>
> I know now, and I have always known, that help comes first from within. I know that if one doesn't somehow come to one's own rescue, then all is lost. I know it is time for me to look at myself. I would rather avoid that. But in order to break free of my own chains, I must look at myself.
>
> I could relate the incidents of my youth. I could tell of the many past failures and what I think caused them. But I won't, for one example will show where I'm at. At the beginning of this summer I set my goals. These goals consisted of the college courses I wanted to complete and where I wanted to be physically and mentally when the summer was over. Listed among the goals to be accomplished were courses I needed in writing and accounting. To help me become at ease with my writing, I took English Composition 101, and to clear up my deficiency in accounting, I took that course a second time. But now, at the end of July, I am so far behind in both courses it looks as if I will fail them both. I ask myself, "Why?" I know that if I work enough I can handle the courses. So, why have I been so lazy? Why is it that the things I seem to want most, I either give up or in some way do not strive for? These are the questions I must try to answer.

I remember when I was about five or six—a little, dreamy boy living in the country—a much older neighbor boy told me one rainy afternoon, just when the rain had stopped and the sun peered with glistening rays of gold through gray and white fluffy clouds, that "there is a pot of gold at the end of the rainbow." And right then a pulsating, glowing rainbow of violets, blues, and golds raced from the clouds and down past the hill. It sent me scampering across the wet, weedy field and up the hill and down the other side, where fields with rows of wet corn stood. There my rainbow had moved a little farther on. I should have known then, but I kept walking through the puddles in the muddy fields watching my rainbow fade farther and farther away with each step. I started home when the rainbow faded, but in the puddles of water I saw little rainbows and dreamed that the next time I would get the pot of gold under the big rainbow.

I think it's time for me to stop chasing rainbows in the sky. It's time to stop looking into the sky waiting for help to arrive. It's time for me to start bailing the rot out of my mind, to stop dreaming and not acting, before I have nothing left to hope for. I can see now that I've never given it the total effort, that I've always been afraid I would fail or not measure up. So I've quit early. Instead of acting on my dreams, I've lain back and just floated along. I've lived too much time in this world unfulfilled. I've got to make my dreams work. I've suffered enough in this world. I must do this now, and all it takes is the doing. Somehow I must learn to succeed at success rather than at failure, and the time to start is now.

Your instructor may ask you to write a paper that responds *in detail* to one of the preceding self-motivation strategies. He or she may stress that in this paper, honesty—the expression of your real thoughts and feelings and experiences in relation to your own motivation—is more important than sentence skills.

Self-motivation plays a big part in being a successful student with a positive attitude. However, being self-motivated is not easy. The following is a list of eight strategies to boost your self-motivation.

Eight Ways to Boost Self-Motivation

1   *Know yourself.* No one knows you better than you do. When it comes to self-motivation, know what your strengths and weaknesses are and how to address both. To get started, make a list of those areas of your life where you are self-motivated—such as getting to work on time or getting regular

exercise—and those areas in which you need improvement—such as wasting valuable time on Facebook instead of sitting down to work on a school assignment. Then, focus in on those areas in need of improvement and come up with ways to address them. For example, you might give yourself a limited amount of time on Facebook after you have spent one hour working on a school assignment.

My Strengths

Ex. I get to work on time.

_____

_____

_____

My Weaknesses (areas where I need to be more self-motivated)

Ex. I waste time on Facebook.

_____

_____

_____

What I Will Do to Improve

Ex. I will give myself a limited amount of time on Facebook after I have spent one hour on a school assignment.

_____

_____

2 *Stay positive.* It is easy to lose motivation when negative thoughts fill our heads. But it is important to remember that entire situations can change simply by changing how we think about them. Thoughts such as "I'll never finish this assignment," "This is too hard," or "I can't do this" often come to mind when our back is against the wall and we feel negativity crowding our thoughts. In these cases, turn negative statements into positive ones. For example, you might say: "I can finish this assignment, I just need to break it down into steps" or "This material is hard, but I'm going to ask my instructor for extra help" or "I can do this."

3 *Surround yourself with positive friends.* When it comes to self-motivation, it is not only important to think positively, it is also important to surround yourself with friends and classmates who have a positive outlook on school and life in general. Think about how you feel when a

friend agrees with you when you say, "I'm no good at this" as opposed to a friend who encourages you when you feel bad about yourself and your abilities. A positive attitude is contagious, just as negativity can spread like a virus.

4   *Follow success.* Are there any friends, relatives, classmates, or instructors whom you admire and who have been particularly successful in their career and life? If so, set some time aside to talk to this person (or persons) about what motivates her or him to be successful and ask for advice on how you might adapt some useful strategies for your life. A good first step is to make a list of those people you admire and then send them a short, to-the-point e-mail (or give them a call) asking when the two of you can meet. Don't be shy about this; think about how good you would feel if someone approached you for advice. The person whom you admire will more than likely feel honored that you took the time to reach out to him or her.

5   *Be patient with yourself.* Patience is truly a virtue. There are many times in life when we just need to give ourselves a break and resolve to get it right next time. So, when your best-laid plans don't come together, and the goals you have set are not met or fall apart completely, be patient with yourself and resolve to try again.

6   *Have a sense of humor.* Another tool toward self-motivation is to have a sense of humor. At times, we all take ourselves or life situations too seriously, and when that happens our ability to think clearly and make important decisions is affected. Think, for example, about those times when something difficult happened in your life and you or someone else found humor in the situation. Perhaps in that humor, for just a moment, your mood lightened enough so that you could think clearly and move forward. Of course, we don't want to think of ourselves and our lives as one big joke; instead, we want to work toward a balance of seriousness and humor.

7   *Start over, and over, and over again.* Being self-motivated is like being on a diet. That is, we need to remind ourselves, over and over again, what our goals are, why we have set those goals, and, many times, start a goal over because we have lost our way.

8   *Start and end your day with a goal.* One of the best ways to stay motivated is to start with a goal for the day and steps toward meeting that goal—such as, "I will take careful notes during each of my classes, and to do so I will make sure that I have all of the necessary materials—pencil, pen,

highlighter, notebook, and so on." Then, at the end of the day, go back over your day and the goal you set to see if you were able to achieve that goal. If, for example, you took notes in half of your classes, then give yourself a pat on the back for doing so, and resolve to take notes in all of your classes next time. There are a couple of good ways to remind yourself of goals you have set—you can, for example, stick a Post-it note on your computer or car dashboard with the starting goal and put a note on your bedside table with a reminder of that goal. You might also use a computer device—such as a smartphone—to put your goals in a computerized calendar that buzzes in the a.m. and p.m.

Setting Goals for Yourself

If you asked a cross section of students why they are in college, you would probably get a wide range of responses. Following are some reasons people give for going to college. Check the reasons that you feel apply to you. Be honest; think a bit about each reason before you go on to the next one.

Reasons Students Go to College	Apply in My Case
• To have some fun before getting a job.	_____
• To prepare for a specific career.	_____
• To please their families.	_____
• To educate and enrich themselves.	_____
• To be with friends who are going to college.	_____
• To fill in time until they figure out what they want to do.	_____
• To take advantage of an opportunity they didn't have before in their lives.	_____
• To find a husband or wife.	_____
• To see if college has anything to offer them.	_____
• To do more with their lives than they've done so far.	_____
• To take advantage of VA benefits or other special funding.	_____
• To earn the status that they feel comes with a college degree.	_____
• To get a new start in life.	_____
• To set an example for their children.	_____
• To be qualified for a promotion at work.	_____

Get together with one or more other students to compare and discuss your responses to this list. Talk about what you feel are the "bottom-line" reasons you are in college. Make a genuine effort to be as honest about yourself as possible.

Now write in the spaces that follow the basic reason or reasons you have for being in college.

_____

_____

_____

_____

If you do not have one or more solid reasons for being in college, you may have trouble motivating yourself to do the hard work that will be required. When difficult moments occur, your concentration and effort will lag unless you can remember that you have good reasons for persisting.

Long-Term Goals

For many students, a main reason for being in college is to prepare themselves for a career—the specific kind of work they intend to do in life. If you have not been thinking actively about this long-range goal, you should begin doing so during your first year at college. Here are four specific steps you can take to start formulating a career goal.

1   If you are not sure of a major, visit the college's counseling center. The center probably administers an *interest inventory* and a *vocational preference test.* The first identifies what you like and can do well; the second points to careers that match your interests and abilities. With this information, the counseling staff at the center can help you decide on a possible major. You should begin taking courses in this prospective major as soon as you can in order to learn for sure that it is right for you.

2   Sometime early in college, make an appointment to talk with a faculty member in the department of your intended major. Most department advisers set aside a certain period of time to meet with students and discuss their course of study. Ask such advisers the following questions:

What courses are required in the major?

What courses are recommended?

What courses, if any, offer practical work experiences?

3   Also, plan to go to the placement office some time during your first year to get specific information on careers. Many students have the notion that placement offices provide this information only to students who are about to graduate, but this is not the case. In fact, waiting until you are about to graduate to start investigating the job field is a poor idea. *It is important for beginning students to speak to the placement staff to obtain updated information about the future of specific fields.* For example, it would make little sense for you to plan to become a history teacher if that particular job market is expected to have few openings at the time you graduate.

4 Go online to see the latest edition of the *Occupational Outlook Handbook,* which is an invaluable source of information about the many kinds of jobs currently available and the best job prospects in the future. The online address is www.bls.gov/oco.

Activity

1. In the *Occupational Outlook Handbook* online, go to the section, "Overview of the 2008–18 Projections" and then select "Employment Change by Detailed Occupation." From Table 1: Occupations with the Fastest Growth, identify three occupations that appeal to you and explain why.

   a. _____

   b. _____

   c. _____

2. Of the 20 fastest-growing occupations as listed in Table 1 (and as explained in the paragraph just before the table), what profession accounts for half of the fastest-growing jobs in the economy? Why is this profession growing so rapidly?

   _____

   _____

3. Scroll down to Table 2, "Occupations with the Largest Numerical Growth," and list the top three occupations with the largest numerical growth.

   _____

4. According to Table 2, what educational degree is required for elementary school teachers?

   _____

5. According to Table 2, what is the average salary for a retail salesperson, computer software engineer, and executive secretary/assistant?

   _____

   _____

Short-Term Goals

There is a familiar saying that the longest journey begins with a single step. To achieve your long-term career goal, you must set and work toward a continuing series of short-term goals. These can be as simple as a list of specific objectives that you have for your present semester in college. Activity 1 provides an example—the short-term goals that one student, Allen, set for himself.

Personal and Study Goals

Activity 1

Specific goals can consist of both *personal* and *study* goals. In the spaces beside the items on Allen's list, indicate whether the goal listed is a personal or a study goal.

Allen's Short-Term Goals

1. To get the name and cell phone number of at least two people in each of my classes (_____)

2. To earn a B in my basic math class (_____)

3. To earn a B or better in my writing class (_____)

4. To earn a B in my basic accounting class (_____)

5. To get my motorcycle running again (_____)

6. To see my writing tutor at least once a week (_____)

7. To go out no more than one night during the school week (_____)

8. To use either Saturday or Sunday as a study day each weekend (_____)

You can help yourself succeed in your present semester of college by setting a series of personal and study goals. The goals must be honest ones that you choose yourself—goals that you truly intend to work on and that you have the time to achieve. If necessary, you can change or add to your goals as needed. What matters is that you have a series of definite targets that will give you direction and motivation during the semester. A list of specific goals will help you do the *consistent* work that is needed for success.

Activity 2

Use the following space to set a series of short-term goals for yourself. Indicate in parentheses whether each goal is a personal or a study goal. Set real targets for yourself. At the same time, be realistic about how much you can achieve in one semester.

Goals for the _____ *Semester, 20____*

1. _____
2. _____
3. _____
4. _____
5. _____
6. _____
7. _____
8. _____
9. _____
10. _____

_____

_____

_____

_____

_____

_____

_____

Use the extra space provided if you decide to change or add to your goals. Refer frequently to your goals as the semester progresses. When a goal is completed, cross it out and write the date beside it.

Steps for Achieving Short-Term Goals

At the same time that you set short-term goals, you should decide on specific steps you must take to achieve those goals. By looking closely at what you must do to reach your goals, you can determine whether they are realistic and practical. You can also get a good sense of just how you will reach them.

Look at some of the specific steps Allen decided he must take to reach his goals:

Goal: <u>To take and earn B's in three courses this semester.</u>

Specific steps for achieving this goal:
I will quit my evening job at the Uni-Mart.
I will tell my boss at my day job that I can't work more than twenty hours
     a week.
I will make weekly grocery lists so I'm not running to the store every day.
I will get up early on weekends so I have time to study as well as do my
     laundry and cleaning.
I will get the cell phone numbers of at least two people in each class, so if I
     ever do have to miss a class, I can find out right away what happened.
I will be in bed by 11 P.M. on weeknights.

Activity 3

Now choose three of your most important goals and list specific steps you must take to achieve each of them.

Goal 1: _____

Specific steps for achieving goal 1:

_____

_____

_____

_____

_____

_____

Goal 2: _____

Specific steps for achieving goal 2:

_____

_____

_____

_____

_____

_____

Goal 3: _____

Specific steps for achieving goal 3:

_____

_____

_____

_____

_____

_____

Activity 4

Your instructor may now put you in a group with one or two other students so that you can compare your goals and discuss the steps you plan to take to achieve them. You should try to give each other feedback on what seems realistic about your goals—and what does not. *Or* your instructor may sit down with you individually to review your goals.

Activity 5

Answer the following questions as honestly as you can.

- How important do you think it is that you set specific goals for yourself and consciously work toward those goals?

  Very important _____

  Fairly important _____

  Somewhat important _____

  Unimportant _____

- How important do you think it is to work out the specific steps that you must take to achieve your goals?

  Very important _____

  Fairly important _____

  Somewhat important _____

  Unimportant _____

- Are you already a disciplined person? Or will you have to make a special effort to work consistently toward your goals during the semester?

  _____

- On the basis of your present situation in life and what you know about yourself, what do you think will be your greatest obstacles in reaching your short-term goals?

  _____

  _____

  _____

- How would you rate your chance of success in achieving your short-term goals?

  Excellent _____

  Good _____

  Fair _____

  Uncertain _____

Learning
Survival
Strategies

Note *Over the years, I have spoken with a number of successful students who started college with a course in reading and study skills and then went on to earn their college degrees. Essentially, what I asked them was, "What would you want to say to students who are just starting out in college? What advice would you give? What experiences would it help to share?" The comments of one student, Jean Coleman, were especially helpful. In several conversations I had with Jean, she identified strategies for surviving in college that other students often spoke of as well. Jean's comments are presented mostly in her own words on the pages that follow.*

The Advice and Experience of a Successful Student

"Be Realistic"

The first advice that I'd give to beginning students is "Be realistic about how college will help you get a job." Some students believe that once they have a college degree, the world will be waiting on their doorstep, ready to give them a wonderful job. But the chances are that, unless they've planned, there will be *nobody* on their doorstep.

I remember the way you dramatized this point in our first class, John. You pretended to be a student who had just been handed a college degree. You opened up an imaginary door, stepped through, and peered around in both directions outside. There was nobody to be seen. I understood the point you were making immediately. A college degree in itself isn't enough. We've got to prepare while we're in college to make sure our degree is a marketable one.

At that time I began to think seriously about (1) what I wanted to do in life and (2) whether there were jobs out there for what I wanted to do. I went to the counseling center and said, "I want to learn where the best job opportunities will be in the next ten years." The counselor told me to go online and check the *Occupational Outlook Handbook,* published by the United States government. The handbook provided good information on the kinds of jobs available now and the career fields that will need workers in the future. The counselor also gave me a vocational interest test to see where my skills and interests lay.

The result of my personal career planning was that I graduated from Atlantic Community College with a degree in accounting. I then got a job almost immediately, for I had chosen an excellent employment area. The firm that I worked for paid my tuition as I went on to get my bachelor's degree. Now, the company is paying for my work toward certification as a CPA, and my salary increases regularly.

By way of contrast, I know a woman named Sheila who majored in French. She earned a bachelor's degree with honors in French. After graduation, she spent several unsuccessful months trying to find a job in which she could use her French degree. Sheila eventually wound up going to a specialized school where she trained for six months as a paralegal assistant. She then got a job on the strength of that training—but her years of studying French were of no practical value in her career at all.

I'm not saying that college should serve only as a training ground for a job. People should take some courses just for the sake of learning and for expanding their minds in different directions. At the same time, unless they have a huge amount of money (and few of us are so lucky), they must be ready at some point to take career-oriented courses so that they can survive in the harsh world outside college.

In my own case, I started college at the age of twenty-seven. I was divorced, had a six-year-old son to care for, and was working full time as a hotel night clerk. If I had had my preference, I would have taken a straight liberal arts curriculum. As it was, I did take some general-interest courses—in art, for example. But mainly I was getting ready for the solid job I desperately needed. What I am saying, then, is that students must be realistic. If they will need a job soon after graduation, they should be sure to study in an area where jobs are available.

"Get Organized"

One of the problems that can start a student off in the wrong direction is failing to get organized right at the beginning of the semester. It's funny, but even a disorganized first day—just one day—can set a negative tone for the semester that just seems to snowball. For instance, I have seen students come to the first day of class as if the first class were some kind of unimportant rehearsal. They don't bother to bring pens or notebooks, and they let the important information they're receiving just float by. You get the feeling that they believe they'll catch up later, but they usually don't.

I think students who are disorganized like this have never learned to take responsibility for their own behavior. They have had parents, teachers, and bosses telling them what to do, so they can't cope when they're placed in an atmosphere that says, "Nobody here is going to protect you from the consequences if you don't take care of things yourself." Students like this miss classes, fail to get the notes they missed, or don't know the most basic information, such as where their instructors' offices are. Then they act surprised when their grades take a nosedive—they feel as if they've been cheated because no one "rescued" them with warnings, reminders, or prodding.

I would tell all students to get organized right at the start of school. To help them do this, I would pass out the following checklist of important items:

- Remember that the first meeting of any class is crucial. Bring two pens and a notebook with you, for many instructors not only distribute basic information about assigned textbooks and requirements—they also start lecturing the first day.

- Don't put off getting your books, even if you have to wait in a long, boring line at the bookstore. You will need your books right away if you don't want to fall behind, so make the sacrifice.

- Find out, early in the semester, the names and phone numbers of some students in the class. Students who feel "funny" about this or are too shy to do it are really hurting themselves. If you miss class, it's your responsibility to go *prepared* to the next class. At the college level, you can't get away with saying to a professor, "I don't have the assignment because I was absent" or "Could you tell me what I missed?" If you have some of your classmates' phone numbers or e-mail addresses, you can find out what happened in class and get the notes or assignments you missed. But of course, if you start missing too many classes or showing up late for your classes, just getting the notes won't help you keep up.

- Have a specific place at home for all your school materials. In other words, have some kind of headquarters. You just can't study when you sit down to work and discover that your biology book is in the trunk of your brother's car, your lab notes are in a locker at school, and you can't find the handout the instructor gave you. All school-related materials should be kept somewhere convenient for you—a desk, a worktable, a closet, or a corner. This kind of very basic organization makes a big difference.

- Decide, right from the start, how much work you can handle. If you are taking five courses, working at a full-time job, and caring for two children, for example, you're asking for a nervous breakdown—no matter how organized you are. I heard a good rule of thumb for this, and it seems accurate: For every ten hours per week you work, deduct one course from a full-time college course load. For example, if you don't work, you can do well in five courses; if you work ten hours, you should attempt only four courses; if you work twenty hours, take three courses maximum; and so on. You might have to bend this rule, however, depending on your family responsibilities and the level of difficulty of the courses you are taking.

I think what all this comes down to is that there seem to be two kinds of students—the ones who have a mature, professional attitude toward being a student and the ones who act like children who have to be taken care of. It's important to realize that college instructors aren't baby-sitters or disciplinarians. They want to teach, but they want to teach adults who meet them halfway and take responsibility for themselves. When I have seen students who have the attitude "I'm sitting in class, so I've done my job—now you make me learn something," I have wanted to ask them, "What are you doing here?" They just never accept, or choose to ignore, the fact that *they*—not the instructors—are the ones who determine whether they will succeed or fail.

"Know How You Learn"

I remember very well writing my first English paper for college. I was determined to do it right. I sat down at my desk with my nice new pen and a blank sheet of paper in front of me—and twenty minutes later I was still sitting there, and the paper was still blank. I began to panic. How was I ever going to get a five-paragraph essay done when I couldn't write a single sentence?

To calm myself down, I walked to the kitchen to make myself a cup of tea. As I waited for the water to boil, I paced around the kitchen, thinking about the paper I had to write. I've always had the habit of talking to myself when I am alone, and in my anxiety about the paper, I began lecturing to myself out loud. "Now, this paper is about *The Great Gatsby*," I told myself. "I read the book. I liked it. What do I want to say about it?" For the next ten minutes or so I walked around my kitchen, sipping my tea and talking to myself about *The Great Gatsby*. Anyone watching me might have thought I was crazy, but I didn't care. I realized that I was doing what I couldn't do when I was sitting at my desk. I was "writing" my paper. By the time I sat down again, I had my essay almost completely composed in my head. All I had to do was write it down.

I had discovered something important about myself. I learn most easily when I'm talking or listening. That's why I have always liked classes that feature plenty of lectures and discussions more than classes that rely heavily on independent reading. As I got to know other students better, I realized that many people favor one learning style over another. For instance, my friend Darlene could never compose a paper by "talking it" as I do. But she is a wizard at the computer keyboard. She tells me, "My thoughts come together as I'm typing. Until I sit down and do the physical act of writing, I honestly don't know what I'm going to say."

I guess a learning specialist would say that I've got an auditory learning style—one that emphasizes hearing. Darlene's learning style is more tactile—she has to touch things, like a pen or the computer keyboard, in order to learn. People who absorb ideas easily through reading have a more visual style—they learn easily through what they see. The point is that not all of us learn in the same ways. If you recognize your own learning style, you can take advantage of it—whether that style emphasizes hearing, touch, sight, or another sense or combination of senses. Don't think that your style is wrong if it happens to be different from your roommate's! The important thing is whether it works for you.

"Persist"

The older I get, the more I see that life visits some hard experiences on us. There are times for each of us when simple survival becomes a deadly serious matter. We must then learn to persist—to struggle through each day and wait for better times to come, as they invariably do.

I think of one of my closest friends, Neil. After graduating from high school with me, Neil spent two years working as a stock boy at a local department store in order to save money for college tuition. He then went to the guidance office at the small college in our town. Incredibly, the counselor there told him, "Your IQ is not high enough to do college work." Neil decided to go anyway, and he earned his degree in five years—with a year out to care for his father, who had had a stroke one day at work.

Neil then got a job as a manager of a regional beauty supply firm. He met a woman who owned a salon, got married, and soon had two children. Three years later he found out that his wife was having an affair. I'll never forget the day Neil came over and sat at my kitchen table and told me what he had learned. He always seemed so much in control, but that morning he lowered his head into his hands and cried. "What's the point?" he kept saying in a low voice over and over to himself.

But Neil has endured. He divorced his wife, won custody of his children, and learned how to be a single parent. Recently, Neil and I got letters informing us of the tenth reunion of our high school graduating class. Included was a short questionnaire for us to fill out that ended with this item, "What has been your outstanding accomplishment since graduation?" Neil wrote, "My outstanding accomplishment is that I have survived." I have a feeling that most of our high school classmates, ten years out in the world, would have no trouble understanding the sad truth of his statement.

I can think of people who started college with me who had not yet learned, like Neil, the basic skill of endurance. Life hit some of them with unexpected low punches and knocked them to the floor. Stunned and dismayed, they didn't fight back and eventually dropped out of school. I remember Yvonne, still a teenager, whose parents involved her in their ugly divorce battle. Yvonne started missing classes and gave up at midsemester. There was Jeff, whose girlfriend broke off their relationship. Jeff stopped coming to class, and by the end of the semester he was failing most of his courses. I also recall Nelson, whose old car kept breaking down. After Nelson put his last $200 into it, the brakes failed and needed to be replaced. Overwhelmed by his continuing troubles with his car, Nelson dropped out of school. And there was Rita, discouraged by her luck of the draw with instructors and courses. In sociology, she had an instructor who wasn't able to express ideas clearly. She also had a mathematics instructor who talked too fast and seemed not to care at all about whether his students learned. To top it off, Rita's adviser had enrolled her in an economics course that put her to sleep. Rita told me she had expected college to be an exciting place, but instead she was getting busywork assignments and trying to cope with hostile or boring instructors. Rita decided to drop her mathematics course, and that must have set something in motion in her head, for she soon dropped her other courses as well.

In my experience, younger students seem more prone to dropping out than do older students. I think some younger students are still in the process of learning that life slams people around without warning. I'm sure they feel that being knocked about is especially unfair because the work of college is hard enough without having to cope with some of life's special hardships.

In some situations, withdrawing from college may be the best response. But there are going to be times in college when students—young or old—must simply determine, "I am going to persist." They should remember that no matter how hard their lives may be, there are many other people out there who are quietly having great difficulties also. I think of Dennis, a boy in my introductory psychology class who lived mostly on peanut butter and discount-store white bread for almost a semester in his freshman year. And I remember Estelle, who came to school because she needed a job to support her sons when her husband, who was dying of leukemia, would no longer be present. These are especially dramatic examples of the faith and hope that are sometimes necessary for us to persist.

"Be Positive"

A lot of people are their own worst enemies. They regard themselves as unlikely to succeed in college and often feel that there have been no accomplishments in their lives. In my first year of college, especially, I saw people get down on themselves all too quickly. There were two students in my developmental mathematics class who failed the first quiz and seemed to give up immediately. From that day on, they walked into the classroom carrying defeat on their shoulders the way other students carried textbooks under their arms. I'd look at them slouching in their seats, not even taking notes, and think, "What terrible things have gone on in their lives that they have quit already? They have so little faith in their ability to learn that they're not even trying." Both students hung on until about midsemester. When they disappeared for good, no one took much notice, for they had already disappeared in spirit after that first test.

They are not the only people in whom I have seen the poison of self-doubt do its ugly work. I have seen others with resignation in their eyes and have wanted to shake them by the shoulders and say, "You are not dead. Be proud and pleased that you have brought yourself here to college. Many people would not have gotten so far. Be someone. Breathe. Hope. Act." Such people should refuse to use self-doubt as an excuse for not trying. They should roll up their sleeves and get to work. They should start taking notes in class and trying to learn. They should get a tutor, go to the learning center, see a counselor. If they honestly and fully try and still can't handle a course, only then should they drop it. Above all, they should not lapse into being "zombie students"—ones who have given up in their heads but persist in hanging on for months, just going through the motions of trying.

Nothing but a little time is lost through being positive and giving school your best shot. On the other hand, people who let self-doubt limit their efforts may lose the opportunity to test their abilities to the fullest.

"Grow"

I don't think that people really have much choice about whether to grow in their lives. Not to be open to growth is to die a little each day. Grow or die—it's as simple as that.

I have a friend, Jackie, who, when she's not working, can almost always be found at home or at her mother's house. Jackie eats too much and watches TV too much. I sometimes think that when she swings open her apartment door in response to my knock, I'll be greeted by her familiar chubby body with an eight-inch-screen television set occupying the place where her head used to be.

Jackie seems quietly desperate. There is no growth or plan for growth in her life. I've said to her, "Go to school and study for a job you'll be excited about." She says, "It'll take me forever." Once Jackie said to me, "The favorite time of my life was when I was a teenager. I would lie on my bed listening to music and I would dream. I felt I had enormous power, and there seemed no way that life would stop me from realizing my biggest dreams. Now that power doesn't seem possible to me anymore."

I feel that Jackie must open some new windows in her life. If she does not, her spirit is going to die. There are many ways to open new windows, and college is one of them. For this reason, I think people who are already in school should stay long enough to give it a chance. No one should turn down lightly such an opportunity for growth.

In Conclusion

Maybe I can put all I've said into perspective by describing briefly what my life is like now. I have inner resources that I did not have when I was newly divorced. I have a secure future with the accounting firm where I work. My son is doing okay in school. I have friends. I am successful and proud and happy. I have my fears and my loneliness and my problems and my pains, to say the least, but essentially I know that I have made it. I have survived and done more than survive. I am tough, not fragile, and I can rebound if hard blows land. I feel passionately that all of us can control our own destinies. I urge every beginning student to use well the chances that college affords. Students should plan for a realistic career, get themselves organized, learn to persist, be positive, and open themselves to growth. In such ways, they can help themselves find happiness and success in this perilous but wonderful world of ours.

■ Questions to Consider

In groups of three or four, discuss the questions that follow. Every person in the group should try to contribute. The more honest you can be in sharing experiences, the more meaningful and valuable the discussion will be.

1. Do you know yet what kind of work you want to do after college? If your answer is *no,* have you visited the counseling center to take a vocational interest test?

2. Are you thinking actively about possible careers and getting information on those careers? If your answer is *yes,* have you checked with the counseling

center or instructors in the field or through your own reading about whether there will be good job opportunities available at the time you graduate?

3. Do you know any people with a recent two- or four-year college degree? How successful have they been in getting jobs? On the basis of their experiences, what areas seem to offer good job opportunities?

4. People often limit themselves by taking only career-oriented courses in college. Are there any courses you plan to take just for the sake of learning?

5. Were you aware of all the tips Jean Coleman discusses in her section on getting organized? Which of her suggestions do you practice, and which ones have you ignored? Describe how well or poorly your actions compare with the habits that Coleman recommends.

6. What is your favorite learning style? Is it like one that Jean Coleman describes, or do you have a learning style that is completely your own? Explain.

7. Are any people you know like the four Jean Coleman describes on page 34 who dropped out of school when their lives became very hard? What do you think might have helped them decide to stay in school?

8. Are there any students you know who continued in school despite tough luck? What kinds of struggles did they have?

9. Do you know any students whose feelings of inferiority are keeping them from making an honest effort to learn in college? What do you think students with self-doubts could do to become more positive?

10. Do you know any "zombie students" like the ones the writer describes on page 35—students who are going through the motions of being college students but are not really committed to study? What are some of the ways they are deluding themselves?

11. Describe one person you know well who is open to growth in life and one person who is not open to such growth. How do they show their willingness or reluctance to grow in their everyday lives?

Your instructor may ask you to write a paper that responds *in detail* to one of the preceding questions.

Part Two
Study Skills

Preview

Part Two presents study skills that you need if you are to do well in your courses. Each skill is explained and illustrated, and a number of activities are given to help you practice and master it. "Taking Classroom Notes" lists a number of hints for note-taking, explains how to study your class notes, and discusses handwriting and listening efficiency. In "Time Control and Concentration," you will learn several ways to make better use of your time and to develop the persistence in your work that is vital to success in school. "Textbook Study I" describes a four-step method you can use to read and study chapters in your textbooks. "Textbook Study II" gives you practice in that method with short and medium-length textbook passages. "Textbook Study III" shows you how to apply the method to an entire textbook chapter. In "Building a Powerful Memory," you will learn seven steps you can take to improve your memory. "Taking Objective Exams" and "Taking Essay Exams" show you how to prepare for both kinds of exams and explain test-taking techniques. Finally, "Using Research Skills" shows you how to use the Internet and the popular search engine Google, how to find books in your library, and how to proceed when writing a research paper.

Taking Classroom Notes

Taking Classroom Notes: In Real Life

Read the profile that follows. Then ask yourself these questions:

- Why does Cheryl believe it's important to write down notes rather than just listen carefully?
- What is one of Cheryl's note-taking tips that I plan to try?
- Have you or someone you know been faced with a learning disability? What ways did you or your friend cope academically?

Student Profile: Cheryl Parker

"If you get a good union job at a factory and work your way up, you'll do okay. You'll be able to support yourself and a family." This was the advice that Cheryl Parker was given in high school. According to the standardized tests she took, she was "slow." She wasn't college material.

Cheryl believed what she was told. As soon as she graduated from high school, she found full-time work with a company that manufactured clothing. Always a hard worker, she eventually moved up into the company's printing department. The years passed. Occasionally Cheryl would see a newspaper article or hear a television news report about learning disabilities—disorders that can keep even highly intelligent people from doing well in school. "I wonder if that's what happened to me," Cheryl would sometimes think.

Continued

Seventeen years after Cheryl started her job, the clothing company declared bankruptcy. "I realized I was at a fork in the road," she says today. "Would I take another full-time job and just keep going the way I'd been going? Or would I challenge myself by going back to school?"

Cheryl made her decision. She approached a counselor at Rio Hondo Community College in Whittier, California, and asked two questions: Could she be tested for a learning disorder? And could she enroll in a remedial English course? The counselor, Judy Marks, encouraged Cheryl on both counts. Cheryl took the test and enrolled in a developmental course taught by Ms. Marks herself. "By the time my test results came back, I was already hooked on school," Cheryl remembers.

Cheryl's test results showed that she was severely dyslexic—a condition that "scrambles" the perception of written words. Suddenly, Cheryl's problems in high school made sense. "It wasn't that I didn't study—I did! It wasn't that I didn't know the material—I did!" she recalls. "But it took me so much longer than the average student to read material and, especially, to write out answers in exams. It was such a relief to know there was a reason, that it wasn't that I was mentally 'slow.'"

Once Cheryl's dyslexia was identified, she and her instructors were able to make the accommodations she needed. She was given extra time to take examinations. She was also allowed to record lectures. Most importantly of all, Cheryl now believed in her own ability. She knew she could find ways around the obstacles that faced her.

Of all the skills Cheryl has developed in her college career, she points to note-taking as perhaps the most important of all. "I've always been an excellent listener. With my disability, I've *had* to become one," she explains. "But I've realized that *no one* can listen well enough to rely on memory alone. There's something about the act of actually writing notes down that helps them stick in your mind. Good notes are absolutely essential to college success."

Continued

Cheryl has a number of tips to share regarding note-taking:

- "First, I sit in the front row of every class. And not only in the front row, but in the *middle* of the front row," she explains. "I need not only to *hear* what the instructor's saying but to *see* everything—her gestures, her posture, her facial expressions. Her body language is as important as her words in telling me what is most important about what she's saying."

- "Next, I record lectures. Even though I've taken notes throughout class, I replay the lecture that same night while it's still fresh in my mind and fill in anything that I've missed. Because I can stop and restart the recording, I can write very clearly, without hurrying."

- "When the instructor uses the blackboard, I write down everything she writes, whether it seems important at the moment or not. When an instructor bothers to write something on the board, it's often in the form of a list—and chances are good that this list is going to show up on the next exam."

- "This may not apply to people who aren't dyslexic, but occasionally I just won't be able to recognize a word on the board, even if I'm familiar with it. When that happens, I ask a classmate what it says. But rather than say 'I'm dyslexic and I can't read that,' I'll fake it a little by saying, 'I can't make that out—is that *a* or *e* or *o*?'"

- "If the instructor uses an overhead projector, I can rarely take complete notes on a transparency before she removes it. Rather than panic because I can't get it all, I ask to borrow it once she's finished. I stay a few minutes after class and copy it down."

- "My notes are full of symbols to myself. I'll write a big star to emphasize an important word. Or I'll underline or circle major points. I'll write a question mark in the margin to remind myself to ask the instructor to clarify something later."

- "Occasionally I'll ask a classmate who I know takes good notes to share his or her notes with me. I'll just compare our notes to make sure we're picking up the same major points. If so, I feel reassured, and if I'm missing something the other student has, I know I need to check into that."

Continued

- "After an exam, even if I've done well on it, I go back to my notes to compare how closely they mirror what was on the test. If they don't overlap a lot with what was on the exam, then I know I have to change my strategy for taking notes in that class. I hear a lot of students say, 'Well, that test is over and there's nothing I can learn from it anymore.' There's always something you can learn, especially from your mistakes."

Cheryl graduated from Rio Hondo College with a 4.0 grade point average during her career there. She went on to study at California State Long Beach University, working toward a bachelor's degree in criminal justice.

Cheryl Parker slow? Yeah—slow like a race horse.

The Importance of Attending Class

If you really want to do well in a course, you must promise yourself that you will go to class faithfully and take good notes. This chapter will offer a series of tips on how to take effective classroom notes. However, the hints will be of no value if you do not attend class. The importance of *regular class attendance* cannot be emphasized enough. Students who cut class rarely do well in college.

The alternatives to class attendance—reading the text or using someone else's notes—can seldom substitute for the experience of being in class and hearing the instructor talk about key ideas in the course. These ideas are often the ones you will be expected to know on exams.

If you do not attend classes regularly, you may be making an unconscious decision that you do not want to attend college at this time. If you think this may be how you feel, talk to a counselor, an instructor, or a friend. Another person can often help you clarify your own thoughts and feelings so that you can achieve a perspective on your situation.

- Have you made a personal decision (be honest!) to attend all your classes regularly? _____

- If not, are you willing to think about why you are reluctant to make the commitment to college work? _____

Thirteen Hints for Taking Effective Classroom Notes

Hint 1: Keep a Written Record

Whether by hand or by typing on a laptop or other electronic device such as an iPad, keep a written record of each class. It's important that you write down the material covered because forgetting begins almost immediately. Studies have shown that within two weeks you probably will forget 80 percent or more of what you have heard. And in four weeks you are lucky if 5 percent remains! The significance of these facts is so crucial that the point bears repeating: To guard against the relentlessness of forgetting, you must write down much of the information presented in class. Later, you will study your notes so that you understand and remember the ideas presented in class. And the more complete your notes are when you review them, the more likely you are to master the material.

How many notes should you take? If you pay attention in class, you will soon develop an instinct for what is meaningful and what is not. If you are unsure whether certain terms, facts, and ideas are significant, here is a good rule to follow: *When in doubt, write it down.* This doesn't mean you should (or could) get down every word, but you should be prepared to do a good deal of writing in class. Also, do not worry if you don't understand everything you record in your notes. Sometimes an instructor will phrase an idea several different ways, and it may turn out that it is the third version of the idea that you clearly understand. Later, it is easy to cross out the material that you don't need, but it is impossible to recover material you never recorded in the first place. Keep in mind that writing too much, rather than too little, may mean the difference between passing and failing a course or between a higher grade and a lower one.

- Explain briefly why you should keep a written record of each class.

_____

_____

_____

_____

Hint 2: Sit Where You'll Be Seen

Sit where the instructor will always see you, and where you can see the blackboard clearly and easily. Your position near or at the front will help you stay tuned in to what the instructor does in class. If you sit behind someone, are hidden in a corner, or are otherwise out of the instructor's line of vision, it may be a reflection of your attitude—either you are worried that you may be noticed and called on (a common anxiety) or you don't really want to be in the classroom at all (something worth thinking about).

Analyze your attitude. If you're hiding, be aware that you're hiding and try to understand why. It is all right not to want to be in a class; instructors can be boring and subjects uninteresting. However, the danger in such cases is that you may slide into a passive state where you won't listen or take notes. Don't fool yourself. If a class is deadly, there is all the more reason to make yourself take good notes—that way you will pass the course and get out of the class once and for all.

- Explain briefly two reasons why you should sit near the front.

  _____

  _____

  _____

  _____

Hint 3: Do Some Advance Reading

Ideally, read in advance about the topic to be discussed in class. All too often, students don't read assigned textbook material on a topic until after class is over. Lacking the necessary background, they have trouble understanding the new ideas discussed in class. However, if they have made an initial breakthrough on a topic by doing some advance reading, they will be able to listen and take notes more easily and with greater understanding. And they should be able to write more organized and effective notes because they will have a general sense of the topic.

If you don't know what the next topic is going to be, check with your instructor at the end of the preceding class. Simply ask, "Is there a chapter in the textbook that I can read in advance of your next class? I'd like to get a head start on what you're going to cover." At the least, you are going to make a good impression on the instructor, who will appreciate your seriousness and interest.

In particular, try to read the textbook in advance when the subject is very difficult. Reading in advance is also a good idea if you have spelling problems that hinder note-taking. As you read through the text, write down key terms and recurring words that may come up in the lecture and that you might have trouble spelling.

• Explain briefly why you should read your textbook in advance of a lecture.

_____

_____

_____

_____

Hint 4: Record Notes Systematically

1   Use full-size 8½- by 11-inch paper. Do *not* use a small note tablet. As explained below, you will need the margin space provided by full-size paper. Also, on a single page of full-size paper you can often see groups of related ideas that might not be apparent spread over several small pages.

2   Use a ballpoint pen. You will often need to write quickly—something that you cannot do as well with a pencil or a felt-tip pen. (Don't worry about making mistakes with a pen that makes marks you can't erase. Just cross out the mistakes!)

3   Keep all the notes from each course together in a separate section of a notebook. Use a loose-leaf binder with sections indicated by dividers and index tabs, or use a large spiral notebook that has several sections. A spiral notebook is simpler. But a loose-leaf binder has the advantage of letting you insert handout sheets and supplementary notes at appropriate points. If you use a binder, you may want to leave previous notes safe at home and just bring to each class the last day or so of notes and some blank paper.

4   Date each day's notes.

5   Take notes on one side of the page only and leave space at the top of the page and at the left-hand margin. (You might use notebook paper that has a light red line down the left side.) Using only one side of the paper eliminates the bother, when you are studying, of having to flip pages over and then flip them back to follow the development of an idea.

Leaving wide margins gives you space to add to your notes if desired. You may, for example, write in ideas taken from your textbook or other sources. Also, the margins can be used to prepare study notes (see pages 53–56) that will help you learn the material.

6   Write legibly. When you prepare for a test, you want to spend your time studying—not deciphering your handwriting.

7   To save time, abbreviate recurring terms. Put a key to abbreviated words in the top margin of your notes. For example, in a biology class, *ch* could stand for *chromosome;* in a psychology class, *o c* could stand for *operant conditioning.* (When a lecture is over, you may want to go back and fill in the words you have abbreviated.)

Also abbreviate the following common words, using the symbols shown:

+	= and	def	= definition
w/	= with	∴	= therefore
eg	= for example	info	= information
ex	= example	1, 2, 3	= one, two, three, etc.

Note, too, that you can often omit words like *a*, *and*, and *the*.

8   Note prominently exams or quizzes that are announced, as well as assignments that the instructor gives. It's a good idea to circle exam dates and put a large *A* for *assignment* in the margin. (Be sure you have a definite system for keeping track of assignments. Some students record them on a separate small notepad; others record them at the back of the notebook devoted to a given course.)

• What do you consider the three most helpful suggestions for recording notes?

_____

_____

_____

_____

Hint 5: Use an Outline for Notes

Try to write your notes in the form of an outline, as described below. By following the outline form, you'll be able to tell at a glance which are the most important points in your notes and which are less essential, supportive details.

Start writing main points at the margin of the page. Indent (skip a few spaces from the margin) secondary ideas and supporting details. Further indent material subordinate to secondary points.

Main points start at the margin.
 Secondary points and supporting details are indented, like this line.
 Material subordinate to secondary points is indented further.

Definitions, for example, are essential to your understanding of the material, so they should always start at the margin. When a list of terms is presented, the heading should also start at the margin, but each item in the series should be set in slightly from the margin. Examples, too, should be indented under the point they illustrate.

Here is another organizational aid: When the instructor changes topics or moves from one aspect of an idea to another, show this shift by skipping a line or two, leaving a clearly visible white space.

In the fast-paced lecture, you won't always be able to tell what is a main point and what is secondary material. Be ready, though, to use the outline technique of indentation and extra space whenever you can. They are the first steps toward organizing class material.

- Explain briefly what is meant by *indentation*.

_____

_____

_____

_____

Hint 6: Be Alert for Signals

Watch for signals of importance:

1 Write down whatever your instructor puts on the board. Ideally, *print* such material in capital letters. If you don't have time to print, write as you usually do and put the letters *OB* in the margin to indicate that the material was written on the board. Later, when you review your notes, you will know which ideas the instructor emphasized. The chances are good that they will come up on exams.

2 Always write down definitions and enumerations. Most people instinctively write down definitions—explanations of key terms in the subject they are learning. But they often ignore enumerations, which are often equally important. An *enumeration* is simply a list of items (marked 1, 2, 3, etc., or with other symbols) that fit under a particular heading. (See also page 324.)

Instructors use enumerations, or lists, to show the relationships among ideas. Being aware of enumerations will help you organize material as you take notes. Enumerations are signaled in such ways as "The four steps in the process are . . . "; "There were three reasons for . . . "; "Five characteristics of . . . "; "The two effects were . . . "; and so on. When you write a list, always mark the items 1, 2, 3, or use other appropriate symbols. Also, always be sure to include a clear heading that explains what a list is about. For example, if you list and number six kinds of defense mechanisms, make sure you write at the top of the list the heading "Kinds of Defense Mechanisms."

3   Your instructor may say, "This is an important reason . . . "; or "A point that will keep coming up later . . . "; or "The chief cause was . . . "; or "The basic idea here is . . . "; or "Don't forget that . . . "; or "Pay special attention to . . . "; and so on. Be sure to write down the important statements announced by these and other emphasis words, and write in the margin *imp* or some other mark (such as * or ✓ or →) to show their importance.

4   If your instructor repeats a point, you can usually assume it is important. You might write *R* for *repeated* in the margin so that you will know later that your instructor stressed this idea.

5   An instructor's voice may slow down, become louder, or otherwise signal that you are expected to write down exactly what is being said, word for word. Needless to say, do so!

- Which two signals of importance do you think will be most helpful for you to remember?

_____

_____

_____

_____

Hint 7: Write Down Examples

Write down any examples the instructor provides, and mark them with *ex.* The examples help you understand complex and abstract points. If you don't mark them with *ex,* you are likely to forget their purpose when you later review them for study. You may not have to write down every example that illustrates an idea, but you should record at least one example that makes a point clear.

Hint 8: Write Down Details That Connect or Explain

Be sure to write down the details that connect or explain main points. Too many students copy only the major points the instructor puts on the board. They do not realize that as time passes, they may forget the specifics that serve as bridges connecting key ideas. Be sure, then, to record the connecting details the instructor provides. That way you are more apt to remember the relationships among the major points in your notes.

In science and mathematics classes especially, students often fail to record the explanations that make formulas or numerical problems meaningful. Their notes may consist only of the letters and numbers the instructor chalked on the board. But to understand how the letters and numbers are related, they should also write down accompanying explanations and details.

Always take advantage of the connections instructors often make at the beginning or end of a class. They may review material already covered and preview what is to come. Write down such overviews when they are presented and label them *review* or *preview,* as the case may be. An instructor's summaries or projections will help the course come together for you.

- How often do you write down connections between ideas?

    _____ Frequently   _____ Sometimes   _____ Almost never

Hint 9: Leave Some Blank Spaces

Leave blank spaces for items or ideas you miss. Right after class, ask another student (or the instructor) to help you fill in the gaps. Ideally, you should find a person in each course who will agree to be your note-taking partner—someone with whom you can compare and fill in notes after a class. If another person is not available, you might want to tape each class and play back the tape right away to get any missing material. (Don't ever, though, fall into the trap of relying only on a tape recorder to take most of your notes. In no time at all, you'll have hours and hours of tape to go through—time you probably cannot afford to take. Use a tape only to help you fill in occasional gaps.)

When you do fall behind in note-taking during class, don't give up and just stop writing. Try to get down what seem to be the main ideas rather than supporting facts and details. You may be able to fill in the supporting material later.

Hint 10: Ask Questions

Don't hesitate to ask the instructor questions if certain points are confusing to you. Probably, other students have the same questions but are reluctant to ask to have the material clarified. Remember that instructors look favorably on students who show interest and curiosity.

- How often do you ask questions in class?

    _____ Frequently

    _____ Sometimes

    _____ Almost never

Hint 11: Take Notes during Discussions

Do not stop taking notes during discussion periods. Many valuable ideas may come up during informal discussions, ideas that your instructor may not present formally later on. If your instructor puts notes on the board during a class discussion, it's a good sign that the material is important. If he or she pursues or draws out a discussion in a given direction, it's a clue that you should be taking notes. And don't forget the advice in hint 1 on page 45: When in doubt, write it down.

Hint 12: Take Notes Right Up to the End of Class

Do not stop taking notes toward the end of a class. Because of time spent on discussions, instructors may have to cram important points they want to cover into the last minutes of a class. Be ready to write as rapidly as you can to get down this final rush of ideas.

Be prepared, also, to resist the fatigue that may settle in during class. As a lecture proceeds, the possibility of losing attention increases. You do not want to snap out of a daydream only to realize that an instructor is halfway into an important idea and you haven't even begun writing.

- Are you one of the many students whose note-taking slows down at the end of a class? _____

Hint 13: Review Your Notes Soon

Go over your notes soon after class. While the material is still clear in your mind, make your notes as clear as possible. A day later may be too late, because forgetting sets in almost at once.

As far as possible, make sure that your punctuation is clear, that unfinished ideas are completed, and that all words are readable and correctly spelled. You may also want to write out completely words that you abbreviated during the lecture. Wherever appropriate, add connecting statements and other comments to clarify the material. Make sure important items—material on the board, definitions, enumerations, and so on—are clearly marked. Improve the organization, if necessary, so that you can see at a glance the differences between main points and supporting material as well as any relationships among the main points.

This review does more than make your notes clear: It is also a vital step in the process of mastering the material. During class, you have almost certainly been too busy taking notes to absorb all the ideas. Now, as you review the notes, you can roll up your sleeves and wrestle with the ideas presented and think about the relationships among them. You can, in short, do the work needed to reach the point where you can smile and say, "Yes, I understand—and everything I understand is written down clearly in my notes."

- Explain briefly why you should go over your notes soon after class.

_____

_____

_____

_____

How to Study Class Notes

The best time to start studying your notes is within a day after taking them. Because of the mind's tendency to forget material rapidly, a few minutes of study soon after a class will give you more learning for less time and effort than almost any other technique you can practice.

One Effective Method for Studying Class Notes

Here is one effective way to study your notes:

1   Use the margin space at the side (or top) of each page. Jot down in the margin a series of key words or phrases from your notes. These key words or phrases, known as *recall words,* will help you pull together and remember the important ideas on the page.

On page 55 are notes from a business course. Take the time now to look them over carefully. You will notice in the side margin the recall words that the student, Janet, used for studying this page of notes.

2   To test yourself on the material, turn the recall words in the margin into questions. For instance, Janet asked herself, "What is the origin of economics?" After she could recite the answer without looking at it, she asked herself, "What is the definition of economics?" Janet then went back and retested herself on the first question. When she could recite the answers to both the first and second questions, she went on to the third one.

Shown below are most of the questions that Janet asked herself. Fill in the missing questions.

What is the origin of economics?
What is the definition of economics?

_____

What is the definition of economic resources?

What are the two kinds of property resources and their definitions?
What are the three kinds of human resources and their definitions?

Janet tested herself on each of the seven questions and retested herself on those from earlier lectures, until she could recite all of them from memory. (For more information on repeated self-testing, see page 206.)

This approach, if it is pursued regularly, will help you remember the material covered in your classes. With such a study method, you will not be left with a great deal of material to organize and learn right before an exam. Instead, you will be able to devote preexam time to a final intensive review of the subject.

Another Good Method for Studying Class Notes

Some students prefer to write out on separate sheets of paper the material they want to learn. They prepare study sheets that often use a question-and-answer format. The very act of writing out study notes is itself a step toward remembering the material. Shown on page 56 is a study sheet that Janet could have prepared.

Two Special Skills That Help Note-Taking

Two special skills that will help you take effective classroom notes are handwriting efficiency and listening efficiency. The following pages explain and offer practice in these skills.

Increasing Handwriting Efficiency

Activity 1

To check your handwriting efficiency, write as fast as you can for ten minutes. Don't stop for anything. Don't worry about spelling, punctuation, erasing mistakes, or finding exact words. If you get stuck for words, write "I am looking for something to say" or repeat words until something comes. You have two objectives in this rapid-writing activity: to write as many words as you can in ten minutes (you will be asked to count the words later) and to write words legibly enough so that you can still understand them several weeks from now.

Count the number of words you have written in the ten minutes and record the number here: _____.

Janet's Classroom Notes

	Business 101 11-29-08 ec = economic(s) res = resource
Origin of ec	Economics—from Greek words meaning "HOUSE" and "TO MANAGE." Meaning gradually extended to cover management not only of household but of business and governments.
Def of ec	Ec (definition)—STUDY OF HOW SCARCE RESOURCES ARE ALLOCATED IN A SOCIETY OF UNLIMITED WANTS.
	Every society provides goods + services; these are available in limited quantities + so have value.
Imp assumption	One of the most imp. assumptions of ec: Though res of world are limited, wants of people are not. This means ec system can never produce enough to satisfy everyone completely.
Def of ec res	Ec res—all factors that go into production of goods + services.
2 types of ec res	Two types:
	1. PROPERTY RES—2 kinds:
2 kinds of property res + defs	a. LAND—all natural res (land, timber, water, oil, minerals).
	b. CAPITAL—all machinery, tools, equipment, + building needed to produce goods + distribute them to consumers.
3 kinds of human res + defs	2. HUMAN RES—3 kinds
	a. LABOR—all physical and mental talents needed to produce goods + services.
	b. MANAGEMENT ABILITY—talent needed to bring together land, capital, + labor to produce goods + services.
	c. TECHNOLOGY—accumulated fund of knowledge which helps in production of goods + services.

Sample Study Sheet

What is the origin of economics?

From Greek words "house" and "manage." Word gradually extended to include business and government.

What is the definition of economics?

Study of how scarce resources are allocated in a society of unlimited wants.

What is an important assumption of economics?

Resources are limited but people's wants are not.

What is the definition of economic resources?

All the factors that go into production of goods + services.

What are the two types of economic resources?

Property + human resources.

What are the two kinds of property resources and their definitions?

a. Land—all natural resources (land, timber, water, oil, minerals).

b. Capital—all the machinery, tools, equipment, and building needed to produce goods + distribute them to consumers.

What are the three kinds of human resources and their definitions?

a. Labor—all physical and mental talents needed to produce goods + services.

b. Management ability—talent needed to bring together land, capital, + labor to produce goods + services.

c. Technology—accumulated fund of knowledge which helps in production of goods + services.

Handwriting Speed and Legibility   In Activity 1, you should have been able to write at least 250 legible words in ten minutes—and ideally 100 or so more than that. Handwriting speed is important because it is basic to effective note-taking in fast-moving lectures. If you cannot write quickly enough, you are likely to miss valuable ideas presented in such classes. Also, you may have trouble writing out full answers on essay exams. And in either situation, if your handwriting is not legible, there is hardly any point in writing at all.

Improving Speed   There are several steps you can take to improve your handwriting speed.

One step is to practice *rapid writing*—writing nonstop for ten or fifteen minutes at a time about whatever comes into your head. Try to increase the number of pages you fill with words in the limited time period. With several practice sessions, you should be able to increase your handwriting speed significantly.

Another way to increase speed is to use abbreviations. Abbreviate words that occur repeatedly in a lecture class, and put a key for such words in the top margin of your notes. For example, if the name *Linnaeus* keeps recurring in a botany class, at the top of the page write *L = Linnaeus,* and from then on in your notes that day simply use *L.*

- What keys could you make for a psychology class on Skinner and behaviorism?

  _____   _____

Following is a list of other symbols that can be made part of a general "shorthand" for your writing. (Note that you can often omit *a, and, the,* and other connecting words.)

$$+ \ = \ and$$
$$w/ \ = \ with$$
$$eg \ = \ for\ example$$
$$ex \ = \ example$$
$$def \ = \ definition$$
$$imp \ = \ important$$
$$ind \ = \ individual$$
$$info \ = \ information$$
$$sc \ = \ science$$
$$soc \ = \ sociology$$
$$psy \ = \ psychology$$
$$1,\ 2,\ 3, \ = \ one,\ two,\ three,\ (etc.)$$

Finally, you can write faster if you streamline your handwriting by eliminating unnecessary high and low loops in letters. For example,

Instead of	Write	Instead of	Write
b	*b*	*k*	K
d	*d*	*l*	l
f	*f*	*p*	P
g	*g*	*t*	t
h	*h*	*y*	y

You will find that this streamlined, print-style writing is learned easily and will help you write faster.

- Go back and put the numbers 1, 2, and 3 in front of the three methods described for increasing handwriting speed.

Improving Legibility   To improve and maintain legibility, check a sample of your writing for the four common types of faulty handwriting illustrated here. Or give your writing sample to someone else to analyze for handwriting faults.

1   Overlapping letters from one line to the next. For example:

One of the main types of faulty handwriting is the overlapping of letters from one line to the next.

Note the improvement in legibility when this fault is eliminated:

One of the main types of faulty handwriting is the overlapping of letters from one line to the next.

2   Slanting letters in more than one direction. For example:

Another kind of faulty handwriting is to slant letters in all directions instead of just one.

Note how legibility improves when slants are consistent:

Another kind of faulty handwriting is to slant letters in all directions instead of just one.

3 Making decorative capitals or loops. For example:

The use of decorative capitals and loops may result in a script that

You can greatly improve legibility by *printing* capital letters and restraining your loop letters.

4 Miswriting the letters *a*, *e*, *r*, *n*, and *t*. Common errors include writing the letter *e* like *i* (closing the loop) and putting a loop in nonloop letters like *i* and *t*. Check your handwriting to be sure you form these letters clearly. Also, look for other letters that you may miswrite consistently.

To improve legibility, follow two other tips as well. First, always use a ballpoint pen rather than a pencil. A dull-edged pencil will slow down your writing speed and hinder legibility. You can buy a Bic pen for 99 cents. Second, be sure to hold your pen between the thumb and index finger, resting it against the middle finger. Don't grip the pen tightly, but hold it just firmly enough to keep it from slipping. And don't hold it, as some people do, too close to the tip—you won't be able to see what you're writing. Hold it about ¾ inch from the point.

If you follow these suggestions, your handwriting should become more efficient. Clear and rapid handwriting is a mechanical technique; once you decide to learn it and begin to practice, mastery is almost bound to follow. People should not allow a failure to write skillfully to limit their note-taking performance, whether in school or on the job.

Activity 2

Write again for ten minutes without stopping. Try to write more words than you did in Activity 1. At the same time, be sure to keep your words legible.

Number of words in Activity 1: _____   In Activity 2: _____

Increasing Listening Efficiency

Activity 1

To take effective classroom notes, you must be able to listen attentively. This activity will test your ability to listen carefully and to follow spoken directions. The instructor will give you a series of thirteen directions. Listen closely to each one and then do exactly what it calls for. Each direction will be spoken only once.

If you are working on this book independently, get a friend to read the directions to you, or read each direction aloud once to yourself and then try to follow it. Do the same for other activities in this section as well.

Direction 1: Do not say a word at any point during this exercise. Do not raise your hand or look at your neighbor. There will be thirteen directions in the exercise. Follow every one of them except for the last direction, which you should disregard.

Direction 2: Get out a sheet of paper and write your full name in the upper left-hand corner of the paper.

Direction 3: Write the numbers 1 to 8 down the left-hand side of the page.

Direction 4: Write beside space 2 the word *quiet,* which is spelled *q-u-i-e-t.*

Direction 5: Write down the name of the street where you live beside space 3. Do not write down the street number.

Direction 6: Think of the name of the high school that you went to. Do not write it down beside space 1.

Direction 7: Think of the name of the toothpaste that you use. Write it down on the back of your sheet of paper.

Direction 8: Listen to the following set of numbers and then put them down beside space 4. The numbers are 8, 12, 20, 31, 45.

Direction 9: Think of the name of a television show that you like, turn your paper upside down, and write the name of the show beside space 5.

Direction 10: Turn your paper back to the original position. Then count the number of people in the room, including yourself. Write out the number beside space 6.

Direction 11: Print in capital letters your first name or nickname beside space 7.

Direction 12: Write the word *banana*—spelled *b-a-n-a-n-a*—beside space 8. Then draw a picture of a pear on one side of the word *banana* and a picture of an apple under the word *banana.*

Direction 13: This is the last direction. Crumple your paper into a ball and throw it to the front of the room.

If you followed all directions correctly, you have done an effective job of attending closely. It is a skill that will help you be a good listener and note-taker.

Skills in Good Listening   Effective listening and note-taking require not only the ability to attend but other skills as well. At the same time you are writing down what an instructor has said, you must be able to listen to what he or she is now saying and to decide whether it is important enough to write down as well. Also, in a rapid lecture you must be able at times to store one or more ideas in your memory so that you will be able to write them down next. If you can "listen ahead" and process and remember what you hear at the same time that you are writing rapidly, you will be listening efficiently. Your brain will be able to work along with and ahead of your pen.

Activity 2

This activity will give you practice in developing your listening efficiency.

Group A   Your instructor will read each sentence in group A once, at a normal speaking speed. Listen carefully and, after the instructor has read the sentence, see if you can write down what has been said. Before starting the second sentence, the instructor will give you time to finish writing. Do not worry about getting down every word; do try to get down the basic idea. (If there are words you cannot spell, spell them the way they sound. In actual note-taking situations, you can later look up correct spellings in your textbook or dictionary.) There are three practice sentences in group A.

1. Almost one in every seven Americans is affected by hypertension—that is, by high blood pressure.

2. A half hour of TV nightly news, if printed, would not fill one page of *The New York Times*.

3. In 1900 about one in thirteen marriages ended in divorce; today one in two ends in divorce.

Group B   The three examples in group B are almost twice as long as those in group A. They require, then, increased listening efficiency. Your instructor will read the two sentences in each example at a normal speaking rate. You can begin writing as soon as the instructor starts the first sentence. You will have to listen to and remember the second sentence in each example at the same time you are writing the first sentence.

1. The popular idea that you can tell the age of a rattlesnake by the number of rattles on its tail is false. A healthy snake can grow several new rattles in a single year.

2. The usual age of retirement in America is sixty-five. Many experts are now questioning the fairness of a system that removes people from their jobs no matter how qualified they are.

3. People have a great advantage over computers, for we can understand visual images drawn from our environment. Computers can process only facts that are put into numerical form.

Group C   The three examples in group C are about three times as long as those in group A. They create, then, an even more realistic note-taking situation, and they require a further increase in listening efficiency. Again your instructor will read the sentences in each example at a normal rate of speed. You will have to "listen ahead" and remember what you hear at the same time that you are writing rapidly.

1. When trapped in quicksand, do not struggle, or you will be sucked in deeper. The body floats on quicksand, so you should fall on your back, stretching out your arms at right angles, as if floating on water. Then, after working your legs free from the sand, begin rolling your entire body toward safe ground.

2. Political activist Ralph Nader has suggested that voting be required in this country, as it is in several other countries. In Australia, students learn that if they don't vote at age eighteen, they may have to pay a fine equal to about $15 in American money. The result is that about 90 percent of qualified voters go to the polls.

3. Babies seldom cry for no reason at all. They cry because of some discomfort that they feel. In the first year of life in particular, it is important that parents respond to a baby's cries rather than ignore them. A prompt response helps give the baby a sense of security and trust.

In addition to efficient handwriting and listening skills in writing effective classroom notes, if you use an electronic device such as a laptop, you should brush up on your typing skills. There are several software programs that offer typing tutorials, and you can also go to YouTube and type in "how to type faster" to find a range of helpful videos on improving your typing speed.

You will receive additional practice in listening when you take notes on the short lectures that appear on pages 65–71.

Practice in Taking Classroom Notes

Activity 1

Taking Notes   Evaluate your present note-taking skills by putting a check mark beside each of the thirteen note-taking hints that you already practice. Then put a check mark beside those steps that you plan to practice. Leave a space blank if you do not plan to follow a particular strategy.

Now   Plan
Do   to Do

____ ____   1. Take notes on classroom work.

____ ____   2. Sit near the front of the class.

____ ____   3. Read in advance textbook material about the topic to be presented in class.

4. Record notes as follows:

____ ____   a.   Use full-size 8½- by 11-inch paper.

____ ____   b.   Use a ballpoint pen.

Now Do	Plan to Do	
___	___	c. Use a notebook divided into parts.
___	___	d. Date each day's notes.
___	___	e. Take notes on one side of the page only.
___	___	f. Write legibly.
___	___	g. Abbreviate common words and recurring terms.
___	___	h. Indicate assignments and exams.

5. Write notes in outline form as follows:

Now Do	Plan to Do	
___	___	a. Start main points at the margin; indent secondary points.
___	___	b. Use white space to show shift in thought.

6. Watch for signals of importance:

Now Do	Plan to Do	
___	___	a. Write whatever the instructor puts on the board.
___	___	b. Write definitions and enumerations.
___	___	c. Write down points marked by emphasis words.
___	___	d. Record repeated points.
___	___	e. Note the hints given by the instructor's tone of voice.
___	___	7. Write down examples.
___	___	8. Write down connecting details and explanations.

9. Do as follows when material is missed:

Now Do	Plan to Do	
___	___	a. Leave space for notes missed.
___	___	b. Try to get the broad sweep of ideas when you fall behind.
___	___	10. Question the instructor when an idea isn't clear.
___	___	11. Do not stop taking notes during discussion periods.
___	___	12. Do not stop taking notes toward the end of a class.
___	___	13. Go over your notes soon after class.

Studying Notes   Now, evaluate your skills in studying class notes.

Now Do	Plan to Do	
___	___	• Jot in the margin key words to recall ideas.
___	___	• Turn recall words into questions.
___	___	• Use repeated self-testing to learn the material.
___	___	• Apply this study method regularly.

Activity 2

Below is an excerpt from notes taken during an introductory lecture in a sociology class. In the margin of the notes, jot down key words or phrases that could be used to pull together and recall the main ideas on the page.

Sociology 101   11-21-11

In the million years or so of life on earth, human beings have sought truth in many places. FIVE SOURCES OF TRUTH in particular are important to note:

(1) intuition, (2) authority, (3) tradition, (4) common sense, and (5) science.

1. INTUITION—any flash of insight (true or mistaken) whose source the receiver cannot fully identify or explain.
    Ex.—Galen in second century made chart of human body showing exactly where it might be pierced without fatal injury. Knew which zones were fatal through intuition.

2. AUTHORITY—persons who are experts in a specific field.

    Two kinds of authority:
    a. SACRED—rests upon faith that a certain tradition or document—eg, the Bible—is of supernatural origin.
    b. SECULAR—arises from human perception + is of two kinds:
        (1) secular scientific—rests upon empirical observation.
        (2) secular humanistic—rests upon belief that certain "great people" have had special insight.

Activity 3

Turn in to your instructor a copy of one day's notes that you have taken in one of your classes. These notes should fill at least one side of a sheet of paper. If you have never taken a full page of notes in class, add a second or third day's notes until you complete at least one sheet. In the top or left-hand margin of your notes, write down key words or phrases you could use to master the material in the notes.

Activity 4

The activity that follows will give you practice in taking lecture notes. The activity is based on a short lecture on listening given in a speech class. Take notes on the lecture as your instructor or a friend reads it aloud. Items that the original lecturer put on the board are shown at the top of the lecture. As you take your notes, apply the hints you have learned in this chapter. Then answer the questions that follow the selection by referring to your notes but not to the selection itself. Write your answers on separate sheets of paper.

Lecture about Listening

On Board

Problem of losing attention	Spare time
125 wpm = talking speed	Three techniques for concentration
500 wpm = listening speed	Intend to listen

I'm going to describe to you a listening problem that many people have. I'll also explain why many people have the problem, and I'll tell you what can be done about the problem. The listening problem that many people have is that they lose attention while listening to a speaker. They get bored; their minds wander; their thoughts go elsewhere.

Everyone has had this experience of losing attention, but probably few people understand one of the main reasons why we have this trouble keeping our attention on the speaker. The reason is this: There is a great deal of difference between talking speed and listening speed. The average speaker talks at the rate of 125 words a minute. On the other hand, we can listen and think at the rate of about 500 words a minute. Picture it: The speaker is going along at 125 wpm, and we are sitting there ready to move at four times that speed. The speaker is like a tortoise plodding along slowly; we, the listeners, are like the rabbit ready to dash along at a much faster speed. The result of this gap is that we have a lot of spare time to use while listening to a speech.

Unfortunately, many of us use this time to go off on side excursions of our own. We may begin thinking about a date, a sports event, a new shirt we want to buy, balancing our budget, how to start saving money, what we must do later in the day, and a thousand other things. The result of the side excursions may be that when our attention returns to the speaker, we find that we have been left far behind. The speaker has gotten into some new idea, and we, having missed some connection, have little sense of what is being talked about. We may have to listen very closely for five minutes to get back on track. The temptation at this point is to go back to our own special world of thoughts and forget about the speaker. Then we're wasting both our time and the speaker's time. What we must do instead is work hard to keep our attention on the speaker and to concentrate on what is being said.

Here are three mental techniques you can use to keep your concentration on the speaker. First of all, summarize what the speaker has said. Do this after each new point is developed. This constant summarizing will help you pay attention. Second, try to guess where the speaker is going next. Try to anticipate what direction the speaker is going to take, based on what has already been said. This game you play with yourself arouses your curiosity and helps maintain your attention. Third, question the truth, the validity, of the speaker's words. Compare the points made with your own knowledge and experience. Keep trying to decide whether you agree or disagree with the speaker on the basis of what you know. Don't simply take as gospel whatever the speaker tells you; question it—ask yourself whether you think it is true. Remember, then, to summarize what the speaker has said, try to guess where the speaker is going next, and question the truth of what is stated.

All three techniques can make you a better listener. But even better than these techniques, I think, is making a conscious effort to listen more closely. You must intend to concentrate, intend to listen carefully. For example, you should go into your classes every day determined to pay close attention. It should be easier for you to make this important mental decision if you remember how easily attention can wander when someone else is speaking.

Questions on the Lecture

1. What is a listening problem that many people have?

   _____

   _____

2. What are common talking and listening speeds?

   _____

   _____

3. What are three techniques to help you pay attention when someone is talking?

_____

_____

4. What is the most important step you can take to become a better listener?

_____

_____

Activity 5

Follow the directions given for Activity 4.

Lecture about Propaganda Techniques

On Board

Propaganda   Testimonial   Bandwagon   Plain folks   Transfer

We all know that advertising sells products. How many times have you bought a particular item because you saw it advertised on TV? We all have, of course, and that is the power of advertising. One thing that makes ads work is propaganda. Propaganda may be defined as *messages intended to persuade audiences to adopt a certain opinion.* We know that totalitarian governments use propaganda to win people to their side. But propaganda is also used by our own politicians, editorial writers, and advertisers. Today, we will discuss four propaganda techniques often used by advertisers.

The first of these techniques is called the *testimonial.* This means that celebrities are used to pitch an idea or sell a product. For example, you may have seen ads that used celebrities like Ellen DeGeneres for American Express or LeBron James for Nike. The testimonial is a propaganda method because the audience associates the star qualities of the celebrity with the product— whether or not the celebrity knows anything at all about the product. Our good feelings about the person, in other words, spill over to the product. You can all think of famous people who have appeared in TV or magazine or billboard ads to sell products.

Another propaganda technique used by advertisers is the *bandwagon.* This method encourages people to do or buy something because "everyone else is doing it." Advertisers, for example, tell us that "nobody doesn't like Sara Lee" or that we should "make the switch to Burger King" because everyone else (in the ads, at least) is doing just that. Countless ads have begun with the statement "All over America, people are switching to . . . using . . . buying." You are expected to do the same if you don't want to feel "out of it." The bandwagon, then, tells us that by buying a certain product we can get "on board."

Plain folks is a third propaganda method, one in which the product being sold is associated with "ordinary" people—people we can identify with. They're not glamorous types; they're just folks like you and me. When you see "regular" people, the kind who don't seem to be actors, explaining how Tylenol helped their headaches, or how Bounce made their wash softer, or how much better Pepsi tasted than Coke, you are seeing the plain folks method. Advertisers know that consumers will believe people who seem down-to-earth, honest, and just like the folks next door.

A final propaganda technique is called *transfer.* In this method, the product is associated with something else that is attractive, respectable, or admirable. For example, countless advertisements for cars show a gorgeous model leaning over the hood or sliding into a plush interior. The audience will transfer its feeling about the model ("I want to be like her" or "She is beautiful") to the car ("I want it" or "It is beautiful"). Advertisers use transfer, too, when they associate their products with patriotic symbols, such as the bald eagle or the Liberty Bell. When we see an eagle flying over the land while a narrator tells us about the Westinghouse Corporation's philosophy of quality, we transfer our patriotic feelings to the company.

This, then, has been an introduction to some of the propaganda methods that advertisers use to sell their products.

Questions on the Lecture

1. What is propaganda?

   _____

   _____

2. What are four propaganda techniques used by advertisers?

   _____

   _____

3. Explain the bandwagon technique.

   _____

   _____

4. Explain the technique of transfer.

   _____

   _____

Activity 6

Follow the directions given for Activity 4.

Lecture on Effective Writing

On Board

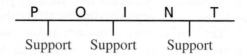

1. Make a point.
2. Support the point (BS).
3. Organize the support.
4. Write clear sentences.

Many people think that writing a good paragraph or paper is a kind of magical skill—one that some people have and others don't. When such people find that they have to do a great deal of writing themselves, either in college or on their jobs, they become angry and frustrated. Why should they have to write? After all, people aren't asked to play the piano or draw a picture if they have no training or talent. Isn't it just as unfair to be asked to write?

Probably the best-kept secret about writing is that it is a skill that can be mastered. That's right—you can learn to write a decent paper, learn to do well in writing assignments in school or on the job, no matter how much trouble you may have had with writing before. Writing consists of a series of steps that you can follow. When you finish, you should have an organized, effective paper.

The first step in writing an effective paper is to *make a point of some kind.* A point is an assertion, a statement that goes beyond a mere fact—a point has your opinion injected into it. We all make points all day long. If we could gather several points from the conversations around us, we might hear things like "That movie was a waste of money"; "Our sociology professor is the best teacher I have ever had"; "I don't vote, because politicians are crooks"; "Going out for an evening is getting to be really expensive." Starting to write means deciding to focus on a point similar to any of these. For example, let's take a subject we all know something about: high school proms. When we were in high school, we all went to proms, or talked about people who went to proms, or stayed home from proms. We could make many points about proms; each of you would have some opinion about them. Let's take one point in particular, though. My point is that proms should be banned. If I said this to you as we were talking, I might go on to give you my reasons, or I might refuse to talk about it anymore, or I might change the subject. In writing, however, once I made this point, I would have to support it.

That's the second step in writing—*supporting your point.* You saw that the first step wasn't too hard; this one isn't either. When I say support your point, I mean back it up. In other words, give reasons, details, examples, anything you can think of to make your point a convincing one. In addition, you should BS a lot. Yes, I said BS. You must remember to BS in your writing if you want to be effective. Of course, you all know what BS stands for— "Be specific." The details that support your point should be exact, precise, particular—not vague and general. In other words, they should be specific.

Let's try to come up with some specific details to support my point about proms. Perhaps I feel proms should be banned, first of all, because they cost too much money. Now I have to develop this reason with specific details. If I write, "All the things a person has to buy to go to the prom are too expensive," I have failed my readers. "Too expensive" is not specific. Instead, I might write, "Attending the prom means buying a gown for $150, a bouquet of flowers for $35, a pair of tickets at $50 apiece, and a set of photographs that can cost $100 and up." Now I'm communicating better, for I have given my readers a clear idea of exactly how much money I'm talking about. Now there's a much better chance that they will eventually agree with my opening point—or at least respect my opinion. You can see, too, that specific details are a lot more interesting and lively than general ones. If you don't want your reader to fall asleep, then remember to BS.

The third step in writing a good paper is *organizing your supporting details.* Without some method of organization, your paper will sound confused and illogical, no matter how good your details are. How do you organize the details? Basically, there are two methods: *time order* and *emphatic order.* Time order means that the details are arranged as they occur in time. For example, if you were writing about a day in your life, you might start with getting up in the morning and end with watching *The Tonight Show* through bleary eyes. My prom paper could be organized this way; I might begin with the preparations for the prom and end with prom night itself. Of course, I would weave in my reasons for banning proms along the way. I might begin with before-prom expenses and end with after-prom drinking.

The other method of organization is, again, emphatic order. Emphatic order means saving the best, most dramatic, or most important detail for last. In other words, you build up to the best. I could decide to use emphatic order for my prom paper. I would make a scratch outline of my reasons for wanting proms banned. Then I would save for last my most important reason for wanting proms banned. For me, that reason would be the drunken driving that often seems to go along with prom night. Drunken driving is more important than prom expenses or anything else.

Finally, after you have made a point, supported it, and organized your supporting details, you have one last step. You must be sure you have written *clear, correct sentences.* This means checking for mistakes in spelling, grammar, and punctuation. The importance of this step should be obvious; it won't matter how good your ideas are if no one can understand them. I can't go into detail about individual grammar skills in the time I have left. Let me just say, then, that a dictionary and an English handbook are essential for this step.

Let's end with a summary. To write an effective paper, you must take the four steps you see on the board:

1. Make a point.
2. Support the point (BS).
3. Organize the support.
4. Write clear sentences.

You can definitely learn how to follow these four steps. It's a matter of practice and a matter of thinking, planning, checking, and rewriting. If you work hard, you will produce clear and effective pieces of writing. And writing is a skill that will help you immeasurably both in school and later in your career.

Questions on the Lecture

1. What are the four steps in effective writing?

   _____

   _____

2. What does BS in writing refer to?

   _____

   _____

3. What are two methods of organizing details in writing?

   _____

   _____

4. What is meant by emphatic order?

   _____

   _____

Time Control and Concentration

This chapter will show you how to manage your time by using

- A course outline
- A large monthly calendar
- A weekly study schedule
- A "to do" list
- Hints on concentration

Time Control and Concentration: In Real Life

Read the profile that follows. Then ask yourself these questions:

- What challenges does Maria Cardenas face in managing her time?
- What solutions has she found to those challenges?
- Are any of the time-control challenges Maria has faced problems for me, too?

Student Profile: Maria Cardenas

As she talks about the challenge of making time for her studies as well as her husband, three school-age children, housekeeping job, and beloved garden, Maria Cardenas—an honor student at Florida Gulf Coast University—sounds more matter-of-fact than flustered. "I just do what I have to do," she says.

Maybe the experience of growing up as a migrant worker with an abusive father puts future difficulties in perspective. The second oldest of eight children, Maria left Rio Verde, Mexico, for the United States at age seven. With the rest of her family, Maria traveled with the harvest, using a series of false names to evade immigration authorities. Laboring like an adult in the fields, Maria often attended three or four schools

Continued

each year. Her school attendance suffered as her father grew more brutal. Eventually at age sixteen, Maria, barely able to read or write, left school to marry a man as abusive as her father.

But by age twenty-nine, Maria had turned her life around. In a solid second marriage, having struggled to acquire the skills she needed to earn her GED, Maria enrolled at Edison Community College in Fort Myers, Florida. There she was a straight-A student and a member of Phi Theta

Kappa, the international honor society for two-year colleges. Now a junior at Florida Gulf Coast, Maria has a high grade-point average and expects to graduate with a B.A. in elementary education. Her goal is to teach other migrant children "to stand on their own two feet, to achieve their dreams."

For Maria, the key to time management is "do a little at a time, all the time." With her weeks consisting of working at least twenty-four hours; attending to her children, now ages eight, thirteen, and eighteen; and taking three college courses, Maria rarely has the luxury of long uninterrupted study sessions. She has become a master of using what time she does have efficiently.

"I study steadily, all through the term," Maria says. "Every day after class, while the material is fresh in my mind, I review my notes and make sure I understand whatever is there. If not, I question the instructor." By never allowing herself to fall behind in class, Maria avoids the need for last-minute cramming for an exam. "I'm prepared by then. All I have to do is spend a little extra time the night before going over my notes."

When a big project or term paper is assigned, Maria approaches it in the same "do it now" fashion. "First, I make sure I know *exactly* what the instructor wants," she says. "I pay very close attention to any handouts, and I ask, ask, ask. Then I do the project a little at a time, staying in close touch with the instructor every step of the way. Whenever possible, I'll get a draft of the project done early and ask the instructor to go over it with me before I hand in a final version." By checking in with her instructor frequently, Maria emphasizes, she saves herself the time and discouragement of having to redo her work.

Continued

As she grabs chunks of study time when and where she can, Maria has two criteria in mind: silence and solitude. "I concentrate best when the house is quiet, so I do most of my studying after the children are in bed," she says. "I sit in the living room or at the kitchen table—with the TV off!" she adds with a laugh. "Best of all is the school library, where I don't have any of the household distractions. At home, it's too easy to think, 'I really should be getting groceries.'"

In order to maintain her concentration and give herself an incentive, Maria knows she must schedule times for breaks. "If I had my way, I'd be in my garden all day with my daughter Jasmine, my gardening buddy," she admits. "So I work it into my schedule. If I've been studying well for a while, I'll tell myself, 'Okay, you can have twenty minutes in the garden.' Or if I reach the point where I cannot read another word, I go for a really fast walk with one of the children. That way, I can clear my head and have some one-to-one conversation at the same time. When I come back in, my mind is rested and I can concentrate again."

Maria has one final trick for making wise use of her study time. Without a conventional high school background, she admits that she is often overwhelmed at first by the material in her textbooks, especially in the humanities. "Renoir, Beethoven, Christopher Columbus—what do I know about any of them?" she asks. "I start to read the textbook chapters, and they mean nothing to me. I could spend hours staring at those words and not understanding them. So, instead, I go to the library" (and here Maria lowers her voice to a confidential whisper) "*to the juvenile section.* I get out children's books about the subject and read them. They're very short, simple, and to the point. *Then* I return to my fat college textbooks with some idea of what's going on!"

With Maria's record of success, nobody is going to argue with her methods.

All of us need free time, hours without demands and obligations, so we can just relax and do what we please. But it is easy to lose track of time and discover suddenly that there aren't enough hours to do what needs to be done. No skill is more basic to survival in college than time control. If you do not use your time well, your college career—and the life goals that depend on how well you do in college—will slip like sand through your fingers. This chapter describes four methods to help you gain control of your time: You will learn how to use a course outline, a large monthly calendar, a weekly study schedule, and a daily or weekly "to do" list. There is also a series of hints on concentration—how to use your study time more effectively.

Your Course Outline

At the beginning of a school semester, each of your instructors will probably pass out a course outline, or syllabus, and often post the syllabus on a separate website. If you do not want to take a giant step to control your time, throw this syllabus away or put it in the back of a notebook and never look at it.

The syllabus is your instructor's plan for the course. Chances are it will explain the instructor's grading system and the factors on which your grade will be based. Chances are it will give you the dates of exams and will tell you when papers or reports are due. Chances are it will outline what topics will be covered in each week of class, and it may list the chapters in the textbook that you may be expected to read. Chances are it will contain important contact information, such as your instructor's e-mail address, so that you can contact her or him with questions.

In other words, the syllabus will put you inside your instructor's head and help you learn exactly what you must do to succeed in the course. The syllabus is often the key to doing well in a course.

Believe it or not, many students ignore the syllabus. Don't make this mistake! Instead, use the syllabus to help organize your work for the course: Move the dates of exams and the due dates of papers to a large monthly calendar. Refer to the syllabus on a regular basis to make sure you are doing just what your instructor expects you to do.

A Large Monthly Calendar

You should buy or make a large monthly calendar. There are also free electronic calendars that you can download online. Google, for example, offers a very useful calendar. To learn more, go to: www.google.com/calendar. Using a calendar is your first method of time control because it allows you, in one quick glance, to get a clear picture of what you need to do in the weeks to come. Be sure your monthly calendar has a good-sized block of white space for each date. Erasable (laminated) calendars are especially helpful because they allow you to easily make corrections to your schedule. As soon as you learn about exam dates and paper deadlines, enter them clearly in the appropriate spots on the calendar. Hang the calendar in a place where you will see it every day, perhaps on your kitchen or bedroom wall. The monthly calendar made up by one student is shown on the next page.

October

Sun.	Mon.	Tues.	Wed.	Thurs.	Fri.	Sat.
				1 Computer quiz	2	3
4	5 Soc test	6	7	8	9 English essay due	10
11	12	13 Bio field trip	14	15 Psych quiz	16	17
18	19 Speech	20	21	22	23 English essay due	24
25	26 Bio test	27	28	29 Business report due	30	31

Activity

In the following spaces, write the names of the courses you are taking. Also, record the dates on which papers or other assignments are due and the dates on which exams are scheduled. Due dates are often listed in a course syllabus as well as announced by a course instructor.

Courses	Paper Due Dates	Exam Dates
_____	_____	_____
_____	_____	_____
_____	_____	_____
_____	_____	_____
_____	_____	_____

Transfer all of this information to a monthly calendar.

- Write here what you think would be the best place for you to post a monthly calendar:

  _____

- *Complete the following statement:*
  A monthly calendar will keep you constantly aware of exam days and paper

  target days so that you can _____
  well in advance.

A Weekly Study Schedule

Evaluating Your Use of Time

A weekly study schedule will make you aware of how much time you actually have each week and will help you use that time effectively. Before you prepare a weekly study schedule, however, you need to get a sense of how you spend your time *each day*. The activity that follows will help you do that.

Activity

The daily schedule of one student, Emily, follows. Emily has three classes. Assuming that every hour of class time should receive at least one hour of study time, how could Emily revise her schedule so that she would have at least three full study hours in addition to time for "rest and relaxation"? Make your suggested changes by crossing out items and adding study time to her schedule. Your instructor may have you compare answers with those of others in the class.

Emily's Daily Schedule

Time	Activity	Time	Activity
6:30–7:30	Get up, shower, breakfast	2–2:30	Read newspaper in library
7:30–8	Travel to school	2:30–3	Drive to work
8–9	Class (English)	3–6	Work at Wal-Mart
9–10	Coffee in student center	6–7:30	Travel home, eat supper, watch news
10–11	Class (Business)	7:30–9	Telephone, go on Internet, English homework
11–1	Lunch in cafeteria	9–11:30	TV
1–2	Class (sociology)	11:30	Bed

Next, use the chart that follows to record a *typical* school day in your life. Be honest: You want to see clearly what you are doing so that you will be able to plan ways to use your time more effectively.

Time	Activity

Now, honestly evaluate your use of time. Write in the number of hours you *actually* used for study in your typical day: _____ hours. Next, go back to your chart and block off time in the day that you *could* have used for study. (Remember to still allow time for "rest and relaxation," which is also needed.) Write in the number of hours you could have used for study in the day: _____ hours.

Note   People sometimes learn from their schedules that they are victims of a time overload, for they have taken too much work on themselves with too little time to do it. If you think this is your case, you should talk with your instructor or a counselor about possibly dropping one or more courses.

Emily's Weekly Schedule

	Mon.	Tues.	Wed.	Thurs.	Fri.	Sat.	Sun.	
6:00 A.M.								6:00 A.M.
7:00	B		B		B			7:00
8:00	Eng	B	Eng		Eng	B		8:00
9:00				B			B	9:00
10:00	Biz	Phys Ed	Biz		Biz	Job		10:00
11:00		↓						11:00
12:00	L	L	L	L	L			12:00
1:00 P.M.	Chem	Lab	Chem		Chem		L	1:00 P.M.
2:00								2:00
3:00			Job		Job			3:00
4:00			↓		↓			4:00
5:00	S	S	↓	S		↓	S	5:00
6:00			S			S		6:00
7:00	Comp Prog			Psych	↓			7:00
8:00	↓				S			8:00
9:00	↓			↓				9:00
10:00								10:00
11:00								11:00
12:00	Bed	Bed	Bed	Bed			Bed	12:00
1:00 A.M.								1:00 A.M.
2:00	④	④	③	⑤	②	⓪	⑤	2:00

B = Breakfast   ■ = Study blocks   Psych = Psychology   Eng = English
L = Lunch   ◯ = Study hours per day   Comp Prog = Computer Programming   Phys Ed = Physical Education
S = Supper   Blanks = Free time   Chem = Chemistry   Biz = Business

Important Points about a Weekly Study Schedule

You are now ready to look over the master weekly schedule, shown on page 80, that Emily prepared to gain control of her time. You should then read carefully the points that follow; all are important in planning an effective weekly schedule. Note that you will be asked to refer to Emily's schedule to answer questions that accompany some of the points.

Point 1: Plan, at first, at least one hour of study time for each hour of class time.

Depending on the course, the grade you want, and your own study efficiency, you may have to schedule more time later. A difficult course, for example, may require three hours or more of study time for each course hour. Remember that learning is what counts, not the time it takes you to learn. Be prepared to schedule as much time as you need to gain control of a course.

- How many class hours, excluding lab and phys ed, does Emily have? _____
- How many study hours has she scheduled? _____

Point 2: Schedule regular study time.

To succeed in your college work, you need to establish definite study hours. If you do not set aside and stick to such hours on a daily or almost daily basis, you are probably going to fail at time control. Jot down in the following spaces the free hours each day that you would use as regular study time. The first column shows Emily's free hours on Monday.

For Emily		*Your Possible Study Hours*					
Mon.	Mon.	Tues.	Wed.	Thurs.	Fri.	Sat.	Sun.
9–10	___	___	___	___	___	___	___
11–12	___	___	___	___	___	___	___
2–4	___	___	___	___	___	___	___

There are many benefits to setting aside regular study hours. First of all, they help make studying a habit. Study times will be programmed into your daily schedule as automatically as, say, watching a favorite television program. You will not have to remind yourself to study, nor will you waste large amounts of time and energy trying to avoid studying; you will simply do it. Another value of regular study time is that you will be better able to stay up to date on work in your courses. You are not likely to find yourself several days before a test with three textbook chapters to read or five weeks of classroom notes to organize and study. Finally, regular study takes advantage of the proven fact that a series of study sessions is more effective than a single long "cram" session.

- How many separate blocks of study time has Emily built into her weekly schedule?

  _____

- How many benefits of regular study hours are described in the preceding paragraph? (*Hint:* Word signals such as "First of all" are clues to each separate value.)

  _____

Point 3: Plan blocks of study time at least one hour long.   If you schedule less than one hour, your study period may be over just when you are fully warmed up and working hard.

- What is the largest single block of study time that Emily has during the week? (Write down the day and the number of hours.)

  _____

- What is the largest single block of study time available to you each week?

  _____

Point 4: Reward yourself for using study time effectively.   Research shows that people work better if they get an immediate reward for their efforts. So, if your schedule permits, try to set up a reward system. Allow yourself to telephone a friend or watch a television show or eat a snack after a period of efficient study. On Emily's schedule, for example, nine to ten o'clock on Tuesday night is free for watching television as a reward for working well in the two-hour study slot before. When you are studying over a several-hour period, you can also give yourself "mini-rewards" of five to ten minutes of free time for every hour or so of study time.

Your reward system won't work if you "cheat," so deprive yourself of such pleasures as television shows when you have not studied honestly.

- Locate the other spots where Emily has built free time into her schedule after

  study periods and indicate the hours here: _____

  _____

  _____

- Do you think it is a good idea for Emily to reward herself with one day in the

  week (Saturday) free from study? Why or why not? _____

  _____

  _____

  _____

Point 5: Try to schedule study periods before and after classes.

Ideally, you should read a textbook chapter before an instructor covers it; what you hear in class will then be a "second exposure," so the ideas are likely to be a good deal more meaningful to you. You should also look over your notes from the preceding class in case the instructor discusses the material further. Similarly, if you take a few minutes to review your notes as soon after class as possible, you will be able to organize and clarify the material while it is still fresh in your mind.

- If a new textbook chapter is to be covered in Emily's psychology class on Thursday, where in her schedule should she plan to read it?

Point 6: Work on your most difficult subjects when you are most alert.

Save routine work for times you are most likely to be tired. You might, for example, study a new and difficult mathematics chapter at 8 P.M. if you are naturally alert then, and review vocabulary words for a Spanish class at 11 P.M., when you may be a little tired.

- Assuming that Emily is most alert early in the day and that chemistry is her most difficult subject, in what time slots should she schedule her work on that subject? _____

- At what time of day do you consider yourself most alert? _____

Point 7: Balance your activities.

Allow free time in your schedule for family, friends, sports, television, and so on. Note that there is a good deal of free time (empty space) in Emily's schedule, even with her classes, work, and study hours.

- Where is the biggest block of free time in Emily's schedule? _____

- Where do *you* plan to have a substantial block of free time? _____

Point 8: Keep your schedule flexible.

When unexpected events occur, trade times on your weekly timetable. Do not simply do away with study hours. If you find that your schedule requires constant adjustment, revise it. (Your instructor may be able to give you extra copies of the following schedule.) After two or three revisions, you will have a realistic, practical weekly schedule that you can follow honestly.

- If Emily went to a family reunion on Sunday at 1 P.M. and didn't get back until eight o'clock that evening, where in her schedule could she make up the missed hour of study time? _____

Your Weekly Schedule

	Mon.	Tues.	Wed.	Thurs.	Fri.	Sat.	Sun.	
6:00 A.M.								6:00 A.M.
7:00								7:00
8:00								8:00
9:00								9:00
10:00								10:00
11:00								11:00
12:00								12:00
1:00 P.M.								1:00 P.M.
2:00								2:00
3:00								3:00
4:00								4:00
5:00								5:00
6:00								6:00
7:00								7:00
8:00								8:00
9:00								9:00
10:00								10:00
11:00								11:00
12:00								12:00
1:00 A.M.								1:00 A.M.
2:00								2:00

Activity

Keeping the preceding points in mind, use the form provided on page 84 to make up your own realistic weekly study schedule. Write in your class and lab periods first; next, add in your hours for job and meals; and then fill in the study hours that you need in order to do well in your courses. At the bottom of your schedule, make up a key that explains the symbols you have used in the schedule. Also, add up and circle the total number of study hours you realistically plan to set aside each day.

A Daily or Weekly "To Do" List

How to Make a "To Do" List

A "to do" list is simply a list of things a person wants to accomplish within a limited period. Many successful people make the "to do" list a habit, considering it an essential step in making the most efficient use of their time each day. A "to do" list, made up daily or weekly, may be one of the most important single study habits you will ever acquire. In addition to handwritten lists, you can find free electronic "to do" list programs online. For example, Remember The Milk, www.rememberthemilk.com, allows users to make multiple "to do" lists and share them with others.

Emily's "To Do" List

<u>To Do</u>   <u>Monday</u>

1. Make up outline for English research paper
2. Read Chapter 6 of business text
3. Review notes for chemistry test on Wednesday
4. Reserve time in computer lab to type psych report
5. Return DVDs
6. Buy cat food!!
7. Find article on Internet booksellers for business class
8. Buy gym shorts
9. Call Jen; get English notes from class missed Friday
10. Do laundry
11. Answer Dan's e-mail
12. Make lunch date with Kate and Melanie
13. Review chemistry notes again before bed

Important Notes about the "To Do" List

Point 1: Carry the list with you throughout the day. An electronic organizer, a small notebook, or a four- by six-inch slip of paper can be kept in a purse, pocket, or wallet.

You may also want to keep your "to do" list in a *daily planner* (also called a *datebook* or *time organizer*). A daily planner is an inexpensive purchase at any bookstore or office supply store. It combines a calendar with space for a daily "to do" list. If you actively use the planner—carrying it with you every day and consulting it and adding or crossing out items on a regular basis—it will definitely help you organize your time.

Point 2: Decide on priorities. Making the best use of your time means focusing on top-priority items—things that will really have a negative impact if they're not done—rather than spending hours on low-priority activities. When in doubt about what to do at any time in the day, ask yourself, "What are the highest priority items on my list?" and choose one of them.

- Look at Emily's "to do" list and label each of the items *A*, *B*, or *C* to indicate what you think is a reasonable priority level for it.

Point 3: Cross out items as you finish them. Don't worry unnecessarily about completing your list; what is not done can often be moved to the next day's list. What is important is that you make the best possible use of your time each day. Focus on top-priority activities!

Activity

Use this space to make up your own "to do" list for tomorrow. If you cannot think of at least seven items, then put down as well things that you want to do over the rest of the week. Label each item as *A, B,* or *C* in priority.

Your "To Do" List

To Do

Concentration

A monthly calendar, a weekly study schedule, and a "to do" list are essential methods of organizing your study time. Unfortunately, though, all your effort in creating them is useless if you waste the study time you have set aside. Unless you master the art of *concentrating* on your work, you will learn very little.

Is concentration difficult? The answer is both *yes* and *no*. The skill of concentration somewhat resembles a beating heart. When it works, we take it for granted and are hardly aware of it; any malfunction, however, is painfully obvious. For example, you probably find it very easy to concentrate on something you are extremely interested in—a suspenseful movie, a sporting event, a conversation with a friend. But concentration may seem impossible when you are studying a biology chapter or mathematics problems.

- Name an activity on which you can easily concentrate:

  _____

- Name an activity on which you can concentrate only with great difficulty:

  _____

Why People Can't Concentrate

Why is it often so difficult to concentrate on studying? There are several reasons; one or more of them may apply to you.

You equate studying with punishment. If you have a history of doing poorly in school, or if you have often received poor grades even though you tried to study, you will naturally have a negative reaction every time you sit down with your books. After all, you may think, the work is hard and probably not worthwhile. You are conditioned to see studying as torture. All your negative experiences have created a study block that hinders your ability to concentrate.

- Do you think you have a block about studying because of past school experiences? _____

- If so, are you ready to break through your block by applying the study skills in this book? _____

You put everything off until the last minute. The Procrastinators Club holds its Christmas party in February. However, putting off your studies until the last minute is not as harmless and amusing as the Procrastinators' social schedule.

Trying to study ten hours today for an exam tomorrow or starting at nine o'clock in the morning to write a paper that is due by three o'clock in the afternoon is like trying to work with a gun at your head: Concentration is difficult at best.

- Are you a procrastinator? _____

- If so, what do you do to avoid studying? _____

- Does procrastination make you feel anxious and guilty, as it does for most people? _____

You don't feel comfortable or settled.   You're dying of thirst. The chair you're sitting in is sending shooting pains up your spine. Your head is pounding or your eyes are drooping. Your body feels so exhausted that it seems impossible to remain upright any longer. At the same time, dozens of other thoughts may crowd into your mind: next weekend's trip, the argument you had with your mother, the dirty laundry piling up in your closet. Such physical and mental distractions will soon overwhelm any concentration you may have been able to achieve.

- Of the three reasons for not concentrating just listed, which one applies most in your case? _____

Ways to Concentrate

When you can't concentrate, you can take either of two courses. You can give in to defeat by rationalizing your failures. You can tell yourself, for example, "Nobody could understand this textbook" or "I hate this course anyway and I don't care if I fail" or "I don't know why I'm in school" or "I'll really concentrate next time." The better route to take is to decide that you will do everything you can to aid your concentration. Here are practical hints that will help you fix your attention on the studying you have to do.

Hint 1: Work on Having a Positive Attitude.   It is a rare student who has a deep interest in every one of his or her college courses. Most students find that at least some of the studying they have to do involves uninteresting material. In such cases, it is essential to examine your priorities and goals. Don't let some less-than-stimulating courses block your route to the college degree you want. Decide that you will do the studying because, someday, the course will be forgotten, but your college education and degree will be benefiting your life.

- What are the most unpleasant study tasks you will have this semester?

  _____

- Is your college degree important enough for you to do these unpleasant tasks?

  _____

Hint 2: Prepare to Work by Setting Specific Study Goals.

Don't stare at a foot-high pile of thick textbooks and wonder how you'll ever make it through the semester. Instead, go over your assignments and jot down a list of practical goals for the period of study time you have available. These will be the study items on your day's "to do" list. This technique helps you get organized; it also breaks your large, overwhelming study task into manageable units that you can accomplish one at a time. Here are typical study items from one student's daily "to do" list:

> Read pages 125–137 in history text.
>
> Do Internet research on possible topics for psych paper.
>
> Memorize three chemistry formulas.
>
> Review notes for English quiz.

You may want to work first on the assignments that seem easiest, or least painful, to you. It's a good feeling to cross something off your list; knowing you've finished at least *one* thing can often give you the confidence you need to continue.

- Jot down four specific assignments you must complete in the next school week.

  _____

  _____

  _____

  _____

Hint 3: Keep Track of Your Lapses of Concentration.

When you start studying, jot down the time (for example, "7:15") at the bottom of your "to do" list of study items. When you find yourself losing interest or thinking about something else, put the time (for example, "7:35") on that same piece of paper. Catching yourself like this can help train your mind to concentrate for longer and longer periods. You should soon find that you can study for a longer span of time before the first notation appears. The notations, too, should become fewer and fewer.

- Record the time here whenever you have a lapse in concentration while reading the rest of this chapter.

_____

Hint 4: Create a Good Study Environment.   Choose a room that is, first of all, quiet and well-lighted. To avoid glare, make sure that light comes from above or over your shoulder, not from in front of you. Also, you should have more than one light source in the room. For example, you might use a ceiling light in addition to a pole lamp behind your chair.

- Do you think that the place where you study is well lighted? _____
- If not, what might you do to improve the lighting? _____

_____

Second, you should have a comfortable place to sit. Do not, however, try to study in a completely relaxed position. Slight muscular tension promotes the concentration needed for study. So sit on an upright chair or sit in a cross-legged position on your bed with a pillow behind you. Keep in mind, also, that you do not have to study while sitting down. Many students stay alert and focused by walking back and forth across the room as they test themselves on material they must learn.

- What is your usual position when you study? _____

_____

- Are your muscles slightly tense in this position, or are they completely relaxed?

_____

Make sure you have all the materials you will need: ballpoint pens, highlighter pens, pencils, loose-leaf or typing paper, and a small memo pad. It would be ideal (though not essential) to have computer access and a calculator as well.

Finally, to avoid interruptions in your study place, ask your family and friends to please keep away during study hours. Tell them that you will return telephone calls and answer e-mail after you finish studying. Preparing a good environment in advance ensures that when you do achieve concentration, nothing will interrupt you.

If you do not have a room where you can study, use a secluded spot in the library or student center, or find some other quiet spot. If you have one particular place where you usually do most of your studying, you will almost automatically shift into gear and begin studying when you go to that place.

Hint 5: Stay in Good Physical Condition.

You do not want to tire easily or have frequent illnesses. Eat nourishing meals, starting with breakfast—your most important meal of the day. For some students, breakfast is simply coffee and doughnuts or a soda and cookies from a vending machine. But a solid breakfast is not merely a combination of caffeine and sugar. It is, instead, protein, as in milk, yogurt, or a whole-grain cereal. Protein will supply the steady flow of blood sugar needed to keep you mentally alert through the entire day.

Try to get an average of eight hours of sleep a night unless your system can manage with less. Also, try to exercise on a regular basis. A short workout in the morning (if only five minutes of running in place) will help sustain your energy flow during the day. Finally, do not hesitate to take a fifteen- to thirty-minute nap at some point during the day. Research findings show that such a nap can provide a helpful energy boost.

- What is your typical breakfast? How could you realistically improve it?

  _____

- What other steps do you take—or should you take—to stay in good physical condition? _____

Hint 6: Vary Your Study Activities.

Study sessions need not be four-hour marathons devoted to one subject. When you cannot concentrate anymore, don't waste time staring unproductively at, say, a mathematics problem. Switch over to your English paper or biology report. The change in subject matter and type of assignment can ease mental strain by stimulating a different part of your brain—verbal ability, for instance—while the other part (mathematical ability) rests. By varying your activities, you will stay fresh and alert longer than you would if you hammered away at one subject for hours.

Hint 7: Practice the Study Skills in This Book.

Many students can't concentrate on their studies because they don't know *how* to study. They look at the brief notes they took during a class lecture and wonder what to do with them. They start reading a textbook as casually as if they were reading the sports page of the newspaper, and then they wonder why they get so little out of it. They have perhaps been told that taking good notes and then reciting those notes are keys to effective study, but they are not sure how to apply these skills. Learning and practicing study skills will help you become deeply involved in your assignments. Before you know it, you are concentrating.

- Of all the study skills in this book, which are the three most important for you to practice? _____ _____ _____

Hint 8: Use Outside Help When Needed.   Some people find that study-ing with a friend or friends helps concentration. Others, however, find it more of a distraction than an aid because they spend more time chatting than studying cooperatively. Use the technique of team study only if you think it will be of real value to you. Also, find out if your school has a tutoring service. If so, do not hesitate to use the service to get help in a particular subject or subjects. Having a good tutor could make a significant difference in your grade for a course. And determine if your school, like many schools, has a learning center where you may work on developing skills in writing, reading, study, mathematics, and computers. Finally, learn the office hours of your instructors and find out whether you can see them if you need additional help.

- Does your school have a tutoring service? _____
- Does your school have a learning center? _____
- If so, where is each located? _____

Some Final Thoughts

You now have several practical means of gaining control of your time: a course outline, a monthly calendar, a master study schedule, and a "to do" list. In addition, you have learned useful hints for aiding concentration. Use whatever combination of techniques is best for you. These tools, combined with your own determination to apply them, can reduce the disorder of everyday life, where time slips quickly and silently away. Through time planning, you can achieve the consistency in your work that is absolutely vital for success in school. And through time control and steady concentration, you can take command of your life and accomplish more work than you have ever done before.

Practice in Time Control and Concentration

Activity 1

Several time-control skills and study and concentration habits are listed below. Evaluate yourself by putting a check mark beside each of the skills or habits that you already practice. Then put a check mark beside those steps that you plan to practice. Leave a space blank if you do not plan to follow a particular strategy.

Now Do	Plan to Do	
____	____	• Use course outlines.
____	____	• Use a large monthly calendar.
____	____	• Use a weekly study schedule.
____	____	• Use a daily or weekly "to do" list.
____	____	• Have regular study hours.
____	____	• Schedule as many hours as needed for a particular course.
____	____	• Have rewards for using study time effectively.
____	____	• Work on difficult subjects at times when you are most alert.
____	____	• Balance activities.
____	____	• Try to have a positive attitude about each course.
____	____	• Set goals before starting work.
____	____	• Create a good study environment (comfortable but nondistracting).
____	____	• Stay in good physical condition.
____	____	• Vary your study activities.
____	____	• Use outside help when needed.

Activity 2

Several weeks into the semester, your instructor will ask you to hand in copies of the following:

• One month from your monthly calendar.
• Your weekly study schedule.
• Your most recent daily or weekly "to do" list.

Do not simply pass in copies of the materials you have prepared while doing this chapter; instead, pass in recent and updated materials. And be honest; if you are not using one or more of these methods of time control, don't pretend you are. Instead, write a short essay explaining why you have decided not to use one or more of the time-control methods in this chapter.

Activity 3

Write a short paper about some aspect of concentration skills. Here are some suggestions.

Option 1   Write a paragraph about the problems you've had concentrating in one particular class. Describe the reasons you may not have concentrated effectively. For example, you might have had a poor attitude about school in general or this subject in particular; you might have procrastinated a good deal; you might have lacked certain study skills; you might have had a poor study environment. Use specific details to give a clear picture of your study habits in that class.

Option 2   Write a narrative paragraph about your last study session. Be specific about how well *or* how poorly you concentrated and why.

Option 3   Write a paragraph detailing three specific changes you are planning to make in the place where you study.

Option 4   Write a paragraph on the mistakes the students you see around you make when they study. Note, for example, where you see students studying, the conditions under which they are trying to study, how they are going about studying, and so on.

The PRWR Study Method

This chapter will show you how to study a textbook chapter by

- **Previewing the chapter**
- **Reading the chapter**
- **Taking notes on the chapter**
- **Studying your notes**

Textbook Study: In Real Life

Read the profile that follows. Then ask yourself these questions:

- How did Ryan expect to feel about his college textbooks? How was he surprised?
- What techniques does Ryan use to study his textbooks?
- Which of Ryan's textbook-study techniques sound most helpful to me?

Student Profile: Ryan Klootwyk

Ryan Klootwyk didn't go straight from high school to college.

He took what he now refers to as "a tiny fourteen-year break" first.

The 34-year-old graduate of Grand Valley State University in Allentown, Michigan , had spent his last three years of high school "bouncing between the normal school and the alternative school for troubled kids. Usually I didn't go to either of them; I hung out at the library, reading."

Ryan had grown up amid a chaos of heroin addiction, drinking, and abuse at the hands of his mother's vicious boyfriend. He kept his grades

Continued

high through most of it, but when he was a teenager, the strain became too much. Turning his back on school, Ryan embraced a life of alcohol, drugs, and petty crime. After barely earning his high school degree, he went to work as a manual laborer. Days of backbreaking, low-paying work might have deadened his mind except for one thing: He'd never stopped reading. He found himself drawn to historical accounts of soldiers and prisoners of war, people who'd battled their way out of mental or physical prisons and emerged stronger men. Finally, at age twenty-nine, Ryan was ready to break out of his own self-imposed captivity. He enrolled for his first class at Muskegon Community College.

Although he knew going back to school at his age would be difficult, Ryan also brought a certain cockiness to the endeavor. "I went into college thinking this'd be a piece of cake," he admits today. "I'd always thought of myself as having more on the ball than the average guy. I was a great reader; I knew my comprehension was excellent, so I'd just whip through this stuff, right?"

Wrong. When Ryan got his first look at college textbooks, he was floored. "They were wordy and high-falutin', and they seemed to convey a message that was over my head. I consider myself an intelligent person, but they were just plain *frustrating*." Fortunately, Ryan's momentum carried him through this initial discouragement. He began to seek out help—help from tutors, help from his instructors. "I got into the habit of taking my books to them and saying, 'What *is* this?"

Gradually, thanks to the help from those outside sources and his own drive to succeed, Ryan worked out effective methods for dealing with the intimidating texts. He begins the process as soon as he gets a new book.

"First, I find some quiet time and place to look through the whole thing," he says. "I don't try to plow in and read it. I get the big picture first. I leaf through it, look at the illustrations, the captions, the headings, the titles, and try to get a sense of the book as a whole."

Continued

After he's gotten acquainted with the textbook, Ryan begins studying with highlighter in hand, marking key words and phrases—but the important word here is *key*. "I highlight *very restrictively*," he says emphatically. "Before I touch the highlighter to the page, I search out the absolutely most essential ideas. Textbooks tend to overload you with tiny details, and if you treat them all as equally important, you'll drive yourself crazy." When Ryan saves money by buying used textbooks, he is amazed to see how much of the text the previous user has highlighted. "Sometimes there is more material highlighted than not," he says. "Highlighting like that would be of absolutely no help to me."

Another of Ryan's habits is to make notes in the margins of his textbooks as he studies. "I jot down main ideas, key words, paraphrases of the most important themes," he says. "In a pinch, if I'm running short of time to study for an exam, I can just read the highlighted material and my margin notes and be in decent shape."

A final trick of Ryan's is to keep his textbook open during class lectures. As his instructor presents ideas that are related to textbook material, Ryan jots down notes right there on the textbook page. "That way, I don't forget the relationship between the lecture and the book, the way I might if I just wrote the notes in my notebook."

Each of Ryan's textbook-study techniques is designed with the same goal in mind: to help him thoroughly understand main concepts, rather than mindlessly memorize less important details. "I don't want to overload my poor old middle-aged brain," Ryan says with a laugh. "I'd rather know five things well than sort of know ten."

Ryan must be choosing the right things to "know well." With solidly good grades, he has graduated from Grand Valley with a degree in secondary education. He now has a job teaching high school history. Like those prisoners of war Ryan read about so long ago, he has freed himself from the chains that bound him.

Using Your Textbook: A Caution

To begin this chapter on textbook study, let me share an experience with you. When I first began teaching, I was still studying for my advanced degree in reading at a nearby state college. I remember especially a class in statistics I had every Monday night. I would travel to the college after a long day of teaching. I'd be exhausted, and I'd have to sit through a class that was hardly my favorite subject.

There was a textbook, but I didn't understand much of it. I remember looking through it when I bought it and thinking, "Good grief! How in the world am I going to survive this?"

As it turned out, the instructor didn't require us to do anything with the textbook. I wasn't too surprised at that, because in many of my undergraduate courses, although we had to buy a textbook, most of the learning actually took place in the classroom. The instructor's attitude seemed to be "Here is the textbook as a resource. But I'm going to present to you in class the most important ideas."

My statistics instructor did a lot of presenting in class. I remember sitting next to another student whose name was John also. We were a study in contrasts: He was very active in class, constantly asking questions and volunteering answers. In fact, he was so active that he didn't take many notes except to write down what the instructor put on the board. I said very little because I was so tired and neither my heart nor my head was in the subject. I did little but sit there and take lots of notes. I wrote down not just everything the instructor put on the board but also the connections between those ideas. As the instructor explained things, I didn't just listen; I wrote it all down. My attitude was "I can't understand any of this stuff now, but later—when I don't feel turned off and brain-dead—I'll be able to go through it and try to make sense of it."

When I began to prepare for my midsemester exam, I was surprised to see that I had written some ideas down three or even four times. The instructor had repeated them, and I, getting everything down on paper, had repeated them as well. I had so many notes that I was able to make sense of the material. The instructor had done his job: He had used class time to help us understand a difficult subject. His explanations were very clear, and I had gotten them all down on paper. All I needed to study for that exam was right there in my notes. I didn't even open the textbook.

Do you want to guess who got the higher score in the midsemester exam—the other John or me? I got an 86; the other John got a 74. He saw my paper and felt, I think, a little chagrined. If he had asked me my secret, I would have said, "Take lots of notes."

The point of my story is this: *Don't underestimate the importance of taking class notes in doing well in a course.* If the truth be told, in a number of courses, good class notes will be enough to earn you a decent grade. In many courses, the textbook is only a secondary source of information for the ideas you need to know on exams.

Some students fail to take many notes in class because they think, "I'll get what else I need by reading the textbook." Whatever you do, don't make that mistake. An idea you can get down in five minutes in class might take you two hours to get out of a textbook—if it's there at all! Learn how to use the textbook, but don't *ever* make the mistake of trying to use it as a substitute for classroom note-taking.

- In a chapter on textbook study, why do you think so much space should be

  devoted to a story about classroom note-taking? _____

PRWR: A Textbook-Study Method

To become a better reader—of a textbook or any other material—you should systematically develop a whole series of important reading skills, presented in Part Four. This chapter will give you a plan of attack for dealing with a textbook assignment. It explains four steps needed for studying a chapter. The two chapters that follow give you practice in applying these four steps.

The four-step study method is known as PRWR, and variations of it (the most familiar is known as SQ3R) are taught by many reading instructors. The letters stand for the four steps in the process: (1) Preview, (2) Read, (3) Write, and (4) Recite.

Step 1: Preview

A *preview* is a rapid survey that gives you a bird's-eye view of what you are reading. It involves taking several minutes to look through an entire chapter before you begin reading it closely.

Here is how to preview a selection:

- Study the *title*. The title gives you in a few words the shortest possible summary of the whole chapter. Without reading a line of text, you can learn in a general way what the material is about. For example, if the assigned chapter in a psychology text is titled "Stress and Coping with Stress," you know that everything in the chapter is going to concern stress and how to deal with it.

- Quickly read over the *first and last several paragraphs*. These paragraphs may introduce and summarize some of the main ideas covered in the chapter.

- Then page through the chapter and look at the different levels of *headings*. Are there two levels of headings? Three levels? More? Are any relationships obvious among these headings? (For more detail on this, see "Recognizing Headings and Subheadings" in Part Four.)

- Look briefly at words marked in **boldface** and *italics* and in color; such words may be set off because they are important terms. (For more on this, see "Recognizing Definitions and Examples" in Part Four.)

- Glance at *pictures, charts, and boxed material* in the chapter.

Many students have never been taught to preview. They plunge right into a chapter rather than taking a minute or two to do a survey. But remember that it can help to get the "lay of the land" before beginning to read.

Activity 1

Answer the following questions.

1. Were you taught to preview as part of your reading instruction in school? _____

2. Do you think that previewing seems like a good idea? _____

3. What part of the preview do you think might be most helpful for you?

   _____

Activity 2

Take about two minutes to preview the following textbook selection; then answer the questions that follow it.

Alternatives to Conflict

The conflict process may operate at so great a cost that people often seek to avoid it. Conflict is often avoided through some form of three other processes: *accommodation*, *assimilation*, and *amalgamation.*

Accommodation

It threw me when my folks got a divorce right after I graduated. I guess I took them for granted. Our home always seemed to me like most others. At graduation, Dad took me aside and said that he and Mom were calling it quits. He said that they had bugged each other for years, but now that I would be on my own, they were going to separate.

The above story, adapted from a student's life history, is an example of accommodation, a process of developing temporary working agreements between conflicting individuals or groups. It develops when persons or groups find it necessary to work together despite their hostilities and differences. In accommodations, no real settlement of issues is reached; each group retains its own goals and viewpoints but arrives at an "agreement to disagree" without fighting. Two forms of accommodation are described below.

Displacement. Displacement is the process of suspending one conflict by replacing it with another. A classic example is the threat of war to end internal conflicts and bring national unity.

Finding a scapegoat is a favorite displacement technique. The term refers to an ancient Hebrew ceremony in which the sins of the people were symbolically heaped upon a goat that was then driven into the wilderness. Unpopular minorities often become scapegoats. For example, in newly independent countries, all problems may be blamed upon the remaining "colonial influences."

Toleration. In some conflicts, victory is impossible and compromise undesirable. Toleration is an agreement to disagree peaceably. Religious conflict is a classic example of this situation. In Europe at the time of the Reformation, both Protestants and Catholics were positive that they had the "true" version of the Christian faith. Neither group was willing to compromise, and in spite of severe conflict, neither group could destroy the other. Adjustment was made on the basis of toleration; each church ceased to persecute other churches while continuing to hold that these other churches were in error.

Assimilation

Whenever groups meet, some mutual interchange or diffusion of culture takes place. This two-way process by which persons and groups come to share a common culture is called assimilation. Assimilation reduces group conflicts by blending different groups into larger, culturally homogeneous groups. The bitter riots against the Irish and the discrimination against the Scandinavians in the United States disappeared as assimilation erased group differences and blurred the sense of a separate group identity.

Amalgamation

Amalgamation is the biological interbreeding of two groups until they become one. For instance, wholesale amalgamation ended the conflicts of the Anglo-Saxons with the Norman invaders of England. An incomplete amalgamation, however, generally creates a status- and conflict-filled system where status is measured by blood "purity" as in Central America and parts of South America.

1. What is the selection about? (You can answer this question by studying the title.) _____

2. What are the three alternatives to conflict? (You can answer this question by looking at the relationship between the title and the main headings.)

   a. _____ b. _____ c. _____

3. What are the two forms of accommodation? (You can answer this question by looking at the relationship between the heading "Accommodation" and the two subheadings under it.)

   a. _____ b. _____

The purpose of this activity is probably clear to you: Often a preview alone can help you key in on important ideas in a selection.

Step 2: Read

Read the chapter straight through. In this first reading, don't worry about understanding everything. There will be so much new information that it will be impossible to comprehend it all right away. You just want to get a good initial sense of the chapter. If you hit snags—parts that you don't understand at all—just keep reading. After you have gotten an overall impression of the chapter by reading everything once, you can go back to reread parts that you did not at first understand.

Read the chapter with a pen in hand. Look for and mark off what seem to be important ideas and details. In particular, mark off the following:

- *Definitions* of terms—underline definitions.
- *Examples* of those definitions—put an *Ex* in the margin.
- Items in major *lists* (also called *enumerations*)—number the items *1, 2, 3,* and so on.
- What seem to be other *important ideas*—use a star or *Imp* in the margin.

(For more detail, see the skills presented in Part Four on recognizing definitions and examples, enumerations, and main ideas.)

Notes about Marking   The purpose of marking is to set off points so that you can easily return to them later when you take study notes. Material can be marked with a pen or pencil, or it can be highlighted with a felt-tip pen.

Here is a list of useful marking symbols:

Symbol	Explanation
_____	Set off a definition by underlining it.
Ex	Set off helpful examples by writing *Ex* in the margin. Do not underline examples.
1, 2, 3	Use numbers to mark enumerations (items in a list).
☆ **Imp**	Use a star or *Imp* to set off important ideas.
|	Put a vertical line in the margin to set off important material that is several lines in length. Do not underline these longer sections, because the page will end up being so cluttered that you'll find it difficult to make any sense of the markings.
✓	Use a check to mark off any item that *may* be important.
?	Use a question mark to show material you do not understand and may need to reread later.

Marking should be a *selective* process. Some students make the mistake of marking almost everything. You have probably seen textbooks, for example, in which almost every line has been highlighted. But setting off too much material is no better than setting off too little.

Activity 1

Answer the following questions.

1. Why should you mark off definitions, examples, and enumerations when reading? _____

2. Why do you think you should *not* underline examples? _____

_____

Activity 2

Go back and read and mark the textbook selection you previewed in Activity 2 on pages 100–101. Remember to be selective. Mark only the most important points: definitions, key examples, enumerations, and what seem to be other important ideas.

Step 3: Write

I can still remember the time when I really learned how to study. I was taking an introductory history course. For our first test, we were responsible for three chapters in the textbook plus an abundance of classroom notes. I spent about two hours reading the first chapter—about thirty pages—and then I started to "study." My "studying" consisted of rereading a page and then looking away and reciting it to myself. After a half hour or so, I was still on the first page! "This is not going to work," I muttered. "I need a faster way to do this."

Here's what I did. I went through the first chapter, rereading and thinking about the material and making decisions about what were the most important points. I then wrote those points down on separate sheets of paper. In a nutshell, I went through a large amount of information and reduced it to the most important points. The very act of deciding what was most important and writing that material down was a valuable step in understanding the material. It took me a couple of hours to prepare my study sheets. Then I was able to close the book and just concentrate on studying those sheets.

I used that study technique successfully through college and graduate school. And when I began my own professional work in reading and study skills, I discovered that almost all successful students use some variation of the same basic strategy.

The third step, then, is to *write*. Following are specific directions for taking good notes.

What to Write

1   Write the *title* of the chapter at the top of your first sheet of paper. Then write down each *heading* in the chapter. Under each heading, take notes on what seem to be the important points.

2   Rewrite headings as *basic questions* to help you locate important points. For example, if a heading is "One-Parent Families," you might convert it to the question "How many one-parent families are there?" Then write down the answer to that question if it appears in the text. If a heading is "Choosing a Mate," you could ask "How do we choose a mate?" and write down the answer to that question.

3   Look for *definitions of key terms,* usually set off in color, **boldface,** or *italics.* Write down each term and its definition.

4   Look for *examples* of definitions. The examples will help make those definitions clear and understandable. Write down one good, clear example for each definition.

5   Look for *major items in a list* (enumerations). Write them down and number them *1, 2, 3,* and so on. For example, suppose the heading "Agents of Socialization" in a textbook is followed by four subheads, "The Family," "Peers," "School," and "The Mass Media." Write down the heading. Then write the four subheads under it and number them *1, 2, 3,* and *4.*

6   Remember that your goal is to take a large amount of information in a chapter and reduce it to the most important points. Try not to take too many notes. Instead, use headings, definitions, examples, and enumerations in the chapter to help you focus on what is most important.

How to Write

1   Write your notes on letter-size sheets of paper (8½ by 11 inches). By using such paper (rather than note cards), you will be able to see *relationships* among ideas more easily, because more ideas will fit on a single page.

2   Make sure your handwriting is clear and easy to read. Later, when you study your notes, you don't want to have to spend time trying to decipher them.

3   Leave space in the left-hand margin and top margin of your study sheet so that you can write down key words to help you study the material. Key words will be described on page 107 of this chapter.

4   Don't overuse outlining symbols when you take notes. To show enumerations, use a simple sequence of numbers (1, 2, 3, and so on) or letters (a, b, c, and so on). Often, indenting a line or skipping a space is enough to help show relationships among parts of the material. Notice, for example, that very few outlining symbols are used in the sample study sheet on page 106, yet the organization is very clear.

5 Summarize material whenever you can. In other words, reduce it to the fewest words possible while still keeping the ideas complete and clear. For instance, in the sample study sheet, the example for "accommodation" has been summarized so that it reads simply, "Parents agree not to separate until child graduates."

Activity 1

Answer the following questions.

1. When you are taking notes on a chapter, how many of the headings in the chapter should you write down? _____

_____

2. What are enumerations? _____

_____

3. In "What to Write" on page 104, what do you consider the three most helpful guidelines?

   a. _____

   _____

   b. _____

   _____

   c. _____

   _____

4. In "How to Write" on page 104, what do you consider the three most helpful tips?

   a. _____

   _____

   b. _____

   _____

   c. _____

   _____

Activity 2

A sample study sheet for the selection "Alternatives to Conflict" appears on the next page. Refer to the selection (on pages 100–101) to fill in the notes that are missing.

Sociology, Chapter 14: "Social Processes"

Three Alternatives to Conflict

1. Accommodation—process of developing temporary working agreements between conflicting individuals or groups.

    Ex.—Parents agree not to separate until child graduates.

Two forms of accommodation:

    a. Displacement—process of suspending one conflict by replacing it with another.

    Ex.—

    Favorite displacement technique: find a scapegoat.

    Ex.—blame problems of new nation on "colonial influences."

    b. Toleration—agreement to disagree peaceably.

    Ex.—Protestants and Catholics during Reformation came to tolerate rather than persecute each other.

2. Assimilation—

    Ex.—riots against Irish in the United States ceased as they were assimilated.

3. Amalgamation—

    Ex.—Anglo-Saxon and Norman invaders of England became one, ending conflicts.

Step 4: Recite

Let's review what you need to do to study a textbook chapter. First you *preview* the chapter. Then you *read* it through once, marking off what appear to be important ideas. Third, you reread it, decide on the important ideas, and *write* study notes. Fourth, you need to learn your notes. How can you do this?

To learn your notes, you *recite* the material to yourself. Using key words and phrases—also known as *recall words*—will help you do this. Write the recall words in the margins of your notes. For example, look at the recall words in the margin of the following notes:

	Three Alternatives to Conflict
	1. Accommodation—process of developing temporary working agreements between conflicting individuals or groups.
	Ex.—Parents agree not to separate until child graduates.
	Two forms of accommodation:

After you have written the recall words, use them to study your notes. To do so, turn each recall word into a question and go over the material until you can answer the question without looking at the page. For example, look at the recall words "3 alternatives to conflict" and see if you can recite those three alternatives to yourself without looking at the material. You'll find out immediately whether or not you know the material. Go back and reread the items if necessary. Then look away again and try once more to recite the material. Next, look at "Def + ex of accommodation" and see if you can say the definition and give an example of accommodation without looking at the page.

After you finish a section, go back and review previous sections. For instance, after you can recite to yourself the definition and example of accommodation, go back and make sure you can also recite the three alternatives to conflict. Continue like this—studying, reciting, and reviewing—as you move through all the material.

You will discover that recitation helps you pay attention. There is simply no way you can sleepwalk your way through it. Either you do it or you don't. Recitation is, in fact, a surefire way of mastering the material you need to learn. More information about recitation is given in the chapter "Building a Powerful Memory" (page 201).

Activity

Answer the following questions.

1. In the past, have you studied material mainly by reading and rereading it or mainly by reading and reciting? _____

2. A number of experiments have found that students who spend 25 percent of their time reading and 75 percent reciting remember much more than students who spend all their time reading. Will this fact make you spend more of your study time reciting? _____

3. Suppose you learn a group of four definitions until you can say them without looking at them. Then you go on and learn a group of several more definitions. What should you do after learning the second group of definitions?

   _____

4. What are recall words? _____

   _____

5. Where should you write recall words? _____

   _____

Learning to Use PRWR

The following activities will give you practice in the four steps of PRWR: previewing, reading, writing notes, and reciting.

Activity 1: A Short Passage from a Speech Text

Preview   Take about thirty seconds to preview the following short textbook passage. The title tells you that the passage is about _____.
How many terms are set off in *italics* within the passage? _____

Noise

A person's ability to interpret, understand, or respond to symbols is often hurt by noise. *Noise* is any stimulus that gets in the way of sharing meaning. Much of your success as a communicator depends on how you cope with external, internal, and semantic noises.

External noises are the sights, sounds, and other stimuli that draw people's attention away from intended meaning. For instance, during a student's explanation of how a food processor works, your attention may be drawn to the sound of an airplane overhead. The airplane sound is external noise. External noise does not have to be a sound. Perhaps during the explanation, a particularly attractive classmate glances toward you, and for a moment your attention turns to that person. Such visual distraction to your attention is also external noise.

Internal noises are the thoughts and feelings that interfere with meaning. Have you ever found yourself daydreaming when someone was trying to tell you something? Perhaps you let your mind wander to thoughts of the good time you had at a dance club last night or to the argument you had with someone this morning. If you have tuned out the words of your friend and tuned in a daydream or a past conversation, then you have created internal noise.

Semantic noises are those alternative meanings aroused by certain symbols that inhibit meaning. Suppose that a student mentioned that the salesman who sells food processors at the department store seemed like a "gay fellow." If you think of "gay" as a word for *homosexual*, you would miss the student's meaning entirely. Since meaning depends on your own experience, others may at times decode a word or phrase differently from the way you intended. When this happens, you have semantic noise.

Read (and Mark)   Read the passage straight through, underlining the four definitions you will find. Also, number the three kinds of noises as 1, 2, and 3, respectively. Put an *Ex* in the margin beside each example of a definition.

Write   Complete the following notes about the passage "Noise":

Noise—_____

_____

Kinds of noises:

1. External—_____

_____

Ex.— _____

2. Internal—_____

_____

Ex.— _____

3. Semantic—_____

_____

Ex.— _____

Note that the keys to the main idea here are an enumeration and definitions.

Recite   What recall words could you write in the margin to help you study this passage? _____

After you can recite to yourself the definition of *noise,* you should study until you can say to yourself the definition and an example of *external noises.* What should you then do? _____

Activity 2: A Short Passage from a Sociology Text

Preview   Take about thirty seconds to preview the following short textbook passage. The title tells you that the passage is about _____. How many terms are set off in **boldface** within the passage? _____

The Crowd

The crowd is one of the most familiar and at times spectacular forms of collective behavior. It is a temporary, relatively unorganized gathering of people who are in close physical proximity. Since a wide range of behavior is encompassed by the concept, the sociologist Herbert Blumer distinguishes among four basic types of crowd behavior. The first, a **casual crowd,** is a collection of people who have little in common except that they may be participating in a common event, such as looking through a department-store window. The second, a **conventional crowd,** is a number of people who have assembled for some specific purpose and who typically act in accordance with established norms, such as people attending a baseball game or concert. The third, an **expressive crowd,** is an aggregation of people who have gotten together for self-stimulation and personal gratification, such as at a religious revival or a rock festival. And fourth, an **acting crowd** is an excited, volatile collection of people who are engaged in rioting, looting, or other forms of aggressive behavior in which established norms carry little weight.

Read (and Mark)   Read the passage straight through, underlining the five definitions you will find. Number the types of crowd behavior 1, 2, 3, and 4.

Write   Complete the following notes about the passage "The Crowd":

Crowd—_____

_____

Types of crowd behavior:

1. Casual crowd—_____

_____

2. Conventional crowd—_____

_____

3. Expressive crowd—_____

_____

4. Acting crowd—_____

_____

Recite   To help you study this passage, you could write "crowd" in the margin as one recall word and _____ as the other recall words.

Activity 3: A Short Passage from a Psychology Text

Preview   Take about thirty seconds to preview the following short textbook passage. The title tells you that the passage is about _____. How many terms are set off in *italics* within the passage? _____

Four Types of ESP

Parapsychologists (psychologists who study claims of more-than-normal happenings) have proposed four types of extrasensory perception, or ESP, each of which is said to occur without using the physical senses. *Telepathy* is one person's sending thoughts to another. For example, in an experiment, one person may look at a picture and try to "send" this picture to a "receiver" in another room. *Clairvoyance* is perceiving distant events, such as sensing that one's child has just been in a car accident. *Precognition* is "preknowing" (foretelling) future events, such as the assassination of a political leader. *Psychokinesis* is "mind over matter"—for example, levitating a table or, in an experiment, influencing the roll of a die by concentrating on a particular number.

Read (and Mark)   Read the passage straight through, underlining the four definitions you will find. Number them 1, 2, 3, and 4, respectively. Put an *Ex* in the margin beside each example of a definition.

Write   Complete the following notes about the passage "Four Types of ESP":

1. Telepathy—_____

   Ex.—_____

2. Clairvoyance—_____

   Ex.—_____

3. _____

   Ex.—_____

4. _____

   Ex.—_____

Recite   What recall words could you write in the margin to help you study this passage? _____

After you can recite to yourself the definition and an example of *telepathy,* you should then study until you can say to yourself the definition and an example of *clairvoyance.* What should you then do? _____

_____

Activity 4: A Short Passage from a Social Psychology Text

Preview   Take about thirty seconds to preview the following short textbook passage. The title tells you that the passage is about _____.
What words are set off in *italics* within the passage? _____

Seeing Ourselves Favorably

It is widely believed that most of us suffer from low self-esteem: the "I'm not OK—you're OK" problem. For example, the counseling psychologist Carl Rogers concluded that most people he has known "despise themselves, regard themselves as worthless and unlovable." As the comedian Groucho Marx put it, "I'd never join any club that would accept a person like me." The evidence, however, indicates that the writer William Saroyan was closer to the truth: "Every man is a good man in a bad world—as he himself knows."

Although social psychologists are debating the reason for this *self-serving bias*—that is, the tendency to perceive oneself favorably—there is general agreement regarding its reality, its prevalence, and its potency.

Experiments have found that people readily accept credit when told they have succeeded (attributing the success to their ability and effort), yet often attribute failure to such external factors as bad luck or a problem's inherent "impossibility." Similarly, in explaining their victories, athletes commonly credit themselves; but they are more likely to attribute losses to something else: bad breaks, bad officiating, the other team's super effort.

And how much responsibility do you suppose car drivers tend to accept for their accidents? On insurance forms, drivers have described their accidents in words like these: "An invisible car came out of nowhere, struck my car and vanished." "As I reached an intersection, a hedge sprang up, obscuring my vision, and I did not see the other car." "A pedestrian hit me and went under my car." Situations that combine skill and chance (for example, games, exams, job applications) are especially prone to the phenomenon: Winners can easily attribute their successes to their skill, while losers can attribute their losses to chance. When I win at Scrabble, it's because of my verbal dexterity; when I lose, it's because "Who could get anywhere with a Q but no U?"

Read (and Mark)   Read the passage through, underlining the one definition you will find. Put *Ex* in the margin beside an example of the definition.

Write   Complete these notes about "Seeing Ourselves Favorably" by filling in the definition and then *summarizing* one example in your own words. Summarizing the example will help you understand it and reduce it in size.

Self-serving bias— _____

Ex.—_____

_____

_____

Recite   After you can say the definition without looking at it, make sure that you can say the _____ without looking at it.

Activity 5: A Short Passage from a Business Text

Preview   Take about thirty seconds to preview the following short textbook passage. The title tells you that the passage is about _____. How many words are set off in *italics* within the passage? _____

Factors of Production

A society's resources are referred to by economists as the factors of production. One factor of production, *land,* includes not only the real estate on the earth's surface but also the minerals, timber, and water below. The second, *labor,* consists of the human resources used to produce goods and services. The third factor of production is *capital,* the machines, tools, and buildings used to produce goods and services, as well as the money that buys other resources. A fourth factor of production is embodied in people called *entrepreneurs.* They are the ones who develop new ways to use the other economic resources more efficiently. They acquire materials, employ workers, invest in capital goods, and engage in marketing activities. In some societies, entrepreneurs risk losing only their reputations or their positions if they fail. In our society, they also risk losing their own personal resources. On the other hand, our entrepreneurs reap the benefits if they succeed; this possibility is what motivates them to take the risk of trying something new.

Read (and Mark)   Read the passage straight through. As you do, underline the five definitions you will find. Also, number as 1, 2, 3, and 4 the four definitions that fit into a group with one another.

Write   Complete the following notes about the passage "Factors of Production":

Factors of production—_____

1. Land—_____

_____

2. Labor—_____

_____

3. Capital—_____

_____

4. Entrepreneurs—_____

_____

Recite   Simply putting the three recall words _____
in the margin would be enough to help you study your notes. Seeing those recall words, you would try to recite to yourself the definition of *factors of production* as well as the "four factors of production" and their definitions.

Using PRWR

This chapter will provide further practice in the PRWR study system explained in "Textbook Study I." You'll use PRWR with ten readings, longer than the readings in "Textbook Study I" and with more varied activities. Readings 1 to 5 will give you guided practice: Each of these passages appears on a left-hand page, with activities and comments on the facing right-hand page. Readings 6 to 10 will give you more independent practice: These are still longer passages with introductory hints, for which you'll do note-taking on your own.

Before you start on the readings, you should master two valuable memory techniques that will help you recite and learn your notes after you have read and taken notes on a passage. *Catchwords* and *catchphrases* will therefore be explained briefly here. (They are also described in detail on pages 208–210, in the chapter "Building a Powerful Memory.")

Two Memory Aids for PRWR

Catchwords

In "Textbook Study I," you took notes on four kinds of crowds (page 110): (1) casual, (2) conventional, (3) expressive, (4) acting. Chances are that you might forget at least one of these four types. To help ensure that you remember all four types, you could create a catchword.

A *catchword* is a word that is made up of the first letters of several words you want to remember. For example, the first letters of the terms for the four kinds of crowds are

C   (casual)
C   (conventional)
E   (expressive)
A   (acting)

Use these letters to form an easily recalled catchword, rearranging them if necessary. The catchword can be a real word, or it can be a made-up word. For example, you might remember the letters C, C, E, A with the made-up word CACE.

After you create a catchword, test yourself until you are sure that each letter stands for a key word in your mind. For these types of words, you'd make sure that C stands for *casual,* A for *acting,* C for *conventional,* and E for *expressive.* In each case, the first letter serves as a "hook" to help you pull an entire idea into your memory.

This memory device is a proven method for remembering a group of items. Learn to use and apply it!

- In "Textbook Study I," you also took notes on the four factors of production (page 114). The first letters of these four factors are L (land), L (labor), C (capital), and E (entrepreneurs). Make up a catchword that would help you remember these four factors.

    Catchword: _____

Catchphrases

Sometimes you can't easily make up a catchword. In such cases, create a catchphrase instead. A *catchphrase* is a series of words, each beginning with the first letter of a word you want to remember.

Look at the passage on noise in "Textbook Study I" (pages 108–109). The first letters of the three kinds of noise are

E   (external)

I   (internal)

S   (semantic)

You might not be able to make a good catchword out of E, I, and S, but you could create an easily remembered catchphrase. For example, I have a friend named Ed, and I quickly came up with the catchphrase "I shot Ed." This is an outrageous sentence, since I do not expect to shoot Ed or anyone, or even put a gun in my hand. The point is that because I created the sentence and because it is outrageous, I would automatically remember it. That's what you want to do: Create a sentence you'll be sure to remember. The catchphrase does not have to be a model of grammar or make perfect sense. It can be so outrageous that you would not want anyone else to know what it is. All that matters is creating a line that will stick in your memory.

The purpose of the catchphrase is to give you the first letters of the words you want to remember. After you create a phrase, test yourself until you are sure each letter stands for the right word in your mind. If you were studying the kinds of noise and used the catchphrase "I shot Ed," you'd make sure that *I* helped you recall *internal, S* helped you recall *semantic,* and *E* helped you recall *external.*

If you were then given a test question asking you to list and describe the three kinds of noise, you would think immediately, "I shot Ed." You would have the first letters *I, S,* and *E.* The letter *I* would be a memory hook to help you remember that one kind of noise is *internal, S* would help you remember that another kind of noise is *semantic,* and *E* would help you remember that the third kind of noise is *external.*

- In "Textbook Study I," you took notes on the four kinds of ESP (page 111). The first letters of these four types are T (telepathy), C (clairvoyance), P (precognition), and P (psychokinesis). Make up a catchphrase that would help you remember the letters T-C-P-P. (Note that you can put the letters in any order when creating your sentence.)

Catchphrase: _____

Guided Practice in PRWR

Reading 1: A Passage from a Marketing Text

Stages of the Business Cycle

The traditional business cycle goes through four stages: prosperity, recession, depression, and recovery. However, economic strategies adopted by the federal government have averted the depression stage in the United States for about sixty years. Consequently, today we think of a three-stage **business cycle**—prosperity, recession, and recovery—then returning full cycle to prosperity. Marketing executives need to know which stage of the business cycle the economy currently is in, because a company's marketing program usually must be changed from one stage of the business cycle to another.

Prosperity is a period of economic growth. During this stage, organizations tend to expand their marketing program as they add new products and enter new markets.

A *recession* is a period of retrenchment for consumers and businesses—we tighten our economic belts. People can become discouraged, scared, and angry. Naturally, these feelings affect our buying behavior, which, in turn, has major marketing implications for companies, often leading to economic losses. In a recession, consumers cut back on eating out and entertainment outside the home. As a result, firms catering to these needs face serious marketing challenges.

For some companies, though, a recession can present profitable marketing opportunities. For example, during the recession in 1991, Campbell Soup Company spotted a trend away from the more expensive, ready-to-serve soups and toward lower-priced cook-at-home products. The company took its new cream of broccoli soup out of the higher-priced Gold Label can, cut the price, and put it in Campbell's familiar red-and-white can. Furthermore, the label included recipes for using the soup as a base for homemade meals. The result: It became the first new soup since 1935 to be among the top ten Campbell best-sellers.

Recovery is the period when the economy is moving from recession to prosperity. The marketers' challenge is to determine how quickly prosperity will return and to what level. As unemployment declines and disposable income increases, companies expand their marketing efforts to improve sales and profits.

Source: Michael J. Etzel, Bruce J. Walker, and William J. Stanton, *Marketing*, 11th ed. (New York: Irwin/McGraw-Hill).

Activity for Reading 1

Preview   Take about thirty seconds to preview Reading 1 on the previous page. The title tells you that the passage is about _____. How many other headings are in the passage? _____ How many terms are set off in **boldface** in the passage? _____ How many terms are set off in *italics*? _____

Read and Mark   Read the passage straight through. As you do, underline the definitions you find. Mark with an *Ex* in the margin an example that makes each definition clear for you. Also, number the items in an enumeration that you'll find in the passage.

Write   On separate paper, take notes on "Stages of the Business Cycle":

1. Write down the definitions of the three stages of today's business cycle.
2. Also, add details of note by answering these questions:
   a.   What emotional effects does a recession typically have on consumers?
   b.   What challenge faces marketers during a period of recovery?
   c.   When it repackaged its cream of broccoli soup, what stage in the business cycle was Campbell Soup taking advantage of?
   d.   How do organizations typically respond to a period of prosperity?

Recite   To remember the three stages of today's business cycle, create a *catchphrase,* a short sentence made up of the first letters of the three stages: P for *prosperity,* R for *recession,* and R for *recovery:*

Comments on Reading 1   After you have created a catchphrase, use those first letters as "hooks" to help you pull into memory the words they stand for. Test yourself, then, to make sure that P stands in your head for *prosperity,* R stands in your head for *recession,* and R stands in your head for *recovery.*

Reading 2: A Passage from a Psychology Text

Anger

Anger is indeed an unpleasant emotion. Think of the last time you felt angry with yourself or someone else. Anger usually is aroused by *frustration*, a feeling that results whenever you cannot reach a desired goal. For example, assume you had a long, hard day at work and are anxious to get home at a reasonable hour. Your car engine will not turn over. You have no idea what is wrong, and there is nothing you can do about it. You feel frustrated, and your frustration leads to anger. Frustration occurs whenever you cannot reach a desired goal. Psychologists have found that frustration often results in some form of anger or resentment. If you become irritated and kick the car, your behavior is fairly normal.

There are many possible reasons why you cannot reach a desired goal. Sometimes you simply lack the ability. For example, in the case of your car's failing to start, you were unable to diagnose the problem and correct it. In addition to feeling irritation toward the car, you may have been annoyed with yourself for not learning ways to troubleshoot engine problems. Often people aspire to goals far beyond their abilities. A shy man may wish to be a supersalesman, or a woman with limited finances and intelligence may wish to become a nuclear physicist.

Frustration can also result from confusion about goals. Sometimes people feel pulls in more than one direction. Kurt Lewin specified three types of goal confusion or conflict that people experience. Each of these three types of conflicts leads to a feeling of frustration.

Approach-Approach Conflicts Of the three types of conflicts, these are the least frustrating. An *approach-approach* conflict is one that results from having to choose between two desirable goals. You cannot possibly reach both of them at the same time. Maybe there are two good parties in different parts of town at the exact same time on the same night. You must miss one, but which one? Or assume a rich aunt hands you $50,000 to buy yourself a new car. Both a Mercedes and a Porsche look appealing. You must make a choice, but indeed it is a pleasant dilemma. In an approach-approach conflict, you always win, even if you must lose another appealing alternative. As a result, approach-approach conflicts are only mildly frustrating.

Avoidance-Avoidance Conflicts These are the most frustrating of the three types of conflicts. Here the conflict results from being forced to choose between two undesirable goals. Did your mother ever tell you to clean your messy closet or go to bed? Assuming you disliked cleaning closets and were not tired, you experienced an *avoidance-avoidance* conflict. The thought of wasting hours cleaning a cluttered closet was dreadful, but the notion of suffering hours of boredom was also unappealing. The usual reaction to an avoidance-avoidance conflict is to attempt to escape. Perhaps you threatened to run away from home. When no escape is possible, facing the conflict is inevitable. The result is being forced to make an unpleasant choice. The choice is accompanied by intense frustration and anger.

Approach-Avoidance Conflicts These are the most common of the three types of conflicts. The conflict results from weighing the positive and negative aspects of a single goal. Eating a piece of chocolate fudge will provide a delicious taste. But it will also cause tooth decay and, perhaps, unwanted pounds. Studying for an exam will result in a better grade, but it will require an evening away from friends.

Source: Virginia Nichols Quinn, *Applying Psychology*, 2nd ed. (New York: McGraw-Hill).

Activity for Reading 2

Preview   Take about thirty seconds to preview Reading 2 on the previous page. The title tells you that the passage is about _____. How many other headings are in the passage? _____ How many terms are set off in *italics*? _____

Read and Mark   Read the passage straight through. As you do, underline the definitions you find. Mark with an *Ex* in the margin an example that makes each definition clear for you. Also, number the items in an enumeration that you'll find. And note what seem to be important details.

Write   On separate paper, take notes on "Anger":

1. Write down the definition of *frustration.*
2. Write down the definitions and examples of the three types of conflict.
3. Also, note which is the *least frustrating* conflict, the *most frustrating* conflict, and the *most common* conflict.

Recite   To remember the three kinds of conflict, you might want to create a line like "At least approach Lola since it is most frustrating to avoid her."

This line will help you remember that the first kind of conflict is *approach–approach* and that it is the least frustrating of conflicts. And it will help you remember that the second kind of conflict is *avoidance–avoidance* and that it is the most frustrating of conflicts. All that's left, then, is for the last conflict to be *approach–avoidance* and for it to be the most common conflict.

See if you can come up with a line of your own that will help you remember the same information: _____

_____

Comments on Reading 2   After you have a line that you automatically remember in order to "anchor" your study, test yourself until you can recite from memory the definition of *frustration* as well as the kinds of conflict, their definitions, examples, and an important detail about each.

Reading 3: A Passage from a Sociology Text

Norms

All societies have ways of encouraging and enforcing what they view as appropriate behavior while discouraging and punishing what they consider to be improper conduct. "Put on some clean clothes for dinner" and "Thou shalt not kill" are examples of norms found in American culture, just as respect for older people is a norm in Japanese culture. *Norms* are established standards of behavior maintained by a society.

In order for a norm to become significant, it must be widely shared and understood. For example, when Americans go to the movies, we typically expect that people will be quiet while the film is showing. Because of this norm, an usher can tell a member of the audience to stop talking so loudly. Of course, the application of this norm can vary, depending on the particular film and type of audience. People attending a serious artistic or political film will be more likely to insist on the norm of silence than those attending a slapstick comedy or horror movie.

Types of Norms Sociologists distinguish between norms in two ways. First, norms are classified as either formal or informal. *Formal norms* have generally been written down and involve strict rules for punishment of violators. In American society, we often formalize norms into laws, which must be very precise in defining proper and improper behavior. In a political sense, *law* is the "body of rules, made by government for society, interpreted by the courts, and backed by the power of the state." Laws are an example of formal norms, although not the only type. The requirements for a college major and the rules of a card game are also considered formal norms.

By contrast, *informal norms* are generally understood but are not precisely recorded. Standards of proper dress are a common example of informal norms. Our society has no specific punishment or sanction for a person who comes to school or to college dressed quite differently from everyone else. Making fun of nonconforming students for their unusual choice of clothing is the most likely response.

Norms are also classified by their relative importance to society. When classified in this way, they are known as *mores* and *folkways.*

Mores (pronounced "MOR-ays") are norms deemed highly necessary to the welfare of a society, often because they embody the most cherished principles of a people. Each society demands obedience to its mores; violation can lead to severe penalties. Thus, American society has strong mores against murder, treason, and child abuse that have been institutionalized into formal norms. *Folkways* are norms governing everyday behavior whose violation raises comparatively little concern. For example, walking up a "down" escalator in a department store challenges our standards of appropriate behavior, but it will not result in a fine or a jail sentence. Society is more likely to formalize mores than it is folkways. Nevertheless, folkways play an important role in shaping the daily behavior of members of a culture.

Source: Richard T. Schaefer and Robert P. Lamm, *Sociology,* 4th ed. (New York: McGraw-Hill).

Activity for Reading 3

Preview   Take about thirty seconds to preview the textbook passage on the previous page. The title tells you that the passage is about _____. How many other headings are in the passage? _____ How many terms are set off in **boldface** in the passage? _____

Read and Mark   Read the passage straight through. As you do, underline the definitions you find. Write *Ex* in the margin beside an example that makes each definition clear for you. Also, number the items in the two enumerations that you'll find.

Write   On separate paper, take notes on "Norms":

1. Write down the definition of *norms* and an example of a norm.
2. Write down and number the two ways in which sociologists distinguish between types of norms. Include definitions and examples.

Recite   To remember the four norms, create a *catchphrase*: a short sentence made up of the first letters of the four norms: *f* for *formal*, *i* for *informal*, *m* for *mores*, and *f* for *folkways*:

Your sentence: *F*_____ *I*_____ *M*_____ *F*_____

Comments on Reading 3   After you can say the definition and an example of *norm* to yourself without looking at them, go on and see if you can say the four norms to yourself. Doing this should be easy because you will have created a catchphrase that will automatically give you the first letters (F, I, M, F) of those four norms. You can then use the first letters as "hooks" to help you pull the words themselves into memory. Test yourself, then, to make sure that the first *F* stands in your head for *formal*, *I* stands for *informal*, *M* stands for *mores*, and the second *F* stands for *folkways*.

Reading 4: A Passage from a Health Text

Illnesses Associated with Long-Term Alcohol Use

Alcohol is linked with many serious illnesses that can destroy the body's most important organs and sometimes result in death.

Gastrointestinal Disorders Alcohol stimulates secretion of digestive acid throughout the gastrointestinal system, irritating the lining of the drinker's stomach and the linings of the esophagus and intestines. It is not unusual for alcoholics to develop bleeding ulcers in the stomach and intestines, and sometimes lesions in the esophagus. Alcohol can give "binge drinkers" diarrhea. It may inhibit the pancreas's production of enzymes that are crucial for the digestion of food. When heavily abused, it can also lead to **pancreatitis** (inflammation of the pancreas).

Malnutrition A common myth holds that alcohol, being made from fruit or grain, is food. It is not. Worse, alcohol actually starves the body of essential nutrients. It does consist of calories, so it produces energy, but it does not contain any of the chemical substances the body needs to build and repair tissue. Alcohol abuse has been reported as the most common cause of vitamin deficiency in this country. An alcoholic may undereat; or, because the digestive system is disrupted, he or she may be unable to process properly the nutrients that are eaten. Alcoholics may also suffer nutritional imbalances because of diarrhea, loss of appetite, and vomiting. In short, alcoholism can be a form of slow starvation.

Liver Damage The liver is one of the organs most vulnerable to alcohol abuse. Alcohol changes the way the liver processes important substances; it can also contribute to infections and other disorders. If the liver is disturbed or infected, the body's immune system and ability to flush out poisons are affected. Damage to the liver can also harm other organs, because the liver is essential to the production and modification of many substances the body needs.

Many alcoholics suffer **cirrhosis of the liver**, a chronic inflammatory disease of this organ in which healthy liver cells are replaced by scar tissue. Cirrhosis of the liver caused more than 27,000 deaths in 1983; it was the ninth leading cause of death that year. Drinking can also cause **alcoholic hepatitis**, in which the liver becomes swollen and inflamed. It may also lead to a "fatty liver" condition by changing the way the liver processes fats.

Glandular (Endocrine) Disorders Excessive drinking can damage the body's glandular system, which regulates such important functions as moods and sexuality. Men who drink too much may suffer impotence and reduced levels of the hormone testosterone; in one study, researchers found that the second most frequent reason for impotence among men was excessive drinking. Women may also throw their hormonal system out of balance through heavy drinking; recent studies indicate that alcohol abuse can lead to early menopause.

Source: Marvin R. Levy, Mark Dignan, and Janet H. Shirreffs, *Essentials of Health,* 5th ed. (New York: McGraw-Hill).

Activity for Reading 4

Preview   Take about thirty seconds to preview Reading 4 on the previous page. The title tells you that the passage is about _____.

How many other headings are in the passage? _____ How many terms are set off in **boldface** in the passage? _____

Read and Mark   Read the passage straight through. As you do, underline the definitions you find. Notice that each of the headings under the title is part of an enumeration, so number those headings. Also, place a check beside details that seem important under each heading.

To decide what is important, turn each heading into a basic question and read to find details that answer it. For example, turn the heading "Gastrointestinal Disorders" into the question "What are examples of gastrointestinal disorders?" Turn the heading "Malnutrition" into the question "How does alcohol cause malnutrition?" Turn the heading "Liver Damage" into the questions "How is the liver damaged?" and "What are the kinds of liver damage?"

The technique of turning headings into basic questions starting with words like *What*, *How*, *When*, and *In what ways* is a good way to locate and focus on important details within a section.

Write   On separate paper, take notes on "Illnesses Associated with Long-Term Alcohol Use":

1. Write down the four illnesses associated with long-term alcohol use, along with important details about each illness.

2. Be sure to include the definitions of *pancreatitis*, *cirrhosis of the liver*, and *alcoholic hepatitis*.

Recite   To remember the four kinds of long-term alcohol-related illness, create a *catchphrase*, a short sentence made up of the first letters of the four kinds of illness: *G* for *gastrointestinal*, *M* for *malnutrition*, *L* for *liver*, and *G* for *glandular (endocrine) disorders*.

Your four-word sentence with the letters *G, M, L,* and *G* (in any order):

_____

Comments on Reading 4   In a passage such as this one, there are an enumeration and some definitions. At the same time, you must turn headings into questions to help yourself focus on the major points presented in each section. Asking questions that are based on headings can be an excellent way to get inside a block of material. The questions help you understand the material and pick out what might be most important.

Reading 5: A Passage from a Biology Text

Building Blocks of All Matter

Two basic principles of chemistry emerged from the work of the French chemist Antoine Lavoisier, the English chemist John Dalton, and others in the late 1700s and early 1800s.

• All matter, living and nonliving, is made up of **elements**, substances that cannot be decomposed by chemical processes into simpler substances. There are ninety-two chemical elements in nature, and thirteen more have been created in the laboratory. Some examples of elements are hydrogen (symbolized H), oxygen (O), sulfur (S), gold (Au), iron (Fe), and carbon (C).

• Each element is composed of identical particles called **atoms**, the smallest units of matter that still display the characteristic properties of the element. All the atoms in a brick of pure gold, for example, are identical to one another but different from all the atoms in a lump of carbon, an ingot of iron, or a sample of other elements. The properties of an element, such as the dense, shiny, metallic nature of gold or the dull black quality of carbon, are based on the structure of its individual atoms, as we shall see.

The Elements of Life   A natural question arose from the pioneering work of Lavoisier and Dalton: Are living things made up of the same elements as rocks, planets, and stars, or is our chemical makeup different? Living things, it turns out, display a special subset of the ninety-two naturally occurring elements in the earth's crust, but the elements occur in very different proportions. Fully 98 percent of the atoms in the earth's crust are the elements oxygen, silicon (Si), aluminum (Al), iron, calcium (Ca), sodium (Na), potassium (K), and magnesium (Mg), with the first three predominating. In a typical organism, however, 99 percent of the atoms are the markedly different subset carbon, hydrogen, nitrogen (N), and oxygen, with sodium, calcium, phosphorus (P), and sulfur making up most of the remaining 1 percent, plus a few other elements present in trace amounts.

Biologists are not certain why the chemical subsets of living and nonliving things are so different, but they do know that atomic architecture determines the physical properties of elements and, in turn, the properties of living organisms.

Atomic Structure   Atoms are extremely small: about three million atoms sitting side by side would probably cover the period at the end of this sentence. The physicist Gerald Feinberg once calculated that there are more atoms in the human body than there are stars in the known universe. Although minuscule in size, each atom is made up of three types of subatomic particles: protons, neutrons, and electrons. **Protons** have a positive (+) charge; **neutrons** have no electrical charge (they are neutral); and **electrons** have a negative (–) charge. Since these subatomic particles are only parts of atoms, none of them displays properties of elements. The protons and neutrons are clustered in a small dense body at the center of the atom called the *nucleus* (the diameter of an atom is about 100,000 times larger than that of the nucleus). The outer limits of the atom are defined by the paths of its electrons, which continuously race about the nucleus in cloudlike orbits. Electrons, protons, and neutrons are themselves made up of a dozen or more smaller subatomic particles held together by special forces.

Source: Janet L. Hopson and Norman K. Wessells, *Essentials of Biology* (New York: McGraw-Hill).

Activity for Reading 5

Preview   Take about thirty seconds to preview Reading 5 on the previous page. The title tells you that the passage is about _____. How many other headings are in the passage? _____ How many words are set off in **boldface** in the passage? _____ What word is set off in *italics*? _____

Read and Mark   Read the passage straight through. As you do, underline the definitions you find. Where appropriate, set off an example of a definition with an *Ex* in the margin. Also, number the items in the two enumerations. Finally, jot down what seem to be important details within the passage.

Write   On separate paper, take notes on "Building Blocks of All Matter":

1. Write down the two basic principles of chemistry.
2. Write down examples of elements and atoms.
3. Note whether living things are made up of the same elements as nonliving things.
4. Note the size of atoms.
5. Note the definitions of the three types of subatomic particles and of the nucleus.

Recite   Write here key words that you might put in the margin of your notes to help you study the material:

_____

_____

After you can recite the first scientific principle (involving elements) without looking at it, study until you can say to yourself the second scientific principle (involving atoms) without looking at it. Then go back and review the first principle. Remember that constant review is a key to effective study.

Comments on Reading 5   Remember that a good way of taking notes is to write down all the headings and then place notes under those headings. Textbook authors carefully organize their information through a series of major and minor headings. By writing those headings down, you help organize your own notes.

Like most scientific materials, this passage is densely packed with information. But once again, you have seen how a combination of headings, definitions, and enumerations can help you get down the important information in a textbook selection.

Independent Practice in PRWR

Following are several longer textbook passages. Apply the PRWR method—preview, read, write, recite—to study the material in each passage. Use your own paper to take study notes. Hints for note-taking are provided at the start of each selection.

Reading 6: A Passage from a Psychology Text

Hints   Definitions, examples, and answers to questions provided by the authors are the keys to important ideas in this selection.

Remember that a good way of taking notes is to write down all the headings and then place notes under those headings. Textbook authors carefully organize their information through a series of major and minor headings. By writing those headings down, you help organize your own notes.

Development of Social Attachments

"I don't believe you. I know that a baby can't do much more than cry, eat, and sleep. You're saying that your baby recognizes your face. A baby's brain isn't big enough to do that." The neighbor had finished talking and stood there with her arms crossed, looking down at the ten-week-old infant. The mother smiled, "OK, I'll show you. You stand on the left side of the crib and I'll stand on the right. Then we'll play peekaboo. If the baby spends more time looking at me, it means that she recognizes my face. If she spends more time looking at you, it means that she doesn't." The mother took her place on the right and the neighbor walked over and stood on the left side of the crib. The neighbor and the mother alternately played peekaboo. There was little doubt about the results. The baby spent more time looking at her mother's face. The neighbor was shaking her head from side to side. "Could be a coincidence. I still don't believe that tiny Kim really recognizes your face."

Whom would you believe, the mother or the neighbor? In a study similar to the peekaboo game played by the mother and the neighbor, Tiffany Field and her associates reported that four-day-old infants initially spent more time looking at their mother's face than a stranger's. Field concluded that even newborns can learn some distinctive features of their mother's face.

Lewis Lipsitt says that until recently, parents were told that their infants were mostly blind at birth and could not taste, smell, feel pain, learn, or remember. Now we know that newborns can see, taste, feel pain, detect their mother's odor, and show taste and flavor preferences. Even more remarkable, Lipsitt has shown that infants can learn and remember. The first time Kim hears a new sound, her heart accelerates briefly. But after the sound is present a number of times, her heart no longer accelerates. This indicates that she "remembers" or recognizes the sound, a process called *habituation.* Lipsitt has also shown that newborn Kim can learn to turn her head at the sound of a tone but not a buzzer to get a taste of sugar water. This is an example of *associative learning.* All these studies indicate that newborn Kim's senses and brain are functioning to a remarkable degree. One way that researchers could assess normal brain development is by analyzing Kim's crying to see whether it fits a normal or abnormal pattern. If her brain development is normal, within months she will develop further sensory and cognitive functions and form attachments to her parents.

Forming Attachments

Between four and six weeks, rhythmically moving stimuli, such as the nodding head of a puppet or a rotating mobile, will cause Kim to smile. Then gradually, between the ages of two and three months, a human face becomes the most effective stimulus for eliciting a smile. Because this smile is directed toward another person, it is called **social smiling.** Psychologists believe that Kim's social smiling may be increased by parental reinforcement. But her social smiling also serves a very important social function, that of communication. The emergence of social smiling is thought to mark the beginning of a period during which the infant forms social attachments with caretakers.

By six months, Kim will recognize her parents' faces. Soon she will begin to give them happy greetings when they reappear after a short absence. When Kim's father comes home from work, she may smile and gurgle, bounce up and down in her highchair, and hold out her arms to him. In a few more months, when Kim is able to crawl, she will begin to follow her parents wherever they go. At the same time, Kim will begin to show distress whenever her mother and father temporarily leave her in the care of someone else. This reaction, called **separation anxiety,** may include loud protests, crying, and agitation, as well as despair and depression when the separation is very long. Both separation anxiety and joyous greetings on reunion are signs that Kim is developing strong affectional bonds toward her parents, bonds called **social attachments**. A social attachment will form toward whoever is a child's primary caretaker—whether mother, father, grandparent, or any other caring adult.

By studying the reactions of infants to being separated from and reunited with their mothers, Mary Ainsworth found that infant–mother attachments vary greatly in quality. When placed in an unfamiliar room containing many interesting toys, a **securely attached** infant tends to explore freely as long as the mother looks on. If the mother leaves, most of these babies cry and become upset. But when mother returns, they greet her happily and are very easily soothed. In contrast, an **anxiously attached** infant does not respond positively when the mother comes back to the room. Some show great ambivalence toward her, one minute clinging and wanting to be held, and the next minute squirming and pushing away.

Other anxiously attached infants simply avoid the mother upon her return; they turn their heads in another direction or move away from her.

There is some relationship between the security of the infant–caretaker attachment and the child's later behaviors. For example, the more secure the infant–caretaker attachment, the less dependence the child later shows and the better he or she copes with the stress of attending kindergarten. The development of the infant–caretaker attachment is important because it establishes an initial pattern of trust and understanding in the infant's life.

Why does the quality of infant–caretaker attachments vary so greatly? The answer lies in a complex interaction between traits of the parent, traits of the baby, and the kind of environment in which they both live. For instance, researchers have found that mothers of securely attached infants tend to be more sensitive to their baby's needs than mothers of anxiously attached infants. When the child is crying and upset, these mothers usually respond quickly and offer comfort until the baby is soothed. This style of mothering is called *sensitive care.* Mothers of anxiously attached infants, in contrast, are less likely to respond right away when their baby is distressed and are more apt to let the infant "cry it out." These women may also have more negative feelings toward motherhood and are more tense and irritable toward their child.

At the same time, many infants who become insecurely attached start life with certain characteristics that make them harder for an adult to respond to. For example, anxiously attached infants in general have been found to be less active, less alert, and less socially engaging as newborns. Outside conditions may also enter into the development of an insecure attachment. When a woman with a difficult baby has many additional stresses in her life and little emotional support from others, the relationship between mother and child may get off to a bad start. The development of attachments is a very complex process that involves many interacting factors.

Although psychologists have long studied the infant–mother attachment, they have only recently studied the infant–father attachment. Researchers found that mothers were more likely to interact with their infants during routine caretaking, such as feeding or bathing, and to pick up their infants at these times. In contrast, fathers were more likely to interact with their infants for the sole purpose of play. The researchers concluded that infants become attached to their fathers as well as to their mothers, and that fathers provide different kinds of stimulation and activities from mothers.

As you can see, the kind of attachment a child develops with a mother, a father, or another adult depends on a complex interaction among a host of factors. When this interaction goes very badly, the result can be tragic, as in the development of child abuse.

Source: Rod Plotnik, *Introduction to Psychology,* 2nd ed. (New York: McGraw-Hill).

Reading 7: A Passage from a Speech Text

Hints   Enumerations, headings, and subheadings are the keys to important ideas here. Notice that each heading under "How to Become a Better Listener" is part of an enumeration. When you take notes, number these headings. You will also find another enumeration in this passage that is formed from *subheadings* (headings that fit under a larger heading); be sure to number these subheadings.

How to Become a Better Listener

Take Listening Seriously

The first step to improvement is always self-awareness. Analyze your shortcomings as a listener and commit yourself to overcoming them. Good listeners are not born that way. They have *worked* at learning how to listen effectively. Good listening does not go hand in hand with intelligence, education, or social standing. Like any other skill, it comes from practice and self-discipline.

You should begin to think of listening as an active process. So many aspects of modern life encourage us to listen passively. We "listen" to the radio while studying or "listen" to the television while moving about from room to room. This type of passive listening is a habit—but so is active listening. We can learn to identify those situations in which active listening is important. If you work seriously at becoming a more efficient listener, you will reap the rewards in your schoolwork, in your personal and family relations, and in your career.

Resist Distractions

In an ideal world, we could eliminate all physical and mental distractions. In the real world, however, this is not possible. Because we think so much faster than a speaker can talk, it's easy to let our attention wander while we listen. Sometimes it's very easy—when the room is too hot, when construction machinery is operating right outside the window, when the speaker is tedious. But our attention can stray even in the best of circumstances—if for no other reason than a failure to stay alert and make ourselves concentrate.

Whenever you find this happening, make a conscious effort to pull your mind back to what the speaker is saying. Then force it to stay there. One way to do this is to think a little ahead of the speaker—try to anticipate what will come next. This is not the same as jumping to conclusions. When you jump to conclusions, you put words into the speaker's mouth and don't actually listen to what is said. In this case you *will* listen—and measure what the speaker says against what you had anticipated.

Another way to keep your mind on a speech is to review mentally what the speaker has already said and make sure you understand it. Yet another is to listen between the lines and assess what a speaker implies verbally or says nonverbally with body language. Suppose a politician is running for reelection. During a campaign speech to her constituents she makes this statement: "Just last week I had lunch with the President, and he assured me that he has a special concern for the people of our state." The careful listener would hear this implied message: "If you vote for me, there's a good chance more tax money will flow into the state."

To take another example, suppose a speaker is introducing someone to the audience. The speaker says, "It gives me great pleasure to present to you my very dear friend, Nadine Zussman." But the speaker doesn't shake hands with Nadine. He doesn't even look at her—just turns his back and leaves the podium. Is Nadine really his "very dear friend"? Certainly not.

Attentive listeners can pick up all kinds of clues to a speaker's real message. At first you may find it difficult to listen so intently. If you work at it, however, your concentration is bound to improve.

Don't Be Diverted by Appearance or Delivery

If you had attended Abraham Lincoln's momentous Cooper Union speech of 1860, this is what you would have seen:

> The long, ungainly figure upon which hung clothes that, while new for this trip, were evidently the work of an unskilled tailor; the large feet and clumsy hands, of which, at the outset, at least, the orator seemed to be unduly conscious; the long, gaunt head, capped by a shock of hair that seemed not to have been thoroughly brushed out, made a picture which did not fit in with New York's conception of a finished statesman.

But although he seemed awkward and uncultivated, Lincoln had a powerful message about the moral evils of slavery. Fortunately, the audience at Cooper Union did not let his appearance stand in the way of his words.

Similarly, you must be willing to set aside preconceived judgments based on a person's looks or manner of speech. Gandhi was a very unimpressive-looking man who often spoke dressed in a simple white cotton cloth. Helen Keller, deaf and blind from earliest childhood, always had trouble articulating words distinctly. The renowned physicist Stephen Hawking is severely disabled and can speak only with the aid of a voice synthesizer. Yet imagine if no one had listened to them. Even though it may tax your tolerance, patience, and concentration, don't let negative feelings about a speaker's appearance or delivery keep you from listening to the message.

On the other hand, try not to be misled if the speaker has an unusually attractive appearance. It's all too easy to assume that because someone is good-looking and has a polished delivery, he or she is speaking eloquently. Some of the most unscrupulous speakers in history have been handsome people with hypnotic delivery skills. Again, be sure you respond to the message, not to the package it comes in.

Suspend Judgment

Unless we listen only to people who think exactly as we do, we are going to hear things with which we disagree. When this happens, our natural inclination is to argue mentally with the speaker or to dismiss everything she or he says, but neither response is fair—to the speaker or to ourselves. In both cases we blot out any chance of learning or being persuaded.

Does this mean you must agree with everything you hear? Not at all. It means you should hear people out *before* reaching a final judgment. Try to understand their point of view. Listen to their ideas, examine their evidence, assess their reasoning. *Then* make up your mind. If you're sure of your beliefs, you need not fear listening to opposing views. If you're not sure, you have every reason to listen carefully. It has been said more than once that a closed mind is an empty mind.

Focus Your Listening

As we have seen, skilled listeners do not try to absorb a speaker's every word. Rather, they focus on specific things in a speech. Here are three suggestions to help you focus your listening.

Listen for Main Points. Most speeches contain from two to four main points. Here, for example, are the main points of a speech delivered by Bill Clinton on the challenges facing the United Nations in the twenty-first century.

1. The first challenge facing the U.N. is to use the benefits of global prosperity to combat poverty and disease in developing nations.
2. The second challenge facing the U.N. is to prevent ethnic cleansing and other incidents of mass killing and displacement.
3. The third challenge facing the U.N. is to ensure that nuclear, chemical, and biological weapons will never be used again.

These three points are the heart of Clinton's message. As with any speech, they are the most important things to listen for.

Unless a speaker is terribly scatterbrained, you should be able to detect his or her main points with little difficulty. Often a speaker will give some idea at the outset of the main points to be discussed in the speech. For example, at the end of his introduction, Clinton said he was going to offer "three resolutions for the new millennium." Noticing this, a sharp listener would have been prepared for a speech with three main points, each dealing with a different resolution. As the speech progressed, Clinton enumerated each main point to help his listeners keep track of them. He also summarized them in his conclusion. After this, only the most inattentive of listeners could have been in the dark about Clinton's main points.

Listen for Evidence. Identifying a speaker's main points, however, is not enough. You must also listen for supporting evidence. By themselves, Clinton's main points are only assertions. You may be inclined to believe them just because they were stated by the President of the United States. Yet a careful listener will be concerned about evidence no matter who is speaking. Had you been listening to Clinton's speech, you would have heard him support his claim about the need to combat poverty and disease with a mass of verifiable evidence. Here is an excerpt:

> We are still squandering the potential of far too many: 1.3 billion people still live on less than a dollar a day. More than half the population of many countries have no access to safe water. A person in South Asia is 700 times less likely to use the Internet than someone in the United States. And 40 million people each year still die of hunger—almost as many as the total number killed in World War II. . . . Over the next ten years in Africa, AIDS is expected to kill more people and orphan more children than all the wars of the twentieth century combined.

There are four basic questions to ask about a speaker's evidence:

Is it *accurate*?
Is it taken from *objective* sources?
Is it *relevant* to the speaker's claims?
Is it *sufficient* to support the speaker's point?

In Clinton's case, the answer to each question is yes. His figures about economic conditions, water quality, Internet use, hunger, and the AIDS epidemic in Africa are well established in the public record and can be verified by independent sources. The figures are clearly relevant to Clinton's claim about the problems of poverty and disease in developing nations, and they are sufficient to support that claim. If Clinton's evidence were inaccurate, biased, irrelevant, or insufficient, you should be wary of accepting his claim.

Listen for Technique. We said earlier that you should not let a speaker's delivery distract you from the message, and this is true. However, if you want to become an effective speaker, you should study the methods other people use to speak effectively. When you listen to speeches—in class and out—focus above all on the content of a speaker's message; but also pay attention to the techniques the speaker uses to get the message across.

Analyze the introduction: What methods does the speaker use to gain attention, to relate to the audience, to establish credibility and goodwill? Assess the organization of the speech: Is it clear and easy to follow? Can you pick out the speaker's main points? Can you follow when the speaker moves from one point to another?

Study the speaker's language. Is it accurate, clear, vivid, appropriate? Does the speaker adapt well to the audience and occasion? Finally, diagnose the speaker's delivery: Is it fluent, dynamic, convincing? Does it strengthen or weaken the impact of the speaker's ideas? How well does the speaker use eye contact, gestures, and visual aids?

As you listen, focus on the speaker's strengths and weaknesses. If the speaker is not effective, try to determine why. If he or she is effective, try to pick out techniques you can use in your own speeches. If you listen in this way, you will be surprised how much you can learn about successful speaking.

Source: Stephen E. Lucas, *The Art of Public Speaking*, 7th ed. (New York: McGraw-Hill).

Reading 8: A Passage from a Communications Text

Hints Definitions, examples, enumerations, and headings and subheadings are all keys to important ideas in this selection.

Remember that a good way of taking notes is to write down all the headings and then to place notes under those headings. Textbook authors carefully organize their information through a series of major and minor headings. By writing those headings down, you help organize your own notes.

Verbal Forms of Information

As you conduct research, you'll be looking for both factual statements and expert opinions. **Factual statements** are those that can be verified. "A recent study confirms that preschoolers watch an average of twenty-eight hours of television a week," "The Macintosh Performa comes with a CD-ROM port," and "Johannes Gutenberg invented printing from movable type in the 1400s" are all statements of fact that can be verified. **Expert opinions** are interpretations and judgments made by authorities in a particular area. "Watching twenty-eight hours of television a week is far too much for young children," "Having a CD-ROM port on your computer is a necessity," and "The invention of printing from movable type was for all intents and purposes the start of mass communication" are all *opinions* based on the previous factual statements. Factual information and expert opinions may be presented in the form of examples and illustrations, statistics, anecdotes and narratives, comparisons and contrasts, and quotable explanations and opinions.

Examples and Illustrations. Examples are specific instances that illustrate or explain a general factual statement. The generalization "American cars are beginning to rival the quality of Japanese cars," for instance, may be illustrated or explained with the following specific example: "The frequency-of-repair records for Dodge Intrepid and Buick Regal in the past year are much closer than in previous years to those of the Nissan Maxima and Toyota Camry." Examples are useful because they provide concrete detail that makes a general statement more meaningful to the audience.

You may also find a good example cast in illustration form. An illustration is an example that has been developed with added detail. The following segment shows the difference between casting the same information in example form and in illustration form.

> **Generalization:** Most people want to accomplish an objective with the least amount of effort.
>
> **Example:** When entering a building, people will wait for an open door rather than use the energy to open a closed door.
>
> **Illustration:** "I remember watching the entrance of a large office building. There were five doors. The one on the far left was open, the rest closed. Almost everybody used the open door, even waiting for people to come out before they could enter just because the door was easier than the effort of pushing another door open. This is true of much of life."

Now let us consider guidelines for selecting and using examples. First, the examples should be specific enough to create a clear picture for the audience. If you exemplified the generalization "American cars are beginning to rival the quality of Japanese cars" with the statement "Some American cars are quite reliable," the audience would still not have a clear idea of the degree of reliability. But if you gave the example "The 1997 Dodge Intrepid reliability record, as shown in the April 1998 issue of *Consumer Reports,* is virtually the same as that of the 1997 Toyota Camry," the point would be clear and specific.

Second, the examples you use should not be misleading. For instance, if the Ford Taurus was the only American car whose frequency-of-repair record was anything like the records of Japanese cars, it would be unethical to start with the generalization "American cars are beginning to rival the quality of Japanese cars."

Third, examples should relate to the generalization. If you say "American cars are beginning to rival the quality of Japanese cars" and then give the example "Chrysler Corporation has run a series of commercials showing the beauty of their leather interiors," the example may concern quality, but it does not show how Chrysler Corporation cars compare with Japanese cars.

Because specifics both clarify and substantiate, it's a good idea to follow this rule of thumb in preparing your speeches: Never let a generalization stand without at least one example.

Statistics. Statistics are numerical facts. Statistical statements, such as "Seven out of every ten local citizens voted in the last election" or "The cost of living rose 2.5 percent in 1997," enable you to pack a great deal of information into a small package. Statistics can provide impressive support for a point, but when they are poorly used in the speech, they may be boring and, in some instances, downright deceiving. Following are some guidelines on using statistics effectively.

1. Taking statistics from only the most reliable source and double-checking any startling statistics with another source will guard against the use of faulty statistics. For example, it is important to double-check statistics that you find in such sources as paid advertisements or publications distributed by special-interest groups. Be especially wary if your source does not itself provide documentation for the statistics it reports.

2. Record only recent statistics so that your audience will not be misled. For example, if you find the statistic that only two of one hundred members of the Senate, or 2 percent, are women (true in 1992), you would be misleading your audience if you used that statistic in a speech. If you want to make a point about the number of women in the Senate, find the most recent statistics. Check for both the year and the range of years to which the statistics apply.

3. Look for statistics that are used comparatively. By themselves, statistics are hard to interpret, but when used comparatively, they have much greater impact.

   In a speech on chemical waste, Donald Baeder points out that whereas in the past chemicals were measured in parts per million, today they are measured in parts per billion or even parts per trillion. Had he stopped at that point, the audience would have had little sense of the immensity of the figures. Notice how he goes on to use comparisons to put the meaning of the statistics in perspective: "One part per billion is the equivalent of one drop—one drop!—of vermouth in two 36,000-gallon tanks of gin, and that would be a very dry martini even by San Francisco standards! One part per trillion is the equivalent of one drop in two thousand tank cars."

4. Do not overuse statistics. Although statistics may be an excellent way to present a great deal of material quickly, be careful not to overuse them. A few pertinent numbers are far more effective than a battery of statistics. When you believe you must use many statistics, try preparing a visual aid, perhaps a chart, to help your audience visualize them.

Ancedotes and Narratives. Ancedotes are brief, often amusing stories; **narratives** are tales, accounts, personal experiences, or lengthier stories. Each presents material in story form. Because holding the audience's interest is so important in a speech and because the audience's attention is likely to be captured by a story, anecdotes and narratives are worth looking for, creating, and using. For a two-minute speech, you have little time to tell a detailed story, so one or two anecdotes or a very short narrative would be preferable.

The key to using stories is to make sure that the point of the story states or reinforces the point you make in your speech. In his speech about telecommunication, Randall Tobias, vice chairman of AT&T, uses a story to make a point about the promise and the threat of technology:

> A lighthearted story I heard from a scientist-colleague illustrates the point.
>
> A theologian asked the most powerful supercomputer, "Is there a God?" The computer said it lacked the processing power to know. It asked to be connected to all the other supercomputers in the world. Still, it was not enough power. So the computer was hooked up to all the mainframes in the world, then all the minicomputers, and then all the personal computers. The theologian asked for the final time, "Is there a God?" And the computer replied: "There is now."

Comparisons and Contrasts. One of the best ways to give meaning to new ideas is through comparison and contrast. **Comparisons** illuminate a point by showing similarities. Although you can easily create comparisons using information you have found, you should still keep your eye open for creative comparisons developed by the authors of the books and articles you have found.

Comparisons make ideas not only clearer but also more vivid. Notice how Stephen Joel Trachtenberg, in a speech to the Newington High School Scholars' Breakfast, uses figurative comparison to demonstrate the importance of being willing to take risks, even in the face of danger.

> The eagle flying high always risks being shot at by some harebrained human with a rifle. But eagles and young eagles like you still prefer the view from that risky height to what is available flying with the turkeys far, far, below.

Whereas comparisons show similarities, **contrasts** show differences. Notice how this humorous contrast dramatizes the difference between "participation" and "commitment":

If this morning you had bacon and eggs for breakfast, I think it illustrates the difference. The eggs represent "participation" on the part of the chicken. The bacon represents "total commitment" on the part of the pig!

Quotations. When you find an explanation, an opinion, or a brief anecdote that seems to be exactly what you are looking for, you may quote it directly in your speech. Because audiences want to listen to your ideas and arguments, they do not want to hear a string of long quotations. However, a well-selected **quotation** might be perfect in one or two key places.

Quotations can both explain and vivify. Look for quotations that make a point in a particularly clear or vivid way. For example, in her speech "The Dynamics of Discovery," Catherine Ahles, vice president for College Relations at Macomb Community College, used the following quotation from Helen Keller to show the detrimental effects of pessimism: "No pessimist ever discovered the secrets of the stars . . . or sailed to an uncharted land . . . or opened a new heaven to the human spirit."

Keep in mind that when you use a direct quotation, it is necessary to credit the person who formulated it. Using any quotation or close paraphrase without crediting its source is plagiarism.

Source: Rudolph F. Verderber, *Communicate!* 9th ed. (New York: Wadsworth).

Reading 9: A Passage from a Business Text

Hints   Definitions, examples, enumerations, headings, and subheadings are all keys to important ideas in this selection.

Remember that a good way of taking notes is to write down all the headings and then to place notes under those headings. Textbook authors carefully organize their information through a series of major and minor headings. By writing those headings down, you help organize your own notes.

Consumer Products

Consumer products can be subdivided into four groups on the basis of how people buy them: (1) convenience products, (2) shopping products, (3) specialty products, and (4) unsought products.

Convenience Products

Convenience products are items that consumers want to buy with the least possible shopping effort. There are three types of convenience products: staples, impulse items, and emergency products.

Staple Items. These are convenience products for which consumers usually do some planning. Food items are good examples. For instance, though consumers don't seek much information about milk, they do buy it often, and they plan to buy it when preparing to go to the grocery store.

Impulse Items. These are purchased not because of planning but because of a strongly felt immediate need. Thus, distribution is an important factor in marketing impulse products. If they are not located conveniently, exchange will not take place. Shoppers tend to react by impulse in deciding to buy, say, *People* magazine.

Emergency Products. These are items that are needed to solve an immediate crisis. Price and quality are not of primary importance, although the product obviously has to be of sufficient quality to meet the emergency. Thus, while the price of an adhesive bandage means little when one is needed, it *does* have to stick.

Shopping Products

Consumers visit several stores to compare prices and quality before buying *shopping products.* Even before going into the store to examine such products, consumers may study magazines like *Consumer Reports,* ask friends for their opinions about certain products, or study advertisements. In other words, before buying shopping products, consumers seek information that will allow them to compare two or more brands or substitute products.

Shopping products can be divided into groups, depending on how consumers perceive them. *Homogeneous products* are perceived as being essentially similar (canned food items and home insurance policies are examples), whereas *heterogeneous products* are seen as essentially different (furniture, draperies, automobiles, and repair services are examples). With heterogeneous products the different styles and aesthetic features are important, while price is less important. But homogeneous products pose problems for marketers, because they are similar and must be differentiated in consumers' minds.

For instance, there are many smoke detectors on the market, and they all serve the same essential function; all are warning devices. From the marketing viewpoint, however, the similarity ends there. Each brand of smoke detector is technically different, performs somewhat differently, and sells for a different price. It is up to the marketers of a particular smoke detector to differentiate their product in the marketplace. Generally, they will try through advertising to show that their product is different from competing brands, and sometimes price will be used to distinguish one product from another. Homogeneous shopping products put demands on consumers because information is needed in order to sort the similar products and make a buying decision. For the same reason, such products require much attention from marketers.

Specialty Products

Specialty products are items for which there are no acceptable substitutes in the consumer's mind. Consumers are willing to search long and hard until they find them. Usually, the buyers of specialty products have investigated the products available and have decided which one they want to buy. And they are willing to search for an outlet for that particular product.

With specialty products, the brand name is extremely important. In fact, that may be most of what consumers are buying. Designer fashions are a good example. People go out of their way to find a store that carries clothes designed by Halston, Anne Klein, or Bill Blass. Such designers attempt to generate demand for their clothing so that people will search for their products and buy nothing else. A similar situation exists with specialty services like dental and medical care. People do not want to accept substitute goods and services.

Unsought Products

Unsought products are items that consumers do not readily realize they want or need. Most new products fall into this category, until marketers promote their benefits and the needs they satisfy. Not so long ago the trash compacter was an unsought product, because people didn't know they had a need for one. But as the compacter was developed and promoted, the need for it came to be recognized.

Hospitals, convalescent homes, and cemetery plots are other examples of unsought products. Consumers do not shop for such things until a need arises. But when the need is recognized, the products are sought.

Source: Charles D. Schewe and Reuben M. Smith, *Marketing* (New York: McGraw-Hill).

Reading 10: A Passage from a Chemistry Text

Hints   Definitions, examples, enumerations, and headings are all keys to important ideas in this densely packed passage from a science text.

Remember that a good way of taking notes is to write down all the headings and then to place notes under those headings. Textbook authors carefully organize their information through a series of major and minor headings. By writing those headings down, you help organize your own notes.

States of Matter

All matter on earth exists in three physical states: **solid**, **liquid**, and **gaseous**. Various physical properties distinguish the three states of matter. The properties most often considered are shape, volume, average density, structure, viscosity, and compressibility. Shape, volume, and density have been discussed previously; the last two properties require some explanation.

Viscosity is a measure of the resistance to flow. Substances with high viscosities do not flow readily, whereas substances with low viscosities flow more readily. If we are told that water is more fluid than motor oil, we know that the viscosity of water is less than that of motor oil. **Compressibility** is the measure of the decrease in volume of a substance with an applied pressure. A substance is deemed compressible if a force exerted on its surface (a pressure) results in a compacting of the substance.

Let's consider each physical state individually, starting with the solid state and proceeding to the liquid and gaseous states. The physical state of a substance depends on its temperature and pressure. Unless otherwise noted, room conditions of 25°C (298 K) and normal atmospheric pressure are assumed. Atmospheric pressure is measured in atmospheres, the atmosphere being a unit of gas pressure. Normal atmospheric pressure is equivalent to one atmosphere.

Solids

Solids have fixed shapes that are independent of their container. The volume of a solid is also fixed and does not change when a pressure is exerted. Solids are almost completely incompressible. Those that seem to be compressible, such as foams or corrugated paper, actually are solids that contain holes, or empty regions, throughout their volume. When these are "compressed," the solid structure fills into the empty regions: the solid itself is not compressed.

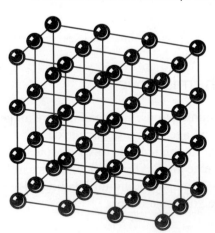

Of the three states of matter, solids have the highest average density. Densities in excess of 1 g/cm³ are the norm for solids. Such is not the case for most liquids and gases. A high average density reflects the fact that the particles within solids are usually packed closer than

Most solids are composed of a regular array of closely packed particles. Particles within solids are usually more organized and packed more tightly than are the particles within liquids and gases.

those in liquids or gases. The tightly packed particles of solids are also highly organized (see the figure above). The regular patterns of particles found in solids are not detected in either liquids or gases.

Solids have practically no ability to flow because the particles that compose a solid are very tightly bonded. Stated in another way: Solids have very high viscosities.

Liquids

Liquids are quite different from solids in many respects, but the two share some characteristics. Like solids, liquids are essentially incompressible; pressure exerted on liquids generally produces little, if any, change in their volumes. When placed in a container, liquids assume the shape of the container to the level they fill (see the figure below).

As previously mentioned, the average density of liquids is less than that of solids but greater than that of gases. Liquid particles are not bonded as strongly as those in solids, and they are less orderly—more randomly distributed. Both of these factors tend to increase the average volume of liquids relative to that of solids. Thus, for equal masses of an average solid and liquid, the volume of the liquid is usually larger than that of the solid, which results in a lower density.

Viscosities of liquids vary over a broad range. Liquids have much lower viscosities than solids; i.e., they are significantly more fluid than solids. However, the viscosities of liquids are greater than those of gases. The gaseous state is the most fluid state of matter.

A liquid completely fills and takes the shape of the bottom of its container.

Gases

Gases bear little resemblance to the more-condensed states of matter, solids and liquids. To a degree, the properties of gases are the opposite of those of solids. Gases completely fill the volume of their containers, are compressible, have a completely disorganized structure, possess the lowest average density of the three states, and have the lowest viscosities.

Matter can change from one physical state to another. For example, solids, when heated, change to liquids. The characteristic temperature at which a particular solid changes to a liquid is called its **melting point**. At the melting point, the solid and liquid states of the substance coexist. Liquids, in turn, change to solids as they are cooled. The temperature at which a liquid becomes a solid is called the **freezing point**. Freezing and melting occur at the same temperature. In one case, the solid changes into a liquid—it melts. Moving in the other direction, a liquid changes into a solid—it freezes.

$$\text{Solids} \underset{\text{freezing}}{\overset{\text{melting}}{\rightleftharpoons}} \text{liquid}$$

For example, water freezes or melts at 0.0°C.

$$\text{Liquid} \underset{\text{condensation}}{\overset{\text{boiling}}{\rightleftharpoons}} \text{liquid}$$

Numerous solids change directly to their vapors without going through the liquid state. This state change is called **sublimation.** At the temperature and pressure at which a substance sublimes, the solid and vapor states coexist.

$$\text{Solid} \xrightarrow{\text{sublimation}} \text{Vapor}$$

A good example of a solid that sublimes is "dry ice," or solid carbon dioxide. At −78°C (195 K), solid carbon dioxide and gaseous carbon dioxide coexist.

Source: Drew H. Wolfe, *Introduction to College Chemistry,* 2nd ed. (New York: McGraw-Hill).

Checking Your Mastery of PRWR: Quizzes

After you study each of the readings in this chapter, you can use the following quizzes to test your understanding of the material. It may take you too much time to study each passage as fully as you would if you were taking a test in a course. However, the very act of reading the material, making decisions on what is important, taking notes, and applying some memory techniques should give you a good basic sense of the material. That is what will be tested in the quizzes that follow.

■ Quiz on Reading 1

1. Into how many stages is today's business cycle divided?

   a. one

   b. two

   c. three

   d. four

2. Which of the following can happen during a recession?

   a. People eat in restaurants less frequently.

   b. Companies often suffer economic losses.

    c.   People can become frightened and angry.

    d.   All of the above.

3. *True or false?* ____ Organizations are most likely to add new products during the beginning of the recovery period.

4. According to the passage, sales of Campbell's cream of broccoli soup increased when the company

    a.   packaged it in a Gold Label can.

    b.   packaged it in a red-and-white can with recipes on the label.

    c.   advertised it as ready to serve.

    d.   announced that it was on the Campbell best-sellers list.

■ Quiz on Reading 2

1. Frustration is caused by

    a.   not being able to reach a desired goal.

    b.   confusion about goals.

    c.   both of the above.

    d.   neither of the above.

2. The most frustrating type of conflict is the

    a.   approach-approach conflict.

    b.   avoidance-avoidance conflict.

    c.   approach-avoidance conflict.

    d.   anger-frustration conflict.

3. The most common type of conflict is the

    a.   approach-approach conflict.

    b.   avoidance-avoidance conflict.

    c.   approach-avoidance conflict.

    d.   anger-frustration conflict.

4. An example of an approach-approach conflict is

    a.   having to choose between a Mercedes and a Porsche.

    b.   having to choose between cleaning a closet and going to bed.

    c.   weighing the advantages and disadvantages of eating chocolate fudge.

    d.   kicking your car when the engine will not turn over.

■ Quiz on Reading 3

1. A society's laws are examples of

   a. folkways.

   b. mores.

   c. informal norms.

   d. formal norms.

2. *True or false?* _____ Folkways are norms considered highly necessary to the welfare of society.

3. *True or false?* _____ Walking up a "down" escalator is a violation of a more.

4. Standards of dress are examples of

   a. folkways.

   b. mores.

   c. informal norms.

   d. formal norms.

■ Quiz on Reading 4

1. The four types of illnesses resulting from long-term alcohol use are gastrointestinal disorders, malnutrition, glandular disorders, and

   a. infections.

   b. cirrhosis of the liver.

   c. liver damage.

   d. chronic inflammatory diseases.

2. *True or false?* _____ Because alcohol provides calories, it can be considered a food.

3. In alcoholic hepatitis,

   a. the pancreas is inflamed.

   b. bleeding ulcers occur.

   c. hormones are disturbed.

   d. the liver becomes swollen and inflamed.

4. Excessive drinking can cause impotence because of damage to the

   a. liver.

   b. pancreas.

   c.   glandular system.

   d.   digestive system.

■ Quiz on Reading 5

1. *True or false?* _____ Chemical processes cannot break elements down into simpler substances.

2. The smallest units of matter that are still characteristic of an element are

   a.   atoms.

   b.   protons.

   c.   neutrons.

   d.   orbits.

3. One of the three subatomic particles is called an

   a.   element.

   b.   atom.

   c.   electron.

   d.   orbit.

4. The small dense body at the center of an atom is called a(n)

   a.   proton.

   b.   element.

   c.   neutron.

   d.   nucleus.

■ Quiz on Reading 6

1. An infant's getting used to a sound that at first made his or her heart beat rapidly is an example of

   a.   habituation.

   b.   associative learning.

   c.   social attachment.

   d.   sensitive care.

2. In social smiling, a baby's smile is always directed toward

   a.   a neighbor.

   b.   a nodding puppet head.

     c.   a mobile.

     d.   another person.

3. Separation anxiety is seen when a baby shows distress or great discomfort at

     a.   loud buzzing noises.

     b.   being left in the care of someone other than the mother or father.

     c.   being in an unfamiliar room.

     d.   the return of the mother to an unfamiliar room.

4. *True or false?* ____ The more secure the infant–caretaker attachment, the better the child's adjustment in kindergarten.

■ Quiz on Reading 7

1. The author has divided his advice on how to become a better listener into how many main suggestions?

     a.   three

     b.   four

     c.   five

     d.   six

2. According to the author, listening between the lines is a way to

     a.   review mentally what the speaker has already said.

     b.   resist distractions.

     c.   agree with what you hear.

     d.   listen for main points.

3. To focus your listening, pay attention to main points, evidence, and

     a.   technique.

     b.   conclusions.

     c.   problems raised by the speaker.

     d.   anecdotes.

4. To judge a speaker's evidence, pay attention to its accuracy, objectivity, relevance, and

     a.   main points.

     b.   technique.

c. efficiency.

d. sufficiency.

■ Quiz on Reading 8

1. The author defines *statistics* as

    a. brief, often amusing stories.

    b. numerical facts.

    c. specific instances that illustrate a statement.

    d. a statement showing how two things are similar.

2. *True or false?* ____ If you paraphrase a quotation, it is unnecessary to credit the person who formulated it.

3. The passage concerning the theologian who asked a computer if God existed was an example of

    a. a comparison.

    b. an anecdote.

    c. statistics.

    d. quotations.

4. *True or false?* ____ The author defines *factual statements* as interpretations and judgments made by authorities in a particular area.

■ Quiz on Reading 9

1. The author classifies consumer products according to

    a. cost.

    b. need.

    c. how they are bought.

    d. how important they are.

2. The four groups of consumer products are convenience products, specialty products, unsought products, and

    a. staple items.

    b. impulse items.

    c. shopping products.

    d. brand-name products.

3. *People* magazine is an example of products that tend to be

    a.   staple items.

    b.   impulse items.

    c.   homogeneous products.

    d.   unsought products.

4. *True or false?* _____ According to the author, emergency products are a type of specialty product.

■ Quiz on Reading 10

1. How many states of matter are there?

    a.   two

    b.   three

    c.   four

    d.   five

2. Particles are usually most tightly packed in

    a.   solids.

    b.   liquids.

    c.   gases.

    d.   oils.

3. A melting point is the characteristic temperature at which a

    a.   gas becomes liquid.

    b.   liquid becomes solid.

    c.   liquid changes to a gas.

    d.   solid changes to a liquid.

4. Dry ice is an example of substances that

    a.   are easily compressed.

    b.   never change their physical state.

    c.   have a melting point.

    d.   undergo sublimation.

Applying PRWR to a Textbook Chapter

This chapter will help improve your textbook study by

- Reviewing the PRWR study method
- Providing note-taking practice on an entire textbook chapter
- Presenting hints and comments on good note-taking

To make your practice at textbook study as realistic as possible, you are now going to apply the PRWR method to an entire chapter from a college textbook. The book, *Sociology: The Core,* by Michael Hughes and Carolyn J. Kroehler, was published in a tenth edition in 2011. This McGraw-Hill book is widely used in colleges throughout the country.

You will read and take notes on the entire chapter by completing the "activities and comments" pages placed at five different spots within the chapter. The work you do will help show you just how the enormous amount of information presented within a chapter can be reduced to a limited number of notes. You will also become aware of the techniques that authors use to help communicate their ideas in an organized way.

Ideally, before studying this chapter, you should work through all the reading skills in Part Four of this book. If you have practiced individual skills such as locating definitions, enumerations, and main ideas, you will be better able to take on an entire textbook chapter. On the other hand, if you need practical guidance right away in how to read and study a textbook, you may want to proceed now with the sample chapter.

A Review of PRWR

To read and study this or any textbook chapter, apply the four steps in the PRWR study method. Following is a summary of those steps.

Step 1: Previewing the Chapter

Note the title and reflect for a moment on the fact that this entire chapter is going to be about "The Family." Then skim the chapter (which goes to page 198) to answer the following questions:

- How many major heads are in the chapter? (You'll note that major heads are set off in especially large type.) _____

- Look at the first major head, "Structure of the Family: A Global View." How many subheads appear under this major head? _____

- What are the first three terms that are set off in **boldface** type in the chapter?

  _____   _____   _____

- What are the first three terms that are set off in *italic* type in the chapter?

  _____   _____   _____

- How many figures, photographs, and boxes are in the chapter? _____
- Does the chapter have an introduction? _____
- Does the chapter have a summary? _____
- Is there a glossary of key terms in the chapter? _____

Step 2: The First Reading

Read the chapter all the way through once. As you do so, mark off as a minimum the following: *definitions* (underline them), *examples* (put an *Ex* in the margin), *major enumerations* (number them 1, 2, 3, and so on), and what seem to be *important ideas* (put a check in the margin).

Remember that while you mark, you should not worry about understanding everything completely. Understanding is a process that will come gradually while you continue to work with the text. Bit by bit, as you reread the text, take notes on it, and study the notes, you will increase your understanding of the material.

Step 3: Writing Notes on the Chapter

As you proceed, write down all the major and minor headings in the chapter. The authors have used these headings to organize their material, and you can use the same headings to help organize your notes. Under the headings, write down definitions, examples, enumerations, and main ideas. (You will be shown just how to take such notes.)

Use common sense when taking textbook notes for your actual courses. Write down only what adds to ideas you have learned in class. Have your class notes in front of you while taking textbook notes. If a good definition of a term has been given to you by the instructor, there may be no need to write down a definition that appears in the textbook.

Step 4: Reciting Your Notes

Use the key words you have placed in the margin of your notes to go over the material repeatedly until you have mastered it.

Studying the Sample Chapter

How to Proceed

Preview, read, and take notes on the textbook chapter that follows. While previewing, you will see that four sets of "activities and comments" appear within the chapter. All the notes you need for the chapter will go on those "activities and comments" pages. Doing the activities will give you a solid, realistic grounding in the skills needed to read and study textbook material.

CHAPTER 10

The Family

[Section 1]
Structure of the Family: A Global View

Forms of the Family
Forms of Marriage
Patterns of Courtship

[Section 2]
Marriage and the Family in the United States

Marriage
Parenthood
Two-Income Families
Beyond the Traditional Nuclear Family

[Section 3]
Challenges for American Families and American Society

Family Violence, Child Abuse, and Incest
Child Care
Divorce
The Elderly

[Section 4]
Sociological Perspectives on the Family

The Functionalist Perspective
The Conflict Perspective
The Interactionist Perspective

BOX 10.1   Sociology Around the World: A Wide Variety in Family Values
BOX 10.2   Social Inequalities: Family Backgrounds and Unequal Childhoods
BOX 10.3   Doing Social Research: Racial Diversity Within Families

In the 1950s, a television sitcom called *Leave It to Beaver* featured an all-American family, Ward and June Cleaver and their sons, Wally and Beaver. In 2010, a television sitcom called *Modern Family* featured three related all-American families: Claire, Phil, and their three children; Claire's father, Jay, his very-much-younger wife, Gloria, and her son, Manny, from a previous relationship; and Claire's brother, Mitchell, his gay partner, Cameron, and their adopted baby, Lily.

Families, and media depictions of them, have changed. At one time in American history, marriage was the primary defining social relationship for adults. As sociologist Paul Amato and his colleagues explain in their book *Alone Together: How Marriage in America Is Changing* (2007:1), getting married was associated with several life events:

- Leaving one's parents
- Creating one's own home
- Achieving economic independence
- Initiating regular sexual activity
- Having children

Today, 51 percent of American women are living without a husband (Roberts, 2007), about half of men and two-fifths of women ages 25–29 have never been married, fewer than a quarter of all households in the United States are married couples with children (U.S. Census Bureau, 2009), American teenagers are becoming sexually active at increasingly younger (unmarried) ages, two-fifths of U.S. children are born to unmarried parents (U.S. Census Bureau, 2009), and between 60 and 70 percent of all married couples cohabit before they marry (Rhoades, Stanley, and Markman, 2009; Stanley, Whitton, and Markman, 2004). Clearly marriage and the family do not hold all of the same meanings they once did.

312   Chapter 10   *The Family*

Whether American lifestyle changes are positive or not is a matter of opinion. Some observers argue that the changes to the family reveal its flexibility and resilience. They agree that the meaning of marriage has been changing, and with it the family institution, and they contend that earlier structures were flawed as conformity-ridden, male-dominated, and oppressive. Others cite gay marriage, easy divorce, the postponement of marriage, a rise in the proportion of the never-married, and the ready availability of contraception as forces that have eroded the family and compromised its "ultimate function"—the licensing of reproduction. No matter what we think family is, most of us think it's tremendously important. "Protecting family" was ranked at the top of 57 personal values by a majority of survey respondents in the United States, Canada, and many other countries (Roper Starch Worldwide, 2000).

Whether the American family was disintegrating or merely changing over the last half of the 20th century, widespread behavioral changes have occurred in the United States and throughout Western societies. Table 10.1 compares the circumstances of American children in 2008 with those in 1960; Figure 10.1 reveals substantial shifts in American family arrangements.

The "family question" is not new. Concerns about the family have a long history (Coontz, 1992), and it is safe to assume that debate will continue. In this chapter we will look first at the structure of the family from a global perspective, including forms of marriage and family and patterns of courtship around the world. We will then focus on marriage and family in the United States, both the traditional nuclear family and other forms of family life. We will look at special challenges American families and American society face, including divorce, family violence and abuse, child care, and care for the elderly. Finally, we will see what the three major sociological perspectives have to offer to our understanding of the family.

[Section 1 begins.]

Structure of the Family: A Global View

What is the family? Even experts on the family have trouble defining it; textbooks for courses on the family offer multiple definitions (e.g., Cherlin, 2010). Many of us still think of the family as a social unit consisting of Mom, Pop, and the kids, living in a comfortable home of their own. But as we will see in the course of the chapter, this definition is too restrictive. Even in the United States, this model of the family—a married couple, breadwinner husband and homemaker wife, raising children—now composes only one in five families. Moreover, in many societies it is the kin group, and not a married couple and their children, that is the basic family unit. With so many Americans living in single-parent households, stepparent households, childless households, gay and lesbian households, and unmarried cohabiting male and

Table 10.1	A Comparison of the State of U.S. Children, 1960 and 2008	
	1960	2008
Children born to unmarried mothers	5%	40.6%
Mothers returning to work within 1 year of a child's birth	17%	57%
Children under 18 living in a one-parent family	10%	26%
Infant mortality (deaths before first birthday)	28/1,000	6.7/1,000
Children under 18 living below the poverty line	27%	18.2%
Married women with children under 6 years old in labor force	18.6%	61.6%

Source: U.S. Census Bureau, 2009; Centers for Disease Control, 2010.

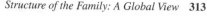

Structure of the Family: A Global View **313**

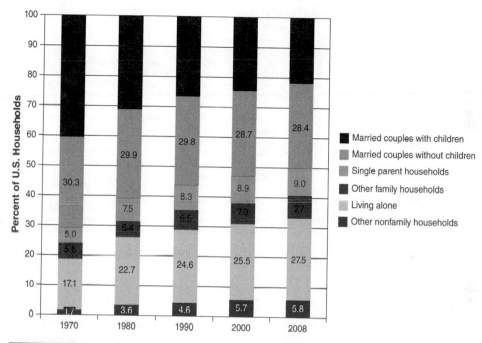

| Figure 10.1 | Today's Families Differ from Those of an Earlier Generation |

Source: Figure generated by the authors using data from the U.S. Census Bureau, 2009.

female households, some sociologists have suggested that it would be better to dispense with the concept of "family" altogether and focus instead upon "sexually bonded primary relationships" (Scanzoni et al., 1989).

Sociologists have traditionally viewed the **family** as a social group whose members are related by ancestry, marriage, or adoption and live together, cooperate economically, and care for the young (Murdock, 1949). Some argue that psychological bonds and intimacy are what families are all about; they see the family as a close-knit group of people who care about and respect one another (e.g., Lauer and Lauer, 2000). The family, then, is a matter of social definition. Because the family is a social construct, family ties are often independent of legal or kin status (Gubrium and Holstein, 1990).

Defining the family is not simply an academic exercise. How we define it determines the kinds of families we will consider normal or deviant and what rights and obligations we will recognize as legally and socially binding. A growing number of judges and legislators are now extending to qualifying domestic partners some of the benefits traditionally accorded married heterosexuals, including health benefits, property and life insurance, bereavement leave, and annuity and pension rights. In 2010 President Obama mandated that hospitals allow patients to designate visitors and to choose who will make end-of-life decisions for them, regardless of traditional family ties (Shear, 2010).

10.1 Sociology Around the World

A Wide Variety in Family Values

The family is among the most important institutions in every society, but exactly how people value the family varies from one society to the next. Compared to other industrialized nations, Americans get married more often, get divorced more often, and get out of relationships more quickly when trouble arises (McCarthy, 2009). A Gallup survey in 16 countries on four continents found a wide variety in attitudes about the importance of parents being married, the ideal number of children to have, preferences for a boy or a girl, and even the degree to which people desire to have children at all (Gallup, 1997).

The ideal number of children for a family varies among countries, from India, where 87 percent of the survey respondents indicated that up to two children was the perfect number, to Iceland, where 69 percent indicated that three or more was the perfect number. Other countries favoring small families (with up to two children as ideal) included Spain, Germany, Colombia, Hungary, Thailand, and Great Britain. Countries favoring three or more children included Guatemala and Taiwan. The United States is divided on the issue of the perfect number of children, with 50 percent favoring up to two children and 41 percent favoring three or more.

Survey respondents also were asked whether, if they could have only one child, they would prefer to have a girl or a boy. Although more than half the respondents replied "no opinion" in many countries (e.g., Tawain, Hungary, Guatemala, Canada, Singapore, Germany, Iceland, and Spain), when respondents did have an opinion they tended to prefer boys. In only a few countries did a preference for girls beat a preference for boys, and only by a slim margin.

Finally, whether children are important to one's sense of fulfillment also varied by country, but in almost every country surveyed, most respondents agreed that they were. In Hungary, 94 percent of the respondents said it was necessary to have a child to feel fulfilled. The United States was at the opposite extreme, with only 46 percent of respondents indicating that having a child was important and 51 percent indicating that it was not. In 2006, 20.4 percent of 40- to 44-year-old U.S. women had not had children, a rate double that from 1980 (U.S. Census Bureau, 2009). Other countries whose respondents felt that having a child was important were India, Taiwan, Iceland, Thailand, Lithuania, and Singapore.

Men and women within each country generally agreed on the various family value questions. The only question on which men and women had clear differences of opinion was gender preference. Women had either no gender preference or a slight preference for boys; men had a strong preference for boys, around the world but especially in the United States and in several less industrialized countries.

Valuing the family may be universal, but family values are not. These findings strongly suggest that, like other cultural traits, family values vary because of differing social, economic, and other factors, such as religion. They also suggest that as our society, economy, and culture change, we are likely to observe more changes in our American family values.

Questions for Discussion

1. How do you account for the small proportion of Americans who believe having a child is important?

2. Why do you think people who express a gender preference for their offspring primarily prefer boys?

In this section we will look at forms of the family, forms of marriage, and patterns of courtship in the United States and around the world.

Forms of the Family

Families are organized in many ways. Individuals differ in their thoughts about whether parents should be married, how many children make a perfect family, whether male or female offspring are preferable, and even whether having children at all is important (see Box 10.1).

More fundamentally, families vary in their composition and in their descent, residence, and authority patterns—characteristics we examine here.

Composition

Social relationships between adult males and females can be organized within families by emphasizing either spouse or kin relationships. In the **nuclear family** arrangement, spouses and their offspring constitute the core relationship;

blood relatives are functionally marginal and peripheral. In contrast, in the **extended family** arrangement, kin—individuals related by common ancestry—provide the core relationship; spouses are functionally marginal and peripheral. Americans typically find themselves members of two nuclear families. First, an individual belongs to a nuclear family that consists of oneself and one's father, mother, and siblings, what sociologists call the **family of orientation**. Second, since over 90 percent of Americans marry at least once, most are or have been members of a nuclear family that consists of oneself and one's spouse and children—the **family of procreation**.

Extended families are found in numerous forms throughout the world. In the Nayara soldiering caste of southwestern India during the pre-British period, spouse ties were virtually absent (Fuller, 1976). When a woman was about to enter puberty, she was ritually married to a man chosen for her by a neighborhood assembly. After three ceremonial days, she was ritually separated from him and was then free to take on a series of visiting husbands or lovers. Although a woman's lovers gave her regular gifts on prescribed occasions, they did not provide support. When a woman had a child, one of the men—not necessarily the biological father—paid a fee to the midwife and thus established the child's legitimacy. However, the man assumed no economic, social, legal, or ritual rights or obligations toward the child. It was the mother's kin who took responsibility.

For some time sociologists assumed that industrialization undercut extended family patterns while fostering nuclear family arrangements. A closer look shows a different pattern. By virtue of high mortality rates, the nuclear family had come to prevail in England before the Industrial Revolution got under way (Laslett, 1974, 1976; Stearns, 1977; Quadagno, 1982). When Tamara K. Hareven (1982) examined family life in a textile community in 19th-century

New Hampshire, she discovered that industrialism promoted kin ties. Not only did different generations often reside together in the same household, but they provided a good deal of assistance to one another. Indeed, economic dislocations and the increased availability of nonnuclear kin may actually have encouraged the formation of extended family households in the early industrialization of England and the United States (Ruggles, 1987). Overall, a growing body of research suggests that a large number of factors—in addition to the nature of the political economy—interact with one another to produce a diversity of family life patterns (Cherlin, 2010; Taylor et al., 2010; Kertzer, 1991).

Descent

Societies trace descent and pass on property from one generation to the next in one of three ways. Under a **patrilineal** arrangement, a people reckon descent and transmit property through the line of the father. Under a **matrilineal** arrangement, descent and inheritance take place through the mother's side of the family. Under the **bilineal** arrangement, both sides of an individual's family are equally important. Americans are typically bilineal, reckoning descent through both the father and the mother; however, the surname is transmitted in a patrilineal manner.

Residence

Societies also differ in where couples take up residence after marriage. In the case of **patrilocal residence**, the bride and groom live in the household or community of the husband's family. The opposite pattern prevails in **matrilocal residence**. For example, among the Hopi of the Southwest, the husband moves upon marriage into the dwelling of his wife's family, where he eats and sleeps. In the United States, newlyweds tend to follow **neolocal residence** patterns, in which they set up a new place of residence independent of either of their parents or other relatives.

316   Chapter 10 *The Family*

Authority

Although the authority a man or woman enjoys in family decision making is influenced by their personalities, societies nonetheless dictate who is expected to be the dominant figure. Under **patriarchal authority**, the eldest male or the husband fills this role. The ancient Hebrews, Greeks, and Romans and the 19th-century Chinese and Japanese provide a few examples. Logically, the construction of a **matriarchal authority** family type is very simple and would involve the vesting of power in women. Yet true matriarchies are rare (Hutter, 1998), and considerable controversy exists about whether the balance of power actually rests with the wife in any known society (Stephens, 1963). Matriarchies can arise through default upon the death of or desertion by the husband. In a third type of family, the **egalitarian authority** arrangement, power and authority are equally distributed between husband and wife. This pattern is on the increase in the United States.

Forms of Marriage

Marriage refers to a socially approved sexual union between two or more individuals that is undertaken with some idea of permanence. The parties to a marriage must be members of two different kin groups, which has crucial implications for the structuring of the family. Indeed, the continuity, and therefore the long-term welfare, of any kin group depends on obtaining spouses for the unmarried members of the group from other groups. A kin group has a stake in retaining some measure of control over at least a portion of its members after they marry (Lee, 1977). In

this section we will define and discuss exogamy, endogamy, incest taboos, monogamy, polygyny, polyandry, and group marriage.

Exogamy and Endogamy

All societies regulate the pool of eligibles from which individuals are expected to select a mate. A child's kin generally have more in mind than simply getting the child married. They want the child married to the right spouse, especially where marriage has consequences for the larger kin group. Two types of marital regulations define the "right" spouse: endogamy and exogamy. **Endogamy** is the requirement that marriage occur within a group. Under these circumstances people must marry within their class, race, ethnic group, or religion. **Exogamy** is the requirement that marriage occur outside a group. Whether or not marriages should take place outside of specific groups can change rapidly, as in Iraq, where Sunni–Shiite marriages

Norms that govern marriage in many ethnic groups, including those among Orthodox Jews, specify endogamy, the requirement that marriage occur within the group.

went from symbolizing a tolerant society to being the source of conflict, hatred, and family breakdown (Raghavan, 2007).

Regulations relating to exogamy are based primarily on kinship and usually entail **incest taboos**, rules that prohibit sexual intercourse with close blood relatives and exist today in virtually every society (Olson and DeFrain, 1997). Such relationships not only are prohibited but also bring reactions of aversion and disgust. At one time social scientists singled out incest taboos as the only universal norm in a world of diverse moral codes. But sociologist Russell Middleton (1962) found that brother–sister marriage was not only permitted but frequently practiced by the ancient Egyptians. He speculated that brother–sister marriage served to maintain the power and property of a family and prevented the splintering of an estate through inheritance. A similar arrangement apparently occurred among the royal families of Hawaii, the Inca of Peru, and the Dahomey of West Africa.

There have been numerous attempts to account for both the existence and the prevalence of incest taboos. Some have argued that incest taboos came about because of real or imagined negative effects of "inbreeding." However, the incest taboo has been found even in cultures where people were unaware of the father's role in reproduction (Hutter, 1998). Anthropologist Claude Lévi-Strauss (1956) suggested that incest taboos promote alliances between families and reinforce their social interdependence; the Zulu have a saying: "They are our enemies, and so we marry them."

Types of Marriage

The relationships between a husband and wife may be structured in one of four ways: **monogamy**, one husband and one wife; **polygyny**, one husband and two or more wives; **polyandry**, two or more husbands and one wife; or **group marriage**, two or more husbands and two or more wives. Monogamy appears in all societies, although other forms may be not only permitted but preferred. Monogamy was the preferred or ideal type of marriage in fewer than 20 percent of 862 societies included in one cross-cultural sample (Murdock, 1967).

Polygyny has been widely practiced throughout the world. The Old Testament, for example, records polygynous practices among the Hebrews. In China, India, and the Islamic countries, polygyny has usually been the privilege of the wealthy few. In the United States, it is not legal, but it does exist. A man in Utah with five wives and 29 children was charged with bigamy and rape in 2000. An additional 30,000 polygynists are thought to be practicing "underground" (Arrillaga, 2000). The arrangement tends to be favored where large families are advantageous and women make substantial contributions to subsistence.

In contrast to polygyny, polyandry is exceedingly rare. Polyandry usually does not represent freedom of sexual choice for women; often, it involves the right or the opportunity of younger brothers to have sexual access to the wife of an older brother. If a family cannot afford wives or marriages for each of its sons, it may find a wife for the eldest son only.

Social scientists are far from agreement on whether group marriage has ever existed as a cultural norm. There is some evidence that it did occur among the Kaingang of Brazil, the Marquesans of the South Pacific, the Chukchee of Siberia, and the Todas of India. At times, polyandry appears to slip into group marriage, where a number of brothers share more than one wife (Stephens, 1963).

Patterns of Courtship

Marriage brings a new member into the inner circle of a family, and relatives have a stake in who is to be the spouse. Random mating might jeopardize these interests: If sons and daughters were permitted to "fall in love" with anybody, they might choose the wrong mate. Instead,

318   Chapter 10 *The Family*

courtship in many societies follows specific and traditional patterns, the topic of discussion of this section.

The Social Regulation of Love

Although love has many meanings, we usually think of the strong physical and emotional attraction between a man and a woman as **romantic love**. The ancient Greeks saw such love as a "diseased hysteria," an overwhelming force that irresistibly draws two people together and leads them to become passionately preoccupied with one another.

Sociologist William J. Goode (1959) found that some societies give romantic love more emphasis than others. At one extreme, societies view marriage without love as mildly shameful; at the other, they define strong romantic attachment as a laughable or tragic aberration. The American middle class falls toward the pole of positive approval; the 19th-century Japanese and Chinese fell toward the pole of disapproval; and the Greeks after Alexander and the Romans of the empire took a middle course.

Societies undertake to control love in a variety of ways. One approach is *child marriage,* which was employed at one time in India. A child bride went to live with her husband in a marriage that was not physically consummated until much later. Similarly, in an *arranged marriage* the parents of the bride and groom make the arrangements for the marriage, sometimes when both are too young to marry but also when both are of marriageable ages. The parents of the bride may know of the groom through friends or relatives or may simply answer a newspaper advertisement.

Another approach involves the *social isolation* of young people from potential mates. For instance, the Manus of the Admiralty Islands secluded their young women in a lodge built on stilts over a lagoon. The *close supervision* of couples by chaperones was an arrangement found among 17th-century New England Puritans. Finally, *peer and parental pressures* may

be brought to bear. For example, in the United States parents often threaten, cajole, wheedle, and bribe their children to limit their social contacts to youths with "suitable" ethnic, religious, and educational backgrounds. The net result of these approaches is the same—a person's range of choice is narrowed by social barriers.

Factors in Mate Selection

Given a field of eligible mates, why do we fall in love with and marry one person and not another? A variety of factors are at work. One is **homogamy**—the tendency of like to marry like. People of similar age, race, religion, nationality, education, intelligence, health, stature, attitudes, and countless other traits tend to marry one another to a degree greater than would be found by chance. Although homogamy seems to operate with respect to social characteristics, the evidence is less clear for psychological factors such as personality and temperament.

Physical attractiveness also plays a part in mate selection. We prefer the companionship and friendship of attractive people to that of unattractive people (Feingold, 1990). However, since the supply of unusually beautiful or handsome partners is limited, we tend in real life to select partners who have a degree of physical attractiveness similar to our own (Murstein, 1972, 1976; Feingold, 1988). According to the **matching hypothesis**, we typically experience the greatest payoff and the least cost when we follow this course; individuals of equal attractiveness are those most likely to reciprocate our advances.

The **complementary needs** theory (Winch, 1958) refers to two different personality traits that are the counterparts of each other and that provide a sense of completeness when they are joined. Dominant people find a complementary relationship with passive people, and talkative people find themselves attracted to good listeners. Interpersonal attraction depends on how well each partner fulfills the role expectations of the other and how mutually gratifying they find

Marriage and the Family in the United States **319**

their "role fit" (Bluhm, Widiger, and Miele, 1990; Collins and Read, 1990).

Exchange theory links these three factors. It is based on the notion that we like those who reward us and dislike those who punish us (Molm, 1991; Lawler and Yoon, 1993). Many of our acts derive from our confidence that from them will flow some benefit—perhaps a desired expression of love, gratitude, recognition, security, or material reward. In the course of interacting, we reinforce the relationship by rewarding each other. Thus, people with similar social traits, attitudes, and values mutually reward one another. In selecting partners of comparable physical attractiveness, we minimize the risk of rejection while maximizing the profit from such a conquest. And the parties in complementary relationships offer each other high rewards at low cost to themselves. In sum, exchange theory proposes that people involved in a mutually satisfying relationship will exchange behaviors that have low cost and high reward.

[Section 1 ends.] [Section 2 begins.]

Marriage and the Family in the United States

The American family has become such a debated subject that sociologists sometimes appear to be at war with one another. Some argue that marriage and family have positive effects on children and marriage partners (Glenn, 1997; Popenoe, 1993). Others—perhaps the majority—say that there are both negative and positive effects and that those who extol the virtues of "family" are traditionalists and conservatives (Scanzoni, 1997; Skolnick, 1997; Cherlin, 1997). This section focuses on the issues that underlie this debate. Let's take a brief look at the marriage and family statistics for the United States: In 2008, 57 percent of those aged 20 to 54 were married; 62 percent of married people reported being "very happy" with their marriages;

60 percent of America's children were born to married parents; and 61 percent of America's children were living with their own married parents (NCAAMP, 2009). Turn that around: Pretty close to half of 20- to 54-year-olds are not married; more than a third of married people are less than "very happy"; 40 percent of U.S. births are to unmarried parents; and 39 percent of our children live with single parents or stepparents. In general, compared to 30 years ago, people are getting married later, they are less likely to divorce, and remarriage is less common (Isen and Stevenson, 2010).

In this section we will examine marriage, parenthood, and two-income families. Then we will discuss some of the many types of lifestyles in the United States beyond the traditional nuclear family: singlehood, single parenthood, stepfamilies, cohabitation, and gay and lesbian couples.

Marriage

In the 1980s two landmark studies on marriage appeared—one a look at life within marriage (Blumstein and Schwartz, 1983) and the other a comparison of marriage then with marriage in the 1920s (Caplow et al., 1982; Lynd and Lynd, 1929, 1937). In the first comprehensive study on American marriage since the 1980s, Paul Amato, Alan Booth, David Johnson, and Stacy Rogers (2007) used two data sets to paint a portrait of marriage and the changes it has undergone. The Marital Instability over the Life Course Study was conducted in 1980, and the Survey of Marriage and Family Life in 2000. Similar research designs, target populations, and questionnaires allowed the researchers to use the data from the two studies to compare the quality of people's marriages—how happy they are with their marriages—in 1980 and 2000. In this section we will look at important details from this study.

First, what defines a happy marriage? Amato and his co-authors found that in 2000,

Studying Section 1

Activities for Section 1

Before starting Section 1, notice that the title page of the chapter (chapter page 311) lists all the main heads and subheads within the chapter. The chapter-opening page (opposite the photograph) page shows that the family is examined in four different ways, starting with "Structure of the Family: A Global View" and ending with "Sociological Perspectives on the Family."

Notice also that the chapter ends with four sections. What are the titles of these four sections?

_____

_____

_____

_____

As you will see, the chapter is followed by a detailed summary titled "The Chapter in Brief: The Family," and the summary is then followed by a "Glossary" that includes definitions of all the key terms in the chapter. The third closing section of the chapter, "Review Questions," tests your knowledge of the chapter, and the final closing section, "Internet Connection," provides opportunities to research family values using the Internet. **In a nutshell, these closing sections of the chapter provide you with the most important ideas in the chapter** and opportunities to test your knowledge and do further research.

Use the Summary and Glossary sections as a guide while you go through the chapter, taking notes as you go. In general, as you will see, your notes will consist of definitions and enumerations.

Complete the following notes on the first eight pages of the text (chapter pages 311–319).

(Chapter 10: The Family)

Structure of the Family: A Global View

Traditional sociological definition of the family: _____

_____

_____

Composition:

1. Nuclear Family – _____

    Two types:

    a. Family of orientation – _____

    b. Family of _____

2. Extended family – _____

_____

Descent

Three kinds:

1. Patrilineal – _____

2. _____

3. _____

Authority

Three kinds:

1. _____

2. _____

3. _____

Forms of Marriage

Definition of marriage: _____

_____

Parties must be members of two different kin groups.

Endogamy – _____

_____

Exogamy – _____

_____

Incest taboos – _____

_____

Four types of marriage:

1. Monogamy – one husband and one wife.

2. _____

3. _____

4. _____

Patterns of Courtship

Romantic Love – _____

_____

Ways that societies control marriage:

1. _____ – child bride lives with husband-to-be.

2. _____ – parents of bride and groom make the arrangements for marriage.

3. _____ – keep young people apart.

4. _____ – Example: chaperones used by 17th-century New England Puritans.

5. Peer and parental pressures

Factors in Mate Selection

1. Homogamy – _____

   Example: People of same age or race or religion tend to marry one another.

2. _____ – notion that we typically experience the greatest payoff and the least cost when we select partners who have a degree of physical attractiveness similar to our own.

3. Complementary needs – _____

   _____

4. _____ – view proposing that people involved in a mutually satisfying relationship will exchange behaviors that have low cost and high reward.

Comments on Section 1

- As a general rule, take notes on a chapter by first writing down a given main idea or subheading. Then write down whatever seem to be the most important ideas under that heading. This is an extremely important guideline to keep in mind when taking notes on a chapter. *Remember to write down headings, definitions, by examples, enumerations, and what seem to be other important ideas.*

- Complete the following: Almost all of the notes above consist of headings, _____, and _____. This kind of note-taking is typical with introductory textbooks, where you are often learning the special vocabulary of a subject.

- When taking notes, don't use any more symbols than you need to. When you do use symbols, make sure they really mean something. In the notes above, the symbols "1," "2," etc. show the four types of marriage, the four ways that societies control marriage, and the factors in mate selection.

320   Chapter 10   *The Family*

happy couples were those who were committed to staying married. Happily married couples think that the division of labor in their marriage is fair, and they have nontraditional attitudes toward how labor should be divided. Happy couples get married at older ages, share decision making, and have close friends in common. In addition, they are more likely to attend religious services together on a regular basis and to be affiliated with the same organizations. On the other hand, the researchers found that spouses who had grown up with divorced parents, had lived together before they got married, and were emotionally insecure had poorer-quality marriages. Despite the prevalence of unhappy high-profile marriages splashed on the covers of tabloids and magazines, Amato and his colleagues found no net change in marital happiness over the 20-year period. They discovered that marriages at the end of the century were stronger and more satisfying in some ways and weaker and less satisfying in others than in 1980, with negative changes offset by positive changes.

What does a typical marriage look like today? Amato and his co-authors categorized married couples into five groups. About 13 percent of the couples they surveyed are grouped as "disadvantaged, young, single-earner marriages" (18 percent in 1980). Another 13 percent of marriages (up from 6 percent in 1980) are "upper-middle-class, prosperous, mostly dual-earner marriages." A larger group (18 percent of married couples) is the "working-class/middle-class, traditional, single-earner" category; this group was 30 percent of all married couples in 1980. Even more married couples (26 percent) are in the "working-class, young, dual-earner" group, not much of a change from their 32 percent standing in 1980. The largest category of married couples in the United States today, and the biggest shift since 1980, is the "middle-class, egalitarian, dual-earner" group, 30 percent of all marriages in 2000 but only 14 percent in 1980.

In 1982, Jessie Bernard argued that husbands and wives experience marriage so differently that a marriage should be referred to as "his marriage" and "her marriage." The 2000 survey found that in some respects this is true; wives scored lower than husbands on all five measurements of marital quality. But the differences were very small, and in general the factors that were associated with a high-quality marriage were the same for men and women (Amato et al., 2007). Only one factor was consistently different for husbands and wives, and that was the husband's share of housework. To simplify results: When husbands did more housework, they were less happy with their marriages but wives were *more* happy with their marriages. The survey data showed that in 2000 women were earning about a third of total family income, while men were doing about a third of all the housework. Both husbands and wives had become less traditional in their views about the division of household labor, with women more so than men, and wives were more likely than husbands to feel that the division of labor was unfair to them. (See Chapter 8 for more about the division of labor by gender.)

Amato and his colleagues also found that age of first marriage has increased (see Figure 10.2) and that marrying at later ages is associated with greater marital happiness. The median age at first marriage for U.S. men rose to 28.1 in 2009 from a low of 22.6 in the mid-1950s (U.S. Census Bureau, 2009). For U.S. women the figure rose to 25.9 years, up from a low of 20.2 years. Marrying at a young age, researchers have found, is a good predictor of divorce, with couples who married when they were young reporting more problems (Amato et al., 2007). Those who are young when they marry are less likely than older spouses to be financially secure, and they are less experienced and more naïve about relationships. In addition, those who marry young have spent less time looking for a spouse. Education plays a role:

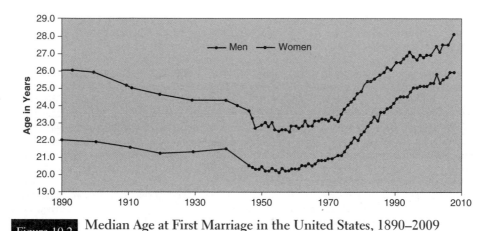

Figure 10.2   Median Age at First Marriage in the United States, 1890–2009

Source: U.S. Census Bureau, Current Population Survey, March and Annual Social and Economic Supplements, 2009 and earlier. Available at www.census.gov/population/socdemo/hh-fam/ms2.xls.

Women with college degrees are more likely to marry in their 30s and 40s, while women without degrees are more likely to be married in their 20s (Isen and Stevenson, 2010).

The 2000 survey also found that the percentage of interracial marriages in the United States had doubled since 1980 (from 1.3 to 2.6). Married couples that included members of different religions also were more common in 2000, as were couples in which the wife was older than the husband. These **heterogamous marriages**, in which spouses have different characteristics, have been found to be associated with reports of less happiness, more quarreling, and less time engaged in positive interaction than for homogamous marriages (Amato et al., 2007).

The importance of marriage appears to differ for different racial and ethnic groups in the United States. In 2008, 75 percent of white families were married couples, while about 20 percent were headed by a woman only and another 5 percent headed by a man only. In contrast, 40 percent of black families were married couples, with 55 percent of families headed by a woman

alone and 5 percent by a man (U.S. Census Bureau, 2009). The numbers for Asian and Pacific Islander families are higher than those for whites (84 percent married couples, 12 percent female-headed, 3 percent male-headed) and those for Hispanic families (70 percent married couples, 26 percent female-headed, 3 percent male-headed). In 2008, 41 percent of African Americans age 18 and over had never been married, compared with 32 percent of Hispanics and 26 percent of whites and Asian Americans.

Public opinion surveys indicate that Americans depend very heavily on marriage for their psychological well-being (Waite and Gallagher, 2000; Gove, Style, and Hughes, 1990; Glenn and Weaver, 1981). Although divorce rates increased dramatically earlier in the century, they have declined gradually since the early 1980s. And almost everyone tries marriage; only about 5 percent of Americans never marry. Most people who get divorced also get remarried.

Although Amato and his colleagues (2007) found a number of significant changes in U.S. marriages over the last 20 years of the 20th

322   Chapter 10 *The Family*

In 2008, 54 percent of African American children were living with a single parent. About 42 percent of all U.S. families headed by a single parent are living below the poverty threshold.

century, in general, married Americans seem to be fairly happy. Nearly half of all married people are "very happy" with the extent of agreement with their spouses, 56 percent describe their feelings of love for their spouse as "very strong," 53 percent are "very happy" with their sex lives, and 68 percent say that their marriage is "better than most."

Parenthood

Married couples who decide to have children find their lives transformed by parenthood. Among other changes, costs go up when children are added to a family: Total annual expenditures per child range from $8,330 to $22,960 (Lino and Carlson, 2009).

Nuclear families that are not disrupted by divorce, desertion, or death typically pass through a series of changes and realignments across time, what sociologists call the **family life course**. These changes and realignments are related to the altered expectations and requirements imposed on a husband and wife as children are born and grow up.

In Chapter 4 you learned about group dynamics and the consequences of adding members to a group. A family typically begins with the husband–wife pair—a dyad—and becomes a triad with the addition of the first child. As the family grows, new roles are created and the number of relationships is multiplied. The family then stabilizes for a time, after which it begins shrinking as each of the adult children is launched. Finally, it returns once more to the husband–wife pair and eventually terminates with the death of a spouse. Decisive economic, social, political, or military events intervene to alter the normal course of events (Elder, 1983), and divorce, desertion, death, remarriage, and the blending of children from one marriage into another all complicate the family life course.

Each change in the role of one family member can affect all the other members. The arrival of the first child compels the reorganization of a couple's life. Parents have to juggle their work roles, alter their time schedules, change their communication patterns, and relinquish some privacy. Parenthood competes with the husband or wife role. After the birth of a first child, husbands and wives who could once focus unlimited attention on their spouses now have to split their attention between spouse and child. The result is that young parents may feel that their spouses are not paying enough attention to them. Not surprisingly, marital adjustment ratings, an indicator of marital satisfaction, typically fall after the birth of a first child (Belsky and Rovine, 1990). The addition of a second child changes the family again, sometimes reducing the mother's participation in the paid labor force, increasing her responsibilities in housework, and making fathers feel more a part of the family (Boodman, 2000). A consistent finding is that the psychological well-being of parents is a little worse than that of childless couples, and it remains lower until children grow up and move out of the household (Evenson and Simon, 2005). Despite the changes a child brings to their lives, most couples report enormous satisfaction with parenthood, ranking their families as more important than work, recreation, friendships, or status.

Clinical psychologists and psychiatrists have stressed the problem parents face when their children leave home. But most couples do not experience difficulty with the "empty nest" period; the majority view this stage as a time of new freedoms. Indeed, national surveys show that middle-aged women whose children have left home experience greater general happiness and enjoyment of life, in addition to greater marital happiness, than middle-aged women with children still living at home (White and Edwards, 1990; Vander Zanden, 1993). With changes in the family life course, the "empty

nest" has become an ill-defined stage; young adults are establishing their own households later and often return to reside for varying lengths of time in their parents' home (Meyer, 2007; Hill and Young, 1999). In 2008, 20 percent of young adults in the United States (ages 25 to 34) lived in a multigenerational household, meaning they lived with their parents or in-laws (Taylor et al., 2010).

Two-Income Families

Between 1980 and 2008, the proportion of wives employed outside the home increased from 50 percent to 61 percent (U.S. Census Bureau, 2009). More than 60 percent of all mothers with children under six years of age are now in the workforce (see Figure 10.3). In 1950 only one in eight were working. In 1998 a record 59 percent of women with infants were employed, a proportion that had dropped a bit to 57.8 percent by 2007 (U.S. Census Bureau, 2009).

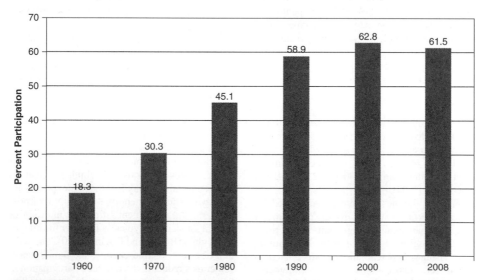

Figure 10.3   Labor-Force Participation Rates for Married Women in the U.S. with Children under Six Years Old, 1960–2008

Source: Figure generated by the authors using data from the U.S. Census Bureau, 2009.

10.2 Social Inequalities

Family Backgrounds and Unequal Childhoods

Sociologists have long known that social class has a powerful impact on children's life chances. In a classic study, sociologist James Coleman and his colleagues (Coleman et al., 1966) found that family background was the most important determinant of educational inequality. But what specific family processes are responsible for the link between parents' social class and children's outcomes? This question was addressed in a study by Annette Lareau (2002). Lareau systematically observed the daily lives of poor, working-class, middle-class, and upper-middle-class families with 9- and 10-year-old children, spending hours at a time with each family. She found that organized activities dominate the lives of middle-class children; their parents engage in what she calls "concerted cultivation"—they manage their children's lives to optimize the cultivation of their talents and abilities. In poor and working-class families, leisure activities are left to the children themselves; their parents facilitate "the accomplishment of natural growth," and the provision of organized leisure activities is not seen as an essential part of good parenting.

Middle- and upper-middle-class children benefit directly from their parents' attempts to cultivate their talents; further, they gain a sense of entitlement and the skills for getting what they want or need from others, Lareau says. The poorer children she followed, on the other hand, learned to "keep their distance from people in positions of authority, to be distrustful of institutions, and . . . to resist officials' authority" (2002:773).

Data from the Census 2000's "A Child's Day" report (Lugaila, 2003) confirm Lareau's observations and bring into sharp focus the disadvantages faced by many American children. Five percent of all kids under 12, for example, had not been taken on an "outing" during the month before parents filled out their census surveys; an outing includes a trip to a park, a church, a playground, or a grocery store, or a visit with friends or relatives. That's 2.4 *million* children who apparently did nothing but go to school and come back home, for an entire month. Eight percent of the nation's 1- to 5-year-olds—1.6 million kids—had not been read to at all in the week before the survey, and only half were read to every day. As Lareau found in her observational study, many children engage in a variety of organized activities such as soccer, baseball, gymnastics, dance, Girl Scouts, Boy Scouts, music lessons, choir, and the like, but many children do not.

For many of the factors in the "Child's Day" report, family background, especially the income and education of the parents, is the critical element. For example, family characteristics that are associated with lower levels of reading to children include living in poverty, having parents with a high school education or less, and having never-married parents. Children who live in poverty do not "go on outings," as the Census Bureau puts it, and they are much less likely to be involved in organized sports, clubs, or lessons. The level of education of the parents plays a major role in a child's participation in extracurricular activities, with about half of the children of parents with advanced degrees participating in sports, clubs, and lessons, compared to 20–30 percent of the children whose parents have a high school education or less. School opportunities are sorted by social class, too; half of the children whose parents have advanced degrees are enrolled in "gifted classes," compared to only 14 percent of the children whose parents have a high school education or less.

In other words, the children who might benefit greatly from extra attention, special activities, and more caring from adults in their lives—children from low-income families, children whose parents have little education, and children from broken homes—are the least likely to get it. As Lareau (2003) says in the book that elaborates her research, America is a land both of opportunity and of inequality.

Questions for Discussion

1. Based on the findings presented here, what sorts of enrichment programs would you recommend for children living in poverty?

2. Are there benefits to a childhood that is not dominated by organized activities?

Dual-income couples evolve new patterns and traditions for family living and face challenges and opportunities not experienced by families with only one breadwinner (Guelzow, Bird, and Koball, 1991; Vannoy and Philliber, 1992). But families seem to be adjusting to the change. In 1980, a wife employed outside the home was correlated with more marital conflict and other sorts of marital problems, while the 2000 data showed that an employed wife was associated with less conflict and fewer other marital problems (Amato et al., 2007). In both 1980 and 2000, however, when a wife spent long hours on the job marital quality suffered. In this section we will consider some of the dynamics of such families: what the effects of employment on women and children are, who cares for the children, and who makes the decisions.

Effects on Women

Women who work outside the home still spend significantly more time on housework than do men (Milkie, Raley, and Bianchi, 2009; Bianchi, Robinson, and Milkie, 2006; Amato et al., 2007; Bittman et al., 2003), working the "second shift" we discussed in Chapter 8 (p. 254). When children enter the equation, the workload increases, and women are penalized in the labor force for their reproductive responsibilities (Dey and Hill, 2007; Budig and England, 2001; England, 2000). Time out of the labor force also carries career penalties (Aisenbrey, Evertsson, and Grunow, 2009). Most women say that mothers in the paid labor force experience more stress than mothers who stay home (Public Agenda, 2001).

Nevertheless, paid employment is typically beneficial to women's mental health and self-esteem, and juggling motherhood and paid employment also seems to be good for women's physical health (McMunn et al., 2006). Studies show that both married women working at a paid job who want to work and married women who are not in the paid labor force and do not want to be have good mental health (Ross, Mirowsky, and Huber, 1983). The problems arise for women who are either working or staying home when they don't want to. Husbands helping with housework and husbands having a positive attitude about their spouse's employment both reduce the psychological distress of working women (Ross, Mirowsky, and Huber, 1983). Sociologist Arlie Russell Hochschild (1997) has argued that unpaid household labor is more demanding than any work anyone does in the paid workplace. Although she also argued that the workplace traditionally has been a refuge for men and was increasingly so for women, other research (Kiecolt, 2003) indicates that this is not the case. Over the past 30 years, home has been more likely to be a haven from work than vice versa for both men and women, and the trend for home to be a haven has increased for women and remained stable for men. Research has shown that although the participation of wives in the labor force has increased, many wives are "not enthusiastic" about this role (Amato et al., 2007). The percentage of women who reported "preferring no job at all" increased between 1980 and 2000.

Who Cares for the Children?

With increasing numbers of mothers in the labor force, two trends have emerged. One is the expansion of nonparental child care, with children being cared for by grandparents or other relatives, babysitters, nannies, family day care, and child care centers (Kids Count, 2006; see the section on child care later in this chapter). Many public schools now provide before- and after-school programs and breakfasts and dinners in addition to the school lunch (Epstein, 2004). Anthropologist Sarah Blaffer Hrdy (2009) thinks that hunter-gatherer populations of humans depended on "child care" long ago, with infants and toddlers spending much of their time being cared for by nonparent individuals. Today, children under 6 whose mothers work spend an average of 37 hours per week in nonparent child care, which is often multiple forms of care patched together; in total, more than 12 million children are in day care (NACCRRA, 2009).

326 Chapter 10 *The Family*

The other trend in care for children is that mothers have reprioritized their activities so that, despite the increase in time spent at work, the amount of time mothers spend with children now is not different from the norm decades ago (Bianchi, Robinson, and Milkie, 2006). An analysis of time diaries kept by parents showed that employed mothers have not given up sleep or leisure time to make time for their children; they have made more of an effort to spend quality time with them by multitasking other responsibilities and by doing less housework. Other survey data have shown that wives' perceptions that they are doing an unfair amount of household labor increase when they become parents (Amato et al., 2007), but the time diary analyses showed that American fathers have nearly tripled the time they spend with their children over the past 40 years (Bianchi, Robinson, and Milkie, 2006). Despite that increase, women still provide most of the at-home child care.

Effects on Children

Research findings are contradictory regarding the effects of maternal employment during a child's first year, with some studies reporting negative cognitive and social outcomes (Baydar and Brooks-Gunn, 1991; Nash, 1997), and others finding only minimal negative outcomes (Parcel and Menaghan, 1994). But in general, maternal employment does not appear to harm children, as long as the hours worked are not excessive (Amato and Booth, 1997), and studies show that parent and family characteristics are more important to the social behaviors, language, and cognitive development of children than are any aspects of child care (NICHD, 2006). High-quality day care and preschool programs have been shown to benefit children (Belsky et al., 2007; Field, 1991); the problem is that only 40 percent of the nation's children have access to such high-quality care (Public Agenda, 2001).

Working mothers provide a different role model for their children, one associated with less traditional gender-role concepts and a higher evaluation of female competence (Hoffman, 1989; Debold, Wilson, and Malave, 1993). Perhaps as a result, their children tend to be more unconventional (Amato and Booth, 1997). In addition, because socioeconomic status affects the ways that families link to the wider society, the benefits of growing up in a two-income family can be considerable (see Box 10.2).

Who Makes the Decisions?

The patriarchal family structure of 50 years ago is quickly disappearing. Paul Amato and his colleagues asked survey respondents whether there were any kinds of decisions made by married couples in which either the wife or the husband had the final word and whether the respondent or the respondent's spouse more often had the final say in decision making (Amato et al., 2007). Shared decision making, in which neither spouse has the final word, increased from the 1980 survey to the 2000 survey, with nearly 65 percent of both husbands and wives reporting shared decision making in 2000. Earlier studies showed that husbands and wives had "areas of expertise" in which their decision making ruled supreme, with traditional gender-role assignments—for example, women decided what to make for dinner and when to clean, and men decided whom to hire to fix the roof. Although the 2000 survey did not ask for details, respondents indicated that they had the final word about some things while their spouses were in charge of other decisions, but the number of marriages in which spouses report either the husband or the wife as having the final say about everything is small. About a quarter of husbands reported that they have the final say, while about a fifth of wives reported that they are in charge of decision making in the household. Amato and his co-authors found that decision making was not affected by how much income the wife contributed to the household.

Family researchers Linda Waite and Maggie Gallagher (2000) say that marriage works best

10.3 Doing Social Research

Racial Diversity Within Families

Some Americans strongly oppose transracial adoption, claiming that children need to be raised by parents of their own race. What does the research show? Social scientist Rita J. Simon (1996) began studying transracial adoptees and their families in 1971 and followed the families until their children reached adulthood. Simon used the research method of intensive interviewing to conduct her study. Each family was visited by a team of one male and one female graduate student in 1971; often one interviewer was white and the other black. Simon and her associates interviewed 204 parents and 366 children during this first stage of her research. In 1979, 1983, and 1991, Simon was able to reinterview a sizable proportion of the parents and children.

What did Simon discover about the children's racial attitudes and racial identity? During 1971 and 1972, she and her associates found a complete absence of a racial preference for whites on the part of all the children. The children correctly identified themselves as black or white, and they showed no preference for white or negative reactions to black. In 1983, self-esteem scores were essentially the same for black adoptees, other transracial adoptees, white adoptees, and white birth children. A family integration scale similarly revealed no significant differences among the four groups of children; adopted children apparently felt as integrated into family life as birth children.

Perhaps the most compelling information about transracial adoption comes from the children themselves when they had reached adulthood. In 1991, Simon told the now-adult transracial adoptees and birth children that the National Association of Black Social Workers and several councils of Native Americans strongly opposed transracial adoption and asked them how they felt about that. Eighty percent of the transracial adoptees and 70 percent of the birth children said that they disagreed; 5 percent of the transracially adopted children said they agreed, and the others said they were not sure. When asked directly what effect being adopted and raised by white parents had on their self-image, a third said it had a positive effect, a third said it had no effect, and a third said they did not know. None of the transracially adopted children responded that it had a negative effect.

It would appear that in most racially diverse families, parents and children, both adopted and birth, do very well.

Questions for Discussion

1. Our society is increasingly characterized by racial diversity. What are some ways families can be racially diverse? Do you expect a decrease or increase in family racial diversity?

2. U.S. society has increased its acceptance of white parents adopting children of other races. What do you think societal reaction would be to parents of other races adopting white children?

---

when wives and husbands need each other, but that these dependencies should be freely chosen. Whether both partners are paid for their work or not, marriage should be viewed as a "true partnership," not a shifting balance of domination and subordination.

Beyond the Traditional Nuclear Family

Family relationships are becoming more varied. Transracial adoption results in families whose diversity reflects that of U.S. society (see Box 10.3). Increasing numbers of children grow up with several sets of parents and an assortment of half brothers and half sisters and stepbrothers and stepsisters, or with unmarried parents. Americans now may have any of a number of **lifestyles**—the overall patterns of living people evolve to meet their biological, social, and emotional needs. In this section we will examine a number of lifestyle options: stepfamilies, singlehood, single parenthood, unmarried cohabitation, and gay and lesbian couples.

Stepfamilies

Remarriage frequently results in stepfamilies, also termed "reconstituted" and "blended" families. Because more than half of remarried persons are parents, their new partners become stepparents. One in six American families are stepfamilies; 35 million Americans live in a

328   Chapter 10 *The Family*

stepfamily, including 20 percent of the nation's children under age 18. About 40 percent of remarriages unite two divorced persons; half of them are a first marriage for one member of the couple. Nine out of 10 stepchildren live with their biological mother and a stepfather.

Andrew Cherlin (1978, 2010) has called remarriage an "incomplete institution." A stepfamily functions differently than the traditional nuclear family (Pill, 1990; Larson, 1992); the stepparent role does not necessarily approximate that of a biological parent, particularly in authority, legitimacy, and respect. The family tree of a stepfamily can be very complex and convoluted, populated not only by children of both spouses but by six sets of grandparents, relatives of former spouses, relatives of new spouses, and the people former spouses marry. It appears, however, that these complicated family situations are becoming much more the norm in U.S. society, and data collected by Paul Amato and his colleagues (2007) support this. Most of the marriages they examined in their 2000 data set involved spouses who had been previously married, and more of the families included stepchildren than in 1980. And attitudes had changed: In 1980, having stepchildren in one's family was associated with lower levels of marital happiness, more conflict, and a higher level of a measure they called "divorce proneness"—a couple's propensity to divorce. In the 2000 survey, however, they found just the opposite—stepchildren were associated with more marital happiness, less marital conflict, and a lower level of divorce proneness.

Stepfathers usually underrate their parenting skills and their contributions to the lives of their stepchildren (Bohannan and Erickson, 1978). Children living with stepfathers apparently do just as well, or just as poorly, in school and in their social lives as children living with natural fathers. And children with stepfathers on the whole do better than children from homes where the father is absent (Beer, 1988; Fine and Kurdek, 1992).

Singlehood

The number of Americans living alone more than doubled (increased 100 percent) between 1970 and 2000, a much greater increase than the 16 percent growth in married couples. By 2008, 32.2 million Americans were living alone; more than one of every four occupied dwelling units had only one person in it. Figure 10.4 shows the percentage living alone by age category in 2008. Divorced (8.8 million), widowed (8.6 million), and never-married (12.9 million) persons constitute distinct groups among adults (in this data set, anyone age 15 or older) who head nonfamily households, including those who live alone (U.S. Census Bureau, 2003). The high incidence of divorce, the ability of the elderly to maintain their own homes alone, and the deferral of marriage among young adults have contributed to the high rate of increase in the number of nonfamily households.

Research strongly suggests that people live alone because they choose to (Michael, Fuchs, and Scott, 1980). People who live alone can avoid unwanted intrusions of others and have more latitude to construct their lives the way they wish to. This is probably why the mental health of persons who live alone is as good as or better than that of unmarried persons living with others (Hughes and Gove, 1981).

In 2008, 58.8 percent of men and nearly 45.5 percent of women ages 25–29 had never been married. This is more than triple the 1970 rate for men and quadruple the rate for women (U.S. Census Bureau, 2009; Saluter, 1996). More liberal sex standards, the high divorce rate, money woes, and the pursuit of education and careers have spurred young adults to marry later than at any time since the Census Bureau started keeping track in 1890. Even so, the population remaining single today is smaller than it was in 1900, when fully 42 percent of all American adult men and 33 percent of adult women were never-marrieds (Kreider, 2008; Kain, 1984).

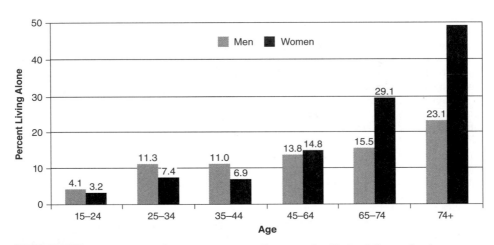

Figure 10.4 Percentage of Persons Living Alone in the United States by Age and Gender, 2009

Source: Figure generated by the authors using data from the U.S. Census Bureau, Current Population Survey, 2009 Annual Social and Economic Supplement. Available at http://www.census.gov/population/www/socdemo/hh-fam/cps2009.html.

For many years research has shown that married people report greater happiness than unmarried, including the never-married. This difference has varied over the years, and some researchers (e.g., Glenn and Weaver, 1988) have argued that a fundamental shift has occurred resulting in the unmarried being nearly as happy as the married. These conclusions were premature, however. Over the period 1972 to 2008, both married men and women consistently reported higher levels of happiness than the never-married. The advantage for the married is even greater when we compare them to the widowed, separated, and divorced (data analyzed by the authors from the General Social Survey, Davis, Smith, and Marsden, 2009).

Single Parenthood

More than one American youngster in four lives with just one parent (Kreider, 2008). Of all such children, 85 percent live with their mothers. However, the number of men raising children on their own has risen; in 2004, 5 percent of the nation's children were living with their fathers only, or 15 percent of the children living in single-parent households (Kreider, 2008). About two-thirds of single fathers are divorced; roughly 25 percent are among the never-married; and only 7.5 percent are widowers. The largest share of youngsters in single-parent homes—38.6 percent—are living with a divorced parent, and 30.6 percent are living with a parent who has never married; others reside with a parent who is married but separated or are offspring of a widowed parent (U.S. Census Bureau, 2003). In 2008, 54 percent of African American children under the age of 18 were living with a single parent. A quarter of Hispanic children, 20 percent of white children, and 12 percent of Asian American children also were in single-parent families (U.S. Census Bureau, 2009).

As we pointed out in Chapter 6 (p. 191), female-headed households are likely to be

330   Chapter 10 *The Family*

low-income households. In 2004, 18 percent of all children lived below the poverty line, compared with 36.5 percent of children living only with their mothers and 16.6 percent of children living only with their fathers. In the case of divorce, marital separation frequently produces a precipitous and sustained decline in household income for the mother and child. The overall financial situation of female-headed households in terms of their net worth is shown in Figure 10.5.

Unwed motherhood is also on the increase. According to the Census Bureau, one in five of the nation's never-married women ages 15–44 have become mothers (Bachu, 1997). Forty percent of all births in the United States were to unwed mothers in 2008 (U.S. Census Bureau, 2009). Though unwed motherhood is more likely to occur among women in the lower class and those in disadvantaged racial minority groups, recent increases in unwed motherhood have been much greater among whites, and rates for teenagers actually fell 11 percent between 1994 and 1998. Such births do not necessarily result in single-parent families; two-fifths of nonmarital births were to cohabiting couples (Ventura and Bachrach, 2000).

Women heading a single-parent family typically experience greater stress than women in two-parent families (Fassinger, 1989; Simons et al., 1993). Lack of job training, loss of skills during the childbearing years, and discriminatory

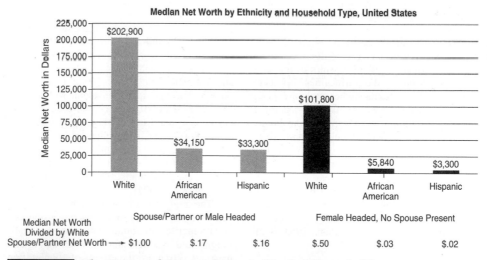

Median Net Worth by Ethnicity and Household Type, United States

	Median Net Worth Divided by White Spouse/Partner Net Worth →
White — $202,900	$1.00
African American — $34,150	$.17
Hispanic — $33,300	$.16
White — $101,800	$.50
African American — $5,840	$.03
Hispanic — $3,300	$.02

Spouse/Partner or Male Headed   Female Headed, No Spouse Present

Figure 10.5 **The Financial Status of Female-Headed Households**
Net worth, or wealth, of a household is all the assets of that household minus all debts. Female-headed households have far less net worth than other households. The situation of African American and Hispanic female-headed households is particularly grave; they have on average 3 and 2 cents, respectively, for every dollar of net worth owned by a white male-headed or spouse/partner household.

Source: Figure generated by the authors using data from the 2007 Survey of Consumer Finances, Board of Governors of the Federal Reserve System.

hiring and promotion patterns often mean that single mothers work for low wages. Female family heads report much lower self-esteem, a lower sense of effectiveness, and less optimism about the future than their counterparts in two-parent settings. But research shows that women who head households on their own may choose not to marry depending on a variety of factors, including mistrust of men, fear of domestic violence, household decision making, respectability, and potential marriage partners who lack stable jobs with decent earnings (Edin, 2000).

Single fathers encounter many of the same problems as single mothers. Research shows that being single and having children to raise is worse on the mental health of men than on that of women (Simon, 1998; Hughes, 1989). Juggling work and child care poses considerable difficulties, especially for fathers with preschool youngsters.

Many families headed by single parents survive their hardships with few ill effects; some even blossom as a result of the spirit of cooperation brought out by their difficulties. But there can be problems. Some studies show that juvenile delinquency is twice as likely to occur in a single-parent home as in a two-parent home. Children of single parents are also more likely to drop out of school, be unemployed when they reach adulthood, have out-of-wedlock children, become sexually active at an earlier age, and cohabit (Musick and Bumpass, 1999). Lack of parental supervision and persistent social and psychological strains are usually complicated by the problems of poverty (Mann, 1983; Bank et al., 1993).

Cohabitation

Marriage is differentiated from other types of intimate relationships by its institutionalized status. The number of unmarried adults who share living quarters with an unrelated adult of the opposite sex—a type of intimate relationship termed **cohabitation**—has increased in recent decades; 5.6 million American households were made up of unmarried couples in 2008, an increase of 16 percent since 2000 (www.census .gov/compendia/statab/2010/tables/10s00 63.xls). More than 10 percent of all unmarried persons were cohabiting in 2008. Five percent of children live in a household that included either their mother's or their father's unmarried partner. Researchers estimate that about 40 percent of all out-of-wedlock births are to cohabiting parents (Bumpass and Lu, 2000). For white and Hispanic teens, living in cohabiting families is worse than living with single mothers; those living with cohabitors are more likely to have school troubles and emotional and behavioral problems (Nelson, Clark, and Acs, 2001). Cohabiting also seems to be less effective than remarriage at providing economic stability for the children of divorce (Morrison and Ritualo, 2000).

Only 2 percent of American women born between 1928 and 1932 cohabited before marrying or attaining age 30; 40 percent of those born between 1958 and 1962 did so (Schoen and Weinick, 1993). Cohabiting before marriage has become quite prevalent, with 41 percent of all married couples surveyed in 2000 having cohabited before they married (Amato et al., 2007), and researchers estimating that 60 to 70 percent of couples today will live together before they get married (Rhoades, Stanley, and Markman, 2009; Stanley, Whitton, and Markman, 2004).

The high proportion of married couples who live together prior to marriage suggests that premarital cohabitation may become institutionalized as a new step between dating and marriage. What are the effects of cohabitation on marriage? While some couples say that they are planning to live together before marriage to see what living together is like, studies show that more couples end up living together without making any real decision to do so or any serious commitment to one another. This "sliding into cohabitation" has been shown to be associated with lower levels

332   Chapter 10   *The Family*

of marital satisfaction, lower levels of male commitment to the spouse, greater likelihood of divorce, and more negative communication in marriage (Stanley and Rhoades, 2009). Amato and his colleagues (2007) also found that couples who had cohabited before marriage reported lower marital quality than those who had not. Stanley attributes this effect to the lack of commitment associated with cohabitation; he and other researchers suggest that marriage after cohabitation may occur more because the couple's financial, social, and emotional lives have become intertwined than because the couple makes a serious decision to get engaged and then married (Stanley and Rhoades, 2009). Couples who become engaged before cohabitation or who do not live together at all before they marry report higher marital satisfaction.

Gay and Lesbian Couples

Homosexuality also serves as the basis for family life, though with some differences from heterosexual couples. In terms of love and relationship satisfaction, heterosexual couples, gay couples, and lesbian couples do not differ (Savin-Williams and Esterberg, 2000). Gay and lesbian couples are more likely than heterosexual couples to be well educated. Their average incomes are similar, but homosexual couples are less likely to own their own homes (Associated Press, 2003). Compared with married couples, gay and lesbian couples are more likely to split up household tasks so that each partner performs an equal number of different tasks. However, lesbian couples tend to share more tasks, whereas gay couples are more likely to have one or the other partner perform the tasks (Kurdek, 1993).

Until recently, cohabitation was the only option for homosexual "family life" in the United States. Unlike Belgium, Denmark, and the Netherlands, where same-sex marriage is legal, the United States has only a handful of states that approve of marriage for homosexual couples. Same-sex marriages are legal in Connecticut, Iowa, Massachusetts, New Hampshire, Vermont, and Washington, DC, and are recognized but not performed in Maryland, New York, and Rhode Island. A 2010 presidential mandate that hospitals allow patients to designate both visitors and medical decision makers regardless of traditional family ties was widely interpreted as legal protection for gay and lesbian couples (Shear, 2010). Some cities and counties also have provisions for unmarried couples to register as domestic partners, with rights conferred ranging from being allowed to visit hospitalized partners to sharing health insurance benefits (Cherlin, 2010).

Population Size of Homosexuals Most estimates of the homosexual population range from 1 to 3 percent (Barringer, 1993; Crispell, 1993), and fewer than half of 1 percent of all "partner households" in the United States are gay or lesbian couples (U.S. Census Bureau, 2009). One study found that 1.4 percent of women and 2.8 percent of men identified themselves as gay, lesbian, or bisexual (Laumann et al., 1994). The percentage of persons who have engaged at some time in homosexual activity may be substantially higher: at least 20 percent of males, according to a Kinsey Institute study (Fay et al., 1989). However, another study puts the figure lower, at 7 percent for men and nearly 4 percent for women (Laumann et al., 1994). The major problem with all these estimates is that they rely on self-reports and therefore almost certainly underestimate rates of homosexual involvement. Many people may be afraid to admit to homosexual activity out of fear of discrimination or ostracism.

What Is Homosexuality? Is homosexuality a condition or characteristic of people, or is it simply a way we have of describing an activity that some people engage in? Kinsey's study

(Kinsey, Pomeroy, and Martin, 1948) revealed the interesting fact that homosexuality/heterosexuality was not a simple dichotomy. Kinsey found people all along the continuum from exclusively homosexual to exclusively heterosexual, combining homosexuality and heterosexuality in a variety of ways. Though he did find the majority to be exclusively heterosexual, he also found people who engaged in homosexual activity in certain periods in the life course and not in others. On the basis of findings like these, many sociologists and psychologists have concluded that it is more reasonable to think about heterosexual and homosexual *practices,* not homosexual *individuals* (Bell, Weinberg, and Hammersmith, 1981; Kirkpatrick, 2000). In this "constructionist" view, homosexuality and heterosexuality are social constructions that describe behaviors, roles that people may play, and identities, not inherent characteristics of persons.

The alternative "essentialist" view argues that homosexual orientation is either inborn or fixed very early in one's development and thus is an inherent part of what an individual is (LeVay, 1996, 1991). LeVay's 1991 study presented evidence that there are differences in the brain structures of homosexual and heterosexual men. Other studies show that identical twins, who share 100 percent of their genes, are more likely to have the same sexual orientation than are fraternal twins, who are as genetically alike as any siblings (Burr, 1996). However, it is still not clear whether findings such as these reflect the fact that homosexual preferences are caused or sustained by biological factors. In 1975 the American Psychological Association urged medical practitioners to stop thinking of homosexuality as a mental illness, and in 1997 it passed a resolution to limit therapy aimed at converting homosexuals to heterosexuals (Weiss, 1997).

What is not controversial is that, for the most part, gay and lesbian people, except for their sexual orientations and practices, represent a cross section of the U.S. population, differing little from their heterosexual counterparts (Bell and Weinberg, 1978; Blumstein and Schwartz, 1983). They are found in all occupational fields, political persuasions, religious faiths, and racial and ethnic groups. Some are married, have children, and lead lives that in most respects are indistinguishable from those of the larger population.

Attitudes Toward Gay Marriage   Two years after the Netherlands legalized gay marriage, nearly 8 percent of weddings were same-sex couples, and the relationships were increasingly seen as commonplace and even "old-fashioned" (Richburg, 2003). What about in the United States? Americans' attitudes toward the morality of homosexuality have been increasingly liberal since 1990, and Americans have become steadily less willing to restrict the civil liberties of homosexuals. Most Americans think homosexuals should have equal rights in terms of job opportunities (Saad, 1996), and in 2004, 52 percent of Americans said that they thought homosexual relations between consenting adults should be legal (Gallup, 2004). Despite the Catholic Church's rejection of homosexual activity, U.S. Catholic bishops have urged parents of homosexuals to accept and love them (Murphy, 1997).

When it comes to marriage and family, Americans are not quite ready to give their full approval to same-sex unions. Although the percentage of Americans who support same-sex civil unions has steadily increased since the early 2000s and stood at 57 percent in 2009, support for gay marriage in 2009 was 39 percent, essentially the same level it was in 2003 (Pew Research Center for the People and the Press, 2009a).

There is a significant religious dimension to much of the opposition to same-sex marriage. When the Episcopal Church gave its bishops the option of allowing priests to bless committed homosexual relationships, polls showed that

334   Chapter 10   *The Family*

"a strong majority" of the public disapproved, especially frequent churchgoers (Morin and Cooperman, 2003). Surveys of specific religious groups show that 79 percent of evangelical Christians, 70 percent of traditional Catholics, 53 percent of mainline Protestants, and 35 percent of liberal Catholics think that marriage should be defined by law as a union between a man and a woman (PBS, 2005).

Except for their sexual preferences and practices, gays and lesbians differ little from their heterosexual counterparts. Some are or have been married, have children, and lead lives that in most respects are indistinguishable from those of the larger population.

[Section 2 ends.]   [Section 3 begins.]

Challenges for American Families and American Society

Some family problems stay in the family; others spill over into society. For example, family violence, child abuse, and incest produce scarred members of society, many of whom go on to have families of their own in which the same terrible acts are repeated. In our society, people express considerable support for family values. But an assessment of parental leave policies in the United States, the availability and quality of child and elder care, the protection of children from abuse and neglect, and other issues suggests that people are less willing to support policies that would ensure the viability of the family. In this section, we will examine the challenges posed by abuse and neglect, child care, divorce, and an increasing population of the elderly.

Family Violence, Child Abuse, and Incest

Mounting evidence suggests that family violence, child abuse, and incest are much more common than most Americans had suspected. In this section we will present and discuss some of the data available about family violence, child abuse, and incest.

Family Violence

Estimates of family violence vary widely. Nearly a quarter of women report having been physically assaulted by an intimate partner, and 8 percent report rape by an intimate partner (Cherlin, 2010). The World Health Organization (WHO) maintains a database on violence against women. In a study of 10 countries, it found that 35–76 percent of women over the age of 15 have been physically or sexually assaulted, most by a partner (Garcia-Moreno et al., 2005). In the United States, 22 percent of women have been assaulted by an intimate partner (WHO, 2000). Two sources

Studying Section 2

Activities for Section 2

Continue your note-taking on the model chapter by completing the partial notes below. These notes cover the marked part of chapter page 319 to the marked part of chapter page 334.

Marriage and the Family in the United States

- How many figures or graphs are included in this part of the chapter? _____ These visuals help reinforce points made in the text.
- The age of first marriage has increased and marrying at later ages is associated with greater marital happiness.
- Nearly 61 percent of all mothers with children under age six are in the paid workforce. In general, maternal employment (working mother) does not appear to harm children, as long as the hours worked are not excessive.
- One in six American families are stepfamilies; 35 million Americans live in a stepfamily, including 20 percent of children under the age of 18.
- Family relationships are becoming more varied. Americans now may have any number of lifestyles—the overall patterns of living people evolve to meet their biological, social, and emotional needs.
- More than one American youngster in four lives with just one parent. Of all such children, 85 percent live with their mothers.

Lifestyle options:

1. Stepfamilies – result of remarriage.
2. _____ – one of four people live alone; their mental health as good as unmarried persons living with others.
3. _____ – more than one in four children live with one parent.
4. _____ – unmarried people living together has increased.
5. _____ – 1 to 3 percent of population.

Comments on Section 2

- The notes above, which cover almost 15 pages, are based on some key details, one definition ("family life course") and an enumeration ("lifestyle options"). One aid to picking out key details is "The Chapter in Brief: The Family" summary on chapter pages 344–345.

- Note that when you add details that seem important, there's no need to number each detail. Simply set off details with a dash or a bullet, as shown in the notes above.

of data suggest that domestic violence may be decreasing in the United States. A survey of married couples showed a decrease in the amount of violence ever occurring in the marriage from 21 percent in 1980 to only 12 percent in 2000, and rates of intimate partner violence (as reported in the National Crime Victimization Surveys) decreased by 41 percent between 1993 and 1999 (Amato et al., 2007).

Although both men and women engage in violence, men typically do more damage than their female partners and many more women than men report victimization (Cherlin, 2010). Women put up with battering for a variety of reasons (France, 2006). The fewer the resources a wife has in the way of education or job skills, the more vulnerable she is in the marriage. And violence is not faced only by young women—survey data suggest that 3–5 million Americans over 50 are in physically abusive relationships (France, 2006).

Child Abuse

One need spend only an hour or so in a supermarket or a shopping mall to observe instances of children being physically or verbally abused. Such public behavior is but the tip of the iceberg. A 2005 PBS survey found that 64 percent of American adults agree that "a good, hard spanking" is sometimes necessary in disciplining a child (PBS, 2005), despite accumulating evidence that children who get spanked regularly are more likely to cheat or lie, to be disobedient at school, to bully others, and to have less remorse for what they do wrong (Straus, Sugarman, and Giles-Sims, 1997). Child abuse goes far beyond unnecessary spanking; abuse cases may involve burning, scalding, beating, and smothering. Neglect of children is a closely related problem. In 2006, there were 905,000 confirmed cases of child maltreatment; 91,278 of these were infants in the first year of their lives (U.S. Department of Health and Human Services, 2008). Neglect has been shown to cause severe short- and long-term harm, including

The functionalist perspective on the family stresses that an important function of the family is care and protection of family members, but evidence on child abuse demonstrates that families do not always serve this function.

many mental and physical health problems, juvenile delinquency, and adult criminality (Dubowitz, 2007), and abuse also has long-term effects, including increased risk of suicide in adulthood (McGowan et al., 2009).

Approximately 1,530 children died in 2006 of abuse or neglect (U.S. Department of Health and Human Services, 2008). The age at which females are most at risk of homicide is from birth to age one, and the perpetrators are nearly always parents, family friends, or guardians

336   Chapter 10   *The Family*

(Tucker, 2000). Although the chances of males being murdered during infancy are even greater than for females, it is not the most dangerous time of life for them; the male homicide rate is more than four times higher at age 21 (Tucker, 2000). Child welfare workers say that risk to infants is related to whether parents and caregivers have any parenting skills and to situational factors including stress and social isolation.

Although exact numbers are hard to obtain, more than 1.5 million children, teenagers, and young adults are living on the streets in the United States (Stand Up for Kids, 2008), and more than 500,000 children are in foster care, living under the temporary care of nonrelated adults (AACAP, 2005). About 30 percent of foster care children have "severe emotional, behavioral, or developmental problems," and many have been abused or suffered neglect.

Incest and Sexual Abuse

The status of incest as a taboo has not kept it from taking place but merely from being talked about. Probably the best available figures on sexual abuse come from a national survey of more than 2,000 adults undertaken in 1985 for the *Los Angeles Times* by psychologist David Finkelhor and his colleagues. They found that 27 percent of the women and 16 percent of the men disclosed a history of some sort of sexual abuse during their childhood (Darnton, 1991). A study of first intercourse experiences found that girls who had sex at age 11 or 12 were much more likely to have partners much older than themselves, and both older partners and early first intercourse were associated with a greater number of problem behaviors (Leitenberg and Saltzman, 2000).

The perpetrator in sexual abuse is commonly the father, uncle, or other male authority figure in the household, "family tyrants" who employ physical force and intimidation to control their families (Finkelhor, 1979; Herman and Hirschman, 1981). The mothers in incestuous families are commonly passive, have a poor self-image, and are overly dependent on their husbands, much the same traits found among battered wives. The victims of molestation are usually shamed or terrified into treating the experience as a dirty secret.

The sexual abuse of children often leads to behavior problems, learning difficulties, sexual promiscuity, runaway behavior, drug and alcohol abuse, gastrointestinal and genitourinary complaints, compulsive rituals, clinical depression, low self-esteem, and suicidal behavior. Victimized women tend to show lifetime patterns of psychological shame and stigmatization (Kendall-Tackett, Williams, and Finkelhor, 1993; Malinosky-Rummell and Hansen, 1993).

Looking to the Future

The problems of family violence, child abuse, and incest have emerged as major public issues. Some, but not all, researchers find that the arrest of offenders is the most effective means for preventing new incidents of wife battery (Berk and Newton, 1985; Sherman et al., 1992). The adoption of no-fault divorce laws is associated with a drop in suicides among women, murder of women by their partners, and domestic violence against both men and women (Wolfers and Stevenson, 2006). A cultural revolution of attitudes and values is required to eradicate the abuse of women and children (Gelles, Straus, and Harrop, 1988; Buzawa and Buzawa, 1990). The drop in spousal violence between 1980 and 2000 (Amato et al., 2007) may suggest that such a cultural revolution is beginning.

Child Care

How children are cared for should be a matter of concern even to those Americans who have no children; they are, as politicians love to point out in speeches, "our future." Over half of all mothers return to work within 6 months of birth, and 64 percent return to work within the first year after birth; a total of 14.5 million American children under age 6 (62 percent) are cared for by someone other than their parents for an average of 36 hours per week (NACCRRA, 2009). Nannies may get the most attention in books and movies, but child care centers and grandparents are the most commonly used form of child care in the United States. About one-fifth of children aged 5 to 14 are home alone after school; the others are in some type of after-school care. The quality and availability of child care resources play an essential role in the rearing of America's children.

High-quality day care and preschools can be good for children (Belsky et al., 2007; Field, 1991; MacKinnon and King, 1988; Kagan, Kearsley, and Zelazo, 1978). Such programs are characterized by small group size, high staff–child ratios, well-trained staffs, good equipment, and attractive and nurturing environments.

Unfortunately, high-quality care is often unavailable. Only 9.4 percent of child care centers (and less than 1 percent of family day cares) are accredited, meaning they meet high enough standards of quality to be accredited by a national organization. Teachers at child care centers are required to undergo training in early childhood education in only 13 states; all child care programs are required to meet licensing standards in only 11 states; and in 8 states, licensed programs are inspected less often than once a year (NACCRRA, 2009). Seventeen states allow family day care providers to have no training, and 43 percent of assistant child care center teachers and 44 percent of family day care teachers have only high school diplomas or less. Some centers hire caregivers without doing background checks and do not require that caregivers be trained in CPR, first aid, or recognizing signs of child abuse. Child care workers rank among the lowest 10 percent of wage earners in the United States, earning less than parking lot attendants, and the high turnover rate of such workers creates low continuity of care for children (Clawson and Gerstel, 2002).

Quality of care is not the only problem. The number of children needing child care exceeds by nearly 4 million the number of available spaces in legally operating care programs (NACCRRA, 2009). About a third of children in child care are in multiple care arrangements, spending time each week with relatives, in a center, with a babysitter, or however parents are able to string together care. And cost is prohibitive for many families: The cost of having an infant in full-time child care exceeds the average annual cost of a public university education (NACCRRA, 2009). An increasing number of women find that they actually have to pay to work, which they may be willing to do in order to avoid losing work time that leads to promotions and retirement benefits (Dvorak, 2010).

No National Policy

Child care advocates warn that failure to develop a national policy toward child care will result in "a generation of neglected children." The United States is one of the few industrialized nations that does not have a comprehensive day care program. Access to early childhood education and care is a statutory right in Denmark, Finland, Sweden, France, Belgium, Italy, Germany, and Britain (Child Policy, 2004), and Japan has a "uniformly excellent" publicly supported day care system (Yamamoto and Struck, 2002). Further, while the United States provides no paid maternity leave by law, more than 140 countries, including most other industrialized nations, do. Recognizing the benefits of retaining experienced employees, some U.S. corporations are beginning to develop their own maternity leave programs (Joyce, 2007).

National policy decisions about caring for the nation's children would need to incorporate standards to ensure that child care centers are not simply what consumer activist Ralph Nader describes as "children's warehouses." The book *The Irreducible Needs of Children* (Brazelton and Greenspan, 2000) describes the essential

338   Chapter 10 *The Family*

ingredients for the emotional and physical health and development of babies and children:

- An ongoing nurturing relationship
- Physical protection, safety, and regulation
- Experiences tailored to individual differences
- Developmentally appropriate experiences
- Limit setting, structure, and expectations
- Stable, supportive communities and cultural continuity
- A protected future

Most parents think public policy should focus on parental leave and other employment programs that would lessen the conflict between work and family (Williams and Boushey, 2010), instead of on child care. Three-quarters of survey respondents believe it is better for children to be at home with a parent, and 81 percent believe that children are more likely to get the affection and attention they need from a stay-at-home parent (Public Agenda, 2001).

Alternatives to Day Care

Increasing numbers of parents are finding alternatives to day care. One alternative is *sequencing*—arranging one's life to provide time to work, time to have children and stay home with them, and time to reenter the workforce again (Cardozo, 1996). But as we discussed in Chapter 8, women pay the price of interrupting their careers to care for children in the forms of loss of job experience, reduced wages, and discrimination from employers. While some people insist that two incomes are essential in the United States, a significant number find that it is possible to live—and even save for the future—on one middle-class income. Another alternative to full-time employment and full-time day care for children is part-time work or work from the home. Some child-friendly employers now allow babies and children to "come to the

office"; one researcher found that 8.9 percent of employed mothers were caring for their children at work (Trost, 1990).

Clinical psychiatrist and pediatrician Stanley I. Greenspan (1997) recommended a "four-thirds solution": Each parent works two-thirds time and spends one-third of the time raising the children. Greenspan also called for government and industry support, including government incentives for employers to provide part-time work options, more flextime, and guaranteed parental leave.

Divorce

Although divorce rates increased sharply from the 1960s to the early 1980s, they have declined almost as dramatically since then (see Figure 10.6). It is unclear why divorce rates have declined since 1981. Two possible factors are the increased age of marriage and increasing education. Recent research shows that women with a college education marry later, have fewer children, are happier in their marriages and family life, and are both the least likely to divorce and have experienced the greatest declines in divorce since the 1970s compared to less educated women (Isen and Stevenson, 2010). People who marry later, have children later, and have personal resources are more likely to be able to arrange their lives in ways that promote their personal well-being, including the nature of their personal relationships. Yet divorce rates still are high in comparison to historical trends, and divorce is a common part of contemporary society. When today's elderly were establishing families, divorce was relatively infrequent. With the number of divorced people increasing over the past 30 years and young people delaying the formation of new unions, the number of divorced people per 1,000 married people has nearly doubled in the past three decades. In 2008 there were 178 divorced people for every 1,000 married people. Societal attitudes toward divorce have changed as well.

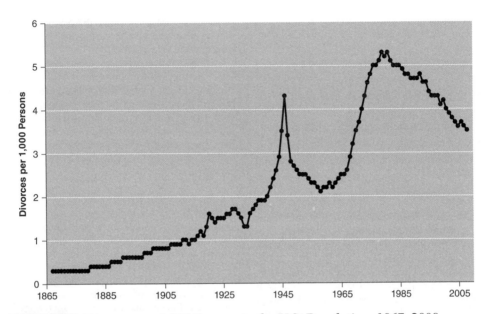

| Figure 10.6 | Divorces per 1,000 Persons in the U.S. Population, 1867–2008 |

Divorce rates in the U.S. increased dramatically in the 20th century. The social disruptions caused by World War II produced a very sharp spike in the immediate postwar years. Rates have been declining since the early 1980s. Divorce rates in this chart from the 19th and very early 20th centuries are based on limited data.

Source: Figure generated by the authors using data from the U.S. Department of Health, Education, and Welfare, 1973; U.S. Department of Health and Human Services, 1996; U.S. Census Bureau, 2009 and earlier (www.census.gov/population/socdemo/hh-fam/ms1.xls); and the National Vital Statistics Reports, available at http://www.cdc.gov/nchs/products/nvsr.htm#vol58.

The Effects of Divorce on the Family

More than half of the couples who divorce have children. Researchers find that children of divorced or single parents have higher levels of anxiety, depression, stress, aggression, and school problems and are more likely to drop out of school and become parents themselves at a young age (Lugaila, 2003).

Financial problems complicate the difficulties of both women and men. Only half of divorced mothers receive any money at all from their children's fathers, and this is seldom much. Most men also experience an economic decline

following divorce (McManus and DiPrete, 2001). Moreover, divorce is not the end of family changes but often the beginning. Most divorced parents remarry, and because the rate of divorce among remarriages is greater than among first marriages, many children experience complex family lives (Furstenberg and Cherlin, 1991).

The notion that divorce has adverse consequences for children influences many couples to remain unhappily married until their youngsters reach adulthood. However, some evidence suggests that staying together for the sake of

340   Chapter 10 *The Family*

the children is not necessarily helpful if the marriage is marred by conflict, tension, and discord. Many of the emotional, behavioral, and academic problems children exhibit after their parents divorce are apparent before the time of the actual breakup of the family. Marital discord has a negative effect on children's emotional bonds with both parents (Amato and Sobolewski, 2001). On the other hand, clinical psychologist Mary Pipher argues that children may not be affected if their parents are unhappy but that divorce "shatters many children" (Pipher, 1994:133). Family sociologist Linda Waite says research supports that view: "As long as Mom and Dad don't fight too much, [children] thrive under the love, attention, and resources two married parents provide" (Waite and Gallagher, 2000:144).

Long-Term Effects

Although divorce may be more commonplace today, it is no more a routine experience for adults than it is for children. In many cases divorce exacts a greater emotional and physical toll than almost any other type of stress, including the death of a spouse (Kitson and Holmes, 1992). Separated and divorced people are overrepresented in mental institutions; more likely to die from cardiovascular disease, cancer, pneumonia, and cirrhosis of the liver; and more prone to die from accidents, homicides, and suicides.

Middle-aged and elderly women are especially devastated by divorce. These women—called *displaced homemakers*—often have dedicated themselves to managing a home and raising children, only to find themselves jettisoned after years of marriage. Within the United States, some 100,000 people over the age of 55 divorce each year.

Grown children of divorce have lower levels of psychological well-being (Amato and Sobolewski, 2001) and die, on average, four years sooner than adults who were raised by

parents who did not divorce (Tucker et al., 1997). Children of divorce are more likely to marry as teens but less likely to marry at all once they get past age 20 (Wolfinger, 2003). On the other hand, adult children of divorced parents are now significantly less likely to divorce than children of a generation or two ago; between 1974 and 1993, the propensity to divorce if one's parents had divorced declined by about 50 percent (Wolfinger, 1999).

After Divorce

Most divorced people remarry. About five of every six divorced men and three of every four divorced women marry again. Divorced men are more likely to remarry than women. Because men usually marry younger women, divorced men have a larger pool of potential partners from which to choose. Divorced men also are more likely to marry someone not previously married. About 61 percent of men and 54 percent of women in their thirties who remarry will undergo a second divorce.

The Elderly

As life expectancy increases and the birth rate decreases, the proportion of elderly people in the United States also has increased, and a population structure in which those over 60 outnumber those under 15 will soon be a feature of U.S. society (Rowe et al., 2009). John Rowe and his colleagues in the MacArthur Foundation Research Network on an Aging Society have been working to identify changes needed to meet the challenges of this shift in age distribution in society. The elderly in the United States also will be characterized by better health and fewer disabilities than in the past, as improvements in medical care have resulted in a faster increase in "active life span" than even the increase in total life span. As asthma, obesity, and diabetes skyrocket among younger people, it's possible that our elderly population will find itself to be more healthy than middle-aged and younger Americans. Rowe and others contend that current approaches to the elderly were designed when being elderly was synonymous with being ill and cognitively or physically disabled and that they limit opportunities for the "new elderly" to be productive members of society.

At some point, of course, many of the elderly need help as they approach the ends of their lives, and this almost always involves the family. As our society ages, care facilities will need to be expanded and improved. Although some facilities for the care of the elderly are adequately staffed and provide adequate care, a government study in 2002 showed that more than half of the nursing homes in the United States are so understaffed that residents cannot be taken care of (Connolly, 2008). Thirty percent of seriously ill elderly survey respondents indicated that they would rather die than live in a nursing home, but seniors aren't always safe at home; elder abuse and neglect can be family problems and may include financial exploitation in addition to physical and psychological neglect and abuse (Connolly, 2008). Even our medical system is unprepared for the growing population of seniors in American society: Estimates for a future need for 30,000 geriatricians compare bleakly to the 9,000 currently in practice in the United States (Connolly, 2008).

Care for the elderly falls most often on daughters and daughters-in-law. These women have historically functioned as our society's "kin-keepers" (Brody, 1990; Brody et al., 1994). Although the average family caregiver is 45 years old, female, and married, 35 percent of caregivers to the elderly are themselves older than 65 years of age, and 10 percent are older than 75.

While some see an aging society as forcing policy makers to choose between investing in youth or investing in the elderly, Rowe and his colleagues point out that these are not mutually exclusive policies (2009:20):

[M]any programs that target the elderly have significant benefits for younger generations and should properly be seen as family programs. Social Security payments to older people relieve their middle-aged children of the economic burden of supporting their parents. But they also help the elderly support their children . . . Such multigenerational win–win opportunities exist in many areas, including education, training and job flexibility, retirement, welfare, and health.

[Section 3 ends.]   [Section 4 begins.]

Sociological Perspectives on the Family

We have been following three major sociological perspectives—the functionalist, conflict, and interactionist—as we move through our introduction to sociology. What do these major theoretical frameworks have to tell us about the family?

The Functionalist Perspective

As we have noted in other chapters, functionalist theorists stress that if a society is to survive and operate with some measure of effectiveness, it must guarantee that certain essential tasks are performed. The performance of these tasks—or *functions*—cannot be left to chance (see Chapter 1, pp. 18–19). To do so would be to run the risk that some activities would not be carried out, and the society would disintegrate. Although acknowledging that families show a good deal of variation throughout the world, functionalists seek to identify a number of recurrent functions families typically perform (Davis, 1949).

Reproduction

If a society is to perpetuate itself, new members have to be created; families perform that function by providing social and cultural supports and motivations for having children.

Studying Section 3

Activities for Section 3

Challenges for American Families and American Society

- Family violence, child abuse, and incest are more common than most people think. The sexual abuse of children often leads to behavior problems.

- Incest and sexual abuse—27 percent of women and 16 percent of men. Perpetrator commonly a male authority figure in household.

- Child care and grandparents—most commonly used form of child care. Quality of child care available is often poor.

- Long-term effects of divorce—greater emotional and physical toll than almost any other type of stress, including death of a spouse. And children raised by single parents are more likely to have problems.

Comments on Section 3

- Note again that when you add details that seem important, there's no need to number each detail. Just set off details with a dash or a bullet, as shown in the notes above. Remember, also, that "The Chapter in Brief" on chapter pages 344–345 will help you identify key details.

342   Chapter 10 *The Family*

Socialization

The family functions as an intermediary in the socialization process between the larger community and the individual. At birth, children are uninitiated in the ways of culture, and thus each new generation subjects society to a recurrent "barbarian invasion" (see Chapter 3). Through the process of socialization, children become inducted into their society's ways, and the family usually serves as the chief culture-transmitting agency.

Care, Protection, and Emotional Support

Human children must be fed, clothed, and provided with shelter well into puberty. Throughout the world, the family has been assigned the responsibility for shielding, protecting, sustaining, and otherwise maintaining not just children, but also the infirm and other dependent members of the community (Rossi and Rossi, 1990). The family also provides an important source for entering into intimate, constant, face-to-face contact with other people. Healthy family relationships afford companionship, love, security, a sense of worth, and a general feeling of well-being.

Assignment of Status

Infants must be placed within the social structure. The family confers ascribed statuses (see Chapter 2, p. 56) that (1) orient a person to a variety of interpersonal relationships, including those involving parents, siblings, and other kin, and (2) orient a person to basic group memberships, including racial, ethnic, religious, class, national, and community relationships.

Regulation of Sexual Behavior

A society's norms regulate sexual behavior by specifying who may engage in sexual behavior with whom and under what circumstances. In no known society are people given total freedom for sexual expression. Although some

70 percent of the world's societies permit some form of sexual license, even those societies typically do not approve of childbirth out of wedlock—this is the **norm of legitimacy**; like other norms, this one is occasionally violated, and those who violate it are usually punished.

Critics of the functionalist perspective point out that these tasks can be performed in other ways. Indeed, by virtue of social change, many of the economic, child care, and educational functions once performed by the family have been taken over by other institutions. Even so, the family tends to be the social unit most commonly responsible for reproduction, socialization, and the other functions we considered.

The Conflict Perspective

Functionalists spotlight the tasks carried out by the family that serve the interests of society as a whole. Many conflict theorists, in contrast, have seen the family as a social arrangement benefiting some people more than others. Friedrich Engels (1884/1902), Karl Marx's close associate, viewed the family as a class society in miniature, with one class (men) oppressing another class (women). He contended that marriage was the first form of class antagonism in which the well-being of one group derived from the misery and repression of another. The motivation for sexual domination was the economic exploitation of a woman's labor.

Women as Sexual Property

Sociologist Randall Collins (1975, 1988a) has said that historically men have been the "sexual aggressors" and women the "sexual prizes for men." Women have been victimized by their smaller size and vulnerability as childbearers. Across an entire spectrum of societies women have been seen as sexual property, taken as booty in war, used by their fathers in economic bargaining, and considered as owned by their husbands.

Sociological Perspectives on the Family   **343**

According to Collins, marriage is a socially enforced contract of sexual property. Within Western tradition, a marriage was not legal until sexually consummated, sexual assault within marriage was not legally rape, and the principal ground for divorce was sexual infidelity. A woman's virginity was seen as the property of her father, and her sexuality as the property of her husband. Thus, rape has often traditionally been seen less as a crime perpetrated by a man against a woman than as a crime perpetrated by one man against another man.

In recent years, however, economic and political changes have improved women's bargaining position. The sexual bargains women strike can focus less on marriage and more on immediate pleasure, companionship, and sexual gratification.

Conflict as Natural and Necessary

Other social scientists have approached the issue of conflict somewhat differently. At the turn of the century psychoanalyst Sigmund Freud (1930/1961) and sociologist Georg Simmel (1908/1955, 1908/1959) also advanced a conflict approach to the family. They contended that intimate relationships inevitably involve antagonism as well as love. Sociologists like Jetse Sprey (1979) developed these ideas and suggested that conflict is a part of all systems and interactions, including the family and marital interactions. Viewed in this fashion, the family is a social arrangement that structures close interpersonal relationships through ongoing processes of negotiation, problem solving, and conflict management. This view is compatible with the interactionist perspective.

The Interactionist Perspective

As we saw in Chapters 2 and 3, symbolic interactionists emphasize that human beings create, use, and communicate with symbols. One way in which families reinforce and rejuvenate their bonds is through the symbolic mechanism of

rituals. Social scientists find that household rituals such as gathering for meals are a hidden source of family strength. It seems that when families preserve their rituals, their children fare better emotionally, even when the family faces other disruptive problems (e.g., alcoholism). Some therapists help families establish rituals as a means to heal family stresses and tensions (Goleman, 1992; Pipher, 1997).

The symbolic interactionist perspective is a useful tool for examining the complexities of a relationship. When the roles of one family member change, there are consequences for other family members. For example, we have seen that parenthood alters the husband–wife relationship by creating new roles and increasing the complexity of the family unit. Likewise, family life is different in homes where a mother is in the paid labor force or where an economic provider is unemployed. And the loss of critical family roles caused by divorce has vast implications for family functioning (Gubrium and Holstein, 1990).

 What Can Sociology Do for You?

This chapter has presented lots of information about families in U.S. society and around the world. Issues related to families provide multiple career opportunities—in social work, in child or elder care, in policy and planning, or in family and marriage counseling, just to name a few. If you've ever thought you might like to be a counselor, you may want to go to **http://www.allpsychologyschools.com/faqs/become_counselor.php** and read this site's information about counseling careers.

If you enjoyed Chapter 10 and are interested in family issues, you might want to take a family course, a marriage and courtship class, a course exploring the implications and challenges of our aging society, or other related classes.

[Section 4 ends.]

Studying Section 4

Activities for Section 4

Sociological Perspectives on the Family

Three perspectives:

1. _____—If society is to survive and succeed, it must guarantee that certain essential tasks or functions are performed. Such functions include reproduction, socialization, care, protection, and emotional support; assignment of status; regulation of sexual behavior.

   _____—the rule that children are not to be born out of wedlock.

2. _____—family seen as social arrangement that benefits some people more than others.

3. _____—families maintain their bonds through rituals—for example, gathering for meals.

Comments on Section 4

- An enumeration and three main definitions are the keys to important ideas in the above notes.

344   Chapter 10 *The Family*

The Chapter in Brief: *The Family*

Structure of the Family: A Global View

The way in which we define the family determines the kinds of **family** we will consider to be normal or deviant and what rights and obligations we will recognize as legally and socially binding.

■ **Forms of the Family**   In the **nuclear family** arrangement, spouses and their offspring constitute the core relationship. In the **extended family** arrangement, kin provide the core relationship. Most Americans will belong to a **family of orientation** and a **family of procreation**. Descent and inheritance can be **patrilineal, matrilineal,** or **bilineal**, and couples may take a **patrilocal, matrilocal,** or **neolocal** residence. Most societies are **patriarchal,** with some industrialized nations becoming more **egalitarian**; none are known that are truly **matriarchal.**

■ **Forms of Marriage**   **Marriage** refers to a socially approved sexual union undertaken with some idea of permanence. Two types of marital regulations define the "right" spouse: **endogamy** and **exogamy**. **Incest taboos** are rules that prohibit sexual intercourse with close blood relatives. Societies further structure marriage relationships in one of four ways: **monogamy, polygyny, polyandry,** and **group marriage**.

■ **Patterns of Courtship**   Societies "control" love through child and arranged marriages, social isolation of young people, close supervision of couples, and peer and parental pressures. A variety of factors operate in the selection of a mate: **homogamy,** physical attractiveness (the **matching hypothesis**), and **complementary needs**.

Exchange theory provides a unifying link among these factors.

Marriage and the Family in the United States

Some see the nuclear family as the source of many modern woes; others see it as the last bastion of morality in an increasingly decadent world.

■ **Marriage**   American couples with better marital quality are those who share decision making, have nontraditional views on the division of labor, and have close friendships and activities in common. Researchers have identified five common types of marriages.

■ **Parenthood**   Nuclear families typically pass through a series of changes and realignments across time, what sociologists call the **family life course**. Altered expectations and requirements are imposed on a husband and wife as children are born and grow up.

■ **Two-Income Families**   More than 60 percent of all mothers with children under age six are in the paid workforce. Such women also do more of the housework and child care than men. Research findings about the effect of working mothers on children are varied. In one-fifth of such couples, the woman is the chief breadwinner.

■ **Beyond the Traditional Nuclear Family**   Americans have a variety of **lifestyles**, the overall pattern of living that people evolve to meet their biological, social, and emotional needs. Among the lifestyles Americans find themselves adopting are singlehood, single parenthood, **cohabitation**, and relationships based on **homosexuality**.

Challenges for American Families and American Society

Some family problems stay in the family; others spill over into society.

■ **Family Violence, Child Abuse, and Incest**   Family violence, child abuse, and incest are more common than most people think. The sexual abuse of children often leads to behavior problems, learning difficulties, sexual promiscuity, runaway behavior, drug and alcohol abuse, and suicidal behavior.

■ **Child Care**   Most child psychologists agree that high-quality day care and preschools provide acceptable child care arrangements. The United States is one of the few industrialized nations that have no comprehensive day care program, and the quality of child care available is often poor.

■ **Divorce**   Divorce exacts a considerable emotional and physical toll from all family members. Children raised by single parents are more likely to drop out of high school, to use drugs, to have teen births, to have illegitimate children, and to be poorer than children raised in two-parent homes. More than half the adults who remarry undergo a second divorce.

■ **The Elderly**   The proportion of elderly people in the United States is increasing such that we will soon have a population structure with more over-60s than under-15s. These elderly will be characterized by better health and fewer disabilities than in the past and will continue to lead productive lives well past traditional retirement age. Resources, policies, and facilities for this increased population of elderly will be required.

Sociological Perspectives on the Family

■ **The Functionalist Perspective**   Functionalists identify a number of functions families typically perform: reproduction; socialization; care, protection, and emotional support; assignment of status; and regulation of sexual behavior through the **norm of legitimacy**.

■ **The Conflict Perspective**   Conflict theorists have seen the family as a social arrangement benefiting men more than women. Some conflict sociologists say that intimate relationships inevitably involve antagonism as well as love.

■ **The Interactionist Perspective**   Symbolic interactionists emphasize that families reinforce and rejuvenate their bonds through the symbolic mechanism of rituals such as family meals and holidays.

Glossary

bilineal   An arrangement based on reckoning descent and transmitting property through both the father and the mother.

cohabitation   An intimate relationship that involves sharing living quarters with an unrelated adult of the opposite sex.

complementary needs   Two different personality traits that are the counterparts of each other and that provide a sense of completeness when they are joined.

egalitarian authority   An arrangement in which power and authority are equally distributed between husband and wife.

endogamy   The requirement that marriage occur within a group.

exchange theory   The view proposing that people involved in a mutually satisfying relationship

346 Chapter 10 *The Family*

will exchange behaviors that have low cost and high reward.

exogamy The requirement that marriage occur outside a group.

extended family A family arrangement in which kin—individuals related by common ancestry—provide the core relationship; spouses are functionally marginal and peripheral.

family Traditionally defined as a social group whose members are related by ancestry, marriage, or adoption and who live together, cooperate economically, and care for the young.

family life course Changes and realignments related to the altered expectations and requirements imposed on a husband and a wife as children are born and grow up.

family of orientation A nuclear family that consists of oneself and one's father, mother, and siblings.

family of procreation A nuclear family that consists of oneself and one's spouse and children.

group marriage The marriage of two or more husbands and two or more wives.

heterogamous marriages Marriages in which spouses have different characteristics, including race or ethnicity, age, or religion.

homogamy The tendency of like to marry like.

homosexuality A preference for an individual of the same sex as a sexual partner.

incest taboos Rules that prohibit sexual intercourse with close blood relatives.

lifestyle The overall pattern of living that people evolve to meet their biological, social, and emotional needs.

marriage A socially approved sexual union between two or more individuals that is undertaken with some idea of permanence.

matching hypothesis The notion that we typically experience the greatest payoff and the least cost when we select partners who have a degree of physical attractiveness similar to our own.

matriarchal authority A family arrangement in which power is vested in women.

matrilineal An arrangement based on reckoning descent and inheritance through the mother's side of the family.

matrilocal residence The residence pattern in which a bride and groom live in the household or community of the wife's family.

monogamy The marriage of one husband and one wife.

neolocal residence The residence pattern in which newlyweds set up a new place of residence independent of either of their parents or other relatives.

norm of legitimacy The rule that children not be born out of wedlock.

nuclear family A family arrangement in which the spouses and their offspring constitute the core relationship; blood relatives are functionally marginal and peripheral.

patriarchal authority A family arrangement in which power is vested in men.

patrilineal An arrangement based on reckoning descent and inheritance through the father's side of the family.

patrilocal residence The residence pattern in which a bride and groom live in the household or community of the husband's family.

polyandry The marriage of two or more husbands and one wife.

polygyny The marriage of one husband and two or more wives.

romantic love The strong physical and emotional attraction between a man and a woman.

Review Questions

1. Differentiate between nuclear and extended families and between family of orientation and family of procreation.

2. Describe the various forms of marriage found around the world.

3. How do courtship patterns control love?

4. What is the family life course?

5. What sorts of lifestyles do Americans adopt besides the traditional nuclear family?

6. Name and describe some of the challenges facing American families today.

7. How do the functionalist, conflict, and interactionist perspectives on the family differ?

Internet Connection   www.mhhe.com/hughes10e

Using a search engine such as **google.com**, do a search on "family values." Choose a number of the sites you find, and explore them further. Write a short report about the many ways "family values" are defined in our society. How is this term thought about differently by different interest and cultural groups, including political and religious groups?

Closing Comments

In the process of taking notes, you have reduced almost forty pages of material to about five pages! These five pages provide an anchor for your understanding of the chapter. Keep in mind that if your instructor intends to test you on just this chapter, you may need to have a very detailed knowledge of the material and may want to do more rereading and add even more notes. On the other hand, if your instructor intends to test you on this and two other chapters, plus several weeks of classroom notes, it may well be that the five pages of notes are more than enough. You will quickly develop skill at making a good judgment call about just how much you need to learn.

• Complete the following description of the final stage of textbook study:

After taking as many notes as you need, your final step is to study the notes. To do so, put _____ words in the margin. For instance, the words "family structure" and "family functions" would help you learn the material on the first page of your notes. Your purpose would be to study until you could _____ to yourself the family structures and family functions without looking at them. You could then go on to study the other four pages of notes. After completing each page of notes, you should go back and _____ the previous pages. Through this process of repeated self-testing, you will effectively learn the material.

Building a
Powerful Memory

This chapter will show you how to develop your memory by

- Organizing the material to be learned
- Intending to remember
- Testing yourself repeatedly
- Using several memory techniques
- Spacing memory work over several sessions
- Overlearning
- Studying before sleep

Building a Powerful Memory:
In Real Life

Read the profile that follows. Then ask yourself these questions:

- How does Joe combine using a highlighter and using index cards as he memorizes?
- Why does Joe read his notes aloud to himself?

Student Profile: Joe Davis

Joe Davis wants to make one thing clear: He has a lousy memory. "It's bad across the board," he admits. "Facts, dates, names, faces. If I work with you and see you every day, I'm fine. But if I meet you today and see you again in a week, I have to ask your name again. That's embarrassed me more than once." He envies people who memorize things easily. "What an advantage a good memory is!" he explains. "You learn more quickly, you test better, you work more efficiently. But I've got to work with what I've got."

Continued

What Joe's got has gotten him pretty far. Joe earned his master's degree in social work from the University of Pennsylvania. He works as a therapist at the John F. Kennedy Mental Health Center in Philadelphia. He is also coordinator of Think First, a program at Magee Rehabilitation Hospital. Think First sends speakers who have suffered spinal-cord and head injuries into local schools. There they share their personal stories, making their audiences aware of the consequences of high-risk behavior.

The story Joe shares with Think First audiences involves years of drug use and crime, behavior that finally resulted in his being on the receiving end of a .22 bullet. The shooting left Joe paralyzed from the chest down. After a long and rocky rehabilitation, marked by continued drug use and an eventual suicide attempt, Joe took a good look at his life and was sickened by what he saw. He enrolled in a vocational rehabilitation program and got his first real job. Then he signed up for a university math class. He didn't do well. Refusing to give up, he enrolled in basic math and English courses at a local community college. Bit by bit, inch by inch, week by week, he struggled to acquire the academic skills he'd never cared about before.

"It was *hard*. It still *is* hard," Joe says today. "But it's worth the work."

As he works to memorize the material he studies, Joe says he'd be lost without two things: his highlighter and a stack of 3- by 5-inch cards. Reading slowly through his textbooks, he highlights definitions, examples, and "anything brand-new; anything that I haven't heard or seen before." Grabbing a pen, he'll scrawl notes to himself in the margin: "Look this up" or "Definition?" Then he'll read through the material yet again, this time copying whatever he's highlighted onto his 3-by-5 cards. Later, he'll read those cards out loud to himself. If they include terms he's not familiar with, he'll look the terms up, then talk

Continued

about them to a colleague or an instructor. "I want to know for sure how to pronounce them and how to use them correctly," he says. "I remember the embarrassment back in college when I mixed up the words 'stigma,' which means a mark of disgrace, and 'astigmatism,' which is an eye disorder. Now I look everything up, and I ask questions."

Joe finds that the combination of writing down new material and speaking it aloud works. "When it's time for me to remember that material, in a discussion or on a test, I can call up that recent memory. I can *see* myself writing it down or *hear* my voice saying it out loud. Studying just by reading the material silently is not nearly as effective for me."

Perhaps you think that memorizing material for a test is a waste of time; you may be convinced that you will forget what you memorize as soon as a test is over. Moreover, because some instructors believe that memorization and learning are incompatible, they may tell you that you shouldn't *memorize* material; rather, you should *understand* it.

Memorization, however, can be an important aid to understanding—and not just in situations where basic, uncomplicated material is involved. Effective memorizing requires that you organize and repeatedly test yourself on the material to be learned. As you do this, you are sure to enlarge your comprehension of the material and notice relationships you have not seen before. In short, memorization and understanding *reinforce* one another. Together, they help you learn—and learning is the goal of education. What you need, then, is a series of strategies, or steps, to help you memorize effectively. The following pages present seven such steps:

1   Organize the material to be learned.
2   Intend to remember.
3   Test yourself repeatedly on the material to be memorized.
4   Use several memory techniques.
5   Space memory work over several sessions.
6   Overlearn the material.
7   Use as a study period the time just before going to bed.

Step 1: Organize the Material to Be Learned

The first key to effective remembering is to organize in some meaningful way the material to be learned.

For example, imagine that your instructor has given you and your fellow students the assignment of memorizing each others' names. In such a situation, students typically begin by introducing themselves in isolated pairs. This doesn't work well for learning all the names, however, and someone usually suggests that the introductions be done in an organized manner. What usually happens then is that, one by one, people take turns giving their names to the entire class. Some students even jot down a rough seating chart (a further organizational device) to help them remember all the names. The point is that some meaningful kind of *organization* is a vital first step in the memorization process. The following two examples should also show how organizing material will aid memory.

Example A   Suppose that you had to memorize these numbers in any sequence:

1, 10, 7, 12, 22, 28, 20

You could eventually memorize the numbers by sheer mechanical repetition. However, you could learn them far more quickly, and remember them far longer, by grouping them in a meaningful and logical way:

$$10 + 12 = 22$$
$$1 + 7 + 20 = 28$$

Example B   Suppose that before you left for school or work, you were asked to look at a shopping list attached to the refrigerator door and to pick up the items later, at the store. To save the time of writing down the items, and to exercise your memory, you look over the list:

Tide	Parmesan cheese
Bic razors	Dawn
spaghetti	Windex
ChapStick	hair gel
garlic bread	

Memorizing the items at random would be difficult. So you organize them into meaningful groupings:

Dinner	*Cleaning Items*	*Personal-Care Items*
spaghetti	Tide	Bic razors
garlic bread	Dawn	hair gel
Parmesan cheese	Windex	ChapStick

The three groups of related items are far easier to study and remember than the nine random items.

To be an effective student, you must learn how to organize the material in classroom lectures and reading assignments. It is easier to remember ideas and details that are related to one another than ideas that are isolated, unorganized, and unrelated. In this book, "Taking Classroom Notes" (pages 41–71) will help you learn how to organize the material in classroom lectures, and the three chapters on textbook study (pages 95–199) will help you tie together ideas and details in reading assignments. You will then be ready to memorize any of the information that is necessary for you to remember.

- Material in your class notes and textbooks should be _____ in some meaningful way before you attempt to memorize it.

Step 2: Intend to Remember

An important aid to memory is *deciding* to remember. This advice appears to be so obvious that many people overlook it. But if you have made the decision to remember something and you then work at mastering it, you *will* remember. Anyone can improve his or her memory by working at it.

When assigned the task of memorizing classmates' names, students are often surprised at their ability to learn the names so quickly and completely. A main reason for their success is that they have decided to learn—for it might be embarrassing if they were the only ones not to have mastered the names when the instructor returns. The lesson here is that *your attitude is crucial in effective memorization.* You must begin by saying, "I am going to master this."

- Do you ever have trouble, as many people do, in remembering the names of persons you are introduced to? _____ Yes   _____ No

- If you do, the reason is probably that you did not consciously decide to remember their names. Suppose you were introduced to a person who was going to borrow money from you. Is it safe to say you would make it a point to remember (and so *would* remember) that person's name? _____ Yes _____ No

Step 3: Test Yourself Repeatedly on the Material to Be Learned

After you have organized the material you intend to learn, memorize it through repeated self-testing. Look at the first item in your notes; then look away and try to repeat it to yourself. When you can repeat the first item, look at the next item; look away and try to repeat it. When you can repeat the second item, *go back* without looking at your notes and repeat the first *and* second items. After you can recall the first two items without referring to your notes, go on to the third item, and so on. In short, follow this procedure: *After you learn each new item, go back and test yourself on all the previous items. This constant review is at the heart of self-testing and is the key to effective memorization.*

- If you were memorizing a list of ten definitions, what would you do after you mastered the second definition? The sixth? The tenth?

_____

_____

Step 4: Use Several Memory Techniques

The following techniques will help you in the self-testing process:

- Use several senses.
- Use key words.
- Use catchwords.
- Use catchphrases.

Catchwords and catchphrases are sometimes called *mnemonic* (nĭ mŏn′ ĭk) devices. (The term is derived from the Greek word for *memory*.) All four techniques are explained and illustrated on the pages ahead.

Use Several Senses

Use several senses in the self-testing process. Research has shown that most people understand and retain information more effectively when several senses are involved in learning the material. Do not, then, merely recite the information silently to yourself. Also repeat it out loud so that you *hear* it, and write it down so that you both *see* and, as it were, *touch* it. These steps will help you learn more than you would if you only repeated the information silently to yourself.

- What senses do you use in studying material? _____

_____

Use Key Words

Key words can be used as "hooks" to help you remember ideas. A *key word* stands for an idea and is so central to the idea that if you remember the word, you are almost sure to remember the entire concept that goes with the word.

Here is an illustration of how key words may function as hooks to help you recall ideas. Assume that your biology instructor has announced that the class will be tested on a textbook chapter dealing with the ecology of urban life. This is one important paragraph taken from that chapter:

> Urban planners who want to replace living plants with plastic ones seem to think that the city does not need to have living plants in it. Actually, plants do many useful things in a city even if they are not producing food for people. Plants improve the quality of the air by giving off oxygen and woodsy-smelling compounds, such as those emitted by pine trees. Smog contains some gases that, in low concentrations, can be used as nutrients by plants. Thus plants can absorb some air pollutants. Evaporation of water from plants cools the air; also, the leaves of plants catch falling dust particles. Trees and shrubs muffle the noise of what otherwise could be the deafening sound of street traffic and construction work. Finally, the roots of plants—even weeds on vacant lots—help to hold earth in place and reduce the number of soil particles blown into the air and washed into sewers.

Since you want to learn this information, you would first prepare study notes that might look something like this:

Uses of Plants in City

1. *Give off oxygen (and pleasant smell)*
2. *Absorb air pollutants (gases used as nutrients)*
3. *Cool the air (evaporation from leaves)*
4. *Catch dust particles*
5. *Muffle noises (traffic, construction)*
6. *Hold earth in place*

It is now necessary for you to memorize the study notes, and to do that you will need a technique. One way to memorize these study notes is to use key words as hooks. What you do is circle a key word from each of the listed items. The word you select should help you pull into memory the entire idea that it represents. Write each of the words, one after the other, under the study notes. Here is how your notes would look:

Uses of Plants in City

1. *Give off oxygen (and pleasant smell)*
2. *Absorb air pollutants (gases used as nutrients)*
3. *Cool the air (evaporation from leaves)*
4. *Catch dust particles*
5. *Muffle noises (traffic, construction)*
6. *Hold earth in place*

Key words: oxygen, pollutants, cool, dust, muffle, earth

After you pick out key words, the next step would be to test yourself repeatedly until you remember each of the six key words *and* the concepts they stand for.

- Take five minutes to study your six key words for the uses of plants in the city. Test yourself until you can recite from memory all the words and the ideas they stand for. Your instructor may then ask you to write from memory the six words and concepts on a sheet of paper.

Use Catchwords

Sometimes people who use key words to pull central ideas into memory can't remember one of the key words, and so they forget the entire concept the word represents. Using catchwords is one way to ensure that you remember an entire series of key words and so the ideas they stand for. *Catchwords* are words made up of the first letters of other words. (See also page 116.)

Follow these guidelines when you create catchwords. First, circle the key words in your study notes. Then write down the first letter of each key word. Here are the first letters for the key words in the paragraph about city plants: O (oxygen), P (pollutants), C (cool), D (dust), M (muffle), and E (earth). Now, if necessary, rearrange the letters to form an easily recalled catchword. It can be a real word or a made-up word. For example, you might remember the letters O-P-C-D-M-E with the made-up word MEDCOP.

What matters is that you create a word that you can automatically remember and that the letters in the word help you recall the key words (and so the ideas the key words represent).

After you create a catchword, test yourself until you are sure each letter stands for a key word in your mind. Here is how you might use the catchword MEDCOP to pull into memory the textbook paragraph about city plants:

MEDCOP
M ≈ muffle
E ≈ earth
D ≈ dust
C ≈ cool
O ≈ oxygen
P ≈ pollutants

Cover the key words (*muffle*, *earth*, etc.) with a sheet of paper, leaving only the first letter exposed. Look at the letter *M* and see if you can recall the key word *muffle* and the idea that plants muffle noise. Next, look at the letter *E* and see if you remember the key word *earth* and the idea that plant roots hold the earth in place. Then do the same for the other four letters. In each case, the letter serves as a hook to pull into memory the key word and then the whole idea.

Here is an illustration of how first letters and key words help you remember ideas. As shown here, the first letter helps you remember the key word, which helps you pull the entire idea into memory.

First Letter	Key Word	Entire Idea
M ⟶	muffle ⟶	muffle noise of traffic and construction
E ⟶	earth ⟶	hold earth in place
D ⟶	dust ⟶	catch dust particles
C ⟶	cool ⟶	cool the air
O ⟶	oxygen ⟶	give off oxygen
P ⟶	pollutants ⟶	absorb air pollutants

- An instructor in a psychology class described the following four techniques used in behavior therapy: (1) extinction, (2) imitation, (3) reinforcement, and (4) desensitization. Make up a catchword that will help you remember the four techniques, and write the word here: _____

Use Catchphrases

Another way to remember key words is to form some easily recalled *catchphrase*. Each word in a catchphrase begins with the first letter of a different key word. For example, suppose you had to remember the six uses of city plants in the exact order in which they are presented in the textbook paragraph (*oxygen, pollutants, cool, dust, muffle, earth*). You would write a six-word phrase with the first word beginning with *O*, the second with *P*, the third with *C*, and so on. Here is a catchphrase you might create to help remember the order of the six letters and the key words they stand for:

Our **p**arents **c**ook **d**inner **m**ost **e**venings.

Your catchphrase does not have to be perfect grammatically; it does not even have to make perfect sense. It simply needs to be a phrase that will stick in your memory and that you will automatically remember.

Once you create a catchphrase, follow the testing process already described above in the section on catchwords. Note that the first letter of each word in the catchphrase pulls into memory a key word and the key word recalls an entire idea. For example, the *O* in *Our* recalls the key word *oxygen* and the idea that plants give off oxygen, the *P* in *parents* helps you remember the key word *pollutants* and the idea that plants absorb air pollutants, and so on.

- Suppose an instructor wants you to learn the following five influences on a child's personality. The influences are listed in order of importance.

Influences on Children
One: Parents
Two: Siblings (brothers and sisters)
Three: Friends
Four: Close relatives
Five: Teachers

Make up a catchphrase that will help you remember in sequence the five influences on children and write the phrase here:

_____

Step 5: Space Memory Work Over Several Sessions

If you try to do a great deal of self-testing at any one time, you may have trouble absorbing the material. Always try to spread out your memory work. For instance, three two-hour sessions will be more effective than one six-hour session.

Spacing memory work over several time periods gives you a chance to review and lock in material you have studied in an earlier session but have begun to forget. Research shows that we forget a good deal of information right after studying it. However, review within a day reduces much of this memory loss. So try to review new material within twenty-four hours after you first study it. Then, if possible, several days later review again to make a third impression or "imprint" of the material in your memory. If you work consistently to retain ideas and details, they are not likely to escape you when you need them during an exam.

- Do you typically try to study the material for a test "all at once," or do you spread out your study over several sessions?

  _____

  _____

- How might you spread out six hours of memory work that you need to do for a biology exam?

  _____

  _____

Step 6: Overlearn the Material

If you study a subject beyond the time needed for perfect recall, you will increase the length of time that you will remember it. You can apply the principle of over-learning by going over several times a lesson you have already learned perfectly. The method of repeated self-testing is so effective partly because it forces you to overlearn. After you study each new idea, the method requires that you go back and recite all the previous ideas you have studied.

Another way to apply the principle of overlearning is to devote some time in each session to review. Go back to restudy—and overlearn—important material that you have studied in the past. Doing so will help ensure that you will not "push out" of memory old ideas at the time you are learning new ones.

- If you memorize a list of ten definitions using the process of repeated self-testing, how many times, at a minimum, will you have tested yourself on the first definition? _____

Step 7: Study before Going to Bed

Study thoroughly the material to be learned. Then go right to sleep without watching a late movie or allowing other activities to interfere with your new learning. Your mind will work through and absorb much of this material during the night. Set your clock a half hour earlier than usual so that you will have time to go over the material as soon as you get up. The morning review will complete the process of solidly fixing the material in your memory.

- Have you ever used this technique and found it to be helpful? _____

_____

- Do you think you should practice the technique daily or use it more as a study aid in the review period before an exam? _____

Practice in Building a Powerful Memory

Activity 1

1. An instructor in a criminal justice class describes the four traditional goals of punishment. Make up a catchword that will help you remember all four goals.

_____

   Retribution
   Deterrence
   Incapacitation
   Rehabilitation

2. An instructor in a psychology class writes on the board the following five characteristics of schizophrenia. Make up a catchword that will help you remember these five characteristics.

_____

Language-thought disturbances

Delusions

Perceptual disorders

Emotional disturbances

Isolation

3. The following six avoidance tactics often used by students were described on pages 17–19 of this book. Circle the first letter of a key word in each of these tactics and then create a catchphrase to help remember the six key words. The key words, in turn, will help you remember the six avoidance tactics.

_____

I can't do it.

I'm too busy.

I'm too tired.

I'll do it later.

I'm bored with the subject.

I'm here, and that's what counts.

4. You have memorized three groups of items individually. Now take ten to fifteen minutes to prepare for a quiz in which you will be asked to write from memory the four goals of legal punishment, the five characteristics of schizophrenia, and the six avoidance tactics.

Activity 2

1. A psychology text explains Abraham Maslow's theory of basic human needs. The five needs, in order of importance, follow. Use a catchphrase to memorize them *in sequence*.

_____

Basic Human Needs

First: Biological needs

Second: Safety needs

Third: Need for companionship

Fourth: Esteem needs

Fifth: Need for self-actualization

2. Many articles and textbooks refer to Holmes and Rohe's scale of specific life experiences that result in stress. Use a catchphrase to memorize *in sequence* the first six experiences on that scale as well as the point value assigned to each.

Death of spouse	100
Divorce	73
Marital separation	65
Jail term	63
Death of close family member	63
Personal injury or illness	53

3. A sociology text describes the following seven steps that are taken in scientific research. Use a catchphrase to memorize the seven steps *in sequence*.

First: Define the problem.

Second: Review the literature.

Third: Formulate the hypotheses.

Fourth: Plan the research design.

Fifth: Collect the data.

Sixth: Analyze the data.

Seventh: Draw conclusions.

4. You have memorized three groups of items individually. Now take ten to fifteen minutes to prepare for a quiz in which you will be asked to write from memory, and *in sequence,* the five human needs, the six sources of stress, and the seven steps in scientific research.

Activity 3

1. Read the following selection from a text on public speaking. Then look over the study notes on the selection.

Analyzing the Audience

A number of factors about the audience should be kept in mind when you are planning your speech. First, how large is the audience? If the group is very small, you can get away with speaking quite informally. But the larger the audience, the more polished and formal your delivery should be. Second, how much interest does your audience have in your topic? Especially if you are addressing a "captive audience" of students, you should take pains to adjust your topic so as to involve your listeners. In addition, how much does your audience already know about your topic? If the audience members are already well-informed, you can speak at a sophisticated level. But if they know little about the topic, you will have to speak in elementary terms. Next, what is the audience's attitude toward the topic? If you are speaking on the subject of abortion rights, for example, and your audience is largely antiabortion, you will need to take a different approach from the one you would take if the audience shared your view. Finally, how does the audience perceive you, the speaker? If the audience members see you as well prepared and well informed, they'll listen to what you have to say more favorably than if they see you as unprepared, ill-informed, or otherwise unbelievable.

Study Notes

Analyzing the Audience

One: How large is the audience?

Two: How much interest does the audience have in the topic?

Three: How much knowledge does the audience have?

Four: What is the audience's attitude toward the topic?

Five: How does the audience perceive the speaker?

Pick out a key word for each of the five tips for analyzing an audience, and then use a catchword or catchphrase to memorize the tips.

2. Read the following selection taken from a psychology textbook. Then look over the study notes on the selection.

Personal Space

In addition to what you wear and how you stand, where you stand can communicate your attitude. One researcher, E. Hall, identified four types of personal zones or spaces. The first type of personal space is intimate distance (from body contact to one foot away). This space is reserved for a limited few, including lovers, parents, children, and close friends. In addition, health professionals, such as doctors, nurses, and dentists, are allowed to enter this space. If anyone else got this close, you would feel very uncomfortable. The second zone is personal distance (one to four feet away). This zone is used for personal conversations with close friends. If you are sitting in a half-empty theater or bus, and someone takes the seat next to you, you will probably feel annoyed. A stranger in our personal zone makes us feel ill at ease. If people must be packed together—as on a crowded bus—they often avoid eye contact as a way of protecting their personal space. The third zone is social distance (four to ten feet). This zone is used for social and casual conversations or for business transactions. The final zone is public distance (ten feet and beyond). Communication within a large lecture hall, or the relationship of an audience to a sports event or performance, takes place at public distance. Often, in these situations, we consider private behavior or comments inappropriate.

Study Notes

Personal zones

One: Intimate distance (body contact to one foot away)

Two: Personal distance (one to four feet)

Three: Social distance (four to ten feet)

Four: Public distance (ten feet and beyond)

Pick out a key word for each of the four personal zones and then use a catchword or catchphrase to memorize the four zones.

3. You have memorized two groups of items individually. Now take ten to fifteen minutes to prepare for a quiz in which you will be asked to write from memory the five tips for analyzing an audience and the four personal zones.

Activity 4

Use catchwords to memorize this outline of a selection on job hunting.

Four Stages in Getting a Job

A. Make contact through
   1. College placement bureau
   2. Want ads and employment agencies
   3. Telephone calls
   4. Personal connections
B. Prepare essential written materials
   1. Résumé
   2. Cover letter

C. Go out on interview
1. Interview etiquette
2. Prepare responses to some typical questions
a. "Why are you interested in this job?"
b. "What are your greatest strengths and weaknesses?"
c. "Tell me about yourself."
d. "Why should we hire you?"
3. Come across as a competent person
D. Follow up on interview with thank-you note

Activity 5

This activity will help you apply memory techniques to different kinds of lecture and textbook notes. Use catchwords or catchphrases to do one or more of the following:

- Learn the four steps in writing a paper (pages 69–71).
- Learn the concentration hints (pages 88–92).
- Learn the two forms of water pollution (page 327).
- Learn the five ways of becoming a better listener (pages 131–135).

Activity 6

From one of your course textbooks or from the class notes for one of your courses, select a list of important items that you will need to remember. Then do these three things and turn in a copy of your work to your instructor.

1. Write the full list on a sheet of paper.
2. Circle key words that will help you remember each item on the list.
3. Make up a catchword or catchphrase for the first letters of the key words.

Activity 7

Select four lists of important items to remember from the sample textbook chapter on pages 154–196. Then do the three things listed in Activity 6.

Taking Objective Exams

This chapter will show you how to

- Prepare for and take tests in general
- Prepare for objective exams
- Take objective exams
- Cram when you have no other choice

Taking Objective Exams: In Real Life

Read the profile that follows. Then ask yourself these questions:

- When Katie knows that a test is coming up, how does she adjust her week's schedule?
- What is one way that Katie eliminates possible answers for a multiple-choice item?

Student Profile: Katie Peacock

Katie Peacock had been home-schooled throughout her high school years, and making the transition to college required certain adjustments for her. No longer could she attend class in her pajamas. No longer could she put off classes until after lunch. And no longer could she avoid taking tests.

Test-taking, then, was a skill that Katie had to learn, and learn quickly. She took advantage of the information provided in her developmental reading course and came up with a strategy that has worked for her.

Katie's strategy for preparing for an objective test includes the following steps:

- She takes careful notes in her classes and reviews them before an exam.
- If her textbook includes end-of-chapter review questions or mastery tests, she makes sure she can complete them successfully.

Continued

- She is sure to attend any review sessions offered by her instructors before exams.

- When she knows a test is coming up, she takes that into account as she schedules her week's work. "I get my other assignments out of the way so that I really have time before the test to study for it," she says. "I want to go into the test well prepared, with the information fresh in my mind."

- She pays attention to an instructor's hints that certain material may be on the test. "Sometimes an instructor will say directly, 'You'll be tested on this,'" Katie says. "But in other cases, I'll just notice when she spends an especially long time talking about a certain point. I'll put a big star beside that material in my notes."

Here are some of Katie's tips for actually taking the test:

- "I don't start filling in answers right away. I look over the entire test first. Then I go back, quickly answer the questions I know for sure, and use the rest of the time to work on the more difficult items."

- "As I look at multiple-choice items, I eliminate answers in a couple of ways. First, the longest answer is often the right one. Of course I have to read it carefully to make sure it makes sense. Also, you can often eliminate answers with words like 'always' and 'never' in them. Answers that include 'often' or 'much of the time' are more likely to be correct."

- "True-and-false questions are often hard for me. They're often written in a way that I find really tricky. I have to take extra time to read them carefully before I answer them."

Katie's mastery of test-taking skills is helping her to do well in all her courses. She expects to graduate from Delaware County Community College with an associate's degree in business management, and then to transfer to Cabrini College, also in Pennsylvania, to earn a bachelor's degree.

Avoiding Exam Panic

A familiar complaint of students is "I'm always afraid I'll panic during an exam. I'll know a lot of the material, but when I sit down and start looking at the questions, I forget things that I know. I'll never get good grades as long as this happens. How can I avoid it?" The answer is that if you are *well prepared*, you are not likely to block or panic on exams.

"How, then," you might ask, "should a person go about preparing for exams?" The answer is plain: You must go to class consistently, read the textbook and any other assigned material, take class and textbook notes, and study and at times memorize your notes. In short, you must start preparing for exams in the first class of the semester. The pages that follow offer a series of practical suggestions to help you use your study time efficiently.

Note   Many of the suggestions offered in this chapter assume that you know how to take effective classroom and textbook notes and that you know how to memorize such notes. If you have not developed these essential skills, refer to the appropriate chapters.

- *Complete the following sentence*: You are unlikely to forget material during exams if you are _____.

What to Study

You will not always know beforehand if a scheduled exam will be an objective test or an essay test (or a combination of both). To be prepared for whichever kind is given, you should, throughout the course, pay attention to the following.

Key Terms   Look for key terms, their definitions, and examples that clarify the meaning of the terms (see also page 317). Look for this material in your class and textbook notes. If your textbook notes are not complete, go back to the original reading material to locate key terms. This information is often set off in *italic* or **boldface** type.

- Which of the courses you are now taking contains a number of new terms you will probably have to know for exams? _____

Enumerations   Look for enumerations (lists of items) in your class and textbook notes (see also page 324). Enumerations are often the basis of essay questions.

Items in a list will probably have a descriptive heading—for example, characteristics of living things, major schools of contemporary psychology, or primary consequences of the Industrial Revolution—and the items may be numbered. Be sure to learn the heading that describes the list as well as the items in the list.

Points Emphasized   Look for points emphasized in class or in the text. Often phrases such as *the most significant*, *of special importance*, *the chief reason*, and so on (see page 50) are used to call attention to important points in a book or a lecture. When you take notes on such material, mark these significant points with an *imp,* an asterisk (*), or some other mark.

Also, as you go through your class notes, concentrate on areas the instructor spent a good deal of time discussing. For example, if the instructor spent a week talking about present-day changes in the traditional family structure, you can reasonably expect to get a question on the emphasized area. Similarly, review your textbook. If many pages in a chapter deal with one area, you may be sure that this subject is important, and you should expect a question about it on an exam.

- Write down here the name of one of your courses and an area that your instructor has spent a good deal of time discussing in the course.

    Course: _____

    Area: _____

Topics Identified by the Instructor   Pay attention to areas your instructors have advised you to study. Some instructors conduct in-class reviews during which they tell students what material to emphasize when they study. Always write down these pointers; your instructors have often made up the test or are making it up at the time of the review and are likely to give valuable hints about the exam. Other instructors indicate the probable emphasis in their exams when they distribute reviews or study guides. You should, of course, consider these aids very carefully.

- One study-skills instructor has said, "I sometimes sit in on classes, and time and again I have heard instructors tell students point-blank that something is to be on an exam. Some students quickly jot down this information; others sit there in a fog." Which group of students do you belong to?

    _____

- What are some specific study aids instructors have given to help you prepare for tests? _____

    _____

Questions on Earlier Tests   Pay attention to questions on past quizzes and reviews as well as tests at the end of textbook chapters.

If you follow these suggestions, you will have identified most, if not all, of the key concepts in the course.

The following hints will help you make the most of your time before a test.

Hint 1   Spend the night before an exam making a final review of your notes. Then go right to bed without watching television or otherwise interfering with the material you have learned. Your mind will tend to work through and absorb the material during the night. To further lock in your learning, get up a half hour earlier than usual the next morning and review your notes.

• Do you already review material on the morning of an exam? _____

  If so, have you found it to be very helpful? _____

Hint 2   Make sure you take with you any materials (pen, paper, eraser, dictionary, and other aids allowed) you will need during the exam.

Hint 3   Be on time for the exam. Arriving late sets you up to do poorly.

Hint 4   Sit in a quiet spot. Some people are very talkative and noisy before an exam. Since you don't want anything to interfere with your learning, you are better off not talking with others during the few minutes before the exam starts. You might want to use those minutes to make one final review of your notes.

• How do you typically spend the minutes in class right before an exam?

  _____

Hint 5   Read over carefully *all* the directions on the exam before you begin. Many students don't take this important step and end up losing points because they fail to do what is required. Make sure you understand how you are expected to respond to each item, how many points each section is worth, and how many questions you must answer. Also, listen carefully to any oral directions or hints the instructor may give. Many students wreck their chances at the start because they do not understand or follow directions. Don't let this happen to you.

• Do you already have the habit of reading all the directions on an exam carefully before you begin? _____

Hint 6   Budget your time. Take a few seconds to figure out roughly how much time you can spend on each section of the test. Write the number of minutes in the margin of your exam paper or on a scratch sheet. Then stick to that schedule. Be sure to have a watch or to sit where you can see a clock.

Exactly *how* you budget your time depends on what kinds of questions you are good at answering (and so can do more quickly) and the point value of different sections of the test. Keep in mind that the reason for budgeting your time is to prevent you from ending up with ten minutes left and a fifty-point essay still to write or thirty multiple-choice questions to answer.

Activity 1

This activity will check your skill at following written directions.

A Test in Following Directions   First read all ten directions carefully. Then follow them.

_____   _____

1. Print your full name, last name first, on the line at the right above.

2. Write your full name, first name last, under the line at the left above.

3. Count the number of *e*'s in this sentence and write out the total number in the margin to the right of this line.

4. Fold this page in half, side to side; then open it again.

5. Read the following question carefully and answer it in the space provided. "A plane crashes on the United States–Canadian border. On which side are the survivors buried?" _____

6. Disregard the fourth instruction.

7. If Kurt and Gail each have $100, how much would Kurt have to give Gail for her to have $10 more than he has? _____

8. How many birthdays does the average hippopotamus have? _____

9. Block out the three-letter words, circle the four-letter words, and underline the five-letter words in this sentence. Then indicate in the space that follows the number of words left unmarked. _____

10. If Glug zorted the rochenelle and hochwinded a swattorg, what fortig dorts Glug?

Activity 2

Here is an activity that will check your skill at budgeting time. Suppose that you had two hours for a test made up of the following sections:

Part 1: 10 true–false questions worth 10 points   (_____ minutes)

Part 2: 40 multiple-choice questions worth 40 points   (_____ minutes)

Part 3: 2 essay questions worth 50 points   (_____ minutes)

In the spaces provided, write how much time you would spend on each part.

One possible division of time is to spend an hour on the first two parts (about ten minutes on the true–false questions and fifty minutes on the multiple-choice questions) and a half hour on each essay question. Because the essay questions are worth half the points on the test, you want at least an hour to work on them.

Preparing for and Taking Objective Exams

Objective exams may include multiple-choice, true–false, fill-in, and matching questions. Perhaps you feel that objective tests do not require as much study time as essay exams do. A well-constructed objective test, however, can evaluate your understanding of major concepts and can demand just as sophisticated a level of thinking as an essay exam. In short, do not cut short your study time just because you know you will be given an objective test.

To do well on objective tests, you must know how to read test items carefully. The pages that follow describe a number of strategies you can use to deal with the special problems posed by objective tests.

Getting Ready for Objective Exams

Hint 1   Be prepared to memorize material when studying for an objective test. The test may include short-answer questions. For example, the instructor may give several technical terms and ask you to define them. Or the instructor may include headings such as "Three Values of the Social Security Act" and expect you to list the values underneath. He or she may include fill-in questions such as "An important leader of the stimulus-response school of psychology has been

_____."

Even objective tests made up only of multiple-choice and true–false questions can include such fine distinctions that memorization may be necessary. In addition, memorization helps keep your study honest: It forces you to truly *understand* the material you are learning.

There is one difference worth noting between the kind of memorizing needed for essay exams and the kind needed for objective tests. In an essay test, you are actually expected to *recall course material.* For example, an essay test might ask you to list and explain three kinds of defense mechanisms. In an objective test, you are expected to *recognize the correctness of course material.* For instance, an objective test might give you a defense mechanism followed by a definition and ask you whether that definition is true or false. In either kind of test, however, memory is required.

• Describe the specific kinds of objective exams that your instructors give:

_____

Hint 2   Ask your instructor what kind of items will be on the test. Not all instructors will provide this information. However, finding out beforehand that an exam will include, let's say, fifty multiple-choice and fill-in items relieves you of some anxiety. At least you know what to expect.

Hint 3   Try to find a test that is similar to the one you will be taking. Some instructors distribute past exams to help students review. Also, some departments keep on file exams given in earlier semesters. Looking at these exams closely can familiarize you with the requirements, format, and items you may reasonably expect on your exam.

Hint 4   Be sure to review carefully all the main points presented in the course. These were detailed in "What to Study" on pages 221–223. To sharpen your understanding of the key material, apply the techniques of repeated self-testing (page 206) to the recall words written in the margin of your class and textbook notes (pages 53 and 55).

Hint 5   Make up practice test items when you study. That way you will be getting into the rhythm of taking the test, and you may even be able to predict some of the questions the instructor will ask.

Taking Objective Exams

Hint 1   Answer all the easier questions first. Don't lose valuable time stalling over hard questions. You may end up running out of time and not even getting a chance to answer the questions you can do easily. Instead, put a light check mark (✓) beside difficult questions and continue working through the entire test, answering all the items you can do right away. You will find that this strategy will help give you the momentum you need to go confidently through the rest of the exam.

Hint 2   Go back and spend the remaining time with the difficult questions you have marked. Often you will find that while you are answering the easier questions, your unconscious mind has been working on questions you at first found very difficult. Or later items may provide just the extra bit of information you need to answer earlier items you found difficult. Once you answer a question, add a mark to the check you have already made (✗) to show you have completed that item.

Hint 3   Answer *all* questions unless the instructor has said that extra points will be deducted for wrong answers. Guess if you must; by doing so, you are bound to pick up at least a few points.

Hint 4   Ask the instructor to explain any item that isn't clear. Not all instructors will provide this explanation, but probably many will. Most experienced instructors realize that test questions may seem clear and unambiguous to them as they make up the exam but that students may interpret certain questions in other and equally valid ways. In short, you can't lose anything by asking to have an item clarified.

Hint 5   Put yourself in the instructor's shoes when you try to figure out the meaning of a confusing item. In light of what was covered in the course, which answer do you think the instructor would say is correct? If a test item is worded so ambiguously that no single response seems correct, you may—in special situations—use the margin of your test paper to explain to the instructor what you feel the answer should be. Obviously, use this technique only when absolutely necessary.

Hint 6   Circle or underline the key words in difficult questions. This strategy can help you untangle complicated questions and focus on the central point in the item.

Hint 7   Express difficult questions in your own words. Rephrasing an item in simpler terms and then writing it down or even saying it to yourself can help you cut through the confusion and get to the core of the question. Be sure, however, not to change the original meaning of the item.

Hint 8   Take advantage of the full time given and go over the exam carefully for possible mistakes. People used to say that it is not a good idea to change the first answer you put down. However, as long as you have a good reason, you *should* change your earlier answers if they seem incorrect. At the same time, be on guard against last-minute anxiety that prompts you to change, without good reason, *many* of your original answers. You should control any tendency you may have to make widespread revisions.

Activity

Write here what you think are the three most important of the preceding hints to remember in taking objective exams.

1. _____

2. _____

3. _____

Specific Hints for Answering Multiple-Choice Questions

1 Remember that in multiple-choice exams, a perfect answer to every question may not be provided. You must choose the best answer *available.*

2 Cross out answers you know are incorrect. Eliminating wrong answers is helpful because it focuses your attention on the most reasonable options. If you think all options are incorrect, the correct answer may be "none of the above"—if that choice is given.

3 Be sure to read all the possible answers to a question, especially when the first answer seems correct. Remember that the other options could also be correct. In this case, "all of the above" would be the correct response—if that choice is given.

4 Minimize the risk of guessing the answer to difficult items by doing either of the following:

   a Read the question and then the first possible answer. Next, read the question again and the second possible answer, and so on until you have read the question with each separate answer. Breaking the items down this way will often help you identify the option that most logically answers the question.

   b When you return to difficult items, try not to look at the answers. Instead, read the question, supply your own answer, and then look for the option on the test that is closest to your response.

5 Use the following clues, which may signal correct answers, *only* when you have no idea of the answer and must guess.

   a The longest answer is often correct.

   • *Use this clue to answer the following question*: The key reason students who are well prepared still don't do well on exams is that they (a) are late to the test, (b) don't have all their materials, (c) forget to jot down catchphrases, (d) haven't studied enough, (e) don't read all the directions before they begin the test.

The correct answer is *e,* the longest answer.

b The most complete and inclusive answer is often correct.

- *Use this clue to answer the following question*: If you have to cram for a test, which of these items should receive most of your attention? (a) The instructor's tests from other years; (b) important ideas in the class and text notes, including such things as key terms, their definitions, and clarifying examples; (c) the textbook; (d) class notes; (e) textbook notes.

  The correct answer is *b,* the most complete and inclusive choice. Note that the most complete answer is often also the longest.

c An answer in the middle, especially if it is longest, is often correct.

- *Use this clue to answer the following question*: Many students have trouble with objective tests because they (a) guess when they're not sure, (b) run out of time, (c) think objective exams are easier than essay tests and so do not study enough, (d) forget to double-check their answers, (e) leave difficult questions to the end.

  The correct answer is *c,* which is in the middle and is longest.

d If two answers have opposite meanings, one of them is probably correct.

- *Use this clue to answer the following question*: Before an exam starts, you should (a) sit in a quiet spot, (b) join a group of friends and talk about the test, (c) review the textbook one last time, (d) read a book and relax, (e) study any notes you didn't have time for previously.

  The correct answer is *a.* Note that *a* and *b* are roughly opposite.

e Answers with qualifiers, such as *generally, probably, most, often, some, sometimes,* and *usually,* are frequently correct.

- *Use this clue to answer the following question*: In multiple-choice questions, the most complete and inclusive answer is (a) never correct, (b) often correct, (c) always correct, (d) all of the above, (e) none of the above.

The correct answer is *b,* the choice with the qualifying word *often.* Note also that answers with absolute words, such as *all, always, everyone, everybody, never, no one, nobody, none,* and *only,* are usually incorrect.

- *Use this clue to answer the following question*: In multiple-choice questions, the answer in the middle with the most words is (a) always correct, (b) always incorrect, (c) frequently correct, (d) never wrong, (e) never right.

The correct answer is *c*; all the other answers use absolute words and are incorrect.

Activity

Write here what you think are the three most helpful clues for you to remember when you are guessing the answer to a multiple-choice question.

1. _____

2. _____

3. _____

Specific Hints for Answering True–False Questions

1 Simplify questions with double negatives by crossing out both negatives and then determining the correct answer.

- *Use this hint to answer the following question: True or false?* _____ You won't be unprepared for essay exams if you anticipate several questions and prepare your answers for those questions.

The statement is true. It can be reworded to read, "You will be prepared for essay exams if you anticipate several questions and prepare your answers to those questions."

2 Remember that answers with qualifiers such as *generally, probably, most, often, some, sometimes,* and *usually* are frequently true.

- *Use this hint to answer the following question*: *True or false?* _____ Some instructors will tell students what kinds of items to expect on an exam.

The statement, which contains the qualifier *Some,* is true.

3 Remember that answers with absolute words such as *all, always, everyone, never, no one, nobody, none,* and *only* are usually false.

- *Use this hint to answer the following question: True or false?* _____ You should never review your notes on the morning of an essay exam.

The statement, which contains the absolute word *never*, is false.

Specific Hints for Answering Fill-In Questions

1 Read the questions to yourself so you can actually hear what is being asked. If more than one response comes to mind, write both responses lightly in the margin. Then, when you review your answers later, choose the answer that feels most right to you.

2 Make sure each answer you provide fits logically and grammatically into its slot in the sentence. For example: An _____ lists ideas in a sequence.

The correct answer is *enumeration*. Note that the word *an* signals that the correct answer begins with a vowel.

3 Remember that not all fill-in answers require only one word. If you feel that several words are needed to complete an answer, write in all the words unless the instructor or the directions indicate that only single-word responses will be accepted.

Specific Hints for Answering Matching Questions

1 Don't start matching items until you read both columns and get a sense of the choices. Often, there's an extra item or two in one column. This means that not all items can be paired. Some will be left over. For example:

1. Sentence-skills mistakes _____	a. compare, explain, analyze
2. Absolute words _____	b. often, usually, most
3. Connecting words _____	c. from, over, in, with
4. Qualifying words _____	d. misspelled and omitted words
5. Direction words in instructions _____	e. all, never, only
	f. first, second, next, also

The correct answers are 1-*d*, 2-*e*, 3-*f*, 4-*b*, and 5-*a*. Item *c* is extra.

2 Start with the easiest items. One by one, focus on each item in one column and look for its match in the other column. Cross out items as you use them.

A Final Note: How to Cram When You Have No Other Choice

Students who consistently cram for tests are not likely to be successful; they often have to cram because they have not managed their time well. However, even organized students may sometimes need to cram because they run into problems that disrupt their regular study routine. If you're ever in this situation, the following steps may help you do some quick but effective studying.

1 Accept the fact that, in the limited time you have, you are not going to be able to study everything in your class notes and textbook. You may even have to exclude your textbook if you know that your instructor tends to base most of a test on class material.

2 Read through your class notes (and, if you have them, your textbook notes) and mark off those ideas that are most important. Use as a guide any review or study sheets that your instructor has provided. Your purpose is to try to guess correctly many of the ideas your instructor will put in the test.

 Important ideas often include definitions, enumerations (lists of items), points marked by emphasis words, and answers to basic questions made out of titles and headings. See also "What to Study" on pages 221–223.

3 Write the ideas you have selected on sheets of paper, using one side of a page only. Perhaps you will wind up with three or four "cram sheets" full of important points to study.

4 Prepare catchwords or catchphrases to recall the material and then memorize the points using the method of repeated self-testing described on page 206.

5 Go back, if time remains, and review all your notes. If you do not have textbook notes, you might skim your textbook. Do not use this time to learn new concepts. Instead, try to broaden as much as possible your understanding of the points you have already studied.

Practice in Test-Taking

Activity 1

Evaluate your present test-preparation and test-taking skills. Put a check mark beside each of the following steps that you already practice. Then put a check mark beside those steps that you plan to practice. Be honest; leave a blank space if you do not plan to follow a particular point.

Now   Plan
Do   to Do   *What to Study*

____ ____   1. Key terms, definitions, and examples.

____ ____   2. Enumerations (lists of items).

____ ____   3. Points emphasized in class.

____ ____   4. Reviews and study guides.

____ ____   5. Questions in past quizzes and textbook chapters.

General Tips before an Exam

____ ____   1. Study right before sleep.

____ ____   2. Take materials needed to the exam.

____ ____   3. Be on time for the exam.

____ ____   4. Sit in a quiet spot.

____ ____   5. Read all directions carefully.

____ ____   6. Budget your time.

Getting Ready for Objective Exams

____ ____   1. Memorize as necessary.

____ ____   2. Ask instructor about makeup of test.

____ ____   3. Look at similar tests.

____ ____   4. Review carefully all main points of course.

____ ____   5. Make up practice test items.

Taking Objective Exams

____ ____   1. Answer all easier questions first.

____ ____   2. Do difficult questions in time remaining.

____ ____   3. Answer all questions.

____ ____   4. Ask instructor to explain unclear items.

____ ____   5. For difficult questions, think of the instructor's point of view.

____ ____   6. Mark key words in difficult questions.

____ ____   7. State difficult questions in your own words.

____ ____   8. Use all the time given.

____ ____   9. Use the specific hints given for multiple-choice, true–false, fill-in, and matching questions.

Activity 2

All the questions that follow have been taken from actual college tests. Answer the questions by using the specific hints for answering multiple-choice and true–false questions that follow. Also, in the space provided, give the letter of the hint or hints used to determine the correct answer.

Hints for Test Taking

a The longest multiple-choice answer is often correct.

b The most complete and inclusive multiple-choice answer is often correct.

c A multiple-choice answer in the middle, especially the one with the most words, is often correct.

d If two multiple-choice answers have the opposite meaning, one of them is probably correct.

e Answers with qualifiers, such as *generally*, *usually*, *probably*, *most*, *often*, *some*, *may*, and *sometimes*, are usually correct.

f Answers with absolute words, such as *all*, *always*, *everyone*, *everybody*, *never*, *no one*, *nobody*, *none*, and *only*, are usually incorrect.

Hint _____   1. *True or false?* _____ Denial and intellectualization always reduce anxiety.

Hint _____   2. Newton's third law of motion is

     a. $x = 2y.$

     b. "force equals mass times acceleration."

     c. "for every force there is an opposing force of equal value."

     d. a measure of inertia.

Hint _____   3. With a policy of exclusive market coverage, a manufacturer

     a. expands the availability of a product.

     b. restricts the availability of a product.

     c. seeks multiple retail outlets.

     d. advertises in low-circulation magazines.

Hint _____   4. *True or false?* _____ Too much thyroxin can often result in tenseness and agitation.

Hint _____   5. Charismatic authority is based on

    a.   law.

    b.   established behavior.

    c.   belief in the extraordinary personal qualities of the ruler.

    d.   religious beliefs.

Hint _____   6. Schizophrenics labeled *paranoid*

    a.   always display "waxy flexibility."

    b.   usually fear that they are being persecuted.

    c.   are invariably the children of schizophrenics.

    d.   always display multiple personalities.

Hint _____   7. Prohibition

    a.   was supported mainly by urban dwellers.

    b.   caused a decrease in crime.

    c.   was an unqualified success.

    d.   failed because of widespread violations, an upsurge in crime, and inadequate enforcement.

Hint _____   8. *True or false?* _____ A charged cloud may cause an induced charge in the earth below it.

Hint _____   9. A covalent bond is

    a.   a bond between two atoms made up of a shared pair of electrons.

    b.   impossible in organic compounds.

    c.   an extremely unstable chemical bond.

    d.   the basis of all inorganic compounds.

Hint _____   10. *True or false?* _____ The only factors influencing the decision of the United States to enter World War I were economic ones.

Taking Essay Exams

This chapter will show you

- **Two key steps in preparing for an essay exam**
- **Three key steps in writing an exam essay**

Taking Essay Exams: In Real Life

Read the profile that follows. Then ask yourself these questions:

- When Rod first started college, what did he consistently do that caused him to lose points on tests?

- According to Rod, there is a question that a student should keep in mind throughout a course in order to prepare for essay exams. What is that question?

Student Profile: Rod Sutton

By the time he was permanently expelled from his junior high school in Newark, New Jersey, Rod Sutton had been suspended fifty-two times. His troubled public-school career ended when the 190-pound youngster got into a shoving match with a teacher who was encouraging him to move along to class.

Amazingly, Rod is now a committed seventh-grade teacher at an inner-city school in Philadelphia. In his previous position as an elementary teacher in Camden, New Jersey, he designed an exciting program which provided positive direction to at-risk boys. He is married, a graduate student, a homeowner, and the father of two treasured children.

The road that led Rod from expulsion to a career as a respected educator took him to St. Benedict's School, a Catholic boys' school in Newark, and on to Franklin and Marshall College in Lancaster, Pennsylvania. It was not a straight path: Two weeks after enrolling at St. Benedict's, he got into a violent chair-throwing fight with another student

Continued

that shattered windows and, Rod believed, his chances for remaining at the school. But the compassionate response from the headmaster—he handed Rod a broom and dustpan, told him to clean up the mess, and never mentioned the incident again—had a powerful effect on Rod. He determined that he was going to succeed in school.

And succeeded he has. Since then—first as a student, next as a teacher, and now as a mentor to less experienced instructors—Rod has learned more about *how* to learn than most of us will ever know.

Rod talks about taking essay exams with the same passion that he brings to all subjects concerning education. He is eager to share his hard-earned knowledge with those it will benefit. "There are two keys to taking essay exams," he says. "The first sounds obvious, but it trips up many students. I know it tripped me up. That is the need to read the questions *carefully,* to understand *exactly* what is being asked. When I was first in college, I was constantly getting tests back with points off and comments like, 'You answered only part of the question,' or 'Good point, but that's not really what was asked.' I slowly, painfully realized that all my wonderful ideas didn't matter if I didn't answer precisely what had been asked."

Key number two, says Rod, "is to anticipate just what *is* going to be asked so that you can focus your preparation for the exam." If that sounds like mind reading, Rod points out that the task isn't really that mysterious. The way he explains it, it's all a matter of putting yourself in the instructor's shoes. "People don't become teachers just because they want to follow a curriculum," he says. "They become teachers because they want to pass on a particular worldview, a particular way of looking at things. The trick is to identify that worldview. As you take the course, keep asking yourself, 'What are the *major ideas* this instructor wants us to take away from this class?' Chances are those ideas will be the focus of the essay questions."

Continued

For example, Rod describes two European history courses he took in college. "In one, the professor constantly referred to the competition between Spain, England, and France. For every event that occurred, he'd point out how those three countries were struggling for the upper hand. It became obvious that if we took nothing else away from that course, the instructor wanted us to understand the importance of that competition. It would have been amazing if that theme *hadn't* been the focus of the final essay exam—and it was.

"In the other history course, the focus was entirely different. The instructor looked at every event from the point of view of 'What was the effect on the common person?' And *that* was the focus of the final essay test."

Anticipate the probable questions. Read the questions carefully. It's part of the technique that has carried Rod Sutton on his long journey from school failure to outstanding success.

Essay exams are perhaps the most common type of writing you will do in school. They include one or more questions to which you must respond in detail, writing your answers in a clear, well-organized manner. Many students have trouble with essay exams because they do not realize there is a sequence to follow that will help them do well on such tests. Here are five steps you should master if you want to write effective exam essays:

1 Anticipate probable questions.
2 Prepare and memorize an informal outline answer for each question.
3 Look at the exam carefully before you start writing.
4 Prepare a brief, informal outline before answering an essay question.
5 Write a clear, well-organized essay.

Each step will be explained and illustrated on the pages that follow.

Step 1: Anticipate Probable Questions

Because exam time is limited, the instructor can give you only a few questions to answer. He or she will reasonably focus on questions dealing with the most important areas of the subject. You can probably guess most of them.

Go through your class notes with a colored pen and mark those areas where your instructor has spent a good deal of time. The more time spent on any one area, the better the chance you'll get an essay question on it. If the instructor spent a week talking about the importance of the carbon molecule, about the advantages of capitalism, or about key early figures in the development of psychology as a science, you can reasonably expect that you will get a question on the emphasized area.

In both your class notes and your textbooks, pay special attention to definitions and examples and to basic lists of items (enumerations). Enumerations in particular are often the key to essay questions. For instance, if your instructor spoke at length about the causes of the Great Depression, or about the long-range effects of water pollution, or about the advantages of capitalism, you should probably expect a question such as "What were the causes of the Great Depression?" or "What are the wide-range effects of water pollution?" or "What are the advantages of capitalism?"

If your instructor has given you study guides, look for probable essay questions there. (Some instructors choose their essay questions from among those listed in a study guide.) For clues to essay questions, look at any short quizzes that you may have been given. Finally, consider very carefully any review that the instructor provides. Always write down such reviews—your instructor has often made up the test or is making it up at the time of the review and is likely to give you valuable hints about the test. Take advantage of them! Note also that if the instructor does not offer to provide a review, do not hesitate to *ask* for one in a friendly way. Essay questions are likely to come from areas the instructor may mention.

- *Complete the following sentence:* Very often you can predict essay questions,

   for they usually concern the most _____ areas of a subject.

Step 2: Prepare and Memorize an Informal Outline Answer for Each Question

Write out each question you have made up and, under it, list the main points to be discussed. Put important supporting information in parentheses after each main point. You now have an informal outline that you can go on to memorize.

If you have spelling problems, make up a list of words you might have to spell in writing your answers. For example, if you are having a psychology test on the principles of learning, you might want to study such terms as *conditioning*, *reinforcement*, *Pavlov*, *reflex*, *stimulus*, and so on.

An Illustration of Step 2   One class was given a day to prepare for an essay exam on the note-taking hints on pages 45–53. The students were told that the question would be "Describe seven helpful hints for taking classroom notes." One student, Tony, made up this outline answer for the question:

Hints to remember when taking class notes:

1   *Read* text *in advance (understand more, take better notes)*
2   *Signals of importance (defs. + enumerations, emphasis words, repeats, tone of voice, blackboard)*
3   *Write* connections *between ideas (need for full understanding; also, previews + reviews)*
4   *Written* record *of class (80% forgetting in 2 weeks)*
5   *Outline form (main points at margin, skip line)*
6   *Discussion notes (may not cover later main ideas that arise)*
7   *Review soon after class (gaps, organization)*

TSCRODR (Tom Smothers's cat ran outside dressing room)

Activity

Complete this explanation of what Tony did to prepare for the essay question.

First, Tony wrote down the heading and then numbered the seven hints under it. Also, in parentheses beside each point he added _____.

Then he picked out and circled a key _____ in each hint, and

below his outline he wrote down the first _____ of each key word. Tony then used the first letter in each key word to make up a catchphrase that

he could easily remember. Finally, he _____ himself over and over until he could recall all seven of the words that the first letters stood for. He also made sure that each word he remembered truly stood for an

_____ in his mind and that he recalled much of the supporting material that went with each idea.

Step 3: Look at the Exam Carefully Before You Start Writing

1   Get an overview of the exam by reading *all* the questions on the test.

2   Note the direction words (*compare*, *illustrate*, *list*, and so on) for each question. Be sure to write the kind of answer that each question requires. For example, if a question says "illustrate," do not "compare." The list on the following page will help clarify the distinctions among various direction words. Notice that, ordinarily, you are not asked for your opinion. Instead, essay questions ask you to give back information you have learned about a given topic.

3   Budget your time. Write in the margin the number of minutes you should spend for each essay. For example, if you have three essays worth an equal number of points and a one-hour time limit, figure twenty minutes for each one. Make sure you are not left with only a couple of minutes to do a major essay.

4   Start with the easiest question. Getting a good answer down on paper will help build up your confidence and momentum. Number your answers plainly so that your instructor will know which question you answered first.

An Illustration of Step 3   When Tony received the exam, he circled the direction word *describe*, which meant that he should explain in detail each of the seven hints. He also jotted a 30 in the margin when the instructor said that students would have a half hour to write the answer.

Activity

Complete the short matching quiz below. It will help you review the meanings of some of the direction words shown in the box on the next page.

1. List _____   a. Tell in detail about something.

2. Contrast _____   b. Give a series of points and number them 1, 2, 3, ...

3. Define _____   c. State briefly the important points.

4. Summarize _____   d. Show differences between two things.

5. Describe _____   e. Give the formal meaning of a term.

Direction Words Used in Essay Questions

Compare	Show similarities between things.
Contrast	Show differences between things.
Criticize	Give the positive and negative points of a subject as well as evidence for these positions.
Define	Give the formal meaning of a term.
Describe	Tell in detail about something.
Diagram	Make a drawing and label it.
Discuss	Give details and, if relevant, the positive and negative points of a subject as well as evidence for these positions.
Enumerate	List points and number them 1, 2, 3, ...
Evaluate	Give the positive and negative points of a subject as well as your judgment about which outweighs the other and why.
Illustrate	Explain by giving examples.
Interpret	Explain the meaning of something.
Justify	Give reasons for something.
List	Give a series of points and number them 1, 2, 3, ...
Outline	Give the main points and important secondary points. Put main points at the margin and indent secondary points under the main points. Relationships may also be described with symbols, as follows:

1. _____

    a. _____

    b. _____

2. _____

Prove	Show to be true by giving facts or reasons.
Relate	Show connections among things.
State	Give the main points.
Summarize	Give a condensed account of the main points.
Trace	Describe the development or history of a subject.

Step 4: Prepare a Brief, Informal Outline before Answering an Essay Question

Use the margin of the examination or a separate piece of scratch paper to jot down quickly, as they occur to you, the main points you want to discuss in each answer. Then decide in what order you want to present these points in your response. Put *1* in front of the first item, *2* beside the second item, and so on. You now have an informal outline to guide you as you answer your essay question.

If there is a question on the exam that is similar to the questions you anticipated and outlined at home, quickly write down the catchphrase that calls back the content of the outline. Below the catchphrase, write the key words represented by each letter in the catchphrase. The key words, in turn, will remind you of the concepts they represent. If you have prepared properly, this step will take only a minute or so, and you will have before you the guide you need to write a focused, supported, organized answer.

An Illustration of Step 4   Tony immediately wrote down his catchphrase, "Tom Smothers's cat ran outside dressing room." He next jotted down the first letters in his catchphrase and then the key words that went with each letter. He then filled in several key details. At that point, he was ready to write his actual essay answer.

Here is what Tony's brief outline looked like:

Tom Smothers's cat ran outside dressing room

T   Text—read in advance
S   Signals (defs. + enumerations, repeats, voice, emphasis words)
C   Connections between ideas
R   Record of the class (80% forgotten in 2 weeks)
O   Outline
D   Discussion notes
R   Review after class

Step 5: Write A Clear, Well-Organized Essay

If you have followed the suggestions to this point, you have done all the preliminary work needed to write an effective essay. Be sure not to wreck your chances of getting a good grade by writing carelessly. Instead, as you prepare your response, keep in mind the principles of good writing: unity, support, organization, and clear, error-free sentences.

First, start your essay with a sentence that clearly states what it will be about. Then make sure that everything in your essay relates to your opening statement.

Second, though you must obviously take time limitations into account, provide as much support as possible for each of your main points.

Third, use transitions to guide your reader through your answer. Words such as *first, next, then, however,* and *finally* make it easy for the reader to follow your train of thought.

Last, leave time to proofread your essay for sentence-skills mistakes you may have made while you concentrated on writing your answer. Look for illegible words; for words omitted, miswritten, or misspelled (if possible, bring a dictionary with you); for awkward phrasings or misplaced punctuation marks; for whatever else may prevent the reader from understanding your thoughts. Cross out any mistakes and make your corrections neatly above the errors. If you want to change or add to some point, insert an asterisk at the appropriate spot, put another asterisk at the bottom of the page, and add the corrected or additional material there.

An Illustration of Step 5   Read through Tony's answer, on the following page, and then do the activity below.

Activity

The following sentences comment on Tony's essay. Fill in the missing word or words in each case.

1. Tony begins with a sentence that clearly signals what his paper _____. Always begin with such a clear signal!

2. Notice the various _____ that Tony made when writing and proofreading his paper. He crossed out awkward phrasings and miswritten words; he used his _____ after he had finished the essay to correct misspelled words; he used insertion signs (^) to add omitted words; and he used an asterisk to add omitted details.

3. The transition words that Tony used to guide his reader, and himself, through the seven points of his answer include

_____   _____   _____

_____   _____   _____

_____   _____

	The seven hints that follow are helpful to remember when
	taking classroom notes. he First, read the textbook in advance.
	This way you understand more of the material given in class.
	Also, you may be able to organize your notes better. A Second, be
	ready for signals of importance. These un include definitions and
	enumerations, emphasis words ("the chief cause . . ."), the teacher's
	tone of voice.* Next, write down the connections between ideas so
	that you will be able to tie together and fully understand your ideas
	later. Write down any previous previews or reviews the teacher
	gives as well. A fourth hint is a written to make you a written
	record of the class. This must done because in only too two weeks
	we forget 80% of what we hear. In added time we about forget just
	about everything. Another hint is to try to outline notes when you
	can. Keep the main points at the margin and indent supporting
	info below information under main points. Also use white space
	to show when the instructor has moved from one topic to another.
	A sixth hint is to keep taking notes during discussion periods.
	Important ideas may come up here that the instructor will not come
	back to later. Finally, review your notes soon after class, when you
	still remember enough to add to the matri material. You can also
	make the organization clearer to yourself, if necessary.
	*and everything the instructor puts on the board.

Practice in Preparing for and Taking Essay Exams

Activity 1

Evaluate your present skills in preparing for and taking essay tests. Put a check mark beside each of the following steps that you already practice. Then put a check mark beside those steps that you plan to practice. Leave a space blank if you do not plan to follow a particular point.

Now Plan
Do   to Do

____ ____   1. List ten or so probable questions.

____ ____   2. Prepare a good outline answer for each question and memorize the outline.

3. Look at the exam carefully and do the following:

____ ____   a. Read *all* the questions.

____ ____   b. Note direction words.

____ ____   c. Start with the easiest question.

____ ____   4. Outline an answer before writing it.

5. Write a well-organized answer by doing the following:

____ ____   a. Have a main-idea sentence.

____ ____   b. Use transitions throughout the answer.

____ ____   c. Write complete sentences.

____ ____   d. Proofread the paper for omitted words, miswritten words, unclear phrasing, punctuation problems, and misspellings.

Activity 2

The student paragraph that follows was written in response to the essay question "Describe seven helpful hints to remember when taking classroom notes." On separate paper, rewrite the paragraph, expanding and correcting it. Begin with a clear opening statement, use transitions throughout your answer, and make sure that each point and the supporting details for that point are clearly presented.

	One of the first things is to be in class. Attending class is often the chief to
	doing well in a course. Read your text book to help notetaking. Always write
	down examples they are good for you and can help you very much. Remember
	that forgetting sets it almost immediate. In two week we forget 80% of what
	we hear. Always try to review your notes after class still fresh in your mind.
	Next, the connections between ideas—label PREVIEW or REVIEW. Last,
	notes at the end of a class are important.

Activity 3

Spend a half hour getting ready to write a one-paragraph essay on the question "Describe seven steps you can take to improve your memory." (Refer to pages 203–212.) Prepare for the test by following the advice given in step 2 on page 240.

Activity 4

Prepare five questions you might be expected to answer on an essay exam in one of your courses. Make up an outline answer for each of the five questions. Memorize one of the outlines, using the technique of repeated self-testing (see page 206). Finally, write a full essay answer, in complete sentences, to one of the questions. Your instructor may ask you to hand in your five outlines and the essay.

Using Research Skills

This chapter will show you how to

- **Use the Internet and the search engine Google**
- **Find books in your library**
- **Proceed in writing a research paper**

Using Research Skills: In Real Life

Read the profile that follows. Then ask yourself these questions:

- What lesson did Matthew learn when he typed the search words "drug use" in the Google search engine?
- For what purposes do you plan to use your school library?

Student Profile: Matthew Sullivan

In grade school in New Jersey, Matthew Sullivan was introduced to the computer, which he at first used just for typing purposes. By the time he was in high school, he had built his own at-home computer, and he was soon going on the Internet. After trying a variety of search engines, he eventually discovered that Google did an especially good job of searching for information on a given topic. "It was the best one to use," he says. "I could rely on it to give me exactly what I wanted most of the time. I just needed to enter in the right keywords."

When Matthew enrolled at Camden County College, where he is now just one course short of graduating with his A.A. degree, he soon found that he was able to use his home computer and the search engine Google for almost all of the research needs of his courses. "I mostly used the college library just as a place to read or study between classes," he said. "Once I checked the library's catalog to see if a certain book

Continued

was available. And once I had to look up a specific journal for one of my science classes. Otherwise, it was just so easy for me to just go home and do all my research there."

Recently he sat down to see how Google would help him do a paper on drug use. When he typed in the words "drug use," he got more than 75 million *hits*, or individual results. He narrowed his topic to "drug use among students" and got 14 million hits. When he further narrowed his topic to "drug use among middle school students," he received more than 4 million hits. He then narrowed down his potential topic even more to "Sudafed drug use among middle school students" and got 192,000 hits. He understood clearly that with so much information available, the challenge is to narrow down one's search to a manageable size. Then it's possible to come up with a research topic that is limited enough to be covered in a ten- or twelve-page paper.

Research on almost any subject can often be done in two simple steps:

1   Use a computer with Internet access.
2   Take advantage of search engines such as Google.

Before explaining the wonders of Google, let's review briefly how the Internet works. The Internet is a giant network that connects computers to educational, scientific, government, and commercial organizations around the world. A large part of this global information system consists of individual sites that are linked together, forming a kind of web. This part of the Internet is called the World Wide Web.

To use the World Wide Web, you need a computer with a connection to it, either a *modem*—a device that sends or receives electronic data over a telephone or cable line—or a high-speed or wireless connection. You also need software (such as Safari, Firefox, or Internet Explorer) that will enable your computer to visit Web sites. And if you have a printer for your computer, you can do a good deal of your research at home, for you can simply print out information that you find. Alternatively, you can use a computer and printer available at your school library.

Once you are online, open up a search engine such as Google or you might also try such popular search engines as Yahoo and Bing. A search engine, as its name suggests, and as the cartoon here humorously implies, is a powerful search tool. In a matter of seconds, it will help you go through a vast amount of information on the Web to find articles about almost any topic.

"Go ask your search engine."

Using Google

Open up Google by typing its Internet address (URL) into the address line of the software that connects you to the Web:

www.google.com

You'll then get a screen similar to the following:

As you can see, a box appears in which you can type one or more keywords—words related to your topic—after which you then click "Google Search."

Examples of Google Searches

Here are ten examples of Google searches. As you read them, you should get a good sense of just how Google may be helpful in your research and schoolwork.

Example 1
Your sociology professor asks you to prepare a paper on hate crimes.

After typing in "hate crimes" and clicking "Google Search," Rachel got a list of 7.5 million hits in less than one second—with each item a link to individual articles, reports, stories, opinion papers, research studies, or even entire Web sites about hate crimes. Of course, all those items cannot be shown on one screen; Rachel would have to keep scrolling for many days to look at each item—let alone clicking, opening up, and reading each one! Fortunately, she didn't have to do this, for Google does a good job of listing first what other people have found to be the most helpful items on a topic.

Rachel then decided to have Google help narrow her search. She typed in "hate crimes against gays." The result was about 1 million items providing information about such hate crimes. Rachel then typed in "how churches can help prevent hate crimes against gays" and got more than 350,000 hits. Several of the first items listed gave her an abundance of information for her paper.

Example 2
Your communications professor asks you to prepare a report on media tycoon Oprah Winfrey.

After typing in "Oprah Winfrey" and clicking "Google Search," Rhonda got a list of more than 89 million items in less than one second. She then decided to have Google narrow her search. Rhonda admired the work Winfrey has done to help others, so she next typed in "Oprah Winfrey as humanitarian" and got 15 million hits. After reading through a few of the items listed, Rhonda decided to focus her report on Winfrey's humanitarian work in South Africa.

Rhonda also wanted to include photographs of Winfrey standing next to the school for disadvantaged girls that she sponsored in South Afirca. To do so, she went to Google again and clicked "Images" (which, as you can see in the illustration on the previous page, appears to the right of the word "Web"). A search box appeared, and she typed in "Oprah Winfrey School in South Africa," and immediately got to choose from more than 53,400 photographs and illustrations of Oprah Winfrey and the school.

Example 3
Your history professor asks you to prepare a paper on World War II. Your professor says that it is up to you to decide which aspect of the war to highlight.

Diego typed in "World War II," which yielded more than 125 million hits, making it difficult for him to decide which part of the war to write about. He then remembered stories his grandfather told him about World War II and typed in "Hispanics in World War II," which produced 17 million links. After reading through a few of the links, he saw the name "Agustin Ramos Calero" come up several times and typed that name into the Google search area, which yielded 539,000 links. Diego decided to write about Calero's involvement in the war and the 22 decorations and honors he received for his actions.

Example 4

Your English professor wants you to prepare a paper on J. D. Salinger's famous novel *The Catcher in the Rye.*

Luisa typed in "The Catcher in the Rye" and got more than 6.4 million hits. She then narrowed her search by typing "interpretations of The Catcher in the Rye" and got 301,000 responses. She had no problem, then, getting a variety of points of view that helped her arrive at her own informed opinion about the book.

Example 5

You want to get current news.

Go to Google and click "News" (which, as you can see in the illustration on page 251, is one of the categories listed on the toolbar at the top of the Google page). When the news of the day comes up, you can type in the search box any current topic you want to investigate. For example, typing in "stem cell research" brought up nearly 2,300 items.

Example 6

You want to find out what books are available online.

Go to Google and type "books online." You'll find enough books online, including many classics that are now out of copyright, for a lifetime of reading. If you are researching a particular topic, such as animal rights, type in "books online about animal rights" to find any books available online on your topic.

Example 7

You want to find other search engines.

Go to Google and type "other search engines." You'll find the names of plenty of other engines you could use to search the Web. As of this writing, however, Google is regarded as one of the best.

Example 8
You want to check the spelling of "jeopardy."

Go to Google and type "spelling of jepordy." Google will respond "Did you mean: spelling of *jeopardy*?" It will do the same for many words you are unsure of how to spell.

Example 9
You want to review sentence fragments, which your English teacher has flagged in your writing.

Go to Google and type "sentence fragments." You'll find explanations and examples.

Example 10
You want to look up the meaning of a word.

Go to Google and type "meaning of stupor" or "meaning of incessant" or whatever word you need defined. You'll get an instant response.

I could go on and on with more examples, but you get the point: Use a first-rate Internet search engine such as Google to help you find information fast. Very often, your challenge will be sorting through too much information rather than finding too little. Always be prepared, then, to experiment with keywords to narrow your topic.

Here are five topics followed by narrowed versions of those topics. A rounded-off number of hits for each keyword is shown at the right. Note that very often when you type in a general topic like "organ donation," the items that come up will give you ideas about how to narrow and focus your topic.

Organ donation	4.3 million
False ideas about organ donation	1.4 million
Organ donation worldwide	618,000
Prison reform in the world	20 million
Drawbacks to prison reform	5.7 million
Prison reform in the U.S.	3.8 million
Best job prospects	14.8 million
Job prospects in health care	3.6 million
Job prospects 2012–2015	26,900

Cremation	31.8 million
Increase in cremation	2 million
Drawbacks of cremation	677,000
Heroes	371 million
Celebrity heroes	48.9 million
Absence of everyday heroes today	6.5 million

Activity

Do a search for the three items below. Suggest two ways of narrowing each search, as in the examples above.

1. Internet dating

   _____

   _____

2. junk foods

   _____

   _____

3. school uniforms

   _____

   _____

Finding Books

To find books on a topic you are researching, you can do two things:

1   Visit booksellers online.
2   Visit your library.

Books Online

To find books on your topic, go online and type in the Web address of one of the large commercial online booksellers:

Amazon at www.amazon.com

Barnes and Noble at www.bn.com

The easy-to-use search functions of both Amazon and Barnes and Noble are free, and you are under no obligation to buy books from them.

After you arrive at a bookstore Web site, go to the search box and type in keywords for the topic you would like to research. For example, I typed "drug abuse among teenagers" in the Amazon search box and got 96 book titles as a result. I then had the option of having the books shown in a list with the bestselling ones first. I clicked one of these books—*Drugs, Lies, & Teenagers*—and was able to browse the table of contents and an excerpt from the book.

Here's the point: Use an online bookstore site to get information quickly about books that might be of value in your research. Just the titles of books can help you decide on ways to narrow the focus of your research project. You can then go to your library to get a copy of books you want. Alternatively, you may be able to order inexpensive used copies of books online.

Books in Your Library

To get a book in your library, you need to know how to use your library. If you don't, and time is short, you can say to someone at the library front desk, "I need such-and-such a book. Can you help me see if the library has it? If so, can you find it for me so I can check it out? I would really appreciate your help." In many cases, a library staff person will be able to help you.

Of course, in the long run you should know how to use your library. Following are guidelines that will help.

Main Desk

The main desk is usually located in a central spot. Find it and ask for a handout or map that describes the layout and services of the library. Or ask if someone can give you a tour.

Activity 1

Make up a floor plan of your college library. Label the main desk, card file or computer terminals that offer access to the online catalog, book stacks, magazine file, and magazine storage area.

Catalog

The *catalog* is a list of all the books in the library and will be your starting point for almost any research project. It may be an actual card catalog: a file of cards alphabetically arranged in drawers. More likely, the catalog is computerized and can be accessed on computer terminals located at different spots in the library. And increasingly, local and college libraries can be accessed online, so you may be able to check their book holdings on your home computer.

Finding a Book—Author, Title, and Subject

There are three ways to look up a book: according to *author*, *title*, or *subject*. For example, suppose you wanted to see if the library has the book *Amazing Grace* by Jonathan Kozol. You could check for the book in any of the following ways:

1   You could go to the *author* section of the book file and look it up there under *K*, or type the author's name into the online catalog's search screen. An author is always listed under his or her last name.

2   You could go to the *title* section of the book file and look it up there under "Amazing," or type *Amazing Grace* into the online catalog's search screen. Note that you always look up a book under the first word in the title, excluding the words *A, An,* or *The*.

3   If you know the subject that the book deals with—in this case, "poor children"—you could go to the *subject* section of the book file and look it up under "Poor." Or you could search the library's online catalog using the keyword "poor children."

Here is the author entry in a computerized card catalog for Kozol's book *Amazing Grace:*

AUTHOR:	Kozol, Jonathan
TITLE:	Amazing Grace
PUBLISHER:	Crown, 1995
SUBJECTS:	1. Poor children—New York (N.Y.) 2. Racism and racial segregation—New York (N.Y.) 3. Children of minorities—New York (N.Y.) 4. AIDS, asthma, illnesses of children.

Call Number	Material	Location	Status
362.709 Koz	Book	Cherry Hill	Available

Note that in addition to giving you the publisher (Crown) and year of publication (1995) the entry also tells you the *call number*—where to find the book in the library. If the computerized card catalog is part of a network of libraries, you may also learn at what branch or location the book is available. If the book is not at your library, you can probably arrange for an interlibrary loan.

Using Subject Headings to Research a Topic

Generally, if you are looking for a particular book, it is easier to use the *author* or *title* section of the card catalog, or to search for the author or title in the online catalog. On the other hand, if you are researching a topic, then the *subject* section or screen is where you should start.

Searching by subject gives you three valuable advantages:

- It will give you a list of books on a given topic.
- It will often provide related topics that might have information on your subject.
- It will suggest to you more limited topics, helping you narrow your general topic.

Chances are you will be asked to do a research paper of about five to fifteen pages. You do not want to choose a topic so broad that it could be covered only by an entire book or more. Instead, you want to come up with a limited topic that can be adequately supported in a relatively short paper. As you search the subject section or search the online catalog, take advantage of ideas you may discover that will help you narrow your topic.

Activity 2

Answer the following questions about the card catalog.

1. Is your library's catalog an actual file of cards in drawers, or is it computerized?

   _____

2. Which section of the catalog will help you research and limit a topic?

   _____

Book Stacks

The *book stacks* are the library shelves where books are arranged according to their call numbers. The *call number,* as distinctive as a Social Security number, always appears on a call file for any book. It is also printed on the spine of every book in the library.

If your library has open stacks (ones that you are permitted to enter), here is how to find a book. Suppose you are looking for *Amazing Grace*, which has the call number HV875 / N48 / K69 in the Library of Congress system. (Libraries using the Dewey Decimal system have call letters made up entirely of numbers rather than letters and numbers. However, you use the same basic method to locate a book.) First, you go to the section of the stacks that holds the H's. After you locate the H's, you look for the HV's. After that, you look for the HV875. Finally, you look for HV875 / N48 / K69, and you have the book.

If your library has closed stacks (ones you are not permitted to enter), you will have to write down the title, author, and call number on a slip of paper. (Such slips of paper will be available near the card catalog or computer terminals.) You'll then give the slip to a library staff person, who will locate the book and bring it to you.

Activity 3

Which system of classifying books is used by your library: the Library of Congress system *or* the Dewey Decimal system?

Notes on Writing a Research-Based Paper

1   **Develop a *limited* topic.**   The paper should be narrow and deep rather than broad and shallow. Therefore, as you search on the Internet, look for ways to limit a general topic.

Do not expect to limit your topic and make your purpose clear all at once. Gradually, through trial and error, you can work out a limited focus for your paper. Note that many research-based papers have one of two purposes:

a. Your purpose might be to make and defend a point of some kind. For example, your purpose might be to provide evidence that gambling should be legalized in your state.

b. Depending on the course and the instructor, your purpose might be to simply present information about a particular subject. For instance, you might be asked to do a paper that describes the most recent scientific finds about what happens when we dream.

2   **Prepare a scratch outline.**   As you read through material you are gathering, think constantly about the content and organization of your paper. Begin making decisions about exactly what information you will present and how you will arrange it. Prepare a scratch outline for your paper that shows both its thesis and the areas of support for the thesis. Try to plan at least three areas of support.

Thesis:

Support: (1)
        (2)
        (3)

Here, for example, is the brief outline that one student prepared for a paper on divorce mediation.

Thesis: Divorce mediation is an alternative to the painful, expensive process of a traditional divorce.

Support: 1. Saves time and money.
        2. Produces less hostility.
        3. Produces more acceptable agreement between ex-spouses.

3   **Take care not to plagiarize.** If you fail to document information that is not your own, you will be stealing. The formal term is *plagiarizing*—using someone else's work as your own, whether you borrow a single idea, a sentence, or an entire essay.

One example of plagiarism is turning in a friend's paper as if it is one's own. Another example is copying an article found in a source on the Internet and turning it in as one's own. By copying someone else's work, you may risk being failed or even expelled. Equally, plagiarism deprives you of what can be a very helpful learning and organizational experience—researching and writing about a selected topic in detail.

Keep in mind, too, that while the Internet has made it easier for students to plagiarize, it has also made it riskier. Teachers can discover that a student has taken material from an Internet source by typing a sentence or two from the student's paper into a powerful search engine like Google; that source is then often quickly identified.

4   **Be careful about your Internet sources.**   Keep in mind that the quality and reliability of information you find on the Internet may vary widely. Anyone with a bit of computer know-how can create a Web site and post information there. That person may be a Nobel Prize winner, a leading authority in a specialized field, a high school student, or a crackpot. Be careful, then, to look closely at your electronic source in the following ways:

   a. *Internet address.* Who is sponsoring the Web site? Look first at the address's extension—the part that follows the "dot." If the extension is *edu* (which indicates an educational institution), *gov* (which indicates a government institution), or *org* (which indicates a nonprofit organization), it is probably a reliable source. If the extension is *com* or *net* (which indicate a commercial or business or private-individual source), reliability may vary.

b. *Author.* What credentials does the author have (if any)? Has the author published other material on the topic?

c. *Internal evidence.* Does the author produce solid, adequate support for his or her views?

d. *Date.* Is the information up-to-date? Check at the top or bottom of the document for copyright, publication, or revision dates. Knowing such dates will help you decide whether the material is current enough for your purposes.

5   Document your sources.   When you take material from a source and use it in your paper, document that source. Here is an example from a paper on divorce mediation:

> Divorce is never easy. Even if two people both want to break up, ending a marriage is a painful experience. In order to become divorced, most people go through a process that increases this pain. Starting with the lawsuit that one partner files against the other, the two take on the roles of enemies. As one author describes it, "You will each hire lawyers who will fight on your behalf like ancient knights, charging each other with lances. But the wounds inflicted don't appear on the other warrior: they appear on you, your spouse, and your children" (James 3).

Within your paper, use only brief citations such as "James 3" above, in which "James" is the author's last name and "3" is the page number where the information was found. Then, at the end of your paper, include a page with the heading "Works Cited." On this page, list each source you drew upon in full. Here is the full source for the James quotation:

James, Paula. <u>The Divorce Mediation Handbook</u>. San Francisco: Jossey-Bass, 1997.

For further information about using research skills to write a paper, visit http://www.mhhe.com/socscience/english/langan/langan and go to the book "Reading and Study Skills, Ninth Edition." Then select "student edition" in the Online Learning Center and choose Part 2, Skill 9, "Using Research Skills."

Final Activity

1. Using Google and Amazon.com, find the titles of three books and three Internet articles about teenage mothers *or* about adoption.

   Three books:

   _____

   _____

   _____

   Three Internet articles:

   _____

   _____

   _____

2. Using Google and Amazon.com, find the titles of three books and three Internet articles about date rape *or* about gambling and youth.

   Three books:

   _____

   _____

   _____

   Three Internet articles:

   _____

   _____

   _____

Part Three

A Brief Guide to Important Word Skills

Preview

In Part Three, the explanations and activities in "Using the Dictionary" will explain the most important kinds of information about words that a good dictionary provides. The chapter "Understanding Word Parts" will help you review sixty of the most common word parts used in forming English words. And "Vocabulary Development" explains three approaches that can increase your word power.

An Important Note

Part Three provides a concise review of important word skills, some of which you may remember from earlier school years. These and other skills, such as word pronunciation and spelling, can be supplemented by the extensive materials usually available in college learning centers.

Using the Dictionary

This chapter will help you use the dictionary to

- **Look up the spelling of words**
- **Find the syllable divisions in a word**
- **Pronounce an unfamiliar word**
- **Obtain other information about words**

The dictionary is a valuable tool. To help you use it, this chapter explains essential information about dictionaries and the information they provide.

Owning Your Own Dictionaries

You can benefit greatly by owning two dictionaries. The first dictionary you should own is a paperback one you can carry with you. Any of the following would be an excellent choice:

The American Heritage Dictionary, Paperback Edition

Random House Webster's Dictionary, Paperback Edition

The Merriam-Webster Dictionary, Paperback Edition

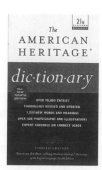 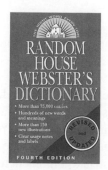 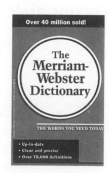

The second dictionary you should own is a desk-size, hardcover edition, which should be kept in the room where you study. All the dictionaries below come in hardbound versions:

 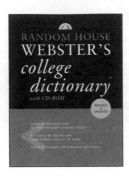 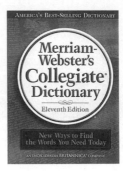

Hardbound dictionaries contain a good deal more information than paperback editions. For instance, a desk-size dictionary defines far more words than a paperback dictionary. And there are more definitions per word, as well. While they cost more, these larger dictionaries are worth the investment, as they are valuable study aids.

Dictionaries are often updated to reflect changes that occur in the language. New words come into use, and old words take on new meanings. So you should not use a dictionary that has been lying around the house for a number of years. Instead, invest in a new dictionary. It is easily among the best investments you will ever make.

Dictionaries on Your Computer

If you use a computer, you have two additional ways to look up a word: online dictionaries and a dictionary that may come with computer software.

Online Dictionaries

If your computer is connected to the Internet, you may find it easy to check words online. Here are three sites with online dictionaries:

www.merriam-webster.com. In addition to an online dictionary, Merriam-Webster online also includes a thesaurus, Spanish/English translations, medical definitions, and an encyclopedia. You can also play word games, learn a new word of the day, and keep up-to-date on new words that may make their way into the dictionary. Also take a moment to click on the "Ask the Editor" section where you will learn history about the English language (among the topics covered).

www.dictionary.com. This online dictionary also offers a thesaurus, English/ Spanish translations, word games, and a translator that translates words from English and dozens of other languages.

www.yourdictionary.com. Also offers a thesaurus and guidance on grammar, language, and much more.

For example, if you go online to www.merriam-webster.com and type in the word *disdain*, this is one of the pages you may see:

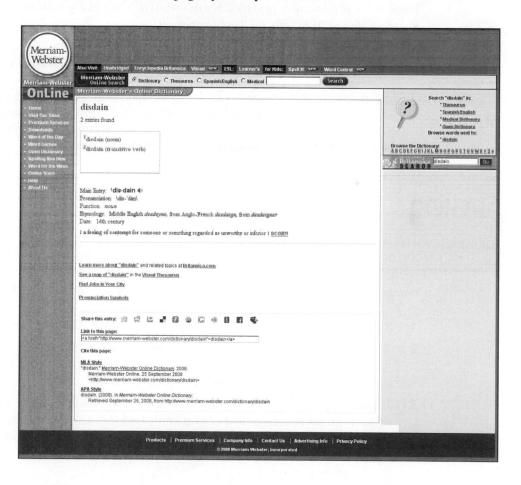

Notice the speaker icon next to the word *disdain*. If you click on this icon, the word will be pronounced for you.

Often, you will also get information on *synonyms* (words with similar meanings to the word you have looked up) and *antonyms* (words with opposite meanings to the word you have looked up).

Software Dictionaries

Some word-processing programs come with a built-in dictionary. For example, if you use Microsoft Word, click on "Tools" and then choose "Dictionary."

Understanding a Dictionary Entry

Look at the information provided for the word *disdain* in the following entry from *Random House Webster's College Dictionary:*

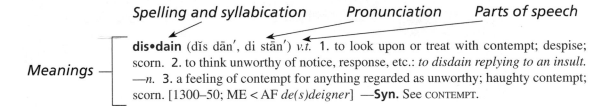

Spelling and syllabication   Pronunciation   Parts of speech

Meanings —

dis•dain (dĭs dān′, di stān′) *v.t.* 1. to look upon or treat with contempt; despise; scorn. 2. to think unworthy of notice, response, etc.: *to disdain replying to an insult.* —*n.* 3. a feeling of contempt for anything regarded as unworthy; haughty contempt; scorn. [1300–50; ME < AF *de(s)deigner*] —**Syn.** See CONTEMPT.

Spelling

The first bit of information, in the **boldface** (heavy-type) entry itself, is the spelling of *disdain*. At times you may have trouble looking up words that you cannot spell. Be sure to pronounce each syllable in the word carefully and write it down the way you think it is spelled. If you still cannot find it, proceed as follows:

1 Try other vowels. For example, if you think the vowel is *e*, try *a*, *o*, *i*, *u*, and *y*.

2 Try doubling consonants. If you think the letter is one *c*, try *cc*; if one *m*, try *mm*; if one *t*, try *tt*; and so on. On the other hand, if you think the word has double letters, try a single letter.

3 If you think a word has the letter or letter combination in the first column of each group that follows but you can't find the word in the dictionary, try looking at the letter or letters in the second column of each group.

c	k, s	g, j	j, g	s	c, z, sh
er, re	re, er	ie, ei	ei, ie	sh, ch	ch, sh
f	v, ph	k	c, ch	shun	tion, sion
		oo	u	y	i, e

Use your dictionary and the preceding hints to correct the spelling of the following words.

guidence	_____	acomplish	_____
writting	_____	acsept	_____
agresive	_____	enviroment	_____
plesent	_____	particuler	_____
akomodate	_____	conscous	_____
progrem	_____	artical	_____
disese	_____	nesessary	_____
begining	_____	chalenge	_____

Syllabication

The second bit of information that the dictionary gives, also in the boldface entry, is the syllabication of *disdain*. Note that a dot separates each syllable (or part) in the word. The syllable divisions help you pronounce a word and also show you where to hyphenate a word as needed when writing a paper.

Use your dictionary to mark the syllable divisions in the following words. Also, indicate how many syllables are in each word.

s p a r k l e	(_____ syllables)
h y p n o t i z e	(_____ syllables)
e x o r c i s m	(_____ syllables)
o p p o r t u n i s t i c	(_____ syllables)

Pronunciation

The third bit of information in the dictionary entry is the pronunciation of *disdain*: (dĭs-dān′). You may already know how to pronounce *disdain*, but if you didn't, the information within the parentheses would serve as your guide. Use your dictionary to complete the following exercises that relate to pronunciation.

Vowel Sounds

You will probably use the pronunciation key in your dictionary mainly as a guide to pronouncing different vowel sounds (vowels are the letters *a*, *e*, *i*, *o*, and *u*). Here is a part of the pronunciation key in the *Random House Webster's College Dictionary:*

| ă bat | ā say | ĕ set | ē bee | ĭ big |

The key tells you, for example, that the sound of the short *a* is like the *a* in *bat*, the sound of the long *a* is like the *a* in *say*, and the sound of the short *e* is like the *e* in *set*.

Now look at the pronunciation key in your dictionary. The key is probably located in the front of the dictionary or at the bottom of every page. What common word in the key tells you how to pronounce each of the following sounds?

ĕ _____   ō _____

ī _____   ŭ _____

ŏ _____   o͞o _____

(Note that the long vowel always has the sound of its own name.)

The Schwa (ə)

The symbol ə looks like an upside-down *e*. It is called a *schwa*, and it stands for the unaccented sound in such words as *ago*, *item*, *edible*, *gallop*, and *circus*. More approximately, it stands for the sound *uh*—like the *uh* speakers may make when they hesitate. Perhaps it would help to remember that *uh*, as well as ə, could often be used to represent the schwa sound.

Here are some of the many words in which the sound appears: *recollect* (rĕk′ə-lĕkt′ *or* rĕk′uh-lĕkt′); *hesitate* (hĕz′ə-tāt *or* hĕz′uh-tāt); *courtesy* (kûr′tə-sē *or* kûr′tuh-sē). Open your dictionary to any page, and you will almost surely be able to find three words that make use of the schwa in the pronunciation that appears in parentheses after the main entry. Write each of the three words and their pronunciations in the following spaces:

1. _____   (_____)

2. _____   (_____)

3. _____   (_____)

Accent Marks

Some words contain both a primary accent, shown by a heavy stroke (′), and a secondary accent, shown by a lighter stroke (′). For example, in the word *discriminate* (dĭs krĭm′ə-nāt′), the stress, or accent, goes chiefly on the second syllable (krĭm′) and to a lesser extent on the last syllable (nāt′).

Use your dictionary to add accent marks to the following words:

connote (kə nōt)

admonish (ăd mŏn ĭsh)

behemoth (bĭ hē məth)

reciprocal (rĭ sĭp rə kəl)

extravaganza (ĕk străv ə găn zə)

polyunsaturated (pŏl ē ŭn săch ə rā tĭd)

Full Pronunciation

Here are ten pronunciations of familiar words. See if you can figure out the correct word in each case. Confirm your answers by checking your dictionary. One is done for you as an example.

kwĭz	_quiz_	kwĕs′chən	_____
tĭk′əl	_____	ĕg′zĭt	_____
wûr′ē	_____	kē′bôrd′	_____
dĭ-zurt′	_____	fĭk-tĭsh′əs	_____
mēt′bôl′	_____	lŭg′zhə-rē	_____

Now use your dictionary to write out the full pronunciation (the information given in parentheses) for each of the following words:

1. cogent _____ə_____　　6. lucrative _____ə_____

2. fiasco _____　　7. nemesis _____ə_____

3. rationale ____ə____　　8. deprecate _____

4. atrophy ____ə____　　9. lethargy _____ə_____

5. trenchant ____ə____　　10. rapacious ___ə___ ___ə___

Now practice *pronouncing* each word. Use the pronunciation key in your dictionary as an aid to sounding out each syllable. Do *not* try to pronounce a word all at once; instead, work on mastering *one syllable at a time.* When you can pronounce each of the syllables in a word successfully, say them in sequence, add the accent, and pronounce the entire word.

Other Information about Words

Parts of Speech

The next bit of information that the dictionary gives about *disdain* is *v.* This label, as the key in the front of your dictionary explains, indicates the *part of speech* and is one of the abbreviations given in the dictionary.

Fill in any meanings that are missing for the following abbreviations:

v. = verb

n. = _____

adj. = adjective

pl. = _____

sing. = _____

Principal Parts of Irregular Verbs

Disdain is a regular verb and forms its principal parts by adding *-ed*, *-ed*, and *-ing* to the stem of the verb. When a verb is irregular, the dictionary lists its principal parts. For example, with *write* the present tense comes first (the entry itself, *write*). Next comes the past tense (*wrote*) and then the past participle (*written*), the form of the verb used with such helping words as *have*, *had*, and *was*. Then comes the present participle (*writing*)—the *-ing* form of the verb.

Look up the parts of the following irregular verbs and write them in the spaces provided. The first one has been done for you.

Present	Past	Past Participle	Present Participle
write	wrote	written	writing
begin	_____	_____	_____

steal   _____   _____   _____

eat   _____   _____   _____

Plural Forms of Irregular Nouns

The dictionary supplies the plural forms of all irregular nouns (regular nouns form the plural by adding -s or -es). Give the plurals of the following nouns. If two forms are shown, write both.

apology   _____

wife   _____

hypothesis   _____

formula   _____

passer-by   _____

Meanings

When a word has more than one meaning, its meanings are numbered in the dictionary, as with *disdain*. In many dictionaries, the most common meanings are presented first. The introductory pages of your dictionary will explain the order in which meanings are presented.

Use the context to try to explain the meaning of the italicized word in each of the following sentences. Write your definition in the space provided. Then look up and record the dictionary meaning of the word. Be sure you pick out the meaning that fits the word as it is used in the sentence.

1. *Effervescent* drinks like soda appeal to children; they enjoy the bubbles that burst below their noses.

   Your definition: _____

   Dictionary definition: _____

2. The actress's *effervescent* personality saved the show from being a disaster.

   Your definition: _____

   Dictionary definition: _____

3. The small border skirmish was merely a *prelude* to the full-scale war that followed.

    Your definition: _____

    Dictionary definition: _____

4. The pianist began the *prelude* in a hesitant manner; then he relaxed and gained confidence.

    Your definition: _____

    Dictionary definition: _____

Etymology

Etymology refers to the history of a word. Many words have origins in foreign languages. For example, you'll notice on page 267 that *disdain* is derived from Middle English and (Anglo-) French words. Information about etymology is more likely to be provided in a hardbound desk dictionary than in a paperback one.

Synonyms

A *synonym* is a word that is close in meaning to another word. Using synonyms helps you avoid unnecessary repetition of the same word in a paper. A paperback dictionary is not likely to give you synonyms for words, but a good desk dictionary or an online dictionary will. You'll notice, for example, that the entry for *disdain* (page 267) ends with a synonym. You might also want to own a *thesaurus*, a book that lists synonyms and *antonyms* (words approximately opposite in meaning to another word). You can also find a thesaurus online—for example, the online entry for *disdain* on page 267 will give you access to a thesaurus. Many word-processing programs have a built-in thesaurus.

Usage Labels

As a general rule, use only standard English words in your writing. If a word is not standard English, your dictionary may give it a usage label such as *informal*, *nonstandard*, or *slang*. Look up the following words and record how your dictionary labels them. Note that a recent hardbound desk dictionary will be the best source of information about usage.

rough (meaning *difficult*)   _____

finagle   _____

hang-up (meaning *inhibition*)   _____

ain't   _____

cool (meaning *composure*)   _____

Practice in Using the Dictionary

Activity 1

Use your dictionary to write the full pronunciation for the following words.

1. encomium _____ ə _____   6. verbatim _____ ə _____

2. caustic _____   7. amorphous ___ ə ___ ə _____

3. conjecture ___ ə ___ ə ___   8. primeval _____ ə _____

4. pernicious ___ ə ___ ə ___   9. machination _____ ə ___

5. Roquefort _____ ə _____   10. disingenuous _____ ə ___

Activity 2

Use your dictionary to answer the questions that follow.

1. How many syllables are in the word *optimist*? _____

2. How many syllables are in the word *rehabilitate?*_____

3. Where is the primary accent in the word *tentative*? _____

4. Where is the secondary accent in the word *discriminate*? _____

5. The first *a* in *blatant* sounds like the *a* in:

   a. *pay*   b. *hat*

6. The *u* in *lucid* sounds like the *oo* in

   a. *cool*   b. *look*

7. Is the word *disrespect* a noun or a verb or both? _____

8. What is the past participle form of the verb *drive*? _____

9. What is the plural form of the noun *enemy*? _____

10. In the sentence "People who rush into marriage often regret their temerity later," what does *temerity* mean? _____

Understanding
Word Parts

This chapter will help you recognize and spell

- **Twenty common prefixes**
- **Twenty common suffixes**
- **Twenty common roots**

One way to improve your pronunciation and spelling of words is to increase your understanding of common word parts. These word parts—also known as *prefixes*, *suffixes*, and *roots*—are building blocks used in forming many English words. The activities in this section will give you practice with sixty of the most common word parts. Working with them will help your spelling, for you will realize how many words are made up of short, often-recurring, easily spelled parts. Increasing your awareness of basic word parts will also help you to pronounce many unfamiliar words and, at times, to unlock their meanings.

Prefixes

A *prefix* is a word part added to the beginning of a word. The prefix changes the meaning of some words to their opposites. For example, when the prefix *in-* is added to *justice*, the result is *injustice*; when the prefix *mis-* is added to *under-standing*, the result is *misunderstanding*. A prefix need not change a word to its opposite, but it will alter the meaning of the word in some way. For instance, when the prefix *re-* (meaning *again*) is added to *view*, the result is *review*, which means *to view again*. When the prefix *mal-* (meaning *bad*) is added to *practice*, the result is *malpractice*, which means *bad* or *improper practice*.

Activity

In the following activities, look carefully at the meanings of the two prefixes presented. Then add the appropriate prefix to the base word (the word in *italics*) in each of the five sentences *a* to *e*. Write your word in the space provided. You will know which prefix to choose in each case if you consider both its meaning and the general meaning of the sentence. Next, you'll see two groups of words separated by a slash line (/). In the spaces provided, write a sentence using one word from the first group and a sentence using one word from the second group.

1 mono   alone, one
2 trans   across, over, beyond

Example   After the full moon rose, Lawrence Talbott was (. . . *formed*) _____*transformed*_____ into the Wolfman.

a.   The interpreter (. . . *lated*) _____ the speech into sign language.

b.   She hates the student in her psychology course who tries to (. . . *polize*) _____ the class discussion time.

c.   As soon as they (. . . *ported*) _____ the stolen cigarettes across the state line, they were guilty of a federal offense.

d.   A (. . . *poly*) _____ occurs when one person or group exerts unfair control over others.

e.   Some people use yoga or other Eastern disciplines to try to (. . . *cend*) _____ everyday cares and difficulties.

Now write a sentence using one of the words before the slash line and a sentence using one of the words that appear after the slash.

monologue monotony mononucleosis / transplant transition transparent

_____

_____

3 **dis** apart, away

4 **pre** before

a. She (. . . *cards*) _____ friends the way some people throw away clothing they no longer want.

b. I would be frightened to go to a fortune-teller if he or she truly had the ability to (. . . *dict*) _____ the future.

c. The speaker was (. . . *composed*) _____ by the conversations that went on during his talk.

d. I sometimes have a tendency to (. . . *judge*) _____ people; only when I meet them do I find out how biased I've been.

e. I worry about germs taking over the house if I don't (. . . *infect*) _____ the bathroom once a week.

disorient dispassionate dissatisfied / presume preliminary prevention

_____

_____

5 **inter** between, among

6 **sub** under, below

a. During the halftime (. . . *val*) _____ at the football game, I ran out to get a pizza.

b. Cold medicines will (. . . *due*) _____ a cold, but they won't cure it.

c. She has the bad habit of (. . . *rupting*) _____ people when they are in the midst of making a point.

d. Seeing whether and how (. . . *heads*) _____ relate to main heads in a text is an important reading skill.

e. My mother would constantly (. . . *fere*) _____ in my relationship with my first girlfriend, who lived next door to us.

interact interject intercom / subdivide subvert submerged

_____

_____

7 ex   out
8 mis   badly, wrong

a. In grade school I shunned the pursuit of grades and majored in (. . . *conduct*) _____.

b. Snakes are often (. . . *represented*) _____ as slimy; in fact, they feel pleasantly dry and cool.

c. If a football player doesn't learn how to (. . . *ecute*) _____, or carry out, a play properly, he will soon lose his job.

d. One day Mel suddenly realized that he had (. . . *treated*) _____ his children in the same way his father had been unfair to him.

e. When Raid wasn't enough, I called in an (. . . *terminator*) _____ to battle the roaches.

exorcist exhaust exclamation / misspelling mismatch misunderstanding

_____

_____

9 con   together, with
10 post after, following, later

a. A (. . . *mortem*) _____ examination was not needed to reveal the obvious cause of death: a wooden stake through the heart.

b. He could hardly walk across the attic floor because of the (. . . *glomeration*) _____ of items piled there.

c. His (. . . *operative*) _____ condition was poor, and so he was put in the intensive care unit.

d. Part of me often wants to (. . . *form*) _____ to the group; the other part of me wants to follow the beat of my own drummer.

e. She feels persecuted and believes that everyone is (. . . *spiring*) _____ against her.

congested   concur   conflict / postnasal   postpone   postscript

_____

_____

11 anti   against

12 pro   before; for (in favor of)

    a.   The (. . . *posal*) _____ to legalize gambling was placed on the state ballot.

    b.   Because I had forgotten to put in (. . . *freeze*) _____, my car's radiator turned into a block of ice one frigid winter morning.

    c.   The main purpose of marriage, according to some religions, is (. . . *creation*) _____—that is, having children.

    d.   Even though the new cold remedy was no more effective than others on the market, millions of dollars were spent to (. . . *mote*) _____ it.

    e.   If an (. . . *dote*) _____ is not given within minutes after the bite of a cobra, death is almost a certainty.

antiseptic antipathy antithesis / proponent promise progress

_____

_____

13 un   not, reverse

14 ad   to, toward

    a.   The (. . . *hesive*) _____ tape stuck to his fingers more than it stuck to the package.

    b.   Because she finds it difficult to tolerate (. . . *certainty*) _____, she quickly closes her mind on many issues.

    c.   (. . . *diction*) _____ to alcohol or other drugs is a major problem in our country.

    d.   The dog continued to run around the neighborhood (. . . *restrained*) _____, and so someone decided to call the police.

    e.   People who feel very depressed are likely to have (. . . *productive*) _____ workdays.

unreasonable unfamiliar uncompromising / address advise advocate

_____

_____

15 in   not, within
16 extra more than

a. The school principal showed (. . . *ordinary*) _____ composure when the first grader threw a rock at him.

b. Students who do well in (. . . *curricular*) _____ activities but earn poor grades are mistaking the sideshow for the main event.

c. Because of (. . . *adequate*) _____ funds, the school athletic program was canceled.

d. The old father in the play was driven mad by the (. . . *gratitude*) _____ of his daughters.

e. The instructor explained that the class would be run in an (. . . *formal*) _____ way, for she wanted students to be relaxed.

incompetent inaudible insatiable / extrasensory extravagance extramarital

_____

_____

17 re   again, back
18 mal   bad

a. In many poor families in Appalachia, you will find children and adults suffering from (. . . *nutrition*) _____.

b. After her (. . . *covery*) _____ from a pulled leg muscle, the tennis pro went on to have a great year.

c. The politician was convicted of (. . . *feasance*) _____ in office and was sentenced to a one-week jail term.

d. Most students agree that they should (. . . *view*) _____ their notes right after class, but few take the time to do so.

e. Psychologists advise parents to give children (. . . *inforcement*) _____—compliments and rewards for doing well.

relapse recount reflect / malpractice malfunction maladjusted

_____

_____

19 com   with, together with
20 de   down, from

a. (. . . *munal*) _____ living is difficult for someone who feels a strong need for privacy.

b. An entire block of houses had been (. . . *molished*) _____ in order to build the shopping center.

c. The man who stopped to help us change our flat tire (. . . *meaned*) _____ himself afterward by asking for $5.

d. If I did not (. . . *ply*) _____ with my parents' household rules, I would be punished.

e. Homes (. . . *preciated*) _____ in value as soon as plans for a nearby airport were publicized.

compatible   combine   companion   /   descend   deplore   detract

_____

_____

Suffixes

A *suffix* is a word part added to the end of a word. While a suffix may affect a word's meaning slightly, it is more likely to affect how the word is used in a sentence. For instance, when the suffix *-ment* is added to the verb *measure*, the result is the noun *measurement*. When the suffix *-less* is added to *measure*, the result is the adjective *measureless*. Very often, one of several suffixes can be added to a single word. Understanding common suffixes is especially helpful when you are learning new words. If you note the suffixes that can be added to a new word, you will learn not just a single word but perhaps three or four other forms of the word as well.

Activity

In the following activities, decide from the context which suffix in each pair should be added to the base word (the word in *italics*) in sentences *a* to *e*. Then write the entire word in the space provided. Alternative forms of some suffixes are shown in parentheses, but you will not have to use alternative forms to complete the spelling of any of the base words. Next, you'll find two groups of words separated by a slash line (/). In the spaces provided, write a sentence using one word from the first group and a sentence using one word from the second group.

1   ion (tion)

2   less

    a.   Heartburn and a knotted feeling in the stomach often develop when people are under a lot of (*tens* . . .) _____.

    b.   The panhandler who everyone thought was (*penni* . . .) _____ turned out to have a $50,000 bank account.

    c.   The dealer I bought the junk car from is a master in the art of (*persuas* . . .) _____.

    d.   One type of (*care* . . .) _____ driver is the person who neglects to signal before making a turn.

    e.   The squirrel sat (*motion* . . .) _____ on the tree trunk, as if made of stone.

Now write a sentence using one of the words before the slash line and a sentence using one of the words that appear after the slash.

    corruption   election   confusion   /   worthless   speechless   restless

_____

_____

3   ant (ent)

4   ness

    a.   Men seem to have more difficulty admitting vulnerability and (*sad* . . .) _____ than women do.

    b.   Popeye was (*reluct* . . .) _____ to swallow the spinach, for he wanted to give his opponent a fighting chance.

    c.   He refuses to use (*deodor* . . .) _____ because he believes that sweating is a natural process.

    d.   The storm broke with such (*sudden* . . .) _____ that the floors were wet before we had time to shut all the windows.

    e.   (*Abund* . . .) _____ practice is the best way of mastering a skill.

    apparent   convenient   dependent   /   togetherness   happiness   loneliness

_____

_____

5 en

6 ize (ise)

a. Some people do not know how to (*memor . . .*) _____ material efficiently.

b. He saw her eyes (*soft . . .*) _____ as she greeted him, and he realized that she loved him.

c. To (*strength . . .*) _____ and tone her muscles, she began doing the Royal Canadian Air Force exercises.

d. The sky began to (*dark . . .*) _____, the wind picked up, and the rain hurtled down.

e. For some people, having children is a way to (*immortal . . .*) _____ themselves.

fasten   weaken   risen   /   theorize   materialize   compromise

_____

_____

7 age

8 ist

a. Approximately one week after their (*marri . . .*) _____, they realized they had made a mistake.

b. At one time in this country, people lost their jobs if they were accused of belonging to the (*Commun . . .*) _____ Party.

c. He was reluctant to go to a medical (*special . . .*) _____, for he was afraid of the expense.

d. Because the bathtub was not caulked, there was water (*leak . . .*) _____ onto the floor below.

e. His favorite things to read in the newspaper are the sports and Abby, the advice (*column . . .*) _____.

overage   breakage   mileage   /   tourist   capitalist   pharmacist

_____

_____

9 ment

10 ful

    a.   Many people are demanding reforms in the tax system of our (*govern . . .*) _____.

    b.   My (*forget . . .*) _____ brother did not leave me the key to the house, and I was locked out.

    c.   She felt both nervousness and (*excite . . .*) _____ when she took her driver's test; her face was flushed and her knees trembled.

    d.   The ten-year-old girl felt (*grate . . .*) _____ to her uncle, who spoke to her as though she were an adult, not a little child.

    e.   As he saw the (*improve . . .*) _____ in his grades, he began to study more; success bred success.

replacement   establishment   movement   /   helpful   useful   hopeful

_____

_____

11 ship

12 able (ible)

    a.   People who are part of an assembly line seldom have pride in their (*work-man . . .*) _____.

    b.   She is not (*comfort . . .*) _____ until she takes off her working shoes and clothes and puts on slippers and a bathrobe.

    c.   Many persons describe their first goal in life as achievement in their work; their second goal is love and (*friend . . .*) _____.

    d.   More and more companies put their products in plastic bottles, even though plastic is not always (*recycl . . .*) _____.

    e.   She never forgot the poverty and (*hard . . .*) _____ her family went through when she was a little girl.

membership   apprenticeship   leadership   /   capable   noticeable   changeable

_____

_____

13 ence (ance)

14 ify (fy)

a. She attempted to achieve (*excell . . .*) _____ in whatever she did.

b. He was cooperative and courteous to his demanding boss because he wanted to use him later as a (*refer . . .*) _____.

c. Many students are afraid to ask questions to (*clar . . .*) _____ an instructor's point.

d. The landlord was not able to (*just . . .*) _____ his neglect of the slum properties that he owned.

e. An animal's (*depend . . .*) _____ on its mother for survival varies from several days to several years.

continuance   acquaintance   assistance   /   verify   notify   rectify

_____

_____

15 ate

16 ly

a. There was not enough good topsoil on their lawn for them to (*cultiv . . .*) _____ a healthy crop of grass.

b. I ate my meal too (*quick . . .*) _____, and my stomach suffered as a consequence.

c. Education is one means of breaking the vicious circle in which slums (*perpetu . . .*) _____ more slums.

d. The restaurant waiter (*final . . .*) _____ served their dinner, but they were so angry about waiting so long that they decided to leave.

e. The television show did not (*gener . . .*) _____ enough interest to keep him awake.

fortunate   populate   aggravate   /   obviously   apparently   carefully

_____

_____

17 ious (ous)

18 or (er)

    a.   They went to a marriage (*counsel . . .*) _____ to try to improve their relationship.

    b.   He had a troubling dream in which he saw a (*myster . . .*)_____ stranger in a dark robe standing by a lake.

    c.   The fact that many students don't follow test directions is an example of how we often overlook the (*obv . . .*) _____.

    d.   Ben Franklin was an (*invent . . .*) _____, a statesman, a philosopher, and a businessman.

    e.   After three years as an unemployed (*act . . .*) _____, I decided on another career.

        dangerous   jealous   glamorous   /   builder   teacher   employer

    _____

    _____

19 ism

20 ery (ary)

    a.   Her (*tomfool . . .*) _____ in grade school classes kept her from getting good marks.

    b.   Some people believe that (*terror . . .*) _____ in the form of kidnapping deserves the death penalty.

    c.   For a long time, (*alcohol . . .*) _____ was regarded as a vice rather than a physical disease.

    d.   It was cold in the (*cemet . . .*) _____, so Dracula decided to move his coffin to a Howard Johnson motel.

    e.   The instructor stopped assigning research projects when she realized that most of her students resorted to (*plagiar . . .*) _____, or stealing, to do their papers.

        realism   socialism   baptism   /   imaginary   dictionary   library

    _____

    _____

Roots

A *root* is a basic word part to which prefixes, suffixes, or both are added. For example, to the root word *port* (meaning *carry*), the prefix *trans-* (meaning *across*) could be added; the resulting word, *transport*, means *to carry across*. Various suffixes could also be added, among them *-ed* (*transported*), *-able* (*transportable*), and *-ation* (*transportation*).

Activity

In the following activities, decide from the context which root in each pair should be added to the word part or parts in italics in sentences *a* to *e*. Then write the entire word in the space provided. Some common roots at times change their spelling slightly, especially in the last one or two letters. Alternative spellings of such roots are shown in parentheses. Note, however, that you will not have to use the alternative spellings to complete any of the following sentences.

Next, you'll find two groups of words separated by a slash line (/). In the spaces provided, write a sentence using one word from the first group and a sentence using one word from the second group.

1   duc (duct)   take, lead
2   mit (miss)   send, let go

  a.   The preface at the beginning of a book often serves as an (*intro . . . tion*) _____, or lead-in, to a subject.

  b.   Copper wire is an excellent (*con . . . tor*) _____ of electricity.

  c.   The collection agency warned me that if I did not (*re . . .*) _____ my payment, I would be harassed day and night.

  d.   News is instantly (*trans . . . ted*) _____ over the Internet.

  e.   The only decision that the (*com . . . tee*) _____ made during the meeting was to call another meeting.

Now write a sentence using one of the words before the slash line and a sentence using one of the words that appear after the slash.

reduce   abduct   conducive   /   submit   missile   commission

_____

_____

3 **port**   carry
4 **voc (vok)**   call

    a. He decided that his (. . . *ation*) _____ in life was to be a plumber, but his guidance counselor wanted him to apply to law school.

    b. She is an (*ad . . . ate*) _____ of the death penalty; her husband is not.

    c. I am going to buy a (. . . *able*) _____ television that I can carry from the living room to the bedroom.

    d. (*Re . . . ers*) _____ channel the news from its source to the general public.

    e. She began reading faster when she learned the difference between main ideas and (*sup . . . ing*) _____ details.

    export   supporter   transport   /   vocal   revoke   avocation

    _____

    _____

5 **tract (trac)**   draw
6 **auto**   self

    a. Simon posted handsome photos of himself, for he wanted to (*at . . .*) _____ more friends on Facebook.

    b. The television, computer, and phone in her room are such strong (*dis . . . ions*) _____ that they pull her away from her studies.

    c. He loves to read (. . . *biographies*) _____, for he is curious about what other people write about themselves.

    d. The Mediterranean design of the wallpaper (*de . . . s*) _____ from the country style in the rest of the room.

    e. Because the thirteen American colonies wanted to form their own (. . . *nomous*) _____ government, they rebelled against British rule.

    attraction   traction   retract   /   automobile   automation   autograph

    _____

    _____

7 path   feeling

8 cept (capt)   take, seize

    a.   The audience felt an embarrassed (*sym . . . y*) _____ for the young comedian who had to continue his performance even though no one was laughing.

    b.   Both political candidates seemed so inferior that many voters were completely (*a . . . etic*) _____ about the election.

    c.   Everyone (*ex . . .*) _____ me seems to have a Twitter account.

    d.   The bad cowboys had a (*re . . . ion*) _____ waiting for the good cowboys—a hail of bullets.

    e.   The parents were gratified that their own children quickly (*ac . . . ed*) _____ the foster child they had decided to adopt.

    pathos   telepathy   pathetic   /   deception   interception   except

_____

_____

9 dict (dic)   say, tell, speak

10 script (scrib)   write

    a.   The article's vivid (*de . . . ion*) _____ of the beauties of Senegal made her want to visit there.

    b.   They bought the magazine because it contained an astrologer's (*pre . . . ions*) _____ for the coming year.

    c.   The (*manu . . .*) _____ was damaged in the mail; fortunately, she had printed out an extra copy.

    d.   One does not (*contra . . .*) _____ him, or he will blow up entirely.

    e.   The (*in . . . ion*) _____ on the tombstone of Henry David Thoreau is simply "Henry."

    diction   indicate   dictator   /   postscript   scripture   subscribe

_____

_____

11 vers (vert)   turn
12 tang (tact)   touch

a.   Children's ideas often get (. . . *led*) _____ together, and they try to say several things at once.

b.   She is a (. . . *atile*) _____ athlete, able to perform in different sports with ease.

c.   The judge dismissed the case for lack of (. . . *ible*) _____ evidence; everything was hearsay.

d.   He had been down on his luck for so long that he felt he deserved a (*re . . . al*) _____ of fortune.

e.   While spending ten hours as a security guard in a lonely warehouse, he does crossword puzzles for (*di . . . ion*) _____.

reversal   subversive   introvert   /   tangent   tactless   tactics

_____

_____

13 cess (ced)   go, move, yield
14 sist   stand

a.   Almost more than any other quality, (*per . . . ence*) _____ is needed for college success.

b.   When the infamous Dr. Frankenstein was killed, his (*as . . . ant*) _____, Igor, got a job as a medical lab technician.

c.   The only part of her grade school days that she enjoyed was (*re . . .*) _____.

d.   With the help of a police escort, the long funeral (*pro . . . ion*) _____ was able to proceed (*suc . . . fully*) _____ through the midday traffic.

e.   An expensive paint is likely to be more weather-(*re . . . ant*) _____ than a cheap paint would be.

precede   intercession   concede   /   consistent   subsistence   insist

_____

_____

15 gress   go
16 pend (pens)   hang, weigh

    a.   To succeed in many businesses, you must be highly (*ag . . . ive*) _____.

    b.   The ruby (*. . . ant*) _____ around her neck was her mother's.

    c.   Our instructor has a tendency to go off on (*di . . . ions*) _____ from his topic that are interesting but not helpful to us.

    d.   Because of the (*im . . . ing*) _____ divorce trial, he was unable to sleep at night.

    e.   He is thirty-two years old but is still entirely (*de . . . ent*) _____ on his mother.

    progress   transgress   regression   /   appendix   suspend   pending

    _____

    _____

17 psych   mind
18 vid (vis)   see

    a.   It was (*e . . . ent*) _____ from the instant replay that the umpire's call had been correct.

    b.   When she began hearing voices inside her head, she realized she was suffering from a severe (*. . . osis*) _____.

    c.   The teenagers in our family spend much of their time watching (*. . . eos*) _____ on YouTube.

    d.   A neighbor of mine who claims to have (*. . . ic*) _____ powers has predicted the end of the world on two occasions.

    e.   Some people try to use pills for body pains that are (*. . . osomatic*) _____ in origin.

    psychology   psychotherapy   psychedelic   /   visual   vision   visibility

    _____

    _____

19 spec (spic)   look
20 graph   write

a.   In (*retro . . . t*) _____, he realized that his decision to go to college right after high school had been a mistake.

b.   She loved her job as a safety (*in . . . tor*) _____ at the bicycle shop.

c.   She believes that (*re . . . t*) _____ is something you buy with money rather than earn with deeds.

d.   Some companies insist on giving regular (*poly . . .*) _____ tests to check on their employees' honesty.

e.   The two essential steps in writing an effective (*para . . .*) _____ are to make a point and to support that point.

perspective spectator respectable / photography biography choreography

_____

_____

Practice in Understanding Word Parts

Activity 1

Draw a single line under the prefix and a double line under the suffix in each of the following words:

transparent	antiseptic	replacement
disorient	preliminary	subdivision
exclamation	malpractice	extrasensory
compatible	confusion	conductive
deceptive	reversal	interpretation

Activity 2

Your instructor will give you a spelling test on all the words used in the prefix activities on pages 278–283. You will be expected to spell the *prefix part of the word* correctly and to do your best with the spelling of the rest of the word. (The word will be marked wrong only if the prefix is spelled incorrectly.) Study carefully, then, the spelling of the twenty prefix parts. You will find that knowing the spelling of a prefix will help you considerably in the spelling of an entire word.

Activity 3

The same instructions apply that were given for Activity 2, except that the test will be on the twenty suffixes on pages 284–288.

Activity 4

The same instructions apply that were given for Activity 2, except that the test will be on the twenty roots on pages 289–294.

Vocabulary Development

This chapter will explain how you can develop your vocabulary by

- **Regular reading**
- **Using context clues**
- **Systematically learning new words**

A good vocabulary is a vital part of effective communication. A command of many words will make you a better writer, speaker, listener, and reader. In contrast, a poor vocabulary can seriously slow your reading speed and limit your comprehension. Studies have shown that students with a strong vocabulary and students who work to improve a limited vocabulary are more successful in school. And one research study found that *a good vocabulary, more than any other factor, was common to people enjoying successful careers.*

The question, then, is not whether vocabulary development is helpful but what the best ways are of going about it. This section describes three related approaches you can take to increase your word power. Remember from the start, however, that none of the approaches will help unless you truly decide in your own mind that vocabulary development is an important goal. Only when you have this attitude can you begin doing the sustained work needed to improve your word power.

- *Complete the following sentence:* Most people who enjoy successful careers have in common a _____.

Regular Reading

The best way to learn words is by experiencing them a number of times in a variety of sentences. Repeated exposure to a word will eventually make it a part of your working language. This method of learning words requires that *you make reading a habit.* You should, first of all, read a daily newspaper. You do not have to read it from first page to last. Instead, you should read the features that interest you. You might, for instance, read the movie and television pages, the sports section, columns on consumer tips, and any news articles or features that catch your eye. Second, you should subscribe to one or more weekly magazines such as *Newsweek*, *Time*, or *People*, as well as monthly magazines suited to your interests. Among monthlies, you might choose from such magazines as *Sports Illustrated*, *Cosmopolitan*, *Science Digest*, *Consumer Reports*, *Ladies' Home Journal*, *Oprah*, *Personal Computing*, *Glamour*, *Redbook*, and many others.

Finally, you should, if possible, try to fit reading for pleasure into your schedule. A number of interesting books are included in the selected list on page 609. You may find such reading especially difficult when you also have textbooks to read. Try, however, to redirect a half hour to an hour of your recreational time to reading books on a regular basis instead of watching television, listening to music, or the like. By doing so, you may eventually reap the rewards of an improved vocabulary *and* discover that reading can be truly enjoyable.

- *Complete the following sentence:* The best way to learn a word is by seeing it in

  several different _____.

- Put a check mark next to each step that you can realistically take to make reading a part of your life.

_____   Begin a subscription to a daily newspaper. What newspaper would be a good choice for you? _____

_____   Begin a subscription to a weekly magazine. What magazine might you want to subscribe to? _____

_____   Go to the library or bookstore and pick out a book you will read for pleasure. (You may want to look at the list of recommended books starting on page 609.) What book might you want to try first?

              _____

_____   Find a time and place that will be suitable for quiet reading. (I, for example, read in bed for a half hour or so before I go to sleep. That's an ideal quiet time for me.) What is one possibility?

              _____

Activity 1

Read through a daily newspaper. Record below the name and date of the paper and the titles and authors (when their names are given) of five different features or articles that you found interesting to read. For this activity you can also look at online newspapers such as *the New York Times*: www.nytimes.com and *the Washington Post*: www.washingtonpost.com.

Name of newspaper: _____ Date: _____
Articles read:

1. _____
2. _____
3. _____
4. _____
5. _____

Bring (or print out) one of the articles to class and give a three-minute talk on it to a small group of other students. Do not read the article to them. Instead, explain what you felt was the main point of the article (the title will often provide a clue). Also, express in your own words some of the details used to support or develop the main point.

Activity 2

Go through a weekly or monthly magazine such as *Time*, *Newsweek*, or *Sports Illustrated*, and read at least five articles that seem interesting to you. Record the following information:

Name of magazine: _____ Date: _____
Articles read (title and author):

1. _____
2. _____
3. _____
4. _____
5. _____

Prepare a three-minute report on one of the articles, to be presented to a small group of students:

- Explain briefly the main point of the article (again, the title often provides a clue to the author's main idea).

- Then present to the group the chief details that are used to support or develop that point.

- As you provide details, quote several sentences (no more than three) from the article.

Activity 3

Obtain one of the books listed on pages 609–614. Fill in the following information about the book:

Title: _____   Author: _____

Place of publication: _____   Publisher: _____   Year: _____

Read a minimum of fifty pages in the book. Prepare a ten-minute oral report on these pages for a small group of your peers. Your purpose in this report is to give them a good sense of the flavor of the book. To do this, you should explain and summarize in your own words how the book begins, who the main characters are, and what specific problems or conflicts are developed. Read at least two passages you like from the book as part of your report. The passages you read should be no more than 20 percent of your entire report.

Alternatively, prepare a written report that you will hand in to your instructor. Follow the same instructions that were given for the oral report. Set off quoted passages longer than three sentences by single-spacing them and by indenting them ten spaces in from the left margin of your paper.

Some Final Thoughts about Regular Reading

Keep in mind that you cannot expect to make an instant habit of reading newspapers, magazines, and books. Also, you should not expect such reading to be an instant source of pleasure. You may have to work at becoming a regular reader, particularly if you have done little reading in the past. You may have to keep reminding yourself of the enormous value that regular reading can have in developing your language, thinking, and communication power. Remember that if you are determined and if you persist, reading can become a rewarding and enjoyable activity.

Using Context Clues

When asked how they should deal with an unknown word they meet in reading, many people answer, "Use the dictionary." But stopping in midsentence to pull out a dictionary and look up a word is seldom a practical—or necessary—solution. You can often determine the meaning of an unknown word by considering the context in which the word appears. The surrounding words and sentences frequently provide clues to the meaning of the word. Notice the italicized word in the following selection:

> A poll showed that the senator's *candor* was appreciated even by the voters who did not agree with him. "I don't go along with some of his views," one voter said. "But it's refreshing to have a politician tell you exactly what he believes."

Even if you do not know the meaning of *candor*, the context helps you realize that it means *openness*, or *honesty*. Much of the time, such context clues in surrounding words or sentences will help you make sense of unknown words in your reading.

If you are a regular reader, you will use context clues on repeated occasions to determine the meaning of a word. Perhaps another time you will read:

> Tony appreciated Lola's *candid* remark that his pants were baggy. And he was pleased with himself for not getting upset when faced with an unflattering truth.

Again, context helps you understand and learn the word. And through repeated use of such context clues to understand an unfamiliar word, you will make that word a natural part of your working vocabulary.

In combination with regular reading, the use of context clues is an excellent way to improve your vocabulary. Unfamiliar words, encountered often enough in context, eventually become part of one's natural working vocabulary. If you develop the habits of reading regularly and using context clues to guess the meanings of unknown words, you will turn many unfamiliar words into familiar ones.

- *Complete the following sentence*: Instead of using a dictionary, you can often

  determine the meaning of an unknown word by looking at _____

  _____.

Activity 1

Read each of the following sentences carefully. Then decide which of the four choices provided comes closest in meaning to the word in *italic* type. Circle the letter of your choice.

1. As a *naive* little boy, I thought elbow grease was something you bought in a store.

   a.   careless

   b.   serious

   c.   unknowing

   d.   easygoing

2. The billionaire J. Paul Getty was so *frugal* that he had a pay telephone for the guests in his home.

   a.   honest

   b.   generous

   c.   sensitive

   d.   thrifty

3. Sue *affected* to like him only until she found a better-looking boyfriend.

   a.   decided

   b.   bothered

   c.   pretended

   d.   agreed

4. My Corvette's *voracious* appetite for gasoline made me decide to trade it in for an economy car, the Chevette.

   a.   huge

   b.   tiny

   c.   finicky

   d.   sensational

5. When I was called on to give an on-the-spot speech in class, I was so surprised that I stood up and recited nothing but *gibberish*.

   a.   stories

   b.   jokes

c. nonsense

d. lies

6. My neighbors are hardly *gregarious*; they keep their blinds drawn and have put a high fence around their property.

a. hostile

b. lonely

c. strange

d. friendly

7. Ted is a *masochist*; he encourages people to criticize and hurt him.

a. one who likes pleasure

b. one who likes pain

c. one who agrees with others

d. one who feels angry

8. School council members often complain about the *apathy* of the student body; they ignore the fact that students have interests other than school government.

a. hostility

b. loneliness

c. discourtesy

d. indifference

9. I felt *vindictive* toward the sales clerk who rudely ignored me, so I decided to complain to the store manager.

a. apologetic

b. jealous

c. sorry

d. inclined to revenge

10. The instructor said my term paper had no *contemporary* references; I should have cited some up-to-date research on my topic.

a. recent

b. scholarly

c. local

d. clear

Activity 2

Use the context to try to explain the italicized word in each of the following sentences. Then check your answers in a dictionary.

1. Sometimes I have *ambivalent* feelings toward my husband; I both love him and hate him.

   Your definition: _____

   Dictionary definition: _____

2. I tried to *emulate* my sister's success in school by studying as hard as she did.

   Your definition: _____

   Dictionary definition: _____

3. The doctor gave a *placebo* to the overworried patient who imagined that she was not taking enough pills for her arthritis.

   Your definition: _____

   Dictionary definition: _____

4. I have never met anyone who has not made *disparaging* comments about certain national politicians.

   Your definition: _____

   Dictionary definition: _____

5. My paper was so *redundant* that my instructor asked me to reduce its number of words by half.

   Your definition: _____

   Dictionary definition: _____

Activity 3

The sentences on the following pages are taken from widely used college textbooks. They should dramatize how context clues are a practical tool for helping you identify the meanings of words you may not know in your college work. Read each sentence carefully. Circle the letter of the choice that comes closest in meaning to the italicized word.

1. The move from stage to stage is not automatic, and Greeley indicates that *regression* to an earlier stage is always a possibility.

   a. progress

   b. advance

   c. expansion

   d. return

2. The *fallacy* of this approach is that it overlooks the extent to which every large organization is a network of small primary groups.

   a. incorrectness

   b. value

   c. cause

   d. result

3. Most of us are *deferential* toward those whose social position we believe to be above ours and look down on those whom we consider socially below us.

   a. open

   b. impolite

   c. bitter

   d. respectful

4. Like reward, punishment serves two major functions in discipline. It *deters* the repetition of socially undesirable acts, and it shows the adolescent what the social group considers wrong.

   a. encourages

   b. discourages

   c. permits

   d. organizes

5. The first stage is denial. The patient refuses to accept the *prognosis*, typically believing that it is a mistake, and consults other doctors or even faith healers.

   a. medical forecast

   b. therapy

   c. medicine

   d. bill

6. America has been called the "*affluent* society" because of its abundance of goods and services.

   a. divided

   b. middle-class

   c. prosperous

   d. anxious

7. For four years, Hitler had concentrated on making northern France the most *impregnable* wall of his fortress.

   a. expensive

   b. unconquerable

   c. inconspicuous

   d. interesting

8. Competition functions as one method of *allocating* scarce rewards. Other methods are possible. We might ration goods on some basis such as need, age, or social status. We might distribute scarce goods by lottery or even divide them equally among all people.

   a. distributing

   b. disputing

   c. collecting

   d. taxing

9. As artificial parts *proliferate*, the need for transplants lessens.

   a. increase

   b. become more expensive

   c. decrease

   d. break down

10. Catholic Democrats who were *adamant* that federal aid should go to parochial schools and Republicans who were *adamant* that aid not go to any school were locked in a stalemate that ended hopes for the passage of any bill.

   a. set in a belief

   b. flexible in a belief

   c. reluctant

   d. agreeable

Systematically Learning New Words

Learning Technical Words

Some of the most important words you must learn and remember are the technical terms used in specific subjects. In a psychology course, for instance, you need to understand such terms as *behaviorism, stimulus, regression, cognition, neurosis, perception,* and so on. With an introductory course in particular, you must spend a good deal of time learning the specialized vocabulary of the subject. Mastering the language of the subject will be, in fact, a major part of mastering the subject.

Textbook authors often define a technical word at the same time they introduce it to you. Here are several examples:

> *Catharsis*, the release of tension and anxieties by acting out the appropriate emotions, has long been recognized as helpful to one's health.
>
> A *capitalist*, then, is an individual who invests money or other assets in a business, hoping to make a profit.
>
> The word *ulcer* is used to designate an open sore in the skin or in the alimentary canal.

If you should come upon a technical word that is not explained, look for its definition in the glossary of words that may appear in the back of the book. Or look for the word in the index that will probably be included in the back of the book. Once introduced and explained, many technical words may then recur frequently in a book. If you do not learn such words when they are first presented, it may be impossible for you to understand later passages where the words are used again. To escape being overwhelmed by a rising flood of unfamiliar terms, you should mark off and master important technical words as soon as they appear.

Your instructor may be your best source of information about important technical terms. He or she will probably introduce a number of these terms to you during class discussions and provide definitions. You should write down each definition and clearly set it off in your notes by underlining the term and perhaps putting *def* beside it in the margin. If you are responsible for textbook material, you should mark off and then write down definitions and other important ideas, as described on page 317. (If an instructor's definition of a term differs in wording from a text definition of the same term, you should study the one that is clearer for you.)

Some students find it helpful not only to set off definitions in their class and text notes but also to keep a list of such definitions at the back of their course notebooks.

What is crucial is that you realize the importance of noting and mastering the definitions of key words in a subject. If you do not do this, you cannot expect to understand fully and master the subject.

The activities on pages 318–323 will give you practice in locating and writing down definitions of technical terms.

- *Complete the following sentences:*

  Courses such as sociology, psychology, and biology have their own specialized

  _____.

  Technical terms are often _____ when they are first introduced; they may also be defined in a _____ or an _____ at the back of a textbook.

  You may find it helpful to keep a list of important definitions at the back of

  _____.

Learning General-Interest Words

General-interest words are not technical terms but words you might come upon in your everyday reading. Perhaps while reading a magazine you encounter the italicized word in the following sentence: "People who vacation in resort towns often have good reason to feel *exploited.*" You may be able to guess the meaning of *exploited* from the context and so feel no need to consider the word any further. However, perhaps it is a word you have seen and been slightly puzzled about before, and a word you think it would be useful for you to master. You should have an organized method of learning words such as *exploited* so that you can not only recognize them but also use them in speaking and writing.

### A Method of Learning New Words	To build your vocabulary, first mark off in your reading words that you want to learn thoroughly. If you are reading a newspaper or magazine, tear out the page on which the word appears and put the page in a file folder. If you are reading a book, jot down the word and the page number on a slip of paper which you have tucked into the book for that purpose. Then, every so often, sit down with a dictionary and look up basic information about each word. Put this information on a vocabulary word sheet like the one that follows.

Vocabulary Word Sheet

1   Word: _____ exploit _____   Pronunciation: _____ (eks ploit´) _____

Meanings: __ v. 1 To take advantage of _____

_____ 2 To make use of selfishly _____

_____

Other forms of the word: _ exploiter   exploitable   exploitative _

Use of the word in context: _ People who vacation in resort towns _

_ often have good reason to feel exploited. _____

Your own sentence using the word: _ I tried to exploit the fact _

_ that my boss was my father-in-law by asking for a raise. ___

2   . . .

Study each word as follows:

- First, make sure you can correctly pronounce the word and its derivations. (Page 270 explains the dictionary pronunciation key that will help you pronounce each word properly.)

- Second, study the main meanings of the word until you can say them without looking at them.

- Finally, spend a moment looking at the example of the word in context.

You should then go on to follow the same process with the second word. Then, after testing yourself on the first and second words, go on to the third word. Continue going back and testing yourself on all the words you have studied after you learn each new word. Such repeated self-testing is the key to effective learning.

An Alternative Method of Accumulating Words
Some people can effectively use three- by five-inch cards, rather than the word sheet shown before, to accumulate words. In this method, you prepare a card for each word, using the following format.

1 *Front of the card*: word; pronunciation; part of speech; forms of the word; example of the word in context.

> exploit   (eks ploit´) v.
>
> exploiter   exploitable   exploitative
>
> People who vacation in resort towns often have good reason to feel exploited.

2 *Back of the card*: different meanings of the word; check (✓) beside the meaning that fits the context in which you found the word; sentence using the word.

> ✓ 1 To take advantage of
>
> 2 To make use of selfishly
>
> I tried to exploit the fact that my boss was my father-in-law by asking for a raise.

An advantage of this method is that the cards can be shuffled and the words can be studied in any order. A drawback of the method is that some people do not find it practical or convenient to keep handy a pack of vocabulary cards. Use whichever method you think will work for you.

Activity

Locate five words in your reading that you would like to master. Enter them on your vocabulary word sheet and fill in all the needed information. Your instructor may then check your word sheet and perhaps give you a quick oral quiz on selected words.

You may receive a standing assignment to add five words a week to a word sheet and to study the words. Note that you can create your own word sheets using loose-leaf paper, or your instructor may give you copies of the word sheet that follows.

1. Word: _____ Pronunciation: _____

   Meanings: _____

   _____

   _____

   Other forms of the word: _____

   Use of the word in context: _____

   _____

2. Word: _____ Pronunciation: _____

   Meanings: _____

   _____

   _____

   Other forms of the word: _____

   Use of the word in context: _____

   _____

3. Word: _____ Pronunciation: _____

   Meanings: _____

   _____

   _____

   Other forms of the word: _____

   Use of the word in context: _____

   _____

4. Word: _____   Pronunciation: _____

    Meanings: _____

    _____

    _____

    Other forms of the word: _____

    Use of the word in context: _____

    _____

5. Word: _____   Pronunciation: _____

    Meanings: _____

    _____

    _____

    Other forms of the word: _____

    Use of the word in context: _____

    _____

Learning through Vocabulary Study Books

A final systematic way of learning new words is to use vocabulary study books. The most helpful of these books present words in more than one sentence context and then provide several reinforcement activities for each word. The more you work with a given word in actual sentence situations, the better your chances of making it part of your permanent word base.

There may also be materials in your college learning center that take a "word in context" approach. The regular use of vocabulary study books and materials, combined with regular reading and with your own ongoing vocabulary word sheets, is a solid way to improve your vocabulary.

Part Four

Reading Comprehension Skills

Preview

Part Four explains and offers practice in ten key reading comprehension skills. All these skills will help you read and take notes on your textbooks and other college materials. The first five skills involve the ability to recognize and use (1) definitions and examples of definitions, (2) enumerations and their headings, (3) the relationship between headings and subheadings, (4) emphasis words and other signal words, and (5) main ideas in paragraphs and short selections. Skills six to eight involve the ability (6) to outline, (7) to summarize, and (8) to understand graphs and tables. And the final two skills, nine and ten, will help increase your ability to make inferences and think critically.

Introduction

One misleading idea that some students have about reading is that comprehension should happen all at once. They believe that a single reading of a textbook selection should result in a satisfactory understanding of that selection. But what such students do not realize is that good comprehension is usually a *process.* Very often, comprehension is achieved gradually, as you move from a general feeling about what something means to a deeper level of understanding.

Ten Key Skills

The purpose of Part Four is to help you learn ten key skills that will increase your understanding of what you read. The skills are as follows:

1 Recognizing definitions and examples
2 Recognizing enumerations and their headings
3 Recognizing headings and subheadings
4 Recognizing emphasis words and other signal words
5 Recognizing main ideas in paragraphs and short selections
6 Knowing how to outline
7 Knowing how to summarize
8 Understanding graphs and tables
9 Making inferences
10 Thinking critically

Your mastery of the ten basic skills will enable you to read and understand the important ideas in articles and textbook chapters.

• *Complete the following statements:*

Good comprehension seldom happens all at once but is usually a

_____.

There are ten skills you can learn to improve your

_____.

Comprehension and Rapid Reading

Another misleading idea that students sometimes have about reading is that an increase in reading *rate*—the purpose of the much-advertised speed-reading courses—means an automatic increase in reading comprehension. Speed-reading courses *may* increase the number of words your eyes take in and "read" per minute. And comprehension may improve because you tend to concentrate more as you read faster. However, with difficult material, understanding is likely to fall as the rate rises. The surest way to achieve reading speed *and* comprehension is to develop reading comprehension skills. Speed will automatically follow as you learn how to identify main ideas and then go quickly over lesser points and supporting details. Speed will also result as you learn how to vary your reading rate according to the nature of the material and your purpose in reading. In summary, by emphasizing comprehension rather than sacrificing it, you will make yourself a more efficient reader and therefore a faster reader.

- What are two misleading ideas that students sometimes have about reading?

  _____

  _____

  _____

- What is the drawback of speed-reading courses?

  _____

  _____

  _____

- What is the surest way to develop reading speed *and* comprehension?

  _____

  _____

  _____

Skill 1: Recognizing Definitions and Examples

 Definitions are often among the most important ideas in a selection. They are particularly significant in introductory courses, where much of your time is spent mastering the specialized vocabulary of the subject. You are, in a sense, learning the "language" of sociology or biology or whatever the subject might be.

Most definitions are abstract, and so they are usually followed by one or more examples that help clarify their meaning. Always select and mark off at least one example that helps make an abstract definition clear for you.

In the following passage from a sociology textbook, underline the definition. Also, locate the two examples and write *ex* in the left-hand margin beside each of them.

Intuition

Galen, a famous Greek physician of the second century, prepared an elaborate chart of the human body showing exactly where it might be pierced without fatal injury. How did he know the vulnerable spots? He just *knew* them. True, he had learned a good deal of human anatomy through his observations and those of his associates, but beyond this, he relied upon his intuition to tell him which zones were fatal. *Intuition* is any flash of insight (true or mistaken) whose source the receiver cannot fully identify or explain. Hitler relied heavily upon his intuition, much to the distress of his generals. His intuition told him that France would not fight for the Rhineland, that England would not fight for Czechoslovakia, that England and France would not fight for Poland, and that England and France would quit when he attacked Russia. He was right on the first two insights and wrong on the last two.

You may have realized that the first lines of the passage are not the definition of intuition but an example. The definition ("Intuition is any flash of insight") is found midway through the paragraph. The examples (of Galen and Hitler) are found at the beginning and end of the paragraph. Underlining the definition and putting *ex* in the margin beside the examples will be helpful later when you are taking study notes on the passage.

- How should you mark off definitions? _____
- Why should you mark off examples? _____
- If a text gives several examples of a definition, which one should you mark off, write down, or both? _____

_____

Activity 1

Read quickly through the following selections, underlining each definition and writing *ex* in the left-hand margin beside an example of the definition. Some definitions will have several examples, but you need mark off only the example that makes the definition clear for you.

Note that textbook authors often call attention to terms they are defining by setting them off in *italic* or **boldface** type.

1.   *Territoriality* refers to persons' assumptions that they have exclusive rights to certain geographic areas, even if these areas are not theirs by legal right. To take a common example: By the end of the first week of class, most students consider a particular seat to be their territory and will show signs of distress or irritation if someone else sits in that seat. What is interesting, even for the simple example we cited, is the subtle ways in which strangers observe certain implicit territorial rights and the emotional mechanisms that regulate this behavior.

Personal space refers not to a geographic area but to the space surrounding our body, a space that moves with us. Persons regard that space as private and try to prevent others from entering it. For example, persons sitting in a public reading room definitely seek to have at least one empty seat between themselves and the next reader. The phenomenon is also evident in less formal settings.

2.   We should not yield to the **allness fallacy**—the attitude that what we know or say about someone or something is all there is to know and say. The more we delve into some subjects, the more we realize there is so much more to learn and to consider. Even authorities on certain subjects humbly admit they don't know all the answers. Though they sometimes disagree among themselves on various topics, they continue to study all available facts. So do conscientious, open-minded business executives, government leaders, educators, students. Unfortunately, it is true of some people that "the less they know, the more sure they are that they know it all." Perhaps you have worked with such persons. A conspicuous example is that of the high school

sophomore chatting casually with a man who (unknown to the student) was a distinguished scientist devoting his lifetime to studying botany. The smug sophomore commented, "Oh, botany? I finished studying all about that stuff last semester." As Bertrand Russell stated, "One's certainty varies inversely with one's knowledge."

3.   Matter can be said to have both potential and kinetic energy. Potential energy is stored-up energy or energy an object possesses due to its relative position. For example, a ball located twenty feet above the ground has more potential energy than another ball located ten feet above the ground and will bounce higher when allowed to fall. Water backed up behind a dam represents potential energy that can be converted into useful work in the form of electrical energy. Gasoline represents a source of stored-up chemical potential energy that can be released during combustion.

Kinetic energy is the energy that matter possesses due to its motion. When the water behind the dam is released and allowed to flow, its potential energy is changed into kinetic energy, which may be used to drive generators and produce electricity. All moving bodies possess kinetic energy. The pressure exerted by a confined gas is due to the kinetic energy of rapidly moving gas particles. We all know the results when two moving vehicles collide—their kinetic energy is expended in the "crash" that occurs.

4.   The fact that you have been going to school for so many years indicates society's faith that you will transfer your training from classroom situations to everyday life situations. There are two fundamentally different types of transfer: positive and negative. Suppose I have learned that in order to keep the attention of my class in introductory psychology, I must tell a joke every ten minutes or so. It seems to be a reasonably successful device, so I try it in my class in personality psychology, and it works there too. This is an example of *positive transfer:* What I have learned to do in one situation applies equally well in another situation. But suppose that I try to carry it one step further and use the technique in a talk that I give at the faculty club. Here I discover that my jokes fall flat and the talk is a failure. This is an example of *negative transfer:* What works in one situation is not applicable to another situation.

Activity 2

Mark off definitions and examples in the following selections. In addition, take brief study notes on each selection on separate paper. Your study notes should consist of the definition or definitions plus one example that makes the definition or definitions clear to you. In each case, try to summarize your example—that is, condense it into the fewest words possible that are still complete and clear. One selection is done for you as an example.

Example

Edwin Sutherland, who popularized the differential association theory discussed earlier, noted that certain crimes are committed by affluent, "respectable" individuals in the course of their daily business activities. Sutherland referred to such offenses as *white-collar crimes.* More recently, the term *white-collar crime* has been widened to include offenses by businesses and corporations as well as by individuals. A wide variety of offenses are included in this classification, such as income tax evasion, stock manipulation, consumer fraud, bribery and extracting "kickbacks," embezzlement, and misrepresentation in advertising.

White-collar crime—offenses by businesses and corporations as well as by "respectable" business individuals
   Ex.—Income tax evasion

1.   The effort to completely exterminate a people by killing all of them is called *annihilation.* It is ironic that the greatest annihilation in recorded history was conducted by a highly civilized Christian state. Between 1933 and 1945, the German Nazis killed about 4.5 million European Jews, marching many of them into gas chambers with a systematic bureaucratic efficiency. Other cataclysms in history may have produced more deaths, but we have no comparable example of such a deliberate, premeditated mass slaughter carried out as a government policy. Several instances of mass slaughter have occurred since then, perhaps the greatest of which accompanied the Hindu-Moslem clashes in India and Pakistan in 1948. Others include the slaughter of the Ibos in northern and western Nigeria in 1966 and of the Communists in Indonesia after their unsuccessful attempt to seize power in 1965.

2.   Often, when faced with a conflict, we engage in the kind of behavior called vacillation—the tendency to be drawn first toward one possible resolution of the conflict, then toward another. Torn between studying and working and going out with friends, we may change our minds several times. At one moment we may lean strongly toward studying, at the next moment toward going out. In an extreme case of vacillation, we may take so long making up our minds that we wind up with very little time left for either of the possibilities.

3.   Behavior therapists have applied their knowledge of operant conditioning to large groups of hospitalized patients. The basic premise in this work is that patients should be treated as normal people capable of learning normal

behavior if they are appropriately rewarded. Normal people are paid money for doing a job. They also receive attention and affection when they interact with other people. If they were not paid, they would not work; if they were ignored, they would not respond socially to others.

In the treatment method known as the *token economy*, hospitalized psychiatric patients receive rewards for performing "normal" behaviors. For example, one patient's job is to work in the hospital laundry each day. He receives fifty "tokens," usually in the form of poker chips, for each day's work. He can then trade in his tokens for his meals, a more comfortable bed than the hospital's standard equipment, weekend passes to leave the hospital, magazines, cigarettes, and so on.

4.   Throw a stone into a lake: water waves move outward from the splash. Clap your hands: sound waves carry the noise all around. Switch on a lamp: light waves illuminate the room. Water waves, sound waves, and light waves are very different from one another in important respects, but all have in common the basic properties of wave motion. A wave is a periodic disturbance—a back-and-forth change of some kind (of water height in the case of water waves, of air pressure in the case of sound waves, of electric and magnetic fields in the case of light waves)—that spreads out from a source and carries energy as it goes. Information, too, can be carried by waves; this is how sights and sounds reach us.

Activity 3

Working with a chapter or chapters in one of your textbooks, find five definitions *and* examples. Choose only definitions for which there are examples. Also, make sure each example is one that helps make a definition clear to you. Use separate paper for this activity. Include the number of the page on which you find each definition and example, in case your instructor wants to refer to the text in reviewing your answers.

Here is a model for Activity 3:

Textbook _Understanding Psychology_____ Author(s): _Feldman_____

Definition: _Personal stressors—major life events that have immediate_

_negative consequences that generally fade with time._____

Example: _Death of a family member_____

Page number: _____

■ **Review Test**

Read these selections, noting definitions and examples of the definitions. In the space provided, write the number of the sentence that contains a definition. Then write the number of the *first* sentence that gives an example of the definition.

1.   ¹Rumors are both a form of collective behavior and an important element in other types of collective behavior. ²A rumor is a difficult-to-verify piece of information that people transmit to one another in relatively rapid fashion. ³Although many rumors are false, some are accurate, or contain a measure of truth (for instance, a local plant will close or a product will be discontinued). ⁴Rumors typically arise in times of tension and sagging economic conditions in which we lack information or distrust official sources of information. ⁵They are a substitute for hard news. ⁶Rumors regarding alleged contamination and conspiracy are quite common. ⁷Unfounded rumors have hurt the sales of some of the nation's largest corporations. ⁸For instance, McDonald's and Wendy's have had to fight rumors that they put earthworms in hamburgers (perhaps suggested by the fact that raw hamburger resembles red worms). ⁹Some people have seen a Communist connection in the bent-elbow, clenched-fist symbol of Arm & Hammer, the baking soda. ¹⁰And Procter & Gamble removed its 135-year-old moon-and-stars trademark from its products when it was unable to dispel the rumor that the symbol is a sign of devil worship.

Definition: _____ Example: _____

2.   ¹You know what happens if you set out a pan of water: In time, the water will "disappear." ²The water did not boil. ³So what did happen? ⁴Remember, particles of matter are always in motion. ⁵Therefore, at the surface of a liquid, some particles will have enough kinetic energy to leave the liquid. ⁶It makes no difference what the temperature is. ⁷The particles that leave the surface are replaced by other particles. ⁸Some of these have enough kinetic energy to leave the surface. ⁹The process continues to go on. ¹⁰Finally, there is no liquid left. ¹¹This change from liquid to vapor (gas) is called *evaporation.*

Definition: _____ Example: _____

3.   ¹Phobias are fears that are out of proportion to the actual danger involved in a situation. ²Some people will not use elevators. ³Yes, the cable could break, the ventilation could fail, you could be stuck in midair awaiting repairs. ⁴But these problems are infrequent, and it would be foolhardy to walk forty flights twice daily to avoid them. ⁵Other people will not receive

injections, even when quite ill. [6]Injections can be painful, but these people would tolerate an even more painful pinch. [7]Phobias can seriously interfere with our lives. [8]People may know that a phobia is irrational yet still experience fear.

Definition: _____ Example: _____

4. [1]Making up excuses or false attributions for potential failures is especially common when we think we might fail at something. [2]For example, a student fails to get enough sleep before an exam, an employee drinks too much at lunch with his boss, an investor says that he never has any luck in the stock market. [3]According to Edward Jones and Steven Berglas, these individuals are making up excuses so that they can blame some external thing if they fail. [4]The student can blame lack of sleep if she does poorly on the exam, the employee can blame drinking too much if he does not get his raise, and the investor can blame a run of bad luck if he loses money on the stock market. [5]Researchers Jones and Berglas call this tendency to make up an excuse for one's potential failure the use of a *self-handicapping strategy*. [6]By attributing to yourself all kinds of handicaps (missing sleep, drinking, bad luck), you can fail without having failure seem to be your own fault.

Definition: _____ Example: _____

Skill 2: Recognizing Enumerations and Their Headings

 Like definitions, enumerations are keys to important ideas. Enumerations are lists of items that may actually be numbered in the text. More often, however, a list of items is signaled by such words as *first of all*, *second*, *moreover*, *next*, *also*, *finally*, and others. Typical phrases that introduce enumerations are "There are three reasons why . . . "; "The two causes of . . . "; "Five characteristics of . . . "; "There are several ways to . . . "; and so on.

In the following selection, number *1*, *2*, and *3* the guidelines for constructive criticism. Note that each of the guidelines will be indicated by a signal word.

> At times people need help so they can perform better. A necessary and yet far too often misused response is constructive criticism. *Constructive criticism* is evaluation of behavior—usually negative—given to help a person identify or correct a fault. Because criticism is such an abused skill, we offer several guidelines that will help you compose criticism that is both constructive and beneficial. First, make sure that the person is interested in hearing the criticism. The safest rule to follow is to withhold any criticism until it is asked for. It will be of no value if a person is not interested in hearing it. Another guideline is make the criticism as specific as possible. The more detailed the criticism, the more effectively the person will be able to deal with the information. Finally, show the person you are criticizing what can be improved. Don't limit your comments to what a person has done wrong. Tell him or her how what was done could have been done better.

You should have put a *1* in front of "make sure that the person is interested in hearing the criticism" (signaled by *First*), a *2* in front of "make the criticism as specific as possible" (signaled by *Another guideline*), and a *3* in front of "show the person you are criticizing what can be improved" (signaled by *Finally*). Develop the habit of looking for and numbering all the enumerations in a chapter.

When you take study notes on enumerations, be sure to include a heading that explains what a list is about. For example, because the following list does not have a descriptive heading, the notes are not as clear:

1. Make sure the person is interested in hearing the criticism.
2. Make the criticism as specific as possible.
3. Show the person you are criticizing what can be improved.

Your notes will be clear and helpful if they include, as the following notes do, a heading describing what the list is about:

Guidelines for Constructive Criticism

1. Make sure the person is interested in hearing the criticism.
2. Make the criticism as specific as possible.
3. Show the person you are criticizing what can be improved.

- Why should you look for and number enumerations? _____

_____

_____

- What do phrases such as *Two effects of*, *Three important results are*, *Five factors to note* tell you? _____

_____

_____

The activities that follow will give you practice in the skill of locating and marking off enumerations.

Activity 1

In the selections that follow, number *1*, *2*, *3*, and so on, the items in each list or enumeration. Remember that words such as *first*, *another*, *also*, and *finally* often signal an enumeration. Also, in the space provided, write a heading that explains what each list is about. Look first at the example and the hints.

Example

Heading: ___Rewards of Schooling_____

In strictly pragmatic terms, schooling yields three rewards, and the amount of each reward increases in proportion to the amount of schooling. First, the individual who is well schooled stands the [1]best chance of getting any job, other things being equal. Thus, the chance of unemployment is reduced. Second, the individual with a good background is the [2]one chosen for advancement and promotion; this enables him or her to earn more over the long run. Third, because of rewards one and two, the educated individual has [3]more personal freedom. Such a person will have more job opportunities from which to choose, is less threatened with unemployment, and can be freer economically because of his or her higher earning power. The decision in favor of further schooling needs to be encouraged if only for the above listed pragmatic reasons.

Hints

a   A selection often contains a phrase that introduces the enumeration. The introductory phrase in the preceding passage is "schooling yields three rewards." Look for such introductory phrases; they will help you write your heading.

b   Every heading that you write should begin with a word that ends in *s*, as in "Rewards of Schooling." As a reminder, the *s* has been added to each of the heading spaces that follow.

1. Heading: _____

An American worker can be said to earn several types of income. Money income is the amount a person receives in actual cash or checks for wages, salaries, rents, interest, and dividends. Real income is what the money income will buy in goods and services; it is purchasing power. If a person's money income rises 5 percent in one year but the cost of purchases increases 8 percent on the average, then real income decreases about 3 percent. Psychic income is an intangible but highly important income factor related to comfortable climate, a satisfying neighborhood, enjoyment of one's job, and so on. Some people prefer to take less real income so that they can live in a part of the country with a fine climate and recreation opportunities—greater psychic income.

2. Heading: _____

Networking is the way people find out about jobs that aren't advertised in the newspaper; it is the way they learn about valuable new developments in their field before the crowd does. There are three main elements in networking. The first is *visibility,* making your presence known. The more people meet you, the more are likely to remember you. The second element is *familiarity,* letting people get to know you. It takes courage to expose your skills, attitudes, and opinions, but people are more likely to deal with you if they have some idea of how to think and react. The third element, *image,* means giving people the impression that you are competent and pleasant to deal with. An optimistic, enthusiastic approach to business—and to life—is magnetic.

3. Heading: _____

Water pollution takes two forms. The first occurs when garbage and chemicals are thrown into the water. These waste materials upset the natural environment and often prove dangerous to the fish and other life in the water. To prevent further deterioration of our waters, business is now treating its wastes before putting them into the water or is looking for other, safer ways to dispose of them.

A second common problem is thermal, or warm-water, pollution. Hydroelectric power plants, in particular, tend to cause this type of pollution. In creating electricity, utilities take water from a nearby lake or river, convert it to steam for turning the plant's turbine engines, change the steam back to water, and then return it to the original lake or river. The problem is that the water is often returned at five to ten degrees above the original temperature. This causes a change in the environment of the lake or river and can be harmful to the aquatic life there.

4. Heading: _____

Three reasons for the existence of stereotypes will be noted. First, they simplify explanations of human behavior. The crudest way to explain a phenomenon is to classify it. Aristotle was asked, for example, "Why do stones fall to Earth?" He answered that stones belong to the class Earth, and objects yearn to return to the class to which they belong. The explanation seems rather foolish in the light of modern physics. However, if you saw someone behaving oddly in a mental hospital, you might inquire of a psychiatrist, "Why does he behave that way?" The psychiatrist might answer, "He is a schizophrenic." You would probably be satisfied. But the answer is no explanation at all. Why is he diagnosed as a schizophrenic? The answer to this question is: Because he acts oddly—in ways characteristic of schizophrenic patients. Explanations by classification all have this quality of circularity. Nonetheless, explanations by classification often put curiosity to rest. Therefore, stereotypes are sometimes comforting pseudo-explanations.

Second, stereotypes often provide a scapegoat for aggression. A scapegoat is a target for abuse. Scapegoats may actually be innocent, but because they can't fight back, they have all sorts of abuse heaped upon them. Minority groups are often unable to fight back, and they serve as an easy target for angry feelings that may have their real roots in other sources. A man who is angry at his boss may pick a fight with his wife; she becomes the scapegoat for his hostile feelings toward his boss. In the same way, it has been argued that the Nazis offered the Jew as a scapegoat to the German people.

Prior to World War II, Germany had numerous economic problems. There was widespread frustration and latent anger. The Jew was blamed for Germany's problems.

Third, stereotypes give members of a dominant group a sense of superiority. The members of the larger group can look at the members of the minority group and say to themselves, "I'm better than they are." These thoughts help individuals compensate for any dominant feelings of inferiority they themselves may possess. To illustrate, poor white Southern sharecroppers, feeling inadequate and incompetent in many ways, can look at black people and feed their egos by thinking, "We're white and they're black."

From the three reasons postulated for the creation of stereotypes, it seems clear that stereotypes exist for very real reasons. They meet human needs for explanation, aggression, and superiority.

Activity 2

In the following selections, number *1, 2, 3,* and so on, the items in each list and underline the words that introduce the list. In addition, take brief study notes on each selection on separate paper. Your notes should consist of a numbered list of items and an accurate heading for that list. Try to summarize the items in each list—that is, condense them to the fewest words possible that are still complete and clear. One selection is done for you as an example.

Example

Studies have indicated <u>a number of values to reading and reciting,</u> as opposed to just reading. For one thing, when you read something with the knowledge that you must soon recite what you have read, you are [1] more likely to be motivated to remember and less likely to become inattentive. Moreover, recitation provides [2] immediate knowledge of results so that you can see how well you are doing and adjust and modify your responses accordingly. Finally, recitation provides [3] active practice in recalling the material you wish ultimately to retain.

Values of Reading and Reciting

1. *More motivation to remember*
2. *Immediate knowledge of results*
3. *Active practice in recalling material*

1.   Private property serves two important functions in capitalism. First, it places in the hands of individuals power over the use of productive resources. Economic activity cannot occur unless someone makes decisions about which goods are to be produced and when and how they are to be produced. The

Model

Textbook: *Alive and Well*   Authors: *A. and H. Eisenburg*

Heading: *Problems of the Elderly*   Pages: *542–544*

    (1) Retirement

    (2) Health

    (3) Finances

■ **Review Test**

Locate and number the enumeration in each selection that follows. Then, in the space provided, summarize the points in each enumeration. Also, write a heading that accurately describes what the enumeration is about.

1.   There are at present three approaches to treating the allergic patient. One approach is to control the environment by removing the offending substances. Such control could be achieved, for example, by keeping the home—especially the bedroom—free of carpeting, upholstery, clutter, and other dust collectors. Another approach to treating the allergic patient is to use drug therapy or chemotherapy. Antihistamine drugs are the most widely used of all allergy drugs. Most effective for nasal allergies, they are often useful in skin and other allergies as well. Corticosteroids, used since 1949 for asthmatic attacks, have many adverse effects and are usually recommended only for life-threatening attacks and for short-term use. Finally, when environmental control and antihistamines fail to bring relief, the physician may consider "desensitizing" the patient. This is accomplished by a series of injections of the allergen in increasing amounts. Unfortunately, even a successful hyposensitization may wear off with time and need to be repeated.

Heading: _____

(1) _____

(2) _____

(3) _____

2.   There are several reasons why children involved in the divorce situation often live disrupted lives. First, they must deal with the trauma of their parents' separation and of one parent's leaving home. "I remember it was near my birthday when I was going to be six that Dad said at lunch he was leaving," one eight-year-old recalled. "I tried to say, 'No, Dad, don't do it,'

but I couldn't get my voice out. I was much too shocked." In addition, the child of divorce now has only one parent to turn to on a day-to-day basis, and that parent—usually the mother—may often be too busy with work, housekeeping, or finding a social life to offer sufficient support and guidance to the child. Children of divorce must also often deal with the continuing conflict between warring parents. This conflict is especially traumatic in cases of child custody battles, in which the parents vie with each other for custody of the child while the child awaits the outcome.

Heading: _____

(1) _____

(2) _____

(3) _____

3.   Human beings are biological organisms. They possess the ability to respond to stimulation, to move, to regulate inputs and outputs of energy, and to reproduce. They proceed physically through the process of development (that is, over time, they move from simple to complex levels of organization). In the *embryonic stage* (the first two months after conception) the organism increases in size from about 0.14 millimeter in diameter to about 1½ inches. Cell layers that become the nervous, circulatory, skeletal, muscular, digestive, and glandular systems are formed and continue to develop. During the *fetal stage* (third month after conception until birth), the organism continues developing in such a manner that it has all the biological equipment necessary to survive at birth. During the *neonatal stage* (roughly the first four weeks after birth), the organism "breaks in" its biological equipment. It begins to breath, to digest, to circulate blood, and so on. By the beginning of *infancy* (about the first two or three years of life), the organism is well designed for sleeping, eating, and eliminating. It is during infancy that the organism truly begins to become human. The process of maturation defines the blank tablet so that experience may imprint a unique identity on it.

Heading: _____

(1) _____

(2) _____

(3) _____

(4) _____

4.   A 2011 study concluded there is a possible link between cell phone use and brain cancer. Even though the results are still not fully conclusive, there are three key preventive measures cell phone users can take to limit their exposure to harmful radio-frequency (RF) waves. First, use a hands-free device such as a corded or cordless earpiece. Earpieces move the antenna away from the user's head, decreasing the amount of RF waves that reach the head. Corded earpieces emit virtually zero RF waves. RF waves from the phone itself, however, can reach parts of the body if close enough, such as in a pocket. Second, choose a phone with a low SAR value (specific absorption rate). Bluetooth® earpieces have an SAR value of around 0.001 watts/kg (less than one thousandth the SAR limit for cell phones as set by the FDA and FCC). Different models of phones can give off different levels of RF waves, so do some research. One way to get information on the SAR level for a specific phone model is to find the FCC identification (ID) number for that model. The FCC ID number is usually somewhere on the phone, sometimes under the battery pack. Once you have the ID number, go to the following Web address: www.fcc.gov/oet/ea/fccid. On this page, you will see instructions for entering the FCC ID number and finding out the SAR value of that phone. The third and most obvious way to limit exposure to RF waves from cell phones is to limit how much you use them. Use your cell phone only for shorter conversations, or use it only when a conventional (land-line) phone is not available. Parents who are concerned about their children's exposure can place limits on how much time they spend on the phone.

Heading: _____

(1) _____

(2) _____

(3) _____

Skill 3: Recognizing Headings and Subheadings

 Headings and subheadings are important visual aids that give you a quick idea of how the information in a chapter is organized. The model below shows a typical use of heads in a selection.

CHAPTER TITLE

The chapter title is set off in the largest print in the chapter. The title represents the shortest possible summary of what the entire chapter is about.

THIS IS A MAIN HEADING

Appearing under the chapter title are a series of main headings. Main heads may be centered or may start at the left margin; they are often set off with capital letters and, sometimes, a different color of ink. They represent a breakdown of the main topics covered in the chapter.

This Is a Subheading

Set off under the main headings are subheadings. They are in smaller type; sometimes they are underlined, italicized, or set in from the left margin. The subheadings represent a breakdown of the different ideas that are explained under the main headings.

Activity

1. Look at the first chapter of this book (pages 11–20).

   How many main heads are there in the chapter? _____

   How many subheads are there? _____

   How do the main heads differ from the subheads? _____

   _____

   _____

   _____

2. Look at the excerpt from a textbook chapter on pages 154–196. The main head is "The Family."

   How many subheads fit under that main head? _____

   One of the subheads is "Marriage and the Family in the United States." How many sub-subheads fit under it? _____

   How do the sub-subheads differ from the subheads? _____

   _____

   _____

   _____

3. Look at a chapter in one of your other textbooks.

   How many main heads are there in the chapter? _____

   How many subheads are there? _____

   How do the subheads differ from the main heads? _____

   _____

   _____

   _____

Using Headings to Locate Important Ideas

There are two methods for using headings to locate key ideas. Each method is explained and illustrated on the following pages.

Method 1: Change Headings into Basic Questions

Change a heading into one or more basic questions. A basic question can be general, starting with the word *What*, *Why*, or *How*. Or it can be specific, starting with the word *When*, *Where*, or *Who*. Use whatever words seem to make sense in terms of the heading and the passage that follows it. Consider, for example, the following textbook selection:

Decline of the Puritan Work Ethic

The Puritan concept of work as necessary for survival and as a duty and virtue in and of itself long dominated our culture. Work, obedience, thrift, and the delay of gratification were valued highly, and people's righteousness was often judged according to how hard they worked and how much they accomplished.

These views have changed, however, at an accelerated pace. Today's workers, particularly young workers, demand much more of themselves and their jobs than simply "filling a slot" and earning a living. The search for a meaningful, fulfilling job has become crucial. Workers increasingly desire to have responsibility and autonomy, to have a voice, and to demand not merely good physical working conditions but also good psychological working conditions. Rigid, authoritarian work structures are increasingly rejected as workers look to their jobs as a significant source of creative self-expression.

• What are two questions that could be made out of the heading "Decline of the Puritan Work Ethic"?

_____

_____

The title could be changed into the two basic questions: "What is the Puritan work ethic?" and "Why has the Puritan work ethic declined?" The answer to the second question especially (the Puritan work ethic has declined because today's workers want meaningful, personally fulfilling jobs) forms the main idea of the passage. This technique of turning headings into basic questions often helps you cut through a mass of words to get to the heart of the matter. Develop the habit of using such questions.

Method 2: See How Subheads Relate to Main Heads

If subheads follow a main head, determine how they are related to the main head. For example, suppose you noted the following main head and subheads spaced out over three pages of a business text:

ADVANTAGES OF THE PRIVATE ENTERPRISE SYSTEM

Freedom of Choice by Consumers
Decentralized Decision Making
High Productivity

Without having read a word of the text, you will have found one of the main ideas: The private enterprise system has three advantages—(1) freedom of choice, (2) decentralized decision making, and (3) high productivity.

Often the relationship between headings and subheads will be as clear and direct as in this example. Sometimes, however, you must read or think a bit to see how a heading and its subheads are related. For instance, in the excerpt from a speech text on page 131, following the main head "How to Become a Better Listener" are the subheads "Take Listening Seriously," "Resist Distractions," and so on. When you realize that the subheads are a list of the different ways to become a better listener, you have found one of the most important ideas on those pages—without having read even a word of the text. Sometimes there will be no clear relationship between the heading and the subheads. You want to be ready, though, to take advantage of a relationship when it is present.

- Why should you change headings into a basic question or questions?

  _____

- Why should you check to see how subheads relate to the main heads?

  _____

- Look at the excerpt from the speech text starting on page 131. How many sub-subheads appear under the subhead "Focus Your Listening"? _____
  What is the relationship between "Focus Your Listening" and the sub-subheads?

  _____

- Look at the excerpt from the business text starting on page 139. How many subheads appear under the heading "Convenience Products"? _____
  What is the relationship between "Convenience Products" and the subheads?

  _____

Activity 1

Read the following selections to find the answer or answers to the basic question or questions asked. Write your answer or answers in the space provided.

1. *Question:* What is an important difference between writing and talking?

An Important Difference between Writing and Talking

In everyday conversation, you make all kinds of points or assertions. You say, "I'm not going out with him anymore," or "She's really generous," or "I hate my job," or "That was a tremendous party." The people you are talking to don't always challenge you to give reasons for your statements. They may know why you feel as you do, or may already agree with you, or may simply not want to put you on the spot, so they don't always ask "Why?" But the people who *read* what you write may not know you, agree with you, or feel in any way obligated to you. So, if you want to communicate effectively with them, you must provide solid evidence for any point that you make. In writing, any idea that you advance must be supported with specific reasons or details.

Answer: _____

_____

_____

2. *Questions:* What is selfish learning? What is an example of selfish learning?

Selfish Learning

How can one explain the star football player who knows fifty plays by heart and the individual movements of all eleven players for most of the plays yet seems incapable of remembering a simple verb conjugation? Then there is the boy who hears the lesson instructions repeated four times yet fails to do the lesson correctly even though he can remember the pretty girl's phone number that he heard only once. At least some of the answers to the problems posed rest in what the author terms "selfish learning." In its simplest form, selfish learning refers to learning that the student accomplishes only for himself or herself—for his or her own ends with little or no regard for extrinsic, or external, reasons (requirements, grades) for the learning. The boy who knows fifty football plays by heart yet cannot conjugate a verb does not suffer from some impairment of his learning process, nor will general learning theory explain this apparent paradox. The explanation is to be found in those factors that activate or bring learning processes into action, namely, motivation, attention, and personal meaningfulness of the material once it is studied.

Answer: _____

_____

_____

3. *Question:* In what ways can job boredom be overcome?

Overcoming Job Boredom

A major problem in the production process is the fact of job boredom. We know from research in industry that many people are bored with their jobs. For example, assembly-line workers who spend their entire day doing the same operation over and over complain that the work is painfully dull and unrewarding. Many of them have no pride in their jobs. On the other hand, without this division of labor in which everyone performs a simple task, industry could never achieve high production. How can the workers and the work be brought together in a meaningful way? Today a number of methods are being tried, including job enlargement and job enrichment. *Job enlargement* involves giving the workers added duties, such as having them perform more operations or move from job to job on an assembly line. By making the work less routine, the company tries to break down the boredom factor. *Job enrichment* involves changing the jobs so as to build into them things that motivate the workers. These include increased responsibility, challenging work, opportunity for advancement and growth, and a greater feeling of personal achievement.

Answer: _____

_____

_____

4. *Questions:* How many people work in service jobs? Which services predominate?

Service Industries in the United States

The United States is the world leader in service industries. It is estimated that more than 65 percent of the labor force in this country is engaged in providing services. Services are provided by government workers such as police officers, firefighters, post office clerks, public school teachers, and state office employees. Services are also provided by those in the nonprofit private sector, such as employees in hospitals, museums, charities, churches, private schools, and private colleges. But the largest employment in service occupations is seen in profit-oriented and marketing-oriented businesses: airlines, banks, hotels and motels, consulting firms, restaurants, real estate agencies, insurance companies, beauty salons, amusements, caterers, and so on. And that listing continues to expand and increase.

Answer: _____

_____

_____

Activity 2

Following are chapter and section headings taken from a variety of college texts. Change each into a *meaningful* basic question or questions, using words like *what*, *why*, *who*, *which*, *when*, *in what ways*, *how*. Note the example.

Example	Alternatives to	a.	*What are alternatives to conflict?*
	Conflict	b.	*Which is the best alternative?*

Sociology

1. Primary and Secondary Groups
   a. _____
   b. _____

2. Prison Abuses and the Reform Movement
   a. _____
   b. _____

3. Barriers to Social Knowledge
   a. _____
   b. _____

4. Beneficial and Negative Impacts of Cities
   a. _____
   b. _____

Psychology

5. Loneliness in Modern Life
   a. _____
   b. _____

6. The Social Dropouts   a. _____

                      b. _____

7. Coping with Frustration   a. _____

                      b. _____

8. The Mentally Retarded   a. _____

                      b. _____

History and Political Science

9. The Dark Ages and the   a. _____
   Glimmer of Light   b. _____

10. The Two Terms of   a. _____
    Theodore Roosevelt   b. _____

11. The Fourteenth Amendment   a. _____

                      b. _____

12. The War of 1812   a. _____

                      b. _____

Business and Economics

13. Types of Economic   a. _____
    Systems   b. _____

14. Pollution and Business   a. _____

                      b. _____

15. Taft-Hartley Act   a. _____

                      b. _____

16. Regulation of Business   a. _____

                      b. _____

Biology and Other Sciences

17. Characteristics of   a. _____
    Living Things   b. _____

18. Cell Development   a. _____

                        b. _____

19. Energy   a. _____

                        b. _____

20. Heart Disease   a. _____

                        b. _____

Activity 3

Using a chapter from one of your textbooks, change five headings into basic questions. Then read the sections under the headings to find concise, accurate answers to the questions.

On a separate sheet of paper, indicate the headings, the questions you ask about the headings, and the answers to the questions. At the top of the first sheet on which you do this activity, give the name of the textbook, the author or authors, and the pages. Turn this activity in to your instructor.

Activity 4

Scrambled in the list that follows are five textbook headings and four subheadings for each of them. Write the headings in the lettered blanks (A, B, C, D, E) and write the appropriate subheadings in the numbered blanks (1, 2, 3, 4).

Conquest of the Plains	The Cattle Kingdom	Frontier Farmers
Cells	Tissues	Freewriting
Preparing a Scratch Outline	Heart and Artery Disease	Organ Systems
Urban Problems	Pollution	Kinds of Body Units
The Sheepherders	Brainstorming	Crowding
Organs	Arthritis	Diabetes
Noncommunicable Diseases	Making a List	Prospectors and Ranchers
Techniques in the Writing Process	Strikes	Slums
	Cancer	

A. _____

    1. _____

    2. _____

    3. _____

    4. _____

B. _____

    1. _____

    2. _____

    3. _____

    4. _____

C. _____

    1. _____

    2. _____

    3. _____

    4. _____

D. _____

    1. _____

    2. _____

    3. _____

    4. _____

E. _____

    1. _____

    2. _____

    3. _____

    4. _____

Activity 5

Using one of your textbooks, find five sets of main heads and subheads that have a clear relationship to each other. Be sure to number the subheads and to find a minimum of two subheads in each case. Also, include the numbers of the pages on which you find your main heads and subheads, in case your instructor wants to refer to the text in reviewing your answers. A model follows.

Example

Textbook:	_Business Today_	Authors:	Rachman and others
Heading:	The Market Mix	Pages:	298–301
	1. Product		3. Place
	2. Price		4. Promotion

Following the main head "The Marketing Mix" are four subheads—titles in smaller print under the main heading. Each subhead, it is clear, is one of the ingredients in a marketing mix. By recognizing the relationship between the main head and the subheads, the reader has found an important idea—without having yet read a word of the text!

■ Review Test

Part A   Answer the basic questions that are asked about the selections below.

1. *Questions:* How much of a problem is teenage drinking? Who are the teenage drinkers?

Teenage Drinking

Drinking patterns are often set in high school. Thus the growing use of alcohol by adolescents and even preadolescents and the high rate of misuse and abuse are of increasing concern. An estimated 1.3 million teenagers and preteens drink to excess. Though casual drinking is found among all groups of teenagers, problem drinking is found more often among students who also engage in other types of deviant behavior, who value and expect achievement less and esteem independence more than nondrinkers, and who are more tolerant of deviant behavior in others. Girls with drinking problems are likely to have parent problems.

Answer: _____

_____

_____

_____

_____

2. *Questions:* What is the myth of acceptance? Why is it a myth?

The Myth of Acceptance

The myth of acceptance states that the way to judge the worth of one's actions is by the approval they bring. Communicators who subscribe to this belief go to incredible lengths to seek acceptance from people who are significant to them, even when they must sacrifice their own principles and happiness to do so. Adherence to this irrational myth can lead to some ludicrous situations:

Remaining silent in a theater when others are disturbing the show for fear of "creating a scene"

Buying unwanted articles so that the salespeople won't think you have wasted their time or think you are cheap

In addition to the obvious dissatisfaction that comes from denying your own principles and needs, the myth of acceptance is irrational because it implies that others will respect and like you more if you go out of your way to please them. Often this simply isn't true. How is it possible to respect people who have compromised important values only to gain acceptance? How is it possible to think highly of people who repeatedly deny their own needs as a means of buying approval? While others may find it tempting to use these people to suit their ends or amusing to be around them, genuine affection and respect are hardly due such characters.

Answer: _____

_____

_____

_____

_____

_____

Part B   Using words such as *what, why, who, which, in what ways,* and *how,* write two meaningful questions for each textbook head that follows.

Our Changing Life Span   a.   _____

                              b.   _____

Children of Divorce   a.   _____

                              b.   _____

Corporate Cover-Ups   a. _____

                        b. _____

Industrial Revolution   a. _____

                        b. _____

Part C   Scrambled in the list that follows are three textbook headings and three subheadings for each of the headings. Write the headings in the lettered blanks (A, B, C), and write the appropriate subheadings in the numbered blanks (1, 2, 3).

Advertising Media	Drug Abuse	Hypnosis
Sleep	Problems of Adolescence	Juvenile Delinquency
Dropping Out of School	Meditation	Altered States of Consciousness
Television	Direct Mail	
	Magazines	

A. _____

   1. _____

   2. _____

   3. _____

B. _____

   1. _____

   2. _____

   3. _____

C. _____

   1. _____

   2. _____

   3. _____

Skill 4: Recognizing Emphasis Words and Other Signal Words

Signal words help you, the reader, follow the direction of a writer's thought. They are like signposts on the road that guide the traveler. Common signal words show emphasis, addition, comparison or contrast, illustration, and cause and effect.

Emphasis Words

Among the most valuable signals for you to know are *emphasis words*, through which the writer tells you directly that a particular idea or detail is especially important. Think of such words as red flags that the author is using to make sure you pay attention to an idea. Look over the following list, which contains some typical words showing emphasis.

important to note	especially valuable	the chief factor
most of all	most noteworthy	a vital force
a significant factor	remember that	above all
a primary concern	a major event	a central issue
the most substantial issue	the chief outcome	a distinctive quality
a key feature	the principal item	especially relevant
the main value	pay particular attention to	should be noted

Activity

Circle the one emphasis signal in each of these selections. Note the example.

Example

The safest and most effective solution to the various approaches to sex education is obviously a course of compromise. Certain sexual needs should be permitted expression; unadorned information about the physiological and psychological aspects of sex should be presented to all; and the Judeo-Christian traditions within which we live must be understood and dealt with sensibly in the framework of present-day society.

1.   Although the resources of our world are limited, the wants of people are not. Indeed, one of the most important assumptions of economics is that total human wants can never be satisfied. No matter how much we have, we seem to want more. As people's incomes increase, so does their desire for more and better goods and services.

2.   Chronic air pollution is expensive to the American public, costing us dearly in terms of both money and health. Air pollution causes buildings and automobiles to deteriorate. Our poisoned air damages crops, livestock, roads, and metals and forces huge cleaning bills for everything from dusty draperies to soot-blackened buildings. It is especially in terms of health, however, that pollution hurts. It is estimated that breathing the air of New York City is the equivalent of smoking two packs of cigarettes a day.

3.   To be happy, adolescents must be realistic about the achievements they are capable of, about the social acceptance they can expect to receive, and about the kind and amount of affection they will receive. Of the three, social acceptance is the most crucial. Well-accepted adolescents will automatically receive affection from those who accept them, and their achievements will win approval if not acclaim.

4.   In practice, a deficiency of just one nutrient, such as protein, is not generally seen. More likely, a combination of protein and calorie malnutrition will occur. Protein and calorie deficiency go hand in hand so often that public health officials have given a name to the whole spectrum of disease conditions that range between the two—*protein-calorie malnutrition* (PCM). This is the world's most widespread malnutrition problem, killing millions of children every year.

Addition Words

Addition words tell you that the writer's thought is going to continue in the same direction. He or she is going to add points or details of the same kind. Addition words are typically used to signal enumerations, as described on pages 324–333.

Look over the following addition words.

also	first of all	last of all	and
another	for one thing	likewise	second
finally	furthermore	moreover	the third reason
first	in addition	next	

Activity

Read the selections that follow. Circle the *three* major addition words in the first passage and the *five* major addition words in the second passage.

1.   There are a few reasons why Lady Gaga is currently called the Queen of Pop. First, she started early in life, learning to play piano at the age of four, and writing her first piano ballad at the age of 13. In high school, Lady Gaga portrayed lead roles as Adelaide in *Guys and Dolls* and Philia in *A Funny Thing Happened on the Way to the Forum.* In addition to her musical talents, she was a dedicated, studious, and disciplined student in her academic life in high school. At the age of 17, Gaga gained early admission to the *New York University's Tisch School of the Arts.* There she studied music and improved her songwriting skills. Lady Gaga's success grew following the release of her debut studio album, *The Fame* (2008), which was a critical and commercial success. Furthermore, her second studio album, *Born This Way,* released on May 23, 2011, topped the charts in more than ten countries. Some may say that Lady Gaga is a "copycat" artist in that she imitates such iconic entertainers as Madonna, Elton John, and Bette Midler; others say that while she has certainly "borrowed" from these musical greats, Lady Gaga's style is all her own.

2.   Here are ways to take some of the danger out of smoking. First of all, choose a cigarette with less tar and nicotine. The difference between brands (including those with filters) can be as much as two to one, even more. See how much you can reduce your tar and nicotine intake by switching. Also, don't smoke your cigarette all the way down. You get the most tar and nicotine from the last few puffs because the tobacco itself acts as a filter. Smoke halfway and you get only about 40 percent of the total tar and nicotine. The last half of the cigarette will give you 60 percent. Another help is to take fewer draws on each cigarette. Just reduce the number of times you puff on each cigarette and you'll cut down on your smoking without really missing it. In addition, you should reduce your inhaling. Remember, you're not standing on a mountain gulping in fresh air, so don't welcome it with open lungs. Don't inhale as deeply; take short shallow drags. Practice on a big cigar. Finally, you

should smoke fewer cigarettes each day. For some people this is easy, but for others it may be the most difficult step of all. Don't think of it as cutting down; think of it as postponing. It's always easier to postpone a cigarette if you know you'll be having one later. Carry your cigarettes in a different pocket; at work, keep them in a desk drawer or a locker—any place where you can't reach for one automatically. The trick is to change your habit patterns.

Comparison or Contrast Words

Comparison words signal that the author is pointing out a similarity between two subjects. They tell you that the second idea is like the first one in some way. Look over the following comparison words.

like	just as	in the same way	similarly
likewise	in like manner	alike	equally
just like	in a similar fashion	similarity	as

Contrast words signal a change in the direction of the writer's thought. They tell you that the author is pointing out a difference between two subjects or statements. Look over the following contrast words.

but	yet	variation	on the other hand
however	differ	still	conversely
in contrast	difference	on the contrary	otherwise

Activity

Circle the *one* comparison and the *one* contrast signal in each passage.

1.   Sleep has always been a fascinating topic. We spend about one-third of our adult life sleeping. Most animals sleep in a similar fashion—they collapse and relax their muscles. In contrast, birds and horses sleep upright, with their antigravity muscles at work.

2.   Between 1860 and 1910, some 23 million foreigners migrated to America. Just as before the Civil War, most of them came in search of better economic

opportunities. But there were new forces at work in the United States and Europe that interacted to attract ever-increasing numbers of immigrants.

3.   Premarital sex does not always result from a desire for intimacy. Peer pressure also seems to be an important factor. For young males, sexual intercourse is often considered a way to prove their manliness. In like manner, young females believe that sexual intimacy will prove they are sexy and desirable. Several studies have found that young women with a poor self-image sometimes use sex as a way to feel better about themselves. On the other hand, females who plan to attend college are less likely to be sexually intimate than females who do not plan to go to college.

4.   The steadily increasing flow of women into the labor force was caused, then, by a number of economic factors. And just as these economic changes were occurring, attitudes were changing as well. Many women no longer felt that being a full-time homemaker was providing them with an adequate sense of fulfillment and self-worth. Still, many career ladders have remained frustratingly difficult for women to climb.

Illustration Words

Illustration words tell you that an example or illustration will be given to make an idea clear. Such words are typically used in textbooks that present a number of definitions and examples of those definitions (see pages 317–323). Look over the following illustration words.

for example	specifically	for instance
to illustrate	once	such as

Activity

Circle the one illustration signal in each selection below.

1.   One purpose for incorporating sexual themes or pictorial material into advertisements is to attract consumers' attention to the ad. However, evidence suggests that use of such material may not always have an easily predictable or desired effect. For example, one study found nonsexual and sexual-romantic themes to have a greater influence on consumers' attention than did nudity.

2.   An interesting point about role playing is the way middle-years and adolescent youngsters play the role of being their age. One eight-year-old

boy, for instance, avidly collected baseball cards and kept track of games and team standings in the sports pages in accordance with the mores of his neighborhood, even though he had never seen a baseball game or expressed the slightest interest in attending one.

3.   Many problems, of course, do not lend themselves to straightforward strategies but rely more on the use of flexible and original thinking. Psychologists sometimes refer to this type of thinking as *divergent* thinking, in contrast to *convergent* thinking. A problem such as a math problem requires convergent thinking—it has only one solution or very few solutions. Problems that have no single correct solution and require a flexible, inventive approach call for divergent thinking.

4.   Short-term memory is like your attention span. If you're distracted, you'll forget whatever is in short-term memory. This can be a nuisance sometimes, but it helps to preserve sanity. Suppose that you remembered every trivial transaction you were involved in all day long. Such information would interfere with your ability to go on with other activities and to take in new material. To illustrate, if you were waiting on tables and could not put the orders of the previous ten customers out of your mind after they had left the restaurant, you would have a hard time remembering the orders of your current customers.

Cause-and-Effect Words

Cause-and-effect words signal that the author is going to describe results or effects. Look over the following cause-and-effect words.

because	reason	since
therefore	effect	as a result
so that	thus	if . . . then
cause	consequently	result in

Activity

Circle the *one* instance of a cause-and-effect word or words in each of the following passages.

1.   One study of the criminal justice system found that in one year over 800,000 felonies were committed in the city. About 104,000 people were arrested and only 1,000 were imprisoned. The great majority got off "scot

free" because many victims refused to testify. When people call the police, they often do so to frighten the offender and show their anger; they cool off when it comes to giving testimony that will send the person to prison.

2.   Thirty years ago, coal miners and workers in cotton mills accepted cancer of the lung as part of life. In a vague way they knew that longtime workers got short of breath and coughed up blood, and they wrote folk songs about brown lung disease. But as a result of a new awareness about occupational diseases and a social movement against cotton dust and coal dust, an accepted fact of life was transformed into an unacceptable illness.

3.   "The hamburger end of the fast-food industry is facing the long-awaited problem of saturation," says analyst Michael Culp at the brokerage firm of Bache Halsey Stuart Shields. "It's increasingly difficult to open more restaurants, and it's harder to sell more hamburgers." Thus, to maintain their growth momentum, the industry's big names are moving aggressively to steal each other's customers, enlarge their menus, and spawn new fast-food concepts.

4.   There are several possible explanations why retail prices are set to end on certain odd or even numbers. The practice is supposed to have started many years ago when retailers priced products so that clerks were forced to record the sale and make change. This discouraged the clerks from pocketing the money from sales. Some people believe that the practice of odd–even pricing continues today because consumers view these prices as bargains. If the price of the shirt is only $14.95, then they are able to spend "less than $15 for a shirt."

Practice in Recognizing Signal Words

Activity 1

Below are some of the signal words that are most often used by writers. Place each word under its proper heading.

for example	in addition
therefore	for instance
moreover	just as
most important	consequently
but	most significant
also	however
differ	such as
alike	similarly
as a result	especially valuable

Emphasis   *Addition*

_____   _____

_____   _____

_____   _____

Comparison   *Contrast*

_____   _____

_____   _____

_____   _____

Illustration   *Cause and Effect*

_____   _____

_____   _____

_____   _____

Activity 2

Circle the signal words in the selections that follow. The number and kind of signal words you should look for are indicated at the start of each selection.

1. One cause-and-effect signal; one contrast signal.

   Many of the restless and dissatisfied sons and daughters of these middle-, upper-middle-, and upper-class homes had never known want or poverty. Consequently, they could not understand their parents' emphasis upon money, status, and work. Parents, on the other hand, could not understand how some of their children could be indifferent, even hostile, to formal education and preparation for work.

2. One emphasis signal; one illustration signal; one contrast signal; one addition signal.

   One of the most persistent desires of human beings has been to indulge in mood-changing and pleasure-giving practices. For instance, diverse cultures have engaged in the drinking of alcoholic beverages of all descriptions. But as with most pleasures, overindulgence can be harmful to oneself and others. Also, not everyone agrees that drinking or using other mood modifiers should be an accepted pleasure.

3. One emphasis signal; one contrast signal; one cause-and-effect signal.

The greatest value of play technique is in the study of personality. Children often cannot or will not explain themselves in the first person. However, they may reveal much of their inner lives in play. The child who will not tell about his or her own fears and conflicts may readily project these feelings onto dolls. Feelings of rejection, insecurity, mixed attitudes about parents, repressed hatred, fears, and aggressions may all be freely revealed in play. As a result, the play technique, when properly handled, offers opportunities for understanding the child that are otherwise difficult to create.

4. Two cause-and-effect signals; four addition signals; one contrast signal.

As you are well aware, bureaucracies, while designed for maximal efficiency, are notorious for their inefficiencies. In practice, Weber's ideal form of bureaucracy is not achieved, for a number of reasons. First, human beings do not exist just for organizations. People track all sorts of mud from the rest of their lives with them into bureaucratic arrangements, and they have a great many interests that are independent of the organization. Second, bureaucracies are not immune to social change. When such changes are frequent and rapid, the pat answers supplied by bureaucratic regulations and rules interfere with a bureaucracy's rational operation. Third, bureaucracies are designed for the "average" person. However, in real life people vary in intelligence, energy, zeal, and dedication so that they are not in fact interchangeable in the day-to-day functioning of organizations. And fourth, in a bureaucracy each person considers anything that falls outside his or her province to be someone else's problem. Consequently, bureaucrats find it easy to evade responsibility.

■ Review Test

Signal words have been removed from each of the following textbook excerpts and placed above it. Fill in the missing signal word or words in the answer spaces provided.

Note that you will have to read each passage carefully to see which words logically fit in each answer space.

1. *In addition   most vital   Yet   however   for instance*

We take plants for granted. The carpet of greenery that blankets the

earth is, to us, an ordinary and everyday thing. Plants, _____,
are the only living things on earth capable of producing life-sustaining

oxygen. _____, plants release moisture into the atmosphere,

which contributes to the climate conditions we know today. Unfortunately, human beings continue to destroy this _____ element of their environment. In the Amazon jungle, _____, vast tracts of rain forest are being leveled; without the moisture-producing plants, the climate there is already undergoing dangerous changes. People are constantly learning more about the delicate interrelation of life on this planet. _____ they persist in these suicidal actions.

2. *important   Consequently   However   For example*

Many Americans view gambling, prostitution, public drunkenness, and use of marijuana as victimless crimes in which there is no "victim" other than the offender. _____, there has been pressure from some groups to decriminalize certain activities. Such groups believe that decriminalization is an _____ step to freeing up the resources of the overburdened criminal justice system. _____, opponents of decriminalization insist that such offenses do indeed bring harm to innocent victims. _____, a person with a drinking problem can become abusive to a spouse or children; a compulsive gambler may steal in order to pursue this obsession.

3. *One   For example   Because   Finally   Another   important*

In an ideal world, we could eliminate all physical and mental distractions. In the real world, however, this is not possible. _____ we think so much faster than a speaker can talk, it's easy to let our attention wander while we listen. Whenever you find this happening, it is _____ that you make a conscious effort to pull your mind back to what the speaker is saying. Then force it to stay there. _____ way to do this is to think a little ahead of the speaker—try to anticipate what will come next. _____ way to keep your mind on a speech is to review mentally what the speaker has already said and make sure you understand it. _____, listen between the lines and assess what a speaker implies verbally or says nonverbally with body language. _____, suppose a speaker is introducing someone to an audience. The speaker says, "It gives me great pleasure to present to you my very dear friend, Mrs. Smith." But the speaker doesn't shake hands with Mrs. Smith. He doesn't even look at her—just turns his back and leaves the podium. Is Mrs. Smith really his "very dear friend"? Certainly not.

4. *Still   But   As a result   Yet   Second   First*

Adolf Hitler was a short, dark man who believed that the tall, blond "Aryan" race was infinitely superior to all others and had to maintain its purity. _____ his view neglected some uncomfortable facts.

_____, there is no such thing as a "pure" race, and certainly no such thing as an "Aryan" race. _____, it is a matter of scientific fact that interbreeding between different human populations is apt to produce offspring that are healthier than either parental stock. _____, Hitler's theories fired Germany with a sense of national identity—and led to gas chambers and concentration camps, to the murder of up to six million Jews, and to a global war. _____, racist ideology was made utterly disreputable, and few people or governments today, whatever their private attitudes, dare to openly endorse a racist attitude. _____ it is worth noting that the United States fought Hitler with a racially segregated army and that German prisoners of war ate in canteens in which black American soldiers were refused service.

Skill 5: Recognizing Main Ideas in Paragraphs and Short Selections

The Two Basic Parts of a Paragraph

 Almost every effective communication of ideas consists of two basic parts: (1) a point is made, and (2) evidence is provided to support that point. The purpose of textbooks is to communicate ideas, and they typically do so by using the same basic structure: A point is advanced and then supported with specific reasons, details, and facts. You will become a better reader by learning to look for and take advantage of this basic structure used in textbooks.

Activity 1

To make sure that you understand the concept of two basic parts in the communication of ideas, take a few minutes to do the following. Make a point about anything at all and then provide at least two bits of specific evidence to support that point. Here are examples.

Point: I dislike the fast-food restaurant in my town.

Support: 1. The hamburgers have a chemical taste.

             2. Prices are high—for example, $1.75 for a small soda.

Point: My neighbors are inconsiderate.

Support: 1. They allow their children to play on my lawn.

             2. They often have their stereo on loud late at night.

Point: There are many inexpensive ways to save energy.

Support: 1. Install a water-saver plug in your showerhead.

             2. Turn down the thermostat of your water heater to 120 degrees.

Point: Marijuana should not be legalized.

Support: 1. Some people who don't use it now will begin using it because of its availability.

           2. Legalization will give a stamp of social approval that no mind-altering drug deserves.

Now write your own point and support for that point:

Point: _____

Support: 1. _____

             _____

           2. _____

             _____

Many textbook paragraphs that you read will be made up of the same two basic parts. The point is usually expressed in one sentence called a *main idea*, or *topic*, *sentence*. The other sentences in the paragraph contain specific details that support or develop the main idea sentence. Learning how to recognize these two basic parts quickly is sure to increase your reading comprehension.

Activity 2

Read the following textbook paragraph and see if you can identify the two major parts. Underline the main idea and put numbers in front of each reason that supports the main idea.

Changes are occurring in the traditional nine-to-five workday. Many employers are exploring new options, such as flextime, compressed workweeks, and job sharing. With flextime, employees have a choice of starting and stopping times for their workdays. As long as they are present during a midday core period of six hours, they can choose to arrive any time between 7 and 9 A.M. and leave any time between 3 and 5 P.M. Compressed workweeks are another option. In this scheme, employees work longer shifts but fewer days. In one bank's computer department, employees work three twelve-hour days, at the end of which they have a four-day "weekend." Shared jobs are also becoming more popular. Two employees split the hours, work, and benefits of a single full-time job—a situation ideal for parents of young children and others who do not want a full-time job. Alternatives such as these may soon help solve the problems of rush-hour commuting and child care as well as increase employees' morale.

The main idea is expressed in the first sentence, and the supporting ideas follow. The outline that follows shows clearly the two basic parts of the paragraph:

Changes are occurring in the traditional nine-to-five workday.

(1) Flextime

(2) Compressed workweeks

(3) Job sharing

The Value of Finding the Main Idea

Finding the main idea is a key to understanding a paragraph or short selection. Once you identify the main idea or general point that an author is making, everything else in the paragraph should click into place. You will know what point is being made and what evidence is being provided to support that point. You will see the parts (the supporting material in the paragraph) in relation to the whole (the main idea).

If the main idea is difficult and abstract, you may want to read all the supporting details carefully to help increase your comprehension. If the main idea is easily understood, you may be able to skip the supporting details or read them over quickly, since they are not needed to comprehend the point.

The main idea is often located in the first sentence of a paragraph. You should thus pay special attention to that sentence when reading a paragraph. However, the main idea sentence may also be at the end, in the middle, or any other place in the paragraph. On occasion, the main idea of a paragraph may appear in slightly different words in two or more sentences in the paragraph—for example, in the first and last sentences. In other cases, the main idea in one paragraph will serve as the central thought for several paragraphs that follow or precede it. Finally, at times the main idea will not be stated directly at all, and the reader will have to provide it by combining parts of several sentences or by looking closely at the evidence presented.

- *Complete the following sentences:* One way to help yourself understand a paragraph or short selection is to look for two basic parts: (1) _____

  and (2) _____.

  The main idea most often appears in the _____ sentence of a paragraph.

Practice in Finding the Main Idea

Activity 1

Locate and underline the main idea in each of the paragraphs that follow. The paragraphs are taken from a variety of articles and college textbooks.

To find the main idea, look for a general statement. Then ask yourself, *"Does most of the material in the paragraph support or develop the idea in this statement?"* Get into the habit of using this question as a test for a main idea.

1.   New research on the topic of anger is showing that popular notions about anger and what to do about it are changing. It is a common belief that we shouldn't bottle up anger and rather we should express it, or we should "vent." If not, it's said, we'll suffer from high blood pressure, continuing stress, or we'll simply become a doormat. We want a quick fix and so it can feel difficult to manage an angry feeling. We want it to stop and we want to blame and lash out at either the person with whom we are angry or some innocent third party (this is called misdirected anger). Previously it was thought that "releasing" anger in this way is supposed to make us feel better, but that behavior ignores the interpersonal consequences of surly behavior and the damage anger can cause to oneself and others. Current research is showing now that these beliefs are wrong and even more important, that they promote behavior that may actually cause higher stress that lasts for longer periods of time. Expressing anger while you feel angry nearly always makes you feel angrier. People who lash out in the heat of anger often stay angry longer and suffer more physical and mental stress than they would if they behaved more moderately. By comparison, people who can manage their anger, calm down, and then express their complaints in an assertive but less heated fashion are more likely to receive understanding and cooperation. In fact, they are more likely to get what they want.

2.   The very idea of a fire in a crowded building is enough to frighten most people. And with good reason: all too often, the cry of "Fire!" causes people to stampede to the nearest exit, trampling each other on the way. Fear seems to break down normal rational behavior. The result is unnecessary injury. Research studies have duplicated this panic behavior. In one experiment several people were given strings to hold, each of which was attached to a spool inside a bottle. The bottleneck was only large enough for one spool at a time to be removed. Told to get the spools out before the bottle filled with water, everyone tried to remove his or her spool at the same time. The resulting traffic jam kept *everyone* from getting the spool out in time. Even worse jams were produced when the experimenters threatened their subjects with electric shocks if they did not get their spools out before the bottle filled.

3.   In our society a person who wishes to marry cannot completely disregard the customary patterns of courtship. If a man saw a woman on the street and

decided he wanted to marry her, he could conceivably choose a quicker and more direct form of action than the usual dating procedure. He could get on a horse, ride to the woman's home, snatch her up in his arms, and gallop away with her. In Sicily, until recently, such a couple would have been considered legally "married," even if the woman had never met the man before or had no intention of marrying. But in the United States any man who acted in such a fashion would be arrested and jailed for kidnapping and would probably have his sanity seriously challenged. Such behavior would not be acceptable in our society; therefore, it could not be considered cultural.

4.   The term *integrity* essentially refers to being honest with oneself and others. But even on a simple level, being honest is not always easy. Suppose your friend asks you if you like her new hairstyle. Even though you may not think it becoming, it may not be very diplomatic to say, "If you really want to know, I think it looks awful." For such a statement would be far from reassuring and would be of little positive value. Perhaps a more diplomatic and supportive answer would be simply, "I would like to get used to it before I render an opinion." If your opinion remains negative, you can tell her your true feelings at a later time—perhaps suggesting an alternative hairstyle that you think would be more attractive. But even here, the answer is not easy; for the moment a person evades the truth, he or she tends to initiate a process of deception that may make a satisfying relationship impossible.

Activity 2

Following each paragraph below are four general statements. Circle the letter of the statement that best expresses the main idea of the paragraph. The statement you choose should be supported by all or most of the material in the paragraph.

1.   Leaving no stone unturned in their search for the killer of two boys in the early 1980s, the Atlanta police turned to psychics. But after hundreds of psychic visions had been scrutinized, the murderer remained at large until, later, the case was solved through tireless police work. Las Vegas casinos skim off only 1.4 percent of money bet at the tables. So a psychic who could beat chance by even 3 percent could make as much profit from the game as the house normally does. But casino owners who, in a sense, perform ESP experiments every night of the week worry little about people who can predict or influence the roll of the dice. The casinos continue to operate, showing, as always, the expected return. Is there, in all the world, a single psychic who can discern the contents of a sealed envelope, move remote objects, or read others' minds? If so, magician James Randi will be surprised—and poorer. For nearly twenty years, he has been offering $10,000 to anyone who can perform just one such feat. To date, nearly six hundred would-be psychics have inquired, fifty-seven of whom submitted to a test. All have failed.

a. Psychics who perform for profit are fakes.

b. The use of psychics in police investigations has a history of failure.

c. Scientists refuse to believe in the existence of ESP.

d. Little scientific evidence exists to support a belief in ESP.

2.   It has been estimated that over 98 percent of American households have at least one television set, and more than half have several. The average American household has the television turned on over six and three-quarters hours a day, or almost half of our waking day. Americans spend more time watching television than doing anything else except sleeping. For some, the time spent watching television equals or surpasses the time spent working. According to media personality and critic Robert MacNeil, "If you fit the statistical averages, by the age of twenty you will have been exposed to something like twenty thousand hours of television. You can add ten thousand hours for each decade you have lived after the age of twenty." By the time you are sixty-five, it is predicted that you will have spent about nine years of your life watching television. Sleeping habits are changed because of TV, mealtimes are altered because of TV, and leisure time is consumed. In fact, one study demonstrated that more than 40 percent of the leisure time we have available to us is spent watching television; that is almost three times the time we spend using all the other mass media.

a. Most American households have at least one TV set.

b. Some people actually watch TV for more hours than they work.

c. TV alters sleeping and eating habits.

d. To a great degree, TV has affected the structure and makeup of daily life.

3.   What kind of illness would civilized people find so repulsive that they would reject the sufferers in the most barbaric fashion and brand them with a stigma that would remain even if a cure were achieved? These unfortunates—the mentally ill—used to be scorned and burned, but in more enlightened times we have built backwoods fortresses for them, presumably to protect ourselves from contagion. They have been executed as witches, subjected to exorcisms, chained, or thrown into gatehouses and prisons to furnish horrible diversion for the other prisoners. In some countries they were gathered together and placed on a "ship of fools" and shipped off to uninhabited lands where they were left to wander on their own. The methods recommended by Celsus, a first-century Roman scholar, established the pattern of treatment for the years to come: "When he [the mentally ill person] has said or done anything wrong, he must be chastised by hunger, chains, and fetters." In line with that approach, throughout human history the mentally ill have been subjected to

misguided, cruel, sadistic, and fear-based treatment ranging from burning at the stake to banishment from society.

a.   Mentally ill people are now treated in a humane way.

b.   The Romans began the pattern of mistreating the mentally ill.

c.   Mental illness is only now beginning to be understood.

d.   The mentally ill have been mistreated throughout history.

4.   Some scientists consider hostility to represent a biological trait that makes aggressive behavior as inevitable a part of the human condition as fighting over territories is for baboons and other animals. Others, probably a majority, believe that hostility is learned and that it stems from the fact that the child cannot have everything he wants. Some of his desires are bound to be frustrated by the rules of society and by the conflicting desires of other people. He cannot always eat when he wants to. He has to learn to control his drive for elimination except when he is in the bathroom. He cannot have the toy that another child owns and is playing with. His mother cannot spend all her time catering to his whims. Other children, bigger than he, push him around.

a.   Aggressive behavior is an inevitable part of the human condition.

b.   Some scientists believe that hostility is biological, but many believe that it is learned.

c.   A child cannot always have everything he wants.

d.   Hostility is learned.

Activity 3

Do one or both of the following assignments, as directed by your instructor.

1. In the sample textbook chapter on pages 154–196, locate four paragraphs in which the main idea is clearly expressed in one sentence. On a separate sheet of paper, write down the page of this book on which each paragraph appears, the first five words of each paragraph you have chosen, and the full sentence within the paragraph that expresses the main idea.

2. In an article or a textbook, locate four paragraphs in which the main idea is clearly expressed in one sentence. Make copies of the paragraphs (using the copying machine in your library), underline the main idea sentences, and hand in the paragraphs to your instructor.

■ Review Test

Locate and underline the main idea sentence in each selection. Then put the number of each main idea sentence in the space provided at the left.

_____ 1.   [1]Traveling can enrich people's lives. [2]It can open our minds to vast possibilities, and provide adventure and relaxation in an increasingly routine and stressful world. [3]Even if you live in a vibrant city such as New York City, Chicago, Dallas, or San Francisco and have an exciting job and active social life, nothing can replace the unique experiences traveling offers. [4]Visiting a foreign country such as Brazil, Egypt, or any of the many countries in Europe, opens our eyes to how the rest of the world lives. [5]Many of us therefore return home with a new appreciation for our own country while gaining a broader worldview in the process. [6]Traveling also teaches us a lot about ourselves. [7]When we have the experience of comparing our own way of doing things with another culture's way of doing things, we can feel lucky for what we have or discover we'd like to make changes in our life. [8]Stretching our minds in this way has enormous benefits. [9]At home we may decide to learn a new language, make new friends, or even change careers. [10]Traveling helps us move out of our routines and habitual ways of looking at ourselves and the world.

_____ 2.   [1]Education for handicapped children has come a long way since the family of Helen Keller, who was deaf and blind, had to travel to distant cities and eventually hire a private tutor for their daughter. [2]But many children with disabilities still are not receiving the education that could help them to become fully functioning members of society. [3]It has been estimated that about half the nation's seven million disabled youngsters are not being educated adequately. [4]These children—about 10 percent of the school-aged population—are deaf, blind, mentally retarded, physically deformed, emotionally disturbed, speech-impaired, or afflicted with other problems. [5]Some do not attend school at all because their local districts are unable or unwilling to meet their needs. [6]Some are placed in regular classes where they cannot keep up or are channeled into the wrong kind of special classes.

_____ 3.   [1]The clearest single statement we can make is that women who smoke during pregnancy are likely to have infants with lower birth weight. [2]This finding has been reported again and again and seems to be reliable. [3]In addition, there are some indications from studies of smoking during pregnancy that women who smoke are more likely to have infants with some kind of malformation or stillborn infants. [4]Some recent research also points to long-term consequences for the infants: in three different studies, seven- to eleven-year-old children whose mothers smoked during pregnancy had more difficulties in school and were more likely to be hyperactive. [5]It seems pretty clear that smoking is harmful not only to the smoker but also to the fetus.

4.   [1]You have probably had the experience of trying to obtain directions to a particular place in an unfamiliar neighborhood. [2]When you think you are at least in the right area, you stop a pedestrian and ask, "How do you get to the stadium from here?" [3]If he or she says, "Go three blocks north, turn to the right, and it's down a block or two on the left-hand side," you can probably process the information easily enough and will reach your destination with little difficulty. [4]But suppose you ask for directions and the local character says to you, "Well, let's see, go three blocks north, turn right at the diner, go five blocks until you come to a Texaco station, turn left until you hit the third stop sign, turn left again . . . " [5]If you are like most people, you will probably go part of the way, wonder where you are, and then seek new directions. [6]Regardless of how well you listen, you can be overloaded with details.

Skill 6: Knowing How to Outline

The five skills already discussed will help you locate and understand the main ideas in your textbooks. Outlining is another skill that will improve your reading comprehension as well as provide additional benefits. Outlining is an organizational skill that develops your ability to think clearly and logically. It will help as you prepare textbook and classroom notes. It will also help as you plan speeches that you have to give or papers that you have to write. You have already learned a good deal about outlining in marking enumerations, noting relationships between heads and subheads, and identifying main ideas in paragraphs. You will now practice this important skill directly.

A Sample Outline

In an outline, you reduce the material in a selection to its main and supporting points and details. Special symbols are used to show how the points and details relate to one another.

To understand the outlining process, read the selection below and study the outline of the selection. Then look carefully at the comments that follow.

> All homeowners can take action if they are serious about saving on energy costs. Those with more than a hundred dollars to spend should consider any of the following steps. First, the sidewalls and especially the ceiling should be fully insulated. Proper insulation can save 30 percent or more of a heating or

cooling bill. Next, storm windows and doors should be installed. They provide an insulating area of still air that may reduce energy loss by 10 percent or more. Finally, a homeowner might consider installing a high-efficiency gas furnace, especially if the existing heating system is an older one.

Homeowners with less than a hundred dollars to spend can take many energy-saving steps as well. To begin with, two kinds of inexpensive sealers can be used to reduce energy leaks around the house. Caulking will seal cracks around outside windows and door frames, and at corners of the house. Weather stripping can be applied to provide a weather-tight seal between the frame and moving parts of doors and windows. Another inexpensive step is to check that a home heating or cooling system is clean. A dirty or clogged filter, for example, can make a furnace or an air conditioner work much harder to heat or cool a house. Next, a "low-flow" shower head can be used to reduce hot water use. A special shower head can be purchased or a small plastic insert available at a hardware store can be added to a regular head to limit water flow. Finally, blinds and curtains can be used to advantage throughout the year. In winter they can be closed at night to reduce heat loss. In summer they can be closed during the day to keep the house cooler. These and other relatively inexpensive steps can produce large savings.

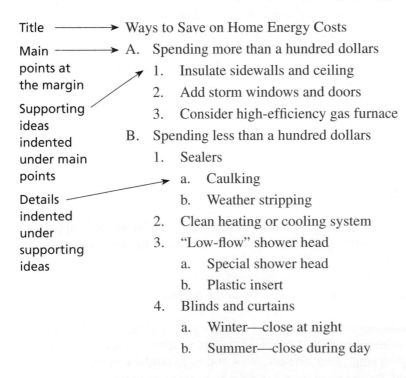

Title ⟶	Ways to Save on Home Energy Costs
Main points at the margin ⟶	A. Spending more than a hundred dollars
	1. Insulate sidewalls and ceiling
Supporting ideas indented under main points	2. Add storm windows and doors
	3. Consider high-efficiency gas furnace
	B. Spending less than a hundred dollars
	1. Sealers
Details indented under supporting ideas	a. Caulking
	b. Weather stripping
	2. Clean heating or cooling system
	3. "Low-flow" shower head
	a. Special shower head
	b. Plastic insert
	4. Blinds and curtains
	a. Winter—close at night
	b. Summer—close during day

Points to Note about Outlining

First   The purpose of an outline is both to summarize material and to show the relationships between different parts of the material. An outline is a summary in which letters and numbers are used to mark the main and supporting points and details.

In outlining, a sequence of symbols is used for the different levels of notes. In the outline above, capital letters (A and B) are used for the first level, numbers (1, 2, 3 . . .) for the second level, and small letters (a, b, c . . .) for the third level.

Second   Put all the headings at each particular level at the same point in relation to the margin. In the outline above, A and B are both at the margin; 1, 2, and 3 are all indented an equal amount of space from the margin; and a, b, and c are all indented an equal, greater amount of space from the margin.

Third   Most outlines do not need more than two or three levels of symbols. In textbook note-taking, two levels will often do. Use a sequence like the following, with subpoints indented under main points.

1. _____
   a. _____
   b. _____
   c. _____
   d. _____
2. _____
3. _____
   a. _____
   b. _____
   c. _____
4. _____
   a. _____
   b. _____

Fourth   Every outline should have a title (such as "Ways to Save on Home Energy Costs") that summarizes the information in the outline.

Activity

To check your understanding of outlining, answer question 1 and complete the statements in items 2 and 3.

1. Why do you think you should always begin main ideas at the margin?

   _____

   _____

2. Supporting ideas must always be _____ main ideas.

3. The material that appears in an outline is summarized in its _____.

Diagramming

Many students find it helpful at times to use *diagramming* (also known as *mapping* or *clustering*) rather than outlining. In diagramming, you create a visual outline of shapes as well as words. Diagrams usually use circles or boxes that enclose major ideas and supporting details. The shapes are connected with lines to show the connections between ideas.

Following are two diagrams of the selection "Ways to Save on Home Energy Costs."

Notice that in the balloon diagram, the main idea is written in the large circle that anchors the entire outline. Each supporting idea occupies one of the balloons attached to the main idea. In the box diagram, the main idea is written in the long box at the top. Below the long box are smaller boxes that contain the supporting ideas.

Activities in this chapter will ask you to use diagrams as well as outlines to make relationships between ideas visually clear. Then, in your own note-taking, you will be able to use either diagrams or outlines, whichever you find more helpful.

Balloon Diagram

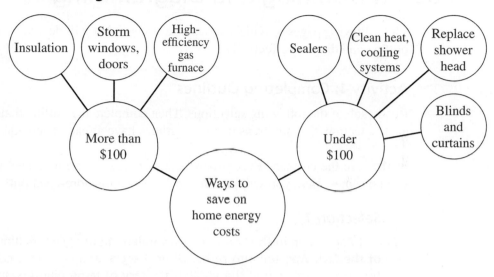

Box Diagram

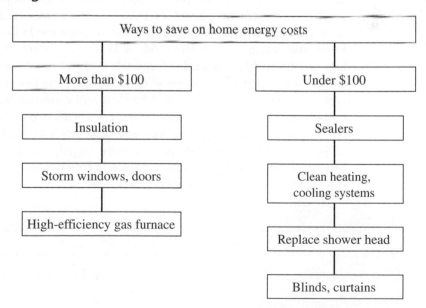

Practice in Outlining and Diagramming

The following pages provide a series of exercises that will develop your ability to outline and diagram effectively.

Activity 1: Completing Outlines

Read each of the following selections. Then complete the outline that comes after each selection. Certain items in some outlines have already been added.

Note   In the chapter "Recognizing Enumerations," you practiced making one-level outlines. Here you will practice making two-or-more-level outlines as well.

Selection 1

Population in the South, which totaled about eleven million on the eve of the Civil War, fell into rather distinct social and economic classes. At the top of the scale stood the small aristocracy of large planters. In 1860 there were 2,292 planters who owned more than a hundred slaves and 10,658 who held over fifty. However, the wealth of this small group gave them social prestige and political power far beyond their numbers. Slightly below the large planters in social and economic status were the lesser planters who had fewer slaves and farmed less land; in 1860 there were 35,616 planters who had twenty to fifty slaves. Professionals and the few business and industrial leaders were also in this general class. Most of the people in the old South were in the middle or lower middle class and were mainly yeoman farmers, skilled mechanics, and tradespeople. The so-called plain people of the old South owned very few slaves, in many cases none at all. They raised a wide variety of crops and livestock and were largely self-sufficient. Below the yeoman farmers were the poor whites and free blacks. And at the bottom of the southern class structure stood the slaves.

_____

1. _____

2. _____

3. _____

4. _____

5. _____

Selection 2

The purchase price of a house is not the only cost that buyers must consider. Buying a house is a major transaction that involves a title search, closing costs, property insurance, and special assessments. A title search is done by a title guaranty company in order to see if a piece of property has any encumbrances. When a title search is done, the history of the property is traced back to the original owners to find out if anyone else has a claim to the property. For example, a power company may have obtained the right to place poles on the property. Any restrictions like this are called encumbrances. Closing costs occur when settlement is made on a piece of property. Costs often include lawyers' fees, the commission due a real estate agent, certain taxes that must be paid in advance, and the expenses in filing records. Property insurance is also essential in purchasing a house. Insurance policies are available for flood, fire, and burglary protection. Insurance is also needed to protect the homeowner against lawsuits, especially if someone is injured on the property. Finally, home buyers may have special assessments that will be charged at settlement. They may have to pay for such services as sewers, sidewalks, and community parks.

Special Costs in Buying a House

1. _____

2. _____

    a. _____

    b. _____

    c. _____

    d. _____

3. _____

    a. _____

    b. _____

    c. _____

    d. _____

4. _____

    a. _____

    b. _____

    c. _____

Selection 3

When you are deciding to go to a professional for psychological help, there are several steps you can take. Begin by asking for recommendations. Talk with your instructor; also, confer with someone in your school's counseling service. Other good sources for recommendations are physicians and members of the clergy. After you have one or two names, try to check out reputations through the professional sources available to you. For instance, if your priest gives you a name, you might check it out with your school counselor. Next, call the professionals and ask about their training, degrees, and experience; a good therapist will not hesitate to give you this information. You might also want to find out what approach they follow and what goals they aim for in treating people. Finally, make your first visit to the professional an exploratory one: learn as much as you can about how he or she does therapy and how your own problems might be dealt with. If you aren't satisfied, go to someone else. One visit to a professional doesn't commit you to further visits. This approach to selecting a professional, while initially somewhat time-consuming, will be well worth it in terms of the quality of help you receive.

Getting Psychological Help _____

1. _____

    a. _____

    b. _____

    c. _____

    d. _____

2. _____

3. _____

    a. _____

    b. _____

4. _____

Activity 2: Completing Diagrams

Read each of the following selections. Then complete the diagram that comes after each selection.

Selection 1

There are several easy ways to lose weight without feeling deprived. If you drink three cups of coffee a day, simply eliminating milk and sugar from the coffee will save approximately two hundred calories a day. If you cut out two hundred calories a day, you'll lose seventeen pounds in a year! Another way to avoid unnecessary calories is to use nonstick pots and pans. You can melt a large pat of butter to cook your eggs, thereby adding one hundred calories. Or you can use a nonstick pan and eliminate those calories. Avoiding calorie-laden salad dressings is another easy way to lose weight. One small spoonful of creamy Russian or blue cheese dressing adds as much as one hundred calories. And how many of us are content with just one small spoonful? That "low-calorie" salad can quickly turn into a diet disaster. Substituting diet dressings, or a dash of lemon and pepper, is an easy way to slash calorie intake. One final way to avoid calories is to substitute broiling or baking for frying. The oil used in frying is absorbed by the food, and oil is high in calories. Broiled or baked chicken, for example, is as delicious as fried chicken, and the saving in calories is enormous.

Selection 2

Research psychologists have identified three kinds of depression. Few of us have not at some time experienced "the blues" because of crises in our lives. This is *normal depression.* Such depression usually clears up by itself in a very short time. But an estimated ten million Americans react to life's problems—most often a loss, disappointment, change, frustration, or threat to identity—with depression deep enough or long-lasting enough to interfere with their functioning. This is *neurotic depression.* Symptoms usually disappear when stress is lifted.

Another six to eight million have medically triggered depression that appears out of the blue, apparently unrelated to life's problems. It may be caused by hereditary factors, hormonal or chemical imbalance, dietary deficiency, or drug or allergic reaction. This *psychotic depression* is more serious and more complex. It is usually divided into two main types: (1) *bipolar depressive disease,* also known as manic-depressive psychosis, in which the individual swings from deep depression to unexplained "highs," during which he or she feels all-powerful and all-wise and becomes difficult to control; (2) *unipolar depressive disease,* in which the patient has bouts of depression and is severely withdrawn and uncommunicative or behaves in an extremely agitated fashion.

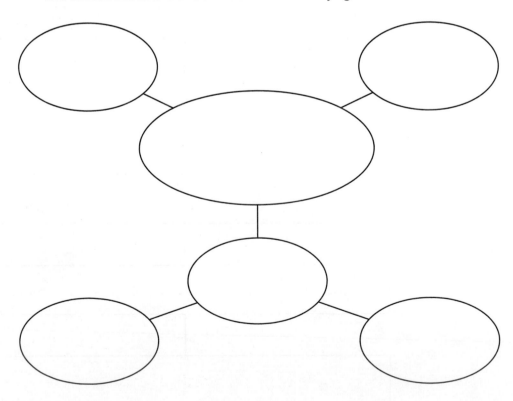

Selection 3

Because alcohol abuse is such a common problem, it is important to recognize the danger signals of alcoholism. Progression from a "social drinker" to a problem drinker to an alcoholic is often subtle. In the *initial* phase, the social drinker begins to turn more frequently to alcohol to relieve tension or to feel good. There are four danger signals in this period that signal excessive dependence on alcohol. The first is increasing consumption. The person drinks more and more and may begin to worry about drinking. The second is morning drinking. Morning drinking is a dangerous sign, particularly when it Is used to combat a hangover or to "get through the day." Next is regretted behavior. The person engages in extreme behavior while drunk that leaves him or her feeling guilty or embarrassed. Finally, there are blackouts. Excessive drinking may be accompanied by an inability to remember what happened during intoxication. The *crucial phase* begins when the person begins to lose control over drinking. At this stage there is usually control over when and where a first drink is taken, but one drink starts a chain reaction leading to a second and a third, and so on. In the *chronic phase,* the alcoholic drinks compulsively and continuously. He or she eats infrequently, becomes intoxicated from far less alcohol than before, and feels a powerful need for alcohol when deprived of it. Work, family ties, and social life all deteriorate. Self-drugging is usually so compulsive that when there Is a choice, the bottle comes before friends, relatives, employment, and self-esteem. The drinker is now an addict.

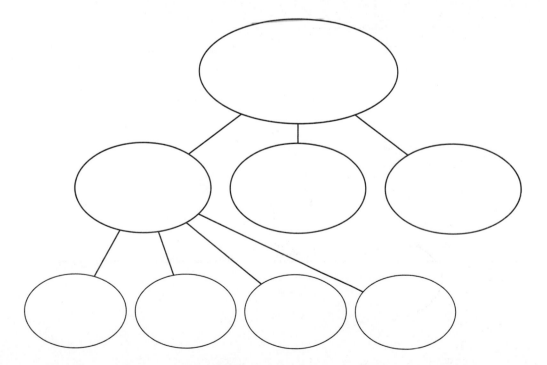

■ Review Test

Complete the diagram or outline for each of the following selections.

Selection 1

By the time students reach high school (their ninth or tenth year of formal education), they are usually well entrenched in a world of their peers. Parents and teachers assume a secondary place as a source of significant values. What is important is what one's crowd thinks. At this age, the crowd is primarily fellow students. Burton R. Clark identifies three types of subcultures; almost every junior and senior high school student belongs to one of them. First is the so-called *fun subculture,* which places utmost emphasis on having a good time. In this subculture, one must have a "good personality" and *savoir-faire* about clothes, automobiles, hangouts, and sports. Books and learning represent drudgery and low status. The second subculture is the *academic,* which places value on being a good student, discussing serious questions and interests of the day, and high educational achievement. This subculture is considerably less popular than the fun subculture in most secondary schools. The least popular but most publicized student subculture is the *delinquent.* Members of this group have contempt for the school and its faculty in addition to a defiant attitude toward any form of regulation and toward anybody not approved by their crowd.

_____

1. _____

2. _____

3. _____

Selection 2

Nonasserters pay in several ways for not expressing themselves. The most obvious costs are social. Shy people make few new acquaintances and have a hard time building friendships with those people they do meet. Even when they do mingle with others, nonexpressive people are often misunderstood.

Nonassertiveness also takes a psychological toll on its victims. Three attitudes often develop in people who are not able to express the full range of their feelings. Some simply withdraw from any kind of meaningful contact with others, taking refuge in impersonal activities such as watching TV for hours at a time or distracting themselves with liquor or other drugs. Other people deal with their inept communications by becoming cynics, claiming that people aren't worth caring about anyway. A third group of nonasserters react to the condition with despair at themselves and at an imperfect world where life is not worth living.

Besides social and psychological consequences, nonassertion also has physiological costs, in the form, first of all, of psychosomatic illnesses. Such illnesses are real, differing in no physical way from organically caused illnesses. Nonassertive people often develop stress-related diseases as well as psychosomatic disorders. Hypertension, or high blood pressure, often has its roots in chronic stress.

1. _____

2. _____

   a. _____

   b. _____

   c. _____

3. _____

   a. _____

   b. _____

Selection 3

There are two types of smog. The first is a *combination of smoke and fog.* Such combinations occur in cities that burn lots of coal. The droplets of fog combine with the smoke particles. The fog acts like a giant sponge in creating this type of smog. The second type of smog is more common. It is properly called *photochemical smog* and is caused by sunlight reacting with certain pollutants. The chemicals in the exhaust of automobile engines are the biggest troublemakers. One of these chemical pollutants is carbon monoxide. In concentrated form, this odorless, colorless gas is a deadly poison. Another pollutant is nitrogen dioxide, a yellow-brown gas that gives photochemical smog its color. Nitrogen dioxide has a sharp odor that is described as "sweetish." Ozone is the other pollutant that results from the photochemical process. Ozone is colorless, but it has a sharp odor. You may have smelled ozone during an electrical storm or when a piece of electrical equipment short-circuited.

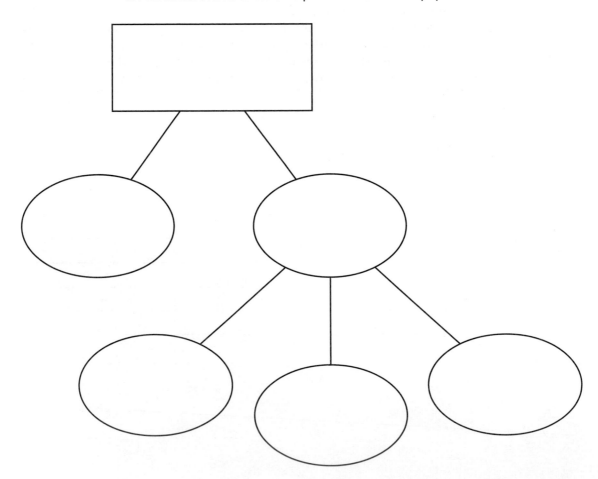

Selection 4

In some ways, there is bound to be some physical decline or slowing down during the years of middle age. A number of signs of aging can be identified. The bone structure, for one thing, stiffens and even shrinks a bit during the course of adulthood. This is the reason why some people may be shorter at their fortieth high school reunion than they were when they were students. Another sign of aging is that skin and muscles begin to lose some elasticity so that, for example, areas of the face and jaws begin to sag. Another sign is the tendency to accumulate more subcutaneous fat, especially in certain areas such as the midriff. There are more sensory defects during the adult years, too. Vision tends to be constant from adolescence to the forties or early fifties, when visual acuity may begin to show signs of decline. However, nearsighted people often are able to see better in middle age than they could as young adults. There is an increased incidence of hearing problems during mid-adulthood, especially hearing loss in the upper frequencies. Long-term exposure to high levels of noise increases the likelihood of hearing loss. Therefore, some factory workers and many city dwellers may be particularly prone to hearing problems In later years.

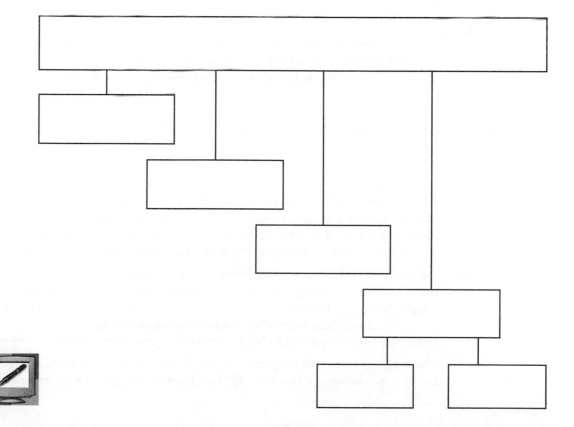

Skill 7: Knowing How to Summarize

To understand the summarizing process, first read the following selection and summary. Then study the points about summarizing that follow.

> In another kind of coping behavior, *rationalization,* an acceptable motive is substituted for an unacceptable one. Put another way, we "make excuses"—we give a different reason from the real one for what we are doing. Rationalization is a common defense mechanism for avoiding the anxiety connected with an unacceptable motive. A student who has sacrificed studying to have a good time may blame his or her failing grades on bad teaching, unfair examinations, or too heavy a workload. A father may beat his child just because he is angry but rationalize it by saying that he is acting for the child's good.

Summary

> Rationalization—a kind of coping behavior in which an acceptable motive is substituted for an unacceptable one.
> Ex.—father rationalizes beating child by saying it's for child's good.

Points to Note about Summarizing

1   A *summary*, like an outline, is a reduction of a large quantity of information to the most important points. Unlike an outline, however, a summary does not use symbols such as A, 1, a, and so on, to indicate the relationships among parts of the original material. The preceding summary includes the most important points—the definition of *rationalization* and an example that makes the definition clear—but the other material is omitted.

2   Summarizing is helpful because it requires that you thoroughly *understand* the material you are reading. You must "get inside" the material and realize fully what is being said before you can reduce it to a few words. Work in summarizing material will help build your comprehension power. It will also markedly improve your ability to take effective classroom and textbook notes.

3   The length of a summary depends on your *purpose* in summarizing. The shortest possible summary is a title. If your purpose requires more information than that, a one-sentence summary might be enough. Longer passages and different purposes might require longer summaries. For example, in writing a report on an article or a book, you might often want to have a summary that is a paragraph or more in length.

In the following practice activities you will be writing title summaries, single- and several-sentence summaries, and one-paragraph summaries. After such varied practice, you should be prepared to write whatever kind of summary you might need to.

- *Complete the following sentences:* A summary _____ a large quantity of material to the most important points. Unless you fully

  _____ the material you are reading, you will not be able to summarize it.

Practice in Summarizing

Activity 1

This activity will give you practice in choosing title summaries and one-sentence summaries. In each case, circle the letter of the title and then of the sentence that best summarize each selection. Your choices should be ones that best answer the question What is this about? Your choices should be as specific and descriptive as possible and at the same time account for all the material in each selection.

Selection A

It is commonly believed that the poor are lazy people who could work if they were willing. In fact, over 60 percent of the poor consist of children under age fourteen, elderly people over age sixty-four, and people of working age who are ill or in school. Another quarter work but do not earn enough to rise above the poverty line. This leaves less than 15 percent of the poor of working age who do not work, and the vast majority of those are mothers of young children. When it comes to work, the poor do not look as bad as their reputation, for most of them are too old, too young, too sick, or too busy caring for children to work.

1. What would be an accurate title for this selection?

    a. Poor Children

    b. Who Are the Poor?

    c. The Working Poor

2. Which sentence best summarizes the selection?

   a.   Most of the poor are too young or too old to work.

   b.   Many people believe that the poor are lazy people who could work if they really wanted to.

   c.   A great majority of the poor either don't work for a good reason or work but are poorly paid.

Selection B

Depending on weather conditions, we may or may not worry about drought in any particular year, but regardless of temporary weather conditions, our nation is using water much faster than the supply is being replenished. One-fourth of the water used in America comes from a system of aquifers—underground areas of porous soils in which water has accumulated through the ages. In some cases, such aquifers are covered by hardpan or rock, through which water penetrates only slowly, even during years of abundant rain. Consequently, although our "bank account" of water is very large, it is being overdrawn. In 1950, the nation pumped 21 trillion gallons from underground; now it pumps more than twice that much each year. In fact, each day, 21 billion more gallons are pumped out than enter the underground aquifers. One water planner notes that the rate of depletion in the Midwest differs from place to place but adds, "Some people project that eventually there will be parts of Nebraska with their water supplies so depleted that farming may never return."

3. What would be an accurate title for this selection?

   a.   Our Vanishing Water Supply

   b.   The Coming Drought in the Midwest

   c.   Sources of Our Water Supply

4. Which sentence best summarizes the selection?

   a.   Weather conditions may lead to temporary droughts.

   b.   We are using up our water supply faster than it is being replenished.

   c.   Eventually it may no longer be possible to farm in Nebraska.

Selection C

Trichinosis is a disease caused by eating pork infested with the larvae (developmental stage) of a worm called the trichina. From the intestinal tract of the human body, the worm larvae enter the blood, reach the muscles, and burrow into them. Muscular pain and fever may develop about seven days after eating the pork; the fever may last for several weeks. Even after these early symptoms have subsided, however, the larvae may lie dormant in the muscles for years. In fact, some of the aches and pains of rheumatism may be caused by trichina larvae in the muscles. The government does not inspect pork for the larvae, and there is no effective treatment for the disease. Therefore, as a precaution, pork and pork products (such as sausage) should always be cooked until they are well-done; thorough cooking will kill any worms that are present.

5. What would be an accurate title for this selection?

   a. Cooking Pork

   b. The Trichina Worm

   c. Trichinosis and Its Prevention

6. Which sentence best summarizes the selection?

   a. Trichinosis, an illness with short- and long-term effects, is caused by a worm in pork that can be killed by thorough cooking.

   b. Trichinosis may last for several weeks and then lie dormant for years.

   c. Entering the body from the intestinal tract, the trichina worm eventually burrows into muscles, causing an illness that may last for several weeks.

Selection D

Did you ever have someone's name on the tip of your tongue, and yet you were unable to recall it? When this happens again, don't try to recall it. Do something else for a few minutes, and the name may pop into your head. The name is there, since you have met this person and learned his or her name. It only has to be dug out. The initial effort to recall *primes* the mind, but it is the subconscious activities that go to work to pry up a dim memory. *Forcing* yourself to recall almost never helps because it doesn't loosen your memory; it only tightens it. Students find the *priming method* helpful on examinations. They read over the questions before trying to answer any of them. Then they answer first the ones of which they are most confident. Meanwhile, deeper mental activities in the subconscious mind are taking place; work is being done on the more difficult questions. By the time the easier questions are answered, answers to the more difficult ones will usually begin to come into consciousness. It is often just a question of *waiting* for recall to be loosened up.

7. What would be an accurate title for this selection?

   a. Memory Techniques

   b. The Priming Method of Memory

   c. Success in Exams

8. Which sentence best summarizes the selection?

   a. The priming method can be very useful to students when taking exams.

   b. In the priming method, the subconscious brings up a memory in response to an initial conscious effort to recall it.

   c. When you have someone's name on the tip of your tongue but can't recall it, trying to force yourself to remember may make it harder to do so.

Activity 2

This activity will give you practice in writing title summaries and one-sentence summaries. Each title and sentence should condense into a few words the essential thoughts of each selection. A good way to proceed is to try to find the fewest words that will answer the question What is this about?

Note when you write the titles that you will be doing exactly the kind of summarizing that textbook authors do when they write headings and subheadings for their work. The experience of "writing labels" should help you appreciate—and take advantage of—the headings given by textbook authors.

Selection A

Instead of letting your mind wander or preparing what you are going to say when you have a chance, you can practice and use active listening skills. *Active listening* includes repeating important details to yourself; questioning; paraphrasing; distinguishing among governing idea, main points, and detail; and, in some situations, note-taking. Active listening involves you in the process of determining meaning. Too often people think of the listening experience as a passive situation in which what they remember is largely a matter of chance. In reality, good listening is hard work that requires concentration and willingness to mull over and, at times, verbalize what is said. Good listening requires using mental energy. If you really listen to an entire fifty-minute lecture, for instance, when the lecture is over you will feel tired because you will have put as much energy into listening as the lecturer put into talking.

Heading: _____

One-sentence summary: _____

_____

_____

Selection B

When Captain Cook asked the chiefs in Tahiti why they always ate apart and alone, they replied, "Because it is right." If we ask Americans why they eat with knives and forks, or why their men wear pants instead of skirts, or why they may be married to only one person at a time, we are likely to get similar and very uninformative answers: "Because it's right." "Because that's the way it's done." "Because it's the custom." Or even "I don't know." The reason for these and countless other patterns of social behavior is that they are controlled by *social norms*—shared rules or guidelines which prescribe the behavior that is appropriate in a given situation. Norms define how people "ought" to behave under particular circumstances in a particular society. We conform to norms so readily that we are hardly aware they exist. In fact, we are much more likely to notice departures from norms than conformity to them. You would not be surprised if a stranger tried to shake hands when you were introduced, but you might be a little startled if he or she bowed, curtsied, started to stroke you, or kissed you on both cheeks. Yet each of these other forms of greeting is appropriate in other parts of the world. When we visit another society whose norms are different, we quickly become aware that things we do this way, they do that way.

Heading: _____

One-sentence summary: _____

_____

_____

Selection C

On the American plains, buffalo were once so numerous that they were counted in the millions. A herd of buffalo could cover the prairie as far as the eye could see. The hoofbeats of an approaching buffalo herd could be heard several miles away. Amazingly, within only a few decades, the vast numbers of buffalo would be reduced to a mere handful by the white man. After railroads reached the plains area, bringing more and more whites, the buffalo were doomed. Special trains would carry passengers into buffalo country; passengers armed with rifles would shoot into the herd from the train window. The "hunters" did not even collect the buffalo carcasses. Thousands of pounds of buffalo meat and hide were left to rot in the sun. Occasionally the buffalo tongue, a delicacy, would be retrieved. After the carcasses had rotted, local farmers would collect wagonloads of bones, in order to sell them as fertilizer at $5 a ton. The buffalo slaughter was so enormous that one hunter, after witnessing the destruction of a herd, wrote, "A man could have walked twenty miles on their carcasses." By the end of the nineteenth century, this wanton waste had made the buffalo practically extinct.

Heading: _____

One-sentence summary: _____

_____

_____

Selection D

The British approach to heroin addiction (heroin maintenance) is fundamentally different from the American approach. The object of the American model is to get addicts "off" heroin by drying up their supplies and imprisoning the addicts. Narcotics control, under this plan, is placed under the jurisdiction of law enforcement authorities. The British plan, in sharp contrast, places control in the hands of medical authorities. Instead of treating addicts as criminals, the British allow doctors to administer drugs to addicts under two conditions: when their complete withdrawal cannot be accomplished and when they can perform satisfactorily if given a controlled dosage. The doctors must notify the British Home Office of all patients under this treatment. When properly registered, those addicts are entitled to receive maintenance doses of heroin; however, if an addict commits a crime, then he or she is treated the same as any other offender. Moreover, if not registered but in possession of opiates, the individual is prosecuted for illegal possession of a dangerous drug.

Heading: _____

One-sentence summary: _____

_____

_____

Activity 3

Read the textbook selection "Defense Mechanisms" on pages 449–452 and then summarize it by answering the questions that follow.

1. Circle the letter of the statement that best summarizes paragraph 1.

   a. Defense mechanisms are methods used to protect one's self-esteem against the many challenges to it.

   b. Getting a new blemish or wrinkle and receiving a low grade are challenges to your self-esteem.

   c. There are numerous ways in which your self-esteem is challenged.

2. Circle the letter of the statement that best summarizes paragraphs 2 and 3.

   a. Going to a movie is a good way to avoid thinking about an argument.

   b. Scarlett O'Hara's line "I'll think about it tomorrow" illustrates the defense mechanism of suppression.

   c. Suppression, useful only for minor problems, is a conscious effort to avoid stressful thoughts.

3. Circle the letter of the statement that best summarizes paragraphs 4 and 5.

   a. Repression is the unconscious forgetting of painful thoughts, which can be "remembered" only through dreams or hypnosis.

   b. Repression of a friend's departure may be the reason you forget to contribute money for a going-away gift.

   c. It is common for people to push thoughts out of the conscious mind.

4. Circle the letter of the statement that best summarizes paragraphs 6–8.

   a. Other unconscious defense mechanisms include withdrawal, or avoidance, a response to fear or frustration that can be positive or negative, depending on its use.

   b. Many famous, likable people have suffered from shyness, a common result of the fear of rejection.

   c. Withdrawal can lead to negative actions, such as quitting jobs, dropping out of school, separating, and divorcing.

5. Circle the letter of the statement that best summarizes paragraph 9.

   a. If used excessively, daydreaming can become an unhealthy substitute for activity.

    b.   Escaping and relaxing through fantasy—for example, through daydreaming or reading a novel—can be healthy if used in moderation and not as a substitute for activity.

    c.   A person can live in a fantasy world in which he or she is always accepted, admired, and loved.

6. Circle the letter of the statement that best summarizes paragraph 10.

    a.   Regression is what occurs when a new baby arrives and an older child returns to previous methods of gaining attention.

    b.   People who behave in a childlike way are likely to do such things as burst into tears, suck their thumbs, throw things, scream, or have a tantrum.

    c.   Regression is a return to earlier ways of handling problems, a response to being deeply upset and unable to handle a problem maturely.

7. Circle the letter of the statement that best summarizes paragraphs 11 and 12.

    a.   Most people are not aware that they rationalize often.

    b.   Rationalization, a common defense mechanism, is a distortion of the truth to maintain self-esteem.

    c.   Richard Nixon rationalized his loss of the 1960 presidential election by commenting that he would have more time to devote to his family.

8. Circle the letter of the statement that best summarizes paragraph 13.

    a.   Projection may explain why a woman who flirts complains that it is the males who are flirting with her.

    b.   Psychological tests may use projection to uncover problems.

    c.   Projection is accusing someone else of your own weaknesses.

9. Circle the letter of the statement that best summarizes paragraph 14.

    a.   Displacement is responding to a problem by victimizing someone else.

    b.   Husbands and wives should avoid controversial topics after either one has had a bad day.

    c.   Using displacement, the rejected person in the cartoon might ridicule and chastise the bartender.

10. Circle the letter of the statement that best summarizes paragraph 15.

    a.   Someone may make up for being a poor student by seeking popularity with clever jokes.

b.   Compensation generally leads to a healthy adjustment to an inadequacy.

c.   Compensation is making up for an inadequacy by doing well in another area, generally a healthy response.

11. Circle the letter of the statement that best summarizes paragraph 16.

a.   Sublimation is channeling unacceptable urges into constructive or creative efforts.

b.   Some of the finest creative works have resulted from the sublimation of members of oppressed groups.

c.   Sublimation is a very positive type of defense mechanism.

Activity 4

Read the following article and then write a one-paragraph summary of 100 to 125 words. Here are some guidelines for summarizing an article:

a Think about the title for a minute or so. The title often summarizes what the article is about.

b Consider any subtitle that may appear. The subtitle, a caption, or other words in large print under or next to the title often provide a quick insight into the meaning of an article.

c Note any subheadings that appear in the article. Subheadings provide clues to the article's main points and give an immediate sense of the content of each section.

d Make an outline of the article before beginning to write.

e Express the author's ideas in your own words—not in the words of the article itself.

f Do not write an overly detailed summary. Remember that the purpose of a summary is to reduce the original material to its main ideas and essential supporting points.

g Do not begin your sentences with expressions like "the author says"; equally important, do not introduce your own opinions into the summary with comments like "another good point made by the author." Instead, concentrate on presenting directly and briefly the author's main points.

When Kids Come Home to an Empty House

Experts Worry about the Effects of "Latchkeyism" and Suggest Some Countermeasures.

Wearing the front-door key on a chain around his neck, eleven-year-old Jeremy Cavin comes home from school each day to an empty house.

"Lonely is the word for it," says Jeremy, an only child who is not allowed to have friends over while his parents are at work.

Says Jeremy's father, Bob: "I don't like the situation. I don't think any parent does." But with no suitable after-school programs in their area of North Carolina, the Cavins feel they have no choice. For as long as both of his parents work, Jeremy will be a so-called *latchkey child.*

The label has been around since the nineteenth century, but the number of latchkey kids between the ages of seven and thirteen has burgeoned in recent decades. Because of the dramatic increases in one-parent and two-paycheck families, there are now more than two million children who fend for themselves for part of every workday. And with two out of every three mothers expected to work outside the home by the end of this decade, the latchkey legion can only grow larger still.

Until recently, little was known about this phenomenon. Now research is under way, "survival" courses geared to latchkey kids are being offered, and some communities are beginning to come up with attractive alternatives.

Some Real Problems

One of the new studies reveals that some latchkey children face very real emotional problems. Dr. Thomas Long, professor of education at the Catholic University of America, and his wife, Dr. Lynette Long, assistant professor of education at Loyola University, interviewed more than fifty latchkey kids in Washington, D.C. One child who lost her key recalled crying on the front porch for hours until her mother returned from work. Another told of climbing into a chair and clutching her shoe as a possible weapon when she heard suspicious noises outside.

Latchkey children can also suffer from being bored, isolated, and confined, the Longs believe. "Where is play for these kids?" asks Thomas Long. "For years these children are denied a social life at a critical time in their development." Kids left alone at home watched up to seven hours of television a day, according to the Longs' study.

But beyond marathon TV watching, the Longs worry about the possible long-term effects of "latchkeyism": feelings of alienation leading to academic failure, violence, vandalism, and experimentation with drugs and alcohol.

Thomas Long says police in his area are seeing more and more latchkey kids in trouble. But he and other experts concede that any conclusive link between latchkey children and delinquency remains hypothetical.

What Can Be Done

What can worried latchkey parents do to minimize the risks? Long suggests that parents help structure empty hours by assigning chores and suggesting a schedule to follow, and by trying to arrange for some after-school activities—scouting, dance lessons, recreation programs—to vary their kids' solo routines. From the comments of children in his study, he also believes that pets can help by providing comfort and companionship in an empty house. Above all, Long suggests that once parents return home, they should put off household duties and "make an extended effort to get into their child's world."

Another study now in progress by Dr. Hyman Rodman, director of the Family Research Center at the University of North Carolina at Greensboro, reveals how nearly twelve hundred latchkey mothers are trying to make the arrangement as *safe* as possible. The women said they worry about fires, forgotten keys, and other frightening possibilities. But most stay in close touch with their children by phone, have a neighbor to turn to in emergencies, and have rules for the kids to follow. Among the most common rules:

- No one is allowed in the house, even friends, without prior special permission.
- The door is not to be opened when someone knocks unless the child is told beforehand that certain persons can be let in or unless it is someone well known to the family.
- Children are given specific tasks that they are expected to do while they care for themselves.
- No use of the stove or other electrical appliances, except the TV, radio, or record player, is allowed.
- No one who calls on the telephone is to be told by the children that they are alone.

Most latchkey mothers who have these rules told Dr. Rodman they were satisfied, if not happy, with the arrangement. Many believed that their children were learning responsibility and self-reliance.

Activity 5

Write a one-paragraph summary of an article in a weekly or monthly magazine. Identify at the start of the summary the title and author of the work. Also, include in parentheses the date of publication. For example, "In an article titled 'Trial-by-Fire' (*Time*, July 22, 2011), Anita Hamilton states . . . ." Then, in your own words, summarize the main point of the article and the key details used to support or develop that point. Finally, be sure to clip or make a copy of the article and attach it to your summary.

Activity 6

Watch a television show of special interest to you. Then prepare a one-paragraph summary of the show. In the first sentence, give basic information about the show by using a format such as "The November 20, 2011, broadcast of CBS's *60 Minutes* examined . . . ."

Activity 7

Write a one-paragraph summary of an important concept from one of your textbooks. Try to choose a general-interest subject such as psychology or sociology rather than a highly specialized field such as anatomy or electronics.

In your summary, first provide the necessary identifying information. For example, "In the chapter 'States of Consciousness' in *Understanding Psychology* (McGraw-Hill, 2008), Robert S. Feldman explains . . . ." Then present the important idea in the chapter, along with key details that support or develop that idea.

■ Review Test

Part A   Circle the letters of the title and the sentence that best summarize each of the following two selections. Remember that the title should be as specific and descriptive as possible and at the same time account for all the material in the selection.

> Sacrifice is a rather widespread ritual. It is generally based on the hope that if an individual gives up something of value to honor a supreme being, he or she will receive a divine blessing. A common sacrificial custom within industrial societies is making a contribution to a religious institution, as in the practice of tithing (giving one-tenth of one's income to a church). Other examples of religious sacrifice include fasting on holy days (such as Yom Kippur, the Day of Atonement for Jews) and giving up worldly pleasures (as Christians do for Lent). The most ancient form of sacrifice—still commonly found throughout the world today—is the burial of goods with a corpse.

Such artifacts as food, clothing, money, and weapons are intended to provide the soul of the deceased with whatever will be needed during an afterlife. In American society, the provision of comfortable coffins for well-dressed corpses and the regular placement of flowers near a grave are forms of sacrifice offered in a similar spirit.

1. What would be an accurate title for this selection?

   a. Tithing

   b. Religious Rituals

   c. Rituals of Sacrifice

2. What sentence best summarizes the selection?

   a. In industrial societies, a common form of sacrifice is making a contribution to a religious institution.

   b. Sacrifice, a widespread ritual, is based on the hope of gaining a blessing by giving up something in honor of a supreme being.

   c. The oldest form of sacrifice, the burial of goods with a corpse, was still common throughout the world in the 1980s.

Eating disorders such as bulimia and anorexia nervosa are widespread in American culture and affect both women (5 to 10 million) and men (1 million). Even though they are well documented, the causes of eating disorders remain mysterious. There is evidence that eating disorders may be linked to other medical and psychiatric disorders such as depression, substance abuse, or anxiety disorders. One study showed that girls with attention-deficit/hyperactivity disorder (ADHD) have a greater chance of developing an eating disorder than those not affected by ADHD. Another study showed that foster girls are more likely to develop bulimia. And still other research shows that for some people there is a genetic reason for developing an eating disorder. Many people with anorexia have coexisting psychiatric and physical illnesses, including depression, anxiety, obsessive behavior, substance abuse, cardiovascular and neurological complications, and impaired physical development. While all these issues may contribute in some part to the cause of eating disorders, many believe that the main cause of eating disorders involves peer pressure and idealized body types seen on television and in newspapers, glossy magazines, and music videos. This idea seems to be substantiated by the fact that eating disorders are increasing all over the globe as Western media images of beauty and the "ideal" body type are projected worldwide.

3. What would be an accurate title for this selection?

    a.   What causes an eating disorder?

    b.   How to treat eating disorders.

    c.   The history of eating disorders in the United States

4. Which sentence best summarizes the selection?

    a.   While all these issues may contribute in some part to the cause of eating disorders, many believe that the main cause of eating disorders involves peer pressure and idealized body types seen on television and in newspapers, glossy magazines, and music videos.

    b.   There is evidence that eating disorders may be linked to other medical and psychiatric disorders such as depression, substance abuse, or anxiety disorders.

    c.   Eating disorders such as bulimia and anorexia nervosa are widespread in American culture and affect both women (5 to 10 million) and men (1 million).

Part B   Circle the letter of the title that best summarizes each of the following two selections. Then write a one-sentence summary of each. If there is a summary sentence in a paragraph, you may use it; one paragraph has such a sentence.

    Sheer proximity is perhaps the most decisive factor in determining who will become friends. Our friends are likely to live nearby. Although it is said that absence makes the heart grow fonder, it also causes friendships to fade. While relationships may be maintained in absentia by correspondence, they usually have to be reinforced by periodic visits, or they dissolve. Several researchers decided to investigate the effects of proximity on friendships. They chose an apartment complex made up of two-story buildings with five apartments to a floor. People moved into the project at random, so previous social attachments did not influence the results of the study. In interviewing the residents of the apartment complex, the researchers found that 44 percent said they were most friendly with their next-door neighbors, 22 percent saw the people who lived two doors away the most often socially, and only 10 percent said that their best friends lived as far away as down the hall. People were even less likely to be friendly with those who lived upstairs or downstairs from them.

5. What would be an accurate title for this selection?

    a.   Proximity

    b.   Factors in Determining Friendships

    c.   Proximity as a Factor in Friendships

6. Summary sentence: _____

_____

_____

   The institutional care we give our older people is a good reflection of the overall attitude of our society toward the aged. In the past few years, nursing homes have received wide attention as boring, meaningless places where people often have little else to do but wait for the end of their lives. Senility wards in mental hospitals are even worse. One of the shocking things about nursing homes has been the unwillingness of people on the outside to show real concern for what happens in these institutions. Even people who are entrusting a parent to the care of a home rarely ask about the nurse–patient ratio, about the kind of creative facilities or physical therapy equipment available, or even about the frequency of doctors' visits. And the government has provided federal money without enforcing high standards of care. In fact, federal standards were lowered in 1974; therefore, in some sense our concern for the aged seems to be moving backward, not forward.

7. What would be an accurate title for this selection?

   a. Institutional Care for the Elderly: A National Disgrace

   b. The Elderly

   c. Government Support of Nursing Homes

8. Summary sentence: _____

_____

_____

Skill 8: Understanding Graphs and Tables

Sometimes, being a skillful reader means more than just having the ability to read words. It can also mean being able to read the visual information presented in graphs and tables. As a student, you will probably encounter many graphs and tables in your textbooks. Such visual material can help you understand important ideas and details as you read. Knowing graphics will probably also help in your career work as well, for occupations in our computerized age increasingly rely on graphics to convey information.

Graphs and tables present information by using lines, images, or numbers as well as words. They often compare quantities or show how things change over a period of time. Reading a graph or table involves four steps:

- *Step 1: Read the title and any subtitles.* This important first step gives you a concise summary of all the information in the graph or table.

- *Step 2: Read any information at the top, at the bottom, and along the sides.* Such information may include an explanatory key to the material presented. It may also include a series of years, percentages, or figures.

- *Step 3: Ask yourself the purpose of the graph or table.* Usually, the title can be turned into a question beginning with *What, How much* or *many*, or *How.* The purpose of the graph or table is to answer that question.

- *Step 4: Read the graph or table.* As you read, keep in mind the purpose of the material.

Using these four steps, let us analyze the sample graph and table that follow.

Sample Graph

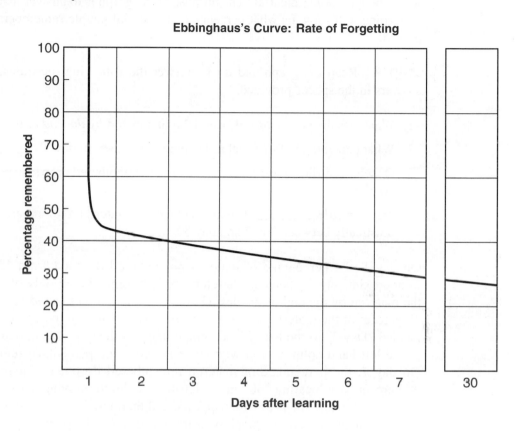

Ebbinghaus's Curve: Rate of Forgetting

Step 1   The title of the graph is "Ebbinghaus's Curve: Rate of Forgetting." Therefore, the information in the graph will show the rate at which people forget material.

Step 2   On one side of the graph is a series of numbers, ranging from 10 to 100 and labeled "Percentage remembered"—this refers to the percentage of material. Along the bottom of the graph is a series of numbers labeled "Days after learning." The numbers are in sequence from 1 to 7; then there is a gap on the graph followed by the number 30. The curved line on the graph will show what percentage of material is remembered on day 1, day 2, and so on—up to day 30.

Step 3   We can turn the title of the graph into the question What is the rate at which people forget material? The purpose of the graph is to answer that question. The graph will show us what percentage of material people remembered as days passed.

Step 4   Read the graph and try to answer the following questions. Put your answers in the spaces provided.

1. What was the percentage of material remembered *by the end of* day 1? _____

2. What percentage of material did people remember on day 3? _____

3. On what day did the percentage of material remembered drop to approximately 30 percent? _____

4. *True or false?* _____ The percentage of material remembered dropped drastically between day 7 and day 30.

On day 1, the percentage of material remembered dropped from 100 percent to approximately 50 percent; therefore, people remembered only 50 percent of the material by the end of the day. On day 3, people remembered approximately 40 percent of the material they had learned. (By moving *up* the graph on the line labeled "Day 3" to the heavy black graph line and then moving *across* the graph to the left-hand column, you will arrive at "40": the percentage remembered.) On day 7, the percentage of material remembered dropped to approximately 30 percent. (By locating "30" in the left-hand column, moving across the graph to the point where the heavy line appears, and then moving down to the series of numbers on the base of the graph, you arrive at day 7.) The percentage of material did not drop drastically between days 7 and 30.

Sample Table

Sound Levels and Human Responses

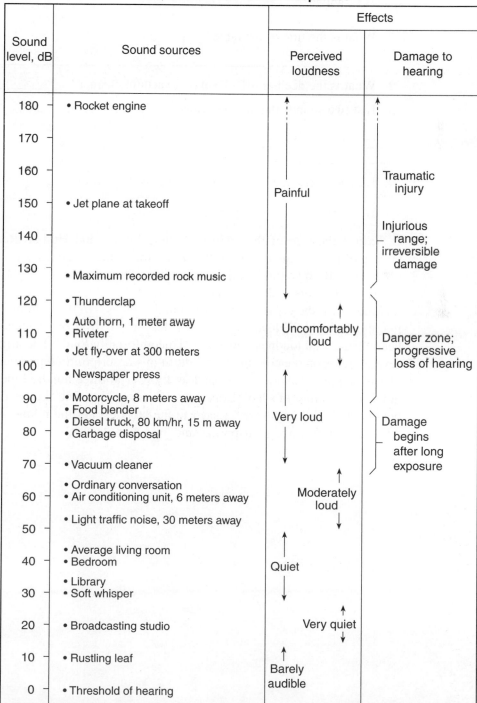

Sound level, dB	Sound sources	Effects	
		Perceived loudness	Damage to hearing
180	• Rocket engine		
170			
160			Traumatic injury
150	• Jet plane at takeoff	Painful	
140			Injurious range; irreversible damage
130	• Maximum recorded rock music		
120	• Thunderclap		
110	• Auto horn, 1 meter away • Riveter • Jet fly-over at 300 meters	Uncomfortably loud	Danger zone; progressive loss of hearing
100	• Newspaper press		
90	• Motorcycle, 8 meters away • Food blender	Very loud	
80	• Diesel truck, 80 km/hr, 15 m away • Garbage disposal		Damage begins after long exposure
70	• Vacuum cleaner		
60	• Ordinary conversation • Air conditioning unit, 6 meters away	Moderately loud	
50	• Light traffic noise, 30 meters away		
40	• Average living room • Bedroom	Quiet	
30	• Library • Soft whisper		
20	• Broadcasting studio	Very quiet	
10	• Rustling leaf	Barely audible	
0	• Threshold of hearing		

Follow the four reading steps listed on page 398, and then answer the following questions about the sample table on the previous page. Put your answers in the spaces provided.

1. What is the title of the table?

    _____

2. What is the decibel (dB) level of a vacuum cleaner? _____

3. List two sounds that are described as "Uncomfortably loud":

    _____

    _____

4. List one item that can lead to hearing damage after long exposure:

    _____

   Since the title of the table is "Sound Levels and Human Responses," the table will answer the question "What are the human responses to various levels of sound?" By reading the information along the top and side of the table, we can locate the answers to the next three questions. We can locate "vacuum cleaner" by looking down the column labeled "Sound sources." In the column to the left, we find the decibel (dB) level of a vacuum cleaner: 70 dB. Looking below the column head "Perceived loudness," we find "Uncomfortably loud." The arrow shows that several items on the column to the left fit this description: thunderclap, auto horn that is one meter away, riveter, and jet fly-over at three hundred meters. Looking down the column labeled "Damage to Hearing," we find the heading "Damage begins after long exposure." Listed to the left of it are the items "food blender," "diesel truck," "garbage disposal," and "vacuum cleaner."

Practice in Reading Graphs and Tables

Activity 1

1. Follow the four reading steps listed on page 398, and then answer the questions about the following graph.

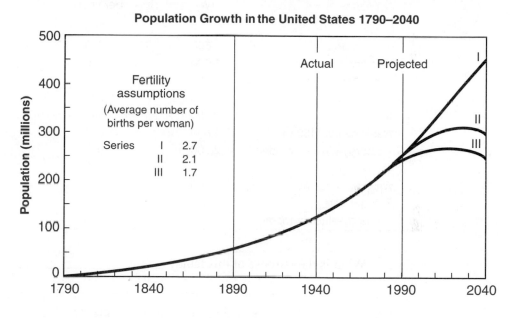

Population Growth in the United States 1790–2040

a. What is the purpose of this graph? _____

_____

b. What (approximately) was the population of the United States in 1940?

_____

c. What (approximately) was the population of the United States in 1990?

_____

d. If we assume that each woman gives birth to 2.7 children between now and 2040, what will the U.S. population be (approximately) in 2040?

_____

e. What will the U.S. population be in 2040 if the projected Series III actually occurs?

_____

2. Follow the four reading steps listed on page 398, and then answer the questions about the following table.

Average Estimated Electrical Energy Use per Year for Typical Household Appliances

Appliance	Power (W)	Average hours used per year	Approximate energy used (kWh/year)
Clock	2	8,760	17
Clothes dryer	4,600	228	1,049
Hair dryer	1,000	60	60
Lightbulb	100	1,080	108
Compact fluorescent	18	1,080	19
Television	350	1,440	504
Water heater (150 L)	4,500	1,044	4,698
Energy-efficient model	2,800	1,044	2,900
Toaster	1,150	48	552
Washing machine	700	144	1,008
Refrigerator	360	6,000	2,160
Energy-efficient model	180	6,000	1,100

a. What is the purpose of this table? _____

_____

b. Which appliance is used for the least hours per year? _____

For the most hours per year? _____

c. Which appliance uses the most energy per year? _____

The least energy per year? _____

d. Which appliance uses more energy per year, a washing machine or a clothes dryer? _____

e. Which appliance is used more, a television or a water heater?

_____

f. About how much energy is saved per year by using an energy-efficient refrigerator instead of a regular model?

____ 100 kW/h ____ 500 kW/h ____ 1,000 kW/h ____ 2,000 kW/h

g. Fill in the blank: A compact fluorescent lightbulb uses as little energy as a *(clock, hair dryer, toaster, regular lightbulb)* _____.

Activity 2

1. Follow the four reading steps listed on page 398, and then answer the questions about the following graph.

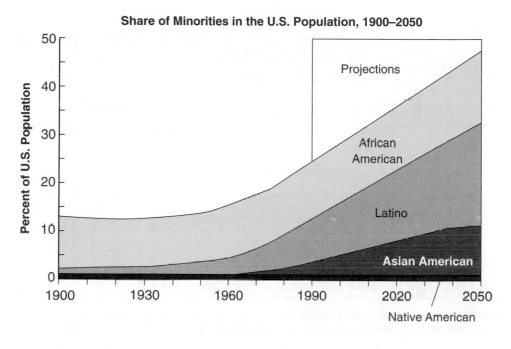

Share of Minorities in the U.S. Population, 1900–2050

a. What is the purpose of the graph? _____

_____

b. In 1900, approximately what percentage of the U.S. population was made up of minorities?

_____ 12 percent _____ 20 percent _____ 30 percent _____ 50 percent

c. By 2050, approximately what percentage of the U.S. population will be made up of minorities?

_____ 12 percent _____ 20 percent _____ 30 percent _____ 50 percent

d. Which minority group will be the largest percentage of the U.S. population in 2050?

_____ African American   _____ Latino

_____ Asian American   _____ Native American

e. Which group will be the smallest percentage of the U.S. population in 2050?

_____ African American   _____ Latino

_____ Asian American   _____ Native American

f. Which group was not a statistically significant percentage of the U.S. population before 1960?

_____ African American   _____ Latino

_____ Asian American   _____ Native American

g. Which *two* groups' shares of the population have remained about the same since 1900?

_____ African American   _____ Latino

_____ Asian American   _____ Native American

2. Follow the four reading steps listed on page 398, and then answer the questions about the following table.

How Different Do Men and Women Think the Sexes Are?

Question: Now I want to ask about some more specific characteristics of men and women. For each one I read, please tell me whether you think it is generally more true of men or more true of women.

Fifteen characteristics most often said to describe men

Fifteen characteristics most often said to describe women

	Total	Opinions of Men	Women		Total	Opinions of Men	Women
1. Aggressive	64%	68%	61%	1. Emotional	81%	79%	83%
2. Strong	61	66	57	2. Talkative	73	73	74
3. Proud	59	62	55	3. Sensitive	72	74	71
4. Disorganized	56	55	57	4. Affectionate	66	69	64
5. Courageous	54	55	53	5. Patient	64	60	68
6. Confident	54	58	49	6. Romantic	60	59	61
7. Independent	50	58	43	7. Moody	58	63	52
8. Ambitious	48	51	44	8. Cautious	57	55	59
9. Selfish	47	49	44	9. Creative	54	48	60
10. Logical	45	53	37	10. Thrifty	52	51	53
11. Easygoing	44	48	40	11. Manipulative	51	54	48
12. Demanding	43	39	46	12. Honest	42	44	41
13. Possessive	42	38	45	13. Critical	42	43	41
14. Funny	40	47	34	14. Happy	39	38	39
15. Levelheaded	39	46	34	15. Possessive	37	43	32

a. What is the purpose of the table? _____

_____

b. Which characteristic do 63 percent of men feel describes women?

_____

c. What percentage of women think that men are disorganized? _____

d. What is the percentage of people (both men and women) who think that creativity is a feminine characteristic? _____

e. What percentage of men think that men are logical? What percentage of women think that men are logical? _____

■ Review Test

1. Study the graph below, and then answer the questions about it.

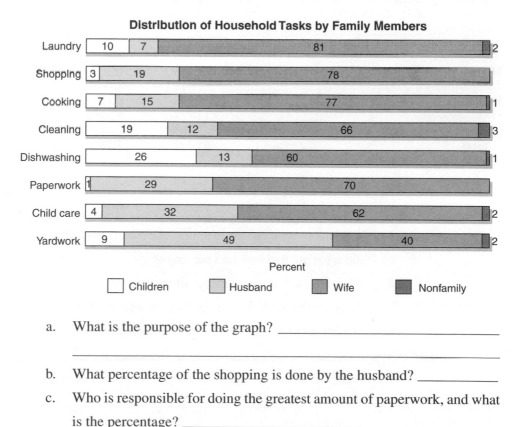

Distribution of Household Tasks by Family Members

Task	Children	Husband	Wife	Nonfamily
Laundry	10	7	81	2
Shopping	3	19	78	
Cooking	7	15	77	1
Cleaning	19	12	66	3
Dishwashing	26	13	60	1
Paperwork	1	29	70	
Child care	4	32	62	2
Yardwork	9	49	40	2

Percent

☐ Children   ☐ Husband   ☐ Wife   ☐ Nonfamily

a. What is the purpose of the graph? _____

_____

b. What percentage of the shopping is done by the husband? _____

c. Who is responsible for doing the greatest amount of paperwork, and what is the percentage? _____

d.   In which area do children contribute the most work, and what is the percentage? _____

e.   What percentage of the cooking is done by nonfamily? _____

f.   What household task is done more by husbands than wives? _____

2. Study the table below, and then answer the questions about it.

Employment and Earnings

| Major Occupation or Longest Job Held | All Workers | | | |
| | Women | | Men | |
	Number (1,000)	Median earnings	Number (1,000)	Median earnings
Executive, administrators, and managerial	6,577	$22,551	9,244	$37,010
Professional specialty	8,814	23,113	8,035	36,942
Technical and related support	2,044	20,312	2,053	28,042
Sales	8,393	7,307	7,871	22,955
Administrative support, including clerical	16,728	14,292	4,141	20,287
Precision production, craft, and repair	1,395	13,377	13,448	22,149
Machine operators, assemblers, and inspectors	3,773	10,983	5,389	19,389
Transportation and material moving	511	10,805	5,056	20,053
Handlers, equipment cleaners, helpers, and laborers	995	8,270	4,885	9,912
Service workers	11,722	5,746	7,801	10,514
Farming, forestry, and fishing	680	3,810	3,548	7,881
Total	**61,732**	**12,250**	**72,348**	**21,522**

a.   What is the purpose of this table? _____
_____

b.   How many women are machine operators, assemblers, and inspectors, and what are their median earnings? _____

c.   What are the median earnings of women who work in sales? _____

d.   What are the median earnings of men who work in sales? _____

e.   In what occupation do the fewest women work? _____
_____

f.   What are the total median earnings of women and the total median earnings of men? _____

Skill 9:
Making Inferences

 You have probably heard the expression "to read between the lines." When you read between the lines, you pick up ideas that are not directly stated. These implied ideas are usually important for a full understanding of what an author means. Discovering the ideas that are not stated directly is called *making inferences* or *drawing conclusions*.

An Introduction to Inferences

You have already practiced making inferences in this book. Do you remember the following sentence from the chapter on vocabulary development? "As a *naive* little boy, I thought elbow grease was something you bought in a store." That sentence does not tell us the meaning of *naive*. But from the general meaning of the sentence, we can infer that *naive* means "unknowing." When you guess what words mean by looking carefully at their context, you are making inferences.

Activity 1

Reread the passage about the influences on the content of dreams, and then answer the inference question that follows.

> There are two strong influences on the content of dreams. One influence is the time of your dream. When you are closest to waking, your dreams are apt to be about recent events. In the middle of the night, however, your dreams are more likely to involve childhood or past events. The other influence on the content of dreams is presleep conditions. In one study, subjects who had six hours of active exercise before sleep tended to have dreams with little physical activity. The researcher concluded that dream content may offset waking experiences to some extent. Other research supports that conclusion. For instance, subjects who had experienced a day of social isolation had dreams with a great amount of social interaction. Also, subjects who had been water-deprived dreamed of drinking.

Which of the following inferences is most soundly supported by the evidence in the passage?

a.   Some people rarely dream.

b.   People don't dream during daytime naps.

c.   A student studying for finals will probably dream about studying.

d.   People who go to bed hungry probably tend to dream of eating.

Explanations

a.   The statement in answer *a* is not supported at all. The passage discusses when and what people dream, not how often.

b.   Statement *b* is also unsupported. Just because the passage doesn't discuss daytime sleeping doesn't mean we don't dream then. Your personal experience, in fact, may tell you that people do dream in the daytime.

c.   According to the passage, dreams don't mirror presleep conditions—they contrast with them. Therefore, a student studying for finals would be less likely to dream about studying.

d.   Answer *d* is most soundly supported by the passage. Because dreams "offset waking experience," a hungry person would tend to dream of eating.

Activity 2

Read the following textbook passage. Then answer the questions about it by circling the letters of the inferences that are most firmly based on the given information.

[1]A twenty-eight-year-old woman named Catherine Genovese was returning home from work one day. [2]Kitty, as she was called by almost everyone in her Queens neighborhood, had just parked her car. [3]Then a man with a knife grabbed her. [4]She screamed, "Oh my God, he stabbed me! [5]Please help me! [6]Please help me!"

[7]For more than half an hour, thirty-eight neighbors watched the killer stalk Kitty. [8]The last time he stabbed her, she was slumped on the foot of the stairs to her apartment. [9]Not one person telephoned the police during the fatal attack. [10]Later, the police gathered statements from the witnesses. [11]Among their comments were "I didn't want to get involved," "We thought it was a lovers' quarrel," and "I was tired. [12]I went back to bed."

1. We can infer that Kitty was attacked

   a.   while she was on vacation.

   b.   in her own neighborhood.

   c.   on her way from work to her car.

2. We can conclude that the man who stabbed Genovese

   a.   was someone she knew.

   b.   intended to kill her.

   c.   was a convicted criminal.

3. We can infer that the witnesses

   a.   might have stopped the attack if they had called the police.

   b.   wanted the man to kill Genovese.

   c.   would not want someone else to get involved if they themselves were being attacked.

Explanations

1. The answer to the first question is *b*. We have solid evidence to conclude that Genovese was attacked in her neighborhood: she was returning home from work and had parked her car. Because she was returning home from work, she was not on vacation. Also, we know she had just parked her car after coming home from work. So the attack could not have taken place before she got into the car to go home.

2. The answer to the second question is *b*. We can conclude that Genovese's attacker wanted to kill her. If his goal was to rob or rape her, he could have done so long before the last time he stabbed her. And no evidence in the passage indicates that Genovese knew her attacker. Finally, although we cannot be sure the attacker was never convicted of a crime, there is absolutely no evidence in the passage to support that conclusion—his past is not referred to at all.

3. The answer to the third question is *a*. The crime took at least a half hour; thus we can conclude that if the police had been called, there is a chance they would have arrived in time to save Genovese. However, we have no reason to believe the witnesses actually wanted the man to kill Genovese. Most people, in fact, would be horrified to see someone stabbed to death. And on the basis of our knowledge of human nature, we can be pretty sure the witnesses would have wanted others to get involved if they were victims.

Guidelines for Making Inferences

The exercises in this chapter provide practice in making careful inferences when you read. Here are three guidelines to that process:

1   Never lose sight of the available information. As much as possible, base your inferences on the facts. For instance, in the paragraph about Kitty Genovese's attack, we are told that she "was returning home from work." On the basis of that fact, we can readily conclude that she was not on vacation.

It's also important to note when a conclusion lacks support. For instance, the idea that the attacker was a convicted criminal has no support in the selection. We are told of only one instance of his criminal behavior, the attack on Genovese.

2   Use your background knowledge, experience, and common sense to help you in making inferences. Our experience with people, for instance, tells us that witnesses would themselves have wanted help if they had been in Genovese's place.

The more you know about a subject, the better your inferences are likely to be. So keep in mind that if your background in a matter is weak, your inferences may be shaky. If you are having problems studying for tests, for example, the inferences of a tutor about what you need to do are likely to be more helpful than those of another student.

3   Consider the alternatives. Don't simply accept the first inference that comes to mind. Instead, consider all the facts of a case and all the possible explanations. For example, the tutor may be aware of many helpful study habits from which to select the best ones for you.

Inferring Purpose and Tone in Reading

An important part of critical reading is to realize that behind everything you read is an author. This author is a person with a reason for writing a given piece and with a personal point of view. To fully understand and evaluate what you read, you must recognize **purpose**—the reason the author writes. You must also be aware of **tone**—the expression of the author's attitude and feeling. Learning an author's purpose and tone requires inference skills.

Purpose in Reading

Authors write with a purpose in mind, and you can better evaluate what is being said by inferring what that purpose is. Three common purposes are

- To inform—to give information about a subject. Authors with this purpose wish to give their readers facts. The following sentence, for instance, was written to inform: "Chocolate is a product of the seed of the cacao tree of Central and South America." The author is simply communicating factual information about chocolate.

- To persuade—to convince the reader to agree with the author's point of view on a subject. Authors with this purpose may give facts, but their main goal is to promote an opinion. This sentence is intended to persuade: "It's about time that our company created a policy of not testing products on animals." The author wishes to persuade people in the company to support a policy of not using animals in testing.

- To entertain—to amuse and delight; to appeal to the reader's senses and imagination. Authors with this purpose entertain in various ways, through fiction and nonfiction. Here's an example of something written to entertain: "My boss is so dumb he once returned a necktie because it was too tight." The exaggerated point of the anecdote is meant mainly to amuse.

Activity 1

Read each of the three selections below and decide whether the author's main purpose is to inform, to persuade, or to entertain. Write what you think is the purpose of each selection in the space provided. Then read the explanations that follow.

1. You must take responsibility to ensure your children's success in school. You should read to your children and also let them see you reading and enjoying books. Then they will approach reading as something fun and desirable.

   Purpose: _____

2. During the Civil War, Clara Barton worked as a volunteer nursing the wounded and sick, often during a battle. Soldiers called her the "angel of the battlefield."

   Purpose: _____

3. I don't know which is harder, taking my body to the doctor or my car to the garage. Both worry me. I'm always afraid they'll find something I didn't know about. The only advantage to taking my body to the doctor over taking my car to the garage is that the doctor never asks me to leave it overnight.

Purpose: _____

Explanations   The purpose of the first paragraph is to persuade parents to give children a head start in learning. The author is trying to encourage parents to contribute to their children's mental development. In contrast, the main purpose of the second item is to inform—it provides information about Clara Barton. The author does not hope that the reader will do or favor anything. In the third passage, the playful comparison between a car and the author's body tells us that the author's main goal is to entertain with humor.

Tone in Reading

A writer's tone reveals the attitude he or she has toward a subject. Tone is expressed through the words and details the writer selects. Just as a speaker's voice can project a range of feelings, a writer's voice can project one or more tones, or feelings: anger, sympathy, hopefulness, sadness, respect, dislike, and so on. Understanding tone is, then, an important part of understanding what an author has written. To infer tone, you must take into account the author's message and choice of words.

To appreciate the differences in tones that writers can use, read the following statements of people who have won a sports event:

"I'm grateful to have won this medal for running. My opponents are wonderful athletes, and I was lucky to beat them today." (Tones: modest, humble; generous)

"Hand over that medal. I've passed the test, and I'm the best." (Tones: arrogant, haughty; humorous, amusing)

"Oh, my God. I won, I won. I can't believe it." (Tones: excited, thrilled; shocked, disbelieving)

Following is a list of words commonly used to describe tone. Note that two different words may refer to the same tone or similar tones—for example, matter-of-fact and objective, or comic and humorous. Brief meanings are given in parentheses for some of the words.

Note   Most of the words in this box reflect a feeling or judgment. In contrast, matter-of-fact (sticking to the facts) and objective (without prejudice, not affected by personal feelings) describe communication that does not express personal bias or feeling.

A List of Words That Describe Tone

objective	matter-of-fact
modest	humble
generous	appreciative
kind	humorous
amusing	confident
surprised	lighthearted
excited	thrilled
sentimental	shocked
disbelieving	uncertain
anxious	depressed
critical	bitter
encouraging	confident
tolerant	sympathetic

arrogant (*conceited*)

optimistic (*looking on the bright side of things*)

pessimistic (*looking on the gloomy side of things*)

ironic (*meaning the opposite of what is expressed*)

sarcastic (*making sharp or wounding remarks; ironic*)

scornful (*looking down on someone or something*)

revengeful (*wanting to hurt someone in return for an injury*)

A Note on Irony   One commonly used tone is that of irony. When writing has an ironic tone, it says one thing but means the opposite. Irony is found in everyday conversation as well as in writing. Following are two examples; notice that the quotation in each says the opposite of what is meant.

> After eating a greasy hamburger with French fries and a few beers, someone might say, "Wow, I'm feeling healthier already."

> A fan might say of Whitney Houston, "Poor woman, born without looks or a singing voice."

Irony also refers to situations in which what happens is the opposite of what we might expect. We could call it ironic, for example, if a man bites a dog. Writing is said to be ironic when it describes such situations. Here are a couple of examples of this type of irony:

A gangster who had many bodyguards to protect him from rivals died by slipping in the bathtub and drowning.

After shopping all day for a special party dress, Emily ended up buying the very first one she had tried on.

Activity 2

Below are three statements expressing different attitudes about a difficult final test. Three different tones are used:

objective	confident	ironic

For each statement, write the tone that you think is present, and then read the explanations.

1. My history final is sure to be lots of fun, and it will last for only three hours.

    _____

2. The history final will include an essay section and a multiple-choice section.

    _____

3. I've kept up with assignments all semester, and I've reviewed all of the important material. So I should do pretty well on my history final.

    _____

Explanations

1. Item 1 has an ironic tone. The speaker is saying the opposite of what he means. He really means that the test will not be fun and that it will last entirely too long.

2. In item 2, the speaker communicates only facts about the test. She reveals no point of view—positive or negative—about those facts. Thus we can say that the speaker's tone is objective.

3. We can describe the tone of item 3 as confident—the speaker is confident about doing well on the final.

Practice in Making Inferences

Activity 1

Read each of the following passages. Then circle the letter of the most logical answer to each question, based on the information given in the passage.

A.   [1]When Oprah Winfrey was a child, she lived with her mother and two younger half-siblings in a Milwaukee apartment without electricity or running water. [2]One Christmas Eve, her mother told her there would be no celebration that year. [3]There was no money to buy presents. [4]"But what about Santa Claus?" Oprah asked. [5]Her mother answered that there wasn't enough money to pay Santa to come. [6]As she went to bed that night, Oprah dreaded the following day. [7]She knew the neighborhood children would be outside playing with their toys and comparing presents. [8]She tried to think of a story she could tell the other kids to explain why she had nothing. [9]Then she heard the doorbell ring. [10]Three nuns had come to the apartment. [11]They brought a turkey, a fruit basket, and toys for the children. [12]"I've never had a stronger feeling of someone lifting me up," she says today. [13]"Their kindness made me feel so much better about myself." [14]Oprah remembers that Christmas as the best she ever had.

1. We can infer that before the nuns came, Oprah dreaded the next day because she

   a.   would not have any new toys to play with at home.

   b.   now knew Santa Claus was not real.

   c.   would be shamed in front of her friends.

2. We can conclude this was Oprah's best Christmas because

   a.   she was so relieved and grateful for what the nuns had done.

   b.   the toys she received were exactly what she had wanted.

   c.   she had never received Christmas presents before.

3. What can we infer Oprah would most likely have done the next day if the nuns had not come?

   a.   She would have been angry and hostile toward her mother.

   b.   She would have made up a lie about the presents somehow being delayed.

   c.   She would have gone out and stolen some toys.

B.   ¹Beware! ²Right now, a movie filled with blood, gore, and severed body parts is on its way to a theater near you. ³The movie's title doesn't matter. ⁴It will follow the same plot as the countless other "slash and gore" movies that have come before it. ⁵These movies are easy to spot. ⁶All involve young, attractive teens having sex and then getting sliced and diced. ⁷The chopping is usually done by an evil villain with bad teeth and a deep, threatening laugh. ⁸And if one of these movies does well at the box office, a sequel will be made— usually with an even larger dose of gore and butchery. ⁹Such movies manage to draw large audiences because they offer date-night appeal. ¹⁰People tend to hold, squeeze, and grab each other when they're scared. ¹¹These movies also offer some privacy to teens intent on making out. ¹²Any sensible adult wouldn't be caught dead at one of these movies.

1. We can conclude that the movies to which the author refers

   a.   attract only adults.

   b.   are uninteresting to teens.

   c.   attract teens.

2. We can infer that the author of the passage feels that the audience of horror movies

   a.   likes to be scared at the movies.

   b.   does not like to be scared at the movies.

   c.   is never scared at the movies.

3. We can infer that the author of the paragraph feels the "slash and gore" plots are generally

   a.   harmful to audiences.

   b.   surprising.

   c.   not very creative.

Activity 2

A.   In the space provided, indicate whether the primary purpose of each sentence is to inform (I), to persuade (P), or to entertain (E).

_____   1. In a country as wealthy as ours, 40 percent of the nation's children should not be living in poverty.

_____   2. Almost all of Antarctica is covered with a sheet of ice about 6,500 feet thick.

_____   3. Do you know where to find the most fish? Between the head and the tail.

B.   Each of the following passages illustrates one of the tones in the box below. In the space provided, put the letter of the tone that applies to each passage. Two tones will not be used.

a. depressed	c. optimistic
b. sentimental	d. sarcastic

_____   4. Let me list some of the reasons I'm happy that my sister Sophie is marrying Tom "Big Shot" Lewis. First, Tom is such a considerate human being. He realizes that doing conventional "nice" things, like remembering his girlfriend's birthday or giving her a Christmas present, would just distract her from the important things in life, like ironing his shirts. Secondly, he's got such potential. It's true that he's not working now; in fact, since we've known him he hasn't held a job for more than two months. But I'm sure any day now his plan to become a traveling disk jockey is going to materialize. Then he'll be able to pay Sophie back all the money she's loaned him.

_____   5. Since I flunked out of school, I haven't felt interested in much of anything. I guess I should be looking for a job or reapplying for admission, but I don't have the energy. I don't know why I did so badly last term. It's not that the work was that hard. I just couldn't concentrate on any of my subjects. After a while it was so much easier to stay in bed than make the effort to get to class. Some of my teachers really tried to help me, but I didn't have much to say to them. They probably think I hate them, but I don't. I just wasn't worth the time they were taking with me.

■ **Review Test**

A. Read the passage and then circle the letter of the most logical answer to each question, based on the information given in the passage.

> [1]The British prime minister Winston Churchill was a master of the elegant put-down. [2]At one fancy dinner party, he was seated next to a favorite target—a woman whose political views were opposed to his own. [3]The two argued more or less continually throughout the meal. [4]Totally annoyed, the lady said, "Sir Winston, if you were my husband, I'd put poison in your coffee!" [5]"Madam," replied Churchill, "if you were my wife, I'd drink it."

1. We can conclude that Churchill

  a. constantly put people down.

  b. liked to put down his political opponents.

  c. was rarely invited to fancy dinner parties.

2. When Churchill said, "If you were my wife, I'd drink it," he meant to imply that

  a. he admired the woman so much he would do whatever she said.

  b. he would never insult the woman by refusing her coffee.

  c. if she were his wife, he would prefer to die.

3. We can conclude that the author of the passage admires

  a. Churchill's politics.

  b. the woman's politics.

  c. Churchill's wit.

B. In the space provided, indicate whether the primary purpose of each sentence is to inform (I), to persuade (P), or to entertain (E).

____   6. The ZIP in zip code stands for the national Zoning Improvement Plan.

____   7. More money should be spent on buying our city police officers up-to-date weapons.

____   8. It's easy to quit smoking; I've done it hundreds of times.

C. Each of the following passages illustrates one of the tones in the box below. In the space provided, put the letter of the tone that applies to each passage. Two tones will not be used.

a. encouraging	c. pessimistic
b. critical	d. tolerant

_____ 9. A successful doctor is scheduled to operate on a patient at 8 A.M., but it has snowed during the night, and driving is difficult. Do you think the doctor will stay home in bed? Not if he or she is professional. This attitude of professionalism is the key to being a successful college student, too. And it is within your reach, no matter how well or how poorly you have done in school up until now. You cannot undo the past, but you can adopt an attitude of professionalism from now on. All you have to do is intend to take school seriously, and the rest will follow. By attending classes, turning in assignments on time, and coming prepared for tests, you will gradually build your skills.

_____ 10. Parents who do not read to their children often excuse themselves by claiming a lack of time. But with few exceptions, their failure to read is a matter of priorities. Most parents find the time to put in a full workday, take a full complement of coffee breaks, eat lunch and dinner, read the newspaper, watch the nightly newscast or ball game, do the dishes, talk on the phone for thirty minutes (mostly about nothing), run to the store for a pack of cigarettes or a lottery ticket, drive to the mall, and never miss that favorite prime-time show. Somehow they find the time for those things—important or unimportant as they are—but can't find time to read to a child, which is much more important than all the other items on a leisure priority list.

Skill 10:
Thinking Critically

Here in a nutshell is what you need to do to become a better reader and thinker: You need to understand clearly the relationship between a point and its support. The **point** is the main idea that a writer is making. The **support** is the evidence that is given to back up this idea. A critical thinker is one who can look at an argument—a point and its support—and decide whether the support is solid or not.

Look at the following point:

Point: Our meal in that new restaurant was unpleasant.

Is there support for this point? Is the person thinking clearly and logically? Let's say the person then goes on to provide the following details:

1. Our meal took forty-five minutes to arrive.

2. The chicken we ordered was tough, and the rice and vegetables were cold.

3. The dessert choices were limited to stale cake and watery Jell-O.

As you can see, the details provide solid support for the point. They give us a basis for understanding and agreeing with the point. In light of the details, we would not be eager to eat at that restaurant.

But what if the person had provided these reasons for saying the meal at the restaurant was unpleasant?

1. We had to wait fifteen minutes for the food to arrive.

2. The chicken we ordered was too juicy, and the vegetables were buttery.

3. The dozen dessert choices did not include my favorite, carrot cake.

We might question whether the above reasons for not liking the restaurant are good ones. To have to wait fifteen minutes is not so bad. Many people would like their chicken juicy and their vegetables buttery, and they would appreciate having a dozen dessert choices.

When evidence is provided, we have a chance to be both logical and critical thinkers: to evaluate for ourselves whether there is enough valid evidence in support of a point. If the reasons above were the only ones given, we might decide to try the restaurant for ourselves.

Practice in Evaluating Arguments

1 Recognizing Point and Support

This first activity will sharpen your sense of the relationship between a point and its support.

Activity 1

In each group of statements, one statement is the point, and the other statement or statements are support for the point. Circle the point in each group.

1. a. Cats refuse to learn silly tricks just to amuse people.
   b. Cats are more sensible than dogs.
   c. Dogs will accept cruel mistreatment, but if a cat is mistreated, it will run away.

2. a. A television is always blaring in one corner of the lounge.
   b. The student lounge is not a place for quiet study.
   c. There are always people there talking loudly to each other.

3. a. High schools need to teach personal finance skills.
   b. Many young people do not know how to budget their money.
   c. More and more people are getting into serious credit-card debt.

4. a. Exercising increases one's sense of well-being and relieves stress.
   b. There are simple ways to manage stress in one's life.
   c. Saying "No" when one's schedule is full keeps stress levels under control.
   d. Getting support from family and friends makes stress more manageable.

5. a. Speaking before a group is a problem for many people.
   b. Stage fright, stammering, and blushing are frequent reactions.
   c. When people are asked to rank their worst fears, they often list public speaking as even worse than death.
   d. Some of us will pretend to be ill so that we do not have to speak publicly.

6. a. It is more economical to cook for yourself than to rely on expensive prepared foods.
   b. When you cook for yourself, you can avoid preservatives and control the amount of fat, sugar, and salt in your food.

    c.   Cooking is a satisfying activity that can draw the family together.

    d.   Cooking is a valuable skill to acquire.

7. a.   People may get irritable and out of sorts because they are eating and drinking too much.

    b.   Old rivalries and tensions between some family members may come to the surface.

    c.   Family celebrations at holiday time can be a strain.

    d.   Expectations for warmth and good cheer are often too high.

8. a.   One diet consists only of water and nine potatoes a day.

    b.   Another diet allows participants to eat only hard-boiled eggs.

    c.   A clever diet permits dieters to eat all they want—but only of foods they hate.

    d.   In their quest to lose weight, people have come up with some strange diets.

9. a.   Almost half of the stores in the shopping mall are empty.

    b.   A deathly hush fills the mall.

    c.   That shopping mall is a depressing place.

    d.   Unhappy-looking store owners stare out at the few passing shoppers.

10. a.   No one knows why we sleep.

    b.   No one knows why we dream when we sleep.

    c.   Large portions of the brain have no apparent function.

    d.   Some basic parts of human life remain mysterious.

2 Identifying Logical Support I

Once you identify a point and its support, you need to decide if the support really applies to the point. The critical thinker will ask, "Is this support logical? Or is it beside the point?" In their enthusiasm to advance a point, people often bring up support that does not apply. For example, a student may wish to make the point that her English instructor is a poor teacher. To support that point, the student may say, "He speaks so softly I can hardly hear him. In addition, he wears ridiculous clothes." A critical thinker will realize that, although a soft voice may in fact interfere with an instructor's effectiveness, what the instructor wears has nothing to do with how well he teaches. The first reason for disliking the English teacher is logical and relevant support, but the second reason is beside the point.

The following activity will sharpen your ability to decide whether evidence truly supports a point. It will help you become a critical reader who can ask and answer the question Is there logical support for the point? Read the point and the three items of "support" that follow. Then circle the letter of the one item that provides logical support for the point.

> **Point:** That woman on the news was courageous.
>
> **Support:**
>
> a. She collected bags of canned and boxed food for months and then brought it to the Golden Door Soup Kitchen to be used for Thanksgiving. Thanks to her efforts, the soup kitchen was able to feed five hundred more people this year than last. That number includes over a hundred children.
>
> b. She had at hand all the facts and figures to back up her statements, citing three different studies by experts in the field. She handled the reporter's questions with ease and confidence.
>
> c. When she saw the child being attacked, she went to his aid without a moment's hesitation. She ran up shouting "Let him go!" and then kicked the ferocious pit bull as hard as she could. When the dog released the child, she grabbed the boy and pushed him to safety, even as the dog turned on her.

Explanation

> a. The information here tells us that this woman was kind and generous with her time. However, nothing she did required her to face danger, so no courage was required. You should not have chosen this item. It is about generosity, not courage.
>
> b. The woman described here showed mastery of her subject and skill in being interviewed, but neither demands great courage. You should not have chosen this item either.
>
> c. The woman referred to here put herself in danger to help a child. Clearly, to do so, she had to be courageous. If you circled the letter of this item, you were correct.

Activity 2

Below is a point followed by three clusters of information. Circle the letter of the one item that provides logical support for the point.

1. **Point:** Greg is irresponsible.

   a. He gives up his bus seat to elderly commuters. When he sees people carrying heavy packages or struggling with squirming children, he rushes to open doors to help them out.

   b. He never pays his bills on time. When he borrows things, he returns them damaged, or not at all. He is usually late for appointments, if he even remembers them at all.

   c. No matter how much trouble I'm having with my English assignment, he refuses to do any of it for me. He says that between his own homework and his job, he doesn't have time. But he always gets B's, and I have trouble getting C's. Furthermore, when I need someone to cover for me at work so that I can see my girlfriend, he's always too busy with something else to help me out.

2. **Point:** That child is very curious.

   a. He was reciting the alphabet when he was only three years old. By age seven, he was doing math at a fourth-grade level. He skipped third and fifth grades.

   b. His favorite word is "NO!" He doesn't start picking up his toys until the fifth or sixth time he is told. Mealtime is a battle to get him to eat properly.

   c. He has taken apart all the clocks in the house to see how they work. He borrowed his father's hammer to break rocks because he "wanted to see what they looked like inside." He is forever asking *how* and *why*.

3. **Point:** Lola is self-centered.

   a. She'll avoid a party invitation to stay home and curl up with a good book. At times, she's so quiet, people forget she's there. When her best friend tried out for the lead in the play, Lola was content to work quietly behind the scenes.

   b. Any time we talk, I hear all about her life, but she never even asks what's new with me. She makes her boyfriend take her to dance clubs and sci-fi movies, but she'll never go to hockey games with him. Every year she throws a birthday party for herself, yet she never even sends her best friends a card on their birthdays.

c. She spends much of her time assisting her grandparents. Several days each week, she takes a bus to their home to help them clean and take care of their house. Many days, she cooks them dinner and talks to them about times when her mother was a child.

3 Identifying Logical Support II

This activity will also develop your skill in thinking clearly about logical support for a given point. Below is a point followed by five statements. Three of the statements logically support the point; two of the statements do not. In the spaces provided, write the letters of the three logical statements of support.

Point: English 102 was the hardest course I ever took.

a. The course included a research paper, five essays, three oral reports, and two major exams.

b. The course was required for my major.

c. The teacher called on students without warning and deducted points when they didn't know an answer.

d. The teacher has been at the school for over twenty years.

e. On average, I had to do at least three hours of homework for every hour in class.

Items that logically support the point: _____   _____   _____

Now read the following comments on the five statements to see which ones you should have chosen and why.

Explanation   The fact that a course is required doesn't make it more difficult, so answer *b* does not support the point. Answer *d* does not support the point either—how long a teacher has been at a school has nothing to do with how hard the course is. So you should have chosen answers *a*, *c*, and *e*. Each one tells about a different difficulty experienced in taking the course.

Activity 3

Each point is followed by three statements that provide logical support and two that do not. In the spaces, write the letters of the three logical statements of support.

1. **Point:** I'm a perfect example of someone who has "math anxiety."

   a.   Fear of math is almost as widespread as fear of public speaking.

   b.   I feel dread every time I sit down to take our Friday math quiz.

   c.   During the math midterm, I "froze" and didn't even try to answer most of the questions.

   d.   I also have a great deal of anxiety when I sit down to write a paper.

   e.   I turned down a job as a salesclerk because I would have had to figure out how much change customers should get back.

   Items that logically support the point: _____ _____ _____

2. **Point:** My kids are getting into the spirit of Halloween.

   a.   Today I found a plastic spider in my soup.

   b.   Last night there was a bloody rubber hand on my pillow.

   c.   Today a cardboard tombstone with my name on it appeared in the backyard.

   d.   My kids also like to decorate the house on Thanksgiving.

   e.   The other day, my oldest daughter said she was too old to go trick-or-treating.

   Items that logically support the point: _____ _____ _____

3. **Point:** Schools should eliminate the summer vacation.

   a.   It costs too much money for school buildings to remain empty in the summer months.

   b.   Children have more energy than adults.

   c.   Year-round school can better prepare students for year-round work in the adult world.

   d.   During summer classes, schools should be air-conditioned.

   e.   Children will learn more if they attend school twelve months a year.

   Items that logically support the point: _____ _____ _____

4 Determining a Logical Point

This activity will develop your ability to come to a logical conclusion. You will look closely at supporting evidence and then decide what point is well supported by that evidence. The skill of making a reasonable judgment based on the information presented is a significant part of clear thinking. Look at the following three items of support:

Support

- Most catalogs have a wide range of high-quality products in choices of colors, styles, sizes, and so forth.
- Catalog products can be ordered over the phone.
- The leading catalogs take pride in delivering their products on time and accepting returns for any reason.

Point: Now see if you can circle the letter of the point that is logically supported by the above evidence:

a. Catalogs offer better-quality products than stores do.

b. Ordering from a catalog can be a convenient way of shopping.

c. Catalogs provide a bigger choice of colors, styles, and sizes than stores do.

d. People should stop shopping in stores.

Explanation

a. The support doesn't compare the quality of catalog products with store products, so you should not have chosen this item.

b. The supporting statements do tell us that shopping by catalog is convenient: It can be done over the phone, delivery is on time, and goods can be returned. The support also tells us that high-quality products are available from most catalogs. This is the statement that is adequately and logically supported, so it is the one you should have chosen.

c. The supporting statements do not compare the choices available through catalogs with those in stores. You shouldn't have chosen this point.

d. The benefits given in the statements of support are not sufficient to support this point. For example, there may be items at a store that are not available through a catalog. Or a store may be offering an item on sale at a price that is cheaper than the catalog price. You should not have chosen this point either.

Activity 4

For each group, read the three items of supporting evidence. Then circle the letter of the point that is most logically supported by that evidence.

Group 1

Support

- Dozens of angry bees attacked people sitting at the picnic table.
- A rain shower made all the food soggy and wet.
- Nearby kids threw a football onto the table, spilling all the drinks.

Point: The point of the above support is:

     a.   Picnics can be a fun way to spend an afternoon.

     b.   The picnic was a disaster.

     c.   Kids should be careful when they play outdoors.

     d.   Everyone loves picnics.

Group 2

Support

- When my dad was called out of town, the man who lives on the corner collected the mail and paper for him every day.
- The young man in the house across the street always shovels my dad's sidewalk when it snows.
- Whenever my dad's car is in the garage for repairs, one of his next-door neighbors drives him around until he gets his car back.

Point: The point of the above support is:

     a.   My dad is nice to his neighbors.

     b.   Neighbors are often very nosy.

     c.   My dad has good neighbors.

     d.   My dad can't do anything for himself.

Group 3

Support

- Before underground plumbing, city people dumped raw sewage out of their windows and into the streets.

- In the days when city vehicles were horse-drawn, manure was piled high in the roadways.

- Before trash collection was available, pigs were set loose in city streets to eat the garbage thrown there.

Point: The point of the above support is:

a.   Cities of the past were probably pleasant places to live.

b.   Cities of the past were not all that different from today's cities.

c.   Cities of the past were troubled with crime.

d.   Cities of the past were very dirty.

■ Review Test

A.   In each of the following groups, one statement is the point, and the other statements are support for the point. Circle the point in each group.

Group 1

a.   My husband is a vegetarian.

b.   My mother, who lives with us, can't digest certain vegetables.

c.   One of my children is allergic to milk, wheat, and eggs.

d.   My family is difficult to cook for.

Group 2

a.   Each year, Americans spend billions of dollars buying cold medications.

b.   Colds cause American business to lose millions of hours of work every year.

c.   The average child misses a week of school each year due to colds.

d.   The common cold has a powerful effect on the nation.

B.   Below is a point followed by three clusters of information. Circle the letter of the one item that provides logical support for the point.

Point: Margo is a very rude worker.

a.   She can barely stay awake while at work. Almost every day, she arrives at the store a half hour late. Her lunch breaks usually lasts twenty minutes longer than anyone else's. She apologizes each time she does something wrong, but she never stops.

b.   She keeps customers waiting while she talks with a coworker. When someone asks her about a sale item, she snaps, "If it isn't on the shelf, we don't have it!" When her boss isn't watching her, she answers the telephone by saying, "Yeah, what do you want?"

c.   She can answer the phone, ring up a customer's purchases, and count large amounts of money all at the same time. She often volunteers to help customers bring their bags to their cars. She does not mind taking time to answer a customer's question or help someone stock a shelf.

C.   The point below is followed by three statements that provide logical support and two that do not. In the spaces, write the letters of the three logical statements of support.

Point: People should be careful when buying used cars.

a.   Many used cars do not come with a guarantee, so you will have to pay if something breaks.

b.   Used cars are much cheaper than brand-new ones.

c.   A used car may have serious mechanical problems and still look fine on the outside.

d.   Some used cars come with a guarantee and are nearly as reliable as new cars.

e.   Used cars whose past owners did not take care of them are more likely to develop problems.

Items that logically support the point: _____ _____ _____

D. Read the three items of supporting evidence below. Then circle the letter of the point that is most logically supported by that evidence.

Support

- A book can be carried anywhere and needs no power source, unlike a laptop computer or other electronic reading device, which needs to be charged every few hours.
- Reading and feeling the actual pages of a book and seeing its illustrations can have a more profound effect on you than seeing the book on a computer screen.
- Books are much cheaper to buy, use, and replace than computers are.

Point: The point of the above support is:

a. Computers still are more expensive to use than books.

b. A book is able to store a great deal of information.

c. Books have certain advantages over computers.

d. Computers will never replace television sets.

Part Five
Skim Reading and Comprehension

Preview

Part Five shows you how to do skimming, or selective reading. You will read quickly through a series of selections, looking for and writing down what seem to be important ideas. To locate the important ideas, you will be asked to apply several of the comprehension skills that you learned in Part Four. Each article or textbook chapter that you skim-read and take notes on will be timed, and you will check your performance by answering questions on the selections afterward. Through a progress chart, you will be able to measure both your skim-reading rate and your comprehension score for each selection.

Introduction

One of the chief myths that students believe about reading is that they must read every word. Consider, though, that the average textbook contains about six hundred pages, or more than 350,000 words. If students have several textbooks and try to read every word of every assignment, they are likely to have little time left to study what they have read—let alone to attend to the essentials of their everyday lives!

Fortunately, not every word in a book must be read, nor must every detail be learned. The purpose of this part of the book is to give you practice in *skimming,* or selective reading. In skimming, you do not read every word; instead, you go quickly and selectively through a passage, looking for and marking off important ideas but skipping secondary material. You can then go back later to read more closely and take notes on important points.

Skim reading will help you when you do not need to read every word of every assignment. Skim reading will also help make you a flexible reader, and this should be your final reading goal. Flexible readers, depending on their purpose in reading and the nature of the material, are able to practice several different kinds of reading: study reading (using the skills learned in Part Four), rapid reading (the concern of Part Six), and skim reading—the subject of this part of the book.

How to Skim-Read

To skim-read effectively, you must be able to apply several of the comprehension skills you learned in Part Four. You must know how to do the following things:

1   *Find definitions:* Remember that they are often signaled by special type, especially *italics*. Look also for one example that makes a definition clear to you.

2   *Locate enumerations:* And remember that locating a numbered series of items is helpful only if you know what *label* the series fits under. So be sure to look for a clear heading for each enumeration.

3   *Look for relationships between headings and subheadings:* Such relationships are often the key to basic enumerations. And when it seems appropriate, you will also want to *change headings into questions* and find the answers to the questions.

4   *Look for emphasis words and main ideas:* If time permits, look for points marked by emphasis words and for main ideas in what seem to be key paragraphs.

•   What is one of the chief myths about reading? _____
_____

•   What is often a real alternative to reading every word of a selection?
_____

•   What are three skills to practice when you are skim reading?

1.   _____

2.   _____

3.   _____

The five reading selections that follow will give you practice in skim reading. You will have a limited amount of time to (1) read and (2) take notes on each selection. At the end of a time period, you will be asked questions about important ideas in the selection, and you can use your notes to answer the questions. You should do well on the quizzes if you have been able to quickly pick out and write down main ideas.

The timed practice will have several benefits. It will teach you skim reading, improve your note-taking and handwriting efficiency, and help you solidify the comprehension skills you practiced in Part Four. By using the progress chart on page 457, you will be able to measure your performance as you move through the selections.

Selection 1

You have ten minutes to skim the following selection for its main points and to take notes on those points. Be sure to time yourself or have your instructor time you as you read and take notes on the selection.

Hint   Definitions and a major enumeration are the keys to the important points in this selection.

Visual Assertion

"Actions speak louder than words" may be an overworn phrase, but it's still true. If you mean what you say, your nonverbal behavior will back up your statements. On the other hand, the most assertive words will lose their impact if expressed in a hesitant, indirect manner. All the following visual elements can be part of assertive communication.

Eye Contact

Inadequate eye contact is usually interpreted in a negative way as anxiety, dishonesty, shame, boredom, or embarrassment. Even when they are not aware of a person's insufficient eye contact, others will often react unconsciously to it by either avoiding or taking advantage of the person exhibiting it. Don't go overboard and begin to stare down everyone you meet—this will just be as distracting as the other extreme—but do be sure to keep your gaze direct.

Distance

Choosing the correct distance between yourself and another person is an important ingredient of assertion. The anthropologist Edward Hall has outlined four distinct distances used by Americans in differing situations. *Intimate distance* ranges from the surface of the skin to about eighteen inches. As its name implies, it is appropriately used for private purposes: expressions of affection, protection, and anger. *Personal distance* runs from eighteen inches to approximately four feet and is used with people we know well and feel relaxed with. As Hall states, this is the range at which we keep someone "at arm's length," suggesting that while there is relatively high involvement here, the immediacy is not as great as that which occurs within intimate distance. *Social distance* ranges from four to twelve feet and is generally appropriate in less personal settings: meeting strangers, engaging in impersonal business transactions, and so on. This is the range at which job interviews are often conducted, customers are approached by salespeople, or newcomers are introduced to us by a third party. We often accuse someone who ought to be using social distance but instead moves into our personal space of being "pushy." Finally, Hall labels as *public distance* the space extending outward from twelve feet. As its name implies, public distance is used in highly impersonal settings and occasions involving larger numbers of people: classrooms, public performances, and so on. Be sure you are using the appropriate range for the message you want to express.

Facial Expression

In the typical assertiveness training group, one or two participants will express confusion as to why they have such trouble being taken seriously. They claim to use the appropriate language, keep eye contact, stand at the proper distance, and so on. When asked to demonstrate how they usually express themselves, the problem often becomes apparent: the facial expression is totally inappropriate to the message. Many communicators, for example, verbally express their dissatisfaction while smiling as if nothing were wrong. Others claim to share approval or appreciation while wearing expressions more appropriate for viewing a corpse.

Gestures and Posture

Like facial expressions, your movements and body positioning can either contribute to or detract from the immediacy of a message. Fidgeting hands, nervous shifting from one foot to another, or slumped shoulders will reduce or even contradict the impact of an assertive message. On the other hand, gestures that are appropriate to the words being spoken and a posture that suggests involvement in the subject will serve to reinforce your words. Watch an effective storyteller, an interviewer, an actor, or some other model and note the added emphasis he or she gives to a message.

Body Orientation

Another way of expressing your attitude is through the positioning of your body in relation to another person. Facing someone head-on communicates a much higher degree of immediacy than does a less direct positioning. In fact, a directly confronting stance in which the face, shoulders, hips, and feet squarely face the other is likely to be interpreted as indicating an aggressive attitude. (To verify this impression, think of the stance used by a baseball player who is furious with an umpire's decision or a Marine drill instructor facing a recruit.) Observation for assertive models will show that the most successful body orientation for most settings is a modified frontal one, in which the communicators are slightly angled away from a direct confrontation—perhaps ten to thirty degrees. This position clearly suggests a high degree of involvement, yet allows occasional freedom from total eye contact, which you have already learned is not to be desired.

When the ten minutes are up, try to answer the questions on page 458 by referring to your notes but *not* referring to the text.

Selection 2

You have ten minutes to skim the following textbook selection for its main points and to take notes on those points.

Science and the Search for Truth

A pathologist after elaborate preparation places a slide under the microscope and adjusts the lens carefully. Members of a Purari war party watch carefully as they place their canoe in the water, for unless it rocks, the raid will not be successful. A man steps from a new station wagon, cuts a forked twig, and carries it around holding it above the ground, while a well-drilling crew stands by, waiting to drill where the twig tells them water will be found. A woman in Peoria, anxious over her teenage daughter, prays to God for guidance. A physician leafs through the pages of a parasitology textbook and tries to identify a patient's puzzling skin rash. A senator scans the latest public opinion poll and wonders how to vote on the farm bill.

Each of these persons is seeking guidance. Their problems vary, and their sources of truth are different. Where shall human beings find truth? How can they know when they have found it? In the million years, more or less, of human life on this earth, people have sought truth in many places. Where are some of them?

Some Sources of Truth

Intuition. Galen, a famous Greek physician of the second century, prepared an elaborate chart of the human body, showing exactly where it might be pierced without fatal injury. How did he know the vulnerable spots? He just *knew* them. True, he had learned a good deal of human anatomy through his observations and those of his associates, but beyond this, he relied upon his intuition to tell him which zones were fatal. *Intuition is any flash of insight (true or mistaken) whose source the receiver cannot fully identify or explain.* Hitler relied heavily upon his intuition, much to the distress of his generals. His intuition told him that France would not fight for the Rhineland, that England would not fight for Czechoslovakia, that England and France would not fight for Poland, and that England and France would quit when he attacked Russia. He was right on the first two insights and wrong on the last two.

Intuition is responsible for many brilliant hypotheses, which can later be tested through other methods. Perhaps intuition's greatest value is in the forming of hypotheses.

Authority.   Two thousand years ago, Galen knew more about human anatomy than any other mortal; as recently as 1800, physicians were still quoting him as an authority. Aristotle stated that a barrel of water could be added to a barrel of ashes without overflowing, and for two thousand years thereafter, a student who might suggest trying it out would be scolded for his impertinence. For many centuries, creative thought was stifled by Aristotelian authority, for since an authority is *right*, any conflicting ideas must be wrong. Authority does not discover new truths, but it can prevent new truths from being discovered or accepted.

Dangerous though authority may be, we cannot get along without it. Our accumulation of knowledge is too great for anyone to absorb, so we must rely upon specialists who have collected the reliable knowledge in a particular field. An authority is a necessary and useful source of knowledge—*in the field in which he is an authority.* Science recognizes no authorities on "things in general."

Authority is of several sorts. *Sacred* authority rests upon the faith that a certain tradition or document—the Bible, the Koran, the Vedas—is of supernatural origin. *Secular* authority arises not from divine revelation but from human perception. It is of two kinds: *secular scientific authority*, which rests upon empirical investigation, and *secular humanistic authority*, which rests upon the belief that certain "great men" have had remarkable insight into human behavior and the nature of the universe. The search for truth by consulting the "great books" is an example of the appeal to secular humanistic authority.

Tradition.   Of all sources of truth, tradition is one of the most reassuring. Here is the accumulated wisdom of the ages, and one who disregards it may expect denunciation as a scoundrel or a fool. If a pattern has "worked" in the past, why not keep on using it?

Tradition, however, preserves both the accumulated wisdom and the accumulated bunkum of the ages. Tradition is society's attic, crammed with all sorts of useful customs and useless relics. A great deal of "practical experience" consists in repeating the mistakes of our ancestors. One task of social science is to sort out our folklore into the true and the merely ancient.

Common Sense.   Common sense and tradition are closely interwoven, with many common-sense propositions becoming part of a people's traditional lore. If a distinction is to be drawn, it may be that traditional truths are those which have long been believed, while common-sense truths are uncritically accepted conclusions (recent or ancient) which are currently believed by one's fellows.

What often passes for common sense consists of a group's accumulation of collective guesses, hunches, and haphazard trial-and-error learning. Many common-sense propositions are sound, earthy, useful bits of knowledge. "A soft answer turneth away wrath" and "Birds of a feather flock together" are practical observations on social life. But many common-sense conclusions are based on ignorance, prejudice, and mistaken interpretation. When medieval Europeans noticed that feverish patients were free of lice while most healthy people were lousy, they made the common-sense conclusion that lice would cure fever and therefore sprinkled lice over feverish patients. Not until the fever subsided would the lice be removed. Common sense, like tradition, preserves both folk wisdom and folk nonsense, and to sort them out one from the other is a task for science.

Science.   Only within the last two or three hundred years has the scientific method become a common way of seeking answers about the natural world. *Science* may be defined as a method of study whereby a body of organized scientific knowledge is discovered. Science has become a source of knowledge about the social world even more recently; yet in the brief period since human beings began to rely upon the scientific method, they have learned more about their world than they learned in the preceding ten thousand years. The spectacular explosion of knowledge in the modern world parallels the use of the scientific method. What makes the scientific method so productive? How does it differ from other methods of seeking truth?

Characteristics of Scientific Knowledge

Verifiable Evidence.   Scientific knowledge is based on verifiable evidence. By *evidence* we mean concrete factual observations that other observers can see, weigh, measure, count, or check for accuracy. We may think the definition too obvious to mention; most of us have some awareness of the scientific method. Yet only a few centuries ago medieval scholars held long debates on how many teeth a horse had, without bothering to look into a horse's mouth to count them.

At this point we raise the troublesome methodological question "What is a fact?" While the word looks deceptively simple, it is not easy to distinguish a fact from a widely shared illusion. Suppose we define a fact as a descriptive statement upon which all qualified observers are in agreement. By this definition, medieval ghosts were a fact, since all medieval observers agreed that ghosts were real. There is, therefore, no way to be *certain* that a fact is an accurate description and not a mistaken impression. Research would be easier if facts were dependable, unshakable certainties. Since they are not, the best we can do is to recognize that a fact is *a descriptive statement of reality that scientists, after careful examination and cross-checking, agree in believing to be accurate.*

Ethical Neutrality. Science is knowledge, and knowledge can be put to differing uses. Atomic fission can be used to power a city or to incinerate a nation. Every use of scientific knowledge involves a choice between values. Our values define what is most important to us. Science tells us that overeating and cigarette smoking will shorten our life expectancy. But can science tell us which we should choose—a longer life or a more indulgent one? Science can answer questions of fact but has no way to prove that one value is better than another.

Science, then, is ethically neutral. Science seeks knowledge, while society's values determine how this knowledge is to be used. Knowledge about group organization can be used to preserve a democracy or to establish a dictatorship.

When the ten minutes are up, try to answer the questions on page 459 by using your notes but *not* referring to the text.

Selection 3

You have ten minutes to skim the following textbook selection for its main points and to take notes on those points. Be sure to time yourself or have your instructor time you as you read and take notes on the selection.

Hint   Definitions and enumerations are the keys to the important points in this selection.

The Nature of Power

Niccolò Machiavelli (1469–1527) wrote *The Prince* as a way of giving advice to Italian princes (such as Cesare Borgia) in their struggle against the pope to establish an Italian state. Machiavelli saw the power of the prince as a means for achieving the moral goal of Italian unification. In the following passage, he makes an important distinction:

> You must know, then, that there are two methods of fighting, the one by law, the other by force: the first method is that of men, the second of beasts; but as the first method is often insufficient, one must have recourse to the second. . . .
>
> Thus it is well to seem merciful, faithful, humane, sincere, religious, and also to be so; but you must have the mind so disposed that when it is needful to be otherwise you may be able to change to the opposite qualities. . . . And therefore, you must have a mind disposed to adapt itself according to the wind, and as the variations of fortune dictate, and, as I said before, not deviate from what is good if possible, but be able to do evil if constrained.

In this celebrated passage, Machiavelli is discussing power. *Power* in society is the *ability to control the behavior of others—against their will if necessary—by using force, authority, or influence.* As the passage indicates, there are different kinds of power. Machiavelli recognized two kinds: force and law. Contemporary sociologists, however, find it more useful to speak of three kinds of power: *force, authority,* and *influence.*

Force

Machiavelli is not a particularly popular person in Italian history, partly because of his favorable attitude toward the use of *force*. Force is *physical coercion or the threat of such coercion.* In Machiavelli's terms, it is the method "of beasts" rather than "of men." Yet he advised his prince to resort to it whenever other means of controlling people's behavior fail. The use of force is at odds with many of our fundamental values, such as equality, freedom, and the importance of the individual personality. Yet there are situations, as illustrated by the aggression of Hitler's Germany or that of a gunman on the loose, where such values are threatened by people willing to use force. Using force to counter force in such situations can protect those values, but it also conflicts with them at the same time.

Authority

A second type of power is *authority*, which may be defined as *legitimate power,* that is, power based on values and norms. Machiavelli contrasted the use of force with the rule of law, and the latter illustrates authority. Authority tends to be a much larger component of most existing power than is force. The socialization process teaches us to conform to a wide variety of norms that allow others—parents, teachers, friends, employers, and officials of all kinds—to direct our behavior.

Three Kinds of Authority.   Max Weber enables us to gain some historical perspective on the nature of authority. At the same time, he distinguishes three kinds of authority: charismatic, traditional, and legal. *Charismatic authority is rule based on belief in the extraordinary personal qualities of the ruler.* Weber illustrates such authority by referring to "the magical sorcerer, the prophet, the leader of hunting and booty expeditions, the warrior chieftain, the so-called 'Caesarist' ruler." For example, we might think of Jesus Christ, Joan of Arc, Adolf Hitler, and Winston Churchill as exercising charismatic authority. They all had qualities of personality that deeply appealed to their followers.

Traditional authority is rule based on conformity to established modes of behavior. It is illustrated by the patriarchal domination of a family by the father or husband, by the rule of the lord over vassals and serfs, or by the rule of the master over slaves. By contrast, *legal authority is rule based on law or formal decrees and regulations.* It is exemplified by the authority of a president, a police officer, a member of Congress, a court official, the head of a government agency, a member of a school board, and a welfare investigator. With the development of industrial society has come a shift from traditional to legal authority. Charismatic authority has existed in the past and continues to exist in the present. It can be combined with the other two kinds of authority.

Influence

The third component of power is *influence,* which may be defined as *the ability to control the behavior of others beyond any authority to do so.* In certain situations, a leader may neither choose to exert force nor have any authority—legal, traditional, or charismatic—yet nevertheless may wish to assert power. He or she may be able to exert our third type of power, influence, simply on the basis of the "exchanges" that can be made. A teacher can influence students to develop interest in a subject by proving to be trustworthy as well as helpful. Such interest cannot be compelled on the basis of the teacher's authority.

The different aspects of power—force, authority, and influence—may be illustrated by Mohandas K. Gandhi's success in leading India toward independence from Great Britain. Gandhi was seen by his followers as a highly charismatic person. Further, his manner of living embodied such traditional ideals as humility, self-sacrifice, and spirituality. He refused to use force and, in its place, developed techniques of passive resistance. Among other things, he trained volunteers to march forward and allow themselves to be struck down by police clubs without defending themselves. Gandhi's leadership illustrates charismatic and traditional authority as well as influence. This was reflected in the title "mahatma" (great soul) that his followers bestowed on him.

Gandhi opposed his authority and influence against the force and legal authority of the British, and that opposition proved to be highly effective. For example, the British exercise of force, although perfectly legal in British terms, came to be seen as immoral not only by Indians but also by large segments of the British population.

The Gandhian approach to conflict influenced Martin Luther King, Jr., to develop his own techniques of passive resistance in the struggle of American blacks against discrimination. For example, black people's boycotts of buses in Montgomery, Alabama, in 1955 (in reaction to the injustice of being forced to sit only in the backs of buses) were almost 100 percent effective. Here King, as Gandhi had done, avoided the use of force and combined charismatic and traditional authority with personal influence to undermine the legal authority of the local government.

When the ten minutes are up, try to answer the questions on page 459 by referring to your notes but *not* referring to the text.

Selection 4

You have ten minutes to skim the following textbook selection for its main points and to take notes on those points.

Defense Mechanisms

Maintaining a good self-concept and high self-esteem is not easy. Each day there are many events that could shatter your self-image. If you notice a new blemish or wrinkle on your face, receive a low grade, or are not invited to lunch by the group, you need to take action to protect your self-esteem. The methods you use to protect your self-esteem are called *defense mechanisms.*

Suppression and Repression

One way to protect your self-esteem is to avoid thinking about your problem. For example, you might intentionally go to a movie to avoid thinking about an argument. This defense mechanism, a deliberate attempt to avoid stressful thoughts, is labeled "suppression." Scarlett O'Hara in *Gone with the Wind* is among the more famous practitioners of suppression. Remember her line "I'll think about it tomorrow"? Scarlett was suppressing her unpleasant thoughts. Have you ever felt lonely and intentionally kept yourself busy with chores, sports, or shopping to avoid thinking about your loneliness? If so, you were using suppression.

Suppression is useful only for minor problems. Usually you can pretend a problem does not exist for only a short period. Thoughts and worries tend to come back and may be even more stressful if they have been bottled up. Suppression requires a conscious and voluntary effort and has limited use as a defense mechanism.

Issues that are deeply wounding to self-esteem may be too painful to reach consciousness. You unconsciously put them out of your mind. Unconsciously motivated forgetting is called "repression." Everyone tends to push unpleasant thoughts out of the conscious mind. Since thoughts that are repressed are not conscious, people can become aware of them only through dreams or hypnosis.

Repression is the most basic defense mechanism. Most other defense mechanisms stem from repression. In its simplest form repression is unconscious forgetting. Suppose you forget to contribute money to a going-away gift for a close friend. Unconsciously you wish your friend were not leaving. Forgetting appointments, birthdays, weddings, and other important events can be a sign of repression. Have you ever met someone who was

"Normally I don't let rejection bother me, but . . ."

The rejection stamped on his forehead may also become buried in
his unconscious. Time for some defense mechanisms . . .

rejecting and cruel to you? If you have difficulty recalling any persons or
names, you may be repressing them! Usually thoughts and feelings that are
repressed bring on other defense mechanisms.

Other Defense Mechanisms

Assuming that the fellow in the cartoon above is deeply worried about
being rejected, he may repress the situation. As a result he could forget the
name of the woman, their entire conversation, what he was drinking, and
where he was that evening. Rather than admit his rejection and suffer, he
could also use a number of other unconscious defense mechanisms.

Withdrawal.   If the man in the cartoon has trouble talking to women in
the future, it could be that he unconsciously fears rejection. *Withdrawal* usually
results when people become intensely frightened or frustrated by a situation.
People who fear rejection often avoid or withdraw from social situations.
Sometimes the result is shyness. Often people fear rejection even when it is
unlikely. Many famous and likable people have suffered from shyness.

If you have ever tried to escape from an unpleasant situation, you have used a withdrawal defense mechanism. If used cautiously, withdrawal can be a healthy defense mechanism. Often, stepping out of a situation can help you gain a better perspective. However, withdrawal can also result in quitting jobs, dropping out of school, separations, and divorces.

Fantasy.   Sometimes people withdraw into a make-believe or *fantasy* world. If the rejected man in the cartoon used a fantasy defense mechanism, he might daydream about his successes with women. He could create his own dream world where he would always be accepted, admired, and loved. Used in moderation, daydreaming and fantasy can be healthy and lead to creative thinking. Everyone daydreams as a method of reducing anxiety. Fantasy can bring a healthy escape from boredom and aid mental relaxation. Reading a novel or watching a soap opera can provide fantasy escapes. However, if fantasy is used excessively, it can become an unhealthy substitute for activity.

Regression.   *Regression* is withdrawal into the past. If the rejected fellow regressed in a childlike way, he would behave like a child. He might burst into tears, or pout, suck his thumb, throw things, scream, and have a tantrum. Regression requires a return to earlier ways of handling problems. It is generally used when a person is deeply upset and cannot cope in a mature manner. Young children who have been toilet-trained and taught to drink from a cup often regress and forget their training when a new baby arrives in their home. The older child does not know how to win parental affection in the new situation. Consequently the child must resort to previous methods for gaining attention and love. The result is regression.

Rationalization.   *Rationalization* is a distortion of the truth to maintain self-esteem. It provides an excuse or explanation for a situation that is really unacceptable. The man in the cartoon might rationalize that the woman was not really his type and that he was delighted to be rid of her so he could arrive home at a reasonable hour. He might even rationalize that he was just having an unlucky day. Failures are often rationalized as being the result of some external factor, but success is deemed the result of personal abilities.

Most people are unaware of how often they rationalize. Although rationalization is indeed a misuse of logic, it can help to reduce anxiety. Have you ever excused yourself from a poor grade by arguing that the test was unfair or that you were feeling sick when you took the test? Rationalization can also allow you to look at the bright side. If an unpleasant event has already occurred, often little or nothing can be done to change it. After losing the 1960 presidential election, Richard Nixon reportedly commented that he would have more time to devote to his family. This was clearly a rationalization but probably aided his acceptance of a painful reality.

Projection.   *Projection* is based on guilt. Rather than accept personal weaknesses, unacceptable features are projected onto another person. The rejected man could project his rejection onto the woman who stamped him. He would then maintain that it was she who was rejected by everyone. Projection permits you to accuse someone else of your weaknesses. Perhaps you have heard complaints from one fraternity that members of another fraternity hated them. They could easily be projecting their own feelings onto the other group. Or maybe you have known a flirt who complained that every male she met flirted with her. Psychologists often use projective tests to uncover problems. It is assumed that individuals will project their own feelings onto the pictures and illustrations in the test material.

Displacement.   *Displacement* requires finding a target or victim for pent-up feelings. The rejected fellow at the bar might ridicule and chastise the bartender for poor drinks or slow service. The chosen victim is usually a safe person, someone who is not likely to deflate self-esteem. Spouses are often selected. As a result, husbands and wives often learn to avoid controversial topics when their mate has had a bad day.

Compensation. *Compensation* allows a person to make up for inadequacies by doing well in another area. Perhaps the rejected fellow at the bar could go back to work and prove himself an outstanding accountant, attorney, or automobile salesman. Compensation allows you to deemphasize your weaknesses and play up your strengths. A child who is a poor student may try learning clever jokes to become popular. Compensation is a reasonable defense mechanism and usually leads to a healthy adjustment.

Sublimation.   *Sublimation* is the most accepted defense mechanism. Unacceptable impulses are channeled into something positive, constructive, or creative. If the man left the bar and wrote a beautiful blues song about rejection and loneliness, he would be sublimating. Some of the finest poetry and folk music have emerged from oppressed groups, an example of their sublimations.

Of the many defense mechanisms, compensation and sublimation are considered the most healthy and acceptable. Since defense mechanisms are unconscious, usually people are completely unaware of them. Think about some of your own behavior. Can you identify the defense mechanisms you choose most often?

When the ten minutes are up, try to answer the questions your instructor gives you by using your notes but *not* referring to the text.

Selection 5

You have ten minutes to skim the following article for its main points and to take notes on those points.

Hint Definitions and enumerations are the keys to the important points in this article.

Fatigue

Fatigue is one of the most common complaints brought to doctors, friends, and relatives. You'd think that in this era of laborsaving devices and convenient transportation, few people would have reason to be so tired. But probably more people complain of fatigue today than in the days when hay was baled by hand and laundry was scrubbed on a washboard. Witness these typical complaints:

"It doesn't seem to matter how long I sleep—I'm more tired when I wake up than when I went to bed."

"Some of my friends come home from work and jog for several miles or swim laps. I don't know how they do it. I'm completely exhausted at the end of a day at the office."

"I thought I was weary because of the holidays, but now that they're over, I'm even worse. I can barely get through the week, and on the weekend I don't even have the strength to get dressed. I wonder if I'm anemic or something."

"I don't know what's wrong with me lately, but I've been so collapsed that I haven't made a proper meal for the family in weeks. We've been living on TV dinners and packaged mixes. I was finally forced to do laundry because the kids ran out of underwear."

The causes of modern-day fatigue are diverse and only rarely related to excessive physical exertion. The relatively few people who do heavy labor all day long almost never complain about being tired, perhaps because they expect to be. Today, physicians report, tiredness is more likely a consequence of underexertion than of wearing yourself down with overactivity. In fact, increased physical activity is often prescribed as a *cure* for sagging energy.

Kinds of Fatigue

There are three main categories of fatigue. These are physical fatigue, pathological fatigue, and psychological fatigue.

Physical. This is the well-known result of overworking your muscles to the point where metabolic waste products—carbon dioxide and lactic acid—accumulate in your blood and sap your strength. Your muscles can't continue to work efficiently in a bath of these chemicals. Physical fatigue is usually a pleasant tiredness, such as that which you might experience after playing a hard set of tennis, chopping wood, or climbing a mountain. The cure is simple and fast: You rest, giving your body a chance to get rid of accumulated wastes and restore muscle fuel.

Pathological. Here fatigue is a warning sign or consequence of some underlying physical disorder, perhaps the common cold or flu or something more serious like diabetes or cancer. Usually other symptoms besides fatigue are present that suggest the true cause.

Even after an illness has passed, you're likely to feel dragged out for a week or more. Take your fatigue as a signal to go slowly while your body has a chance to recover fully even if all you had was a cold. Pushing yourself to resume full activity too soon could precipitate a relapse and almost certainly will prolong your period of fatigue.

Even though illness is not a frequent cause of prolonged fatigue, it's very important that it not be overlooked. Therefore, anyone who feels drained of energy for weeks on end should have a thorough physical checkup. But even if nothing shows up as a result of the various medical tests, that doesn't mean there's nothing wrong with you.

Unfortunately too often a medical workup ends with a battery of negative test results, the patient is dismissed, and the true cause of serious fatigue goes undetected. As Dr. John Bulette, a psychiatrist at the Medical College of Pennsylvania Hospital in Philadelphia, tells it, this is what happened to a woman in Pennsylvania who had lost nearly fifty pounds and was "almost dead—so tired she could hardly lift her head up." The doctors who first examined the woman were sure she had cancer. But no matter how hard they looked, they could find no sign of malignancy or of any other disease that could account for her to be wasting away. Finally, she was brought to the college hospital, where doctors noted that she was severely depressed.

They questioned her about her life and discovered that her troubles had begun two years earlier, after her husband died. Once treated for depression, the woman quickly perked up. She gained ten pounds in just a few weeks, and then she returned home to continue her recovery with the aid of psychotherapy.

Psychological. Emotional problems and conflicts, especially depression and anxiety, are by far the most common causes of prolonged fatigue. Fatigue may represent a defense mechanism that prevents you from having to face the true cause of your depression, such as the fact that you hate your job. It is also your body's safety valve for expressing repressed emotional conflicts, such as feeling trapped in an ungratifying role or an unhappy marriage. When such feelings are not expressed openly, they often come out as physical symptoms, with fatigue as one of the most common manifestations. "Many people who are extremely fatigued don't even know they're depressed," Dr. Bulette says. "They're so busy distracting themselves or just worrying about being tired that they don't recognize their depression."

One of these situations is so common it's been given a name—tired housewife syndrome. The victims are commonly young mothers who day in and day out face the predictable tedium of caring for a home and small children, fixing meals, dealing with repair persons, and generally having no one interesting to talk to and nothing enjoyable to look forward to at the end of their boring and unrewarding day. The tired housewife may be inwardly resentful, envious of her husband's job, and guilty about her feelings. But rather than face them head-on, she becomes extremely fatigued.

Today, with nearly half the mothers of young children working outside the home, the tired housewife syndrome has taken on a new twist: that of conflicting roles and responsibilities and guilt over leaving the children, often with an overlay of genuine physical exhaustion from trying to be all things to all people.

Emotionally induced fatigue may be compounded by sleep disturbance that results from the underlying psychological conflict. A person may develop insomnia or may sleep the requisite number of hours but fitfully tossing and turning all night, having disturbing dreams, and awakening, as one woman put it, feeling as if she "had been run over by a truck."

Understanding the underlying emotional problem is the crucial first step toward curing psychological fatigue and by itself often results in considerable lessening of the tiredness. Professional psychological help or career or marriage counseling may be needed.

What You Can Do about It

There is a great deal you can do on your own to deal with both severe prolonged fatigue and periodic washed-out feelings. Vitamins and tranquilizers are almost never the right answer, sleeping pills and alcohol are counterproductive, and caffeine is at best a temporary solution that can backfire with abuse and cause life-disrupting symptoms of anxiety. Instead, you might try:

Diet.   If you eat a skimpy breakfast or none at all, you're likely to experience midmorning fatigue, the result of a drop in blood sugar, which your body and brain depend on for energy. For peak energy in the morning, be sure to eat a proper breakfast, low in sugar and fairly high in protein, which will provide a steady supply of blood sugar throughout the morning. Coffee and a doughnut are almost worse than nothing, providing a brief boost and then letting you down with a thud.

The same goes for the rest of the day: Frequent snacking on sweets is a false pick-me-up that soon leaves you lower than you were to begin with. Stick to regular, satisfying, well-balanced meals that help you maintain a trim figure. Extra weight is tiring both physically and psychologically. Getting your weight down to normal can go a long way toward revitalizing you.

Exercise.   Contrary to what you may think, exercise enhances, rather than saps, energy. Regular conditioning exercises, such as jogging, cycling, or swimming, help you to resist fatigue by increasing your body's ability to handle more of a workload. You get tired less quickly because your capability is greater. Exercise also has a well-recognized tranquilizing effect, which helps you work in a more relaxed fashion and be less dragged down by the tensions of your day. At the end of the day exercise can relieve accumulated tensions, give you more energy in the evening, and help you sleep more restfully.

Sleep.   If you know you're tired because you haven't been getting enough sleep, the solution is simple: Get to bed earlier. There's no right amount of sleep for everyone, and generally sleep requirements decline with age. Find the amount that suits you best and aim for it. Insomnia and other sleep disorders should not be treated with sleeping pills, alcohol, or tranquilizers, which can actually make the problem worse.

Knowing Yourself.   Try to schedule your most taxing jobs for the time of day when you're at your peak. Some are "morning people" who tire by midafternoon; others do their best work in the evening. Don't overextend yourself trying to climb the ladder of success at a record pace or to meet everyone's demands or expectations. Decide what you want to do and what you can handle comfortably and learn to say no to additional requests. Recognize your energy cycles and plan accordingly. For example, many women have a low point premenstrually, during which time extra sleep may be needed and demanding activities are particularly exhausting.

Taking Breaks.   No matter how interesting or demanding your work, you'll be able to do it with more vigor if now and again you stop, stretch, and change the scenery. Instead of coffee and a sweet roll on your break, try meditation, yoga, calisthenics, or a brisk walk. Even running up and down the staircase can provide refreshment from a sedentary job. If your job is physically demanding, relax in a quiet place for a while. The do-something-different rule also applies to vacations; "getting away from it all" for a week or two or longer can be highly revitalizing, helping you to put things in perspective and enabling you to take your job more in stride upon your return.

When the ten minutes are up, try to answer the questions your instructor gives you by using your notes but *not* referring to the text.

Skim-Reading Progress Chart

On the following chart are skim-reading speeds for the selections in Part Five. The term WPM refers here to the number of words *processed* per minute. (You have not been able to literally *read* every word in the limited time involved.) The reading speeds assume that you have taken one-quarter of your time to read each selection and three-quarters of your time to take notes on what you have read.

Selection	WPM	Comprehension
1 Visual Elements in Assertive Communication (731 words)	505	
2 Science and the Search for Truth (1,464 words)	525	
3 The Nature of Power (1,152 words)	460	
4 Defense Mechanisms (1,625 words)	660	
5 Fatigue (1,957 words)	783	

Note   Reading speed will vary depending on the nature and difficulty of the material. In the five preceding selections, the highest speed is for "Fatigue," an article by the popular health writer Jane Brody, taken from a newspaper. Because the four other selections, all from textbooks, contain more information to process, slightly lower skim-reading rates are suggested.

Questions on
the Skim-Reading
Selections

■ **Selection 1**

1. Name any four elements in visual assertion.

   _____

   _____

   _____

2. What are the four distinct distances that Americans use in differing situations?

   _____

   _____

   _____

   _____

> ***Score***   Number correct (_____) × 12.5 = _____%

■ Selection 2

1. What are the five sources of truth?

   _____   _____   _____

   _____   _____

2. Define intuition. _____

   _____

3. What are the two characteristics of scientific knowledge?

   _____   _____

4. Define science. _____

   _____

5. Define a fact. _____

   _____

Score Number correct (_____) × 10 = _____%

■ Selection 3

1. What are the three kinds of power?

   _____   _____   _____

2. What is force? _____

   _____

3. What are the three kinds of authority?

   _____

   _____

   _____

4. What is influence? _____

   _____

Score Number correct (_____) × 12.5 = _____%

■ **Selection 4**

Your instructor will refer to the Instructor's Manual to give you the questions for Selection 4.

■ **Selection 5**

Your instructor will refer to the Instructor's Manual to give you the questions for Selection 5.

Part Six

Rapid Reading and Comprehension

Preview

Part Six is concerned primarily with developing your comprehension but also with trying to increase the number of words that your eyes take in and "read" per minute. Poor perception habits that may slow down your reading rate are explained, and an activity is provided to show you how your eyes move when they read. You then learn how a conscious effort to increase your speed may be a key to overcoming careless perception habits and achieving a higher reading rate.

A series of ten reading selections then gives you practice in building up your comprehension and perhaps your reading speed as well. Through a progress chart, you will be able to compare your reading rate and comprehension scores as you move through the selections.

Introduction

This part of the book will give you further practice in developing comprehension skills. At the same time, it will help you discover whether you can realistically increase the number of words that your eyes take in and "read" per minute. An increase in reading speed can be valuable, though it is certainly no cure-all for reading problems.

If you feel you are reading your college assignments too slowly or ineffectively, *factors other than reading speed are probably responsible.* For example, perhaps you don't know where and how to look for main ideas and key supporting details in a textbook chapter. You may need to work on the reading comprehension and skim-reading skills presented in Parts Four and Five of this book. Also, you may need to learn more about study skills such as textbook previewing, marking, and note-taking. And you may have to learn how to read flexibly. This means that you adjust your speed and style of reading to accommodate your purpose as well as the level of difficulty of the material.

In summary, there is much more to effective reading than an increase in speed alone. It is also true, however, that some students do benefit from working to improve reading speed. If nothing else, the extra effort and concentration that it takes to increase speed can improve comprehension as well.

- *Complete the following sentence:* _____ reading is only one part of effective reading.

Poor Perception Habits

If you read material of average or less than average difficulty slowly, you can probably significantly increase your present reading speed. In all likelihood, poor perception habits are slowing down your reading. Such habits include *subvocalizing*

463

(pronouncing words silently to yourself as you read); slow and stilted *word-for-word reading*; unnecessary *regressions* (returns to words you have already read); and *visual inaccuracy* (the tendency to misread letters and words on the page). Poor concentration habits often cause this last problem.

• How many bad perception habits are mentioned in the preceding paragraph?

_____

How the Eyes Read

You will understand more clearly how the eyes work during reading when you perform the following experiment. Punch a hole with a pen or pencil through the black dot that follows this paragraph. Hold the page up for another person to see and have him or her read a paragraph or two silently. As the person reads, put your eye close to the hole and watch his or her eye movements. In the space provided here, write down your observations, including a description of how the reader's eyes moved across the lines of print.

●

_____

_____

In performing this activity, you probably observed that the reader's eyes did not move smoothly across the printed lines. Instead, they moved in jerks, making stop-and-go motions across the lines of print. These stops, which you may have been able to count as you peeked through the hole, are called *fixations*, and only during such fixations do you actually read. You may remember as a child trying—and failing—to catch your eyes moving as you looked in a mirror. You never saw them move because the eyes go too quickly between fixations for any clear vision. The eye must fixate, or stop, in order to see clearly. In summary, then, the eye reads by making a number of fixations or stops as it proceeds across a line of print.

In addition to the stops, you probably also noted the sweep of the eyes, like the carriage return of a typewriter, back and down to the beginning of each new line. Possibly you also noticed an occasional backward eye movement, or regression, when the eyes skipped back to reread words or phrases a second time.

Eye reading speed can be increased, in part, by reducing the number of fixations per line. Someone who makes eight stops per line is not reading as quickly as someone who makes four. To read faster, you should learn to take in several words at each stop rather than only one or two. And as this is done, the tendency to subvocalize and to read one word at a time will also be minimized. In addition, speed can be increased by reducing the duration of each pause or stop, by increasing the speed of the return sweep, and by cutting down on the number of backward eye movements or regressions. Finally, with improved concentration, the eyes can be made to read with greater accuracy as well as speed.

The Key to Rapid Reading

Eye speed can be increased and bad perception habits overcome through practice with timed passages in which you consciously *try to read faster.* As you read for speed in the situations that follow, remember that your *mind* is probably not slowing you down; your *eyes* are. The mind is an incredible computerlike instrument that can process words at an extraordinary rate of speed. What holds it back is the limited rate at which your eyes feed in words for it to process. Consciously force your eyes to move and work at ever higher and higher speeds. Your deliberate effort to "turn on" your speed through practice should yield impressive results.

On the following pages are ten selections to use in developing your reading speed. You should read only the first selection at your normal rate of speed. You can then use this rate to measure later increases in speed. As you finish each selection, get your time from your instructor—or time yourself—and record it in the space provided. Then answer the comprehension questions.

Afterward, find your reading rate with the help of the table on pages 522–524. Also, check your answers with the instructor and fill in your comprehension score in the space provided. Finally, record both your reading rate and your comprehension score in the progress chart on page 521.

- Many people have paid hundreds of dollars for speed-reading courses whose message or "secret" can be reduced to four simple words. What are the words?

Rapid Reading and Comprehension: Final Thoughts

You are about to experiment with rapid reading—making your eyes and brain work together to process words at a high rate of speed. It is suggested that you try rapid reading for at least the first five selections that follow. If you feel after doing so that rapid reading works for you, continue it through the final five readings as well. You may then want in general to *try to read faster* as you deal with different kinds of reading material.

At the same time, be sure to keep rapid reading in perspective. It is different from slow, leisurely reading, in which your purpose is pleasure. It is different from skim reading, in which your purpose is to locate the main points in an article or chapter. It is different from the kind of slow study reading that you do to increase your understanding of a difficult selection. It is but one of the many skills of an effective reader, and it is useful at certain times for certain reading purposes.

Finally, if your comprehension drops even after repeated efforts to read quickly, you may reasonably decide that rapid reading is not for you. In that case, you may simply want to focus on developing your comprehension skills, and all ten of the readings in this section of the book will provide you with useful practice.

Selection 1

Read the *Preview* and check the *Words to Watch* below. Then read this first selection at your present comfortable rate of speed. You can use the difference in speeds between this selection and the ones that follow to measure any advances in your reading rate.

From

The Autobiography of Malcolm X

Malcolm X and Alex Haley

■ Preview

While confined to a prison cell, the inspirational African American leader Malcolm X learned to loosen the chains that imprisoned his mind. This excerpt from *The Autobiography of Malcolm X* describes how words were the key to his newfound freedom.

■ Words to Watch

riffling (line 12): flipping through

succeeding (line 28): following

inevitable (line 34): bound to happen

It was because of my letters [which Malcolm X wrote to people outside while he was in jail] that I happened to stumble upon starting to acquire some kind of a homemade education.

I became increasingly frustrated at not being able to express what I wanted to convey in letters that I wrote. . . . And every book I picked up   5
had few sentences which didn't contain anywhere from one to nearly all the words that might as well have been in Chinese. When I skipped those words, of course, I really ended up with little idea of what the book said. . . .

I saw that the best thing I could do was get hold of a dictionary—to study, to learn some words. I requested a dictionary along with some tablets   10
and pencils from the Norfolk Prison Colony school.

I spent two days just riffling uncertainly through the dictionary's pages. I'd never realized so many words existed! I didn't know *which* words I needed to learn. Finally, just to start some kind of action, I began copying.

In my slow, painstaking, ragged handwriting, I copied into my tablet   15
everything printed on that first page, down to the punctuation marks. I believe it took me a day. Then, aloud, I read back to myself everything I'd written on the tablet. Over and over, aloud, to myself, I read my own handwriting.

I woke up the next morning, thinking about those words—immensely proud to realize that not only had I written so much at one time, but I'd   20

467

written words that I never knew were in the world. Moreover, with a little effort, I also could remember what many of these words meant. I reviewed the words whose meanings I didn't remember. Funny thing, from the dictionary's first page right now, that *aardvark* springs to my mind. The dictionary had a picture of it, a long-tailed, long-eared, burrowing African mammal, which lives 25 off termites caught by sticking out its tongue as an anteater does for ants.

I was so fascinated that I went on—I copied the dictionary's next page. And the same experience came when I studied that. With every succeeding page, I also learned of people and places and events from history. Actually, the dictionary is like a miniature encyclopedia. Finally, the dictionary's A 30 section had filled a whole tablet—and I went on into the B's. That was the way I started copying what eventually became the entire dictionary. It went a lot faster after so much practice helped me to pick up handwriting speed.

I suppose it was inevitable that as my word-base broadened, I could for the first time pick up a book and read and now begin to understand what 35 the book was saying. Anyone who has read a great deal can imagine the new world that opened. Let me tell you something: from then until I left the prison, in every free moment I had, if I was not reading in the library, I was reading on my bunk. You couldn't have gotten me out of books with a wedge. Months passed without my even thinking about being imprisoned. 40 In fact, up to then, I never had been so truly free in my life.

Time: _____   *Reading Rate (see page 522):* _____ WPM

■ Reading Comprehension

1. Malcolm X had trouble writing letters and reading books because

    a.   he was not given free time.

    b.   it was too dark in his cell.

    c.   he didn't know enough words.

    d.   he needed eyeglasses.

2. Malcolm compares the dictionary to

    a.   the Bible.

    b.   a miniature encyclopedia.

    c.   a thesaurus.

    d.   an almanac.

3. How much of the dictionary did Malcolm eventually copy?

    a.   A's

    b.   A's and B's

    c.   A through P

    d.   All of it

4. Malcolm's way of learning new words was to

    a. first copy them out on paper.

    b. open up the dictionary at random to a word he didn't know.

    c. study them right off the dictionary page.

    d. recite them silently to himself.

5. *True or false?* _____ One of the first words that Malcolm studied in the dictionary was *anteater.*

6. *True or false?* _____ Only when Malcolm's vocabulary increased was he able to read and understand books.

7. Malcolm says that to know and imagine the new world that books opened up for him, a person would have to

    a. read the same books he did.

    b. read many books.

    c. be in prison.

    d. be as ignorant as he was when he began.

8. Having books to read and knowing how to read them, Malcolm says that he

    a. became truly free even though in prison.

    b. was still bored and restless occasionally.

    c. felt like an educated man.

    d. gained the admiration of his fellow prisoners.

Number Wrong: ____   *Score:* ____

| 0 wrong = 100% | 2 wrong = 75% | 4 wrong = 50% | 6 wrong = 25% |
| 1 wrong = 88% | 3 wrong = 63% | 5 wrong = 38% | 7 wrong = 13% |

■ Critical Thinking and Discussion

1. Malcolm X knew that he wanted to increase his vocabulary. Because he didn't know how else to start, he began copying the dictionary, page by page. What are some other techniques that he might have used to learn new words?

2. What conclusions can you draw about Malcolm X from this selection? What kind of man does he seem to be? What values seem to be important to him?

3. Although he was in prison, Malcolm X says, "I never had been so truly free in my life." In what sense had he become "free"?

Selection 2

Read the *Preview* and check the *Words to Watch* below. Then you should make a deliberate effort to read at a faster rate. You should *will* your eyes to move faster, and you should *will* your brain to process the incoming facts, ideas, and details more quickly.

If you are not already doing so, sit up straight, put your feet flat on the floor, and hold the book at a comfortable angle. Consciously force your eyes to move at a higher rate of speed. Make the decision that you are going to read faster, and do it.

Learning to Keep Your Cool during Tests
Margaret Jerrard

■ **Preview**

If the word *test* fills you with as much anxiety as a visit to the dentist, take heart: Help is available. There are effective ways to deal with test-related anxiety. This selection outlines some of the best.

■ **Words to Watch**

secreted (line 6): formed and released

peripheral sight (line 9): the ability to see beyond the edges of the line of direct sight

optimum (line 30): most favorable

keyed up (line 32): excited or tense

interspersing (line 40): doing at varying intervals

intuitive (line 52): done without reasoning

Have you ever felt so panicky during an examination that you couldn't even put down the answers you *knew*? If so, you were suffering from what is known as test anxiety.

According to the psychologist Ralph Trimble, test anxiety is a very real problem for many people. When you're worried over your performance on an exam, your heart beats faster, your pulse speeds up, hormones are secreted. These reactions trigger others: You may sweat more than you normally do or suffer from a stomachache or headache. Your field of vision narrows and becomes tunnel-like, leaving you with very little peripheral sight. Before you know it, you're having difficulty focusing.   10

5

"What I hear students say over and over again," says Dr. Trimble, who is associated with the Psychological and Counseling Center at the University of Illinois, "is, 'My mind went blank.'"

For a number of years, Dr. Trimble helped many students learn how to function better during exams and to bring up their grades. Some of these students were interested in sharing what they learned and, with Trimble's help, began holding workshops on overcoming test anxiety. For many students, just being in a workshop with other sufferers was a relief. They realized they weren't freaks, that they were not the only ones who had done poorly on tests because of tension. The workshops were so successful that they are still given.

In the workshops, students are taught that anxiety is normal. You just have to prevent it from getting the best of you. The first step is to learn to relax. If before or during an examination you start to panic, stretch as hard as you can, tensing the muscles in your arms and legs; then suddenly relax all of them. This will help relieve tension.

But keep in mind that you don't want to be too relaxed. Being completely relaxed is no better than being too tense. "If you are so calm you don't *care* how you do on an examination, you won't do well," Trimble says. "There is an optimum level of concern when you perform at your best. Some stress helps. There are people who can't take even slight stress. They have to learn that in a challenging situation, being keyed up is good and will help them to do better. But if they label it anxiety and say, 'It's going to hit me again,' that will push them over the edge."

As a student you must also realize that if you leave too much studying until a day or two before the examination, you can't do the impossible and learn it all. Instead, concentrate on what you *can* do and try to think what questions are likely to be asked and what you can do in the time left for studying.

When you sit down to study, set a moderate pace and vary it by interspersing reading, writing notes, and going over any papers you have already written for the course, as well as the textbooks and notes you took in class. Review what you know. Take breaks and go to sleep in plenty of time to get a good night's rest before the exam. You should also eat a moderate breakfast or lunch, avoiding drinks with caffeine and steering clear of fellow students who get tense. Panic is contagious.

Get to the exam room a few minutes early so that you will have a chance to familiarize yourself with the surroundings and get out your supplies. When the examination is handed out, read the directions twice and underline the significant instructions, making sure you understand them. Ask the instructor or proctor to explain if you don't. First answer the easiest questions, then go back to the more difficult. If you are stumped on a multiple-choice question, first eliminate the impossible answers, then make as good an intuitive guess as possible and go on to the next.

On essay questions, instead of plunging right in, take a few minutes to organize your thoughts, make a brief outline, and then start off with a summary 55
sentence. Keep working steadily, and even when time starts to run out, don't speed up.

After the examination is over, don't torture yourself by thinking over all the mistakes you made, and don't start studying immediately for another exam. Instead, give yourself an hour or two of free time.   60

Among the students who are working now as volunteer leaders in the workshops are a number who started out panicky and unable to function on exams. They learned how to deal with test anxiety and are now teaching others. It's almost as easy as ABC.

Time: _____   *Reading Rate (see page 522): _____ WPM*

■ Reading Comprehension

1. Which would be a good alternative title for this selection?

    a.   How to Overcome Test Anxiety

    b.   The Physical Side of Anxiety

    c.   How to Get Better Grades

    d.   Why Students Are Concerned about Grades

2. Which sentence best expresses the main idea of the selection?

    a.   Most students suffer from test anxiety.

    b.   Test anxiety can be controlled.

    c.   Being relaxed is essential to doing well on exams.

    d.   All students should attend stress-management workshops.

3. If you start to panic during a test, you should

    a.   leave the room briefly.

    b.   drink a cup of coffee.

    c.   stretch and then relax your arms and legs.

    d.   skip the essay questions.

4. The first thing to do when you receive the exam is to

    a.   answer the questions you are sure of.

    b.   underline the important instructions.

    c.   make an outline of what you know.

    d.   begin timing yourself.

5. *True or false?* _____ Anxiety can cause a well-prepared student to perform poorly on a test.

6. From the selection we can conclude that

   a.   textbooks make better study guides than class notes do.

   b.   anxiety is learned behavior that can be unlearned.

   c.   students who do poorly in tests may need eyeglasses.

   d.   good students are completely calm before tests.

7. Which of the following tips is *not* mentioned in the article?

   a.   Do easy questions first.

   b.   Organize your thoughts before starting to write an essay answer.

   c.   Ask the instructor to explain unclear directions.

   d.   Budget your time for each part of the test.

8. The author implies that

   a.   you should get to the exam room at the last minute in order to avoid panicky students.

   b.   you should never guess on an exam.

   c.   caffeine can increase anxiety.

   d.   if you have kept up with the work, there's no need to study for the test.

Number Wrong: _____   *Score:* _____

0 wrong = 100%	2 wrong = 75%	4 wrong = 50%	6 wrong = 25%
1 wrong = 88%	3 wrong = 63%	5 wrong = 38%	7 wrong = 13%

■ Critical Thinking and Discussion

1. According to the selection, what are some of the symptoms of test anxiety? What symptoms of anxiety have you most frequently observed in yourself or others?

2. Do you practice any of the anxiety-relieving techniques described in the selection? Can you recommend any others that might be helpful to your fellow students?

3. The selection advises people with test anxiety to avoid fellow students who also get tense, noting "Panic is contagious." Do you think this is true? Does it matter what kind of people surround you as you prepare for or take an exam?

Selection 3

Read the *Preview* and check the *Words to Watch* below. Then you may want to try the following technique. As you read, lightly underline each line of print with your index finger. Do not rest your hand on the page, and do not point to individual words with your finger. Hold your hand slightly above the page and use your finger as a pacer, moving it a little more quickly than your eyes can comfortably follow. Try to glide your finger smoothly across each line of print and to make your eyes follow just as smoothly. If the technique helps you attend closely and read more quickly, use it in other selections as well.

Wired for Touch
Deborah Grandinetti

■ Preview

Human beings can be very strong. We can come back from serious disease and injury and can survive terrible loss. But as strong as we are, we still need physical contact—as the following selection points out.

■ Words to Watch

hesitant (line 11): uncertain

unconditional (line 23): total, absolute

regressed (line 27): went backward

untouchables (line 41): in India, persons of lowest status in society

conceivably (line 67): possibly

He had been a good-looking kid. Nice face. Good bone structure. A well-built, muscular body.

That was before the fire. Afterward, his back, neck, and arms were never the same. He went through a long and painful series of skin grafts. Once he was released from the hospital, he never again left the house without 5 wearing a long-sleeved, collared shirt, even on the hottest of days.

For years, he lived with his mother. She provided him with the tender, loving care only a mother could. In her eyes, he was still the same beautiful young man.

He was 28 when she died. The loss must have been unbearable. And he must have said as much to those who cared about him, because someone 10 urged him to visit a massage therapist. I can only imagine how hesitant he was at first, how scary it must have been to consider the reaction he might get when he took his shirt off for a complete stranger.

But he was in pain and barely hanging on. So he pushed past the fear and asked for referrals. One name kept coming up, and he called this massage therapist even though her office was more than 90 minutes away. He liked what she said and how she sounded, so he made an appointment. 15

The therapist who met with him said later, "When I saw his terrible scars, I had to go very deep within myself to draw strength."

She did. She opened her heart wide, letting go of any feelings of shock 20 and disgust at his appearance. She also said a silent prayer, asking that she be guided to give this client just what he needed. As she did, the energy of loving, unconditional regard for this young man began to flow through her. And this is what her touch communicated as she massaged his damaged skin.

The quality of her touch seemed to relax him. He let down his guard. And 25 then, about halfway through the massage, he wept—tears of loss and release.

"What I felt, under my hands, is that emotionally he had regressed since his mother's death," she said. "I got the sense that he didn't know how to be in the world without her." Part of him feared that he wouldn't be able to survive this second loss. 30

Slowly, but surely, the massage helped him know—at a level deeper than words—that he was seen and fully accepted by a woman other than his mother. It told him that he was still worthy of love and goodness. That knowledge helped give him the strength to go on.

He returned twice after that. Each time he left, he looked a little more 35 relaxed, a little more alive.

Such is the power of touch. Sometimes, it is even more necessary than food to "feed" a person's sense of well-being.

The Nobel Peace Prize winner Mother Teresa knew this. She often said that more people die from lack of love than poverty, hunger, or other physical 40 suffering. That's why she actively reached out to society's "untouchables," often feeding them or tending to their wounds with her own hands. She knew that her caring touch helped restore their sense of dignity.

A San Francisco massage therapist who visited Mother Teresa in India was so inspired by what she saw that she came home with a new sense 45 of purpose. The therapist decided she would make her massage services available to the city's homeless at no charge. She also decided to teach other interested massage therapists how to work with the homeless. She knew that massage was not only a way to help a homeless individual rebuild a sense of self-esteem, but also a way to gain that person's trust, so that he 50 or she might be more willing to take advantage of other available social services. Over ten years ago she opened a Care Through Touch Institute that still provides training and service to the poor.

"When you touch another—whether a person, plant, or animal—you make a connection, and they make a connection with you," the therapist 55 explained. "There is an invisible thread of energy that goes back and forth. Who knows who is giving and who is receiving?"

Clearly, caring touch is a powerful method for healing. It is of benefit for everyone: rich and poor, young and old, healthy and ill. Experts say that caring touch has measurable effects. It can lower blood pressure, raise 60 immunity, and decrease depression. It can also—even if given only briefly— influence behavior, as a number of studies show.

Something as simple as a firm handshake, for instance, can create an instant good impression of the individual who gives it. In fact, a University of Iowa study suggests that a solid handshake may be more important than a 65 résumé for landing a job. The professor who performed the study says the warm handshake sets the tone for the rest of the interview. Conceivably, it could set the tone for any important meeting, so it's a good social grace to master.

Similarly, studies have shown that waitresses who touch the customer's hand or arm in a light, friendly way when they return the check are likely to 70 get higher tips. An even more fascinating study shows that adults who received a friendly pat on the back from a female financial adviser were more willing to take a risk with their money than those who were not touched. Researchers guessed that the woman's touch evoked the feelings of security that comes from a mother's touch. As a result, there was a willingness to take greater risks. 75

What gives touch its power? Why is it that a human being can survive without hearing, or sight, but wither without touch? It could be that we human beings were *designed* to touch and be touched. Consider that we have two eyes and two ears, but five *million* nerve endings embedded in our skin, each ready to be triggered by touch. And we certainly have plenty of touchable skin—roughly 80 18 square feet if it were laid flat—making skin the body's largest organ.

Curious, isn't it, how something so simple can make such a big difference? Or maybe it's not—when you consider those five million nerve endings embedded in human skin. They suggest we are literally wired for touch. With this fact in mind, it may be that all the handshakes and hugs that seem to be 85 part of our culture these days are not just for show. They are also serving a good purpose in keeping us connected with one another.

Time: _____   *Reading Rate (see page 522):* _____ *WPM*

■ Reading Comprehension

1. Which sentence best expresses the central point of the selection?

   a. Massage therapists can help people rebuild a sense of self-esteem.

   b. Our sense of touch develops while we are still in our mother's womb.

   c. Touch, especially caring touch, is of benefit to everyone and can influence health and behavior.

   d. Touch is powerful because we have only two eyes and two ears, but five million nerve endings embedded in our skin.

2. Which sentence best expresses the main idea of paragraphs 17–18?

    a.   Some people are more willing to spend money when someone touches them.

    b.   Touch can be a positive factor in social and business interactions.

    c.   A firm handshake may be more important in getting a job than a résumé.

    d.   Some people feel a sense of security from a female financial advisor's touch.

3. According to the selection, Mother Teresa reached out to society's "untouchables" because

    a.   they were poor.

    b.   of their dangerous wounds.

    c.   she knew her caring touch would help restore their sense of dignity.

    d.   no one else would help them.

4. In the sentence below, the word *evoked* means

    a.   brought to mind.

    b.   destroyed.

    c.   refused.

    d.   decided.

    "Researchers guessed that the woman's touch evoked the feelings of security that comes from a mother's touch."

5. In the excerpt below, the word *wither* means

    a.   grow stronger.

    b.   continue.

    c.   communicate.

    d.   become weak

    "What gives touch its power? Why is it that a human being can survive without hearing, or sight, but wither without touch?"

6. The relationship expressed in the sentence below is one of

    a.   addition.

    b.   cause and effect.

    c.   contrast.

    d.   illustration.

    "It can lower blood pressure, for instance, raise immunity, and decrease depression."

7. The relationship between the two sentences below is one of

   a. cause and effect.

   b. comparison.

   c. time.

   d. illustration.

      "Researchers guessed that the woman's touch evoked the feelings of security that comes from a mother's touch. As a result, there was a willingness to take greater risks."

8. The pattern of organization of paragraphs 2–4 is mainly

   a. time order.

   b. addition.

   c. illustration.

   d. comparison.

Number Wrong: _____   *Score:* _____

| 0 wrong = 100% | 2 wrong = 75% | 4 wrong = 50% | 6 wrong = 25% |
| 1 wrong = 88% | 3 wrong = 63% | 5 wrong = 38% | 7 wrong = 13% |

■ Critical Thinking and Discussion

1. Why do you think Grandinetti begins the selection with the anecdote about the young man who had been badly burned? How does this anecdote relate to her central point?

2. Grandinetti mentions people such as waitresses and financial advisors who make a point of gently touching their clients. How would you feel about being touched in such situations? Do you think it would make you more willing to give a higher tip or take a risk with your money? Or might you react in some other way? Explain.

3. Some families often express affection through touch, while others don't. What was (or is) true of your family? Do you think that their expression of affection through touch (or lack of it) has affected you? Explain.

4. Most people would say that sight and hearing are the most important senses. However, Grandinetti feels differently. Do you agree with Grandinetti's conclusion that we are indeed "wired for touch"? Why or why not?

Selection 4

 Read the *Preview* and check the *Words to Watch* below. Then read the selection that follows. Remember that it is your deliberate effort to read faster, along with extensive practice, that will make you a faster reader. Keep this fact in mind as you read the following selection.

The Scholarship Jacket
Marta Salinas

■ Preview

She had earned the beautiful scholarship jacket. But at the last minute, it seemed that it would be stolen away from her. Marta Salinas remembers a painful, but ultimately triumphant, experience as a young Mexican American girl in south Texas.

■ Words to Watch

agile (line 14): able to move quickly

fidgeted (line 57): moved nervously

muster (line 66): bring together

mesquite (line 77): a sweet-smelling tree

gaunt (line 115): thin

adrenaline (line 133): a hormone that raises the blood pressure and stimulates the heart

The small Texas school that I attended carried out a tradition every year during the eighth grade graduation: a beautiful gold-and-green jacket, the school colors, was awarded to the class valedictorian, the student who had maintained the highest grades for eight years. The scholarship jacket had a big gold S on the left front side, and the winner's name was written in gold letters on the pocket. 5

My oldest sister, Rosie, had won the jacket a few years back, and I fully expected to win also. I was fourteen and in the eighth grade. I had been a straight-A student since the first grade, and the last year I had looked forward to owning that jacket. My father was a farm laborer who couldn't 10 earn enough money to feed eight children, so when I was six I was given to

479

my grandparents to raise. We couldn't participate in sports at school because there were registration fees, uniform costs, and trips out of town; so even though we were quite agile and athletic, there would never be a sports school jacket for us. This one, the scholarship jacket, was our only chance.   15

In May, close to graduation, spring fever struck, and no one paid any attention in class; instead, we stared out the windows and at each other, wanting to speed up the last few weeks of school. I despaired every time I looked in the mirror. Pencil-thin, with not a curve anywhere, I was called "Beanpole" and "String Bean," and I knew that's what I looked like. A flat   20 chest, no hips, and a brain, that's what I had. That really isn't much for a fourteen-year-old to work with, I thought, as I absentmindedly wandered from my class to the gym. Another hour of sweating during basketball and displaying my toothpick legs was coming up. Then I remembered that my P.E. shorts were still in a bag under my desk where I'd forgotten them. I had   25 to walk all the way back and get them. Coach Thompson was a real bear if anyone wasn't dressed for P.E. She had said I was a good forward and once she even tried to talk Grandma into letting me join the team. Grandma, of course, said no.

I was almost back at my classroom door when I heard angry voices and   30 arguing. I stopped. I didn't mean to eavesdrop; I just hesitated, not knowing what to do. I needed those shorts and I was going to be late, but I didn't want to interrupt an argument between my teachers. I recognized the voices: Mr. Schmidt, my history teacher, and Mr. Boone, my math teacher. They seemed to be arguing about me. I couldn't believe it. I still remember the shock that   35 rooted me flat against the wall as if I were trying to blend in with the graffiti written there.

"I refuse to do it! I don't care who her father is, her grades don't even begin to compare to Martha's. I won't lie or falsify records. Martha has a straight A-plus average and you know it." That was Mr. Schmidt, and he   40 sounded very angry. Mr. Boone's voice sounded calm and quiet.

"Look, Joann's father is not only on the Board, he owns the only store in town; we could say it was a close tie and—"

The pounding in my ears drowned out the rest of the words; only a word here and there filtered through. ". . . Martha is Mexican . . . resign . . . won't   45 do it. . . ." Mr. Schmidt came rushing out, and luckily for me went down the opposite way toward the auditorium, so he didn't see me. Shaking, I waited a few minutes and then went in and grabbed my bag and fled from the room. Mr. Boone looked up when I came in but didn't say anything. To this day I don't remember if I got into trouble in P.E. for being late or how I made   50 it through the rest of the afternoon. I went home very sad and cried into my pillow that night so Grandmother wouldn't hear me. It seemed a cruel coincidence that I had overheard that conversation.

The next day when the principal called me into his office, I knew what it would be about. He looked uncomfortable and unhappy. I decided I wasn't 55 going to make it any easier for him, so I looked him straight in the eye. He looked away and fidgeted with the papers on his desk.

"Martha," he said, "there's been a change in policy this year regarding the scholarship jacket. As you know, it has always been free." He cleared his throat and continued. "This year the Board decided to charge fifteen 60 dollars—which still won't cover the complete cost of the jacket."

I stared at him in shock and a small sound of dismay escaped my throat. I hadn't expected this. He still avoided looking in my eyes.

"So, if you are unable to pay the fifteen dollars for the jacket, it will be given to the next one in line."   65

Standing with all the dignity I could muster, I said, "I'll speak to my grandfather about it, sir, and let you know tomorrow." I cried on the walk home from the bus stop. The dirt road was a quarter of a mile from the highway, so by the time I got home, my eyes were red and puffy.

"Where's Grandpa?" I asked Grandma, looking down at the floor so she 70 wouldn't ask me why I'd been crying. She was sewing on a quilt and didn't look up.

"I think he's out back working in the bean field."

I went outside and looked out at the fields. There he was. I could see him walking between the rows, his body bent over the little plants, hoe in 75 hand. I walked slowly out to him, trying to think how I could best ask him for the money. There was a cool breeze blowing and a sweet smell of mesquite in the air, but I didn't appreciate it. I kicked at a dirt clod. I wanted that jacket so much. It was more than just being a valedictorian and giving a little thank-you speech for the jacket on graduation night. It represented eight 80 years of hard work and expectation. I knew I had to be honest with Grandpa; it was my only chance. He saw me and looked up.

He waited for me to speak. I cleared my throat nervously and clasped my hands behind my back so he wouldn't see them shaking. "Grandpa, I have a big favor to ask you," I said in Spanish, the only language he knew. He 85 still waited silently. I tried again. "Grandpa, this year the principal said the scholarship jacket is not going to be free. It's going to cost fifteen dollars and I have to take the money in tomorrow; otherwise, it'll be given to someone else." The last words came out in an eager rush. Grandpa straightened up tiredly and leaned his chin on the hoe handle. He looked out over the field 90 that was filled with the tiny green bean plants. I waited, desperately hoping he'd say I could have the money.

He turned to me and asked quietly, "What does a scholarship jacket mean?"

I answered quickly; maybe there was a chance. "It means you've earned   95
it by having the highest grades for eight years and that's why they're giving
it to you." Too late I realized the significance of my words. Grandpa knew
that I understood it was not a matter of money. It wasn't that. He went back
to hoeing the weeds that sprang up between the delicate little bean plants.
It was a time-consuming job; sometimes the small shoots were right next to   100
each other. Finally he spoke again.

"Then if you pay for it, Marta, it's not a scholarship jacket, is it? Tell your
principal I will not pay the fifteen dollars."

I walked back to the house and locked myself in the bathroom for a long
time. I was angry with Grandfather even though I knew he was right, and I   105
was angry with the Board, whoever they were. Why did they have to change
the rules just when it was my turn to win the jacket?

It was a very sad and withdrawn girl who dragged into the principal's
office the next day. This time he did look me in the eyes.

"What did your grandfather say?"   110

I sat very straight in my chair.

"He said to tell you he won't pay the fifteen dollars."

The principal muttered something I couldn't understand under his
breath and walked over to the window. He stood looking out at something
outside. He looked bigger than usual when he stood up; he was a tall, gaunt   115
man with gray hair, and I watched the back of his head while I waited for
him to speak.

"Why?" he finally asked. "Your grandfather has the money. Doesn't he
own a small bean farm?"

I looked at him, forcing my eyes to stay dry. "He said if I had to pay for   120
it, then it wouldn't be a scholarship jacket," I said and stood up to leave. "I
guess you'll just have to give it to Joann." I hadn't meant to say that; it had
just slipped out. I was almost to the door when he stopped me.

"Martha—wait."

I turned and looked at him, waiting. What did he want now? I could   125
feel my heart pounding. Something bitter and vile tasting was coming up
in my mouth; I was afraid I was going to be sick. I didn't need any sympathy
speeches. He sighed loudly and went back to his big desk. He looked at me,
biting his lip, as if thinking.

"OK, damn it. We'll make an exception in your case. I'll tell the Board,   130
you'll get your jacket."

I could hardly believe it. I spoke in a trembling rush. "Oh, thank you,
sir!" Suddenly I felt great. I didn't know about adrenaline in those days, but
I knew something was pumping through me, making me feel as tall as the
sky. I wanted to yell, jump, run the mile, do something. I ran out so I could   135

cry in the hall where there was no one to see me. At the end of the day, Mr. Schmidt winked at me and said, "I hear you're getting the scholarship jacket this year."

His face looked as happy and innocent as a baby's, but I knew better. Without answering I gave him a quick hug and ran to the bus. I cried on the walk home again, but this time because I was so happy. I couldn't wait to tell Grandpa and ran straight to the field. I joined him in the row where he was working and without saying anything I crouched down and started pulling up the weeds with my hands. Grandpa worked alongside me for a few minutes, but he didn't ask what had happened. After I had a little pile of weeds between the rows, I stood up and faced him. 140

145

"The principal said he's making an exception for me, Grandpa, and I'm getting the jacket after all. That's after I told him what you said."

Grandpa didn't say anything; he just gave me a pat on the shoulder and a smile. He pulled out the crumpled red handkerchief that he always carried in his back pocket and wiped the sweat off his forehead. 150

"Better go see if your grandmother needs any help with supper."

I gave him a big grin. He didn't fool me. I skipped and ran back to the house whistling some silly tune.

Time: _____   *Reading Rate (see page 522):* _____ WPM

■ **Reading Comprehension**

1. Which sentence best expresses the main idea of this selection?

   a. When she went to pick up her gym clothes, Marta overheard a conversation between two teachers that shocked and saddened her.

   b. At Marta's school, the eighth-grade valedictorian was traditionally awarded a beautiful green-and-gold jacket.

   c. Although Marta had earned the scholarship jacket, she almost lost it to a less deserving student.

   d. Marta's older sister had won the scholarship jacket, and Marta deeply wanted to win it as well.

2. Which of the following statements is *false*?

   a. Marta was being raised by her grandparents because her parents were dead.

   b. Mr. Schmidt was angry at the attempt to give the scholarship jacket to someone less deserving than Marta.

    c.   Marta's grandfather refused to give her the money for the scholarship jacket.

    d.   Joann's grades were not nearly as good as Marta's.

3. Marta's grandparents supported themselves by

    a.   running the only store in town.

    b.   teaching high school.

    c.   working on their own farm.

    d.   working as hired labor on other people's farms.

4. *True or false?* _____ Marta could not look the principal in the face after he called her into his office.

5. After her second conversation with the principal, Marta felt

    a.   humiliated.

    b.   overjoyed.

    c.   disappointed.

    d.   confused.

6. The relationship between the two sentences below is one of

    a.   time.

    b.   contrast.

    c.   comparison.

    d.   cause-effect.

         Another hour of sweating during basketball and displaying my toothpick legs was coming up. Then I remembered that my P.E. shorts were still in a bag under my desk where I'd forgotten them.

7. The author implies that Mr. Boone

    a.   had a strong personal dislike for Marta.

    b.   knew Marta was not really as intelligent as other people thought.

    c.   felt that, while Joann's grades were not as good as Marta's, Joann had more leadership ability.

    d.   was more concerned about pleasing Joann's father than being fair to Marta.

8. By saying, ". . . it's not a scholarship jacket, is it?" Marta's grandfather was implying that

   a.   the jacket was not worth fifteen dollars.

   b.   a real award should not have to be bought with money.

   c.   Marta did not deserve to win the scholarship jacket.

   d.   he did not understand what a scholarship jacket was.

Number Wrong: _____   *Score:* _____

| 0 wrong = 100% | 2 wrong = 75% | 4 wrong = 50% | 6 wrong = 25% |
| 1 wrong = 88% | 3 wrong = 63% | 5 wrong = 38% | 7 wrong = 13% |

■ Critical Thinking and Discussion

1. Why was winning the scholarship jacket so important to the Salinas children?

2. What difference did it make to Mr. Boone whether Marta or Joann won the scholarship jacket? What can you infer about his reasons?

3. Why do you think Marta's grandfather asked her, "What does a scholarship jacket mean?" Do you think he did not understand the meaning of the jacket himself?

Selection 5

Read the *Preview* and check the *Words to Watch* below. Then, in this selection and the selections that follow, continue trying to read for both speed *and* understanding. Your effort to concentrate more and increase your speed is very likely to help your comprehension as well. Only if you decide at some point that the effort to improve your speed is *not* working should you return to your normal reading rate.

Dare to Think Big
Ben Carson

■ Preview

Benjamin Carson, growing up poor with his single mother in inner-city Detroit, was considered the "dummy" of his fifth-grade class. The realization that he could learn and, in fact, do brilliantly in school fueled an amazing journey that has led Dr. Carson to become one of the world's most respected surgeons. In this excerpt from his book *The Big Picture,* Dr. Carson shares a message with young people of today.

■ Words to Watch

prevalent (line 8): widespread

deplorable (line 8): deserving of scorn

dire (line 11): extreme in a negative way

cavernous (line 15): wide and empty, like a cave

graphically (line 38): vividly

gratification (line 39): satisfaction

bevy (line 44): group

perspective (line 71): point of view

I do not speak only to parent groups. I spend a lot of time with students, such as those I encountered not long ago on a memorable visit to Wendell Phillips High School, an inner-city school on Chicago's south side.

Before I spoke, the people who invited me to the Windy City held a reception in my honor. There I met and talked with school officials and local religious leaders, many of whom informed me about the troubled

5

neighborhood where the school is located. They indicated that gang influence was prevalent, living conditions were deplorable in the surrounding public housing developments, dropout statistics were high, and SAT scores were low.

It sounded like a lot of other high schools I have visited around the country. 10 Yet so dire were these warnings that, on the crosstown drive to the school, I could not help wondering what kind of reception I would receive from the students.

I need not have worried. When I walked into Wendell Phillips High School, its long, deserted hallways gave the building a cavernous, empty feel. 15 The entire student body (1,500 to 2,000 strong) had already been excused from class and was assembled quietly in the school's auditorium. A school administrator, who was addressing the audience, noted my entrance through a back door and abruptly interrupted his remarks to announce, "And here's Dr. Carson now!" 20

All eyes turned my way. Immediately students began to applaud. Some stood. Suddenly they were all standing, clapping, and cheering. The applause continued the entire time I walked down the aisle and climbed the steps onto the auditorium stage. I couldn't remember ever receiving a warmer, more enthusiastic, or more spontaneous reception anywhere in my entire life. 25

I found out later that a local bank had purchased and distributed paperback copies of my autobiography, *Gifted Hands*, to every student at Wendell Phillips. A lot of those teenagers had evidently read the book and felt they already knew me. By the time I reached the microphone, the noise faded away. I felt overwhelmed by their welcome. 30

I did what I often do when facing such a young audience. I wanted them thinking seriously about their lives and futures. So I quickly summarized my earliest years as a child, about my own student days back at Southwestern High School in Detroit. I referred briefly to the incident when my anger nearly caused a tragedy that would have altered my life forever. I recounted 35 my struggles with peer pressure, which sidetracked me for a time.

Then I talked about the difference between being viewed as *cool* and being classified as a lowly *nerd*. I find that serves as a graphically relevant illustration for my message on *delayed gratification*—a theme I hit almost every time I speak to young people. 40

The *cool* guys in every school are the ones who have earned a varsity letter in some sport—maybe several sports. They wear the latest fashions. They know all the hit tunes. They can converse about the latest blockbuster movies. They drive sharp cars and seem to collect a bevy of beautiful girlfriends. 45

The *nerds* are the guys always hauling around an armload of books, with more in their backpacks. They wear clean clothes—and often big, thick glasses. They even understand the science experiments. They ride the school bus, or worse yet, their parents drive them to school. Most of the popular girls would not be caught dead speaking to them in the hallway between classes. 50

The years go by, and graduation draws near. Often the cool guy has not done well in school, but his personality wins him a job at the local fast-food franchise, flipping hamburgers and waiting on customers. The nerd, who has won a scholarship, goes off to college.

A few more years go by. The cool guy is still flipping burgers. Maybe he 55 has even moved up to Assistant Shift Manager by now. The girls who come in to eat lunch may notice and smile at him. He is still cool.

The nerd finishes up at college and does very well. Upon graduation he accepts a job offer from a Fortune 500 company. With his first paycheck, he goes to the eye doctor, who replaces those big, old, thick glasses with a pair 60 of contacts. He stops at the tailor and picks out a couple of nice suits to wear. After saving a big chunk of his first few paychecks, he makes a down payment on a new Lexus. When he drives home to visit his parents, all the young women in the old neighborhood say, "Hey, don't I know you?" Suddenly, they do not want to talk to the guy behind the fast-food counter anymore. 65

The first guy—the cool guy—had everything back in high school. So what did he get for all that?

The other guy was not cool at all—but he was focused. Where did he go in the long run?

"And that," I told my audience, "is how we have to learn to think about 70 life! With a long-term view. A Big-Picture perspective!"

Those students at Chicago's Wendell Phillips High School could not have been more attentive as I recounted the things this former *nerd* has seen and done. They listened to me explain and illustrate the incredible potential that resides in the average human brain. They even seemed receptive to 75 my challenge that they begin to use those brains to plan and prepare for the future. So, as I wrapped up my talk by daring them to THINK BIG, I did something I had never done before, though I realized it could backfire if I had read this audience wrong. But since they had been such a responsive group, I decided to risk it. 80

I concluded by asking that auditorium full of high school students for a show of hands. "How many of you are ready, here today, to raise your hands and say to me, to your teachers, and to your peers, 'I want to be a nerd.'"

Although many of them laughed, almost all the students of Wendell Phillips High School raised their hands as they stood and applauded and 85 cheered even louder than when I had walked in.

Time: _____   *Reading Rate (see page 522):* _____ *WPM*

■ **Reading Comprehension**

1. Which of the following would be the best alternative title for this selection?

   a. An Inner-City School

   b. An Encouraging Talk

   c. High School Popularity

   d. Cool Guys in High School

2. Which sentence best expresses the main idea of this selection?

   a. In a talk to high school students, Ben Carson encouraged them to focus on long-term goals.

   b. The student body of a tough inner-city high school listened politely to Ben Carson's talk.

   c. Benjamin Carson, a famous surgeon, was considered a nerd in high school.

   d. Guys who earn varsity letters, know all the current music, and drive sharp cars seem to collect the most girlfriends in high school.

3. A lot of the students at Wendell Phillips High School

   a. had already read Ben Carson's autobiography.

   b. skipped school on the day that Dr. Carson spoke.

   c. had unusually high SAT scores.

   d. worked in fast-food restaurants.

4. Peer pressure

   a. sidetracked Dr. Carson for a while during his teenage years.

   b. never affected Dr. Carson during his teenage years.

   c. was less of a problem during Dr. Carson's teen years than it is now.

   d. affected Dr. Carson in positive ways during his teenage years.

5. *True or false?* _____ Dr. Carson expected to receive a warm welcome at Wendell Phillips High School.

6. *True or false?* _____ Dr. Carson often ended his talks to high school audiences by inviting them to say, "I want to be a nerd."

7. From the article, the reader might conclude that

   a. Dr. Carson was considered cool in high school.

   b. planning for the future can mean giving up some pleasure today.

    c.   Dr. Carson hardly ever speaks to parent groups.

    d.   The visit to Wendell Phillips High School was Dr. Carson's first to Chicago.

8. Dr. Carson implies that

    a.   girls in high school aren't impressed by cool guys.

    b.   the cool guy in high school wasn't thinking about his future.

    c.   the cool guy in school had a "Big-Picture" perspective on his life.

    d.   when the nerd got his first paychecks, he should have saved them instead of spending them as he did.

Number Wrong: _____   *Score:* _____

| 0 wrong = 100% | 2 wrong = 75% | 4 wrong = 50% | 6 wrong = 25% |
| 1 wrong = 88% | 3 wrong = 63% | 5 wrong = 38% | 7 wrong = 13% |

■ Critical Thinking and Discussion

1. As Dr. Carson drove to Wendell Phillips High School, he worried about "what kind of reception" he would receive from the students. Why do you think he was concerned? What kind of reception do you think he imagined he might find?

2. Why do you think Dr. Carson admitted to the students that his hot temper had once nearly caused a tragedy and that he was "sidetracked" by peer pressure for a while? Wouldn't it set a better example if he revealed only the positive parts of his life?

3. In your experience, is it true that "cool," popular guys in high school generally do less well academically than hardworking "nerds"? Do you agree with Dr. Carson that the cool guys will do less well in the long run of life?

Selection 6

Winning the Job Interview Game
Marcia Prentergast

■ Preview

Job interviews, like final exams, can cause self-doubts and upset stomachs. You may feel that interviews are even worse than finals since you can't prepare for them. In the reading below, however, Marcia Prentergast explains that there is much you can do to get ready for job interviews—and to make yourself stand out from the crowd of other applicants.

■ Words to Watch

personable (line 6): friendly

conservative (line 19): customary, traditional

flustered (line 24): nervously confused

potential (line 73): possible

Few things in everyday life are dreaded more than going to a job interview. First you have to wait in an outer room, which may be filled with other people all applying for the same job you want. You look at them and they look at you. Everyone knows that only one person is going to get the job. Then you are called into the interviewer's office, where you have to sit 5 in front of a complete stranger. You have to try to act cool and personable while you are asked all sorts of questions. The questions are highly personal, or confusing, or both. *"What are your strengths and weaknesses?"* *"Where do you see yourself in five years?"* The interview may take twenty minutes, but it may seem like two hours. Finally, when you're done, you get to go 10 home and wait a week or so to find out if you got the job.

The job-interview "game" may not be much fun, but it is a game you can win if you play it right. The name of the game is standing out of the crowd—in a positive way. If you go to the interview in a Bozo the Clown suit, you may stand out of the crowd, all right, but not in a way that is likely to 15 get you hired.

A few basic hints can help you play the interview game to win:

1. Dress as if you're in charge. That means wearing business clothing: usually a suit and tie or a conservative dress or skirt suit. Don't dress casually or sloppily, but don't overdress—remember, you're going to a business 20 meeting, not a social affair. Business attire will impress the interviewer. More than that, it will actually help *you* to feel more businesslike, more in charge. As the old saying goes, clothes make the man (or woman).

2. Plan to arrive early. This will keep you from getting hurried and flustered, and also help you avoid the disaster of being late. Give yourself a few minutes 25 to catch your breath and mentally go over your application or résumé.

3. Expect to do some small talk first. Knowing what to expect can put you ahead of the game. When the interviewer calls you in, you will probably spend a minute or so in small talk before getting down to the actual interview questions. This small talk is a good time to make a positive 30 impression, though. Follow the interviewer's lead, and if he or she wants to discuss the weather, let's say, by all means do so for a little bit.

4. Be prepared. Certain questions come up regularly in job interviews. *You should plan for all these questions in advance!* Here are common questions, what they really mean, and how to answer them: 35

"Tell me about yourself." This question is raised to see how organized you are. If you give a wandering, disjointed answer, the interviewer may put you down as a scatterbrain. You might talk briefly about where you were born and raised, where your family lives now, where you went to school, what jobs you've had, and how you happen to be here now looking for the challenge of 40 a new job. You should have planned and rehearsed your answer, so you can present this basic information about yourself quickly and smoothly.

This question can also give you a chance to show that you're right for the job. If you're applying for a sales job, for example, you might want to point out that you like being around people.   45

"What are your weaknesses?" This question is asked to put you off your guard, perhaps making you reveal things you might not want to. A good ploy is to admit a "weakness" that employers might actually like—for example, admit to being a workaholic or a perfectionist.

"Why did you leave your last job?" This can be a "killer" question, especially 50 if you were fired, or if you quit because you hated your boss. According to the experts, never bad-mouth anyone when asked this question. If you were fired, talk about personality conflicts, but without blaming anyone. If you hated your boss, say you quit for some other reason—to find a position with more growth opportunities, for example.   55

"Why did you apply for this job?" This question is really asking how eager an employee you will be. The simple answer might be "I need the money"—but that is not what job interviewers and employers want to hear.

They want employees who will work hard and stay with the company. So be honest, but give a suitable response. You might say that this is the sort of work you've always wanted to do, or that you see this company as the kind of place where you would like to create a career. 60

Other typical questions are pure softball—if you're ready. If you are asked, "Are you creative?" or "Are you a leader?" give some examples to show that you are. For instance, you may want to discuss your organizational role in one of your college clubs. Perhaps you helped recruit new members 65 or came up with ideas to increase attendance at events. If you are asked, "What are your greatest strengths?" be ready to talk about your abilities that fit the job. Perhaps you'll mention your ability to learn quickly, your talent for working with others, your skill with organizing time efficiently, or your ability to solve problems. 70

No amount of preparation is ever going to make job interviews your favorite activity. But if you go in well-prepared and with a positive attitude, your potential employer can't help thinking highly of you. And the day will come when you will be the one who wins the job.

Time: _____   *Reading Rate (see page 522):* _____ *WPM*

■ **Reading Comprehension**

1. Which statement best expresses the central point of the selection?

   a. Interviewers may ask some difficult and highly personal questions.

   b. When going to an interview, dress in business clothing, mentally go over your application or résumé, and go in with a positive attitude.

   c. There are several things you can do to make yourself stand out in a positive way at job interviews.

   d. Employers may ask you why you left your last job.

2. What is the main point of paragraph 8 (lines 36–42)?

   a. Your answer to the question "Tell me about yourself" can demonstrate that you are well organized.

   b. You should tell the interviewer where you were born and raised, where your family lives now, and so on.

   c. You should have planned and rehearsed your answers to common interview questions.

   d. The interviewer may put you down as scatterbrained.

3. What statement best expresses the main point of paragraph 13 (lines 62–70)?

    a. It is a good idea to back up any mention of your college activities with specific examples of what you did.

    b. An interviewer may ask questions such as "Are you creative?" or "Are you a leader?"

    c. You should possess the skills of learning quickly, organizing time efficiently, and being able to solve problems.

    d. "Softball" questions give you the opportunity to describe your good points and how they fit the job.

4. If you were fired from your last job, the author advises you

    a. to make sure your interviewer realizes how unfair your former boss was.

    b. not to blame anyone for the firing.

    c. not to tell the truth, but to convince the interviewer that you quit.

    d. to tell your interviewer a lot of people were fired by the same boss.

5. According to the author, some advantages of arriving early to an interview are:

    a. You will not be flustered or late, and you'll have time to review your application or résumé.

    b. You will have time for small talk with the interviewer.

    c. You will have time to see all the other people applying for the same job.

    d. You will have time to check your appearance and to speak to the interviewer's secretary.

6. In the opinion of the author, what do interviewers really want to know when they ask, "Why did you apply for this job?"

    a. How much money you want to earn.

    b. If you are eager to be hired and will stay with the company.

    c. If you are creative and a leader.

    d. If you were fired from your last job and are desperate for another one.

7. In the sentence that follows, what kind of signal word is used to show the relationship of the second sentence to the first?

    a. Illustration

    b. Addition

    c. Time

    d. Cause and effect

If you are asked, "Are you creative?" or "Are you a leader?" give some examples to show that you are. For instance, you may want to discuss your organizational role in one of your college clubs. (Lines 62–65)

8. We can infer from paragraph 11 (lines 50–55) that

   a.   if you blame someone else for your troubles at work, interviewers may think that you may be a difficult employee.

   b.   most people who quit a job do so because they hate the boss.

   c.   as long as you are telling the truth, it is all right to tell the whole story of why you were fired or quit.

   d.   honesty is always the best policy.

Number Wrong: _____   *Score:* _____

| 0 wrong = 100% | 2 wrong = 75% | 4 wrong = 50% | 6 wrong = 25% |
| 1 wrong = 88% | 3 wrong = 63% | 5 wrong = 38% | 7 wrong = 13% |

■ Critical Thinking and Discussion

1. What advice does Prentergast give if you are asked, "Why did you leave your last job?" If you could ask her just why she gives this advice, what do you think she might say?

2. What, according to the author, is the real purpose of "small talk" at the beginning of the interview?

3. In your experience, are job interviews usually as "dreaded" as the author suggests? What has made the difference (for you) between a pleasant interview and an awful one?

Selection 7

A Door Swings Open

Roxanne Black

■ **Preview**

In this selection from a recent autobiography, the author, Roxanne Black, describes her reactions when, as a teenager, she learned she had an incurable disease. Read the selection, and then answer the questions that follow.

■ **Words to Watch**

wincing (line 14): a quick movement as the result of pain

ominous (line 42): something that is threatening

chronic (line 45): lasting for a long time; continuing to occur

biopsy (line 71): the removal of sample tissue for laboratory examination

intoned (line 80): said something in a slow and serious way

I sat at my bedroom window in my wheelchair, watching my high-school rowing team pull away from the shore, eight friends smiling and waving as they moved into the choppy water. Not long ago, I'd been one of them.

I loved everything about rowing, the feeling of freedom, the teamwork, the sense of strength and accomplishment. When I rowed, I was at peace 5
and forgot about my problems. Not that I'd had many then. In most ways, I was a typical New Jersey teenager; a shy high-school freshman who lived with her mother in a small row house that overlooked Lake's Bay. My mother and I didn't have two dimes to rub together, but with that view from our windows, we considered ourselves rich. 10

It was after rowing one afternoon that I had the first warning that something might be wrong with me—a sharp stab of back pain that took my breath away.

"What's the matter?" my mother asked when she saw me wincing.

"I don't know," I said, stretching. "I guess I strained a muscle." 15

By evening, the pain was almost too painful to bear. My mother filled a hot bath with Epsom salts, and later gave me a heating pad. I took a couple of Tylenol and decided I'd stay away from crew practice for a few days. In my

496

young life, this had been the antidote for any ailment. Eventually everything passed, given time and a little rest.   20

But not this time. Instead of decreasing, the pain grew so intense that I could barely sit up in bed the next morning.

My mother took one look at me and said, "I'm taking you to the doctor."

But by the time we arrived at the office, the pain had subsided and the   25
doctor advised that we simply continue with the heating pad and baths.

Two days later, I developed chest pains that by evening were so acute I could barely breathe. Now I was beginning to worry.

This time the doctor prescribed antibiotics, thinking I might have an infection. The pains intensified over the next few days; then they too   30
vanished.

Although the doctor tracked my reports, took bloodwork, and examined me closely, he couldn't figure out what was wrong. My symptoms were elusive; it was hard to pin them down.

Finally he referred me to a specialist. By the day of my appointment, all   35
my symptoms had subsided except for my swollen ankles. My mother and I arrived at his office, expecting this new doctor would prescribe another medication for what was probably an allergic reaction.

After a routine examination, he studied my bloodwork, then touched my ankles, which were so full of fluid they could be molded like lumps of clay.   40

Then he looked up and a strange word floated from his mouth. Lupus. I saw it, like in a cartoon caption, odd and ominous, hanging in the air.

The word meant nothing to me, but my mother's reaction did; she covered her face with her hands. In her work as a nurse, she'd spent years caring for patients with chronic illness. As I watched her sniff and take out a   45
Kleenex, it hit me that this must be serious, something that Tylenol and bed rest weren't going to solve.

How had this disease that only affected one in many hundreds in the United States ended up in Atlantic City, residing in a teenager like me?

For that, there was no answer.   50

"There's always one moment in childhood when the door opens and lets the future in," Graham Greene wrote. I don't know if most people remember that moment, but I do.

At the children's hospital, I shared a room with a three-year-old girl with a charming face and shiny black hair cut in a bob. She was so energetic and   55
lively, I assumed she was someone's daughter or sister, until I glimpsed a tiny hospital ID bracelet on her wrist.

Her name was Michelle, and we bonded from the moment we met. She brought a herd of plastic ponies to my bedside, and we brushed their manes and made up stories.   60

"Why's she here?" I asked when her parents arrived, looking drawn and worried.

"She has a hole in her heart," her mother told me. "She's having open-heart surgery tomorrow."

I'd never known a sick child before, and now I was in a hospital full 65
of them. It seemed unnatural seeing toddlers on IV's, babies on ventilators, adolescents with leg braces, struggling to walk. A parade of pediatric malfunction passed my door, children smashed in motor accidents, suffering from muscular dystrophy and leukemia. This alternate world had existed all along, behind my formerly sunny, innocent life.   70

The next day I was to find out the results of my kidney biopsy, and Michelle was headed to surgery. Before she left, she walked over and hugged me so tightly that I could smell the baby shampoo in her hair. Then she solemnly handed me a drawing she'd made of a house, a girl, and a tree.

"This is you, isn't it?"   75

She nodded.

"Well it's beautiful, thanks. I'll see you later."

Early in the evening, I was talking on the pay phone in the hallway when an alarm sounded, and doctors began running down the hall from all directions. A woman's voice intoned a code over the loudspeakers, a foreign 80 babble.

Shortly after I returned to my room, a young floor nurse walked in. Her sad face was statement enough, but then she told me. Michelle hadn't made it. She'd suffered a heart attack and died.

So there it was, and I had to face it: Life wasn't fair. Prayers weren't 85 always answered. The young and innocent could be lost. The door had swung open, and I had been pushed through to the other side.

Time: _____   *Reading Rate (see page 522):* _____ *WPM*

■ **Reading Comprehension**

1. The central idea of the selection is that

   a.   Black was shocked to learn that she had a chronic disease.

   b.   Black was saddened when a little girl she met in the hospital died.

   c.   before becoming ill with lupus, Black had been in excellent health.

   d.   as the result of her own chronic illness and the death of a child, Black realized that life isn't fair.

2. Which sentence best expresses the main idea of paragraph 2?

   a.   When Black rowed, she forgot about her problems.

   b.   Black lived with her mother in a small row house overlooking Lake's Bay.

   c.   In most ways, Black, who loved rowing, was a typical teenager.

   d.   Although Black and her mother didn't have much money, they considered themselves rich.

3. Black first thought the intense pain she was experiencing was

   a.   an insect bite.

   b.   an allergic reaction.

   c.   an infection.

   d.   a muscle strain.

4. When the doctor tells Black she has lupus, her mother

   a.   tells the doctor he's wrong.

   b.   screams and then breaks out into loud sobs.

   c.   covers her face with her hands and takes out a Kleenex.

   d.   says she knew it all along.

5. Michelle was in the hospital because she had

   a.   leukemia.

   b.   a hole in her heart.

   c.   a brain tumor.

   d.   been injured in an auto accident.

6. In the excerpt below, the word *antidote* means

   a.   explanation.

   b.   cure.

   c.   cause.

   d.   symptom.

      "I took a couple of Tylenol and decided I'd stay away from crew practice for a few days. In my young life, this had been the antidote for any ailment."

7. In the excerpt below, the word *subsided* means

   a.   became less.

   b.   gotten worse.

   c.   returned.

   d.   stayed the same.

"My mother took one look at me and said, 'I'm taking you to the doctor.'

But by the time we arrived at the office, the pain had subsided, and the doctor advised that we simply continue with the heating pad and baths."

8. In the sentence below, the word *acute* means

    a.   effortless.

    b.   sharp.

    c.   mild.

    d.   predictable.

"Two days later, I developed chest pains that by evening were so acute I could barely breathe."

Number Wrong: _____   *Score:* _____

0 wrong = 100%	2 wrong = 75%	4 wrong = 50%	6 wrong = 25%
1 wrong = 88%	3 wrong = 63%	5 wrong = 38%	7 wrong = 13%

■ Critical Thinking and Discussion

1. When Black enters the hospital, she becomes aware of an "alternate world" that "had existed all along, behind my formerly sunny, innocent life." What is this "alternate world"? What, in particular, does she find surprising about it?

2. Black quotes Graham Greene, who wrote, "There's always one moment in childhood when the door opens and lets the future in." What might this statement mean? According to Black's story, when did this experience happen to her? Why do you think she was so upset afterward?

3. Have you ever known anyone who, like Black, suffers from chronic illness? If so, how does it affect his or her life? What adjustments has the person made in order to live with this condition?

4. Do you remember a moment in *your* life when "the door opened and let the future in"? Describe the event, and explain what it made you realize.

Selection 8

From Nonreading to Reading
Stacy Kelly Abbott

■ Preview

As an adult, married and a father, Stacy Abbott had to face the fact that he could not read well enough to function in society. In this selection, Abbott tells why he grew up a nonreader and describes his struggle to gain the reading skills he needed.

■ Words to Watch

reinforcement (line 31): support

peers (line 53): people of the same class, age, etc., such as classmates

taunting (line 59): insulting in a sarcastic way

jargon (line 73): the specialized vocabulary of a given field

retain (line 99): keep in mind, remember

abstractly (line 100): concerning general ideas (not specific things), theoretically

Reading is the key to success in American society. Everything our society is and does depends on that one word. In addition to the thousands of illiterates we hear about on television and in magazines, there is an unspoken and silent category of people never mentioned. This is the group of people who can read, but not quite well enough to feel comfortable or successful with it.   5
According to *Time* magazine, "There are over seventy-five million illiterate people in America. Another forty million are termed 'marginal readers.'" This is the group that I fit into. I am not totally comfortable with reading, but I am able to get by. Slowly and gradually the role of reading in my life is changing from nonexistent to partially existent to existent.   10
As early as I can remember, there were never any recreational books in our home. They just were not something that was thought to be needed—or wanted, for that matter. My wife tells me that the most important thing for preschoolers to have is exposure to reading. They need to have books to look at and "play" read. She has bought our daughter—who is only a   15
year old—an entire library. Sometimes, when I think about it, I think, "It's not fair! Why didn't my parents buy me books and read to me the way my

501

wife reads to our daughter?" Of course, until my wife told me, I never knew books were supposed to be a part of your early childhood. I had absolutely no exposure to any type of stories, poetry, or even picture books before I 20 entered kindergarten. This was my very first setback in reading. It was my first step on a road to nonreading.

I remember being excited when I entered kindergarten. In my memory, I was not slower than or behind the other children. First grade was about the same. I kept up fairly well, and—although I do not remember learning the 25 actual mechanics of reading—I still learned to read at the first-grade level. The thing to remember is that this was twenty-three years ago, and school has gotten much harder now. I probably would not be able to keep up now, because schools give homework.

What I learned in school was the end of it. I had absolutely no 30 reinforcement at home of what I learned at school. It was at this point that drugs and alcohol were entering my life. My father was an alcoholic, and my three brothers and sisters were all teenagers at this time in my life. My two brothers had already dropped out of school, and my sister was well on her way too. Drugs and alcohol were not considered wrong at my house. They 35 were an everyday part of my life. I did not know that everyone else's home was not like this. It was inevitable that I try them when they were so readily available. This was my next step on the road to nonreading.

Second grade was where major problems began surfacing. I was held back in second grade, and my second year I was placed in "resource" classes. 40 I could no longer fit into regular classes. I could not read past a first-grade level. Most of my memories of early school are of second grade. It was here that my self-esteem plummeted. I realized that I was slower than the other children. Sometimes children can be really cruel. They teased me and told me I was stupid. 45

School and my self-esteem continued on this downward path for several years. During junior high, everything seemed to get worse. This is when "resource" became an embarrassment. It was shameful to be so "stupid." It was not so bad when I was in the resource class, because most of the others were about on my level. Reading aloud in front of this group was sort of 50 calming. It was not bad at all. But I still had to take some regular classes. This was where the humiliation was horrible. I could read a little, but reading in front of this group of peers was impossible. I just stuttered along. This is how the remainder of my school career went. Resource was satisfying, but regular classes were awful. Somehow, though, I stuck with school and did not quit. 55

All my brothers and sisters had dropped out, but they still lived at home. Drugs and alcohol were still readily available. I do not recall exactly when, but sometime while I was in high school one of my brothers found out that I could not read. He began teasing and taunting me. It was horrible. I was one of those millions of marginal readers who graduated from high school 60

barely able to function in American society. I made sure I maintained a job 65
where no reading was required. Life was fine for several years, but I was still
continuing down the road to nonreading.

About the beginning of the change in my life came when I became active in
my church. It is common for young men in my church to serve a mission.
This idea was not so bad, except that all the reading and learning required 70
to be successful was overwhelming. My desire to get my life in order finally
convinced me to serve a mission. I learned to read much better, but only on
church-related subjects. It was like learning a jargon for a job. I really still did
not read very well at all.

About a year after I came home from my mission, I got married. It was 75
then that I realized what bad shape I was really in. I had accumulated several
delinquent bills simply because I could not read the late-notice letters. I even
almost lost my home. By this time in my life, my fear of reading aloud haunted
me. In school, I had more of a "don't care" attitude and really had not cared
what other people thought. Now I did care what people thought of me. I did 80
not want my wife to think any less of me because of my problem. My wife
convinced me that I was OK and she could help me learn to read better.

At her urging, I began college in the summer of 1990. I had been
married for a year and had a daughter who was one week old. I read on an
elementary school level, and my fear of reading aloud was a nightmare. My 85
wife assured me that she had been through four years of college and had
never had to read aloud. I took her word for it. I was taking a developmental
reading class, and the very first day of class the instructor called on me to
read a passage aloud. Somehow I struggled through it, humiliated and all.
When I told my wife what happened, she could not believe it! But she still 90
reassured me that I could do it. I went and spoke with the instructor about
my problem, and she was very understanding. All during the summer and
fall my wife helped me by reading all my material on tape and making notes
for me. I was quickly seeing all the benefits of reading. Those few years had
started me on the path to becoming a reader. 95

I struggled with school and worked really hard. We discovered that the
Texas Rehabilitation Commission could help with fees and tutors for reading.
The commission sent me for testing, and it was discovered that I had a visual-
spatial learning disability. This explained why it was so hard for me to retain
information and think abstractly—two skills that are required in college. Once 100
the problem was discovered, I found it easier to deal with. Now I knew I was
not stupid; I just had to learn to get around this. Though this explained the
problem, it did not solve it. I still had to learn to read at a higher level. I have
received all my textbooks on tape to help me read them. I have purchased
a phonics program to help me with my reading, and it is going slowly but 105
steadily. I am making my way down the road of active reading.

As I look back over the past four years, I see all the things that have happened to make me understand how important reading is. I am not where I want to be yet, but I will be in a year or two. I can say this with confidence now. I see reading now as a key to unlocking my whole future, especially 110 my financial future. No more will there be the fear of having to fill out an application for employment in front of someone. I will be able to fill it out with ease, because I will know how to *read.* No more will there be the fear that my daughter will ask me to read her a book and I will have to say, "Not right now." No more will there be the fear of delinquency letters because 115 of my inability to read. Reading has truly been transformed from a totally nonexistent part of my life to an existent and very essential part. Reading has simply helped me "to be."

Time: _____   *Reading Rate (see page 522):* _____ *WPM*

■ Reading Comprehension

1. Which of the following would be the best alternative title for this selection?

   a. Stacy Abbott

   b. Illiteracy in America

   c. The Story of a Marginal Reader

   d. The Importance of Reading to Children

2. Which sentence best expresses the main idea of this selection?

   a. There were no recreational books in the author's home while he was growing up.

   b. Abbott has improved his reading by getting his textbooks on audiotape and by using a phonics program.

   c. There are forty million marginal readers in the United States.

   d. Despite coming from an unsupportive home and having a learning disability, Abbott is learning to read.

3. Abbott implies in paragraph 2 (lines 11–22) that

   a. he thinks his wife is foolish for buying books for their baby daughter.

   b. he respects his wife's judgment when she buys books for their daughter.

   c. there were not many story, poetry, or picture books published for children when he was a child.

   d. his daughter can already read.

4. Which sentence best expresses the main idea of paragraph 4 (lines 30–38)?

   a.   Drugs and alcohol were not considered wrong in Abbott's home.

   b.   One obstacle to Abbott's reading was his family's lack of support for school and the family members' use of drugs and alcohol.

   c.   Abbott's brothers dropped out of school, and his sister was on her way to doing the same.

   d.   Children often imitate what they see their parents or siblings doing.

5. According to this selection, marginal readers

   a.   are completely illiterate.

   b.   are rare in the United States.

   c.   can read only enough to get by.

   d.   are very comfortable with reading and often attend college.

6. *True or false?* _____ Abbott's poor reading prevented him from serving a mission for his church.

7. The sentence below expresses a relationship of

   a.   time.

   b.   addition.

   c.   contrast.

   d.   illustration.

       I read on an elementary level, and my fear of reading aloud was a nightmare.

8. Abbott implies that a person with a learning disability

   a.   is unlikely to ever learn to read.

   b.   may deal better with the disability once it is fully identified.

   c.   is probably mentally ill as well.

   d.   should not expect to go to college.

Number Wrong: _____   *Score:* _____

0 wrong = 100%	2 wrong = 75%	4 wrong = 50%	6 wrong = 25%
1 wrong = 88%	3 wrong = 63%	5 wrong = 38%	7 wrong = 13%

■   ## Critical Thinking and Discussion

1. What were some of the "steps along the road to nonreading" in Stacy Abbott's life? In your opinion, were some of those steps more damaging to him than others?

2. Abbott writes that realizing he had a specific learning disability made it easier for him to deal with his reading problem. Why do you think this made a difference to him?

3. "Reading is the key to success in American society." Do you think that is true? In what ways would inability to read make success in today's world difficult?

Selection 9

The Certainty of Fear
Audra Kendall

■ Preview

What are you afraid of? Were your fears different five years ago? According to this essay, every stage of life brings its particular fears. Do you fit the pattern?

■ Words to Watch

provocation (line 34): irritation

conspicuous (line 61): noticeable

intoxicated (line 84): drunk

obsessed (line 87): constantly preoccupied

turmoil (line 103): confusion

priorities (line 114): what a person considers most important

frailty (line 123): physical weakness

I had all the usual childhood fears. I couldn't go to sleep unless the light in my bedroom closet was on. I dreaded that someday when my mother was distracted, Crazy Betty (our local small-town oddball) would grab me in the grocery store. On the hottest summer nights, my feet had to be wrapped tightly in my bedsheets; if one of them hung bare over the side of the bed, who knew what might grab it in its cold, slimy claw? 5

But all other frights paled before the Great Fear, the *Titanic* of my childhood terrors. That fear—and I admit, I feel a tightening in my stomach typing the words even today—was that something would happen to Monk-Monk. 10

507

Looking at Monk-Monk today, you wouldn't see what I see. You'd see a torn, discolored sock monkey, very much past his prime, stuffing leaking from his stumpy tail, holes on his sock-body inexpertly stitched up with thread that doesn't match. I see my dearest childhood friend, my companion of a thousand nights. When I was only two and very ill, an aunt made him for 15 me and delivered him to the hospital. I bonded with him fiercely and rarely let him out of my sight. When no one else was around, Monk-Monk played endless games with me, soaked up my tears, and listened to my secrets.

And then Uncle Ken came to visit. I didn't know Uncle Ken well, and I didn't like him very much. I had the feeling he didn't really like me, either. He 20 clearly thought it was pretty silly that a big first-grader was dragging a sock monkey around, and he teased me by saying he thought he'd take Monk-Monk home to Ohio with him. I clutched Monk-Monk more tightly.

I was at school a few days later when Uncle Ken left. When I came home, I couldn't find Monk-Monk anywhere. I can hardly describe the depths of my 25 panic. I don't think I cried; my terror was beyond that. I could barely breathe. My thoughts raced like a wild animal in a tiny cage. Where was Monk-Monk? What had Uncle Ken done to him? Was he safe somewhere, or had Uncle Ken (and this thought made my heart nearly stop) thrown him out the car window? Was Monk-Monk lying in a weedy strip along the interstate, lonely 30 and cold, never to be loved again?

When we found Monk-Monk wedged behind the sofa (could Uncle Ken really have been mean enough to do that? I never found out), I was limp with relief. For days afterwards I was shaken, crying at the least provocation.

As far as I can remember, that near-loss of Monk-Monk was my first 35 encounter with real, deep-down fear. I felt the threatened loss of something precious to me. And that, I think, is the essence of fear—the threat of loss.

Small children fear the loss of a favorite toy. The fears of adolescents are different. Above almost anything, adolescents fear losing their cool— looking "stupid." They will risk almost anything in order to maintain the 40 illusion that they are cool, composed, and in control.

Let me give you an example. A friend of mine had the opportunity to work in Florence, Italy, for a few months. While he was gone, he arranged for his two teenage sons to visit him for a week. The excited boys arrived at the airport and checked in. After sitting down to wait for their flight, one 45 nudged the other. "Look at the tickets," he told his brother. "They don't say 'Florence.'" Indeed, the tickets did not list Florence as the destination. They said "Firenze."

Now, it so happens that Firenze is the Italian name for Florence, so everything was fine. But the boys didn't know that. They thought that 50 through some error, they were being put on the wrong plane for the wrong destination.

So what did they do?

Nothing.

At the appointed time, they unhappily boarded the plane for Firenze, 55
sat down, and worried silently for six hours that they were going to end
up in, oh, maybe South America. Possibly Asia. They had no idea. But the
thought of admitting to a ticket agent that they didn't know what "Firenze"
meant was more terrifying than the prospect of being dumped, alone, in a
strange city on an unknown continent. 60

The fear of being conspicuous does not usually land teenagers on jet
airplanes bound for unknown destinations. But for many adolescents, it rules
their daily lives. Such fear is rooted in the enormous self-consciousness that
afflicts many adolescents. Psychologist David Elkind has come up with what
he calls the "Imaginary Audience Theory" to help explain this period of life. 65

During adolescence, Elkind says, kids are changing so much so fast
(physically, mentally, and emotionally) that they become intensely self-
centered. It is literally difficult for them to remember that other individuals
have their own lives, thoughts, and feelings, and that they are not focusing
their attention on the adolescents. According to Elkind, the adolescent feels 70
as though he or she is on an enormous stage before a watchful audience that
is noticing every aspect of his or her behavior. As a result, the adolescent is
terrified of doing or saying something that will attract scorn or criticism. As
a result, we end up with the teenager whose life is "ruined" by an outbreak
of acne, an adolescent who won't leave the house on a bad hair day, or 75
the teen who refuses to return to school after making an embarrassing slip
during a speech.

In general, typical adolescent fears don't do great harm. Kids mature
and eventually realize a moment's embarrassment isn't that big a deal, and
that, in fact, most people aren't paying much attention to them at all. But the 80
fear of being conspicuous can have serious, even tragic results. Adolescents
can be so fearful of being criticized that they sometimes go along with
the crowd when it is in their best interests not to. Teens get into cars with
obviously intoxicated drivers; they go along with the crowd on a shoplifting
expedition; they engage in risky sexual behavior, etc., in large part because 85
they are afraid to speak up and risk the scorn of the "audience."

In midlife, we generally become more confident and less obsessed with
what others are thinking of us. But underneath that veneer of confidence,
a new kind of fear grips many middle-aged people. That fear has been
expressed in timeless fashion by the Italian poet Dante in his famous poem 90
The Inferno: "In the middle of the road, I found myself in a dark wood, with
no clear path through."

The key word here is "middle." As people enter middle age, they face
the unsettling fact that their lives are halfway over. They are no longer

youngsters, looking ahead at decades filled with unlimited potential. In 95
looking back at what they have accomplished, many people feel unsatisfied.
They may not have achieved the career success they had hoped for. They
fear they do not have time to reach goals that they had once dreamed of.
They become critical of their own aging bodies. As their parents die and their
children grow up and leave home, they feel adrift, no longer certain of their 100
roles in life. Frightening thoughts press in: "My life is heading downhill. I'm
running out of time."

The result of all this inner turmoil is what is often termed a midlife crisis.
Movies and sitcoms often present such a crisis in tragicomic style: the middle-
aged guy dumps his wife, dyes his hair, buys a sports car, and begins romancing 105
a woman young enough to be his daughter. The middle-aged woman gets
liposuction and a facelift and has an affair with a young personal trainer.

There is plenty of evidence that such behavior does occur. Many long-
term marriages break up as a result of one or both partners' midlife crisis.
The panicky feelings that can result from thinking "Is this all there is?" can 110
make even a formerly happy marriage seem suffocating.

However, most midlife crises do not have such dramatic results. More
typically, the midlife crisis is a time of inner exploration, of reconsidering
one's priorities. It may involve a period of depression, but, fortunately, most
people emerge from a midlife crisis feeling relatively satisfied. They come to 115
terms with the idea that youth and its promise are behind them, and learn
to appreciate the perhaps quieter joys of mature life.

Those joys and a sense of certainty about life's priorities often carry over
into the elderly years. Senior citizens' self-knowledge often allows them to
state their opinions and explore new interests in a way they did not feel free 120
to in their younger years.

But along with the relief from self-consciousness comes another set of
fears for the elderly. Those fears center around the increasing frailty of the
body and the accompanying loss of independence.

Some years ago, a television ad featured an elderly woman saying, 125
"Help! I've fallen and I can't get up." The ad became the punch line of many
jokes, but the message was serious. Many elderly people report falling as
their greatest fear. They are not simply concerned with the injury they might
suffer. They worry that a fall might lead to being institutionalized, a step
that many elderly people fear deeply. After a lifetime of independence and, 130
often, of taking care of others, they dread the idea of being helpless, even a
burden to their families.

As a result, many elderly people—especially after having suffered a fall
or another injury—become increasingly reluctant to go out into the world to
try new things and keep up with friends. Afraid of being hurt, they become 135
hermit-like, staying within the confines of their homes. Ironically, this isolation

and lack of exercise can actually hasten the dreaded loss of independence. Mental and physical activity are both key elements in keeping elderly people in good health.

Benjamin Franklin once wrote, "In this world nothing is certain but 140 death and taxes." Franklin might have added, "and fears." Every stage of life brings them; while we may say goodbye to childish fears, there are always others in the wings, waiting to take their place. By being aware of them, we can keep their dark shadows from adversely affecting our lives.

Time: _____   *Reading Rate (see page 522):* _____ *WPM*

■ Reading Comprehension

1. Which sentence best expresses the central point of the selection?

   a. It is impossible to be totally fearless.

   b. Many people allow their fears to affect their behavior negatively.

   c. People fear different things at different stages in their lives.

   d. Some people handle fear better than others.

2. Which sentence best expresses the main idea of paragraph 16?

   a. In general, typical adolescent fears don't do great harm.

   b. Teenagers eventually realize that most people aren't paying much attention to them at all.

   c. Some teens engaged in risky behavior such as getting into cars with drunken drivers, going on shoplifting expeditions, and engaging in risky sexual behavior.

   d. Adolescent fear of criticism can have serious, even tragic results.

3. Which sentence best expresses the main idea of paragraphs 17–21?

   a. In midlife, people generally become more confident and less obsessed with what others think of them.

   b. The midlife period may involve fear, turmoil, crisis, and depression, but most people are able to emerge from it relatively satisfied.

   c. Middle-aged people often fear that they're running out of time and experience a midlife crisis.

   d. Some middle-aged people learn to appreciate the quiet joys of mature life.

4. According to the selection, the thing that adolescents fear most of all is

   a. looking "stupid."

   b. flying to overseas destinations.

   c. appearing to be self-conscious.

   d. engaging in risky behavior.

5. According to the selection, elderly people

   a. are better off leading a quiet existence.

   b. need both mental and physical activity to stay healthy.

   c. sometimes feel relief when they are institutionalized.

   d. have less to fear than adolescents and middle-aged people.

6. The sentences below express a relationship of

   a. contrast.

   b. cause and effect.

   c. addition.

   d. time.

   "I was at school a few days later when Uncle Ken left. When I came home, I couldn't find Monk-Monk anywhere."

7. The relationship of the second sentence below to the first is one of

   a. contrast.

   b. cause and effect.

   c. addition.

   d. time.

   "In midlife, we generally become more confident and less obsessed with what others are thinking of us. But underneath that veneer of confidence, a new kind of fear grips many middle-aged people."

8. On the basis of paragraphs 4–6, we can infer that Uncle Ken was

   a. an insensitive, mean-spirited man.

   b. kind-hearted, but silly.

   c. wise to conclude that a first-grader should not be dragging around a sock monkey.

   d. probably a child molester.

9. On the basis of paragraphs 20–21, we can infer that the author

   a.   strongly disapproves of middle-aged people who have affairs with younger partners.

   b.   respects middle-aged people who do new things, like taking up with younger partners, buying sports cars, and having plastic surgery.

   c.   is not yet middle-aged.

   d.   believes it is important for middle-aged people to learn to appreciate the quieter joys of mature life.

10. Paragraph 26 suggests that

   a.   recognizing our fears helps us to keep them from becoming crippling.

   b.   Ben Franklin was himself fearless.

   c.   all fears are childish.

   d.   it is possible, with effort, to become completely fearless.

Number Wrong: _____   *Score:* _____

| 0 wrong = 100% | 1 wrong = 90% | 2 wrong = 80% | 3 wrong = 70% |
| 4 wrong = 60% | 5 wrong = 50% | 6 wrong = 40% | 7 wrong = 30% |

■ Critical Thinking and Discussion

1. Did you, like the author, have a beloved toy or doll when you were a small child? Why was it so special to you? How would you have responded if you had lost it?

2. What do you think of psychologist David Elkind's "Imaginary Audience Theory" of adolescence? Did you feel the kind of self-consciousness he describes when you were an adolescent? Do you observe that kind of behavior in other teens?

3. The author writes, "And that, I think, is the essence of fear—the threat of loss." Do you agree with her? What are some examples you can think of in which fears are caused by the threat of loss?

Selection 10

What You Need to Know to Succeed at Math
Paul Nolting

■ Preview

Common sense and a positive attitude go a long way toward helping students do well in most college courses. But mathematics courses have requirements all their own. In this excerpt from his textbook *Winning at Math,* Dr. Paul Nolting spells out some important hints to help college students do well in math courses.

■ Words to Watch

sequential (line 12): occurring in a necessary order

enhances (line 61): increases

kamikaze (line 78): suicidal (from the Japanese air attack corps in World War II assigned to make suicidal crashes on targets)

subjective (line 96): based on opinion

The Importance of Practice

Because mathematics courses are so unlike other college courses, they require different study procedures. Passing most of your other college courses requires only that you read and understand the subject material. However, to pass mathematics, an extra step is required: *applying* the material in order to solve problems.   5

Example: Political science courses require that you learn about politics and public service. But your instructor isn't going to make you run for governor to pass the course.

In mathematics you must not only understand the material but apply the material.   10

Sequential Learning Pattern

Another way that learning mathematics is different from learning other subjects is its sequential learning pattern. Sequential learning means that the material learned on one day is used the next day, and the next day, and so forth.

A similar sequential pattern is seen in the building of a house. A house must be built foundation first, walls second, and roof last. Math learning, too, must follow a specific order. If you study Chapter One and understand it, study Chapter Two and understand it, and study Chapter Three and *do not understand it,* then you're not going to understand Chapter Four either.

This is not the case in most subjects. In a history class, if you understand Chapter One and Chapter Two, do *not* understand Chapter Three, but study and understand Chapter Four, you could pass the course. Understanding Chapter Four in history is not totally based on comprehending Chapter Three.

To succeed in mathematics, you need to understand each chapter before continuing on to the next chapter.

Math as a Foreign Language

Another way to understand studying for mathematics is to consider it a foreign language. Looking at mathematics as a foreign language can improve your study procedures. In the case of a foreign language, if you do not practice it, what happens? You forget it. If you do not practice mathematics, what happens? You are likely to forget it too. Students who excel in a foreign language study it and practice it *at least* every other day. The same study habits apply to mathematics.

Like a foreign language, mathematics has unfamiliar vocabulary words or terms to be put in sentences called expressions or equations. Understanding and solving a mathematics equation is similar to speaking and understanding a foreign language. Mathematics sentences use symbols (which are actually spoken words) such as equal (=), less (−), and unknown (*a*).

Learning how to speak mathematics as a language is the key to success.

Math—The Unpopular Subject

Math is not a popular topic. You do not hear the nightly news anchor on television talking in mathematics formulas. Instead, you hear him or her talking about major events to which we can relate politically, geographically, and historically. Through television we learn about English, humanities, speech, social studies, and natural sciences, but rarely mathematics. Mathematics concepts are not constantly reinforced the way English and some other subject areas are reinforced in our everyday lives. Mathematics has to be learned independently. Therefore, it requires more study time.

Example: In basketball, the way to improve your free throw is to *see and understand* the correct shooting form and then to *practice* the shots yourself. Practicing the shots improves your free-throwing percentage. However, if you simply listened to your coach describe the correct form and saw him demonstrate it but did not practice the correct form yourself, you would not improve your shooting percentage.   50

Math works the same way. You can go to class, listen to your instructor, watch the instructor demonstrate skills, and understand everything that is said. However, if you leave the class *and do not practice*—by working and successfully solving the problems—you will not learn math.   55

High School versus College Math

Mathematics as a college-level course is far more difficult than high school mathematics. In college, the fall and spring math class time has been cut to three hours a week. High school math gives you five hours a week. Furthermore, college courses cover twice the material in the same time frame as high school courses. What is learned in one year in high school is learned   60 in one semester (four months) in college. This enhances study problems for the college mathematics student; you are receiving less instructional time and proceeding twice as fast. The responsibility for learning mathematics has now shifted from the school to the student, and most of your learning will have to occur outside the college classroom.   65

Summer versus Fall or Spring Semesters

Mathematics courses taught in summer semesters are more difficult than courses given in the fall or spring semesters. Students in a six-week summer session must learn math two and a half times as fast as regular semester students. Though you receive the same amount of instructional classroom time, there's less time to understand the material between class   70 sessions. Summer semester classes are usually two hours a day and four days a week. If you don't understand the lecture on Monday, then you have only Monday night to learn the material before progressing to more difficult material on Tuesday. Since mathematics is a sequential learning experience where every building block must be understood, you can fall   75 behind quickly and never catch up. In fact, some students become *lost* during the first half of a math lecture and never understand the rest of the lecture. Such an accelerated course is called *kamikaze* math, since most students don't survive it.

If you *must* take a summer mathematics course, take a ten- or twelve-   80 week session so that you have more time to process the material between classes.

Course Grading System

The course grading system for college mathematics is different from that for high school mathematics. In high school, if you make a D or borderline D-F, the teacher more than likely will give you a D and you may go on to the next course. However, in some college mathematics courses, students cannot make a D, or if a D is made, the course will not count toward graduation. Also, college instructors are more likely to give an N (no grade), W (withdraw from class), or F for barely knowing the material, because the instructors know you will be unable to pass the next course. 85 90

The grading system for math courses is very precise compared with the systems in English or humanities courses. In a math course, if you have a 79 percent average and 80 percent is a B, you will get a C in the course. If you made a 79 percent in English, you might be able to talk your instructor into giving you extra-credit work to earn a B. Since math is an exact science and not as subjective as English, do not expect to talk your math instructor into extra work to earn a better grade. 95

Your First Math Test

Making a high grade on the first major math test is more important than making a high grade on the first major tests in other college subjects. The first major math test taken is the easiest and most often least prepared for. 100

Students feel that the first major math test is mainly review and they can make a B or C without much study. These students are overlooking an excellent opportunity to make an A on the easiest major math test of the semester. At the end of the semester, these students sometimes do not pass the math course (or perhaps just miss making an A) because their first major test grade was not high enough to pull up a low test score on one of the remaining major tests. 105

Studying hard for the first major math test and obtaining an A has several advantages. A high score on this test can

- Compensate for a low score on a more difficult fourth or fifth math test— and all major tests have equal value in the final grade calculations. 110

- Provide assurance that you have learned the basic skills required to pass the course. This means you will not have to spend time relearning the misunderstood material covered on the first major test while learning new material for the next test. 115

- Motivate you to do well. Improved motivation can cause you to increase your math study time, allowing you to master the material.

- Raise your confidence. With more confidence you are more likely to work harder on the difficult math homework assignments, which will increase your chances of doing well in the course.   120

You and Your Instructor

College math instructors treat students differently from high school mathematics instructors. High school mathematics teachers warn you about your grades and offer help or makeup work. But college instructors expect *you* to keep up with how well or poorly you are doing. You must take responsibility and make an appointment to seek help from your instructor.   125

Sometimes there are more part-time than full-time math faculty members. This problem can restrict students' and instructors' interaction. Full-time faculty members have regular office hours and are required to help students a certain number of hours per week in their office or math lab. However, part-time faculty members are only required to teach their mathematics courses;   130 they don't have to meet students after class, even though some part-time instructors will provide this service. Since mathematics students usually need more assistance from the instructor after class than other students, having a part-time math instructor could require you to find another source of course help. *Try to select a full-time math faculty member as your instructor.*   135

Time: _____   *Reading Rate (see page 522):* _____ *WPM*

■ Reading Comprehension

1. Which of the following would be a good alternative title for this selection?

   a.   Math: A Tough Subject

   b.   Keys to Doing Well in Math

   c.   High School Math versus College Math

   d.   Why So Many Students Fail Math

2. Which sentence best expresses the main idea of the selection?

   a.   College math instructors have higher expectations for their students than high school instructors do.

   b.   It is helpful to think of math as a foreign language.

   c.   Math is one subject that is not reinforced in daily life as subjects like English or social studies are.

   d.   Successful math students understand that math must be approached differently from other subjects.

3. According to the author, which of the following is *not* a way that math is different from other school subjects?

   a.   Math is rarely useful in everyday life.

   b.   Math must be learned in a sequential pattern.

   c.   Math is forgotten if it is not practiced regularly.

   d.   Math courses require that you not only understand what you've learned but apply it as well.

4. Compared with high school math teachers, college math instructors

   a.   are more likely to warn students who are in danger of failing the course.

   b.   expect students to take more responsibility for their own success.

   c.   offer more office hours and other opportunities to meet with students.

   d.   prefer teaching courses in the summer, rather than in the spring or fall.

5. *True or false?* _____ Students often do poorly on their first major math test because it is one of the most difficult tests of the semester.

6. The author compares learning math to

   a.   anchoring a news program.

   b.   running for governor.

   c.   building a house.

   d.   doing extra credit work in English class.

7. *True or false?* _____ If possible, you should take math classes during a six-week summer session.

8. From the selection you can conclude that

   a.   part-time instructors don't know math well enough to help students.

   b.   many students fail in math because they approach it like other courses.

   c.   English courses are taught through a sequential learning pattern.

   d.   learning a foreign language helps one learn math more quickly.

Number Wrong: _____   *Score:* _____

| 0 wrong = 100% | 2 wrong = 75% | 4 wrong = 50% | 6 wrong = 25% |
| 1 wrong = 88% | 3 wrong = 63% | 5 wrong = 38% | 7 wrong = 13% |

■ Critical Thinking and Discussion

1. In what way does Nolting contrast studying math with studying political science? How does he compare it with studying a foreign language?

2. Why does Nolting refer to an accelerated summer math course as *kamikaze* math? How does that term relate to his earlier comparison between studying math and building a house?

3. In what ways, according to the author, are high school and college math instructors different? Have you found these differences in your own experience?

Rapid Reading Progress Chart

Reading Selection (shortened titles)	Speed (WPM)	Comprehension (%)
1 Malcolm X		
2 Tests		
3 Wired for Touch		
4 Jacket		
5 Think Big		
6 Job Interview		
7 Door Swings Open		
8 Nonreading		
9 Fear		
10 Math		

Initial Reading Rate ("Malcolm X")

Speed _____ WPM; comprehension _____%

Final Reading Rate ("Math")

Speed _____ WPM; comprehension _____%

Reading Rate Table

You can use the following table to find the number of words you read per minute in each of the ten selections in Part Six and in the mastery test on page 580. Suppose, for example, that you read Selection 4 in three minutes thirty seconds (3:30). To locate your WPM, go across the 3:30 column until you come to column 4. The place where the two columns meet gives your WPM—in this case, 559.

Enter your WPM and your comprehension score for a selection into the progress chart on the preceding page.

Time	1 Malcolm X	2 Tests	3 Wired for Touch	4 Jacket	5 Think Big	6 Job Interview	7 Door Swings Open	8 Nonreading	9 Fear	10 Math	Detention Camps
1:00	510	800	1109	1958	1041	966	971	1557	1727	1592	770
1:10	437	689	951	1679	893	827	832	1335	1480	1365	660
1:20	382	602	832	1472	783	724	728	1171	1295	1197	578
1:30	340	533	739	1305	694	644	647	1038	1151	1061	513
1:40	306	482	665	1175	627	579	583	935	1036	959	462
1:50	278	437	605	1068	568	523	530	849	942	869	420
2:00	255	400	555	979	521	483	486	779	864	796	385
2:10	235	370	512	904	481	445	448	719	797	735	355
2:20	218	343	475	840	447	414	416	668	740	683	330
2:30	204	320	444	783	416	386	388	623	691	637	308
2:40	191	301	416	736	391	362	364	585	648	598	288
2:50	180	283	391	691	367	340	343	550	610	562	271
3:00	170	267	370	653	347	322	324	519	576	531	256
3:10	161	253	350	618	329	305	307	492	545	503	243

Time	1 Malcolm X	2 Tests	3 Wired for Touch	4 Jacket	5 Think Big	6 Job Interview	7 Door Swings Open	8 Nonreading	9 Fear	10 Math	Detention Camps
3:20	152	240	333	588	313	289	291	468	518	478	231
3:30	145	229	317	559	297	276	277	445	493	455	220
3:40	139	219	302	535	284	263	265	425	471	435	210
3:50	133	209	289	511	272	252	253	406	451	415	200
4:00	127	200	277	490	260	241	243	389	432	398	192
4:10	122	192	266	470	250	231	233	374	414	382	184
4:20	117	185	256	452	240	222	224	360	399	368	177
4:30	113	178	246	435	231	214	216	346	384	354	171
4:40	109	172	238	420	223	206	208	334	370	342	165
4:50	105	166	229	405	215	199	201	322	357	329	159
5:00	102	160	222	392	208	193	194	311	345	318	154
5:10	98	155	215	379	202	186	188	301	334	308	149
5:20	95	150	208	367	195	181	182	292	324	299	144
5:30	92	145	202	356	189	175	166	283	314	289	140
5:40		141	196	346	184	170	171	275	305	281	135
5:50		137	190	336	178	165	166	267	296	273	132
6:00		133	185	326	174	161	162	260	288	265	128
6:10		130	180	318	169	156	157	253	280	258	124
6:20		126	175	309	164	152	153	246	273	252	121
6:30		123	171	301	160	148	149	240	266	245	118
6:40		120	166	294	156	144	146	234	259	239	115
6:50		117	162	287	152	141	142	228	253	233	112
7:00		114	158	280	149	138	139	222	247	227	110

Time	1 Malcolm X	2 Tests	3 Wired for Touch	4 Jacket	5 Think Big	6 Job Interview	7 Door Swings Open	8 Nonreading	9 Fear	10 Math	Detention Camps
7:10		112	155	273	145	134	135	217	241	222	107
7:20		109	151	267	142	131	132	212	236	217	105
7:30		107	148	261	139	128	129	208	230	212	102
7:40		104	145	256	136	126	127	203	225	208	100
7:50		102	142	250	133	123	124	199	220	203	98
8:00			139	245	130	120	121	195	216	199	
8:10			136	240	127	118	119	191	211	195	
8:20			133	235	125	115	117	187	207	191	
8:30			130	230	122	113	114	183	203	187	
8:40			128	226	120	111	112	180	199	184	
8:50			126	222	118	109	110	176	196	180	
9:00			123	218	116	107	108	173	192	177	
9:10			121	214	114	105	106	170	188	174	
9:20			119	210	112	103	104	167	185	171	
9:30			117	206	110	101	102	164	182	168	
9:40			115	203	108	99	100	161	177	165	
9:50			113	199	106	98	99	158	176	162	
10:00			111	196	104	96	97	156	173	159	

Part Seven
Mastery Tests

Preview

Part Seven consists of a series of mastery tests for many of the skills in the book. Such tests can be used as homework assignments, supplementary activities, in-class quizzes at the end of a section, or review tests at any point during the semester. As much as possible, the tests are designed so that they can be scored objectively, using the special box at the end of each test.

Note to Instructors   Another complete set of mastery tests for use with *Reading and Study Skills* is included in the Instructor's Manual.

Motivational Skills

■ **Mastery Test**

Answer the following questions.

1. An inner commitment to doing the work that college demands
    a. is impossible when your life is confusing and difficult.
    b. is the most important factor in doing well in school.
    c. will help solve your personal and family problems.
    d. guarantees that you will get A and B grades.

2. To achieve a long-term career goal, a person must first set and work toward a continuing series of _____ goals.

3. *True or false?* _____ One way you can begin to set a career goal is by visiting the college counseling center.

4. Career-oriented courses should be
    a. the only courses you take.
    b. geared toward an area with promising employment opportunities.
    c. entertaining, not boring.
    d. studied in specialized, vocational-type schools.

5. *True or false?* _____ Because the author spent most of his first college years in the student game room, he had to drop his mathematics and chemistry courses.

6. According to Jean Coleman's recommendation, a student with a forty-hour-a-week job should take
    a. four courses.
    b. no courses.
    c. two courses.
    d. one course.

7. *True or false?* _____ According to Jean Coleman, younger students are more prone to dropping out of school than older students are.

8. Jean Coleman sees two kinds of students each semester: those with a childish attitude toward school and those with a _____ attitude.

9. Withdrawing from college

   a. never helps.

   b. shows a weak character.

   c. is sometimes the best response.

   d. will solve your personal problems.

10. Which of the following is *not* one of the avoidance tactics described in the section about students' attitudes?

    a. "I'll do it later."

    b. "I'm too disorganized."

    c. "I can't do it."

    d. "I'm bored with the subject."

Score   Number correct (_____) × 10 = _____%

Taking Classroom Notes

■ **Mastery Test**

Some of the questions that follow are true–false or multiple-choice questions, and some require you to write short answers.

1. To guard against forgetting, it is essential to _____ the material that you hear in class.

2. What symbol should you use in the margin of your notes to mark examples that you have written down? _____

3. To get a head start on understanding a topic to be presented in class, you should read about it in advance in your _____.

4. Which of the following methods might an instructor use to signal the importance of an idea?

   a. repetition of a point

   b. emphasis signals

   c. tone of voice

   d. enumerations

   e. all of the above

5. Often the most important single step you can take to perform well in a course is to

   a. sit where the instructor can see you and listen carefully.

   b. write down definitions and examples.

   c. be there and take effective notes.

   d. not stop taking notes during discussion periods or at the end of a class.

6. *True or false?* _____ Some instructors present important ideas during discussion periods rather than in a formal lecture.

7. Circle the two methods that are effective ways of studying your classroom notes.

    a.   Record them on a tape and listen to the recording after class.

    b.   Pick out key recall words on each page and write them in the margin.

    c.   Make up brief study notes on each page of notes.

    d.   Rewrite the notes as neatly as possible.

8. As far as possible, take notes in outline form by starting main points at the margin and by _____ secondary points.

9. *True or false?* _____ Taking too few rather than too many notes in class is one reason students have trouble doing well in their courses.

10. How would you abbreviate the term *self-actualization* during a fast-moving psychology lecture? _____

Score   Number correct (_____) × 10 = _____%

Time Control and Concentration

■ **Mastery Test**

Some of the questions that follow are true–false or multiple-choice questions, and some require you to write short answers.

1. What dates should you mark off on a large monthly calendar?

   _____

2. What are the four principal steps that you should take to gain control of your time?

   a.   Watch your health.

   b.   Use a daily or weekly "to do" list.

   c.   Try to study each class day.

   d.   Use a large monthly calendar.

   e.   Keep your schedule flexible.

   f.   Make up a weekly study schedule.

   g.   Consult course outlines.

3. *True or false?* _____ During a study session, you should try to ignore lapses of concentration.

4. You can probably study most effectively in a

   a.   very tense position.

   b.   slightly tense position.

   c.   completely relaxed position.

5. Studying may be most effective in time blocks of

   a.   15 minutes.

   b.   30 minutes.

   c.   60 minutes.

   d.   120 minutes.

6. The value of regular study hours is that

   a.   you will make studying a habit.

   b.   you will stay up-to-date on courses.

   c.   you will learn more effectively by spacing your study sessions.

   d.   all of the above will happen.

7. Where should you place your monthly calendar and weekly study schedule?

   _____

8. When you make up a "to do" list, you should

   a.   schedule one-hour blocks of study time.

   b.   mark down exam deadlines.

   c.   decide on priorities.

   d.   hang it on your wall.

9. *True or false?* _____ As a general rule, you should not reward yourself after a period of effective study time.

10. One benefit of setting specific study goals at the start of a study session is that

   a.   you work on one subject during an entire study session.

   b.   you keep track of your lapses of concentration.

   c.   you avoid working on difficult subjects.

   d.   your task is broken down into manageable units.

Score   Number correct (_____) × 10 = _____%

Textbook Study I

■ **Mastery Test**

Some of the questions that follow are true–false or multiple-choice questions, and some require you to write short answers.

1. Circle the one thing you do *not* do when previewing a selection.

    a.   Study the title.

    b.   Read over the first and last paragraphs.

    c.   Write down important ideas.

    d.   Look for relationships between headings and subheadings.

2. *True or false?* _____ Many students mark off too much material when reading a textbook.

3. *True or false?* _____ Your first reading of a chapter should proceed slowly, and you should stop as often as necessary to reread material until you are sure you understand it all.

4. Examples should be

    a.   underlined.

    b.   circled.

    c.   labeled *Ex* in the margin.

    d.   underlined and labeled *Ex* in the margin.

5. You should set off definitions in the text by _____ them.

6. Use _____ to mark off each point in an enumeration (list of items).

7. *True or false?* _____ Every note that you write down should have a symbol in front of it, such as *A, B, 1, 2, a, b*, or the like.

8. To study a textbook chapter, first you *preview* the chapter. Then you _____ it through once, marking off what appear to be important ideas.

9. As the third step in studying a chapter, you reread, decide on the important ideas, and _____ study notes. Finally, you recite the material to yourself, over and over, until you have learned it.

10. Leave space in the margin of your notes so that you can write key _____ to help you study the notes.

Textbook Study II

■ **Mastery Test**

This selection is from a sociology textbook. Complete the four-step study process that follows it.

Statuses

A *status* is a position an individual occupies in a social structure. In a sense, a status is a social address. It tells people where the individual "fits" in society—as a mother, college professor, senior citizen, or prison inmate. Knowing a person's status—knowing that you are going to meet a judge or a janitor, a ten-year-old or a fifty-year-old—tells you something about how that person will behave toward you and how you are expected to behave toward him or her. Misjudging status is a frequent cause of embarrassment—as when a woman invites a man she assumes is a bachelor to an intimate dinner and discovers he is married.

Social statuses can be divided into two groups. Some social statuses are *achieved*, or attained through personal effort. For example, individuals achieve the status of senator or sanitation-man, concert pianist or soccer coach, wife or divorcee, through their own choices and behavior. The statuses of convict, junkie, and high school dropout are also achieved. Other social statuses are *ascribed*, or assigned to the individual at birth or at different stages in the life cycle. For instance, men and women, blacks and whites, occupy different statuses in American society because of "what they are," not because of anything they do. Age is another ascribed status. Children occupy one position in society, adults another, elderly people still another. Individuals at each level are expected to act their age. It is important to note that while individuals have considerable control over achieved statuses, they have little or no control over ascribed statuses. The Prince of Wales, for example, was born to his position; he is a prince whether he likes it or not; there is almost nothing he can do to change his "social address."

Step 1: *Preview.* Take about fifteen seconds to preview the passage above. The title tells you that the passage is about _____. How many terms are set off in italics in the passage? _____

Step 2: *Read and Mark.*   Read the passage straight through. As you do, underline the definitions you find. Mark with an *Ex* in the margin an example that makes each definition clear for you. Also, number the items in the basic enumeration in the passage.

Step 3: *Write.*   Complete the following study notes on "Statuses":

Status—_____

_____

Two kinds of _____

_____

Ex—_____

_____

Ex—_____

Individuals can control achieved statuses but not ascribed ones. E.g., Prince of Wales has ascribed status from birth.

Step 4: *Recite.*   Jot down in the spaces below the recall words that could help you recite the material to yourself.

_____   _____

Score   Number correct (_____) × 10 = _____%

Textbook Study III

■ Mastery Test

This selection is from a psychology textbook. Complete the four-step study process that follows it.

Reasons for Forgetting

Forgetting can be embarrassing, inconvenient, and unpleasant. The kind of forgetting of greatest concern to psychologists is of items or events that have been stored in long-term memory and that have become difficult to retrieve. Several explanations have been given to describe why this type of retrieval problem occurs.

Repression

One possible explanation for being unable to retrieve memories is *repression*. Repression is unconsciously motivated forgetting; it is an unconscious blocking of things that are frightening or threatening. Traumatic events and anxiety-provoking people and situations can be painful if they are retrieved from long-term memory. Everyone has encountered some form of repression. Any time you refuse to talk or think about an unpleasant happening, you are experiencing a type of repression. According to Freud, it is a way of protecting yourself from remembering things that are distressing.

Suppression

Have you ever wanted to forget something? Perhaps you did something embarrassing or foolish and wanted to suppress the memory. *Suppression* is a conscious effort to avoid thinking about an event. Since you are aware of the event, suppression is different from repression.

Amnesia

Amnesia is a disorder that displays the most extreme form of repression. It is a loss of memory or a memory gap that includes forgetting personal information that would normally be recalled. Because of the dramatic effect, amnesia patients have been used as the subjects of novels, films, and soap operas. While amnesia victims forget almost all basic information, they do retain basic memories. They remember how to add, subtract, read, write, dress, and cook.

Like repression, amnesia is a limited explanation of why forgetting occurs. It is not nearly as common as the media suggest and can account for only a tiny percentage of forgetting.

Interference

Interference is the most popular explanation for why forgetting occurs. You forget because other information interferes with your memory. According to the interference description of forgetting, there are two types of obstructions to remembering: proactive interference and retroactive interference.

Proactive Interference. Proactive means "acting forward." *Proactive interference* refers to instances when previous memories block the recall of more recent learning. Suppose you meet a new psychology instructor named Professor Kassel, who reminds you of your old girlfriend, Flora Belle. You may have difficulty remembering the professor's correct name and want to call her Flora Belle. In proactive interference, earlier learning interferes with new learning.

Retroactive Interference. Retroactive means "acting backward." *Retroactive interference* refers to instances where recent learning blocks the recall of previous memories. If the next time you meet your old girlfriend Flora Belle, you have difficulty remembering her name and have an urge to call her "Professor," retroactive inhibition will be contributing to your forgetting.

Step 1: *Preview.* Take about thirty seconds to preview the passage above. The title tells you that the passage is about the reasons for forgetting. How many subheads are there in the passage? _____ How many terms are set off in italics in the passage? _____

Step 2: *Read and Mark.* Read the passage straight through. As you do, underline the definitions you find. Mark with an *Ex* in the margin any example that helps make a definition clear. Also, number the items in the two enumerations in the passage.

Step 3: *Write.* Complete the following study notes on "Reasons for Forgetting":

Reasons for forgetting:

Repression—_____

_____

Suppression—_____

_____

Amnesia—_____

_____

Interference—Forget because other information interferes with your learning.

    a.   Proactive interference— _____

    _____

    Ex—Want to call new Professor Kassel by name of your old girlfriend Flora Belle.

    b.   Retroactive interference— _____

    _____

    Ex—_____

Step 4: *Recite.* To remember the four reasons for forgetting, create a *catchword*: a word made up of the first letters in the four reasons for forgetting. Write your catchword here:

_____

To remember the two kinds of interference, create a *catchphrase*: a two-word sentence in which the first word begins with P (for *proactive*) and the second word begins with R (for *retroactive*). Write your catchphrase here:

_____

Score   Number correct (_____) × 10 = _____%

Building a Powerful Memory

■ Mastery Test

Some of the questions that follow are true–false or multiple-choice questions, and some require you to write short answers.

1. The first step in effective remembering is to _____ the material to be learned.

2. The best way to avoid passive studying is to

    a.   study right before bed.

    b.   test yourself on the material to be learned.

    c.   copy several times the material to be learned.

    d.   review material in the morning.

3. *True or false?* _____ Material is best studied in a single long session rather than spaced out over several sessions.

4. Overlearning is

    a.   unnecessary memorization.

    b.   going over a lesson you already know.

    c.   incompatible with learning.

    d.   a way to "push out" old ideas so that you can learn new ones.

5. If you reduce ideas to key words and memorize the key words, they will often serve as _____ that will help you pull the ideas into memory.

6. What aid to memory is illustrated by the fact that someone will always remember the name of a person who owes him or her money?

    a.   spacing memory work

    b.   intending to learn

    c.   using key words as hooks

    d.   overlearning

7. To gain the overall understanding you need in order to learn material effectively, you should

    a.   attend class lectures regularly.

    b.   read textbook assignments.

    c.   take classroom and textbook notes.

    d.   do all of the above.

8. One memory aid is to include as a study period the time just before

    _____.

9. Write a catchword that will help you remember the first letters of the following kinds of defense mechanisms: *projection, repression, identification.*

    _____

10. Write a catchphrase that will help you remember the following kinds of taxes: *self-employment, income, sales, property.* _____

    _____

Score   Number correct (_____) × 10 = _____%

Taking Objective Exams

■ Mastery Test

All the questions that follow have been taken from actual college tests. Answer the questions by using the specific hints for multiple-choice and true–false questions that are listed below. Also, in the space provided, give the letter of the hint used to determine the correct answer.

Test-Taking Hints

a The longest multiple-choice answer is often correct.

b A multiple-choice answer in the middle, especially one with the most words, is often correct.

c Answers with qualifiers, such as *generally*, *probably*, *most*, *almost*, *often*, *may*, *some*, and *sometimes*, are usually correct.

d Answers with absolute words, such as *all*, *always*, *everyone*, *everybody*, *never*, *no one*, *nobody*, *none*, and *only*, are usually incorrect.

Hint _____   1. *True or false?* _____ IQ tests are always reliable measures of intelligence.

Hint _____   2. *True or false?* _____ After June 1944, the Allies had almost completely eliminated the German submarine threat in the Atlantic.

Hint _____   3. A good justification for establishing a new business would be

     a.   a strong personal desire to run a business.

     b.   a shrinking market.

     c.   successful businesses nearby.

     d.   an expanding market combined with the presence of inefficient firms.

Hint _____   4. Diabetics lack

     a.   vitamins.

     b.   insulin, an enzyme needed to use sugar properly.

     c.   amino acids.

     d.   epinephrine.

Hint _____   5. *True or false?* _____ Generally, single-story buildings are preferred for most types of factory operations.

Hint _____   6. During World War II, black Americans

     a.   achieved social equality.

     b.   lived mostly in the South.

     c.   found more job opportunities open and benefited from the movement for equality fostered by the war.

     d.   served in fully integrated service units.

Hint _____   7. *True or false?* _____ The only function of the hypothalamus is to activate the sympathetic nervous system.

Hint _____   8. Affective explanations are statements intertwined with

     a.   altruistic behavior.

     b.   love and intimacy.

     c.   emotions, values, or expectations regarding self-control.

     d.   antisocial behavior.

Hint _____   9. *True or false?* _____ There are no gaps between scientific ideals and the realities of any actual research project.

Hint _____   10. In an attempt to deal with unemployment, President Hoover

     a.   established the NRA.

     b.   began a welfare program.

     c.   created unemployment insurance.

     d.   established the Reconstruction Finance Corporation to make loans to business.

Score   Number correct (_____) × 10 = _____%

Taking Essay Exams

■ Mastery Test

Spend a half hour getting ready to write a one-paragraph essay on the subject "Describe eight points to remember when planning a weekly study schedule." The eight points are presented on pages 81–83.

Study Hint: First summarize each of the eight points in the spaces below. Then study the points by following the advice given in step 2 on pages 240–241.

Important Points about a Weekly Study Schedule

1. _____

_____

2. _____

_____

3. _____

_____

4. _____

_____

5. _____

_____

6. _____

_____

7. _____

_____

8. _____

_____

When the half hour is up, write your essay answer on the other side of this sheet.

Sample Essay Answer

_____

_____

_____

_____

_____

_____

_____

_____

_____

_____

_____

_____

_____

_____

_____

_____

_____

_____

_____

_____

_____

_____

_____

_____

_____

Score Number correct (_____) × 12.5 = _____%

Taking Objective and Essay Exams

■ **Mastery Test**

You have five kinds of questions to answer on this quiz: following directions, matching, sentence completion, true–false, and multiple-choice.

Following Directions   Print your full name, last name first, under the line at the right-hand side below. Write your full name, first name last, on the line at the left-hand side below.

1. _____   2. _____

Matching: Enter the appropriate letter in the space provided next to each definition.

3. Show similarities between two things. _____   a. Define

4. Explain by giving examples. _____   b. Contrast

5. Give the formal meaning of a term. _____   c. Direction words

6. Words that tell you exactly what to do. _____   d. List

7. Give a series of points and number   e. Compare

   them 1, 2, 3, and so on. _____   f. Illustrate

8. Give a condensed account of the main points. _____   g. Summarize

Fill-Ins: Write the word or words needed to complete each of the following sentences.

9. You should _____ consistently in order to avoid last-minute cramming that may cause exam panic.

10. On either an objective or an essay exam, you will build up confidence and momentum if you do the easier questions _____.

11. Because time is limited on an essay exam, instructors can give you only a few questions to answer. They will reasonably focus on questions dealing with the _____ areas of the subject.

12. Before starting an objective or essay test, you should _____ your time.

True or False: Write the word *true* or *false* to the left of the following statements.

_____   13. Often the main reason that students choke, or block, on exams is that they are not well prepared.

_____   14. When studying for an essay test, prepare a good outline answer for each question and memorize the outlines.

_____   15. If you have to cram, you should try to study everything in your class notes and textbook.

_____   16. You should spend the night before an exam organizing your notes.

Multiple Choice: Circle the letter of the answer that best completes each of the following statements.

17. One step that is *not* necessarily recommended in preparing for and taking an essay exam is to

   a.   list ten or so probable questions.

   b.   prepare an outline answer for each question.

   c.   concentrate on details in your class and text notes.

   d.   understand direction words.

18. When taking an objective test, remember that absolute statements are

   a.   always false.

   b.   often false.

   c.   rarely false.

   d.   never false.

19. When taking an essay exam, you should

   a.   outline your answers before you begin to write.

   b.   be direct when you write.

   c.   use signal words to guide your reader through the answer.

   d.   do all of the above.

20. In preparing for an objective or essay exam, pay attention to

    a.   key terms and their definitions.

    b.   major lists of items.

    c.   points emphasized in class or in the text.

    d.   all of the above.

Score Number correct (_____) × 5 = _____%

Using Research Skills

■ **Mastery Test**

1. Google is a search engine that will locate articles on almost any subject in a matter of

    a.   seconds.

    b.   minutes.

    c.   hours.

    d.   days.

2. *True or False?* _____ To do an effective search on the Web, you must learn how to use keywords to widen your topic.

3. *True or False?* _____ To narrow an Internet search to a reasonable number of entries, use more than one keyword.

4–5.   Suggest two ways to narrow the topic "energy conservation":

    _____

    _____

6. To instantly get information about a book,

    a.   visit a local bookstore.

    b.   visit an online bookstore.

    c.   visit your library.

7. In order to locate a book called *The Worst Journey in the World* in a card or computerized catalog, what kind of search should you do?

    a.   Title search under *The*

    b.   Title search under *W* for *Worst*

    c.   Title search under *J* for *Journey*

    d.   Subject search under *J* for *Journey*

8. *True or False?* _____ A good way to find more than one book about the same topic is to do a search by subject.

9. If you use specialized information or ideas that are not your own and you do

    not give the author credit, you are _____.

10. A research paper should be narrow and deep rather than broad and shallow. Which of the following topics would be most suited for a research paper of about ten pages?

    a.   Crime

    b.   Punishments

    c.   The death penalty

    d.   Economic benefits of the death penalty

Score Number correct (_____) × 10 = _____%

Using the Dictionary

■ **Mastery Test**

Use your dictionary to answer the following questions.

1. What is the correct spelling of the word *inscrutible*? _____

2. What is the correct spelling of the word *accelarate*? _____

3. How many syllables are in the word *cajole*? _____

4. How many syllables are in the word *phenomenon*? _____

5. Where is the primary accent in the word *cogent*? _____

6. Where is the secondary accent in the word *emphysema*? _____

7. The *i* in *diatribe* is pronounced like the *i* in

    a.   hi.   b.   sit.

8. What is the past participle of the verb *ride*? _____

9. What is the plural form of the word *variety*? _____

10. In the sentence "My grandmother is the most *volatile* person I know," what does *volatile* mean? _____

Score   Number correct (_____) × 10 = _____%

Understanding Word Parts

■ Mastery Test

Complete the italicized word in each sentence by adding the correct word part. Use the meaning of the word part and the sentence context to determine the correct answer in each case.

---

port—carry   *psych*—mind   *trans*—across   *mis*—badly   *in*—not

tract—draw   *tact*—touch   *inter*—between   *post*—after   *dis*—apart

---

1. The (. . . *ition*) _____ from prison to life on the "outside" can cause psychological problems.

2. To show his (. . . *content*) _____ with the restaurant meal, Fred dumped his dinner onto the floor.

3. When two burly customers started to fight, the skinny bartender was afraid to (. . . *vene*) _____.

4. The (*re . . . able*) _____ ballpoint pen leaked red ink all over the inside of my purse.

5. A blind person's (. . . *ile*) _____ sense is highly developed; the fingertips transmit a wealth of information.

6. Mark, enrolled in five difficult courses, felt he had been (. . . *guided*) _____ by his college counselor.

7. In a (. . . *script*) _____ to his will, the crazy old man left a million dollars to the Internal Revenue Service.

8. The (. . . *er*) _____ was told to bring a mop and a pail to the lobby; a bottle of orange juice had smashed on the floor.

9. (. . . *iatrists*) _____ must qualify as medical doctors before specializing in studies of the mind.

10. The (. . . *edible*) _____ pancakes oozed a sticky white batter as they lay on the plate.

Score   Number correct (_____) × 10 = _____%

Vocabulary Development

■ Mastery Test

Read each of the following sentences carefully. Then decide which of the four choices comes closest in meaning to the word in italic type. Circle the letter of your choice.

1. Because of the *brusque* manner of the waitress, I decided to leave no tip.

    a. slow

    b. courteous

    c. rude

    d. passive

2. We kept our plans *tentative,* so we could quickly change them in case there were new developments.

    a. fixed

    b. indefinite

    c. superficial

    d. honest

3. I could not tolerate an *austere* apartment like the one she lives in; I need plants, pictures, and plenty of furnishings.

    a. bare

    b. lavish

    c. expensive

    d. small

4. She is a *tenacious* person; even though she failed her first biology tests, she kept studying and eventually passed the course.

    a. humorous

    b. stingy

    c. softhearted

    d. persistent

5. Among the many *paradoxes* in the Bible are that the meek shall inherit the earth and the first shall be last.

   a. famous passages

   b. verses

   c. apparent contradictions

   d. prayers

6. His clothes are neat and tasteful, but his hair, *incongruously*, is unkempt and oily.

   a. boldly

   b. inconsistently

   c. apologetically

   d. consistently

7. My English paper had many good details but lacked *coherence*; the instructor said I had a lot to learn about how to structure my ideas.

   a. unity

   b. support

   c. sentence skills

   d. organization

8. I used to be a three-letter athlete in school; now I enjoy sports in a *vicarious* way by watching them on television.

   a. curious

   b. dangerous

   c. substitute

   d. inexpensive

9. My progress in school was *impeded* by poor study habits and a poor attitude.

   a. aided

   b. increased

   c. hindered

   d. reinforced

10. The counselor listened in a *perfunctory* way as she doodled on her notepad; I felt she wasn't really interested in my problem.

    a.   indifferent

    b.   responsive

    c.   intense

    d.   apologetic

Score   Number correct (_____) × 10 = _____%

Definitions and Examples

■ Mastery Test

In the spaces provided, write the number of the sentence in each selection that contains a definition. Then write the number of the sentence that provides the *first* example of the definition.

1.   [1]Admittedly a good deal of our social interaction is motivated by self-interest. [2]You may offer to run an errand for a professor because you hope that he or she will take that help into account when awarding grades. [3]Or you may offer to take care of the neighbors' dog while they are away on vacation because you want them to take care of your cat when you go on vacation. [4]But if behavior that benefits others is *not* linked to personal gain, it is called **altruistic behavior**. [5]For example, many people go to considerable trouble to help a sick neighbor, take in a family left homeless by fire, or serve as hospital aides. [6]Charitable contributions are often directed at strangers and made anonymously.

Definition: _____   Example: _____

2.   [1]Generally, nurses work directly with patients. [2]However, in some instances, they function as *patients' advocates*; that is, they work indirectly on behalf of the patient or intercede for the patient. [3]For example, the nurse who lobbies in the legislature in support of programs of benefit to the consumer of health services functions as a patient advocate. [4]A few other examples are the nurse who seeks the services of other health practitioners on behalf of a patient; the nurse who intercedes for patients by helping them obtain services from various community health agencies; and the nurse who intercedes for the patients by interpreting their needs to family. [5]Nurses become patient advocates also as they plan total health care while serving as a member of the health team.

Definition: _____   Example: _____

3.   [1]Price lining is based on the fact that most retailers have more than one product to price, and a number of substitute products or brands within each product category. [2]For instance, a women's clothing store may offer a variety of wool scarves. [3]But consumers will not respond to a series of minor price differences, such as scarves at $6.50, $6.60, $6.70, $6.90, $7.00, and

so on. [4]Instead, buyers prefer a *few* prices that seem to differentiate the product into "lines" based on some attribute such as quality or prestige. [5]For instance, there may be scarves priced at $5, $8, $10, and $16. [6]These prices clearly indicate that there are scarves for the economy-minded at $5, medium-quality scarves at $8 and $10, and top-of-the-line scarves at $16. [7]Price lining means, then, that a limited number of prices are established for the products or brands within a product class.

Definition: _____   Example: _____

4.   [1]When teachers feel that a certain child will do well in school, that child probably will do well. [2]The *self-fulfilling prophecy*, by which people act as they are expected to, has been documented in many different situations. [3]In the "Oak School experiment," some teachers in this California school were told at the beginning of the term that some of their pupils had shown unusual potential for intellectual growth. [4]Actually, the children had been chosen at random. [5]Yet several months later many of them—especially first- and second-graders—showed unusual gains in IQ. [6]And the teachers seemed to like the "bloomers" better. [7]Their teachers do not appear to have spent more time with them than with the other children or to have treated them differently in any obvious ways. [8]Subtler influences may have been at work, possibly in the teachers' tone of voice, facial expression, touch, and posture.

Definition: _____   Example: _____

5.   [1]Resocialization differs from other types of adult socialization in that it points to a rapid and drastic change, usually one that is forced on the individual to some degree. [2]Military service involves resocialization, since it is a deliberate attempt to remold a person's life and personality in certain respects. [3]The recruit is stripped of previous status and gains a new status only by meeting the demands of the military. [4]A more extreme example is that of religious conversion, in which the person may feel completely reoriented—experiencing a sense of rebirth into a new personality or of having been "born again." [5]Both the recruit and the convert experience a change from an old lifestyle to a new one that is willingly accepted and not seen as abandoning old loyalties.

Definition: _____   Example: _____

Score   Number correct (_____) × 10 = _____%

Enumerations

■ Mastery Test

Locate and number the enumerations in the selections that follow. Then, in the space beneath each selection, summarize briefly the points in the enumeration. Note that headings have already been provided for you.

1.   Credit cards can be divided into three basic groups. One type, the easiest to obtain, is the retail credit card. These are the cards issued by department stores, boutiques, and gasoline companies. Interest is charged on an unpaid balance, but the minimum payment required per month may vary; department stores usually require the highest monthly payments. Another type of credit card is the bank card, such as MasterCard or Visa. Overall, these credit corporations issue more cards than anyone else, but a card must be obtained from a local bank. Like retail cards, bank cards require a minimum monthly payment and charge about 18 percent interest annually on the balance. Some also charge an annual membership fee. These cards may be used in a wide variety of places for items from food to clothes to college tuition payments. A third type of card is that offered by American Express, Carte Blanche, and Diners' Club. Unlike the other types, these companies expect payment in full every month. They also charge a yearly membership fee to card owners. Such cards are usually the most difficult to obtain, since these companies look for more affluent customers capable of meeting all monthly charges.

Types of Credit Cards

(1) _____

(2) _____

(3) _____

2.   As you might guess, pollutants do their greatest damage to the organs of the breathing system. There are several kinds of damage that can occur. The tubes and passages of the breathing system are lined with hairlike structures called cilia. The cilia are constantly moving back and forth; they function like a broom that sweeps out foreign material inhaled from the air. Some pollutants can slow down these cilia—or stop them altogether. This leaves the lungs with one of their protective devices out of order.

    Besides the cilia, the air passages and tubes are also lined with a sticky fluid called mucus, which traps particles that have been inhaled. Mucus production greatly increases when certain pollutants are inhaled. This is a defensive response by the body. Normally, the cilia would sweep out the mucus and much of the foreign matter. But when they do not function, the mucus builds up and narrows the tubes and air passages. Coughing results, and breathing is more difficult.

Pollutants can also cause muscle spasms in the tubes of the lungs. During the spasms, the muscle contracts and gets thicker. This narrows the passageway in the tubes and makes breathing more difficult. Along with the muscle spasms, the membranes inside the tubes may swell. This results in more narrowing of the tubes and more difficulty in breathing.

Ways That Pollutants Damage the Breathing System

(1) _____

(2) _____

(3) _____

3.   There are numerous advantages associated with franchising. One of the most important Is the training and guidance given by the franchisor. One of the best-known training programs is that offered by McDonald's, which sends the owner to "Hamburger U." Here the individual learns how to make hamburgers, control inventory, keep records, handle human relations problems, and manage the unit.

Another advantage is the customer appeal associated with buying a well-known name. Many franchisors advertise on television and radio and have catchy jingles that attract customers to the unit. Just think of some you have heard during this past week from Pizza Hut, Holiday Inn, and Kentucky Fried Chicken.

A third advantage is that the franchise, assuming it is an established one, is a proven idea. There is no need to worry about whether people will like the food being sold or the auto service being provided. There are many other successful franchised units selling the same goods and services.

Finally, there is the financial assistance angle. Some bankers will not be willing to lend money to get a small business started but will change their mind when they find that it is a Dairy Queen franchise, a Holiday Inn, or a Jack-in-the-Box.

Advantages of Franchising

(1) _____

(2) _____

(3) _____

(4) _____

Score   Number correct (_____) × 10 = _____%

Headings and Subheadings

■ **Mastery Test**

Part 1:   Answer the questions below about the selection that follows.

Questions: What is meant by *burnout*? What are the results of burnout?

"Burnout" in the Professions

While professional-level jobs provide prestige, a relatively high income, and other benefits, they are far from perfect. Boredom and alienation are associated with certain types of professional work. Poverty-program lawyers, physicians, prison personnel, social workers, clinical psychologists, psychiatric nurses, and other professionals who work extensively with human problems often feel unable to cope continually with distress. Eventually, they may see themselves as "burned out." Behavioral scientists have found that many handled "burned-out" feelings by distancing themselves from clients and treating suffering people in detached, dehumanizing ways. As emotions grew increasingly negative, these workers experienced severe tension-related problems, including alcoholism.

Answers: _____

_____

_____

Part 2:   Using words such as *what*, *why*, *who*, *which*, *in what ways*, and *how*, write two meaningful questions for each of the textbook heads that follow.

1. Emotional Problems in Childhood   a. _____

   b. _____

2. Reconstruction in the South   a. _____

   b. _____

3. Infectious Diseases   a. _____

   b. _____

4. Our Business System: a. _____

   Its Expansion and Regulation   b. _____

Part 3:   Scrambled together in the list that follows are three textbook headings and three subheadings for each of the headings. Write the headings in the lettered blanks (A, B, C) and write the appropriate subheadings in the numbered blanks (1, 2, 3). Two items have already been inserted for you.

Paranoia   The Muscular System   Sherman's March

The Siege of   Schizophrenia   Major Events of the
Petersburg   Civil War
                            Behavior Disorders
Cardiac Muscle   Skeletal Muscle
                            Smooth Muscle
The Battle of   Psychosis
Gettysburg

A. _____

   1. _____

   2. _____

   3. *Smooth Muscle* _____

B. _____

   1. _____

   2. _____

   3. _____

C. _____

   1. _____

   2. _____

   3. *Psychosis* _____

Score   Number correct (_____) × 5 = _____%

Signal Words

■ **Mastery Test**

In the spaces provided, write the major signal words used in the following selections. The number and kinds of signal words that you should look for are shown at the start of each selection.

Selection 1:   Two contrast signals; one cause-and-effect signal; one addition signal.

The elderly age segment is a growing market that presents many opportunities for marketers. Demand will continue to rise for health care and services, books, nursing homes, travel, retirement housing, and many leisure-time activities. But people in this age group do not like to be stereotyped, and marketers must be sensitive in communicating with them. Several years ago, the H. J. Heinz Company test-marketed a line of "Senior Foods"—lamb, beef, and chicken dishes in eight-ounce containers. The products were dropped six months later; the reason was that older people did not like to see their age reflected in the product's name. On the other hand, the marketing focus of Gerber Products Company does not inhibit older consumers from purchasing and consuming (for dietary reasons) an estimated 6 percent of its baby food. Also, a study conducted by Dannon Yogurt found that 25 percent of the company's sales were made to people over age fifty-five. Clearly, the elderly have unique needs that marketers must try to satisfy.

1. _____

2. _____

3. _____

4. _____

Selection 2:   One emphasis signal; one cause-and-effect signal; two addition signals; two contrast signals.

Speed-reading courses often claim that an increase in speed will mean an automatic increase in comprehension. But this claim is simply not true. With difficult material, understanding is likely to fall as rate rises. Speed-reading courses may increase the number of words your eyes take in and "read" per minute. In addition, comprehension may improve while you take such a course. The cause for this, however, is that you tend to concentrate more as you read faster. The best way to increase reading speed *and* comprehension is to develop reading comprehension skills. Speed will come as you learn how to identify main ideas and go quickly over lesser points and supporting details. Also, speed will come as you learn how to vary your reading rate according to the nature of the material and your purpose in reading.

5. _____

6. _____

7. _____

8. _____

9. _____

10. _____

Score   Number correct (_____) × 10 = _____%

Main Idea

■ Mastery Test

Locate and underline the main-idea sentence in each selection that follows. Then, in the spaces provided in the margin, put the number of each sentence you underlined.

_____ 1.   ¹Violence surrounds us—not only in real life but in our entertainment. ²Films emphasize it—as those who saw *The Godfather* and its sequels know. ³In fact, violence is big at the box office. ⁴A drive-in favorite was *The Texas Chainsaw Massacre,* which graphically portrayed a series of murders perpetrated by unemployed cattle butchers. ⁵Indeed, the realism with which film violence is staged is ever increasing. ⁶Improved techniques allow close-ups of realistically bruised and mutilated bodies. ⁷Television, in both its news reports and its entertainment, provides a steady diet of violence. ⁸Riots, uprisings, wars, terrorists' raids—all are a part of our daily lives in the evening news. ⁹Even children's toys can encourage aggression.

_____ 2.   ¹One of childhood's saddest figures is the child who is chosen last for every team, hangs around the fringes of every group, walks home alone after school, is not invited to any of the birthday parties, and sobs in despair, "Nobody wants to play with me." ²There are many reasons why this child and other children can be unpopular. ³Sometimes such children are withdrawn or rebellious. ⁴They are often the youngsters who walk around with a "chip on the shoulder," showing unprovoked aggression and hostility. ⁵Or they may act silly and babyish, "showing off" in immature ways. ⁶Or they may be anxious and uncertain, exuding such a pathetic lack of confidence that they repel other children, who don't find them any fun to be with. ⁷Extremely fat or unattractive children, children who behave in any way that seems strange to the others, and slow-learning youngsters are also outcasts.

_____ 3.   ¹Companies are constantly changing the packaging that covers their products. ²At times, however, the changes backfire and reduce rather than increase customers' satisfaction with the product in question. ³One of the most successful packages has been the Camel cigarette pack, which shows a camel, two pyramids, and three palm trees. ⁴An executive at R. J. Reynolds some years ago decided that the package would be more striking if the pyramids and trees were removed. ⁵The surgery was performed, but the public howled. ⁶Camel sales fell off instantly, and, not surprisingly, Reynolds quickly returned the camel's props.

_____   4.   ¹Colonial farmers in America grew all their own food, with the exception of certain imported luxury items, such as coffee, tea, and sugar. ²Farm animals such as sheep, pigs, and cows provided milk and meat. ³Clothing was made from plant and animal sources. ⁴The flax plant's fibers were dyed with berry juices, spun into thread, woven into cloth, and sewn into shirts and dresses. ⁵Sheep provided wool for heavier clothing, and the hides of pigs and cows were tanned into leather. ⁶Leather could be cut and crafted into shoes, boots, gloves, shirts, and leggings; leather was also needed for harnesses, bridles, whips, and reins. ⁷The abundant forests of a young America were filled with timber for houses and fuel. ⁸Colonists chopped down trees and corded wood in order to cook and to heat their homes. ⁹Only a few necessary items, such as glass and iron, were bought by the farmers. ¹⁰Luxuries such as books, china, and lace were purchased when it was possible; they were by no means considered essential items. ¹¹This self-sufficiency, or ability to provide for themselves, was a characteristic of many early American settlers.

_____   5.   ¹A bottle of cologne on a department store counter catches your eye. ²It is beautifully packaged in a handsome bottle and shiny box. ³You check the price tag, which reads "$37.50," and walk away wondering how two ounces of cologne can be so expensive. ⁴After all, cologne is made from only a few pennies' worth of alcohol and essential oils mixed with a good amount of water. ⁵How can a department store charge so much for it? ⁶The price on the cologne box reflects not only the cost of the raw materials but a variety of additional costs. ⁷The department store is paying the salary of the salesperson behind the counter and the cost of the space needed to store the cologne inventory. ⁸The department store also provides services such as charge accounts; the cost of each piece of merchandise is raised accordingly. ⁹The manufacturer of the cologne may have spent more on its fancy bottle and box than on the fragrance itself. ¹⁰The packaging caught your eye, as the manufacturer wanted, but you are going to pay for it. ¹¹You'll also pay for the advertising done by the nationally known cosmetics company and the cost of the transportation used to ship the cologne to the store. ¹²And if the cologne was made in and shipped from France, the price goes up even more!

Score   Number correct (_____) × 20 = _____%

Outlining

■ **Mastery Test**

Part A: Read the selection below and then complete the outline that follows.

Stress is a factor in all our lives. Learning to deal with stress in a positive, intelligent way is essential to good health. One way to combat stress is to work it off in physical activities. Anything from jogging around the neighborhood to a workout on the dance floor can relieve stress and, surprisingly, give you more energy to cope with life. Stress can also be controlled by changing your mental attitude. Learn to accept things; fighting against the unavoidable or the inevitable is useless. Learn to take one thing at a time. Rather than trying to do everything at once, deal with more important problems first, and leave the rest to another day. Learn to take your mind off yourself. Since stress is self-centered, doing something for others helps reduce it. Finally, talking about stress is important. When events in your life seem overwhelming, talk about your troubles. This can be done informally, by opening up to your family. You can also set aside special time to confide in friends. When your emotional life is severely shaken, however, formal help may be needed. Seek out a psychologist who has been recommended to you by a reliable source. Alternatively, find a professional counselor who will assess your difficulties and help you deal with them.

A. _____

B. _____

    1. _____

    2. _____

    3. _____

C. _____

    1. _____

        a. _____

        b. _____

    2. _____

        a. _____

        b. _____

Part B: Read the selection below and then complete the diagram that follows.

Credit cards have both advantages and disadvantages, depending on how the credit-card holder chooses to use them. One of the benefits of credit cards, for example, is that they can be used to obtain interest-free loans for up to two months. By purchasing goods just after the close of one billing cycle, taking advantage of the grace period of twenty-five days or so for payment, and then paying the bill in full, you have borrowed the amount of your purchase with no interest fee. Another advantage of credit cards is that they are convenient. You can buy anywhere without the hassle of carrying large amounts of money or trying to use a personal check. Credit cards, however, do have disadvantages. Occasionally, billing mix-ups occur, and customers may be overcharged or charged for items they never purchased. The major problem presented by credit cards, though, is the fact that they tempt some consumers to overspend. Such people find it easy to charge items they would probably not purchase for cash; when the bills arrive, they have trouble making the payment. Or they find themselves trapped in a cycle of making minimum payments and thereby paying high finance charges on a never-shrinking balance.

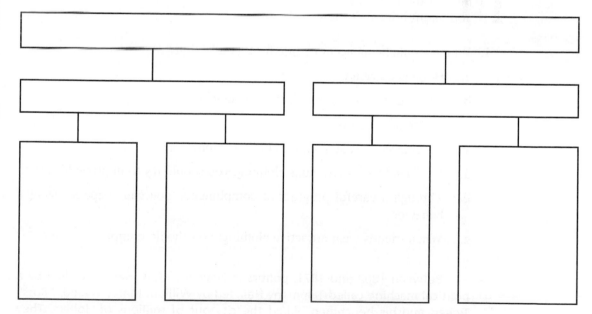

Score   Number correct (_____) × 5 = _____%

Summarizing

■ Mastery Test

Part A: Circle the letter of the title and then of the sentence that best summarizes each of the following three selections. Remember that the title and sentence should be as specific and descriptive as possible and at the same time account for all the material in the selection.

> Suppose a friend of yours has the habit of wearing absolutely atrocious clothes. You decide to go on a campaign to help reform his taste. How do you go about it? Your friend has just one outfit in which he looks great—but which he rarely wears. Every time he wears a shirt the same color as the one you like, you compliment him, and perhaps you also mention the shirt you're trying to "promote." After *that* shirt appears more frequently for a while, you "reinforce" only it—not the less attractive ones of the same color. At the same time, you try to suggest that your favorite shirt looks so good on him that he really should get more like it. And when he does, you compliment him on the new outfits. Gradually, you are "shaping his behavior," though you might not call it that.

1. Which would be an accurate title for this selection?

    a.   Helping a Friend

    b.   Shaping Behavior through Reinforcement

    c.   Differences in Taste

2. Which sentence best summarizes the selection?

    a.   If a friend wears atrocious clothing, you should try to improve his taste.

    b.   Through a careful program of compliments, you can shape someone's behavior.

    c.   When friends wear attractive clothing, you should compliment them.

> Between 1862 and 1871, politics in New York City was controlled by a political machine called Tammany Hall, led by William Marcy Tweed. "Boss" Tweed and his henchmen bilked the city out of millions of dollars. They

usually sold contracts for city work to corrupt companies. These companies would overcharge the city government for the job and "kick back" a fee to the political machine. Once, one of Tweed's friends billed the city for $179,729.60 for three tables and forty chairs. Of course, the Tweed Ring received a good share of that money. Gradually, the press began to take notice. Especially damaging to Tweed were the political cartoons by Thomas Nast. Nast drew cartoons showing Tweed and his men as vultures preying on the body of New York. Tweed's Ring eventually collapsed, and Tweed died in jail while awaiting trial.

3. Which would be an accurate title for this selection?

   a.   Political Corruption

   b.   Thomas Nast

   c.   Boss Tweed and Tammany Hall

4. Which sentence best summarizes the selection?

   a.   Tammany Hall, a corrupt nineteenth-century New York City political machine led by "Boss" Tweed, was defeated by the press.

   b.   Tammany Hall was led by "Boss" Tweed, who cheated New York City out of millions of dollars.

   c.   The cartoonist Thomas Nast depicted "Boss" Tweed and his men as vultures preying on the body of New York City.

The Leboyer method of childbirth seeks to protect a newborn's delicate senses from the shock of bright lights, harsh sounds, and rough handling. After the baby's head has begun to emerge, lights are dimmed and the delivery room is quieted. The baby is not held by the ankles and slapped to encourage the first breath; Leboyer states that since the fetus's spinal column has never been in a straight position, this kind of handling is a severe shock to the infant. Instead, the baby, with the umbilical cord still attached, is gently placed on the mother's abdomen until breathing begins naturally. At this point, the baby is rinsed in a tepid bath, rather than weighed on a cold scale. Babies born this way are usually relaxed and smiling, not tense and screaming. Some studies of Leboyer babies and standard-delivery babies have shown that Leboyer children are slightly more physically advanced and quicker to learn. Parents of Leboyer children, in general, saw the birth as a positive, exhilarating experience.

5. Which would be an accurate title for this selection?

   a.   Types of Delivery Rooms

   b.   A Baby's First Moments

   c.   The Leboyer Method

6. Which sentence best summarizes the selection?

   a.   The usual method of childbirth subjects newborns to bright lights, harsh sounds, and rough handling.

   b.   In the Leboyer method of childbirth, a newborn's first breath is never encouraged by the common process of holding the infant by the ankles and slapping it.

   c.   The Leboyer method of childbirth, designed to protect a newborn's delicate senses from the shock of standard deliveries, has positive effects.

Part B: Circle the letter of the title that best summarizes each of the following two selections. Then write a one-sentence summary of each. If there is a summary sentence in a paragraph, you may use it; one paragraph has such a sentence.

> We are all familiar with a slogan spoken by a stern bear in a forest ranger's hat: "Only you can prevent forest fires!" For many years, an extensive advertising campaign has been conducted, using symbols like Smokey the Bear and Woodsy Owl, to warn the public about the dangers of forest fires. We are told that forest fires are ugly, destructive, and dangerous. However, despite the advertising campaigns, forest fires are actually beneficial to forest ecologies. First of all, they clear out underbrush and debris on the forest floor. The fire consumes this unnecessary material, and the larger, more resistant trees are spared. Without regular, small forest fires, the dry tinder of brush and fallen limbs on the forest floor builds to a high level. Then, if a fire starts, it will be intense enough to destroy every tree, large and small. Forest fires also eliminate undesirable species of trees that take root in the forest from wind-borne seeds. Some special forests are actually dependent on fire to exist. In New Jersey's Pine Barrens, seeds are liberated from tightly closed pine cones by the intense heat of a fire. The cones pop open as the fire passes, and a new generation of trees begins.

7. Which would be an accurate title for this selection?

   a.   Advertising Campaigns and Forest Fires

   b.   Dangers of Forest Fires

   c.   Benefits of Forest Fires

8. Summary sentence: _____

_____

The large, gleaming refrigerator is the focal point of most American kitchens. It holds enough food to last many days, and even for months in the freezer. It is cold enough to preserve that food well. It can provide ice cubes, ice chips, and ice water. Its advantages are clear. But that big refrigerator has its drawbacks as well. First of all, a large refrigerator encourages the hoarding of food and leads to obesity and other eating problems. Also, it has destroyed the pleasant custom, still common in Europe, of going to market each day. Picking out one's fresh produce daily while chatting with friends and neighbors is no longer a part of our lives. In addition, people's desire to buy huge amounts of groceries just a few times a month has encouraged the growth of supermarkets and destroyed local grocery stores. Other victims of the giant refrigerator have been small local farmers, who can't compete against the mega-producers favored by the supermarkets.

9. Which would be an accurate title for this selection?

   a.   The Modern Refrigerator: Pluses and Minuses

   b.   The Advantages of the Modern Refrigerator

   c.   Victims of the Modern Refrigerator

10. Summary sentence: _____

_____

| *Score*   Number correct (_____) × 10 = _____% |

Understanding Graphs and Tables

■ Mastery Test

1. Study the table below from the sample textbook chapter on page 156 and answer the questions about it.

A Comparison of the State of U.S. Children, 1960 and 2008		
	1960	2008
Children born to unmarried mothers	5%	40.6%
Mothers returning to work within 1 year of a child's birth	17%	57%
Children under 18 living in a one-parent family	10%	26%
Infant mortality (deaths before first birthday)	28/1,000	6.7/1,000
Children under 18 living below the poverty line	27%	18.2%
Married women with children under 6 years old in labor force	18.6%	61.6%

Source: U.S. Census Bureau, 2009; Centers for Disease Control, 2010.

a. Are more or fewer children born to unmarried mothers in this century?

_____

b. Are more or fewer children living below the poverty line in this century?

_____

c. Are more or fewer children under 18 living in one-parent families in this century? _____

d. How many married women with children under 6 years old are in the labor force today, compared with the last century? _____

2. Study the table below from the sample textbook chapter on page 175 and answer the questions about it,

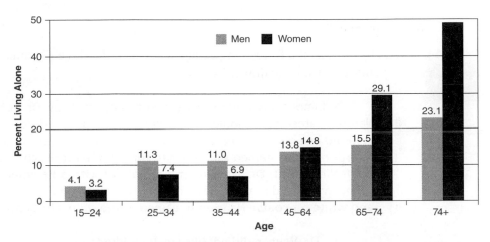

Percent of Persons Living Alone in the United States by Age and Gender, 2009

Source: Figure generated by authors using data from the U.S. Census Bureau, Current Population Survey, 2009 Annu Social and Economic Supplement. Available at http://www.census.gov/population/www/socdemo/hh-fam/cps2009.html.

a. In which age group are the fewest men and women living alone? _____

b. Are more men or women between the ages of 35 and 44 living alone?

   _____

c. In which age group do more women than men start living alone?

   _____

d. In which age group are the most women living alone? _____

Score   Number correct (_____) × 12.5 = _____%

Making Inferences

■ **Mastery Test**

A. (1–3.) Read the following passage and check the three (3) inferences that can most logically be drawn from it.

> [1]A famous psychology experiment conducted by Dr. John B. Watson demonstrates that people, like animals, can be conditioned—trained to respond in a particular way to certain stimulations. [2]Watson gave an eleven-month-old baby named Albert a soft, furry white rat. [3]Each time Albert tried to stroke the rat, Dr. Watson hit a metal bar with a hammer. [4]Before long, Albert was afraid not only of white rats but also of white rabbits, white dogs, and white fur coats. [5]He even screamed at the sight of a Santa Claus mask.

____ 1. Dr. Watson did not like small children.

____ 2. Before the experiment, Albert was not afraid of white rats.

____ 3. Albert had been familiar with rats before the experiment.

____ 4. If he had seen a black fur coat, Albert would have screamed.

____ 5. Albert connected the loud noise of the hammer striking the metal bar with the white rat.

____ 6. Albert was afraid of unexpected loud noises from the beginning.

B. (4–7.) Label each item according to its main purpose: to inform (I), to persuade (P), or to entertain (E).

____ 4. Professional athletes do not deserve their inflated salaries, nor does their behavior merit so much media attention.

____ 5. The best approach to take when you feel the urge to exercise is to lie down quickly in a darkened room until the feeling goes away.

____ 6. On average, women dream more than men, and children dream more than adults.

____ 7. Billboard advertising is a form of visual pollution and should be banned.

C. (8–10.) Each of the following passages illustrates a tone from the following box. In the space provided, put the letter of the tone that applies to each passage. One tone will not be used.

a. sympathetic	b. pessimistic
c. critical	d. curious

___ 8. Whatever happened to the practice of saving up for what you want? It seems nobody has that kind of patience anymore. Many Americans buy what they want when they want it and worry about paying for it later. The average American spends significantly more than he or she earns, much to the enjoyment of the credit-card companies. Apparently people need to reach a financial crisis before they realize that it's downright stupid to neglect to balance their budgets and to save for a rainy day.

___ 9. When people are unemployed, two major sources of stress come into play. One is the loss of income, with all the financial hardships that this brings. Suddenly there are the difficulties of paying the monthly rent or mortgage, of making the car payment and paying credit-card bills, of dealing with utility costs, and the fundamental matter of putting enough food to eat on the table. The other source of stress is the effect of the loss of income on workers' feelings about themselves. Workers who derive their identity from their work, men who define manhood as supporting a family, and people who define their worth in terms of their work's dollar value lose more than their paychecks when they lose their jobs. They lose a piece of themselves; they lose their self-esteem.

___ 10. During my last physical, the doctor found a little lump in my throat. I'm going into the hospital tomorrow so that they can check out what it is. The doctor said it was most likely a harmless cyst, but of course he would say that. What's he going to say: "Sorry—looks like cancer to me"? He also said that if it is cancer, it's probably of a kind that is easily treated. Right, I thought. He's trying to be nice, I know, but I also know how these things go. First he'll say it's nothing; then he'll say it's cancer but no big deal; and finally he'll tell me the truth. I'm done for.

Score Number correct (_____) × 10 = _____%

Thinking Critically

■ Mastery Test

A. (1–2.) In each of the following groups, one statement is the point, and the other statements are support for the point. Circle the point in each group.

Group 1

a.   The only character we liked was killed halfway through the film.

b.   The movie we saw last night was not very good.

c.   We were able to figure out the ending long before the movie was over.

d.   The most exciting scene was filmed with so little light that we could not see what was happening.

Group 2

a.   The storm flooded the creek, which filled the basements of several homes.

b.   The recent storm did a lot of damage to the neighborhood.

c.   Storm winds knocked down a large tree, which broke through the roof of one house.

d.   The storm knocked down wires, leaving many houses without electricity for two days.

B. (3.) Below is a point followed by three clusters of information. Circle the letter of the cluster that logically supports the point.

Point: Neil is a hypocrite, often saying one thing but meaning another.

a.   He spent forty-five minutes talking and laughing with someone yesterday, then later confided to me, "I can't stand that man!" He lectures his son about the dangers of drug addiction, then sits down to watch the ball game with a case of beer and a carton of cigarettes.

b.   He waits until December to put in winter storm windows, and his Christmas tree is still up in March. He usually pays his bills a few days after they are due, and he does not get his car's 10,000-mile checkup until the car has gone 25,000 miles.

c.   After thirty-seven years of marriage, he still writes love letters to his wife. He took early retirement so that he could stay home and care for her when an illness left her bedridden. He never leaves the house without bringing her back something special.

C. (4.) The point below is followed by three statements that provide logical support and two that do not. In the spaces, write the letters of the three logical statements of support.

Point: I do not trust my sister's new boyfriend.

a.   He likes one of my favorite bands very much and has seen it in concert three times.

b.   He refuses to give my sister his phone number, saying that he'll call her.

c.   When anyone asks what he does for a living, he just says, "I have a lot of projects going on."

d.   My sister met him at the electronics store where she works.

e.   When I saw him in a restaurant with another girl, he acted very embarrassed and left before I could say hello.

Items that logically support the point: _____ _____ _____

D. (5.) Read the three items of supporting evidence below. Then circle the letter of the point that is most logically supported by that evidence.

Support

• A study showed that regular churchgoers had lower blood pressure than nonchurchgoers.

• Researchers have found lower rates of depression among religious people.

• A study found that patients who have strong faith have a much greater chance of surviving heart surgery than those who do not.

Point: The point of the above support is:

a.   Scientists have some evidence that religious faith is good for one's health.

b.   Studies show that religious people are more intelligent than nonreligious people.

c.   Medical science rejects the idea that religion can help people.

d.   Today, many hospitals encourage people to express their religious feelings openly.

Score   Number correct (_____) × 20 = _____%

Skim Reading

■ Mastery Test

Take five minutes to skim-read the following selection and to take notes on it. Then see if you can answer the questions that follow by referring to your notes but *not* referring back to the text.

The Hospice Program
Objectives of the Hospice Program

The hospice program is a fairly new method of caring for the dying. While there is no solid definition of *hospice,* it is generally considered a program with two objectives. The first objective is to keep patients free from pain on a continuous basis. The second objective is to provide the dying with a homelike atmosphere in which to spend their final days.

How Hospices Reach Their Goals

Hospices reach their goals through one of several approaches. Some hospices work on an outpatient basis and thus have no physical facility from which to work. Outpatient hospices depend on team efforts of professionals from several institutions. An outpatient team could consist of a member of the clergy, social workers, nurses, doctors, and psychologists. A second approach some hospices have adopted is to work on an inpatient basis, using a building that is set up to have a homelike atmosphere. These buildings include some sort of sleeping quarters, eating facilities, and lounges or some other recreational area. In these inpatient facilities, the patients decide when to eat, sleep, and relax. Still other hospices use a combination of inpatient and outpatient services. Services are provided in the home when possible and in the hospice facility when necessary.

How Hospices Differ from Other Health Care Facilities

Even if a hospice operates only on an inpatient basis, it still differs from hospitals and nursing homes. Hospices differ from other health care facilities in four major ways. First, there is a lack of scheduling and structure in hospices. For one thing, there are no time schedules (with the exception of medication schedules) forced on hospice patients. This means open-ended visiting hours, mealtimes, bedtimes, and so on. Patients can adjust more easily to their condition if they are allowed to live by their own life patterns in the "no-schedule" atmosphere. Lack of structure means something else too: no restrictions on diet or activity. If a patient wants to have a favorite dessert at every meal or if a visitor brings a patient a special snack, the patient is allowed to have the food. If patients desire to try a strenuous activity one day and the activity tires them out so much that they must spend the next day in bed, so be it. The patient's schedule is what he or she wants it to be.

Another aspect of hospices that differs from other care facilities is that the facility personnel concentrate solely on the patient and don't become involved in side activities such as research and teaching. Patients' psychological needs, for example, are a main concern to hospice personnel. If a patient needs to talk over his or her feelings with someone in the middle of the night, personnel are there to listen. Personnel have time to be with patients because they have no other duties to distract or detain them.

View of pain control is another aspect of hospice care that sets it apart from care in hospitals and other facilities. In traditional health care institutions, patients may be expected to bear pain until it is unbearable. In hospices, patients are given medication as often as necessary to keep pain from surfacing at all.

Finally, unlike the philosophy of most health care facilities, the hospice theme includes the patient's family in the care cycle. Family needs are mainly psychological. Hospices provide the family members with counseling to help them accept the eventual death of their relative. Once the family member has died, hospices also provide the family with bereavement follow-up services.

Questions about the Selection

What are the two objectives of the hospice program?

1. _____

2. _____

What are three ways that hospices reach their goals?

3. _____

4. _____

5. _____

What are three ways that hospices differ from other health care facilities?

6. _____

7. _____

8. _____

Score   Number correct (_____) × 12.5 = _____%

Rapid Reading Passage

■ Mastery Test

Read this selection as rapidly as you can without sacrificing comprehension. Then record your time in the space provided and answer the comprehension questions that follow.

America's Detention Camps

John is a junior college English teacher. When he was three years old, the United States government sent him, and his family, to a detention camp. Howard, a newspaper publisher, spent eight months imprisoned with his wife and children in a one-room tarpaper shack. He had committed no crime; his imprisonment was legal. Jeanne, an author, was sent to a prison camp when she was seven. She spent three years there and now says: "All I knew was that we were in camp, behind barbed wire. Everything had fallen apart. No more Christmas, Thanksgiving."

John, Howard, and Jeanne had all been in America; neither they nor their families had committed, been tried for, or been convicted of a crime. They were imprisoned in "internment camps" simply because their parents or grandparents (or even great-grandparents) had come to America from Japan. They had Japanese faces.

In December 1941, the Japanese attacked Pearl Harbor and destroyed America's Pacific fleet. The rallying cry in America was "Remember Pearl Harbor!" and the country was plunged into a wave of anti-Japanese sentiment. On February 19, 1942, President Franklin Roosevelt signed Executive Order 9066. It allowed the military to move Japanese American civilians to ten relocation camps, stretching from California to Arkansas. Most Japanese Americans lived on the West Coast, and the government acted on fears that they would become saboteurs and spies for Japan.

Eventually, almost 110,000 civilians, over two-thirds of whom were American citizens, were forced to move. Laws were passed penalizing those who disobeyed military orders. Indeed, the Supreme Court ruled that the confinement of these people, based only on race, was legal; the Court also upheld rulings on curfews and travel restrictions for Japanese Americans.

Many of those who were interned left families, prosperous businesses, farms, and personal possessions behind. The resettlement was swift; money was lost in the shuffle or confiscated by the government. One California bank, in 1942, estimated the loss by Japanese Americans at $400 million. Japanese American homes were searched without warrants, and workers were fired for no reason.

The Japanese, of course, were not America's only enemies in World War II; we also fought Germans and Italians. However, none of these immigrants or their children received the treatment that the Japanese did. They were not interned or taken to "safe" locations. Strong racial prejudice against the Japanese seemed to be at work. Earl Warren (later to become Chief Justice of the United States Supreme Court) was then attorney general of California. Even Warren, who became known as a strong fighter for civil liberties, appeared to show racial bias. In 1942, he said: "We believe that when we are dealing with the Caucasian race we have methods that will test the loyalty of them . . . but when we deal with the Japanese we are in an entirely different field and we cannot form any opinion that we believe to be sound."

During the war, second-generation Japanese Americans (called Nisei) were eventually allowed to join the army; they made up a special unit, the 442nd Regimental Combat Team, that fought in the European theater, especially the Italian campaign. Many of these men came out of internment camps to fight for the country they loved, the country that had so wronged them. The Nisei won more decorations than any regiment in history and suffered an extremely high casualty rate. Senator Daniel Inouye, who served on the Watergate investigation committee, is a Nisei who lost an arm in the war.

When the war ended, the Japanese Americans were released. They went back to their homes and attempted to pick up the pieces of their lives. The Evacuation Claims Act of 1948 was to compensate them for their economic losses, but it returned only $38 million to the internees—less than 10 percent of the estimated losses.

How do Japanese Americans feel about this treatment now? One, an army sergeant, says:

> I was born in [a camp] in 1944. Living quarters were small, and they never had enough blankets. . . . The guns around the camp were always pointed into the camp, not outward. . . . My folks say they want to forget this ever happened. They lost a lot of relatives who went to Europe with the 442nd Combat Team.

Some Japanese Americans feel that a financial repayment is called for. Others feel that money is no longer important, but justice is. Since their rights were violated, since they were denied the privileges of citizens, they want an apology. One woman says: "It is the gesture, the recognition, the honor that is restored. It is the symbolic gesture of the government standing up and saying it was wrong." Since no other immigrant group has ever been singled out for such harsh and unfair treatment, this seems to be the least our government could do.

Time: _____   *Reading Rate (see page 522):* _____ WPM

Reading Comprehension

1. *True or false?* _____ Japanese Americans were not allowed to fight in World War II.

2. On February 19, 1942, President Franklin Roosevelt signed Executive Order 9066, which

    a. imposed curfews.

    b. imposed travel restrictions.

    c. allowed the military to move Japanese Americans.

    d. confiscated the property of Japanese Americans.

3. Two-thirds of the interned Japanese Americans were

    a. American citizens.

    b. farm owners.

    c. from the West Coast.

    d. homeowners.

4. Economic losses of Japanese Americans were estimated at

    a. $20 million.

    b. $40 million.

    c. $200 million.

    d. $400 million.

5. The word *Nisei* means

    a. second-generation Japanese Americans.

    b. a Japanese American combat regiment.

    c. a Japanese American senator.

    d. an internment camp.

6. The Evacuation Claims Act of 1948

    a. fully restored all financial losses.

    b. partially restored financial losses.

    c. declared that Japanese Americans should be interned.

    d. was signed by President Roosevelt.

7. The main idea in the selection is that

    a. Japanese Americans are bitter about their treatment.

    b. the government's action against the Japanese was unfair and unjust.

    c. Germans and Italians should have received the same treatment as the Japanese did.

    d. Americans were hysterical during the war.

8. The government feared the Japanese Americans would

    a. hide their money.

    b. defect to Japan.

    c. join the armed services.

    d. spy for Japan.

9. The 442nd Regimental Combat Team

    a. fought in the Pacific theater.

    b. won more decorations than any other regiment.

    c. had a low casualty rate.

    d. fought the internment policy.

10. The writer suggests that Japanese Americans

    a. were reasonably compensated for their losses.

    b. wish to forget the detention camps.

    c. deserve an official apology.

    d. lacked patriotism during the war.

Score   Number correct (_____) × 10 = _____%

Part Eight
Additional Learning Skills

Preview

Part Eight takes up some extra learning skills that will help you get more out of your studies. In "Studying Mathematics and Science," you'll find tips that will help you deal more effectively with math and science courses. A related chapter is "Reading Literature and Making Inferences," which provides some guidelines that will better equip you to read literary works. Next, "Reading for Pleasure: A List of Interesting Books" offers short descriptions of a number of widely admired books that will give you reading practice and may provide you with some of the most pleasurable and illuminating experiences of your life. Finally, "Writing Effectively" is a brief guide that shows you how to write effective paragraphs and essays, describes relationships between writing and reading, and provides some writing assignments.

Studying Mathematics and Science

For many people, mathematics and science courses are terrifying. There are several very understandable reasons for this feeling. Many of us, first of all, come to class weak in the basics we need to know to handle such courses. A college mathematics or biology instructor, for example, may expect students to know how to handle fractions, decimals, proportions, and simple algebra. Some of the students, in contrast, have forgotten (or never learned) these skills. Without this kind of foundation, the work in the class starts out on a difficult level indeed.

Another reason students dread these courses is that there is no way to pass them without doing a great deal of hard work. Mathematics and science courses *demand* excellent attendance, complete notes, extensive homework, and intensive study sessions. Students looking for courses they can just "slide by" in are naturally wary of mathematics and science. But other students—ones who need chemistry or calculus, for example, to become medical technicians, nurses, or computer programmers—are willing to work hard; the problem is that they don't know how to deal with such courses. Their note-taking and study skills just don't seem adequate for mathematics and science.

Doing well in mathematics and science courses *is* possible. But you must be aware of the adjustments you should make when you switch to mathematics and science from your less technical subjects. The pointers that follow will help you gain control over these subjects.

- *In mathematics and science, knowledge is cumulative.* The learning that you do in mathematics and science courses is cumulative—each fact or formula you learn must rest on a basic structure of all you have learned before. You have to begin with the essentials and build your knowledge in a methodical, complete way. For this reason, *absences from class or weaknesses that are never corrected can be academically fatal.* You will not understand a simple algebra equation, for example, if you are not sure what a "variable" is. It is essential to stay current in such courses and to attack your weak points early. If you don't understand something, ask your instructor for help or visit the tutoring center. Every day you wait makes it more likely that you will do poorly in the course.

- *In mathematics and science, great emphasis is placed on specialized vocabulary, rules, and formulas.* Mathematics and science deal in precision. Everything has a specific name, and every problem can be solved with specific rules and formulas. In a way, this quality makes such courses easier because there is little fuzziness involved and few individual interpretations are required. If you know the vocabulary and have the rules down pat, you should do well.

  An important study technique for mathematics and science is the use of flash cards. These are three- by five-inch index cards that help you memorize and test yourself on terms and formulas. On one side of the card, write the term, rule, or formula you need to know (for instance, "photosynthesis," "Bohr's energy law," or "formula for weight density"). On the other side, write the information that you must memorize. Flash cards enable you to study the material conveniently and to discover quickly what you know and what exactly you are unsure of.

- *In mathematics and science, special emphasis is placed on homework.* In many mathematics and science classes, you will be given numerical problems to solve outside class. Often, these problems will not be checked by the instructor; their purpose is to give you practice in the kinds of material you will find on tests. Many students do a hurried job on—or skip completely—any work that is not graded. If you are not conscientious about this homework, however, you will be panicky before tests and unprepared for what is on them. If you want to pass your mathematics and science classes, you *must* take the responsibility for much of the necessary learning yourself by doing the problems and asking questions in class about problems that puzzle you.

- *Taking clear notes in class is crucial.* In your class notes for mathematics and science, you will often be copying problems, diagrams, formulas, and definitions from the blackboard. In addition, you will be trying to follow your instructor's train of thought as he or she explains how a problem is solved or how a process works. Such classes obviously demand intense concentration. As you copy material from the board, be sure to include in your notes any information the instructor gives that can help you see the *connections between steps or the relationship of one fact to another.* For example, if an instructor is explaining and diagramming human blood circulation patterns, you should copy the diagram; you should also be sure you have definitions ("alveoli," "aorta") and any important connecting information ("blood moves from artery to capillaries").

As soon as possible after a mathematics or science class, you should clarify and expand your notes while the material is still fresh in your mind.

- *Mathematics and science require patient, slow reading.* The information in mathematics and science tests is often densely packed; texts are filled with special terms that are often unfamiliar; blocks of text are interspersed with numerical formulas, problems to solve, charts, diagrams, and drawings. Such textbooks cannot be read quickly; for this reason, you have to keep up with the assigned reading. It is impossible to read and understand fifty pages—even ten pages—the night before a test.

   The good news about mathematics and science textbooks is that they are usually organized very clearly. They also have glossaries of terms and concise reviews at the ends of chapters. When you are reading mathematics and science books, proceed slowly. Do not skip over any unfamiliar terms; check the index or the glossary in the back of the book for the definition. With mathematics textbooks, spend time going over each sample problem. After you have gone over the sample, you might want to write out the problem on a piece of paper and then see if you remember how to solve it. With science textbooks, be sure to study the visual material that accompanies the written explanations. Study each chart or diagram until you understand it. Being able to visualize such material can be crucial when you are asked to reproduce it or write an essay on it during an exam.

You can succeed in mathematics and science classes if you are organized, persistent, and willing to work. When passing these courses is necessary to achieve your goals, the effort must be made.

Studying a Math Excerpt

Following are the first two pages of a popular college math textbook, *Intermediate Algebra* (McGraw-Hill), by James Streeter, Donald Hutchison, and Louis Hoelzle. Read the text and study the terms and examples in the box. You will be learning the names of properties of addition patterns.

Next, work your way carefully through Example 1, which is a sample practice. To find the answers, compare each item with the examples and explanations in the box. Don't look at an answer in the Solution until you have honestly tried to state the property that applies. (Covering up the answers with a piece of paper will help keep you honest.)

Once you understand the items in Example 1, go on to do Activity 1.

Properties of the Real Numbers

OBJECTIVE

To recognize and apply the properties of the real numbers

Algebra is a system consisting of a set, together with operations that follow certain properties. The set of real numbers is the set we use most often. In this section, we discuss the properties of the operations of addition and multiplication on the set of real numbers.

For the most part, you will find that these properties are familiar from your past experience in working with numbers. As just one example, you know that

$$3 + 5 = 8$$

But it is also true that

$$5 + 3 = 8$$

Your experience tells you that the *order* in which two numbers are added does not matter. This fact is called the *commutative property of addition* and is one of the properties we consider in this section. Let's proceed now with the formal statement of these properties.

PROPERTIES OF ADDITION ON REAL NUMBERS

For any real numbers a, b, and c:

CLOSURE PROPERTY

$a + b$ is a real number

In words, the sum of any two real numbers is always a real number.

COMMUTATIVE PROPERTY

$a + b = b + a$

In words, the *order* in which two numbers are added does not affect the sum.

ASSOCIATIVE PROPERTY

$a + (b + c) = (a + b) + c$

In words, the *grouping* of numbers in addition does not affect the sum.

> **ADDITIVE IDENTITY**
> There exists a unique real number 0 such that
>
> $a + 0 = 0 + a = a$
>
> In words, 0 is the additive identity. No number loses its identity after addition with 0.
>
> **ADDITIVE INVERSE**
> There exists a unique real number $-a$ such that
>
> $a + (-a) = (-a) + a = 0$
>
> In words, $-a$ is the *additive inverse* of a. The sum of a number and its additive inverse is 0.

The additive inverse is also called the opposite of a.

The $\boxed{+/-}$ key on your calculator is an additive-inverse key. Pushing this key gives you the opposite of the number in the display.

Our first example illustrates the use of the properties introduced above.

Example 1

State the property used to justify each statement.

(a) $2 + (4 + 5) = (2 + 4) + 5$
(b) $-8 + 0 = -8$
(c) $(-8) + 5$ is a real number.
(d) $b + (-b) = 0$
(e) $62 + 8 = 8 + 62$

Solution

(a) Associative property of addition   The *grouping* has been changed.
(b) Additive identity
(c) Closure property of addition
(d) Additive inverse
(e) Commutative property of addition   The *order* has been changed.

CHECK YOURSELF 1

State the property (or properties) used to justify each statement.

1. $2x + y = y + 2x$
2. $3n + 0 = 3n$
3. $2x + (3x + 4y) = (2x + 3x) + 4y$
4. $7 + (-10)$ is a real number.
5. $5n + [7 + (-7)] = 5n + 0 = 5n$

Activity 1

State the property (or properties) used to justify each statement. Then read the explanations that follow.

The Property of Addition That Justifies Each Statement

(1) $2x + y = y + 2x$ _____

(2) $3n + 0 = 3n$ _____

(3) $2x + (3x + 4y) = (2x + 3x) + 4y$ _____

(4) $7 + (-10)$ is a real number.   _____

(5) $5n + [7 + (-7)] = 5n + 0 = 5n$ _____

Following is an explanation of each item.

1. Note that in the equation in item (1), *the order of the numbers changes*. Checking the box above, we see that this change in order matches the definition and pattern of the commutative property. So that is the answer for this item.

2. In this equation, $3n$ does not lose its identity after addition with 0—the sum is the same: $3n$. So the answer to this item must be the additive identity. The definition for that property says, "No number loses its identity after addition with 0."

3. Note that this item contains *a change in number groupings*. The pattern and definition in the box that match and justify this equation are for the associative property.

4. The statement "$7 + (-10)$ is a real number" means that the sum of two real numbers—7 and (-10)—is another real number. This statement matches the definition and pattern given for the closure property.

5. *Two* properties justify this equation. First, it shows that adding 7 to -7 equals 0. That part of the equation is justified by the property of additive inverse: "The sum of a number and its additive inverse is 0." The sum of 7 and its additive inverse, -7, is 0.

    The last part of this equation, "$5n + 0 = 5n$," is justified by the property of additive identity: "No number loses its identity after addition with 0." When $5n$ is added to 0, it keeps its identity—the sum is $5n$.

Activity 2

Here is another opportunity to practice using the five properties of addition on real numbers. Feel free to refer to the patterns and definitions in the box on pages 590–591 if necessary. Again, state the property used to justify each statement.

The Property of Addition That Justifies Each Statement

(1) $5n + (-5n) = 0$ _____

(2) $-3 + 0 = -3$ _____

(3) $5y + x = x + 5y$ _____

(4) $(-1) + 2$ is a real number. _____

(5) $7 + (2a + 4) = (4 + 7) + 2a$ _____

Studying a Science Passage

This activity will help you see how well you can actually do in science with careful study techniques. Below are guidelines and questions to help you use the PRWR method (explained in full on pages 99–114) to study a passage about immunity from the college textbook *Life and Health* (McGraw-Hill), by Marvin R. Levey, Mark Dignam, and Janet H. Shirreffs. Work your way through each of the four steps of the activity. Afterward, you can test your understanding of the material by taking a quiz.

Activity

Step 1: *Preview.*   Answer the following questions about the reading below by previewing it: Check the title, read the first paragraph, and look at the headings and highlighted words.

1. The title tells you that the selection is about _____.

2. How many boldfaced terms are there to learn in the reading? _____

Immunity

Immunity is a group of mechanisms that help protect the body against specific diseases. Immunity is the body's most efficient disease-preventing weapon; it can help fight either a viral infection or a bacterial one.

The Role of Lymphocytes

In the immune mechanism, white blood cells become involved in fighting infection. The protective white blood cells are of a type known as **lymphocytes,** including two key subtypes: B and T lymphocytes.

B lymphocytes, or B cells, are believed to originate in the bone marrow (hence the letter B). When foreign or invading pathogens (disease-causing agents) are present in the body, these cells help produce substances called immunoglobulins, or **antibodies**. Antibodies react specifically to the parts of a pathogen that link up to human cells and cause damage. These parts, which are called **antigens**, are thus neutralized. If the invaders are viruses, the antibodies lock on to their antigens and prevent them from entering the target cells. If the invaders are bacteria, the antibodies lock on to them and cause them to clump together, making it easier for certain white blood cells to engulf and digest them. These bacterial-antibody clumps also activate certain bactericidal (bacteria-killing) substances in the blood. Antibodies can also lock on to bacterial toxins to make them less harmful to the body.

T lymphocytes, or T cells, named for their origin in the thymus gland, fight infection in three major ways. First, some T lymphocytes hasten the activity of those white cells that surround and eat foreign substances. Second, some help stimulate the production of antibodies by B lymphocytes. Third, some can attack foreign cells (such as cells in tissues that have been transplanted), cells that have been killed by viruses, and possibly cancer cells.

Natural Immunity

When an invading antigen enters the body, it stimulates the body to produce certain antibodies that can inactivate it. When antigens lock on to specific receptor sites on a body cell's plasma membrane, the immune response is set in motion and antibodies are produced. Antibodies work only on the specific antigens that trigger them: Measles antibodies work only on the measles virus, mumps antibodies on the mumps virus, and so on. There are over a million different specific antibodies, each capable of fighting one antigen. That means that over a million different foreign antigens can stimulate the immune system to take action.

Acquired Immunity

In the past, having a disease was the only way to develop immunity to it (natural immunity through the development of antibodies to fight the current infection and subsequent ones). Today, however, immunity may be induced artificially by means of **vaccines**, which consist of killed or weakened viruses, taken orally or by injection. Several days or weeks after an individual receives a vaccination, the body starts to produce specific antibodies, which circulate in the bloodstream, ready to attack the initiating antigen.

People who contract a disease or receive a vaccine for it usually develop **active immunity**. But what happens if a person is exposed to a serious disease and it is too dangerous to wait for the person's body to produce its own antibodies? In this instance a physician may confer **passive immunity** by giving the person antibodies from another person or an animal. These antibodies are found in certain proteins in the donor's blood that are collectively called **gamma globulin**. Gamma globulin is used to confer passive immunity against infectious hepatitis and other diseases for which an effective vaccine has not been devised.

In general, active immunity is long-term and in some cases lifelong, whereas passive immunity generally lasts only a few weeks or months. Babies have passive immunity at birth because antibodies that pass through the placental membrane become part of the fetus's immune system. Within six weeks after birth, however, passive immunity begins to weaken, and the baby will need to receive vaccinations to start the development of active immunity against certain diseases.

Step 2: *Read.*   Read the passage straight through. As you do, mark the text, using symbols such as those shown on page 102. For example, in the first paragraph, underline the words that follow *immunity*, which explain what that word means, and in the section titled "The Role of Lymphocytes," number the two key subtypes of lymphocytes.

Read as slowly as necessary to understand the material, and don't be discouraged by new terms. You will feel more comfortable with new words as you clarify their meanings to yourself.

Step 3: *Write.*   Complete the following notes on the selection.

Immunity—_____

_____

The Role of Lymphocytes

    Lymphocytes—Certain protective white blood cells

    Two kinds of lymphocytes and their functions:

1. B cells (believed to come from <u>b</u>one marrow) produce antibodies

    Antibodies—Substances that react to and fight antigens

    Antigens—_____

    _____

Pathogens—Disease-causing agents

Ways that antibodies fight the two kinds of pathogens:

    (1) Viruses—_____

_____

    (2) Bacteria—antibodies lock on to bacteria and clump them together for white blood cells to eat up

        —Can also activate bacteria-killer in blood and make bacterial toxins less harmful

  2. T cells (from thymus gland) fight infection in three major ways:

    (1) Spur certain white blood cells to eat foreign substances faster

    (2) Help stimulate production of antibodies by B cells

    (3) _____

_____

Natural Immunity

Natural immunity—Antigens lock on to sites on cell's membrane, producing antibodies, which work only on specific antigens that trigger them

    Ex.—_____

_____

Acquired Immunity

Acquired immunity—Immunity that is brought about artificially

  1. Vaccines—_____

_____

  2. Passive immunity (versus active immunity, gained through illness or vaccine)—Gained from donor antibodies in gamma globulin

    Gamma globulin—a collection of certain proteins in donor blood

    —Lasts only a few weeks or months (versus active immunity, which is long-term or lifelong)

    Ex.—_____

_____

Step 4: *Recite.* Review your notes by reciting to yourself. Use "recall words" to help you: Write words and phrases in the margins of your notes, and turn them into questions that will help you study your notes. Your instructor may wish to have pairs of students spend some time reciting to each other as well. He or she may also ask you to create and use flash cards to help you remember new terms in the reading.

Study Check: By the time you finish studying your notes, you should know the following:

- The meanings of and key information on all the boldfaced words.
- The two types of lymphocytes and their functions.
- What the process of natural immunity is.
- What the two types of acquired immunity are.
- The differences between active immunity and passive immunity.

■ Quiz on the Science Passage

Part A: Write each of the following terms in the blank by its definition.

antigens   gamma globulin   lymphocytes   vaccines

_____ 1. White blood cells that fight infections in various ways.

_____ 2. Substances made up of weakened or killed viruses used to stimulate immunity.

_____ 3. A collection of proteins in donor blood used to provide immunization against some diseases.

_____ 4. Parts of pathogens that link up to human cells and cause damage.

Part B: Circle the letter of your answer choice for each of the following questions.

5. B cells are a type of
   a. antibody.
   b. antigen.
   c. lymphocyte.

6. _____ *True or false?* Antibodies fight disease-causing agents that enter the body and link up to cells.

7. Natural immunity is provided by

   a.   vaccines.

   b.   antibodies.

   c.   donor blood.

8. Acquired immunity is provided by

   a.   vaccines.

   b.   gamma globulin.

   c.   both of the above.

9. Active immunity comes from

   a.   contracting a disease.

   b.   receiving a vaccine.

   c.   both of the above.

10. A baby is born with

   a.   active immunity.

   b.   passive immunity.

   c.   both of the above.

Reading Literature and Making Inferences

 The comprehension skills you've learned in this book apply to everything you read. But to get the most out of literature, you also need to be aware of several important elements that shape fiction. And you need to know how to make inferences. Following, then, are a few guidelines to help you understand fiction more fully.

Key Elements in Literature

Important elements in a work of literature are theme, plot, setting, characters, conflict, climax, narrator, and figures of speech:

- Look for the *theme,* or the overall idea, that the author is advancing. This is the very general idea that is behind the author's entire effort and unifies the work. For example, the theme in much of Katherine Anne Porter's writing is that separateness and misunderstanding are fundamental facts of the human condition.

- Make sure you understand the *plot*—the series of events that take place within the work. For instance, the plot of Philip Roth's short novel *Goodbye, Columbus* is that boy meets girl, they fall in love, and then—because of different values—they fall out of love.

- Observe the *setting*, that is, the time and place of the plot. The setting of *The Adventures of Huckleberry Finn*, by Mark Twain, for instance, is nineteenth-century America.

- Examine the *characters*—the people in the story. Each character will have his or her own unique qualities, behaviors, needs, and values.

- Be alert for the main *conflict* of a story. The conflict is the main struggle of the plot. It may be within a character, between two or more characters, or between one or more characters and some force in the environment. For example, the conflict in *Moby-Dick* is between the hunter Captain Ahab and the animal he hunts—a white whale (the Moby-Dick of the title).

- Watch for the *climax*, the final main turning point of a story. The main conflict of a story is usually solved or explained in a final way at this point in the plot. For example, the climax of Shirley Jackson's story "The Lottery" comes when a woman's neighbors surround her and stone her to death.

- Be aware of the *speaker*, or *narrator*, who tells the story and the *tone* of that speaker. Both strongly influence the character of a work. The speaker is not the author but the fictional voice the author uses to narrate the story. In Mark Twain's *Huckleberry Finn*, for instance, the speaker is the title character, not the author. The tone is the style or manner of a piece. It reflects the speaker's attitude and is strongly related to the author's attitude and purpose as well.

- Note *figures of speech*, expressions in which words are used to mean something other than they usually do. These expressions are often comparisons that make a special point. Examples of figures of speech are "I wandered lonely as a cloud" (William Wordsworth), "my love is like a red, red rose" (Robert Burns), and "the slings and arrows of outrageous fortune" (William Shakespeare).

Making Inferences in Literature

To get the most out of reading literature, it is very important to make *inferences*. In other words, you must "read between the lines" and come to conclusions on the basis of the given information. While writers of factual material often directly *state* what they mean, writers of fiction often *show* what they mean. It is then up to the reader to infer the point of what the writer has said. For instance, a nonfiction author might write, "Harriet was angry at George." But the novelist might write, "Harriet's eyes narrowed when George spoke to her. She cut him off in mid-sentence with the words 'I don't have time to argue with you.'" The author has *shown* us the anger with specific details rather than simply stating its existence abstractly. The reader must observe the details about Harriet and George and infer that she is angry.

The following pages will give you practice in drawing inferences from three kinds of literary material: a poem, a biography, and a novel. In each case, read the literary piece presented and then answer the inference questions that follow.

A Poem

Nowhere is inference more important than in reading poetry. Poetry, by its nature, implies much of its meaning. Implications are often made through figures of speech. For practice, read the poem below. Note that definitions of the more difficult words are provided at the beginning.

When I Was One-and-Twenty
A. E. Housman (1859–1936)

■ Words to Watch

crowns, pounds, guineas: forms of English money

fancy: desire

in vain: with little consequence

rue: sorrow, or regret

> When I was one-and-twenty
> I heard a wise man say,
> "Give crowns and pounds and guineas
> But not your heart away;
> Give pearls away and rubies
> But keep your fancy free."
> But I was one-and-twenty,
> No use to talk to me.
>
> When I was one-and-twenty
> I heard him say again,
> "The heart out of the bosom
> Was never given in vain;
> 'Tis paid with sighs a-plenty
> And sold for endless rue."
> And I am two-and-twenty,
> And oh, 'tis true, 'tis true.

Activity

Answer each question by circling the inference most solidly based on "When I Was One-and-Twenty."

1. To "give . . . your heart away" is a figure of speech meaning

   a. to fall in love.

   b. to be dishonest.

   c. to become ill.

2. To "keep your fancy free" is a figure of speech meaning

   a. don't charge others for your company.

   b. don't be rich.

   c. don't desire only one person.

3. The wise man's advice was:

   a. It's best to be poor.

   b. It's less costly to give riches away than to fall in love.

   c. An expensive romance is never harmful.

4. When the speaker says, "But I was one-and-twenty, / No use to talk to me," the meaning is that he or she

   a. welcomed the wise man's advice.

   b. understood the wise man's advice.

   c. ignored the wise man's advice.

5. When he or she accepted the wise man's advice, the speaker

   a. was twenty-one.

   b. had just fallen in love for the first time.

   c. was twenty-two and had experienced a disappointing romance.

Following is an explanation of each item:

1. To "give . . . your heart away" is a fairly common figure of speech, and so you probably knew right away that it means to fall in love. The answer to this item is *a*.

2. Because *fancy* means "desire," "keep your fancy free" must mean to keep your desire free—of attachments. Thus the answer to this question is *c*—"don't desire only one person."

3. "Crowns and pounds and guineas," "pearls," and "rubies" all represent riches. Thus the wise man's advice was *b*—"It's less costly to give riches away than to fall in love."

4. Because it was "no use" for the wise man to talk to the speaker when he or she was twenty-one, we can infer that at that age, the speaker ignored the wise man's advice. Thus the answer to this question is *c*.

5. At first, the speaker didn't accept the wise man's advice, so we must infer that something happened between the ages of twenty-one and twenty-two to make him or her think differently. From the emotional end of the poem—"And oh, 'tis true, 'tis true"—we can infer that the speaker had an unhappy romance. The answer to this item is thus *c*.

An Excerpt from a Biography

Below is the passage that starts the literary autobiography *Growing Up* by *New York Times* columnist Russell Baker. Inference skills will be helpful in understanding the speaker, the characters, and the setting.

At the age of eighty my mother had her last bad fall, and after that her mind wandered free through time. Some days she went to weddings and funerals that had taken place half a century earlier. On others she presided over family dinners cooked on Sunday afternoons for children who were now gray with age. Through all this she lay in bed but moved across time, traveling among the dead decades with a speed and ease beyond the gift of physical science.

"Where's Russell?" she asked one day when I came to visit at the nursing home.

"I'm Russell," I said.

She gazed at this improbably overgrown figure out of an inconceivable future and promptly dismissed it.

"Russell's only this big," she said, holding her hand, palm down, two feet from the floor. That day she was a young country wife with chickens in the backyard and a view of hazy blue Virginia mountains behind the apple orchard, and I was a stranger old enough to be her father.

Early one morning she phoned me in New York. "Are you coming to my funeral today?" she asked.

It was an awkward question with which to be awakened. "What are you talking about, for God's sake?" was the best reply I could manage.

"I'm being buried today," she declared briskly, as though announcing an important social event.

"I'll phone you back," I said and hung up, and when I did phone back she was all right, although she wasn't all right, of course, and we all knew she wasn't.

She had always been a small woman—short, light-boned, delicately structured—but now, under the white hospital sheet, she was becoming tiny. I thought of a doll with huge, fierce eyes. There had always been a fierceness in her. It showed in that angry, challenging thrust of the chin when she issued an opinion, and a great one she had always been for issuing opinions.

"I tell people exactly what's on my mind," she had been fond of boasting. "I tell them what I think, whether they like it or not." Often they had not liked it. She could be sarcastic to people in whom she detected evidence of the ignoramus or the fool.

"It's not always good policy to tell people exactly what's on your mind," I used to caution her.

"If they don't like it, that's too bad," was her customary reply, "because that's the way I am."

And so she was. A formidable woman. Determined to speak her mind, determined to have her way, determined to bend those who opposed her. In that time when I had known her best, my mother had hurled herself at life with chin thrust forward, eyes blazing, and an energy that made her seem always on the run.

She ran after squawking chickens, an ax in her hand, determined on a beheading that would put dinner in the pot. She ran when she made the beds, ran when she set the table. One Thanksgiving she burned herself badly when, running up from the cellar oven with the ceremonial turkey, she tripped on the stairs and tumbled back down, ending at the bottom in the debris of giblets, hot gravy, and battered turkey. Life was combat, and victory was not to the lazy, the timid, the slugabed, the drugstore cowboy, the libertine, the mushmouth afraid to tell people exactly what was on his mind whether people liked it or not. She ran.

Activity

Now put a check by the six inferences most solidly based on the words and images in the passage. Refer to the passage as needed when making your choices.

_____ 1. Baker's mother knew she was remembering past events.

_____ 2. Baker's mother thought she was actually living at the time of some memories.

_____ 3. The author's mother's last bad fall must have affected her mind.

_____ 4. Baker's mother predicted the day of her own funeral.

_____ 5. Once she imagined that her funeral would take place that day.

_____ 6. In describing the incident in which his mother said, "I'm being buried today," Baker uses the term "all right" with two different meanings.

_____ 7. Baker's mother had been a calm woman with a patient, encouraging manner.

_____ 8. She was an energetic, blunt person.

_____ 9. Baker chose to describe his mother more sentimentally than realistically.

_____ 10. His mother's travels "among the dead decades" caused Baker himself to remember earlier days.

Here are explanations for each of the ten inferences.

1 and 2. Because Baker's mother expected the real Russell to be only two feet high, we know that she was unaware of where she was and that she was mentally experiencing earlier times in her life. Thus, inference 1 is not well supported, but inference 2 is solidly based on the given details.

3. The first sentence of the passage connects Baker's mother's fall with her mind wandering "free through time." Therefore, the details of the passage also support inference 3.

4 and 5. Baker doesn't state that his mother's funeral took place on the day she said it would. This tells us that she did not predict the day of her funeral, but that she only imagined it was about to happen. You thus should have checked 5, but not 4.

6. Because the two uses of the term "all right" seem contradictory ("she was all right, although she wasn't all right"), we can assume that Baker intends them to have different meanings. Thus, the statement is a well-supported inference.

　　In writing "when I did phone back she was all right," Baker refers to his mother having overcome the false belief that she was being buried that day. But when he states "she wasn't all right, of course, and we all knew she wasn't," Baker refers to his mother's generally poor physical and mental condition, which she had not overcome.

7 and 8. The author's description of his mother as someone who had been "always on the run" tells us she was more energetic than calm. And because he describes her as someone with "fierceness in her" who "always told people exactly what was on her mind," sometimes sarcastically, we can conclude that she was more blunt than patient and encouraging. Thus, inference 7 is not well supported, but inference 8 is.

9. This inference is not supported by the passage. In discussing a senile parent, some writers might be tempted to dwell on their warmest, sweetest memories. Because Baker describes his mother as a blunt and impatient person who was often disliked, we can conclude that he has avoided sentimentality.

10. This inference is strongly based on the details of the passage. Baker remembers, for instance, how determined and energetic a person his mother was, running after chickens with an ax and once tumbling down the basement stairs after running up with the Thanksgiving turkey.

An Excerpt from a Novel

Now apply your inference skills to the beginning of Philip Roth's short novel *Goodbye, Columbus.*

From *Goodbye, Columbus*
Philip Roth

The first time I saw Brenda she asked me to hold her glasses. Then she stepped out to the edge of the diving board and looked foggily into the pool; it could have been drained, myopic Brenda would never have known it. She dove beautifully, and a moment later she was swimming back to the side of the pool, her head of short-clipped auburn hair held up, straight ahead of her, as though it were a rose on a long stem. She glided to the edge and then was beside me. "Thank you," she said, her eyes watery though not from the water. She extended a hand for her glasses but did not put them on until she turned and headed away. I watched her move off. Her hands suddenly appeared behind her. She caught the bottom of her suit between thumb and index finger and flicked what flesh had been showing back where it belonged. My blood jumped.

That night, before dinner, I called her.

"Who are you calling?" my Aunt Gladys asked.

"Some girl I met today."

"Doris introduced you?"

"Doris wouldn't introduce me to the guy who drains the pool, Aunt Gladys."

"Don't criticize all the time. A cousin's a cousin. How did you meet her?"

"I didn't really meet her. I saw her."

"Who is she?"

"Her last name is Patimkin."

"Patimkin I don't know," Aunt Gladys said, as if she knew anybody who belonged to the Green Lane Country Club. "You're going to call her if you don't know her?"

"Yes," I explained. "I'll introduce myself."

"Casanova," she said, and went back to preparing my uncle's dinner. None of us ate together: My Aunt Gladys ate at five o'clock, my cousin Susan at five-thirty, me at six, and my uncle at six-thirty. There is nothing to explain this beyond the fact that my aunt is crazy.

"Where's the suburban phone book?" I asked after pulling out all the books tucked under the telephone table.

"What?"

"The suburban phone book. I want to call Short Hills."

"That skinny book? What, I gotta clutter my house with that, I never use it?"

"Where is it?"

"Under the dresser where the leg came off."

"For God's sake," I said.

"Call information better. You'll go yanking around there, you'll mess up my drawers. Don't bother me, you see your uncle'll be home soon. I haven't even fed *you* yet."

"Aunt Gladys, suppose tonight we all eat together. It's hot, it'll be easier for you."

"Sure, I should serve four different meals at once. You eat pot roast, Susan with the cottage cheese, Max has steak. Friday night is his steak night, I wouldn't deny him. And I'm having a little cold chicken. I should jump up and down twenty different times? What am I, a workhorse?"

"Why don't we all have steak, or cold chicken—"

"Twenty years I'm running a house. Go call your girlfriend."

Activity

Now answer each question by circling the inference most solidly based on the material in the excerpt.

1. The narrator of the story is

    a. Aunt Gladys.

    b. Aunt Gladys's nephew.

    c. Philip Roth.

2. The setting of the story is

    a. colonial America.

    b. nineteenth-century America.

    c. twentieth-century America.

3. The figure of speech comparing Brenda's hair to "a rose on a long stem" reflects

   a.   the narrator's concern with flowers.

   b.   the narrator's admiration of Brenda.

   c.   Brenda's occupation.

4. We know that Brenda is

   a.   a good swimmer.

   b.   a lifeguard.

   c.   both of the above.

5. *True or false?* _____ Aunt Gladys's nephew probably wants to call Brenda to ask her out on a date.

6. Aunt Gladys's ideas

   a.   about dating are old-fashioned.

   b.   make perfect sense to her nephew.

   c.   both of the above.

7. Brenda lives

   a.   in the city.

   b.   in the suburbs.

   c.   at the country club.

8. We can assume that Doris

   a.   is related to the narrator.

   b.   is disliked by the narrator.

   c.   both of the above.

9. We can assume that Aunt Gladys

   a.   belongs to the Green Lane Country Club.

   b.   has never met Brenda Patimkin.

   c.   both of the above.

10. We can assume that the members of Aunt Gladys's family

   a.   dislike each other.

   b.   have different tastes in foods.

   c.   have different working hours and so cannot eat together.

Reading for Pleasure:
A List of Interesting Books

On the following pages are short descriptions of some books that might interest you. Some are popular books of the last few years; some are among the most widely read "classics"—books that have survived for generations because they deal with basic human experiences that all people can understand and share.

Nonfiction

I Know Why the Caged Bird Sings, Maya Angelou

> The author writes with love, humor, and honesty about her childhood and what it is like to grow up black and female.

Alicia: My Story, Alicia Appleman-Jurman

> Alicia was a Jewish girl living with her family in Poland when the Germans invaded in 1941. Her utterly compelling and heartbreaking story shows some of the best and worst of which human beings are capable.

Growing Up, Russell Baker

> A giant presence in his life, Russell Baker's mother also insisted that he make something of himself. In his autobiography, the prizewinning journalist shows that he did with an engrossing account of his own family and growing up.

In Cold Blood, Truman Capote

> A frightening true story about the murder of a family, the book is also an examination of what made their killers tick. Many books today tell gripping stories of real-life crimes. *In Cold Blood* was the first book of this type and may still be the best.

Sleepers, Lorenzo Carcaterra

> The author of this autobiography tells of the shocking abuse he suffered while in a detention home for boys and of the elaborate revenge that he and his friends later exacted against the guards. The book becomes impossible to put down, and anyone who reads it is unlikely to ever forget it.

Gifted Hands, Ben Carson, M.D.

This is the inspiring story of an inner-city kid with poor grades and little motivation who turned his life around. Dr. Carson is now a world-famous neurosurgeon at one of the best hospitals in the world; his book tells how he got to where he is today. In *Think Big* and *The Big Picture*, two related books, Dr. Carson tells more of his story and presents the philosophy that helped him make the most of his life.

Move On, Linda Ellerbee

A well-known television journalist writes about the ups and downs of her life, including her stay at the Betty Ford Center for treatment of her alcoholism.

The Diary of a Young Girl, Anne Frank

To escape the Nazi death camps, Anne Frank and her family hid for years in an attic. Her journal tells a story of love, fear, and courage.

Man's Search for Meaning, Viktor Frankl

How do people go on when they have been stripped of everything, including human dignity? In this short but moving book, the author describes his time in a concentration camp and what he learned there about survival.

The Story of My Life, Helen Keller

How Miss Keller, a blind and deaf girl who lived in isolation and frustration, discovered a path to learning and knowledge.

The Autobiography of Malcolm X, Malcolm X and Alex Haley

Malcolm X, the controversial black leader who was assassinated by one of his followers, writes about the experiences that drove him to a leadership role in the Black Muslims.

Makes Me Wanna Holler, Nathan McCall

A dramatic first-person account of how a bright young black man went terribly wrong—and was lured into a life of crime. McCall, now a reporter for *the Washington Post*, eventually found a basis for self-respect different from that of his peers, who are murdered, commit suicide, become drug zombies, or wind up in prison.

Angela's Ashes, Frank McCourt

The most popular nonfiction book published in recent years, this book tells the story of an Irish boy whose father was a drunkard and whose mother tried desperately to hold her family together. The poverty described is heartbreaking, and yet the book is wonderfully moving and often funny. You'll shake your head in disbelief at all the hardship, and at other times you'll laugh out loud at the comic touches.

Dreams from My Father: A Story of Race and Inheritance, Barack Obama

> A lively autobiography by the 44th president of the United States.

My American Journey, Colin Powell

> An interesting look at the life of the former chairman of the Joint Chiefs of Staff from his beginnings in a close-knit neighborhood in the South Bronx to his highly successful military career.

A Hole in the World, Richard Rhodes

> Little more than a year old when his mother killed herself, Rhodes has ever since been conscious of "a hole in the world" where his mother's love should have been. In this true and terrifying account of his boyhood, he describes how he managed to survive.

A Memoir of My Extraordinary, Ordinary Family and Me, Condoleezza Rice

> An account of the life of the first female African American secretary of state.

Down These Mean Streets, Piri Thomas

> Life in a Puerto Rican ghetto is shown vividly and with understanding by one who experienced it.

Fiction

Watership Down, Richard Adams

> A wonderfully entertaining adventure story about rabbits who act a great deal like people. The plot may sound unlikely, but it will keep you on the edge of your seat.

Patriot Games, Tom Clancy

> In a story of thrills and suspense, an agent for the United States government helps stop an act of terrorism. The terrorists then plot revenge on the agent and his family.

The Cradle Will Fall, Mary Higgins Clark

> A country prosecutor uncovers evidence that a famous doctor is killing women, not realizing that she herself is becoming his next target. One typical comment by a reviewer about Clark's books is that they are "a ticket to ride the roller coaster. . . . Once on the track, we're there until the ride is over."

> **Note**   If you like novels with terror and suspense, many of Mary Higgins Clark's books are good choices.

And Justice for One, John Clarkson

In this adventure-thriller, a former Secret Service agent seeks revenge after his brother is almost killed and a woman friend is kidnapped. Because of corruption in the police force, the agent must take the law into his own hands.

Eye of the Needle, Ken Follett

A thriller about a Nazi spy—"The Needle"—and a woman who is the only person who can stop him.

Lord of the Flies, William Golding

Could a group of children, none older than twelve, survive by themselves on a tropical island in the midst of World War Three? In this modern classic, Golding shows us that the real danger is not the war outside but "the beast" within each of us.

Snow Falling on Cedars, David Guterson

This is a unique murder mystery. The story is set in the 1950s in an island community where a fisherman is found dead on his boat and another fisherman is quickly blamed for the death. The accused man is so proud that he refuses to defend himself for a crime he says he did not commit. Like all great stories, it is about more than itself. It becomes a celebration of the mystery of the human heart.

The Silence of the Lambs, Thomas Harris

A psychotic killer is on the loose. To find him, the FBI must rely on clues provided by an evil genius. Like some other books on this list, this was made into a movie that is not as good as the book.

Flowers for Algernon, Daniel Keyes

A scientific experiment turns a retarded man into a genius. But the results are a mixture of joy and heartbreak.

The Shining, Stephen King

A haunted hotel, a little boy with extrasensory perception, and an insane father—they're all together in a horror tale of isolation and insanity. One review says, "Be prepared to be scared out of your mind. . . . Don't read this book when you are home alone. If you dare—once you get past a certain point, there's no stopping."

Note   If you like novels of terror and suspense, many of Stephen King's books are good choices.

Watchers, Dean Koontz

An incredibly suspenseful story about two dogs that undergo lab experiments. One dog becomes a monster programmed to kill, and it seeks to track down a couple who know its secret.

Note If you like novels with a great deal of action and suspense, many of Dean Koontz's books are good choices.

To Kill a Mockingbird, Harper Lee

A controversial trial, involving a black man accused of raping a white woman, is the centerpiece of this story about adolescence, bigotry, and justice. One review describes the book as "a novel of great sweetness, humor, compassion, and of mystery carefully sustained."

The Natural, Bernard Malamud

An aging player makes a comeback that stuns the baseball world.

Waiting to Exhale, Terry McMillan

Four thirty-something black women all hope that Mr. Right will appear, but this doesn't stop them from living their lives. One reviewer writes that McMillan "has such a wonderful ear for story and dialogue. She gives us four women with raw, honest emotions that breathe off the page."

Gone with the Wind, Margaret Mitchell

The characters and places in this book—Scarlett O'Hara, Rhett Butler, Tara—have become part of our culture because they are unforgettable.

A Day No Pigs Would Die, Robert Peck

A boy raises a pig that is intelligent and affectionate. Will the boy follow orders and send the animal off to be slaughtered? Read this short novel to find out.

Harry Potter and the Sorcerer's Stone, J. K. Rowling

The first in a series of award-winning stories that have captured the hearts of young and old alike, around the world. These funny, action-packed, touching books are about a likable boy who is mistreated by the relatives who take him in after his parents are killed. Then Harry discovers that he is a wizard, and his extraordinary adventures begin.

The Catcher in the Rye, J. D. Salinger

The frustrations and turmoil of being an adolescent have never been captured so well as in this book. The main character, Holden Caulfield, is honest, funny, affectionate, obnoxious, and tormented at the same time.

The Help, Kathryn Stockett

> A moving novel of race in America set in Mississippi during the civil rights movement.

The Lord of the Rings, J. R. R. Tolkien

> Enter an amazing world of little creatures known as Hobbits; you, like thousands of other readers, may never want to leave.

Tiny Sunbirds, Far Away, Christie Watson

> A highly readable coming of age story of a 12-year-old girl named Blessing growing up in a small village in Nigeria.

Charlotte's Web, E. B. White

> This best-loved story, for children and adults, is about a little pig named Wilbur and his best friend, a spider named Charlotte. Wilbur is being fattened in order to be killed for a holiday meal; Charlotte must come up with a plan to save him.

Classics

Middlemarch, George Eliot

> A long book that is likely to be one of the peak reading experiences of your life. Eliot writes with extraordinary insight and compassion about the problems that all human beings face in seeing themselves clearly and in coping with the difficulties of their lives.

Invisible Man, Ralph Ellison

> An unforgetable novel of race in America.

The Scarlet Letter, Nathaniel Hawthorne

> A compelling story, set in the days of the Puritans, about a young woman, her illegitimate baby, and the scarlet badge she wears as her punishment.

Moby-Dick, Herman Melville

> Two of the most famous characters in fiction—mad Captain Ahab and Moby-Dick, the white whale—battle it out as hunter and hunted.

The Adventures of Huckleberry Finn, Mark Twain

> A rich book filled with wit, understanding, moral insight, and very human characters—definitely *not* for children only. Many people argue that either this or *Moby-Dick* is the greatest American novel.

Writing Effectively

This section of the book shows you how to write effective paragraphs and essays, describes the relationships between writing and reading, and provides some writing assignments.

What Is a Paragraph?

A *paragraph* is a series of sentences about one main idea, or *point*. A paragraph typically starts with a point, and the rest of the paragraph provides specific details to support and develop that point.

Consider the following paragraph, written by a student named Gary Callahan.

Returning to School

Starting college at the age of twenty-nine was not easy for me. For one thing, I did not have much support from my parents and friends. My father asked, "Didn't you get dumped on enough in high school? Why go back for more?" My mother worried, "Where's the money going to come from?" My friends seemed threatened. "Hey, there's the college man," they would say when I approached. Another reason that starting college was difficult was that I had bad memories of school. I had spent years of my life sitting in classrooms completely bored, watching clocks tick ever so slowly toward the final bell. When I was not bored, I was afraid of being embarrassed. Once a teacher called on me and then said, "Ah, forget it, Callahan," when he realized I did not know the answer. Finally, I soon learned that college would give me little time with my family. After work every day, I have just an hour and ten minutes to eat and spend time with my wife and daughter before going off to class. When I get back, my daughter is in bed, and my wife and I have only a little time together. Then the time on weekends goes by quickly, with all the homework I have to do. But I am going to persist because I believe a better life awaits me with a college degree.

The above paragraph, like many effective paragraphs, starts by stating a main idea, or point. In this case, the point is that starting college at age twenty-nine was not easy. A point is a general idea that contains an opinion.

615

In our everyday lives, we continually make points about all kinds of matters. We express such opinions as "That was a terrible movie" or "My psychology instructor is the best teacher I have ever had" or "My sister is a generous person" or "Eating at that restaurant was a mistake" or "That team should win the playoff game" or "Waitressing is the worst job I ever had" or "Our state should allow the death penalty" or "Cigarette smoking should be banned everywhere." In *talking* to people, we don't always give the reasons for our opinions. But in *writing*, we *must* provide reasons to support our ideas. Only by supplying solid evidence for any point that we make can we communicate effectively with readers.

An effective paragraph, then, not only must make a point but must support it with *specific evidence*—reasons, examples, and other details. Such specifics help prove to readers that the point is reasonable. Even if readers do not agree with the writer, at least they have in front of them the evidence on which the writer has based his or her opinion. Readers are like a jury: They want to see the evidence so that they can make their own judgments.

What Are the Goals of Effective Writing?

Now that you have considered an effective student paragraph, it is time to look at four goals of effective writing:

Goal 1: Make a Point.

It is often best to state your point in the first sentence of your paper, just as Gary did in his paragraph about returning to school. The sentence that expresses the main idea, or point, of a paragraph is called the *topic sentence*.

Goal 2: Support the Point.

To support your point, you need to provide specific reasons, examples, and other details that explain and develop it. The more precise and particular your supporting details are, the better your readers can "see," "hear," and "feel" them.

Goal 3: Organize the Support.

You will find it helpful to learn two common ways of organizing the support in a paragraph—listing order and time order. In "Recognizing Signal Words" on page 347, you learned about signal words, also known as *transitions*, that increase the effectiveness of each method.

Listing Order   The writer organizes the supporting evidence in a paper by providing a list of two or more reasons, examples, or details. Often the most important or interesting item is saved for last because the reader is most likely to remember the last thing read.

Transition words that show a listing order include the following:

one	second	also	next	last of all
for one thing	third	another	moreover	finally
first of all	next	in addition	furthermore	

The paragraph about starting college uses a listing order: It lists three reasons why starting college at twenty-nine is not easy, and each of those three reasons is introduced by one of the above transitions. In the spaces below, write in the three transitions:

_____   _____   _____

The first reason in the paragraph about starting college is introduced with *For one thing*, the second reason by *Another*, and the third reason by *Finally*.

Time Order   Supporting details are presented in the order in which they occurred. *First* this happened; *next* this; *after* that, this; and so on. Many paragraphs, especially ones that tell stories or give a series of directions, are organized in a time order.

Transition words that show time relationships include the following:

first	before	after	when	then
next	during	now	while	until
as	soon	later	often	finally

Read the paragraph below, which is organized in a time order. See if you can underline the six transition words that show the time relationships.

Della had a sad experience while driving home last night. She traveled along the dark, winding road that led toward her home. She was only two miles from her house when she noticed a glimmer of light in the road. The next thing she knew, she heard a sickening thud and realized she had struck an animal. The light, she realized, had been its eyes reflected in her car's headlights. Della stopped the car and ran back to see what she had hit. It was a handsome cocker spaniel, with blond fur and long ears. As she bent over the still form, she realized there was nothing to be done. The dog was dead. Della searched the dog for a collar and tags. There was nothing. Before leaving, she walked to several nearby houses, asking if anyone knew who owned the dog. No one did. Finally Della gave up and drove on. She was sad to leave someone's pet lying there alone.

The main point of the paragraph is stated in its first sentence: "Della had a sad experience while driving home last night." The support for this point is all the details of Della's experience. Those details are presented in the order in which they occurred. The time relationships are highlighted by these transitions: *while*, *when*, *next*, *as*, *before*, and *finally*.

Goal 4: Write Error-Free Sentences.

If you use correct spelling and follow the rules for grammar, punctuation, and usage, your sentences will be clear and well written. But by no means must you have all that information in your head. Even the best writers need to use reference materials to be sure their writing is correct. So when you write your papers, keep a good dictionary and grammar handbook nearby.

In general, however, do not refer to them until you have placed your ideas firmly down in writing. As you will learn on the pages ahead, there will be time enough to make the needed corrections.

How Do You Reach the Goals of Effective Writing?

Even professional writers do not sit down and automatically, in one draft, write a paper. Instead, they have to work on it a step at a time. Writing a paper is a process that can be divided into the following steps:

Step 1: Getting Started through Prewriting

Step 2: Preparing a Scratch Outline

Step 3: Writing the First Draft

Step 4: Revising

Step 5: Proofreading

These steps are described on the following pages.

Step 1: Getting Started through Prewriting

What you need to learn first are strategies for working on a paper. These strategies will help you do the thinking needed to figure out both the point you want to make and the support you have for that point.

There are several *prewriting strategies*—ones that you use before writing the first draft of your paper.

- *Freewriting* is just sitting down and writing whatever comes into your mind about a topic. Do this for ten minutes or so. Write without stopping and without worrying in the slightest about spelling, grammar, or the like. Simply get down on paper all the information about the topic that occurs to you.

- *Questioning* means that you think about your topic by writing down a series of questions and answers about it. Your questions can start with words like *what, when, where, why,* and *how.*

- *Clustering* (also known as *diagramming* or *mapping*; see pages 370–371) is another strategy that can be used to generate material for a paper. It is helpful for people who like to do their thinking in a visual way. In clustering, you begin by stating your subject in a few words in the center of a blank sheet of paper. Then, as ideas come to you, put them in ovals, boxes, or circles around the subject, and draw lines to connect them to the subject. Put minor ideas or details in smaller boxes or circles, and use connecting lines to show how they relate as well. Keep in mind that there is no right or wrong way of clustering. It is a way to think on paper about how various ideas and details relate to one another.

- In *list making,* a strategy also known as *brainstorming*, you make a list of ideas and details that could go into your paper. Simply pile these items up, one after another, without worrying about putting them in any special order. Try to accumulate as many details as you can think of.

  It is natural for a number of such extra or unrelated details to appear as part of the prewriting process. The goal of prewriting is to get a lot of information down on paper. You can then add to, shape, and subtract from your raw material as you take your paper through the series of writing drafts.

Important Notes about Prewriting Strategies   Some writers may use only one of the prewriting strategies. Others may use bits and pieces of all four. Any one strategy can lead to another. Freewriting may lead to questioning or clustering, which may then lead to a list. Or a writer may start with a list and then use freewriting or questioning to develop items on the list. During this early stage of the writing process, as you do your thinking on paper, anything goes. You should not expect a straight-line progression from the beginning to the end of your paper. Instead, there probably will be a continual moving back and forth as you work to discover your point and just how you will develop it.

Finally, remember that you are not ready to begin writing a paper until you know your main point and many of the details that can be used to support it. Don't rush through prewriting. It's better to spend more time on this stage than to waste time writing a paragraph for which you have no solid point and too little interesting support.

Step 2: Preparing a Scratch Outline

A *scratch outline* is a brief plan for the paragraph. It shows at a glance the point of the paragraph and the main support for that point. It is the logical framework upon which the paper is built.

This rough outline often follows freewriting, questioning, clustering, or list making. Or it may gradually emerge in the midst of these strategies. In fact, trying to outline is a good way to see if you need to do more prewriting. If a solid outline does not emerge, then you know you need to do more prewriting to clarify your main point or its support. Once you have a workable outline, you may realize, for instance, that you want to do more list making to develop one of the supporting details in the outline.

Below is the scratch outline that Gary Callahan, after doing a good deal of preliminary writing, prepared for his paragraph on returning to school:

Example of a Scratch Outline

Starting college at age twenty-nine isn't easy.
1. Little support from parents and friends.
2. Bad memories of high school.
3. Not enough time to spend with family.

This helpful outline, with its clear point and solid support, became the foundation of Gary's paragraph.

Step 3: Writing the First Draft

When you do a first draft, be prepared to put in additional thoughts and details that didn't emerge in your prewriting activity. And don't worry if you hit a snag. Just leave a blank space or add a comment such as "Do later" and press on to finish the paper. Also, don't worry yet about grammar, punctuation, or spelling. You don't want to take time correcting words or sentences that you may decide to remove later. Instead, make it your goal to develop the content of your paper with plenty of specific details.

Step 4: Revising

Revising is as much a stage in the writing process as prewriting, outlining, and doing the first draft. *Revising* means that you rewrite a paper, building upon what has been done to make it stronger and better. One writer has said about revising, "It's like cleaning house—getting rid of all the junk and putting things in the right order." A typical revision means writing at least one or two more drafts.

Step 5: Proofreading

Proofreading, the final stage in the writing process, means checking a paper carefully for spelling, grammar, punctuation, and other errors. You are ready for this stage when you are satisfied with your choice of supporting details, the order in which they are presented, and the way they and your topic sentence are worded.

Use a grammar handbook to be sure about your grammar, punctuation, and usage. Also, read through the paper carefully, looking for typing errors, omitted words, and any other errors you may have missed before. Such proofreading is often hard to do—students have spent so much time with their work, or so little, that they want to avoid proofing. But done carefully, this important final step will ensure that your paper looks as good as possible.

Hints for Proofreading

1   One helpful trick at this stage is to read your paper out loud. You will probably hear awkward wordings and become aware of spots where the punctuation needs to be improved. Make the changes needed for your sentences to read smoothly and clearly.

2   Another helpful technique is to take a sheet of paper and cover your paragraph so that you can expose and check carefully just one line at a time.

3   A third strategy is to read your paper backward, from the last sentence to the first. Doing so helps keep you from getting caught up in the flow of the paper and missing small mistakes, which is easy to do, since you're so familiar with what you meant to say.

What Is an Essay?

An essay does the same thing a paragraph does: It starts with a point, and the rest of the essay provides specific details to support and develop that point. However, while a paragraph is a series of *sentences* about one main idea or point, an *essay* is a series of *paragraphs* about one main idea or point—called the *central idea* of the essay. Since an essay is much longer than one paragraph, it allows a writer to develop a topic in more detail. Despite the greater length of an essay, the process of writing it is the same as that for writing a paragraph: prewriting, preparing a scratch outline, writing and revising drafts, and proofreading.

Here are the major differences between a paragraph and an essay:

Paragraph	*Essay*
Made up of sentences.	Made up of paragraphs.
Starts with a sentence containing the main point of the paragraph (*topic sentence*).	Starts with an introductory paragraph containing the central idea of the essay, expressed in a sentence called the *thesis statement* (or *thesis sentence*).
Body of paragraph contains specific details that support and develop the topic sentence.	Body of essay contains paragraphs that support and develop the central idea. Each of these paragraphs has its own main supporting point, stated in a topic sentence.
Paragraph often ends with a closing sentence that rounds it off.	Essay ends with a concluding paragraph that rounds it off.

Later in his writing course, the student Gary Callahan was asked to expand his paragraph into an essay. Here is the essay that resulted:

For a typical college freshman, entering college is a fun and exciting time of life. It is a time not just to explore new ideas in classes but to lounge out on the grass chatting with new friends, to sit having soda and pizza in the cafeteria, or to listen to music and play cards in the student lounge. I see the crowds of eighteen-year-olds enjoying all that college has to offer, and I sometimes envy their freedom. Instead of being a typical freshman, I am twenty-nine years old, and beginning college has been a difficult experience for me. I have had to deal with a lack of support, bad memories of past school experiences, and too little time for my family.

Few people in my life are supportive of my decision to enter college. My father is especially bewildered by the choice I have made. He himself quit school after finishing eighth grade, and he assumes that I should hate school as much as he did. "Didn't you get dumped on enough in high school?" he asks me. "Why go back for more?" My mother is a little more understanding of my desire for an education, but the cost of college terrifies her. She has always believed that college was a privilege only the rich could afford. "Where in the world will all that money come from?" she says. And my friends seem threatened by my decision. They make fun of me, suggesting that I'm going to think I'm too good to hang around with the likes of them. "Ooooh, here comes the college man," they say when they see me approach. "We'd better watch our grammar."

I have had to deal not only with family and friends but also with unhappy memories of my earlier school career. I attended an enormous high school where I was just one more faceless kid in the crowd. My classes seemed meaningless to me. I can remember almost none of them in any detail. What I do remember about high school was just sitting, bored until I felt nearly brain-dead, watching the clock hands move ever so slowly toward dismissal time. Such periods of boredom were occasionally interrupted by moments of acute embarrassment. Once an algebra teacher called on me and then said, "Oh, forget it, Callahan," in a disgusted tone when he realized I didn't know the answer. My response, of course, was to shrink down in my chair and try to become invisible for the rest of the semester.

Furthermore, my decision to enter college has meant I have much less time to spend with my family. I work eight hours a day. Then I rush home and have all of an hour and ten minutes to eat dinner and spend time with my wife and daughter before I rush off again, this time to class. When I return from class, I am dead tired. My little girl is already asleep. My wife and I have only a little time to talk together before I collapse into bed. Weekends are a little better, but not much. That's when I try to get my papers written and catch up on a few chores around the house. My wife tries to be understanding, but it's hard on her to have so little support from me these days. And I'm missing out on a lot of special times in my daughter's life. For instance, I didn't realize she had begun to walk until three days after it happened.

So why do I put myself and my family through all these difficulties? Sometimes I'm not sure myself. But then I look at my little girl sleeping, and I think about the kind of life I am going to be able to give her. My college degree may make it possible for me to get a job that is more rewarding, both financially and emotionally. I believe I will be a better provider for my family, as well as a more well-rounded human being. I hope that the rewards of a college degree will eventually outweigh the problems I am experiencing now.

What Are the Parts of an Essay?

When Gary decided to expand his paragraph into an essay, he knew he would need to write an introductory paragraph, several supporting paragraphs, and a concluding paragraph.

Each of these parts of the essay is explained below.

Introductory Paragraph

A well-written introductory paragraph will often do the following.

1   *Gain the reader's interest.* On pages 625–626 are several time-tested methods used to draw the reader into an essay.

2   *Present the thesis statement.* The thesis statement expresses the central idea of an essay, just as a topic sentence states the main idea of a paragraph. Here's an example of a thesis statement.

> A vacation at home can be wonderful.

An essay with this thesis statement would go on to explain some positive things about vacationing at home.

•   What is the thesis statement in Gary's essay? Find that statement on page 623 and write it here:

_____

_____

You should have written down the next-to-last sentence in the introductory paragraph of Gary's essay.

3 *Lay out a plan of development.* The *plan of development* is a brief statement of the main supporting details for the central idea. These supporting details should be presented in the order in which they will be discussed in the essay. The plan of development can be blended into the thesis statement or presented separately.

> *Blended into a thesis statement:* A vacation at home can be wonderful because you can avoid the hassles of travel, make use of your knowledge of the area, and indulge in special activities.
>
> *Presented separately:* A vacation at home can be wonderful. At home you can avoid the hassles of travel, make use of your knowledge of the area, and indulge in special activities.

Note that some essays lend themselves better to a plan of development than others do. At the least, your introductory paragraph should gain the reader's interest and present the thesis statement.

- What is the plan of development in Gary's essay? Find the sentence on page 623 that states Gary's plan of development and write it here:

_____

_____

You should have written down the last sentence in the introductory paragraph of Gary's essay.

Four Common Methods of Introduction

1 *Begin with a broad statement and narrow it down to your thesis statement.* Broad statements can capture your reader's interest while introducing your general topic. They may provide useful background material as well. The writer of the introductory paragraph below begins with a broad statement about her possessions. She then narrows the focus down to the three possessions that are the specific topic of the paper.

> I have many possessions that I would be sad to lose. Because I love to cook, I would miss several kitchen appliances that provide me with so many happy cooking adventures. I would also miss the wonderful electronic equipment that entertains me every day, including my flat-screen television set and my Wii games. I would miss the two telephones on which I have spent many interesting hours chatting in every part of my apartment, including the bathtub. But if my apartment were burning down, I would most want to rescue three things that are irreplaceable and hold great meaning for me—the silverware set that belonged to my grandmother, my mother's wedding gown, and my giant photo album.

2 *Present an idea or a situation that is the opposite of what will be written about.* One way to gain the reader's interest is to show the difference between your opening idea or situation and the one to be discussed in the essay.

> The role of computers in schools is constantly growing. Such growth is based on a widespread faith that computers can answer many of the learning needs of our students. Many people believe that it is just a matter of time before computers do all but take the place of human teachers. However, educators should be cautious about introducing computers into curriculums. Computers may interfere with the learning of critical language skills, they may move too fast for students to digest new concepts, and they are a poor substitute for certain real-world experiences.

3 *Tell a brief story.* An interesting incident or anecdote is hard for a reader to resist. In an introduction, a story should be no more than a few sentences, and it should relate meaningfully to—and so lead the reader toward—your central idea. The story you tell can be an experience of your own, of someone you know, or of someone you have read about. For instance, in the following introduction, the writer tells a simple personal story that serves as background for his central idea.

> I remember the September morning that I first laid eyes on Jill. I'd been calling clients at my desk at work when I heard a warm, musical laugh. There was something so attractive about the sound that I got up to get a cup of coffee and to find the source of that laugh. I discovered the voice to be that of a young, auburn-haired woman we had just hired from a temporary agency. Soon after, Jill and I began going out, and we spent the next two years together. Only recently have we decided to break up because of disagreements about finances, about children, and about our relationship with her family.

4 *Ask one or more questions.* The questions may be ones that you intend to answer in your essay, or they may show that your topic relates directly to readers. In the following example, the questions are designed to gain readers' interest and convince them that the essay applies to them.

> Does your will to study collapse when someone suggests getting a pizza? Does your social life compete with your class attendance? Is there a huge gap between your intentions and your actions? If the answers to these questions are *yes*, *yes*, and *yes*, read on. You can benefit from some powerful ways to motivate yourself: setting goals and consciously working to reach them, using rational thinking, and developing a positive personality.

- Which of the four methods of introduction described above does Gary use in his essay?

_____

_____

Gary begins with an idea that is the opposite of what he is writing about. His essay is about his difficulties with college life, but he begins with the idea that college "is a fun and exciting time" for some students.

Supporting Paragraphs

The traditional college essay has three supporting paragraphs. But some essays will have two supporting paragraphs, and others will have four or more. Each supporting paragraph should have its own topic sentence that states the point to be developed in that paragraph.

Notice that each of the supporting paragraphs in Gary's essay has its own topic sentence. For example, the topic sentence of his first supporting paragraph is "Few people in my life are supportive of my decision to enter college."

- What is the topic sentence for Gary's second supporting paragraph?

_____

- What is the topic sentence for Gary's third supporting paragraph?

_____

In each case, Gary's topic sentence is the first sentence of the paragraph.

Concluding Paragraph

An essay that ended with its final supporting paragraph would probably leave the reader wondering if the author is really done. A concluding paragraph is needed for a sense of completion. Here are two common methods of conclusion.

Two Common Methods of Conclusion

1 *Provide a summary and a final thought.* Using wording that is different from your introduction, restate your thesis and main supporting points. This review gives readers an overview of your essay and helps them remember what they've read. A final thought signals the end of the paper, as in the following concluding paragraph from the essay about personal possessions.

If my home ever really did burn down, I would hope to be able to rescue some of the physical things that so meaningfully represent my past. My grandmother's silver set is a reminder of the grandparents who enriched my childhood, my mother's wedding gown is a glamorous souvenir of two important weddings, and my photo album is a rich storage bin of family and personal history. I would hate to lose them. However, if I did, I would take comfort in the fact that the most important storage place for family and personal memories is my own mind.

2   *Focus on the future.* A focus on the future often involves a prediction or a recommendation. This method of conclusion may refer in a general way to the central idea, or it may include a summary. The following conclusion from the essay about self-motivation combines a summary with a prediction. The prediction adds further support for the central idea.

So get your willpower in gear, and use the three keys to self-motivation—set goals and work to reach them, think rationally, and develop a positive personality. You will find that a firm commitment to this approach becomes easier and easier. Progress will come more often and more readily, strengthening your resolve even further.

- Which kind of conclusion does Gary use to end his essay?

_____

In his conclusion, Gary refers to his central idea in the context of the future. He makes hopeful points about what his and his family's life will be like after he gets a college degree.

Activity

Answer each of the following questions by filling in the blank or circling the answer you think is correct.

1. An effective paragraph or essay is one that

   a.   makes a point.

   b.   provides specific support.

   c.   makes a point and provides specific support.

   d.   does none of the above.

2. The sentence that states the main idea of a paragraph is known as the _____ sentence; the sentence that states the central idea of an essay is known as the _____ statement.

3. Prewriting can help a writer find

    a.   a good topic to write about.

    b.   a good main point to make about the topic.

    c.   enough details to support the main point.

    d.   all of the above.

4. *True or false?* _____ During the freewriting process, you should not concern yourself with spelling, punctuation, or grammar.

5. One step that everyone should use at some stage of the writing process is to prepare a plan for the paragraph or essay. The plan is known as a(n)

_____.

6. When you start writing, your first concern should be

    a.   spelling.

    b.   content.

    c.   grammar.

    d.   punctuation.

7. Two common ways of organizing a paragraph are _____ order and _____ order.

8. A thesis statement

    a.   is generally part of an essay's introduction.

    b.   states the central idea of the essay.

    c.   can be followed by the essay's plan of development.

    d.   all of the above.

Relationships between Reading and Writing

You may wonder why a section on writing is included in a book called *Reading and Study Skills*. Perhaps you felt that you were capable of becoming a good reader and skilled student without having the additional burden of producing written assignments placed on you. Reading and writing, however, are so closely interconnected that it is virtually impossible to be competent at one without being competent at the other. The two abilities work together in several ways:

- *Reading and writing are interrelated language skills.* Through reading, you learn, almost subconsciously, how good writers put sentences together and organize ideas. In addition, you acquire new vocabulary words. Through writing, you begin to use what you have learned by reading. You also gain intensive practice in being logical, a skill that is essential to understanding more difficult reading material.

- *Both reading and writing are processes.* You become a better reader, or a more skillful writer, by treating each task as a process. You preview, read, and reread. Or you prewrite, write, and rewrite. With each step, your skills become sharper and the end product—your understanding of what you have read or the paper you have written—becomes finer.

- *Both reading and writing are vital for communication.* Competence in reading and writing is an essential skill if you wish to make your voice heard and your ideas known. Shutting yourself off from either one can damage your life in two ways. First, your verbal abilities suffer because you have few language models and few chances to extend your word skills. Second, your message—whatever it may be, either in your personal life or on the job—is lost because you cannot get it across to other people.

Reading and writing, then, are so closely linked that practicing one helps the other—and neglecting one damages the other. This is why writing assignments have a role in this book, and why writing should be an important priority in your life as a student.

Writing Assignments

Following are a number of assignments based on chapters or reading selections in the book. Before attempting any of these assignments, reread the guide on pages 616–618.

1. Consider this study situation:

   Howard has trouble taking notes in all his classes. He is seldom sure about what is important enough to write down. Also, he has trouble organizing material when he does write it down. Often the only points he records are the ones the instructor puts on the board. The connections between these points are usually clear to him in class, for he spends most of his time listening carefully to the instructor rather than taking notes. However, several weeks later, when he is studying for a test, he has trouble remembering many of the relationships among points. His notes do not provide a complete, unified understanding of the subject but seem instead to consist of many isolated bits of information.

One course that gives Howard special problems is sociology. In class the instructor asks students questions and uses their comments as takeoff points for discussing course ideas. Sometimes she is five minutes into an important idea before Howard realizes it is important—and he hasn't taken a single note on that point. He often winds up with such a frustrating shortage of notes that he decides not to go to class at all. In another course, biology, the instructor talks so fast that Howard cannot keep up. Also, Howard misspells so many words that it is often impossible for him to understand his notes when he tries to read them over weeks later, before an exam.

Write a paper in which you respond in detail to Howard's situation. Apply what you have learned in the chapter titled "Taking Classroom Notes" to explain at least three specific steps that Howard could follow to become an effective note-taker.

2. Consider this study situation:

Cheryl has trouble managing her study time. She claims that the only time she can make herself study is right before a test. "If I'm not in a crisis situation with a test just around the corner," she says, "I usually won't study. When I'm in the right mood, I do try to study a bit to keep things from piling up. But most of the time I'm just not in the mood. Some mornings I get up and say to myself, 'Tonight you will do at least two hours of schoolwork.' Then, 95 percent of the time, I let something distract me." Cheryl recently had to face the shortcomings of her cramming method. She found herself with only one night to prepare for two exams and a report; the result was several disastrous grades.

Write a paper in which you respond in detail to Cheryl's situation. Apply what you have learned in the chapter titled "Time Control and Concentration" to explain at least three specific steps that Cheryl could take to control her time effectively.

3. Consider this study situation:

For tomorrow's test in his Introduction to Business course, Gary has to know three chapters from the textbook. At 1:30 P.M. yesterday, he sat down with a yellow marking pen and started reading the first chapter. At 3 P.M. he wasn't even halfway through the first chapter, and he felt bored and worn out. The sentences were long and heavy and loaded with details. Gary's head became so packed with information that as soon as he read a new fact, it seemed to automatically push out the one before it. When he looked back at what he had covered, he realized he had set off most of the text in yellow. Gary decided then to stop marking and just read. But the more he read, the sleepier he got, and the more his mind kept wandering. He kept thinking about all the things he wanted to do once the test was over. At 5:15 P.M. he had just finished reading the first chapter, but he felt completely defeated. He still had to study the chapter, and he had no idea exactly what to study. On top of that, he had to plow through two more chapters and study them as well. He felt desperate and stupid—because he had waited so long to start with the text and because he was having such a hard time reading it.

Write a paper in which you respond in detail to Gary's situation. Apply what you have learned in the chapter titled "The PRWR Study Method" to explain at least three specific steps that Gary could take to study effectively through previewing, textbook marking, and note-taking.

4. Consider this study situation:

In two days, Steve will have a biology quiz in which he will have to write the definitions of ten terms that have been discussed in the course. As a study aid, the instructor has passed out a list of thirty terms that students should know thoroughly. Steve has gone through his class notes and textbook and copied down the definitions of the thirty terms. He tries to study the terms by reading them over and over, but he has trouble concentrating and merely keeps on "reading words." He decides to write out each definition until he knows it. Hours later, he has written out ten definitions a number of times and is still not sure he will remember them. He begins to panic because he is spending such an enormous amount of time for such meager results. He decides to play Russian roulette with the terms—to study just some of them and hope they are the ones that will be on the test.

Write a paper in which you respond in detail to Steve's situation. Apply what you have learned in the chapter titled "Building a Powerful Memory" to explain at least three specific steps that Steve could take to improve his memory.

5. Consider this study situation:

Most of the exams Rita takes include both multiple-choice and true–false questions as well as at least one essay question. She has several problems with such tests. She often goes into the test in a state of panic. "As soon as I see a question I can't answer," she says, "big chunks of what I do know just fly out the window. I go into an exam expecting to choke and forget."

Another problem is her timing. "Sometimes I spend too much time trying to figure out the answer to tricky multiple-choice or true–false questions. Then I end up with only fifteen minutes to answer two essay questions." Rita's greatest difficulty is writing essay answers. "Essays are where I always lose a lot of points. Sometimes I don't read a question the right way, and I wind up giving the wrong answer to the question. When I do understand a question, I have trouble organizing my answer. I'll be halfway through an answer and then realize that I skipped some material I should have put at the start or that I already wrote down something I should have saved for the end. I have a friend who says that essays are easier to study for because she can usually guess what the questions will be. I don't see how this is possible. Essay tests really scare me, since I never know what questions are coming."

Write a paper in which you respond in detail to Rita's situation. Apply what you have learned in the chapters titled "Taking Objective Exams" and "Taking Essay Exams" to explain at least three specific steps that Rita could take to improve her performance on exams.

6. Consider this study situation:

Pete had been out of school for ten years before he enrolled in college. During his first semester, his sociology instructor asked him to "compile a list of ten books and articles about single-parent families." In addition, Pete's business instructor asked him to do a research paper on "benefits of the Japanese quality circle in American companies." Pete dreaded these projects because he had no idea where or how to begin them. Before class one night, he walked into his college library and wandered around for a while, aimlessly and shyly. He felt especially intimidated by the people who sat typing in front of computer screens and seemed to know exactly what they were doing. Pete felt completely out of his element—like a visitor in a foreign land. He didn't even know what questions to ask about how to use the library.

Write a paper in which you respond in detail to Pete's situation. Apply what you have learned in the chapter titled "Using Research Skills" to explain at least three specific steps that Pete could take to do a good job on his research assignments.

7. Read the selection about propaganda on pages 67–68. Then write a paper about an ad you have seen recently that uses several of the propaganda techniques discussed in the selection. Show specifically—by mentioning the name of the product and describing the language, slogans, characters, and settings in the ad—how the ad uses particular propaganda methods.

8. Review the section on effective writing on pages 69–71. An example given in the section to illustrate a "point" is "Proms should be banned." Write your own paper that presents a variation on this idea. Your point should be, "_____ should be banned for several reasons." The topic you choose could be one of the following or something similar: smoking, grades, ads for alcoholic beverages on television, commercials aimed at children, hitchhiking, loud radios.

9. Read the section on concentration skills on pages 87–92. Then write a paper based on the idea that many students—from the youngest to the oldest—find it difficult to pay attention in school. Why might this be true? What aspects of school make it hard to pay attention? (Is it the setting? The teachers? The subject matter? The pressures? The boredom?) Write a paper on the steps a teacher could take to make it easier for students to pay attention. Make your steps practical ones that a concerned teacher at a specific level (primary school, high school, college) could take.

10. Read the selection, "Wired for Touch" starting on page 474. Then write a paper about your own feelings about the power of touch. Consider the following questions when writing: Did your family display affection as you were growing up? That is, did you receive warm, supportive, loving touch from other family members? If you did, what effect do you think this type of touch has on you as an adult? If you did not, what effect has the lack of touch had on you as an adult? Do you consider yourself an affectionate person? Have you witnessed situations in which touching someone in a supportive way (such as a gentle pat on the back, a warm hug, etc.) actually changed a situation for the better? Would you like to be a more affectionate person toward friends and family? Why or why not? As you write, use specific details to explain your experiences with touch.

Acknowledgments

From *The Autobiography of Malcolm X.* Copyright © 1964 by Alex Haley and Betty Shabazz. Reprinted by permission of Random House, Inc. Selection on page 467.

Stacy Kelly Abbott, "From Nonreading to Reading." Reprinted by permission. Selection on page 501.

Ronald B. Alder, "Visual Elements in Assertive Communication." Adapted from *Talking Straight.* Copyright © 1977 by Holt, Rinehart, and Winston. Reprinted by permission of Holt, Rinehart, and Winston, CBS College Publishing. Selection on page 439.

Russell Baker, from *Growing Up.* Reprinted by permission of Don Congdon Associates, Inc. ©1982 by Russell Baker. Selection on page 603.

Roxanne Black, "A Door Swings Open." Reprinted by permission. Selection on page 496.

Jane Brody, "Fatigue." From Jane Brody's *The New York Times Guide to Personal Health.* Copyright © 1976, 1982 by The New York Times Company. Reprinted by permission. Selection on page 453.

Dr. Benjamin Carson and Gregg A. Lewis, "Dare to Think Big." Taken from *The Big Picture* by Dr. Benjamin Carson with Gregg A. Lewis. Copyright © 1999 by Benjamin Carson. Used by permission of Zondervan Publishing House. Selection on page 486.

Jean Coleman and John Langan, adapted from "Learning Survival Skills," in *Groundwork for College Reading,* 3rd ed. Copyright © 2000 by Townsend Press. Material in Part One on pages 29–36.

Gayle Edwards and John Langan, adapted from "Preview, Read, Write, Recite," in *Ten Steps to Improving College Reading Skills,* 3d ed. Copyright © 1997 by Townsend Press. Material on PRWR study system on pages 97–108.

Michael J. Etzel et al., "Stages of the Business Cycle." Adapted from *Marketing,* 11th ed. Copyright © 1997 by Irwin-McGraw-Hill. Selection on page 118.

Deborah Grandinetti, "Wired for Touch." Reprinted by permission of Townsend Press. Selection on page 474.

Janet L. Hopson and Norman K. Wessells, from *Essentials of Biology.* Copyright © 1990 by McGraw-Hill. Reprinted by permission. Selection on page 126.

Paul B. Horton and Chester L. Hunt, adapted from *Sociology,* 4th ed. Copyright © 1976 by McGraw-Hill, Inc. Selection on page 98; Selection 2 on page 442.

Michael Hughes and Carolyn J. Kroehler, "The Family," from *Sociology: The Core,* 10th ed. Copyright © 2011 by McGraw-Hill. Reprinted with permission of the McGraw-Hill Companies. Selection starting on page 154. [Actual pages in *The Core* textbook are 310–347.]

Margaret Jarrard, "Learning to Keep Your Cool during Tests." Copyright © 1985 by Gannet Family Weekly, Inc. *Family Weekly* is a registered trademark of Gannet Family, Inc. Issue of February 10, 1980. Selection 3 on page 470.

Audra Kendall, "The Certainty of Fear." Reprinted by permission of Audra Kendall and Townsend Press. Selection on page 507.

John Langan, adapted from *Ten Steps to Improving College Reading Skills,* 3d ed., et al. Copyright © 1997–2001 by Townsend Press. Material on using course syllabus and a daily planner on pages 76–86; student profiles on pages 41–44, 73–75, 95–97, 201–203, 219–220, 237–239, and 249–250; questions following selections on pages 479–486, 486–491, 496–513, 501–507, and 514–521; material on literature and inferences on pages 599–608; list of books on pages 609–614.

John Langan, adapted from *Ten Steps to Building College Reading Skills,* 4th ed., Copyright © 2004 by Townsend Press. Material on making inferences and thinking critically on pages 409–433.

Susan Lapinski, "Latchkey Blues." Copyright © 1985 by Gannet Family Weekly, Inc. *Family Weekly* is a registered trademark of Gannet Family, Inc. Issue of September 12, 1982. Selection on page 392.

Marvin R. Levey, Mark Dignam, and Janet H. Shirreffs, from *Life and Health,* 5th ed. Copyright © 1986 by McGraw-Hill. Reprinted by permission. Selection 1 on page 124; Selection 2 on page 593.

Stephen E. Lucas, from *The Art of Public Speaking,* 7th ed. Copyright © 2000 by McGraw-Hill, Inc. Reprinted by permission. Selection on page 131.

Paul Nolting, "What You Need to Know to Succeed at Math." Reprinted by permission. Selection on page 514.

Bernard Phillips, "The Nature of Power," from *Sociology.* Copyright © 1979 by McGraw-Hill, Inc. Selection on page 446.

Rod Plotnik, from *Introduction to Psychology,* 2d ed. Copyright McGraw-Hill, Inc. Reprinted by permission. Selection on page 128.

Marcia Prentergast, "Winning the Job Interview Game." Reprinted by permission of the author and Townsend Press. Selection on page 491.

Virginia Nichols Quinn, from *Applying Psychology,* 2d ed. Copyright © 1984 by McGraw-Hill Book Company. Reprinted by permission. Selections on pages 120 and 449.

Philip Roth, from *Goodbye, Columbus.* Copyright © 1959 by Philip Roth. Reprinted by permission of Houghton Mifflin Company. Selection on page 606.

Marta Salinas, "The Scholarship Jacket," from *Nosotras: Latina Literature Today,* edited by María del Carmen Boza, Beverly Silva, and Carmen Valle. Copyright © 1986 by Bilingual Press/Editorial Bilingüe, Arizona State University, Tempe, AZ. Selection on page 479.

Richard T. Schaefer and Robert P. Lamm, from *Sociology,* 4th ed. Copyright © 1992 by McGraw-Hill, Inc. Selection on page 122.

Charles D. Schewe and Reuben M. Smith, from *Marketing.* Copyright © 1980 by McGraw-Hill, Inc. Reprinted by permission. Selection on page 139.

Rudolph E. Verderber, from *Communicate!* 9th ed. Copyright © 1999 by Wadsworth, Inc. Reprinted by permission of the publisher. Selection on page 135.

Drew H. Wolfe, from *Introduction to College Chemistry,* 2d ed. Copyright © 1988 by McGraw-Hill. Reprinted by permission. Selection on page 142.

Index

Abbreviations, 47–48, 57
able, 285
abstractly, 501
Accent marks, 271
ad, 281
adamant, 306
Addition words, 348–350
Additional learning skills, 585–634
  inferences, 600–608
  interesting books, 609–614
  literature. *See* Literature
  mathematics and science, 587–597
  overview, 586
  writing. *See* Writing
adrenaline, 479
Advance reading, 46–47
Adventures of Huckleberry Finn, The
  (Twain), 614
affected, 302
affluent, 306
age, 284
agile, 479
Aids to memory. *See* Memory aids
Alcoholism, 124
Alicia: My Story (Appleman-
  Jurman), 609
allocating, 306
Alternatives to conflict, 100–101
ambivalent, 304
American Heritage Dictionary, 265, 266
America's detention camps, 580–581
Analyzing the audience, 214–215
ance, 287
And Justice for One (Clarkson), 612
Anecdote, 626
Angela's Ashes (McCourt), 610
Anger, 120
ant, 284
anti, 281
Antonym, 274
apathy, 303
Applying Psychology (Quinn), 120
Art of Public Speaking, The (Lucas), 135
ary, 287
Ask questions, 51, 626
ate, 286
Attending class, 44
Attitude, 11–20
  defeatist, 17–18
  discovering commitment to
    work, 14–15
  doing the work, 11–14
  positive, 20, 35
  running from commitment, 16–17
Audience analysis, 214–215
Author, 412
auto, 290
Autobiography of Malcolm X,
  The (Malcolm X/Haley),
  467–468, 610

Balance your activities, 83
Balloon diagram, 370, 371
Baseline knowledge. *See* Self-assessment
Basic structure (textbooks), 358
bevy, 486
Biographical sketches.
  See Student profiles
Biography, 603–606
biopsy, 496
Blackboard material, 49
Blocks of study time, 82

Book, overview, 2, 7, 8
Book passages. *See* Excerpts/passage/
  lectures
Book stacks, 258–259
Books online, 255–256
Bookstore Web sites, 256
Box diagram, 370, 371
Brainstorming, 619
Breakfast, 91
Broad statements, 625
Business cycle, 118

Calendar, 76–78
Call number, 258
Callahan, Gary, 615, 620, 622
Capsule biographies. *See* Student profiles
Card catalog, 257
Cardenas, Maria, 73–75
Catalog, 257
Catcher in the Rye, The (Salinger), 613
Catchphrases, 117, 210
Catchwords, 116, 208–210
Cause-and-effect words, 352–353
cavernous, 486
cept (capt), 291
"Certainty of Fear, The" (Kendall),
  507–511
cess (ced), 292
Chapter title, 334
Charlotte's Web (White), 614
chronic, 496
Citing sources, 260, 261
Clark, Mary Higgins, 611
Class attendance, 44
Classroom notes. *See* Taking
  classroom notes
Climax, 600
Closed stacks, 259
Clustering, 370, 619
Coleman, Jean, 29
College
  counseling center, 22
  learning center, 92, 264, 312
  placement office, 22–23
  reasons for attending, 21
College learning center, 92, 264, 312
com, 283
.com, 261
Commercial online booksellers, 255, 256
Communicate! (Verderber), 139
compare (essay exam), 243
Comparison words, 350
Comprehension. *See* Reading
  comprehension skills
con, 280
conceivably, 474
Concentration, 87–92
Conflict, alternatives to, 100–101
Connecting details, 50
conservative, 491
conspicuous, 507
Consumer products, 139–141
Consumer Reports (magazine), 298
contemporary, 303
Context cues, 301–306
contrast (essay exam), 243
Contrast words, 350
Cosmopolitan (magazine), 298
Counseling center, 22
Course outline, 76
Cradle Will Fall (Clark), 611
Cramming, 232

Critical thinker, 422
criticize (essay exam), 243
Crowds, 110
crowns, 601

Daily planner, 86
Daily schedule, 78–79
"Dare to Think Big" (Carson), 486–488
Datebook, 86
Davis, Joe, 201–203
Day No Pigs Would Die, A (Peck), 613
de, 283
Defense mechanisms, 449–451
deferential, 305
define (essay exam), 243
Definitions and examples, 317–323
deplorable, 486
describe (essay exam), 243
Desk-size dictionaries, 266
deters, 305
Dewey decimal system, 259
diagram (essay exam), 243
Diagramming, 370–381, 619
Diary of a Young Girl, The (Frank), 610
dict (dic), 291
Dictionary, 265–275
  accent marks, 271
  etymology, 274
  mastery test, 551
  meanings, 273
  online, 266–267
  own your own, 265–266
  parts of speech, 272
  plural forms, 273
  principal parts (irregular verbs),
    272–273
  pronunciation, 269, 271–272
  sample entry, 268
  schwa, 270
  software, 268
  spelling, 268–269
  syllabication, 269
  synonyms, 274
  usage label, 274–275
  vowel sounds, 270
dignity, 474
dire, 486
Direction words (essay exam), 243
dis, 279
Discovering commitment to
  work, 14–15
discuss (essay exam), 243
disparaging, 304
Document your sources, 260, 261
Doing the work, 11–14
"Door Swings Open, A" (Black),
  496–499
Down These Mean Streets
  (Thomas), 611
Draft, 621
Drawing conclusions, 409–421
Dreams from My Father: A Story of Race
  and Inheritance (Obama), 611
duc (duct), 289

.edu, 260
embedded, 474
Emphasis words, 347–348
emulate, 304
en, 284
ence, 286
enhances, 514

ent, 284
Entertain (purpose), 413
enumerate (essay exam), 243
Enumeration, 49, 221–222, 324–333
er, 287
Erasable (laminated) calendar, 76
Error-free sentences, 618
ery, 287
ESP, 111
Essay, 622–629. *See also* Writing
  concluding paragraph, 627–628
  final thought, 627–628
  introductory paragraph, 624–627
  paragraph, contrasted, 622
  supporting paragraphs, 627
Essay exams. *See* Taking essay exams
Essentials of Biology (Hopson/
  Wessells), 126
Essentials of Health (Levy et al.), 124
Etymology, 274
evaluate (essay exam), 243
Evaluating arguments, 423
ex, 280
Exam panic, 221, 470–472
Exams. *See* Taking essay exams;
  Taking objective exams
Excerpts/passages/lectures
  alcoholism, 124
  alternatives to conflict, 100–101
  America's detention camps, 580–581
  analyzing the audience, 214–215
  anger, 120
  autobiography, 603–604
  building blocks of all matter, 126
  business cycle, 118
  consumer products, 139–141
  crowds, 110
  dare to think big, 486–488
  defense mechanisms, 449–451
  ESP, 111
  factors of production, 114
  family. *See* Textbook chapter (family)
  fatigue, 453–456
  fear, 507–511
  forgetting, 537–538
  hospice program, 578–579
  income, 326
  incurable disease, 496–499
  intuition, 317
  job boredom, 339
  job interview, 491–493
  latchkey children, 392–393
  learning to read, 501–504
  listening, 65–66, 131–135
  Malcolm X, 467–468
  math textbooks, 590–591
  mathematics courses, 514–518
  myth of acceptance, 345
  networking, 326
  noise, 108–109
  norms, 122
  novel, 606–607
  personal space, 215–216
  poem, 601
  power, 446–448
  propaganda techniques, 67–68
  Puritan work ethic, 336
  returning to school, 615
  scholarship jacket, 479–483
  science and search for truth, 442–445
  science textbooks, 594–595
  scratch outline, 620

Excerpts/passages/lectures—*Cont.*
  seeing ourselves favorably, 124
  selfish learning, 338–339
  service industries, 339–340
  social attachments, 128–130
  social status, 535
  states of matter, 142–144
  stereotypes, 327–328
  teenage drinking, 344
  test anxiety, 470–472
  verbal forms of information, 135–139
  visual assertion, 439–441
  water pollution, 327
  wired for touch, 474–478
  writing, 69–71
  writing/talking, compared, 338
extra, 282
Extra learning skills.
        See Additional learning skills
Eye of the Needle (Follett), 612
Eye reading speed, 465

Factors of production, 114
fallacy, 305
fancy, 601
Fatigue, 453–456
Fear, 507–511
fidgeted, 479
Figures of speech, 600
Fill-in questions, 231
Finding a book (library), 257–259
Fixations, 464
Flexible readers, 437, 463
Flowers for Algernon (Keyes), 612
flustered, 491
Focus on the future, 628
foreboding, 496
Forgetting, 537–538
Four-step study method. *See* PRWR
frailty, 507
Frame of mind. *See* Attitude
Free time, 83
Freewriting, 619
Freshman orientation, 12
"From Nonreading to Reading"
        (Abbott), 501–504
frugal, 302
ful, 285
Full pronunciation, 271
fy, 286

gaunt, 479
General-interest words, 308
General point (main idea), 358–366
Getting something for nothing, 19
gibberish, 302
Gifted Hands (Carson), 610
Glamour (magazine), 298
Goal setting, 21–28
  long-term goals, 22–23
  personal goals, 24
  short-term goals, 24–28
  study goals, 24
Gone with the Wind (Mitchell), 613
Goodbye, Columbus (Roth), 606
Google searches
  books online, 253
  Catcher in the Rye, 253
  current news, 253
  hate crimes, 252
  meaning of a word, 254
  search engines, 253
  sentence fragments, 254
  spelling ("jeopardy"), 254
  Winfrey, Oprah, 252
  World War II, 252–253
.gov, 260–261
grafts, 474
Grammar handbook, 621
graph, 294
graphically, 486

Graphs, 398–408
gratification, 486
gregarious, 303
gress, 293
Growing Up (Baker), 603, 609
guineas, 601

Handwriting, 54–59
Hard work, 19
Hardbound dictionaries, 266
Harry Potter and the Sorcerer's Stone
        (Rowling), 613
Headings and subheadings, 334–346
Help, The (Stockett), 614
hesitant, 474
Hole in the World, The (Rhodes), 611
Hospice program, 578–579

I Know Why the Caged Bird Sings
        (Angelou), 609
ible, 285
ify, 286
illustrate (essay exam), 243
Illustration words, 351–352
impregnable, 306
in, 282
In Cold Blood (Capote), 609
in vain, 601
Income, 326
Incurable disease, 496–499
Index cards, 309–310, 588
inevitable, 467
Inferences, 409–421, 600–608
  biography, 603–606
  context clues, 409
  irony, 415–416
  mastery test, 574–575
  novel, 606–608
  poetry, 601–603
  purpose, 412, 413
  tone, 414–416
Inform (purpose), 413
Instructor
  course outline, 76
  office hour, 92
  repetition, 50
  summaries/projections, 51
  voice/tone, 50
inter, 279
Interest inventory, 22
Interesting books
  classics, 614
  fiction, 611–614
  nonfiction, 609–611
Intermediate Algebra (Streeter et al.), 589
Internet
  connecting to, 250–251
  evaluate the sources, 260–261
  Google, 251–255
  search engines, 251
  what is it, 250
  World Wide Web, 250
Internet address, 260–261
interpret (essay exam), 243
interspersing, 470
intoned, 496
intoxicated, 507
Introduction to College Chemistry
        (Wolfe), 144
Introduction to Psychology
        (Plotnik), 130
Intuition, 317
Intuitive, 470
Invisible Man (Ellison), 614
ion, 284
ious, 287
Irony, 415–416
Irregular verbs, 272–273
ise, 284
ism, 287
ist, 284
ize, 284

Japanese American detention camps, 580–581
jargon, 501
Job boredom, 339
Job interview, 491–493
justify (essay exam), 243

kamikaze, 514
Key terms, 221
Key words, 207–208
keyed up, 470
King, Stephen, 612
Klootwyk, Ryan, 95–97
Know yourself, 20

Ladies' Home Journal (magazine), 298
Laminated calendar, 76
Latchkey children, 392–393
lavish, 474
"Learning to Keep Your Cool during
        Tests" (Jerrard), 470–472
Learn how you learn, 32–33
Learning center, 92, 264, 312
Lectures. *See* Excerpts/passages/lectures
less, 284
Library
  catalog, 257
  finding a book, 257–259
  main desk, 256
  stacks, 258–259
  subject headings, 258
Library of Congress classification
        system, 259
Life and Health (Levey et al.), 593
list (essay exam), 243
List making, 619
List of items, 324. *See also*
        Enumeration
Listening, 59–62, 65–66, 131–135
Listing order, 617
Literature
  biography, 603–606
  climax, 600
  conflict, 600
  figures of speech, 600
  novel, 606–608
  plot, 599
  poetry, 601–603
  setting, 599
  speaker/narrator, 600
  theme, 599
Logical point, 429–433
Logical support, 424–428
Long-term goals, 22–23
Loose-leaf binder, 47
Lord of the Flies (Golding), 612
Lord of the Rings, The (Tolkien), 614
ly, 286

Magazines, 298
Main desk (library), 256
Main heading, 334
Main idea, 358–366
Main idea sentence, 360
Makes Me Wanna Holler (McCall), 610
Making inferences, 409–421.
        See also Inferences
mal, 282
Malcolm X, 467–468
Managing your time. *See* Time
        management
Man's Search for Meaning
        (Frankl), 610
Mapping, 370, 619
Marketing (Etzel et al.), 118
Marketing (Schewe/Smith), 141
Marking, 102–103
Marking symbols, 102
masochist, 303
Mastery tests, 525–583
  classroom notes, 529–530
  definitions and examples, 556–557

dictionary, 551
enumerations, 558–559
essay exams, 544–545, 546–548
graphs, 573
headings and subheadings, 560–561
main idea, 564–565
memory aids, 540–541
motivational skills, 527–528
objective exams, 542–543, 546–548
outlining, 566–567
overview (uses), 526
rapid reading, 580–583
research skills, 549–550
signal words, 562–563
skim reading, 578–579
summarizing, 568–571
tables, 572
textbook study, 533–539
thinking critically, 576–577
time management, 531–532
vocabulary development, 553–555
word parts, 552
Matching questions, 231
Mathematics and science, 587–597
  cumulative nature of knowledge, 587–588
  homework, 588
  math excerpt, 589–593
  notes, 588–589
  PRWR, 593–597
  reading requirements, 589
  science excerpt, 593–598
  specialized terminology, 588
Mathematics courses, 514–518
*Memoir of My Extraordinary, Ordinary
        Family and Me, A* (Rice), 611
Memory aids, 201–217
  attitude, 205–206
  catchphrases, 117, 210
  catchwords, 116, 208–210
  key words, 207–208
  mastery test, 540–541
  morning review, 212
  organization, 204–205
  overlearning, 211–212
  reading (analyzing the audience), 214–215
  reading (personal space), 215–216
  repeated self-testing, 206
  senses, 207
  space work over time, 211
  student profile, 201–203
  study before bed, 212
ment, 285
Merriam-Webster Dictionary, 265, 266
mesquite, 479
Middlemarch (Eliot), 614
mis, 280
mit (*miss*), 289
Mnemonic devices, 206. *See also*
        Catchphrases; Catchwords
Moby-Dick (Melville), 614
Modem, 250
mono, 278
Monthly calendar, 76–78
Monthly magazines, 298
Most difficult subjects, 83
Motivational skills, 9–37
  attitude, 11–20
  goal setting, 21–28
  mastery test, 527–528
  overview, 10
  survival strategies, 29–37
Move On (Ellerbee), 610
Multiple-choice questions, 228–230
muster, 479, 496
My American Journey (Powell), 611
Myth of acceptance, 345

naive, 302
Nap, 91
Natural, The (Malamud), 613

ness, 284
.net, 261
Networking, 326
Newsweek (magazine), 298, 299
Noise, 108–109
Norms, 122
Note-taking. *See* Taking classroom notes
Novel, 606–608

Objective exams. *See* Taking objective exams
obsessed, 507
Occupational Outlook Handbook, 23
One-paragraph summary, 391–394
One-sentence summary, 383–388
Online bookstore sites, 255–256
Online dictionaries, 266–267
Open stacks, 259
Oprah (magazine), 298
optimum, 470
or, 287
.org, 261
Organization, 30–32, 204–205
ous, 287
Outline
    reading comprehension, 367–381, 566–567
    research paper, 259–260
    writing, 620
outline (essay exam), 243
Outline form (notes), 48–49
Outlining (reading comprehension), 367–381
    format, 369
    levels, 369
    mastery test, 566–567
    purpose, 369
    sample outline, 368
    titles, 369
Outside help, 92
Overlearning, 211–212
Overview of book, 2, 7, 8

Paragraph, 615–616, 622
Parker, Cheryl, 41–44
Parts of speech, 272
Passages. *See* Excerpts/passages/lectures
path, 291
Patriot Games (Clancy), 611
Peacock, Katie, 219–220
peers, 501
Pen, 47, 59
pend (pens), 293
People (magazine), 298
Perception habits, 463–464
peripheral sight, 470
Persistence, 33–34
personable, 491
Personal Computing (magazine), 298
Personal goals, 24
Personal space, 215–216
perspective, 486
Persuade (purpose), 413
Physical condition, 91
placebo, 304
Placement office, 22–23
Plagiarism, 260
Plan of development, 625
Poetry, 601–603
Point, 422
port, 290
Positive attitude, 20, 35, 88
post, 280
potential, 491
pounds, 601
Power, 446–448
pre, 279
Prefix, 277–283
prevalent, 486
Preview, 99
Prewriting, 619–620
Principal parts (irregular verbs), 272–273

Principles of good writing, 245
Priorities, 86
priorities, 507
pro, 281
prognosis, 305
proliferate, 306
Pronunciation, 269, 271–272
Proofreading, 621–622
Propaganda techniques, 67–68
Protein, 91
prove (essay exam), 243
provocation, 507
PRWR, 99–108. *See also* Textbook study
    marking, 102–103
    science excerpt, 593–597
    step 1 (preview), 99
    step 2 (read), 102
    step 3 (write), 103–105
    step 4 (recite), 107
    summary, 152–153
psych, 293
Puritan work ethic, 336
Purpose, 412, 413

Questions/questioning, 51, 619, 626

Random House Webster's Dictionary, 265, 266
Rapid reading, 461–524
    comprehension, 316
    deliberately "turn on" your speed, 465
    eye movement, 464
    how to improve reading speed, 465
    index finger, 474
    mastery test, 580–583
    other types of reading, contrasted, 466
    overview, 462
    perception habits, 463–464
    progress chart, 521
    reading (dare to think big), 486–488
    reading (fear), 507–511
    reading (incurable disease), 496–499
    reading (job interview), 491–493
    reading (learning to read), 501–504
    reading (Malcolm X), 467–468
    reading (mathematics courses), 514–518
    reading (scholarship jacket), 479–483
    reading (test anxiety), 470–472
    reading (wired for touch), 474–478
    reading rate table, 522–524
Rapid reading progress chart, 521
Rapid writing, 57
re, 282
Reading
    biography, 603–606
    classics, 614
    eye movement, 464
    fiction books, 611–614
    interesting books. *See* Interesting books
    literature. *See* Literature
    mathematics and science, 589
    myth about, 437
    nonfiction books, 609–611
    novel, 606–608
    perception habits, 463–464
    poetry, 601–603
    process, as, 630
    selective. *See* Skim reading
    speed. *See* Rapid reading
    study. *See* Reading comprehension skills
    vocabulary development, 298–300
    writing, compared, 629–630
Reading comprehension skills, 313–433
    definitions and examples, 317–323
    diagramming, 370–381
    enumerations, 324–333
    graphs, 398–408

headings and subheadings, 334–346
inferences, 409–421. *See also* Inferences
main idea, 358–366
outlining, 367–381. *See also* Outlining (reading comprehension)
    overview, 314, 315
    rapid reading, 316
    signal words, 347–357. *See also* Signal words
    summarizing, 382–397. *See also* Summarizing
    tables, 398–408
    thinking critically, 422–433
Reading every word, 437
Reading rate table, 522–524
Reading selections. *See* Excerpts/passages/lectures
Real-life profiles. *See* Student profiles
Recall words, 53, 107
Recitation, 107
recoil, 474
Redbook (magazine), 298
redundant, 304
regressed, 474
Regression, 464
regression, 305
reinforcement, 501
relate (essay exam), 243
Remember The Milk, 85
remission, 306
Repeated self-testing, 206
Research skills, 249–262
    books online, 255–256
    document your sources, 260, 261
    Google, 251–255
    Internet. *See* Internet
    library, 256–259
    limit your topic, 259
    mastery tests, 549–550
    plagiarism, 260
    scratch outline, 259–260
    student profile, 249–250
    subject headings, 258
retain, 501
Returning to school, 615
Review tests. *See* Mastery tests
riffling, 467
Roots, 289–294
rue, 601
Running from commitment, 16–17

Sample chapter. *See* Textbook chapter (family)
Samples/illustrations. *See also* Excerpts/passages/lectures
    catchphrases, 210
    catchwords, 209
    classroom notes, 55
    daily schedule, 78
    dictionary entry, 268
    Google searches, 252–254
    graph, 399
    index card, 310
    key words, 208
    outline, 368
    recall words, 107
    study sheet, 56, 106
    summary, 382
    table, 401
    "to do" list, 85
    vocabulary word sheet, 309
    weekly schedule, 80
Scarlet Letter, The (Hawthorne), 614
"Scholarship Jacket, The" (Salinas), 479–483
School. *See* College
Schwa, 270
Science. *See* Mathematics and science
Science and search for truth, 442–445
Science Digest (magazine), 298

Scratch outline, 259–260, 620, 620.
    See also Outline
script (scrib), 291
Search engines, 251
secreted, 470
Self-assessment, 2–8
    attitude about studying, 3
    classroom notes, 3–4
    memory training, 5
    other reading and study skills, 8
    other reading skills, 7–8
    taking tests, 5–6
    textbook study, 4–5
    time control and concentration, 4
    using Internet/library, 6
    word skills, 6–7
Self-motivation
    follow success, 20
    friends, 20
    goal setting, 20
    know yourself, 20
    patience, 20
    positive attitude, 20
    restart, 20
    sense of humor, 20
Selfish learning, 338–339
sequential, 514
Service industries, 339–340
Setting goals. *See* Goal setting
Shining, The (King), 612
ship, 285
Short-term goals, 24–28
Signal words, 347–357
    addition words, 348–350
    cause-and-effect words, 352–353
    comparison or contrast words, 350–351
    emphasis words, 347–348
    illustration words, 351–352
    mastery test, 562–563
Signals of importance, 49–50
Silence of the Lambs, The (Harris), 612
sist, 292
Sit where you'll be seen, 45–46
Skim reading, 435–460
    definitions, 438
    emphasis words, 438
    enumerations, 438
    headings and subheadings, 438
    main ideas, 438
    mastery test, 578–579
    myth (reading every word), 437
    progress chart, 457
    purpose, 466
    questions, 458–460
    reading (defense mechanisms), 449–451
    reading (fatigue), 453–456
    reading (power), 446–448
    reading (science and search for truth), 442–445
    reading (visual assertion), 439–441
Skim reading progress chart, 457
Sleep, 91
Sleepers (Carcaterra), 609
Sleepiness syndrome, 18
Snow Falling on Cedars (Guterson), 612
Social attachments, 128–130
Social status, 535
Sociology (Schaefer/Lamm), 122
Sociology: The Core (Hughes/Kroehler), 151
Software dictionaries, 268
spec (spic), 294
Speed reading. *See* Rapid reading
Speed reading courses, 316
Spelling, 268–269
Spiral notebook, 47
Sports Illustrated (magazine), 298, 299
SQ3R, 292
Stacks, 258–259
Standard English, 274

state (essay exam), 243
States of matter, 142–144
Stereotypes, 327–328
Story/anecdote, 626
Story of My Life, The (Keller), 610
Student profiles
  Cardenas, Maria, 73–75
  Davis, Joe, 201–203
  Klootwyk, Ryan, 95–97
  Parker, Cheryl, 41–44
  Peacock, Katie, 219–220
  Sullivan, Matthew, 249–250
  Sutton, Rod, 237–239
Study environment, 90
Study goals, 24, 89
Study reading. *See* Reading
  comprehension skills
Study schedule, 78–85
Study skills, 39–262
  classroom notes. *See* Taking
    classroom notes
  essay exams, 237–248
  Internet. *See* Internet
  library, 256–259
  managing time. *See* Time management
  memory aids. *See* Memory aids
  objective exams. *See* Taking
    objective exams
  overview, 40
  plagiarism, 260
  PRWR, 99–108
  research skills. *See* Research skills
  student profiles. *See* Student profiles
  textbook study. *See* Textbook study
Studying your notes, 53–54
sub, 279
Subheadings, 334–336
subjective, 514
Subvocalizing, 463–464
succeeding, 467
Suffix, 283–288
Sullivant, Matthew, 249–250
summarize (essay exam), 243
Summarizing, 382–397
  guidelines/hints, 391
  length of summary, 382–383
  mastery test, 568–571
  one-sentence summary, 383–388
  purpose, 391
  title summary, 383–388
  what is it, 382
  why important, 382
Support/supporting details, 422, 616
Survival strategies, 29–37
  growth, 35–36
  learn how you learn, 32–33
  organization, 30–32
  persistence, 33–34
  positive attitude, 35
  realistic, 29–30
Sutton, Rod, 237–239
Syllabication, 269
Syllabus, 76
Synonyms, 274

Tables, 398–408
Taking classroom notes, 41–71
  abbreviations, 47–48, 57
  advance reading, 46–47
  ask questions, 51
  assignments/quizzes, 48
  attending class, 44
  blackboard material, 49
  blank spaces, 51
  connecting details, 50
  definitions/enumerations, 49
  discussion periods, 52
  end of class, 51, 52
  examples, 50
  format, 48–49
  handwriting, 54–59
  listening, 59–62

lists, 49
mastery tests, 529–530
notebook, 47
outline form, 48–49
overviews/summaries, 51
paper, 47
pen, 47, 59
review your notes, 52–53
signals of importance, 49–50
sit where you'll be seen, 45–46
student profile, 41–44
studying your notes, 53–54
typing skills, 62
written record, 45, 98
Taking essay exams, 237–248
  anticipated probable questions,
    239–240
  direction words, 243
  informal outline, 240, 244
  introductory sentence, 245
  mastery tests, 544–545, 546–548
  objective exams, contrasted, 226
  principles of good writing, 245
  proofreading, 245
  review exam before starting, 242
  spelling, 240
  steps, listed, 239
  student profile, 237–239
  supporting detail, 245
  transitions, 245
  what to study, 221–223
Taking objective exams, 219–235
  budget your time, 224
  cramming, 232
  difficult questions, 227
  essay exams, contrasted, 226
  exam panic, 221
  fill-in questions, 231
  getting ready, 225–226
  key words, 227
  mastery tests, 542, 543, 546–548
  matching questions, 231
  multiple-choice questions, 228–230
  pre-exam hints, 223–224
  review your answers, 227
  student profile, 219–220
  true–false questions, 230–231
  what to study, 221–223
tang (tact), 292
taunting, 501
Technical words, 307–308
Teenage drinking, 344
terse, 496
Test anxiety, 221, 470–472
Test taking
  essay exams. *See* Taking Essay exams
  exam panic, 221, 470–472
  mastery tests. *See* Mastery tests
  objective exams. *See* Taking
    objective exams
Textbook chapter (family), 151–199
  activities/comments (section 1),
    163–165
  activities/comments (section 2),
    181–182
  activities/comments (section 3), 190
  activities/comments (section 4), 193
  closing comments/activities, 197
  quiz, 198–199
  reading, 154–196
Textbook excerpts. *See* Excerpts/
    passages/lectures
Textbook study, 95–199
  four-step study method. *See* PRWR
  mastery tests, 533–539
  quizzes, 144–150
  reading (alcoholism), 124
  reading (alternatives to conflict),
    100–101
  reading (anger), 120
  reading (building blocks of all
    matter), 126

reading (business cycle), 118
reading (consumer products), 139–141
reading (crowds), 110
reading (ESP), 111
reading (factors of production), 114
reading (family). *See* Textbook
    chapter (family)
reading (listening), 131–135
reading (noise), 108–109
reading (norms), 122
reading (seeing ourselves favorably),
    112–113
reading (social attachment), 128–130
reading (states of matter), 142–144
reading (verbal forms of
    information), 135–139
  student profile, 95–97
Textbooks, basic structure, 358
The Catcher in the Rye (Salinger), 613
The Help (Stockett), 614
The Natural (Malamud), 613
The Shining (King), 612
Thesaurus, 274
Thesis statement, 622, 624
Thinking critically, 422–433
  logical point, 429–433
  logical support, 424–428
  mastery test, 576–577
  point/support, 422–424
Time (magazine), 298, 299
Time management, 73–94
  balance your activities, 83
  blocks of study time, 82
  concentration, 87–92
  flexibility, 83
  mastery test, 531–532
  monthly calendar, 76–78
  most difficult subjects, 83
  outside help, 92
  physical condition, 91
  priorities, 86
  reward yourself, 82
  schedule regular study time, 81
  schedule study periods before/after
    class, 83
  student profile, 73–75
  study environment, 90
  study goals, 89
  study schedule, 78–85
  syllabus, 76
  "to do" list, 85–86
  vary your study activities, 91
Time order, 617–618
Time organizer, 86
Time overload, 79
Tiny Sunbirds, Far Away (Watson), 614
tion, 284
Title summaries, 383–388
"To do" list, 85–86
To Kill a Mockingbird (Lee), 613
Tone, 412, 414–416
Topic sentence, 616, 622
trace (essay exam), 243
tract (trac), 290
trans, 278
Transitions, 245, 616, 617.
    See also Signal words
True–false questions, 230–231
turmoil, 507
Tutor, 92
Typing skills, 62

un, 281
unconditional, 474
untouchables, 474
Usage label, 274–275

Verbal forms of information, 135–139
vers (vert), 292
vid (vis), 293
vindictive, 303
Visual assertion, 439–441

Visual inaccuracy, 464
voc (vok), 290
Vocabulary development, 297–312
  context cues, 301–306
  general-interest words, 308
  index cards, 309–310
  mastery test, 553–555
  methodology, 308–310
  reading, 298–300
  technical words, 307–308
  vocabulary study books, 312
Vocabulary study books, 312
Vocational preference test, 22
voracious, 302
Vowel sounds, 270

Waiting to Exhale (McMillan), 613
Watchers (Koontz), 613
Water pollution, 327
Watership Down (Adams), 611
Weekly magazines, 298
Weekly study schedule, 78–85
What skills do you need to master?.
    See Self-assessment
What to study
  emphasized points, 222
  enumerations, 221–222
  key terms, 221
  questions on past exams, 223
  topics identified by instructor, 222
"What You Need to Know to Succeed
    at Math" (Nolting), 514–518
"When I Was One-and-Twenty"
    (Housman), 601
Winning at Math (Nolting), 514
"Winning the Job Interview Game"
    (Prentergast), 491–493
"Wired for Touch" (Grandinetti),
    474–478
Word-for-word reading, 464
Word parts, 277–295
  mastery test, 552
  prefix, 277–283
  roots, 289–294
  suffix, 283–288
Word power. *See* Vocabulary development
Word skills, 263–312
  dictionary. *See* Dictionary
  overview, 264
  prefixes, 277–283
  roots, 289–294
  suffixes, 283–288
Workout, 91
Works Cited, 261
World Wide Web, 250
Writer's voice, 414–416
Writing, 615–630
  draft, 621
  error-free sentences, 618
  essay. *See* Essay
  make a point, 616
  organize the support, 616–618
  paragraph, 615–616, 622
  prewriting, 619–620
  process, as, 630
  proofreading, 621–622
  reading, compared, 629–630
  revising, 621
  scratch outline, 620
  support the point, 616
Writing assignments, 630–634
Writing/talking, compared, 338
www.amazon.com, 256
www.bn.com, 256
www.dictionary.com, 267
www.google.com, 251–255
www.google.com/calendar, 76
www.merriam-webster.com, 266
www.nytimes.com, 299
www.rememberthemilk.com, 85
www.washingtonpost.com, 299
www.yourdictionary.com, 267